# THE CITY OF NEW YORK

## Summary and Detailed Statements of Revenues and Expenditures for the Years 1910 to 1914, inclusive

PREPARED FOR THE

## CONSTITUTIONAL CONVENTION 1915

*By*

THE DEPARTMENT OF FINANCE
BUREAU OF MUNICIPAL INVESTIGATION AND STATISTICS
*and*
NEW YORK BUREAU OF MUNICIPAL RESEARCH

THE TROW PRESS
NEW YORK



2775, '15, 1M (T)

# TABLE OF CONTENTS

# INDEX

**Note.**—Figures and Symbols at Head of Columns Indicate Statements as Outlined in Table of Contents. the Particular Kind of Information Desired, relative to Any

# INDEX

The Figures in the Columns under the Respective Headings Denote the Pages on which May be Found Department, etc., as Indicated in the Table of Contents.

(See Note on first

*Continued*

page of Index)

| LINE No. | 3D2 | 3D3 | 3D4 | 3D5 | 3E1 | 3E2 | 3E3 | 3E4 | 3E5 | 3F1 | 3F2 | 3F3 | 3F4 | 3F5 | 4 | 5 |
|---|---|---|---|---|---|---|---|---|---|---|---|---|---|---|---|---|
| 1 | .. | .. | .. | .. | .. | .. | .. | .. | .. | .. | .. | .. | .. | .. | 149 | .. |
| 2 | .. | .. | .. | .. | .. | .. | .. | .. | .. | .. | .. | .. | .. | .. | 156 | .. |
| 3 | 46 | 50 | 54 | .. | .. | .. | .. | .. | .. | .. | .. | .. | .. | .. | 90 | .. |
| 4 | 47 | 51 | 55 | 59 | .. | .. | .. | .. | .. | .. | .. | .. | .. | .. | 122 | .. |
| 5 | 46 | 50 | 54 | .. | .. | .. | .. | .. | .. | 67 | 70 | .. | 76 | 79 | 98 | .. |
| 6 | .. | .. | .. | .. | .. | .. | .. | .. | .. | 67 | 70 | .. | .. | .. | 87 | .. |
| 7 | .. | 51 | 55 | .. | .. | .. | .. | .. | .. | .. | .. | .. | .. | .. | 109 | .. |
| 8 | .. | .. | 56 | 60 | .. | .. | .. | .. | .. | .. | .. | .. | .. | .. | 164 | .. |
| 9 | .. | 51 | 55 | .. | .. | .. | .. | .. | .. | .. | .. | .. | .. | .. | 145 | .. |
| 10 | .. | .. | .. | 59 | .. | .. | .. | .. | .. | .. | .. | .. | .. | .. | 137 | .. |
| 11 | .. | .. | 56 | .. | .. | .. | .. | .. | .. | .. | .. | .. | .. | .. | 153 | .. |
| 12 | .. | .. | .. | .. | .. | .. | .. | .. | .. | .. | .. | .. | .. | .. | 158 | .. |
| 13 | .. | .. | 54 | .. | .. | .. | .. | .. | .. | .. | .. | .. | .. | .. | 88 | .. |
| 14 | .. | .. | .. | .. | .. | .. | .. | .. | .. | .. | .. | .. | .. | .. | 147 | .. |
| 15 | .. | 51 | 55 | .. | .. | .. | .. | .. | .. | .. | .. | .. | .. | .. | 139 | .. |
| 16 | .. | .. | .. | .. | .. | .. | .. | .. | .. | .. | .. | .. | .. | .. | 140 | .. |
| 17 | 46 | 50 | 54 | .. | .. | .. | .. | .. | .. | .. | .. | .. | .. | .. | 81 | .. |
| 18 | .. | .. | .. | .. | .. | .. | .. | .. | .. | .. | 70 | 73 | .. | .. | 109 | .. |
| 19 | .. | .. | .. | .. | .. | .. | .. | .. | .. | .. | .. | .. | .. | .. | 113 | .. |
| 20 | .. | 50 | .. | .. | .. | .. | .. | .. | .. | .. | .. | .. | .. | .. | 101 | .. |
| 21 | 47 | .. | 55 | .. | .. | .. | .. | .. | .. | .. | .. | .. | .. | .. | 115 | .. |
| 22 | 47 | .. | 55 | 59 | .. | .. | .. | .. | .. | .. | .. | .. | .. | .. | 114 | .. |
| 23 | .. | .. | .. | .. | .. | .. | .. | .. | .. | .. | .. | .. | .. | .. | 115 | .. |
| 24 | .. | .. | .. | .. | .. | .. | .. | .. | .. | .. | .. | .. | .. | .. | 116 | .. |
| 25 | .. | 51 | 55 | 59 | .. | .. | .. | .. | .. | .. | .. | .. | .. | .. | 114 | .. |
| 26 | 46 | 50 | 54 | 58 | 61 | 62 | 63 | 64 | 65 | 67 | 70 | 73 | 76 | 79 | 201 | .. |
| 27 | .. | .. | .. | 60 | .. | .. | .. | .. | .. | .. | .. | .. | .. | .. | 161 | .. |
| 28 | 48 | 51 | 55 | 59 | .. | .. | .. | .. | .. | .. | .. | .. | .. | .. | 142 | .. |
| 29 | 48 | .. | .. | 59 | .. | .. | .. | .. | .. | .. | 71 | 74 | 77 | .. | 134 | .. |
| 30 | 48 | 52 | 56 | 60 | .. | .. | .. | .. | .. | .. | .. | .. | .. | .. | 150 | .. |
| 31 | 48 | 52 | 56 | 60 | .. | .. | .. | .. | .. | .. | .. | .. | .. | .. | 156 | .. |
| 32 | .. | .. | .. | .. | .. | .. | .. | .. | .. | .. | .. | .. | .. | .. | 116 | .. |
| 33 | 47 | 51 | 55 | 59 | .. | .. | .. | .. | .. | .. | .. | .. | .. | .. | 117 | .. |
| 34 | 47 | 51 | 55 | 59 | .. | .. | .. | .. | .. | .. | .. | .. | .. | .. | 117 | .. |
| 35 | .. | .. | .. | 60 | .. | .. | .. | .. | .. | .. | .. | .. | .. | .. | 162 | .. |
| 36 | 48 | 51 | 55 | 59 | .. | .. | .. | .. | .. | .. | .. | .. | .. | .. | 143 | .. |
| 37 | .. | 52 | 56 | .. | .. | .. | .. | .. | .. | .. | .. | .. | .. | .. | 150 | .. |
| 38 | 48 | 52 | 56 | .. | .. | .. | .. | .. | .. | .. | .. | .. | .. | .. | 157 | .. |
| 39 | 47 | .. | .. | .. | .. | .. | .. | .. | .. | .. | .. | 73 | 77 | 79 | 108 | .. |
| 40 | .. | .. | .. | .. | .. | .. | .. | .. | .. | .. | .. | .. | .. | .. | 151 | .. |
| 41 | 47 | .. | .. | .. | .. | .. | .. | .. | .. | .. | .. | .. | .. | .. | 118 | .. |
| 42 | .. | 51 | 55 | 59 | .. | .. | .. | .. | .. | .. | .. | .. | .. | .. | 135 | .. |
| 43 | 47 | 51 | 55 | 59 | .. | .. | .. | .. | .. | .. | .. | .. | .. | .. | 118 | .. |
| 44 | .. | 51 | 55 | 59 | .. | .. | .. | .. | .. | .. | .. | .. | .. | .. | 135 | .. |
| 45 | .. | .. | .. | .. | .. | .. | .. | .. | .. | .. | .. | .. | .. | .. | 136 | .. |
| 46 | 48 | 51 | 55 | 59 | .. | .. | .. | .. | .. | .. | .. | .. | .. | .. | 143 | .. |
| 47 | .. | 52 | 56 | .. | .. | .. | .. | .. | .. | .. | .. | .. | .. | .. | 151 | .. |
| 48 | .. | .. | 56 | .. | .. | .. | .. | .. | .. | .. | .. | .. | .. | .. | 157 | .. |
| 49 | .. | .. | .. | 60 | .. | .. | .. | .. | .. | .. | .. | .. | .. | .. | 162 | .. |
| 50 | 48 | 51 | .. | 59 | .. | .. | .. | .. | .. | .. | .. | .. | .. | .. | 144 | .. |
| 51 | 48 | 51 | 55 | 59 | .. | .. | .. | .. | .. | .. | .. | .. | .. | .. | 136 | .. |
| 52 | 47 | .. | .. | .. | .. | .. | .. | .. | .. | .. | .. | .. | .. | .. | 120 | .. |
| 53 | .. | .. | .. | .. | .. | .. | .. | .. | .. | .. | .. | .. | .. | .. | 131 | .. |
| 54 | 46 | 50 | 54 | 58 | 61 | 62 | 63 | 64 | 65 | 67 | 70 | 73 | 76 | 79 | 82 | 167 |
| 55 | 46 | 50 | 54 | 58 | 61 | 62 | 63 | 64 | 65 | 67 | 70 | 73 | 76 | 79 | 84 | 201 |
| 56 | 46 | 50 | 54 | 58 | .. | .. | .. | .. | .. | 67 | 70 | 73 | 76 | 79 | 85 | 171 |
| 57 | 46 | 50 | 54 | 58 | 61 | 62 | 63 | 64 | 65 | 67 | 70 | 73 | 76 | 79 | 99 | .. |
| 58 | 46 | .. | .. | .. | .. | .. | .. | .. | .. | .. | .. | .. | .. | .. | 103 | .. |
| 59 | 46 | 50 | 54 | 58 | .. | .. | .. | .. | .. | 67 | 70 | 73 | 76 | 79 | 86 | 198 |
| 60 | 46 | 50 | 54 | 58 | 61 | 62 | 63 | 64 | 65 | 67 | 70 | 73 | 76 | 79 | 86 | 175 |
| 61 | 46 | 50 | 54 | 58 | .. | .. | .. | .. | .. | .. | .. | .. | .. | .. | 87 | .. |

INDEX—

(See Note on first

*Continued*

page of Index)

| LINE No. | 3D2 | 3D3 | 3D4 | 3D5 | 3E1 | 3E2 | 3E3 | 3E4 | 3E5 | 3F1 | 3F2 | 3F3 | 3F4 | 3F5 | 4 | 5 |
|---|---|---|---|---|---|---|---|---|---|---|---|---|---|---|---|---|
| 1 | 46 | .. | .. | .. | 61 | 62 | 63 | .. | 65 | 67 | 70 | 73 | 76 | 79 | 93 | 194 |
| 2 | 46 | 50 | 54 | 58 | 61 | 62 | 63 | 64 | 65 | 67 | 70 | 73 | 76 | 79 | 92 | 190 |
| 3 | 46 | 50 | 54 | 58 | .. | .. | .. | .. | .. | 67 | 70 | 73 | 76 | 79 | 93 | 196 |
| 4 | 46 | 50 | 54 | 58 | .. | .. | .. | .. | .. | 67 | 70 | 73 | 76 | 79 | 92 | 192 |
| 5 | 46 | 50 | 54 | 58 | .. | .. | .. | .. | .. | 67 | 70 | 73 | 76 | 79 | 94 | .. |
| 6 | 46 | 50 | 54 | 58 | .. | .. | .. | .. | .. | 67 | 70 | 73 | 76 | 79 | 94 | .. |
| 7 | 46 | 50 | 54 | 58 | .. | .. | .. | .. | .. | 67 | 70 | 73 | 76 | 79 | 95 | 178 |
| 8 | 46 | 50 | 54 | 58 | .. | .. | .. | .. | .. | 67 | .. | .. | .. | .. | 95 | .. |
| 9 | 46 | 50 | 54 | 58 | 61 | 62 | 63 | 64 | 65 | 67 | 70 | 73 | 76 | 79 | 96 | 169 |
| 10 | .. | .. | .. | .. | .. | .. | .. | .. | .. | .. | .. | .. | .. | .. | 133 | .. |
| 11 | .. | .. | .. | 60 | .. | .. | .. | .. | .. | .. | .. | .. | .. | .. | 163 | .. |
| 12 | 48 | 51 | 55 | 59 | .. | .. | .. | .. | .. | .. | .. | .. | .. | .. | 145 | .. |
| 13 | 48 | 51 | 55 | 59 | .. | .. | .. | .. | .. | .. | .. | .. | .. | .. | 137 | .. |
| 14 | 48 | 52 | 56 | 60 | .. | .. | .. | .. | .. | .. | .. | .. | .. | .. | 152 | .. |
| 15 | 48 | .. | 56 | 60 | .. | .. | .. | .. | .. | .. | .. | .. | .. | .. | 158 | .. |
| 16 | 46 | 50 | 54 | 58 | .. | .. | .. | .. | .. | 67 | 70 | 73 | 76 | 79 | 85 | 171 |
| 17 | 46 | 50 | 54 | 58 | 61 | 62 | 63 | 64 | 65 | 67 | 70 | 73 | 76 | 79 | 99 | .. |
| 18 | .. | 51 | 55 | 59 | .. | .. | .. | .. | .. | .. | .. | .. | .. | .. | 112 | .. |
| 19 | 47 | .. | .. | .. | .. | .. | .. | .. | 65 | .. | .. | .. | .. | .. | 112 | .. |
| 20 | .. | .. | .. | .. | .. | .. | .. | .. | .. | .. | 70 | 73 | .. | .. | 109 | .. |
| 21 | .. | .. | 54 | 58 | .. | .. | .. | .. | .. | .. | .. | .. | .. | .. | 85 | .. |
| 22 | .. | .. | .. | .. | 61 | 62 | 63 | 64 | 65 | .. | .. | .. | .. | .. | 123 | .. |
| 23 | 46 | 50 | 54 | 58 | .. | .. | .. | .. | .. | .. | .. | .. | .. | .. | 91 | .. |
| 24 | 46 | .. | .. | .. | .. | .. | .. | .. | .. | .. | .. | .. | .. | .. | 103 | .. |
| 25 | 46 | 50 | 54 | 58 | .. | .. | .. | .. | .. | 67 | 70 | 73 | 76 | 79 | 86 | 198 |
| 26 | .. | .. | .. | .. | .. | .. | .. | .. | .. | .. | .. | .. | .. | .. | 119 | .. |
| 27 | .. | 51 | 55 | 59 | .. | .. | .. | .. | .. | .. | .. | .. | .. | .. | 135 | .. |
| 28 | .. | .. | .. | .. | .. | .. | .. | .. | .. | 67 | 70 | .. | 76 | 79 | 83 | .. |
| 29 | .. | .. | .. | .. | .. | .. | .. | .. | .. | .. | .. | .. | .. | .. | 123 | .. |
| 30 | 46 | 50 | 54 | 58 | 61 | 62 | 63 | 64 | 65 | 67 | 70 | 73 | 76 | 79 | 86 | 175 |
| 31 | 46 | 50 | 54 | 58 | .. | .. | .. | .. | .. | 67 | 70 | 73 | 76 | 79 | 98 | 173 |
| 32 | .. | .. | .. | .. | .. | .. | .. | .. | .. | 67 | 70 | .. | .. | .. | 87 | .. |
| 33 | .. | 51 | .. | .. | .. | .. | .. | .. | .. | .. | .. | .. | .. | .. | 125 | .. |
| 34 | 46 | 50 | 54 | 58 | .. | .. | .. | .. | .. | .. | .. | 73 | 76 | .. | 102 | .. |
| 35 | .. | .. | .. | .. | .. | .. | .. | .. | .. | 67 | 70 | .. | .. | .. | 87 | .. |
| 36 | .. | .. | .. | .. | .. | .. | .. | .. | .. | .. | .. | .. | .. | .. | 124 | .. |
| 37 | .. | .. | 56 | 60 | .. | .. | .. | .. | .. | .. | .. | .. | .. | .. | 164 | .. |
| 38 | .. | 51 | 55 | .. | .. | .. | .. | .. | .. | .. | .. | .. | .. | .. | 145 | .. |
| 39 | .. | .. | .. | 59 | .. | .. | .. | .. | .. | .. | .. | .. | .. | .. | 137 | .. |
| 40 | .. | .. | 56 | .. | .. | .. | .. | .. | .. | .. | .. | .. | .. | .. | 153 | .. |
| 41 | .. | .. | .. | .. | .. | .. | .. | .. | .. | .. | .. | .. | .. | .. | 158 | .. |
| 42 | 46 | 50 | 54 | 58 | .. | .. | .. | .. | .. | .. | .. | .. | .. | .. | 87 | .. |
| 43 | .. | .. | .. | 60 | .. | .. | .. | .. | .. | .. | .. | .. | .. | .. | 163 | .. |
| 44 | .. | .. | .. | .. | .. | .. | .. | .. | .. | .. | .. | .. | .. | .. | 144 | .. |
| 45 | .. | .. | .. | .. | .. | .. | .. | .. | .. | .. | .. | .. | .. | .. | 151 | .. |
| 46 | 46 | 50 | 54 | 58 | .. | .. | .. | .. | .. | .. | .. | .. | .. | .. | 89 | .. |
| 47 | .. | .. | 54 | .. | .. | .. | .. | .. | .. | .. | .. | .. | .. | .. | 88 | .. |
| 48 | .. | 51 | 55 | .. | .. | .. | .. | .. | .. | .. | .. | .. | .. | .. | 109 | .. |
| 49 | 47 | 50 | 54 | 58 | .. | 62 | 63 | 64 | 65 | 67 | 70 | 73 | 76 | 79 | 104 | 179 |
| 50 | .. | .. | .. | .. | .. | .. | .. | .. | .. | .. | .. | .. | .. | .. | 88 | .. |
| 51 | 46 | 50 | 54 | 58 | .. | .. | .. | .. | .. | .. | .. | .. | .. | .. | 89 | .. |
| 52 | 46 | 50 | .. | .. | .. | .. | .. | .. | .. | .. | .. | .. | .. | .. | 89 | .. |
| 53 | .. | .. | .. | .. | .. | .. | .. | .. | .. | .. | .. | .. | .. | .. | 124 | .. |
| 54 | .. | .. | .. | .. | .. | .. | .. | .. | .. | 67 | 70 | 73 | 76 | .. | 90 | .. |

*Continued*

page of Index)

| LINE No. | 3D2 | 3D3 | 3D4 | 3D5 | 3E1 | 3E2 | 3E3 | 3E4 | 3E5 | 3F1 | 3F2 | 3F3 | 3F4 | 3F5 | 4 | 5 |
|---|---|---|---|---|---|---|---|---|---|---|---|---|---|---|---|---|
| 1 | 47 | 51 | 55 | 59 | .. | .. | .. | .. | .. | 68 | 71 | 74 | 77 | 80 | 125 | .. |
| 2 | .. | .. | .. | .. | .. | .. | .. | .. | .. | .. | .. | .. | .. | .. | 164 | .. |
| 3 | 48 | .. | .. | .. | .. | .. | .. | .. | .. | .. | .. | .. | .. | .. | 146 | .. |
| 4 | 48 | 51 | 55 | .. | .. | .. | .. | .. | .. | .. | .. | .. | .. | .. | 138 | .. |
| 5 | 48 | .. | .. | .. | .. | .. | .. | .. | .. | .. | .. | .. | .. | .. | 153 | .. |
| 6 | 48 | .. | .. | .. | .. | .. | .. | .. | .. | .. | .. | .. | .. | .. | 159 | .. |
| 7 | 46 | 50 | 54 | .. | .. | .. | .. | .. | .. | .. | .. | .. | .. | .. | 90 | .. |
| 8 | 46 | 50 | 54 | 58 | .. | .. | .. | .. | .. | .. | .. | .. | .. | .. | 91 | .. |
| 9 | .. | .. | .. | .. | .. | .. | .. | .. | .. | .. | .. | .. | .. | .. | 126 | .. |
| 10 | .. | .. | .. | .. | .. | .. | .. | .. | .. | .. | .. | .. | .. | .. | 165 | .. |
| 11 | .. | .. | .. | .. | .. | .. | .. | .. | .. | .. | .. | .. | .. | .. | 146 | .. |
| 12 | .. | .. | .. | .. | .. | .. | .. | .. | .. | .. | .. | .. | .. | .. | 138 | .. |
| 13 | .. | .. | .. | .. | .. | .. | .. | .. | .. | .. | .. | .. | .. | .. | 154 | .. |
| 14 | .. | .. | .. | .. | .. | .. | .. | .. | .. | .. | .. | .. | .. | .. | 159 | .. |
| 15 | .. | .. | .. | .. | .. | .. | .. | .. | .. | .. | .. | .. | .. | .. | 126 | .. |
| 16 | .. | .. | .. | .. | .. | .. | .. | .. | .. | .. | .. | .. | .. | .. | 127 | .. |
| 17 | 47 | .. | 55 | 59 | .. | .. | .. | .. | .. | 68 | 71 | 74 | 77 | 80 | 129 | .. |
| 18 | .. | .. | .. | .. | .. | .. | .. | .. | .. | .. | .. | .. | .. | .. | 128 | .. |
| 19 | .. | .. | .. | .. | .. | .. | .. | .. | .. | .. | .. | .. | .. | .. | 127 | .. |
| 20 | .. | .. | 54 | .. | .. | .. | .. | .. | .. | 67 | 70 | 73 | 76 | 79 | 99 | .. |
| 21 | .. | .. | .. | .. | .. | .. | .. | .. | .. | .. | .. | .. | .. | .. | 91 | 189 |
| 22 | 46 | 50 | 54 | 58 | .. | .. | .. | .. | .. | 67 | 70 | 73 | 76 | 79 | 92 | 192 |
| 23 | 46 | .. | .. | .. | 61 | 62 | 63 | .. | 65 | 67 | 70 | 73 | 76 | 79 | 93 | 194 |
| 24 | 46 | 50 | 54 | 58 | 61 | 62 | 63 | 64 | 65 | 67 | 70 | 73 | 76 | 79 | 92 | 190 |
| 25 | 46 | 50 | 54 | 58 | .. | .. | .. | .. | .. | 67 | 70 | 73 | 76 | 79 | 93 | 196 |
| 26 | .. | .. | .. | .. | .. | .. | .. | .. | .. | .. | .. | .. | .. | .. | 119 | .. |
| 27 | .. | .. | .. | .. | .. | .. | .. | .. | .. | .. | .. | .. | .. | .. | 102 | .. |
| 28 | .. | .. | 54 | 58 | .. | .. | .. | .. | .. | .. | .. | .. | .. | .. | 85 | .. |
| 29 | 46 | 50 | 54 | 58 | .. | .. | .. | .. | .. | 67 | 70 | 73 | 76 | 79 | 94 | .. |
| 30 | 47 | 50 | 54 | 58 | .. | .. | .. | .. | .. | .. | .. | .. | .. | .. | 107 | .. |
| 31 | 47 | 50 | 54 | 58 | 61 | 62 | 63 | 64 | 65 | 67 | 70 | 73 | 76 | 79 | 105 | 181 |
| 32 | 47 | 50 | 54 | 58 | 61 | 62 | 63 | 64 | 65 | 67 | 70 | 73 | 76 | 79 | 105 | 183 |
| 33 | 47 | 50 | 54 | 58 | .. | 62 | 63 | 64 | 65 | 67 | 70 | 73 | 76 | 79 | 104 | 179 |
| 34 | 47 | 50 | 54 | 58 | 61 | 62 | 63 | 64 | 65 | 67 | 70 | 73 | 76 | 79 | 106 | 186 |
| 35 | 47 | 50 | 54 | 58 | 61 | 62 | 63 | 64 | 65 | 67 | 70 | 73 | 76 | 79 | 106 | .. |
| 36 | .. | .. | .. | 60 | .. | .. | .. | .. | .. | .. | .. | .. | .. | .. | 165 | .. |
| 37 | .. | 51 | 55 | 59 | .. | .. | .. | .. | .. | .. | .. | .. | .. | .. | 147 | .. |
| 38 | .. | .. | 55 | .. | .. | .. | .. | .. | .. | .. | .. | .. | .. | .. | 139 | .. |
| 39 | .. | .. | .. | .. | .. | .. | .. | .. | .. | .. | .. | .. | .. | .. | 154 | .. |
| 40 | 46 | 50 | 51 | 58 | .. | .. | .. | .. | .. | 07 | 70 | 73 | 76 | 79 | 94 | .. |
| 41 | .. | .. | .. | 59 | .. | .. | .. | .. | .. | 68 | 71 | 74 | 77 | 80 | 128 | .. |
| 42 | 47 | .. | 55 | 59 | .. | .. | .. | .. | .. | 68 | 71 | 74 | 77 | 80 | 129 | .. |
| 43 | .. | .. | 55 | .. | .. | .. | .. | .. | .. | 68 | .. | .. | .. | .. | 129 | .. |
| 44 | .. | .. | .. | .. | .. | .. | .. | .. | .. | .. | .. | .. | .. | .. | 128 | .. |
| 45 | .. | .. | 54 | 58 | .. | .. | .. | .. | .. | .. | .. | .. | .. | .. | 103 | .. |
| 46 | 47 | 51 | 55 | 59 | .. | .. | .. | .. | .. | 67 | 70 | 73 | 77 | 79 | 110 | .. |
| 47 | .. | .. | 55 | .. | .. | .. | .. | .. | .. | 68 | .. | .. | .. | .. | 129 | .. |
| 48 | 47 | 50 | 54 | 58 | 61 | 62 | 63 | 64 | 65 | 67 | 70 | 73 | 76 | 79 | 106 | 186 |
| 49 | .. | .. | .. | .. | .. | .. | .. | .. | .. | .. | .. | .. | .. | .. | 147 | .. |
| 50 | .. | 51 | 55 | .. | .. | .. | .. | .. | .. | .. | .. | .. | .. | .. | 139 | .. |
| 51 | .. | .. | .. | 60 | .. | .. | .. | .. | .. | .. | .. | .. | .. | .. | 166 | .. |
| 52 | .. | 51 | .. | .. | .. | .. | .. | .. | .. | .. | .. | .. | .. | .. | 148 | .. |
| 53 | 48 | .. | .. | .. | .. | .. | .. | .. | .. | .. | .. | .. | .. | .. | 140 | .. |
| 54 | .. | .. | .. | .. | .. | .. | .. | .. | .. | .. | .. | .. | .. | .. | 113 | .. |
| 55 | 47 | 50 | 54 | 58 | 61 | 62 | 63 | 64 | 65 | 67 | 70 | 73 | 76 | 79 | 106 | .. |
| 56 | .. | .. | .. | .. | .. | .. | .. | .. | .. | 67 | 70 | 73 | 76 | .. | 90 | .. |
| 57 | .. | .. | .. | 60 | .. | .. | .. | .. | .. | .. | .. | .. | .. | .. | 166 | .. |

(See Note on first

*Continued*

page of Index)

| LINE No. | 3D2 | 3D3 | 3D4 | 3D5 | 3E1 | 3E2 | 3E3 | 3E4 | 3E5 | 3F1 | 3F2 | 3F3 | 3F4 | 3F5 | 4 | 5 |
|---|---|---|---|---|---|---|---|---|---|---|---|---|---|---|---|---|
| 1 | 48 | 51 | 55 | 59 | .. | .. | .. | .. | .. | .. | .. | .. | .. | .. | 148 | .. |
| 2 | 48 | 51 | 55 | .. | 61 | 62 | 63 | 64 | 65 | .. | .. | .. | .. | .. | 141 | .. |
| 3 | 48 | 52 | 56 | .. | .. | .. | .. | .. | .. | .. | .. | .. | .. | .. | 155 | .. |
| 4 | 48 | 52 | 56 | 60 | .. | .. | .. | .. | .. | .. | .. | .. | .. | .. | 160 | .. |
| 5 | .. | .. | .. | .. | .. | .. | .. | .. | .. | .. | .. | .. | .. | .. | 113 | .. |
| 6 | .. | 51 | 55 | 59 | .. | .. | .. | .. | .. | .. | .. | .. | .. | .. | 135 | .. |
| 7 | .. | .. | .. | .. | .. | .. | .. | .. | .. | .. | .. | .. | .. | .. | 136 | .. |
| 8 | .. | .. | .. | .. | .. | .. | .. | .. | .. | .. | .. | .. | .. | .. | 144 | .. |
| 9 | .. | .. | .. | .. | .. | .. | .. | .. | .. | .. | .. | .. | .. | .. | 151 | .. |
| 10 | .. | 52 | 56 | .. | .. | .. | .. | .. | .. | .. | .. | .. | .. | .. | 151 | .. |
| 11 | .. | .. | 56 | .. | .. | .. | .. | .. | .. | .. | .. | .. | .. | .. | 157 | .. |
| 12 | 48 | 51 | 55 | 59 | .. | .. | .. | .. | .. | .. | .. | .. | .. | .. | 143 | .. |
| 13 | .. | .. | .. | 60 | .. | .. | .. | .. | .. | .. | .. | .. | .. | .. | 162 | .. |
| 14 | 48 | 51 | .. | 59 | .. | .. | .. | .. | .. | .. | .. | .. | .. | .. | 144 | .. |
| 15 | 48 | 51 | 55 | 59 | .. | .. | .. | .. | .. | .. | .. | .. | .. | .. | 136 | .. |
| 16 | .. | .. | .. | 60 | .. | .. | .. | .. | .. | .. | .. | .. | .. | .. | 152 | .. |
| 17 | 48 | .. | 56 | .. | .. | .. | .. | .. | .. | .. | .. | .. | .. | .. | 157 | .. |
| 18 | .. | .. | .. | .. | .. | .. | .. | .. | .. | .. | .. | .. | .. | .. | 130 | .. |
| 19 | .. | .. | .. | .. | .. | .. | .. | .. | .. | .. | .. | .. | .. | .. | 133 | .. |
| 20 | 46 | 50 | 54 | 58 | .. | .. | .. | .. | .. | 67 | 70 | 73 | 76 | 79 | 95 | 178 |
| 21 | .. | .. | .. | .. | .. | .. | .. | .. | .. | 68 | 71 | 74 | 77 | 80 | 132 | .. |
| 22 | .. | .. | .. | .. | .. | .. | .. | .. | .. | 68 | 71 | 74 | 77 | 80 | 132 | .. |
| 23 | 46 | 50 | 54 | 58 | .. | .. | .. | .. | .. | .. | .. | .. | .. | .. | 95 | .. |
| 24 | 46 | .. | .. | 58 | .. | .. | .. | .. | .. | .. | .. | .. | .. | .. | 96 | .. |
| 25 | .. | .. | .. | .. | .. | .. | .. | .. | .. | .. | .. | .. | .. | .. | 130 | .. |
| 26 | .. | .. | .. | .. | 61 | 62 | 63 | 64 | 65 | .. | .. | .. | .. | .. | 104 | .. |
| 27 | .. | .. | .. | .. | .. | .. | 63 | 64 | 65 | .. | .. | .. | .. | .. | 97 | .. |
| 28 | .. | .. | .. | .. | .. | .. | .. | .. | .. | 67 | .. | .. | .. | .. | 110 | .. |
| 29 | .. | .. | .. | .. | .. | .. | .. | .. | .. | 67 | 70 | 73 | 76 | 79 | 100 | .. |
| 30 | 46 | 50 | 54 | 58 | 61 | 62 | 63 | 64 | 65 | 67 | 70 | 73 | 76 | 79 | 96 | 169 |
| 31 | 46 | 50 | .. | .. | .. | .. | .. | .. | .. | .. | .. | .. | .. | .. | 89 | .. |
| 32 | .. | .. | .. | .. | .. | .. | .. | .. | .. | .. | .. | .. | .. | .. | 127 | .. |

July 6, 1915.

HON. MORGAN J. O'BRIEN, *Chairman*

Constitutional Convention Commission,
Albany, N. Y.

*Dear Judge O'Brien:*

At the request of the Constitutional Convention Commission, I undertook two months ago to prepare for the use of the Constitutional Convention detailed comparative statements of the revenues and expenditures of the City of New York, covering a five-year period, from 1910 to 1914, inclusive.

These statements have now been completed and are presented herewith, in a printed volume, in summary and in detail, together with an explanatory note setting forth, in brief, a description of the contents of the volume.

In connection with the preparation of this volume, I desire to record my appreciation of the very valuable assistance and co-operation rendered by the Bureau of Municipal Research.

Sincerely yours,

(Signed) WM. A. PRENDERGAST,
*Comptroller.*

# THE CITY OF NEW YORK

## DEPARTMENT OF FINANCE

WILLIAM A. PRENDERGAST, *Comptroller*

## EXPLANATORY NOTE

The financial statements contained in this volume have been compiled and arranged with the purpose in view of presenting in a quickly digestible form, summary and detailed information for the five years from 1910 to 1914, inclusive, relating to expenditures, revenues collected and other cash receipts, taxes levied and collected, and deficiencies in taxes.

The aim has been to make this information comprehensive and complete and to provide a basis for comparison, which would be helpful to anyone desirous of obtaining information relating to the city's finances.

**The order of presentation is as follows:**

SECTION I—Summary and Detailed Statements of Expenditures of the city as a whole.

SECTION II—Detailed Statements of Unit Costs and Functional Expenses of the principal larger departments.

SECTION III—Summary and Detailed Statements of Revenues Collected and Other Cash Receipts.

SECTION IV—Summary and Detailed Statements of Taxes Levied and Collected, and Deficiencies in Taxes.

**Expenditures.**—Section I, pages 1 to 166, consists of summary and detailed statements relating to the expenditures of the city as a whole. These statements present analyses of expenditures in two ways, viz.: (1) by organization units; and (2) by objects of expenditure. The term "organization units" is here used to mean subdivisions of the city and county governments, i.e., departments, boards, commissions, courts, etc. The term "objects of expenditure," as here used, means the kind of things purchased by the city. The classification is as follows: (1) personal service; (2) supplies; (3) equipment; (4) materials; (5) contract or open order service; (6) contingencies; (7) fixed charges and contributions; (8) unclassified. The plan that has been followed throughout of grouping together departments, boards, commissions, etc., according to the division of responsibility for expenditures, is intended to indicate in a general way the controlling authority that ultimately must be looked to, to initiate and effect the needed economies in the conduct of the business of the individual units of organization comprised within the several groups. The expenditures for the year 1910 as set forth in the statements under Section I, not only include the disbursements during that year applicable to that year's expenses, but also include all disbursements made up to March 31, 1915, which were applicable to the expenses of 1910. To the sum thus produced was added all liabilities unliquidated (i.e., unpaid) at March 31, 1915, but which represent expenditures applicable to the year 1910. The expenditures under each of the other years were similarly computed. There is one respect in which the total expenditures for the respective years do not represent accurate costs, namely, the accounts are on the basis of amounts paid out and the differences between the inventory (i.e., the value of commodities in stores) at the beginning and end of the year have not been taken into account, as this information was not available.

Section II, pages 167 to 202, consists of a series of tabulations setting forth in detail unit costs of operation and expenses of the principal larger departments, classified according to functions performed. In the cases of the department of water supply, gas and electricity and the department of docks and ferries, the income derived from the sale of water and from the leasing of dock and wharfage privileges and the earnings from the operation of municipal ferries is also shown, contrasted with the cost of operation. The expenditures as set forth in the statements under this section are not on the basis of amounts paid out, but are on the basis of things used, and hence more accurately represent costs.

## Revenues Collected and Other Cash Receipts

Section III, pages 203 to 219, relating to receipts, attempts to show all moneys received by or on account of the city and county governments, or by any of the following classes of funds:

1 City treasury—general fund.

2 City treasury—special and trust funds.

3 Sinking funds.

4 Funds not deposited with or administered by the central financial offices of the city government.

Receipts of the fourth class of funds, above named, are shown in the statement and supporting schedules on pages 216 to 219. The total amount of these receipts is comparatively not large, but the fact that they are collected and expended without the audit of the comptroller, or the direction of the board of estimate and apportionment, is significant.

The receipts of the treasury and of the sinking funds are shown in the summary statement on page 203, and in the following detailed statement on pages 204 to 215. These statements present in the first column an outline of the revenues and other receipts of the treasury or of the sinking funds. The remaining columns are used to show with reference to each item in the first column the following facts:

1 The collecting department, bureau or office.

2 The statutory authorization.

3 Amount collected in each of the years, 1910–1914, inclusive.

4 The total amount collected in the five years from 1910–1914, inclusive.

5 Whether the moneys collected were received into the general fund, into the special and trust funds or into the sinking funds.

Attention is called to the fact that in order to show the entire receipts of these three classes of funds, it is necessary to include certain items which do not represent net receipts of the city as a unit, but which are merely payments from one class of funds into another class. On account of this fact, the footing of the total column cannot be used as the amount of the total receipts of the city.

Illustrations of these transfers between funds are found in the following items:

1 Proceeds of New York City bonds sold.
2 Interest on New York City bonds held by the sinking funds.
3 Redemption of New York City bonds held by sinking funds.
4 Budget appropriations for annual installments to the sinking funds.
5 Transfers from water revenue, Brooklyn, to water sinking fund of the city of Brooklyn.

In the summary statement it is attempted to distinguish between revenues and other receipts.

## Taxes Levied and Collected and Deficiencies in Taxes

Section IV, pages 220 to 229, consists of summary and detailed statements having to do with the levy and collection of taxes, and with losses through uncollectable taxes, and with the provisions that have been made for making good the deficiencies occasioned thereby. These statements cover the period from consolidation, January 1, 1898, to December 31, 1913. They show that in this period the losses from uncollectable taxes amounted to $94,000,000 and that practically $63,000,000 of this total arose from taxes on personal property. The credit side of the summary statement shows that up to December 31, 1913, $68,000,000 had been applied towards funding this deficiency and that in addition $13,000,000 of corporate stock had been authorized for this purpose, but was at that time unissued. These two items with some minor credits make up a total of $86,000,000 authorized for funding deficiencies in taxes, leaving an estimated deficit of $8,000,000, of which $6,112,092 has been provided for in the 1915 budget.

# SECTION I

---

## SUMMARY AND DETAILED STATEMENTS OF EXPENDITURES OF THE CITY AS A WHOLE

# THE CITY OF

**Recapitulation of Comparative Summary Statement Showing the Total Annual 1914, Inclusive, Grouped to Indicate**

| | Line No. |
|---|---|
| City Departments, Offices, Courts, Etc. | |
| Mayor and Subordinate Departments, Bureaus and Offices: | |
| Mayor's Office and Departments whose executive heads are appointed by the Mayor and who are removable at his pleasure | 1 |
| Departments whose heads are appointed by the Mayor for a term of office greater than his own, and who are removable only upon charges | 2 |
| Boards and Commissions, majority of which are appointed by the Mayor and for which no other elected City Official shares responsibility | 3 |
| Total Mayor and Subordinate Departments, Bureaus and Offices | 4 |
| Comptroller and Finance Department, excluding the Chamberlains Office | 5 |
| Borough Presidents and Subordinate Departments: | |
| President, Borough of Manhattan | 6 |
| President, Borough of The Bronx | 7 |
| President, Borough of Brooklyn | 8 |
| President, Borough of Queens | 9 |
| President, Borough of Richmond | 10 |
| Total, Borough Presidents | 11 |
| Board of Aldermen, President of Board and City Clerk | 12 |
| Boards, Commissions, etc., whose members are not elected by popular vote and who are not appointed by any elected City official | 13 |
| Boards, Commissions, etc., of mixed responsibility, i.e., ex-officio bodies representing two or more bodies of preceding branches | 14 |
| Courts, including Board of Parole and General Interpreters of Brooklyn | 15 |
| Total City Departments, Offices, Courts, etc | 16 |
| Debt Service | 17 |
| Fixed Charges other than Debt Service, Subsidies, Contributions, Payments to Private and State Institutions, Expenditures not Allotted to Departments | 18 |
| Deficiencies in Taxes | 19 |
| Borough Assessments | 20 |
| Advances for Local Improvements | 21 |
| Total for City Purposes | 22 |
| Direct State Taxes | 23 |
| County Expenditures | |
| New York County | 24 |
| Kings County | 25 |
| Queens County | 26 |
| Richmond County | 27 |
| Bronx County | 28 |
| Total for County Purposes | 29 |
| Total for all Purposes | 30 |

# NEW YORK

EXPENDITURES FROM REVENUE AND CORPORATE STOCK FUNDS FOR THE YEARS 1910 TO THE DIVISION OF RESPONSIBILITY:

| LINE No. | Refer to Page | 1910 | 1911 | 1912 | 1913 | 1914 |
|---|---|---|---|---|---|---|
| 1 | 2 | $79,785,039 09 | $84,622,020 49 | $76,039,102 30 | $84,351,334 37 | $74,953,461 54 |
| 2 | 2 | 54,937,821 25 | 63,405,860 84 | 65,805,860 36 | 65,865,637 29 | 61,097,839 35 |
| 3 | 2 | 93,088 57 | 100,441 83 | 192,203 56 | 169,786 35 | 136,981 74 |
| 4 | 2 | **$134,815,948 91** | **$148,128,323 16** | **$142,037,166 22** | **$150,386,758 01** | **$136,188,282 63** |
| 5 | 3 | **$1,480,584 57** | **$1,379,582 70** | **$1,465,235 93** | **$1,672,732 14** | **$1,548,255 08** |
| 6 | 3 | $4,759,780 42 | $5,203,199 66 | $5,978,881 06 | $5,870,167 80 | $5,009,511 50 |
| 7 | 3 | 1,978,854 25 | 1,507,567 48 | 2,031,536 60 | 2,180,866 28 | 1,837,387 08 |
| 8 | 3 | 3,794,473 92 | 3,588,603 79 | 4,292,329 13 | 4,189,227 50 | 3,190,997 67 |
| 9 | 3 | 1,765,724 21 | 1,699,606 46 | 2,224,604 96 | 2,643,639 81 | 2,572,513 13 |
| 10 | 3 | 1,212,643 84 | 1,157,061 41 | 1,374,896 06 | 1,616,915 61 | 1,058,637 47 |
| 11 | 3 | **$13,511,476 64** | **$13,156,038 80** | **$15,902,247 81** | **$16,500,817 00** | **$13,669,046 85** |
| 12 | 3 | **$281,815 63** | **$326,660 73** | **$397,368 75** | **$345,750 97** | **$357,446 11** |
| 13 | 3 | **$7,699,905 33** | **$11,604,045 77** | **$13,345,489 57** | **$29,342,319 59** | **$27,791,266 62** |
| 14 | 3 | **$2,837,451 15** | **$2,414,645 22** | **$3,278,990 04** | **$3,346,248 02** | **$3,708,998 82** |
| 15 | 3 | **$2,061,229 15** | **$2,352,063 07** | **$2,429,050 99** | **$2,523,003 81** | **$2,586,057 83** |
| 16 | 3 | **$162,688,411 38** | **$179,361,359 45** | **$178,855,549 61** | **$204,117,629 54** | **$185,849,353 94** |
| 17 | 3 | ***$44,743,741 92** | ***$49,550,488 56** | ***$50,218,374 43** | ***$54,533,439 05** | ***$52,491,846 15** |
| 18 | 4 | **$12,895,797 87** | **$10,981,649 96** | **$11,649,620 98** | **$12,391,841 05** | **$16,671,338 00** |
| 19 | 4 | **†$4,000,000 00** | **†$10,000,000 00** | **†$3,287,366 74** | **†$2,300,000 00** | **†$2,500,000 00** |
| 20 | 4 | .......... | .......... | .......... | .......... | **$520,015 06** |
| 21 | 4 | **$16,085,308 01** | **$13,095,611 67** | **$15,200,511 22** | **$17,877,055 22** | **$20,779,517 54** |
| 22 | 4 | **$240,413,259 18** | **$262,989,109 64** | **$259,211,422 98** | **$291,219,964 86** | **$278,812,070 69** |
| 23 | 4 | .......... | .......... | **$4,301,345 65** | **$7,947,031 96** | **$4,576,303 43** |
| 24 | 5 | $3,319,978 27 | $3,530,105 98 | $3,719,929 84 | $3,857,528 36 | $3,857,815 20 |
| 25 | 5 | 1,594,864 36 | 1,676,995 10 | 1,701,040 45 | 1,767,380 30 | 1,841,120 93 |
| 26 | 5 | 341,462 70 | 356,695 67 | 379,511 61 | 426,733 40 | 447,656 36 |
| 27 | 5 | 111,470 72 | 109,185 22 | 119,498 76 | 132,831 48 | 141,872 11 |
| 28 | 6 | .......... | .......... | .......... | 14,501 45 | 537,359 93 |
| 29 | 6 | **$5,367,776 05** | **$5,672,981 97** | **$5,919,980 66** | **$6,198,974 99** | **$6,825,824 53** |
| 30 | 6 | **$245,781,035 23** | **$268,662,091 61** | **$269,432,749 29** | **$305,365,971 81** | **$290,214,198 65** |

*N.B.—These amounts include the redemption of Special Revenue Bonds issued to defray expenditures during the year prior to their redemption, as follows:

*$5,208,150 00*   *$7,264,625 00*   *$5,970,164 92*   *$7,038,065 51*   *$6,319,225 00*

† In addition to these amounts provided through the budget there were also provided through application of the proceeds from the sales of corporate stock, under chapter 208 laws of 1906, the following amounts:

*$3,038,303 75*   *$7,045,529 04*   *$5,036,851 60*   *$5,000,000 00*   *$...........*

COMPARATIVE SUMMARY STATEMENT SHOWING THE TOTAL ANNUAL EXPENDITURES FROM REVENUE AND
FOR I. CITY DEPARTMENTS, OFFICES, COURTS, ETC., GROUPED TO INDICATE THE DIVISION OF
OTHER THAN DEBT SERVICE; IV. DEFICIENCIES IN TAXES; V. BOROUGH ASSESSMENTS; VI.

| | LINE No. |
|---|---|
| I. CITY DEPARTMENTS, OFFICES, COURTS, ETC. | |
| Mayor and Subordinate Departments Bureaus and Offices: | |
| Mayor's Office and Departments whose executive heads are appointed by the Mayor and are removable at his pleasure: | |
| Commissioner of Accounts | 1 |
| Board of Ambulance Service | 2 |
| Board of Assessors | 3 |
| Department of Bridges | 4 |
| Brooklyn Grade Crossing Commission | 5 |
| City Chamberlain | 6 |
| Change of Grade Damage Commission | 7 |
| Department of Correction | 8 |
| Department of Docks and Ferries | 9 |
| Examining Board of Plumbers | 10 |
| Fire Department | 11 |
| Department of Health | 12 |
| Commission for the Improvement and Development of Jamaica Bay | 13 |
| Law Department | 14 |
| Commissioner of Licenses | 15 |
| Mayoralty—Adminstration | 16 |
| Mayoralty—Bureau of Licenses | 17 |
| Mayoralty—Bureau of Weights and Measures | 18 |
| Metropolitan Sewerage Commission | 19 |
| Municipal Civil Service Commission | 20 |
| Municipal Explosives Commission | 21 |
| Park Board | 22 |
| Department of Parks—Manhattan and Richmond | 23 |
| Department of Parks—The Bronx | 24 |
| Department of Parks—Brooklyn | 25 |
| Department of Parks—Queens | 26 |
| Police Department | 27 |
| Department of Public Charities | 28 |
| Department of Street Cleaning | 29 |
| Department of Taxes and Assessments | 30 |
| Tenement House Department | 31 |
| Department of Water Supply, Gas and Electricity | 32 |
| Department of Water Supply, Gas and Electricity—Water Meter Fund | 33 |
| Total | 34 |
| Departments whose heads are appointed by the Mayor for a term of office greater than his own, and who are removable only upon charges: | |
| Aqueduct Commission | 35 |
| Bellevue and Allied Hospitals | 36 |
| College of the City of New York | 37 |
| Department of Education | 38 |
| Normal College of the City of New York | 39 |
| Board of Water Supply | 40 |
| Total | 41 |
| Boards and Commissions majority of which are appointed by the Mayor and for which no other elected City official shares responsibility: | |
| Art Commission | 42 |
| Brooklyn Disciplinary Training School for Boys | 43 |
| Committee on Congestion of Population | 44 |
| Board of Inebriety | 45 |
| Permanent Census Board | 46 |
| Public Recreation Commission | 47 |
| Total | 48 |
| Total, Mayor and Subordinate Departments, Bureaus and Offices | 49 |

# NEW YORK

Corporate Stock Funds for the Years 1910 to 1914, Inclusive, Classified to Show Expenditures
Responsibility for each Group; II. Debt Service; III. Fixed Charges, Contributions, etc.,
Advances for Local Improvements; VII. Direct State Taxes; VIII. County Expense:

| Line No. | Year | | | | |
|---|---|---|---|---|---|
| | 1910 | 1911 | 1912 | 1913 | 1914 |
| 1 | $206,139 64 | $215,398 94 | $214,664 46 | $195,977 82 | $219,940 04 |
| 2 | 628 39 | 9,430 14 | 11,581 09 | 76,863 55 | 79,910 51 |
| 3 | 42,525 67 | 42,256 47 | 42,883 68 | 41,364 34 | 40,150 52 |
| 4 | 9,854,606 36 | 15,980,942 70 | 5,642,472 10 | 5,687,421 96 | 3,910,726 72 |
| 5 | 200,000 00 | 330,000 00 | .......... | 262,500 00 | 365,000 00 |
| 6 | 54,273 86 | 61,382 66 | 61,437 60 | 62,134 14 | 59,568 47 |
| 7 | 36,835 71 | 798,203 96 | 410,846 42 | 173,132 49 | 7,156 63 |
| 8 | 1,563,756 13 | 1,334,221 68 | 1,301,689 06 | 1,507,014 23 | 1,419,418 77 |
| 9 | 8,034,419 58 | 5,086,910 67 | 4,624,730 42 | 11,817,421 91 | 4,520,171 40 |
| 10 | 6,920 48 | 5,373 50 | 5,586 46 | 5,350 58 | 3,908 42 |
| 11 | 8,365,116 27 | 8,402,019 58 | 9,522,989 00 | 10,755,012 98 | 10,373,509 67 |
| 12 | 3,011,892 49 | 2,959,497 71 | 3,474,352 87 | 3,575,308 83 | 3,585,046 76 |
| 13 | 40,793 10 | 460 00 | .......... | .......... | .......... |
| 14 | 770,000 94 | 802,469 75 | 804,112 35 | 862,078 90 | 855,199 96 |
| 15 | 51,647 87 | 50,284 54 | 50,498 25 | 50,592 28 | 28,231 22 |
| 16 | 53,066 44 | 53,695 55 | 54,738 69 | 55,595 28 | 62,083 83 |
| 17 | 44,984 04 | 83,137 77 | 82,093 03 | 115,764 35 | 137,812 61 |
| 18 | 37,558 80 | 65,483 05 | 72,158 60 | 64,686 35 | 76,964 27 |
| 19 | 39,916 17 | 41,820 72 | 46,721 54 | 43,422 52 | 24,997 13 |
| 20 | 149,279 61 | 156,655 66 | 189,983 09 | 211,715 97 | 200,792 38 |
| 21 | 3,970 37 | 16,467 50 | 9,878 93 | 14,516 25 | 8,966 17 |
| 22 | 25,512 19 | 25,310 74 | 31,646 66 | 29,884 36 | 29,222 30 |
| 23 | 1,597,906 50 | 1,714,329 05 | 2,047,038 93 | 2,108,399 57 | 1,474,672 46 |
| 24 | 819,243 95 | 683,988 00 | 692,345 64 | 607,890 01 | 513,289 98 |
| 25 | 1,179,104 55 | 1,258,943 39 | 1,464,497 02 | 1,566,700 37 | 1,230,697 30 |
| 26 | .......... | 3,768 44 | 172,232 43 | 197,424 62 | 192,449 78 |
| 27 | 15,314,568 80 | 16,155,203 76 | 16,683,821 51 | 17,260,940 78 | 17,658,479 24 |
| 28 | 4,159,400 87 | 4,244,072 42 | 4,960,395 64 | 5,606,653 11 | 4,651,116 19 |
| 29 | 9,967,991 67 | 8,221,914 22 | 8,615,744 65 | 7,964,323 94 | 10,158,835 40 |
| 30 | 510,777 88 | 587,947 37 | 636,999 87 | 632,918 76 | 635,441 50 |
| 31 | 804,108 52 | 789,760 30 | 776,988 56 | 762,036 81 | 727,100 57 |
| 32 | 12,838,002 21 | 14,440,670 25 | 13,325,107 30 | 12,023,734 10 | 11,603,242 60 |
| 33 | .......... | .......... | 8,866 45 | 12,553 21 | 9,358 74 |
| 34 | **$79,785,039 09** | **$84,622,020 49** | **$76,039,102 30** | **$84,351,334 37** | **$74,953,461 54** |
| 35 | $1,316,228 48 | $1,109,534 04 | $11,600 67 | $51,225 10 | .......... |
| 36 | 1,906,953 73 | 1,790,212 81 | 1,976,801 57 | 2,699,367 59 | $2,157,973 02 |
| 37 | 631,477 71 | 682,065 15 | 630,363 72 | 691,063 42 | 700,209 00 |
| 38 | 31,318,787 51 | 33,472,978 53 | 38,927,238 35 | 40,401,779 06 | 43,511,022 83 |
| 39 | 371,956 33 | 402,504 38 | 675,879 95 | 669,780 25 | 621,138 91 |
| 40 | 19,392,417 49 | 25,948,565 93 | 23,583,976 10 | 21,352,421 87 | 14,107,495 59 |
| 41 | **$54,937,821 25** | **$63,405,860 84** | **$65,805,860 36** | **$65,865,637 29** | **$61,097,839 35** |
| 42 | $7,587 79 | $7,573 00 | $7,552 45 | $7,551 11 | $7,132 82 |
| 43 | 56,783 63 | 55,477 25 | 56,731 06 | 54,267 79 | 29,013 78 |
| 44 | .......... | .......... | 1,457 12 | .......... | .......... |
| 45 | .......... | 887 19 | 77,494 25 | 15,178 73 | 25,688 49 |
| 46 | 28,717 15 | 36,504 39 | 36,669 65 | 73,474 96 | 54,717 04 |
| 47 | .......... | .......... | 12,299 03 | 19,313 76 | 20,429 61 |
| 48 | **$93,088 57** | **$100,441 83** | **$192,203 56** | **$169,786 35** | **$136,981 74** |
| 49 | **$134,815,948 91** | **$148,128,323 16** | **$142,037,166 22** | **$150,386,758 01** | **$136,188,282 63** |

# THE CITY OF

COMPARATIVE SUMMARY STATEMENT SHOWING THE TOTAL ANNUAL EXPENDITURES FROM REVENUE AND FOR I. CITY DEPARTMENTS, OFFICES, COURTS, ETC., GROUPED TO INDICATE THE DIVISION OF OTHER THAN DEBT SERVICE; IV. DEFICIENCIES IN TAXES; V. BOROUGH ASSESSMENTS; VI. AD

| | LINE No. |
|---|---|
| I. CITY DEPARTMENTS, OFFICES, COURTS, ETC.—*Continued* | |
| Comptroller and Finance Department, excluding the Chamberlain's Office: | |
| Department of Finance | 1 |
| Wallabout Market Funds | 2 |
| Total | 3 |
| Borough Presidents and Subordinate Departments: | |
| President, Borough of Manhattan | 4 |
| President, Borough of The Bronx | 5 |
| President, Borough of Brooklyn | 6 |
| President, Borough of Queens | 7 |
| President, Borough of Richmond | 8 |
| Total | 9 |
| Board of Aldermen, President of Board and City Clerk | 10 |
| Boards, Commissions, etc., whose members are not elected by popular vote and who are not appointed by any elected City official: | |
| Bronx Parkway Commission | 11 |
| Board of Building Examiners | 12 |
| Court House Board | 13 |
| Commissioners of Estimate and Appraisal | 14 |
| Commission on Lunacy | 15 |
| Public Service Commission | 16 |
| Water Pollution Commission | 17 |
| Total | 18 |
| Boards, Commissions, etc., of mixed responsibility, i.e., ex-officio bodies representing two or more preceding branches: | |
| Armory Board | 19 |
| Board of City Record, City of New York | 20 |
| * Board of Elections | 21 |
| Board of Estimate and Apportionment | 22 |
| Board of Revision of Assessments | 23 |
| Commissioners of the Sinking Fund | 24 |
| Total | 25 |
| Courts, including Board of Parole and General Interpreters, Brooklyn: | |
| Coroners, Borough of Manhattan | 26 |
| Coroners, Borough of The Bronx | 27 |
| Coroners, Borough of Brooklyn | 28 |
| Coroners, Borough of Queens | 29 |
| Coroners, Borough of Richmond | 30 |
| City Court of New York | 31 |
| City Magistrate's Court, First Division | 32 |
| City Magistrate's Courts, Second Division | 33 |
| Municipal Courts, City of New York | 34 |
| Court of Special Sessions | 35 |
| General Interpreters, Brooklyn | 36 |
| Board of Parole | 37 |
| Total | 38 |
| Total City Departments, Offices, Courts, etc | 39 |
| II. DEBT SERVICE | 40 |

* The Board of Elections is placed in this group for the reason that in the first two years covered by this statement it was responsible to the Mayor and in the last three years to the Board of Aldermen.

## NEW YORK

Corporate Stock Funds for the Years 1910 to 1914, Inclusive, Classified to Show Expenditures Responsibility for each Group; II. Debt Service; III. Fixed Charges, Contributions, etc., vances for Local Improvements; VII. Direct State Taxes; VIII. County Expense:—*Continued*

| Line No. | Year | | | | |
|---|---|---|---|---|---|
| | 1910 | 1911 | 1912 | 1913 | 1914 |
| 1 | $1,462,726 97 | $1,378,185 90 | $1,460,258 67 | $1,671,242 42 | $1,548,195 08 |
| 2 | 17,857 60 | 1,396 80 | 4,977 26 | 1,489 72 | 60 00 |
| 3 | **$1,480,584 57** | **$1,379,582 70** | **$1,465,235 93** | **$1,672,732 14** | **$1,548,255 08** |
| 4 | $4,759,780 42 | $5,203,199 66 | $5,978,881 06 | $5,870,167 80 | $5,009,511 50 |
| 5 | 1,978,854 25 | 1,507,567 48 | 2,031,536 60 | 2,180,866 28 | 1,837,387 08 |
| 6 | 3,794,473 92 | 3,588,603 79 | 4,292,329 13 | 4,189,227 50 | 3,190,997 67 |
| 7 | 1,765,724 21 | 1,699,606 46 | 2,224,604 96 | 2,643,639 81 | 2,572,513 13 |
| 8 | 1,212,643 84 | 1,157,061 41 | 1,374,896 06 | 1,616,915 61 | 1,058,637 47 |
| 9 | **$13,511,476 64** | **$13,156,038 80** | **$15,902,247 81** | **$16,500,817 00** | **$13,669,046 85** |
| 10 | **$281,815 63** | **$326,660 73** | **$397,368 75** | **$345,750 97** | **$357,446 11** |
| 11 | .......... | $5,408 91 | $31,206 80 | $796,618 12 | $1,159,103 87 |
| 12 | $9,423 53 | 9,340 29 | 9,108 47 | 8,702 03 | 9,038 96 |
| 13 | 1,591 73 | 572 40 | 32,247 62 | 6,485,390 98 | 183,440 09 |
| 14 | 21,220 24 | 16,523 16 | 15,472 56 | .......... | .......... |
| 15 | .......... | .......... | 3,590 30 | 1,120 80 | .......... |
| 16 | 7,666,255 43 | 11,572,201 01 | 13,253,864 12 | 22,050,487 66 | 26,439,683 70 |
| 17 | 1,414 40 | .......... | .......... | .......... | .......... |
| 18 | **$7,699,905 33** | **$11,604,045 77** | **$13,345,489 87** | **$29,342,319 59** | **$27,791,266 62** |
| 19 | $636,481 21 | $479,535 93 | $723,680 51 | $820,703 51 | $758,481 15 |
| 20 | 1,084,596 62 | 828,534 54 | 865,849 77 | 920,152 39 | 915,646 16 |
| 21 | 959,889 36 | 926,305 38 | 1,395,828 00 | 1,186,804 05 | 1,492,016 88 |
| 22 | 153,229 71 | 176,965 32 | 286,618 15 | 414,760 32 | 539,204 70 |
| 23 | .......... | 104 75 | .......... | .......... | 88 00 |
| 24 | 3,254 25 | 3,199 30 | 7,013 61 | 3,827 75 | 3,561 93 |
| 25 | **$2,837,451 15** | **$2,414,645 22** | **$3,278,090 04** | **$3,346,248 02** | **$3,708,998 82** |
| 26 | $64,194 29 | $67,154 13 | $62,675 31 | $63,483 00 | $63,480 32 |
| 27 | 29,754 98 | 30,241 26 | 29,985 44 | 30,559 19 | 30,315 89 |
| 28 | 32,989 87 | 36,481 41 | 34,578 73 | 35,323 71 | 31,362 53 |
| 29 | 19,154 66 | 18,660 55 | 19,422 59 | 19,903 22 | 19,951 82 |
| 30 | 12,151 79 | 12,134 37 | 12,090 52 | 12,077 89 | 12,054 59 |
| 31 | 233,768 20 | 235,537 60 | 246,774 69 | 254,862 24 | 255,754 63 |
| 32 | 291,653 25 | 373,843 38 | 381,949 84 | 414,332 59 | 449,732 14 |
| 33 | 250,520 43 | 339,546 57 | 360,562 06 | 370,911 62 | 388,244 52 |
| 34 | 894,695 56 | 908,377 52 | 927,241 80 | 930,515 56 | 929,492 36 |
| 35 | 219,178 26 | 316,909 08 | 340,390 84 | 373,409 79 | 388,224 03 |
| 36 | 10,200 00 | 10,200 00 | 9,148 27 | 9,000 00 | 8,800 00 |
| 37 | 2,967 86 | 2,977 20 | 4,230 90 | 8,625 00 | 8,645 00 |
| 38 | **$2,061,229 15** | **$2,352,063 07** | **$2,429,050 99** | **$2,523,003 81** | **$2,586,057 83** |
| 39 | **$162,688,411 38** | **$179,361,359 45** | **$178,855,549 61** | **$204,117,629 54** | **$185,849,353 94** |
| 40 | ***$44,743,741 92** | ***$49,550,488 56** | ***$50,218,374 43** | ***$54,533,439 05** | ***$52,491,846 15** |

* N. B.—These amounts include the Redemption of Special Revenue Bonds issued to defray expenditures during the year prior to their redemption, as follows:

*$5,208,150 00*　　*$7,264,625 00*　　*$5,970,164 92*　　*$7,038,065 51*　　*$6,319,225 00*

Comparative Summary Statement Showing the Total Annual Expenditures from Revenue and for I. City Departments, Offices, Courts, etc., Grouped to Indicate the Division of other than Debt Service; IV. Deficiencies in Taxes; V. Borough Assessments; VI. Ad

| | Line No. |
|---|---|
| III. Fixed Charges, other than Debt Service, Subsidies, Contributions, Payments to Private and State Institutions, Expenditures not allotted to Departments: | |
| American Museum of Natural History | 1 |
| Botanical Garden and Arboretum | 2 |
| Charitable Institutions—City | 3 |
| Children's Museum, Brooklyn | 4 |
| Claims | 5 |
| Excise Taxes, Special Account | 6 |
| Grant's Tomb | 7 |
| Jumel Mansion | 8 |
| Metropolitan Museum of Art | 9 |
| Miscellaneous—City | 10 |
| Inactive Accounts, Miscellaneous | 11 |
| Museum of Arts and Sciences | 12 |
| New York Aquarium | 13 |
| New York Botanical Garden | 14 |
| New York Zoological Garden | 15 |
| New York Public Library Building | 16 |
| Brooklyn Public Library | 17 |
| New York Public Library | 18 |
| Queensborough Public Library | 19 |
| Staten Island Association of Art and Sciences | 20 |
| United States Volunteer Life Saving Corps | 21 |
| Total | 22 |
| IV. Deficiencies in Taxes | 23 |
| V. Borough Assessments: | |
| Manhattan | 24 |
| Brooklyn | 25 |
| Total Borough Assessments | 26 |
| VI. Advances for Local Improvements: | |
| Fund for Street and Park Openings | 27 |
| Street Improvement Fund | 28 |
| Total Advances for Local Improvements | 29 |
| Total for City Purposes | 30 |
| VII. Direct State Taxes: | |
| New York County | 31 |
| Kings County | 32 |
| Queens County | 33 |
| Richmond County | 34 |
| Total Direct State Taxes | 35 |
| VIII. County Expenditures: | |
| New York County: | |
| Charitable Institutions | 36 |
| Board of City Record | 37 |
| County Clerk | 38 |
| Courts, General Sessions | 39 |
| Courts, Supreme, First Department | 40 |
| Courts, Supreme, First Department, Maintenance Appellate Division Court House | 41 |
| Courts, Surrogates' | 42 |
| District Attorney | 43 |
| Commissioner of Jurors | 44 |
| Miscellaneous | 45 |
| National Guard and Naval Militia | 46 |

Corporate Stock Funds for the Years 1910 to 1914, Inclusive, Classified to Show Expenditures Responsibility for each Group; II. Debt Service; III. Fixed Charges, Contributions, etc., vances for Local Improvements; VII. Direct State Taxes; VIII. County Expense:—*Continued*

| Line No. | Year 1910 | 1911 | 1912 | 1913 | 1914 |
|---|---|---|---|---|---|
| 1 | $185,757 00 | $189,757 00 | $195,000 00 | $200,000 00 | $200,000 00 |
| 2 | .......... | 14,741 31 | 25,782 40 | 29,459 22 | 37,636 08 |
| 3 | 4,511,647 65 | 4,362,537 93 | 4,431,326 77 | 4,550,374 28 | 5,184,610 06 |
| 4 | 11,861 29 | 11,900 39 | 12,499 43 | 13,121 35 | 13,227 21 |
| 5 | 1,780,056 75 | 287,795 36 | 1,582,360 56 | 1,780,061 72 | 4,392,750 73 |
| 6 | 1,216,161 58 | 1,343,648 71 | 1,340,403 12 | 1,389,008 64 | 1,383,323 53 |
| 7 | 7,000 00 | 7,000 00 | 6,817 15 | 4,692 64 | 4,927 27 |
| 8 | 4,129 85 | 4,487 48 | 5,437 45 | 4,410 96 | 4,163 21 |
| 9 | 200,000 00 | 200,000 00 | 200,000 00 | 200,000 00 | 200,000 00 |
| 10 | 2,071,078 70 | 2,216,367 27 | 1,968,852 23 | 2,345,525 88 | 3,313,940 94 |
| 11 | .......... | .......... | 1,850 72 | .......... | .......... |
| 12 | 93,555 59 | 93,334 00 | 97,623 48 | 102,181 86 | 106,744 33 |
| 13 | 45,974 86 | 47,567 22 | 46,597 08 | 47,335 62 | 46,995 53 |
| 14 | 82,936 32 | 85,981 40 | 90,072 46 | 103,222 19 | 107,163 00 |
| 15 | 167,632 00 | 174,579 74 | 179,272 87 | 189,570 36 | 200,000 00 |
| 16 | .......... | .......... | 10,000 00 | 17,999 37 | 48,500 00 |
| 17 | 418,915 69 | 421,716 86 | 447,814 54 | 552,492 13 | 468,708 45 |
| 18 | 1,965,610 33 | 1,365,195 03 | 841,420 06 | 684,455 94 | 785,624 36 |
| 19 | 118,488 80 | 135,040 26 | 143,997 99 | 155,374 71 | 152,028 37 |
| 20 | 3,991 46 | 9,000 00 | 9,448 44 | 9,318 74 | 8,639 79 |
| 21 | 11,000 00 | 11,000 00 | 13,044 23 | 13,235 44 | 12,355 14 |
| 22 | **$12,895,797 87** | **$10,981,649 96** | **$11,649,620 98** | **$12,391,841 05** | **$16,671,338 00** |
| 23 | ***$4,000,000 00** | ***$10,000,000 00** | ***$3,287,366 74** | ***$2,300,000 00** | **$2,500,000 00** |
| 24 | .......... | .......... | .......... | .......... | $144,448 63 |
| 25 | .......... | .......... | .......... | .......... | 375,566 43 |
| 26 | .......... | .......... | .......... | .......... | **$520,015 06** |
| 27 | $8,530,644 12 | $6,300,963 84 | $7,916,073 05 | $8,286,777 28 | $4,855,640 93 |
| 28 | 7,554,663 89 | 6,794,647 83 | 7,284,438 17 | 9,590,277 94 | 15,923,876 61 |
| 29 | **$16,085,308 01** | **$13,095,611 67** | **$15,200,511 22** | **$17,877,055 22** | **$20,779,517 54** |
| 30 | **$240,413,259 18** | **$262,989,109 64** | **$259,211,422 98** | **$291,219,964 86** | **$278,812,070 69** |
| 31 | .......... | .......... | $3,211,557 62 | $5,736,005 10 | $3,308,080 34 |
| 32 | .......... | .......... | 847,328 81 | 1,684,598 71 | 959,311 91 |
| 33 | .......... | .......... | 200,986 53 | 445,609 98 | 263,332 56 |
| 34 | .......... | .......... | 41,472 69 | 80,818 17 | 45,578 62 |
| 35 | .......... | .......... | **$4,301,345 65** | **$7,947,031 96** | **$4,576,303 43** |
| 36 | $113,875 22 | $112,995 01 | $105,153 59 | $102,928 80 | $78,905 98 |
| 37 | 34,984 60 | 38,614 40 | 39,882 29 | 41,389 61 | 34,203 26 |
| 38 | 150,588 53 | 159,835 33 | 232,157 85 | 191,848 10 | 193,736 08 |
| 39 | 292,318 27 | 314,139 08 | 351,901 91 | 378,996 31 | 404,724 90 |
| 40 | 823,294 42 | 858,978 84 | 918,868 42 | 976,589 75 | 990,529 66 |
| 41 | 30,780 02 | 30,613 14 | 27,374 34 | 30,812 63 | 28,792 71 |
| 42 | 176,862 30 | 175,787 12 | 184,348 10 | 203,676 02 | 193,683 54 |
| 43 | 371,242 25 | 409,108 45 | 450,536 90 | 469,877 03 | 522,847 74 |
| 44 | 50,341 57 | 52,548 46 | 52,122 28 | 52,782 22 | 57,181 14 |
| 45 | 575,347 82 | 587,591 28 | 449,071 18 | 482,962 87 | 475,295 09 |
| 46 | 185,828 75 | 200,132 25 | 212,527 50 | 223,931 00 | 221,101 00 |

* In addition to these amounts provided through the budget there were also provided through the application of the proceeds of sales of corporate stock, under chapter 208 of the laws of 1906, the following amounts:

*$3,038,303 75* *$7,045,529 04* *$5,036,851 60* *$5,000,000 00* $..........

COMPARATIVE SUMMARY STATEMENT SHOWING THE TOTAL ANNUAL EXPENDITURES FROM REVENUE AND FOR I. CITY DEPARTMENTS, OFFICES, COURTS, ETC., GROUPED TO INDICATE THE DIVISION OF OTHER THAN DEBT SERVICE; IV. DEFICIENCIES IN TAXES; V. BOROUGH ASSESSMENTS; VI. AD

| | LINE No. |
|---|---|
| **VIII.** COUNTY EXPENDITURES—*Continued* | |
| New York County:—*Continued* | |
| Public Administrator | 1 |
| Commissioner of Records | 2 |
| Commissioner of Records, Surrogates' Court | 3 |
| Register | 4 |
| Sheriff | 5 |
| Total | 6 |
| Kings County: | |
| Charitable Institutions | 7 |
| City Record | 8 |
| County Clerk | 9 |
| Courts, County | 10 |
| Courts, Supreme, Second Department | 11 |
| Courts, Supreme, Library | 12 |
| Courts, Surrogate's | 13 |
| District Attorney | 14 |
| Commissioner of Jurors | 15 |
| Miscellaneous | 16 |
| National Guard and Naval Militia | 17 |
| Public Administrator | 18 |
| Commissioner of Records | 19 |
| Register | 20 |
| Sheriff | 21 |
| Total | 22 |
| Queens County: | |
| Charitable Institutions | 23 |
| City Record | 24 |
| County Clerk | 25 |
| Courts—County | 26 |
| Courts—Supreme | 27 |
| Courts—Supreme, Library | 28 |
| Courts—Surrogate's | 29 |
| District Attorney | 30 |
| Commissioner of Jurors | 31 |
| Miscellaneous | 32 |
| National Guard and Naval Militia | 33 |
| Public Administrator | 34 |
| Sheriff | 35 |
| Total | 36 |
| Richmond County: | |
| Charitable Institutions | 37 |
| City Record | 38 |
| County Clerk | 39 |
| Courts—County and Surrogate's | 40 |
| Courts—Supreme | 41 |
| District Attorney | 42 |
| Commissioner of Jurors | 43 |
| Miscellaneous | 44 |
| National Guard and Naval Militia | 45 |
| Sheriff | 46 |
| Total | 47 |

## NEW YORK

CORPORATE STOCK FUNDS FOR THE YEARS 1910 TO 1914, INCLUSIVE, CLASSIFIED TO SHOW EXPENDITURES
RESPONSIBILITY FOR EACH GROUP; II. DEBT SERVICE; III. FIXED CHARGES, CONTRIBUTIONS, ETC.,
VANCES FOR LOCAL IMPROVEMENTS; VII. DIRECT STATE TAXES; VIII. COUNTY EXPENSE:—*Continued*

| LINE No. | YEAR | | | | |
|---|---|---|---|---|---|
| | 1910 | 1911 | 1912 | 1913 | 1914 |
| 1 | $26,096 50 | $26,284 87 | $25,377 42 | $26,784 06 | $27,261 86 |
| 2 | 70,243 37 | 72,461 81 | 96,523 35 | 100,300 62 | 96,680 42 |
| 3 | .......... | .......... | 44,817 93 | 49,691 25 | 47,517 17 |
| 4 | 228,750 64 | 310,302 35 | 317,650 04 | 314,615 92 | 279,280 05 |
| 5 | 189,424 01 | 180,713 59 | 211,616 74 | 210,342 18 | 206,074 60 |
| 6 | **$3,319,978 27** | **$3,530,105 98** | **$3,719,929 84** | **$3,857,528 36** | **$3,857,815 20** |
| 7 | $55,735 46 | $57,911 99 | $58,343 57 | $55,192 99 | $51,042 74 |
| 8 | 19,035 52 | 19,967 45 | 17,967 15 | 18,518 32 | 18,809 71 |
| 9 | 88,661 57 | 89,670 80 | 98,868 13 | 104,777 13 | 104,290 81 |
| 10 | 135,531 10 | 145,356 99 | 161,701 06 | 172,217 84 | 194,819 52 |
| 11 | 371,824 57 | 375,855 58 | 407,005 14 | 427,993 31 | 466,314 53 |
| 12 | 9,191 67 | 9,400 00 | 9,400 00 | 9,208 77 | 9,199 69 |
| 13 | 92,661 24 | 91,423 92 | 102,396 12 | 104,787 35 | 109,309 33 |
| 14 | 118,229 69 | 131,673 08 | 113,944 87 | 129,896 16 | 140,028 28 |
| 15 | 37,335 10 | 37,615 12 | 41,846 42 | 40,261 44 | 40,973 03 |
| 16 | 126,103 74 | 174,540 02 | 127,689 95 | 141,000 60 | 146,846 34 |
| 17 | 135,867 50 | 141,277 50 | 144,797 25 | 144,108 25 | 154,855 75 |
| 18 | .......... | .......... | 12,613 83 | 12,128 06 | 12,057 13 |
| 19 | 98,844 68 | 98,706 32 | 97,878 01 | 99,384 24 | 98,730 49 |
| 20 | 220,241 08 | 216,472 89 | 218,223 69 | 216,268 06 | 197,880 05 |
| 21 | 85,601 44 | 87,123 44 | 88,365 26 | 91,637 78 | 95,963 53 |
| 22 | **$1,594,864 36** | **$1,676,995 10** | **$1,701,040 45** | **$1,767,380 30** | **$1,841,120 93** |
| 23 | $5,244 05 | $6,415 41 | $5,920 50 | $6,374 61 | $5,668 71 |
| 24 | 3,648 58 | 3,062 83 | 2,157 27 | 3,780 61 | 3,989 95 |
| 25 | 27,212 54 | 37,086 02 | 77,643 53 | 107,228 67 | 127,866 34 |
| 26 | .......... | 33,139 66 | 39,904 23 | 43,022 73 | 42,428 26 |
| 27 | 146,779 64 | 69,953 19 | 73,714 73 | 94,715 94 | 95,586 38 |
| 28 | .......... | .......... | 2,272 65 | 2,566 43 | 2,308 06 |
| 29 | 17,822 67 | 23,348 18 | 23,793 60 | 23,946 59 | 26,898 03 |
| 30 | 30,740 49 | 38,319 94 | 32,176 02 | 35,872 22 | 40,747 17 |
| 31 | 11,708 16 | 11,779 12 | 10,732 04 | 12,626 86 | 12,253 88 |
| 32 | 14,296 30 | 51,899 64 | 33,517 90 | 38,242 52 | 38,801 57 |
| 33 | 5,020 00 | 5,110 00 | 5,124 00 | 5,110 00 | 5,110 00 |
| 34 | 1,200 00 | 1,200 00 | 1,200 00 | 1,200 00 | 1,306 00 |
| 35 | 77,790 27 | 75,381 68 | 71,355 14 | 52,046 22 | 44,692 01 |
| 36 | **$341,462 70** | **$356,695 67** | **$379,511 61** | **$426,733 40** | **$447,656 36** |
| 37 | $1,179 45 | $1,518 83 | $1,566 41 | $1,289 18 | $1,068 39 |
| 38 | 2,712 72 | 1,490 24 | 2,529 45 | 2,434 39 | 1,720 69 |
| 39 | 20,297 94 | 18,786 07 | 18,743 30 | 22,715 45 | 21,231 32 |
| 40 | 18,618 56 | 18,399 15 | 23,166 68 | 21,509 51 | 21,562 55 |
| 41 | 10,962 51 | 12,726 45 | 12,962 68 | 18,328 55 | 19,219 73 |
| 42 | 12,220 43 | 12,657 86 | 13,533 17 | 15,242 51 | 24,773 75 |
| 43 | 4,137 18 | 4,172 57 | 4,250 14 | 4,273 57 | 4,208 78 |
| 44 | 17,891 13 | 11,648 12 | 12,505 00 | 12,505 00 | 9,858 00 |
| 45 | .......... | .......... | .......... | 1,460 00 | 5,969 00 |
| 46 | 23,450 80 | 27,785 93 | 30,241 93 | 33,073 32 | 32,259 90 |
| 47 | **$111,470 72** | **$109,185 22** | **$119,498 76** | **$132,831 48** | **$141,872 11** |

COMPARATIVE SUMMARY STATEMENT SHOWING THE TOTAL ANNUAL EXPENDITURES FROM REVENUE AND FOR I. CITY DEPARTMENTS, OFFICES, COURTS, ETC., GROUPED TO INDICATE THE DIVISION OF OTHER THAN DEBT SERVICE; IV. DEFICIENCIES IN TAXES; V. BOROUGH ASSESSMENTS; VI. AD

| | LINE No. |
|---|---|
| VIII. COUNTY EXPENDITURES—*Continued* | |
| Bronx County: | |
| Charitable Institutions | 1 |
| City Record | 2 |
| County Clerk | 3 |
| Courts—County | 4 |
| Courts—Supreme, First Department | 5 |
| Courts—Surrogate's | 6 |
| District Attorney | 7 |
| Bronx County Law Library | 8 |
| Commissioner of Jurors | 9 |
| Miscellaneous | 10 |
| National Guard and Naval Militia | 11 |
| Public Administrator | 12 |
| Register | 13 |
| Sheriff | 14 |
| Total | 15 |
| Total for County Purposes | 16 |
| Total for All Purposes | 17 |

NEW YORK

Corporate Stock Funds for the Years 1910 to 1914, Inclusive, Classified to Show Expenditures Responsibility for each Group; II. Debt Service; III. Fixed Charges, Contributions, etc., vances for Local Improvements; VII. Direct State Taxes; VIII. County Expense:—*Continued*

| Line No. | Year 1910 | 1911 | 1912 | 1913 | 1914 |
|---|---|---|---|---|---|
| 1 | .......... | .......... | .......... | .......... | $24,621 52 |
| 2 | .......... | .......... | .......... | .......... | 11,799 30 |
| 3 | .......... | .......... | .......... | .......... | 64,743 72 |
| 4 | .......... | .......... | .......... | .......... | 37,260 01 |
| 5 | .......... | .......... | .......... | .......... | Included in New York County |
| 6 | .......... | .......... | .......... | .......... | 35,039 17 |
| 7 | .......... | .......... | .......... | .......... | 90,188 79 |
| 8 | .......... | .......... | .......... | .......... | 5,328 38 |
| 9 | .......... | .......... | .......... | $14,501 45 | 23,864 09 |
| 10 | .......... | .......... | .......... | .......... | 14,146 38 |
| 11 | .......... | .......... | .......... | .......... | 29,052 00 |
| 12 | .......... | .......... | .......... | .......... | 5,708 52 |
| 13 | .......... | .......... | .......... | .......... | 97,318 11 |
| 14 | .......... | .......... | .......... | .......... | 98,289 94 |
| 15 | .......... | .......... | .......... | **$14,501 45** | **$537,359 93** |
| 16 | **$5,367,776 05** | **$5,672,981 97** | **$5.919,980 66** | **$6,198,974 99** | **$6,825,824 53** |
| 17 | **$245,781,035 23** | **$268,662,091 61** | **$269,432,749 29** | **$305,365,971 81** | **$290,214,198 65** |

**Recapitulation of Comparative Summary Statement Showing Separately the Expenditures Made to Indicate the**

| | Refer to Page | 1910 Revenue Expenditures | 1910 Corporate Stock Expenditures | 1911 Revenue Expenditures | Line No. |
|---|---|---|---|---|---|
| City Departments, Offices, Courts, Etc. | | | | | |
| Mayor and Subordinate Departments, Bureaus and Offices: | | | | | |
| Mayor's Office and Departments, whose executive heads are appointed by the Mayor and who are removed at his pleasure. | 9 | $57,921,554 81 | $21,863,484 28 | $57,692,383 04 | 1 |
| Departments whose heads are appointed by the Mayor for a term of office greater than his own and who are removable only upon charges | 9 | 30,816,247 65 | 24,121,573 60 | 31,302,359 70 | 2 |
| Boards and Commissions, majorities of which are appointed by the Mayor and for which no other elected City Official shares responsibility | 9 | 93,088 57 | .......... | 100,441 83 | 3 |
| Total Mayor and Subordinate Departments, Bureaus and Offices | 9 | **$88,830,891 03** | **$45,985,057 88** | **$89,095,184 57** | 4 |
| Comptroller and Finance Department, excluding the Chamberlain's office | 9 | **$1,480,584 57** | .......... | **$1,379,582 70** | 5 |
| Borough Presidents and Subordinate Departments: | | | | | |
| President, Borough of Manhattan | 9 | $2,671,661 06 | $2,088,119 36 | $2,724,537 28 | 6 |
| President, Borough of The Bronx | 9 | 1,136,667 56 | 842,186 69 | 1,066,497 23 | 7 |
| President, Borough of Brooklyn | 9 | 2,156,603 26 | 1,637,870 66 | 2,038,207 61 | 8 |
| President, Borough of Queens | 10 | 1,373,024 95 | 392,699 26 | 1,356,075 79 | 9 |
| President, Borough of Richmond | 10 | 774,567 39 | 438,076 45 | 742,412 55 | 10 |
| Total, Borough Presidents | 10 | **$8,112,524 22** | **$5,398,952 42** | **$7,927,730 46** | 11 |
| Board of Aldermen, President of Board and City Clerk | 10 | **$281,815 63** | .......... | **$326,660 73** | 12 |
| Boards, Commissions, etc., whose members are not elected by popular vote and who are not appointed by any elected City Official | 10 | **$1,227,197 66** | **$6,472,707 67** | **$1,110,373 56** | 13 |
| Boards, Commissions, etc., of mixed responsibility, i.e., ex-officio bodies representing two or more of preceding branches. | 10 | **$2,306,328 35** | **$531,122 80** | **$2,077,168 99** | 14 |
| Courts, including Board of Parole and General Interpreters of Brooklyn | 11 | **$2,061,229 15** | .......... | **$2,352,063 07** | 15 |
| Total City Departments, Offices, Courts, etc | 11 | **$104,300,570 61** | **$58,387,840 77** | **$104,268,764 08** | 16 |
| Debt Service | 11 | ***$44,743,741 92** | †.......... | ***$49,550,488 56** | 17 |
| Fixed Charges other than Debt Service, Subsidies, Contributions, Payments to Private and State Institutions, Expenditures not Allotted to Departments | 11 | **$11,520,839 72** | **$1,374,958 15** | **$10,047,634 20** | 18 |
| Deficiencies in Taxes | 12 | **$4,000,000 00** | .......... | **$10,000,000 00** | 19 |
| Borough Assessments | 12 | .......... | .......... | .......... | 20 |
| Advances for Local Improvements | 12 | .......... | **$16,085,308 01** | .......... | 21 |
| Total for City Purposes | 12 | **$164,565,152 25** | **$75,848,106 93** | **$173,866,886 84** | 22 |
| Direct State Taxes | 12 | .......... | .......... | .......... | 23 |
| County Expenditures: | | | | | |
| New York County | 12 | $3,319,978 27 | .......... | $3,510,828 43 | 24 |
| Kings County | 13 | 1,594,864 36 | .......... | 1,676,995 10 | 25 |
| Queens County | 13 | 341,462 70 | .......... | 356,695 67 | 26 |
| Richmond County | 13 | 111,470 72 | .......... | 109,185 22 | 27 |
| Bronx County | 14 | .......... | .......... | .......... | 28 |
| Total for County Purposes | 14 | **$5,367,776 05** | .......... | **$5,653,704 42** | 29 |
| Total for all Purposes | 14 | **$169,932,928 30** | **$75,848,106 93** | **$179,520,591 26** | 30 |

*** N.B.—These amounts include the redemption of Special Revenue Bonds issued to defray**

| | | | | |
|---|---|---|---|---|
| | | *$5,208,150 00* | .......... | *$7,264,625 00* |

†—Proceeds from the sales of Corporate Stock were applied, under Chap. 208 Laws of 1906,

| | | | | |
|---|---|---|---|---|
| | | ........... | *$3,038,303 75* | ........... |

# NEW YORK

FROM REVENUE AND FROM CORPORATE STOCK FUNDS, FOR THE YEARS 1910 TO 1914, INCLUSIVE, GROUPED
DIVISION OF RESPONSIBILITY:

| LINE No. | 1911 | 1912 | | 1913 | | 1914 | |
|---|---|---|---|---|---|---|---|
| | Corporate Stock Expenditures | Revenue Expenditures | Corporate Stock Expenditures | Revenue Expenditures | Corporate Stock Expenditures | Revenue Expenditures | Corporare Stock Expenditures |
| 1 | $26,929,637 45 | $60,602,736 27 | $15,436,366 03 | $61,532,072 42 | $22,819,261 95 | $64,189,279 00 | $10,764,182 54 |
| 2 | 32,103,501 14 | 36,461,211 14 | 29,344,649 22 | 38,275,589 12 | 27,590,048 17 | 40,706,438 51 | 20,391,400 84 |
| 3 | .......... | 120,661 15 | 71,542 41 | 166,261 35 | 3,525 00 | 136,981 74 | .......... |
| 4 | **$59,033,138 59** | **$97,184,608 56** | **$44,852,557 66** | **$99,973,922 89** | **$50,412,835 12** | **$105,032,699 25** | **$31,155,583 38** |
| 5 | .......... | **$1,465,235 93** | .......... | **$1,672,732 14** | .......... | **$1,548,255 08** | .......... |
| 6 | $2,478,662 38 | $2,636,178 74 | $3,342,702 32 | $2,762,007 20 | $3,108,160 60 | $2,754,310 30 | $2,255,201 20 |
| 7 | 441,070 25 | 1,117,659 00 | 913,877 60 | 1,205,911 97 | 974,954 31 | 1,204,216 35 | 633,170 73 |
| 8 | 1,550,396 18 | 2,140,031 36 | 2,152,297 77 | 2,071,981 41 | 2,117,246 09 | 2,088,345 45 | 1,102,652 22 |
| 9 | 343,530 67 | 1,740,008 68 | 484,596 28 | 1,970,000 97 | 673,638 84 | 2,064,621 32 | 507,891 81 |
| 10 | 414,648 86 | 770,886 17 | 604,009 89 | 837,878 69 | 779,036 92 | 719,261 79 | 339,375 68 |
| 11 | **$5,228,308 34** | **$8,404,763 95** | **$7,497,483 86** | **$8,847,780 24** | **$7,653,036 76** | **$8,830,755 21** | **$4,838,291 64** |
| 12 | .......... | **$397,368 75** | .......... | **$345,750 97** | .......... | **$357,446 11** | .......... |
| 13 | **$10,493,672 21** | **$1,371,201 79** | **$11,974,288 08** | **$1,890,369 20** | **$27,451,950 39** | **$2,976,992 01** | **$24,814,274 61** |
| 14 | **$337,476 23** | **$2,850,018 13** | **$428,971 91** | **$2,775,627 97** | **$570,620 05** | **$3,194,795 46** | **$514,203 36** |
| 15 | .......... | **$2,429,050 99** | .......... | **$2,523,003 81** | .......... | **$2,586,057 83** | .......... |
| 16 | **$75,092,595 37** | **$114,102,248 10** | **$64,753,301 51** | **$118,029,187 22** | **$86,088,442 32** | **$124,527,000 95** | **$61,322,352 99** |
| 17 | †.......... | ***$50,218,374 43** | †.......... | ***$54,533,439 05** | †.......... | ***$52,491,846 15** | †.......... |
| 18 | **$934,015 76** | **$11,185,782 10** | **$463,838 88** | **$11,828,768 28** | **$563,072 77** | **$15,208,110 56** | **$1,463,227 44** |
| 19 | .......... | **$3,287,366 74** | .......... | **$2,300,000 00** | .......... | **$2,500,000 00** | .......... |
| 20 | .......... | .......... | .......... | .......... | .......... | **$520,015 06** | .......... |
| 21 | **$13,095,611 67** | .......... | **$15,200,511 22** | .......... | **$17,877,055 22** | .......... | **$20,779,517 54** |
| 22 | **$89,122,222 80** | **$178,793,771 37** | **$80,417,651 61** | **$186,691,394 55** | **$104,528,570 31** | **$195,246,972 72** | **$83,565,097 97** |
| 23 | .......... | **$4,301,345 65** | .......... | **$7,947,031 96** | .......... | **$4,576,303 43** | .......... |
| 24 | $19,277 55 | $3,672,340 66 | $47,589 18 | $3,850,888 17 | $6,640 19 | $3,857,815 20 | .......... |
| 25 | .......... | 1,701,040 45 | .......... | 1,767,380 30 | .......... | 1,841,120 93 | .......... |
| 26 | .......... | 379,511 61 | .......... | 426,733 40 | .......... | 447,656 36 | .......... |
| 27 | .......... | 119,498 76 | .......... | 132,831 48 | .......... | 141,872 11 | .......... |
| 28 | .......... | .......... | .......... | 14,501 45 | .......... | 537,359 93 | .......... |
| 29 | **$19,277 55** | **$5,872,391 48** | **$47,589 18** | **$6,192,334 80** | **$6,640 19** | **$6,825,824 53** | .......... |
| 30 | **$89,141,500 35** | **$188,967,508 50** | **$80,465,240 79** | **$200,830,761 31** | **$104,535,210 50** | **$206,649,100 68** | **$83,565,097 97** |

expenditures during the year prior to their redemption, as follows:

| .......... | *$5,970,164 92* | .......... | *$6,319,225 00* | .......... | *$7,038,065 51* | .......... |
|---|---|---|---|---|---|---|

to deficiencies in taxes, as follows:

| *$7,045,529 04* | ............ | *$5,036,851 60* | ............ | *$5,000,000 00* | ............. | ......... |
|---|---|---|---|---|---|---|

Comparative Summary Statement Showing Separately the Expenditures made from Revenue and
tures for I. City Departments, Offices, Courts, etc., Grouped to Indicate the Division of
other than Debt Service; IV. Deficiencies in Taxes; V. Borough Assessments; VI.

| | 1910 | | 1911 | | |
|---|---|---|---|---|---|
| | Revenue Expenditures | Corporate Stock Expenditures | Revenue Expenditures | Corporate Stock Expenditures | Line No. |
| I. City Departments, Offices, Courts, Etc. | | | | | |
| Mayor and Subordinate Departments, Bureaus and Offices. | | | | | |
| Mayor's Office and Departments whose executive heads are appointed by the Mayor and are removable at his pleasure: | | | | | |
| Commissioner of Accounts.. | $206,139 64 | .......... | $215,398 94 | .......... | 1 |
| Board of Ambulance Service. | 628 39 | .......... | 9,430 14 | .......... | 2 |
| Board of Assessors......... | 42,525 67 | .......... | 42,256 47 | .......... | 3 |
| Department of Bridges..... | 1,532,683 60 | $8,321,922 76 | 1,424,579 43 | $14,556,363 27 | 4 |
| Brooklyn Grade Crossing Commission............ | .......... | 200,000 00 | .......... | 330,000 00 | 5 |
| City Chamberlain......... | 54,273 86 | .......... | 61,382 66 | .......... | 6 |
| Change of Grade Damage Commission............ | .......... | 36,835 71 | .......... | 798,203 96 | 7 |
| Department of Correction.. | 1,254,375 04 | 309,381 09 | 1,219,095 91 | 115,125 77 | 8 |
| Department of Docks and Ferries............... | 2,533,737 78 | 5,500,681 80 | 2,575,836 58 | 2,511,074 09 | 9 |
| Examining Board of Plumbers | 6,920 48 | .......... | 5,373 50 | .......... | 10 |
| Fire Department.......... | 7,981,989 58 | 383,126 69 | 8,122,089 12 | 279,930 46 | 11 |
| Department of Health...... | 2,804,976 05 | 206,916 44 | 2,780,022 18 | 179,475 53 | 12 |
| Commission for the Improvement and Development of Jamaica Bay............ | .......... | 40,793 10 | .......... | 460 00 | 13 |
| Law Department.......... | 770,000 94 | .......... | 802,469 75 | .......... | 14 |
| Commissioner of Licenses... | 51,647 87 | .......... | 50,284 54 | .......... | 15 |
| Mayoralty, Administration. | 53,066 44 | .......... | 53,695 55 | .......... | 16 |
| Mayoralty, Bureau of Licenses | 44,984 04 | .......... | 83,137 77 | .......... | 17 |
| Mayoralty, Bureau of Weights and Measures... | 37,558 80 | .......... | 65,483 05 | .......... | 18 |
| Metropolitan Sewage Commission................ | .......... | 39,916 17 | .......... | 41,820 72 | 19 |
| Municipal Civil Service Commission................ | 149,279 61 | .......... | 156,655 66 | .......... | 20 |
| Municipal Explosives Commission................ | 3,970 37 | .......... | 16,467 50 | .......... | 21 |
| Park Board.............. | 25,512 19 | .......... | 25,310 74 | .......... | 22 |
| Department of Parks, Manhattan and Richmond.... | 1,057,806 73 | 540,099 77 | 999,935 53 | 714,393 52 | 23 |
| Department of Parks, The Bronx.................. | 413,428 44 | 405,815 51 | 411,712 48 | 272,275 52 | 24 |
| Department of Parks, Brooklyn.................... | 994,524 82 | 184,579 73 | 942,611 22 | 316,332 17 | 25 |
| Department of Parks, Queens | .......... | .......... | 3,768 44 | .......... | 26 |
| Police Department......... | 15,069,255 88 | 245,312 92 | 15,655,041 83 | 500,161 93 | 27 |
| Department of Public Charities.................. | 2,919,373 13 | 1,240,027 74 | 3,218,150 19 | 1,025,922 23 | 28 |
| Department of Street Cleaning.................. | 9,930,102 65 | 37,889 02 | 8,142,560 54 | 79,353 68 | 29 |
| Department of Taxes and Assessments............ | 510,777 88 | .......... | 587,947 37 | .......... | 30 |
| Tenement House Department.................. | 804,108 52 | .......... | 789,760 30 | .......... | 31 |
| Department of Water Supply, Gas and Electricity...... | 8,667,906 41 | 4,170,185 83 | 9,231,925 65 | 5,208,744 60 | 32 |

# NEW YORK

from Corporate Stock Funds for the Years 1910 to 1914, Inclusive, Classified to Show Expendi-
Responsibility for each Group; II. Debt Service; III. Fixed Charges, Contributions, etc.,
Advances for Local Improvements; VII. Direct State Taxes; VIII. County Expense:

| LINE No. | 1912 | | 1913 | | 1914 | |
|---|---|---|---|---|---|---|
| | Revenue Expenditures | Corporate Stock Expenditures | Revenue Expenditures | Corporate Stock Expenditures | Revenue Expenditures | Corporate Stock Expenditures |
| 1 | $214,664 46 | .......... | $195,977 82 | .......... | $219,940 04 | .......... |
| 2 | 11,581 09 | .......... | 76,863 55 | .......... | 79,910 51 | .......... |
| 3 | 42,883 68 | .......... | 41,364 34 | .......... | 40,150 52 | .......... |
| 4 | 1,446,171 37 | $4,196,300 73 | 1,368,549 25 | $4,318,872 71 | 1,273,983 88 | $2,636,742 84 |
| 5 | .......... | .......... | .......... | 262,500 00 | .......... | 365,000 00 |
| 6 | 61,437 60 | .......... | 62,134 14 | .......... | 59,568 47 | .......... |
| 7 | .......... | 410,846 42 | .......... | 173,132 49 | .......... | 7,156 63 |
| 8 | 1,297,047 94 | 4,641 12 | 1,358,812 62 | 148,201 61 | 1,378,177 57 | 41,241 20 |
| 9 | 2,735,671 10 | 1,889,059 32 | 2,742,878 45 | 9,074,543 46 | 2,510,827 42 | 2,009,343 98 |
| 10 | 5,586 46 | .......... | 5,350 58 | .......... | 3,908 42 | .......... |
| 11 | 8,673,738 51 | 849,250 49 | 9,050,682 33 | 1,704,330 65 | 9,396,341 68 | 977,167 99 |
| 12 | 3,073,242 15 | 401,110 72 | 3,298,082 28 | 277,226 55 | 3,326,155 24 | 258,891 52 |
| 13 | .......... | .......... | .......... | .......... | .......... | .......... |
| 14 | 804,112 35 | .......... | 862,078 90 | .......... | 855,199 96 | .......... |
| 15 | 50,498 25 | .......... | 50,592 28 | .......... | 28,231 22 | .......... |
| 16 | 54,738 69 | .......... | 55,595 28 | .......... | 62,083 83 | .......... |
| 17 | 82,093 03 | .......... | 115,764 35 | .......... | 137,812 61 | .......... |
| 18 | 72,158 60 | .......... | 64,686 35 | .......... | 76,964 27 | .......... |
| 19 | .......... | 46,721 54 | .......... | 43,422 52 | .......... | 24,997 13 |
| 20 | 189,983 09 | .......... | 211,715 97 | .......... | 200,792 38 | .......... |
| 21 | 9,878 93 | .......... | 14,516 25 | .......... | 8,966 17 | .......... |
| 22 | 31,646 66 | .......... | 29,884 36 | .......... | 29,222 30 | .......... |
| 23 | 1,134,149 70 | 912,889 23 | 1,126,524 71 | 981,874 86 | 1,083,772 24 | 390,900 22 |
| 24 | 452,834 58 | 239,511 06 | 464,895 14 | 142,994 87 | 469,586 19 | 43,703 79 |
| 25 | 877,014 18 | 587,482 84 | 867,234 36 | 699,466 01 | 826,273 18 | 404,424 12 |
| 26 | 153,418 40 | 18,814 03 | 182,562 22 | 14,862 40 | 184,397 67 | 8,052 11 |
| 27 | 16,450,647 22 | 233,174 29 | 16,781,054 55 | 479,886 23 | 17,439,827 77 | 218,651 47 |
| 28 | 3,219,029 05 | 1,741,366 59 | 3,719,089 17 | 1,887,563 94 | 3,682,980 96 | 968,135 23 |
| 29 | 8,599,366 23 | 16,378 42 | 7,936,099 58 | 28,224 36 | 10,132,163 33 | 26,672 07 |
| 30 | 636,999 87 | .......... | 632,918 76 | .......... | 635,441 50 | .......... |
| 31 | 776,988 56 | .......... | 762,036 81 | .......... | 727,100 57 | .......... |
| 32 | 9,436,288 07 | 3,888,819 23 | 9,441,574 81 | 2,582,159 29 | 9,310,140 36 | 2,383,102 24 |

COMPARATIVE SUMMARY STATEMENT SHOWING SEPARATELY THE EXPENDITURES MADE FROM REVENUE AND TURES FOR I. CITY DEPARTMENTS, OFFICES, COURTS, ETC., GROUPED TO INDICATE THE DIVISION OF OTHER THAN DEBT SERVICE; IV. DEFICIENCIES IN TAXES; V. BOROUGH ASSESSMENTS; VI. AD

| | 1910 | | 1911 | | |
|---|---|---|---|---|---|
| | Revenue Expenditures | Corporate Stock Expenditures | Revenue Expenditures | Corporate Stock Expenditures | LINE No. |
| I. CITY DEPARTMENTS —*Continued* | | | | | |
| Department of Water Supply, Gas and Electricity, Water Meter Fund—Special Account | .......... | .......... | .......... | .......... | 1 |
| Total | **$57,921,554 81** | **$21,863,484 28** | **$57,692,383 04** | **$26,929,637 45** | 2 |
| Departments whose heads are appointed by the Mayor for a term of office greater than his own, and are removable only upon charges: | | | | | |
| Aqueduct Commission | .......... | $1,316,228 48 | .......... | $1,109,534 04 | 3 |
| Bellevue and Allied Hospitals | $1,167,430 50 | 739,523 23 | $1,261,537 28 | 528,675 53 | 4 |
| College of the City of New York | 607,816 21 | 23,661 50 | 624,786 55 | 57,278 60 | 5 |
| Department of Education | 28,676,143 68 | 2,642,643 83 | 29,044,085 99 | 4,428,892 54 | 6 |
| Normal College of the City of New York | 364,857 26 | 7,099 07 | 371,949 88 | 30,554 50 | 7 |
| Board of Water Supply | .......... | 19,392,417 49 | .......... | 25,948,565 93 | 8 |
| Total | **$30,816,247 65** | **$24,121,573 60** | **$31,302,359 70** | **$32,103,501 14** | 9 |
| Boards and Commissions majorities of which are appointed by the Mayor and for which no other elected City official shares responsibility: | | | | | |
| Art Commission | $7,587 79 | .......... | $7,573 00 | .......... | 10 |
| Brooklyn Disciplinary Training School for Boys | 56,783 63 | .......... | 55,477 25 | .......... | 11 |
| Committee on Congestion of Population | .......... | .......... | .......... | .......... | 12 |
| Board of Inebriety | .......... | .......... | 887 19 | .......... | 13 |
| Permanent Census Board | 28,717 15 | .......... | 36,504 39 | .......... | 14 |
| Public Recreation Commission | .......... | .......... | .......... | .......... | 15 |
| Total | **$93,088 57** | .......... | **$100,441 83** | .......... | 16 |
| Total Mayor, Subordinate Departments, Bureaus and Offices | **$88,830,891 03** | **$45,985,057 88** | **$89,095,184 57** | **$59,033,138 59** | 17 |
| Comptroller and Finance Department, excluding the Chamberlain's office: | | | | | |
| Department of Finance | $1,462,726 97 | .......... | $1,378,185 90 | .......... | 18 |
| Wallabout Market Fund | 17,857 60 | .......... | 1,396 80 | .......... | 19 |
| Total Comptroller and Finance Department | **$1,480,584 57** | .......... | **$1,379,582 70** | .......... | 20 |
| Borough Presidents and Subordinate Departments: | | | | | |
| President, Borough of Manhattan | $2,671,661 06 | $2,088,119 36 | $2,724,537 28 | $2,478,662 38 | 21 |
| President, Borough of The Bronx | 1,136,667 56 | 842,186 69 | 1,066,497 23 | 441,070 25 | 22 |
| President, Borough of Brooklyn | 2,156,603 26 | 1,637,870 66 | 2,038,207 61 | 1,550,396 18 | 23 |

NEW YORK

from Corporate Stock Funds for the Years 1910 to 1914, Inclusive, Classified to Show Expendi-
Responsibility for each Group; II. Debt Service; III. Fixed Charges, Contributions, etc.,
vances for Local Improvements; VII. Direct State Taxes; VIII. County Expense:—*Continued*

| LINE No. | 1912 | | 1913 | | 1914 | |
|---|---|---|---|---|---|---|
| | Revenue Expenditures | Corporate Stock Expenditures | Revenue Expenditures | Corporate Stock Expenditures | Revenue Expenditures | Corporate Stock Expenditures |
| 1 | $8,866 45 | .......... | $12,553 21 | .......... | $9,358 74 | .......... |
| 2 | **$60,602,736 27** | **$15,436,366 03** | **$61,532,072 42** | **$22,819,261 95** | **$64,189,279 00** | **$10,764,182 54** |
| 3 | .......... | $11,600 67 | .......... | $51,225 10 | .......... | .......... |
| 4 | $1,299,348 56 | 677,453 01 | $1,453,030 29 | 1,246,337 30 | $1,437,612 02 | $720,361 00 |
| 5 | 630,363 72 | .......... | 657,321 19 | 33,742 23 | 675,046 00 | 25,163 00 |
| 6 | 34,139,765 22 | 4,787,473 13 | 35,670,393 99 | 4,731,385 07 | 38,073,785 53 | 5,437,237 30 |
| 7 | 391,733 64 | 284,146 31 | 494,843 65 | 174,936 60 | 519,994 96 | 101,143 95 |
| 8 | .......... | 23,583,976 10 | .......... | 21,352,421 87 | .......... | 14,107,495 59 |
| 9 | **$36,461,211 14** | **$29,344,649 22** | **$38,275,589 12** | **$27,590,048 17** | **$40,706,438 51** | **$20,391,400 84** |
| 10 | $7,552 45 | .......... | $7,551 11 | .......... | $7,132 82 | .......... |
| 11 | 56,688 65 | $42 41 | 54,267 79 | .......... | 29,013 78 | .......... |
| 12 | 1,457 12 | .......... | .......... | .......... | .......... | .......... |
| 13 | 5,994 25 | 71,500 00 | 11,653 73 | $3,525 00 | $25,688 49 | .......... |
| 14 | 36,669 65 | .......... | 73,474 96 | .......... | 54,717 04 | .......... |
| 15 | 12,299 03 | .......... | 19,313 76 | .......... | 20,429 61 | .......... |
| 16 | **$120,661 15** | **$71,542 41** | **$166,261 35** | **$3,525 00** | **$136,981 74** | .......... |
| 17 | **$97,184,608 56** | **$44,852,557 66** | **$99,973,922 89** | **$50,412,835 12** | **$105,032,699 25** | **$31,155,583 38** |
| 18 | $1,460,258 67 | .......... | $1,671,242 42 | .......... | $1,548,195 08 | .......... |
| 19 | 4,977 26 | .......... | 1,489 72 | .......... | 60 00 | .......... |
| 20 | **$1,465,235 93** | .......... | **$1,672,732 14** | .......... | **$1,548,255 08** | .......... |
| 21 | $2,636,178 74 | $3,342,702 32 | $2,762,007 20 | $3,108,160 60 | $2,754,310 30 | $2,255,201 20 |
| 22 | 1,117,659 00 | 913,877 60 | 1,205,911 97 | 974,954 31 | 1,204,216 35 | 633,170 73 |
| 23 | 2,140,031 36 | 2,152,297 77 | 2,071,981 41 | 2,117,246 09 | 2,088,345 45 | 1,102,652 22 |

Comparative Summary Statement Showing Separately the Expenditures made from Revenue and tures for I. City Departments, Offices, Courts, etc., Grouped to Indicate the Division of other than Debt Service; IV. Deficiencies in Taxes; V. Borough Assessments; VI. Ad

| | 1910 | | 1911 | | |
|---|---|---|---|---|---|
| | Revenue Expenditures | Corporate Stock Expenditures | Revenue Expenditures | Corporate Stock Expenditures | Line No. |
| I. City Departments—*Continued.* | | | | | |
| President, Borough of Queens | $1,373,024 95 | $392,699 26 | $1,356,075 79 | $343,530 67 | 1 |
| President, Borough of Richmond | 774,567 39 | 438,076 45 | 742,412 55 | 414,648 86 | 2 |
| Total Borough Presidents | **$8,112,524 22** | **$5,398,952 42** | **$7,927,730 46** | **$5,228,308 34** | 3 |
| Board of Aldermen, President of Board and City Clerk | **$281,815 63** | .......... | **$326,660 73** | .......... | 4 |
| Boards, Commissions, etc., whose members are not elected by popular vote and who are not appointed by any elected city official: | | | | | |
| Bronx Parkway Commission | .......... | .......... | .......... | $5,408 91 | 5 |
| Board of Building Examiners | $9,423 53 | .......... | $9,340 29 | .......... | 6 |
| Court House Board | 1,591 73 | .......... | 572 40 | .......... | 7 |
| Commissioners of Estimate and Appraisal | .......... | $21,220 24 | .......... | 16,523 16 | 8 |
| Commission on Lunacy | .......... | .......... | .......... | .......... | 9 |
| Public Service Commission | 1,216,182 40 | 6,450,073 03 | 1,100,460 87 | 10,471,740 14 | 10 |
| Water Pollution Commission | .......... | 1,414 40 | .......... | .......... | 11 |
| Total Boards, Commissions, etc | **$1,227,197 66** | **$6,472,707 67** | **$1,110,373 56** | **$10,493,672 21** | 12 |
| Boards, Commissions, etc., of mixed responsibility, i.e., ex-officio bodies representing two or more of preceding branches: | | | | | |
| Armory Board | $105,358 41 | $531,122 80 | $142,059 70 | $337,476 23 | 13 |
| Board of City Record—City of New York | 1,084,596 62 | .......... | 828,534 54 | .......... | 14 |
| *Board of Elections | 959,889 36 | .......... | 926,305 38 | .......... | 15 |
| Board of Estimate and Apportionment | 153,229 71 | .......... | 176,965 32 | .......... | 16 |
| Board of Revision of Assessments | .......... | .......... | 104 75 | .......... | 17 |
| Commissioners of the Sinking Fund | 3,254 25 | .......... | 3,199 30 | .......... | 18 |
| Total | **$2,306,328 35** | **$531,122 80** | **$2,077,168 99** | **$337,476 23** | 19 |
| Courts, including Board of Parole and General Interpreters, Brooklyn: | | | | | |
| Coroners, Borough of Manhattan | $64,194 29 | .......... | $67,154 13 | .......... | 20 |
| Coroners, Borough of The Bronx | 29,754 98 | .......... | 30,241 26 | .......... | 21 |
| Coroners, Borough of Brooklyn | 32,989 87 | .......... | 36,481 41 | .......... | 22 |
| Coroners, Borough of Queens | 19,154 66 | .......... | 18,660 55 | .......... | 23 |
| Coroners, Borough of Richmond | 12,151 79 | .......... | 12,134 37 | .......... | 24 |
| City Court of New York | 233,768 20 | .......... | 235,537 60 | .......... | 25 |
| City Magistrates' Courts, First Division | 291,653 25 | .......... | 373,843 38 | .......... | 26 |

*The Board of Elections is placed in this group for the reason that in the first two years covered

NEW YORK

FROM CORPORATE STOCK FUNDS FOR THE YEARS 1910 TO 1914, INCLUSIVE, CLASSIFIED TO SHOW EXPENDI-
RESPONSIBILITY FOR EACH GROUP; II. DEBT SERVICE; III. FIXED CHARGES, CONTRIBUTIONS, ETC.,
VANCES FOR LOCAL IMPROVEMENTS; VII. DIRECT STATE TAXES; VIII. COUNTY EXPENSE:—*Continued*

| LINE No. | 1912 | | 1913 | | 1914 | |
|---|---|---|---|---|---|---|
| | Revenue Expenditures | Corporate Stock Expenditures | Revenue Expenditures | Corporate Stock Expenditures | Revenue Expenditures | Corporate Stock Expenditures |
| 1 | $1,740,008 68 | $484,596 28 | $1,970,000 97 | $673,638 84 | $2,064,621 32 | $507,891 81 |
| 2 | 770,886 17 | 604,009 89 | 837,878 69 | 779,036 92 | 719,261 79 | 339,375 68 |
| 3 | **$8,404,763 95** | **$7,497,483 86** | **$8,847,780 24** | **$7,653,036 76** | **$8,830,755 21** | **$4,838,291 64** |
| 4 | **$397,368 75** | .......... | **$345,750 97** | .......... | **$357,446 11** | .......... |
| 5 | .......... | $31,206 80 | $17,385 05 | $779,233 07 | $42,032 02 | $1,117,071 85 |
| 6 | $9,108 47 | .......... | 8,702 03 | .......... | 9,038 96 | .......... |
| 7 | .......... | 32,247 62 | .......... | 6,485,390 98 | .......... | 183,440 09 |
| 8 | .......... | 15,472 56 | .......... | .......... | .......... | .......... |
| 9 | 3,590 30 | .......... | 1,120 80 | .......... | .......... | .......... |
| 10 | 1,358,503 02 | 11,895,361 10 | 1,863,161 32 | 20,187,326 34 | 2,925,921 03 | 23,513,762 67 |
| 11 | .......... | .......... | .......... | .......... | .......... | .......... |
| 12 | **$1,371,201 79** | **$11,974,288 08** | **$1,890,369 20** | **$27,451,950 39** | **$2,976,992 01** | **$24,814,274 61** |
| 13 | $294,708 60 | $428,971 91 | $250,083 46 | $570,620 05 | $244,277 79 | $514,203 36 |
| 14 | 865,849 77 | .......... | 920,152 39 | .......... | 915,646 16 | .......... |
| 15 | 1,395,828 00 | .......... | 1,186,804 05 | .......... | 1,492,016 88 | .......... |
| 16 | 286,618 15 | .......... | 414,760 32 | .......... | 539,204 70 | .......... |
| 17 | .......... | .......... | .......... | .......... | 88 00 | .......... |
| 18 | 7,013 61 | .......... | 3,827 75 | .......... | 3,561 93 | .......... |
| 19 | **$2,850,018 13** | **$428,971 91** | **$2,775,627 97** | **$570,620 05** | **$3,194,795 46** | **$514,203 36** |
| 20 | $62,675 31 | .......... | $63,483 00 | .......... | $63,480 32 | .......... |
| 21 | 29,985 44 | .......... | 30,559 19 | .......... | 30,315 89 | .......... |
| 22 | 34,578 73 | .......... | 35,323 71 | .......... | 31,362 53 | .......... |
| 23 | 19,422 59 | .......... | 19,903 22 | .......... | 19,951 82 | .......... |
| 24 | 12,090 52 | .......... | 12,077 89 | .......... | 12,054 59 | .......... |
| 25 | 246,774 69 | .......... | 254,862 24 | .......... | 255,754 63 | .......... |
| 26 | 381,949 84 | .......... | 414,332 59 | .......... | 449,732 14 | .......... |

by this statement it was responsible to the Mayor, and in the last three years to the Board of Aldermen.

COMPARATIVE SUMMARY STATEMENT SHOWING SEPARATELY THE EXPENDITURES MADE FROM REVENUE AN TURES FOR I. CITY DEPARTMENTS, OFFICES, COURTS, ETC., GROUPED TO INDICATE THE DIVISION O OTHER THAN DEBT SERVICE; IV. DEFICIENCIES IN TAXES; V. BOROUGH ASSESSMENTS; VI. A

| | 1910 | | 1911 | | |
|---|---|---|---|---|---|
| | Revenue Expenditures | Corporate Stock Expenditures | Revenue Expenditures | Corporate Stock Expenditures | LINE No |
| I. CITY DEPARTMENTS—*Continued* | | | | | |
| City Magistrates' Courts, Second Division | $250,520 43 | .......... | $339,546 57 | .......... | |
| Municipal Courts, City of New York | 894,695 56 | .......... | 908,377 52 | .......... | |
| Court of Special Sessions | 219,178 26 | .......... | 316,909 08 | .......... | |
| General Interpreters, Brooklyn | 10,200 00 | .......... | 10,200 00 | .......... | |
| Board of Parole | 2,967 86 | .......... | 2,977 20 | .......... | |
| Total, Courts, etc. | **$2,061,229 15** | .......... | **$2,352,063 07** | .......... | |
| Total, City Departments, Offices, Courts, etc. | **$104,300,570 61** | **$58,387,840 77** | **$104,268,764 08** | **$75,092,595 37** | |
| II. DEBT SERVICE | ***$44,743,741 92** | .......... | ***$49,550,488 56** | .......... | |
| III. FIXED CHARGES OTHER THAN DEBT SERVICE, SUBSIDIES, CONTRIBUTIONS, PAYMENTS TO PRIVATE AND STATE INSTITUTIONS, EXPENDITURES NOT ALLOTED TO DEPARTMENTS: | | | | | |
| American Museum of Natural History | $185,757 00 | .......... | $189,757 00 | .......... | 9 |
| Botanical Garden and Arboretum | .......... | .......... | 14,741 31 | .......... | 10 |
| Charitable Institutions, City | 4,511,647 65 | .......... | 4,362,537 93 | .......... | 11 |
| Children's Museum, Brooklyn | 11,861 29 | .......... | 11,900 39 | .......... | 12 |
| Claims | 1,780,056 75 | .......... | 287,795 36 | .......... | 13 |
| Excise Taxes—Special Account | 1,216,161 58 | .......... | 1,343,648 71 | .......... | 14 |
| Grant's Tomb | 7,000 00 | .......... | 7,000 00 | .......... | 15 |
| Jumel Mansion | 4,129 85 | .......... | 4,487 48 | .......... | 16 |
| Metropolitan Museum of Art | 200,000 00 | .......... | 200,000 00 | .......... | 17 |
| Miscellaneous—City | 2,043,612 97 | $27,465 73 | 1,986,140 72 | $230,226 55 | 18 |
| Inactive Accounts—Miscellaneous | .......... | .......... | .......... | .......... | 19 |
| Museum of Arts and Sciences | 93,555 59 | .......... | 93,334 00 | .......... | 20 |
| New York Aquarium | 45,974 86 | .......... | 47,567 22 | .......... | 21 |
| New York Botanical Garden | 82,936 32 | .......... | 85,981 40 | .......... | 22 |
| New York Zoological Garden | 167,632 00 | .......... | 174,579 74 | .......... | 23 |
| New York Public Library Building | .......... | .......... | .......... | .......... | 24 |
| Brooklyn Public Library | 418,696 71 | 218 98 | 421,156 86 | 560 00 | 25 |
| New York Public Library | 618,361 89 | 1,347,248 44 | 661,965 82 | 703,229 21 | 26 |
| Queensboro Public Library | 118,463 80 | 25 00 | 135,040 26 | .......... | 27 |
| Staten Island Association of Arts and Sciences | 3,991 46 | .......... | 9,000 00 | .......... | 28 |
| United States Volunteer Life Saving Corps | 11,000 00 | .......... | 11,000 00 | .......... | 29 |
| Total Fixed Charges | **$11,520,839 72** | **$1,374,958 15** | **$10,047,634 20** | **$934,015 76** | 30 |

* N.B.—These amounts include the redemption of Special Revenue Bonds,

| | *$5,208,150 00* | | *$7,264,625 00* | | |
|---|---|---|---|---|---|

NEW YORK

FROM CORPORATE STOCK FUNDS FOR THE YEARS 1910 TO 1914, INCLUSIVE, CLASSIFIED TO SHOW EXPENDI-
RESPONSIBILITY FOR EACH GROUP; II. DEBT SERVICE; III. FIXED CHARGES, CONTRIBUTIONS, ETC.,
VANCES FOR LOCAL IMPROVEMENTS; VII. DIRECT STATE TAXES; VIII. COUNTY EXPENSE:—*Continued*

| LINE No. | 1912 | | 1913 | | 1914 | |
|---|---|---|---|---|---|---|
| | Revenue Expenditures | Corporate Stock Expenditures | Revenue Expenditures | Corporate Stock Expenditures | Revenue Expenditures | Corporate Stock Expenditures |
| 1 | $360,562 06 | .......... | $370,911 62 | .......... | $388,244 52 | .......... |
| 2 | 927,241 80 | .......... | 930,515 56 | .......... | 929,492 36 | .......... |
| 3 | 340,390 84 | .......... | 373,409 79 | .......... | 388,224 03 | .......... |
| 4 | 9,148 27 | .......... | 9,000 00 | .......... | 8,800 00 | .......... |
| 5 | 4,230 90 | .......... | 8,625 00 | .......... | 8,645 00 | .......... |
| 6 | **$2,429,050 99** | .......... | **$2,523,003 81** | .......... | **$2,586,057 83** | .......... |
| 7 | **$114,102,248 10** | **$64,753,301 51** | **$118,029,187 22** | **$86,088,442 32** | **$124,527,000 95** | **$61,322,352 99** |
| 8 | ***$50,218,374 43** | .......... | ***$54,533,439 05** | .......... | ***$52,491,846 15** | .......... |
| 9 | $195,000 00 | .......... | $200,000 00 | .......... | $200,000 00 | .......... |
| 10 | 25,782 40 | .......... | 29,459 22 | .......... | 37,636 08 | .......... |
| 11 | 4,431,326 77 | .......... | 4,550,374 28 | .......... | 5,184,610 06 | .......... |
| 12 | 12,499 43 | .......... | 13,121 35 | .......... | 13,227 21 | .......... |
| 13 | 1,582,360 56 | .......... | 1,780,061 72 | .......... | 4,392,750 73 | .......... |
| 14 | 1,340,403 12 | .......... | 1,389,008 64 | .......... | 1,383,323 53 | .......... |
| 15 | 6,817 15 | .......... | 4,692 64 | .......... | 4,927 27 | .......... |
| 16 | 5,437 45 | .......... | 4,410 96 | .......... | 4,163 21 | .......... |
| 17 | 200,000 00 | .......... | 200,000 00 | .......... | 200,000 00 | .......... |
| 18 | 1,763,660 49 | $205,191 74 | 1,944,463 37 | $401,062 51 | 1,913,424 90 | $1,400,516 04 |
| 19 | 1,850 72 | .......... | .......... | .......... | .......... | .......... |
| 20 | 97,623 48 | .......... | 102,181 86 | .......... | 106,744 33 | .......... |
| 21 | 46,597 08 | .......... | 47,335 62 | .......... | 46,995 53 | .......... |
| 22 | 90,072 46 | .......... | 103,222 19 | .......... | 107,163 00 | .......... |
| 23 | 179,272 87 | .......... | 189,570 36 | .......... | 200,000 00 | .......... |
| 24 | 10,000 00 | .......... | 17,999 37 | .......... | 48,500 00 | .......... |
| 25 | 413,628 47 | 34,186 07 | 436,494 31 | 115,997 82 | 444,202 23 | 24,506 22 |
| 26 | 616,958 99 | 224,461 07 | 638,443 50 | 46,012 44 | 747,419 18 | 38,205 18 |
| 27 | 143,997 99 | .......... | 155,374 71 | .......... | 152,028 37 | .......... |
| 28 | 9,448 44 | .......... | 9,318 74 | .......... | 8,639 79 | .......... |
| 29 | 13,044 23 | .......... | 13,235 44 | .......... | 12,355 14 | .......... |
| 30 | **$11,185,782 10** | **$463,838 88** | **$11,828,768 28** | **$563,072 77** | **$15,208,110 56** | **$1,463,227 44** |

issued to defray expenditures during the year prior to their redemption., as follows:

| | 1912 | 1913 | 1914 |
|---|---|---|---|
| | *$5,970,164 92* | *$7,038,065 51* | *$6,319,225 00* |

COMPARATIVE SUMMARY STATEMENT SHOWING SEPARATELY THE EXPENDITURES MADE FROM REVENUE AND TURES FOR I. CITY DEPARTMENTS, OFFICES, COURTS, ETC., GROUPED TO INDICATE THE DIVISION OF OTHER THAN DEBT SERVICE; IV. DEFICIENCIES IN TAXES; V. BOROUGH ASSESSMENTS; VI. AD

| | 1910 | | 1911 | | LINE No. |
|---|---|---|---|---|---|
| | Revenue Expenditures | Corporate Stock Expenditures | Revenue Expenditures | Corporate Stock Expenditures | |
| IV. DEFICIENCES IN TAXES | **$4,000,000 00** | †.......... | **$10,000,000 00** | †.......... | 1 |
| V. BOROUGH ASSESSMENTS: | | | | | |
| Manhattan | .......... | .......... | .......... | .......... | 2 |
| Brooklyn | .......... | .......... | .......... | .......... | 3 |
| Total Borough Assessments | .......... | .......... | .......... | .......... | 4 |
| VI. ADVANCES FOR LOCAL IMPROVEMENTS: | | | | | |
| Fund for Street and Park Openings | .......... | *$8,530,644 12 | .......... | $6,300,963 84 | 5 |
| Street Improvement Fund | .......... | *7,554,663 89 | .......... | 6,794,647 83 | 6 |
| Total Advances for Local Improvements | .......... | **$16,085,308 01** | .......... | **$13,095,611 67** | 7 |
| Total for City Purposes | **$164,565,152 25** | **$75,848,106 93** | **$173,866,886 84** | **$89,122,222 80** | 8 |
| VII. DIRECT STATE TAXES: | | | | | |
| New York County | .......... | .......... | .......... | .......... | 9 |
| Kings County | .......... | .......... | .......... | .......... | 10 |
| Queens County | .......... | .......... | .......... | .......... | 11 |
| Richmond County | .......... | .......... | .......... | .......... | 12 |
| Total Direct State Taxes | .......... | .......... | .......... | .......... | 13 |
| VIII. COUNTY EXPENDITURES: | | | | | |
| New York County: | | | | | |
| Charitable Institutions | $113,875 22 | .......... | $112,995 01 | .......... | 14 |
| Board of City Record | 34,984 60 | .......... | 38,614 40 | .......... | 15 |
| County Clerk | 150,588 53 | .......... | 140,557 78 | $19,277 55 | 16 |
| Courts—General Sessions | 292,318 27 | .......... | 314,139 08 | .......... | 17 |
| Courts—Supreme, First Department | 823,294 42 | .......... | 858,978 84 | .......... | 18 |
| Courts—Supreme, First Department, Maintenance of Appellate Division Court House | 30,780 02 | .......... | 30,613 14 | .......... | 19 |
| Courts—Surrogate's | 176,862 30 | .......... | 175,787 12 | .......... | 20 |
| District Attorney | 371,242 25 | .......... | 409,108 45 | .......... | 21 |
| Commissioner of Jurors | 50,341 57 | .......... | 52,548 46 | .......... | 22 |
| Miscellaneous | 575,347 82 | .......... | 587,591 28 | .......... | 23 |
| National Guard and Naval Militia | 185,828 75 | .......... | 200,132 25 | .......... | 24 |
| Public Administrator | 26,096 50 | .......... | 26,284 87 | .......... | 25 |
| Commissioner of Records | 70,243 37 | .......... | 72,461 81 | .......... | 26 |
| Commissioner of Records, Surrogate's Court | .......... | .......... | .......... | .......... | 27 |
| Register | 228,750 64 | .......... | 310,302 35 | .......... | 28 |
| Sheriff | 189,424 01 | .......... | 180,713 59 | .......... | 29 |
| Total | **$3,319,978 27** | .......... | **$3,510,828 43** | **$19,277 55** | 30 |

* Includes expenditures from proceeds of Assessment Bonds.

† Proceeds from the sales of Corporate Stock were applied, under Chap. 208, Laws of 1906, to

*$3,038,303 75* *$7,045,529 04*

NEW YORK

FROM CORPORATE STOCK FUNDS FOR THE YEARS 1910 TO 1914, INCLUSIVE, CLASSIFIED TO SHOW EXPENDI-
RESPONSIBILITY FOR EACH GROUP; II. DEBT SERVICE; III. FIXED CHARGES, CONTRIBUTIONS, ETC.,
VANCES FOR LOCAL IMPROVEMENTS; VII. DIRECT STATE TAXES; VIII. COUNTY EXPENSE:—*Continued*

| LINE No. | 1912 | | 1913 | | 1914 | |
|---|---|---|---|---|---|---|
| | Revenue Expenditures | Corporate Stock Expenditures | Revenue Expenditures | Corporate Stock Expenditures | Revenue Expenditures | Corporate Stock Expenditures |
| 1 | **$3,287,366 74** | †.......... | **$2,300,000 00** | †.......... | **$2,500,000 00** | .......... |
| 2 | .......... | .......... | .......... | .......... | $144,448 63 | .......... |
| 3 | .......... | .......... | .......... | .......... | 375,566 43 | .......... |
| 4 | .......... | .......... | .......... | .......... | **$520,015 06** | .......... |
| 5 | .......... | $7,916,073 05 | .......... | $8,286,777 28 | .......... | $4,855,640 93 |
| 6 | .......... | 7,284,438 17 | .......... | 9,590,277 94 | .......... | 15,923,876 61 |
| 7 | .......... | **$15,200,511 22** | .......... | **$17,877,055 22** | .......... | **$20,779,517 54** |
| 8 | **$178,793,771 37** | **$80,417,651 61** | **$186,691,394 55** | **$104,528,570 31** | **$195,246,972 72** | **$83,565,097 97** |
| 9 | $3,211,557 62 | .......... | $5,736,005 10 | .......... | $3,308,080 34 | .......... |
| 10 | 847,328 81 | .......... | 1,684,598 71 | .......... | 959,311 91 | .......... |
| 11 | 200,986 53 | .......... | 445,609 98 | .......... | 263,332 56 | .......... |
| 12 | 41,472 69 | .......... | 80,818 17 | .......... | 45,578 62 | .......... |
| 13 | **$4,301,345 65** | .......... | **$7,947,031 96** | .......... | **$4,576,303 43** | .......... |
| 14 | $105,153 59 | .......... | $102,928 80 | .......... | $78,905 98 | .......... |
| 15 | 39,882 29 | .......... | 41,389 61 | .......... | 34,203 26 | .......... |
| 16 | 184,568 67 | $47,589 18 | 185,207 91 | $6,640 19 | 193,736 08 | .......... |
| 17 | 351,901 91 | .......... | 378,996 31 | .......... | 404,724 90 | .......... |
| 18 | 918,868 42 | .......... | 976,589 75 | .......... | 990,529 66 | .......... |
| 19 | 27,374 34 | .......... | 30,812 62 | .......... | 28,792 71 | .......... |
| 20 | 184,348 10 | .......... | 203,676 02 | .......... | 193,683 54 | .......... |
| 21 | 450,536 90 | .......... | 469,877 03 | .......... | 522,847 74 | .......... |
| 22 | 52,122 28 | .......... | 52,782 22 | .......... | 57,181 14 | .......... |
| 23 | 449,071 18 | .......... | 482,962 87 | .......... | 475,295 09 | .......... |
| 24 | 212,527 50 | .......... | 223,931 00 | .......... | 221,101 00 | .......... |
| 25 | 25,377 42 | .......... | 26,784 06 | .......... | 27,261 86 | .......... |
| 26 | 96,523 35 | .......... | 100,300 62 | .......... | 96,680 42 | .......... |
| 27 | 44,817 93 | .......... | 49,691 25 | .......... | 47,517 17 | .......... |
| 28 | 317,650 04 | .......... | 314,615 92 | .......... | 279,280 05 | .......... |
| 29 | 211,616 74 | .......... | 210,342 18 | .......... | 206,074 60 | .......... |
| 30 | **$3,672,340 66** | **$47,589 18** | **$3,850,888 17** | **$6,640 19** | **$3,857,815 20** | .......... |

leficiencies in taxes, as follows:

| 1912 | 1913 | 1914 |
|---|---|---|
| *$5,036 851 60* | *$5,000,000 00* | ........... |

COMPARATIVE SUMMARY STATEMENT SHOWING SEPARATELY THE EXPENDITURES MADE FROM REVENUE AND TURES FOR I. CITY DEPARTMENTS, OFFICES, COURTS, ETC., GROUPED TO INDICATE THE DIVISION OF OTHER THAN DEBT SERVICE; IV. DEFICIENCIES IN TAXES; V. BOROUGH ASSESSMENTS; VI AD

| | 1910 | | 1911 | | LINE No. |
|---|---|---|---|---|---|
| | Revenue Expenditures | Corporate Stock Expenditures | Revenue Expenditures | Corporate Stock Expenditures | |
| VIII. COUNTY EXPENDITURES—*Con.* | | | | | |
| Kings County: | | | | | |
| Charitable Institutions | $55,735 46 | .......... | $57,911 99 | .......... | 1 |
| City Record | 19,035 52 | .......... | 19,967 45 | .......... | 2 |
| County Clerk | 88,661 57 | .......... | 89,670 80 | .......... | 3 |
| Courts—County | 135,531 10 | .......... | 145,356 99 | .......... | 4 |
| Court—Supreme, Second Department | 371,824 57 | .......... | 375,855 58 | .......... | 5 |
| Court — Supreme Court Library | 9,191 67 | .......... | 9,400 00 | .......... | 6 |
| Court—Surrogate's | 92,661 24 | .......... | 91,423 92 | .......... | 7 |
| District Attorney | 118,229 69 | .......... | 131,673 08 | .......... | 8 |
| Commissioner of Jurors | 37,335 10 | .......... | 37,615 12 | .......... | 9 |
| Miscellaneous | 126,103 74 | .......... | 174,540 02 | .......... | 10 |
| National Guard and Naval Militia | 135,867 50 | .......... | 141,277 50 | .......... | 11 |
| Public Administrator | .......... | .......... | .......... | .......... | 12 |
| Commissioner of Records | 98,844 68 | .......... | 98,706 32 | .......... | 13 |
| Register | 220,241 08 | .......... | 216,472 89 | .......... | 14 |
| Sheriff | 85,601 44 | .......... | 87,123 44 | .......... | 15 |
| Total | **$1,594,864 36** | .......... | **$1,676,995 10** | .......... | 16 |
| Queens County: | | | | | |
| Charitable Institutions | $5,244 05 | .......... | $6,415 41 | .......... | 17 |
| City Record | 3,648 58 | .......... | 3,062 83 | .......... | 18 |
| County Clerk | 27,212 54 | .......... | 37,086 02 | .......... | 19 |
| Courts—County | .......... | .......... | 33,139 66 | .......... | 20 |
| Courts—Supreme | 146,779 64 | .......... | 69,953 19 | .......... | 21 |
| Courts—Supreme Court Library | .......... | .......... | .......... | .......... | 22 |
| Courts—Surrogate's | 17,822 67 | .......... | 23,348 18 | .......... | 23 |
| District Attorney | 30,740 49 | .......... | 38,319 94 | .......... | 24 |
| Commissioner of Jurors | 11,708 16 | .......... | 11,779 12 | .......... | 25 |
| Miscellaneous | 14,296 30 | .......... | 51,899 64 | .......... | 26 |
| National Guard and Naval Militia | 5,020 00 | .......... | 5,110 00 | .......... | 27 |
| Public Administrator | 1,200 00 | .......... | 1,200 00 | .......... | 28 |
| Sheriff | 77,790 27 | .......... | 75,381 68 | .......... | 29 |
| Total | **$341,462 70** | .......... | **$356,695 67** | .......... | 30 |
| Richmond County: | | | | | |
| Charitable Institutions | $1,179 45 | .......... | $1,518 83 | .......... | 31 |
| City Record | 2,712 72 | .......... | 1,490 24 | .......... | 32 |
| County Clerk | 20,297 94 | .......... | 18,786 07 | .......... | 33 |
| Courts—County and Surrogate's | 18,618 56 | .......... | 18,399 15 | .......... | 34 |
| Courts—Supreme | 10,962 51 | .......... | 12,726 45 | .......... | 35 |
| District Attorney | 12,220 43 | .......... | 12,657 86 | .......... | 36 |
| Commissioner of Jurors | 4,137 18 | .......... | 4,172 57 | .......... | 37 |
| Miscellaneous | 17,891 13 | .......... | 11,648 12 | .......... | 38 |
| National Guard and Naval Militia | .......... | .......... | .......... | .......... | 39 |
| Sheriff | 23,450 80 | .......... | 27,785 93 | .......... | 40 |
| Total | **$111,470 72** | .......... | **$109,185 22** | .......... | 41 |

# NEW YORK

from Corporate Stock Funds for the Years 1910 to 1914, Inclusive, Classified to Show Expendi-
Responsibility for each Group; II. Debt Service; III. Fixed Charges, Contributions, etc.,
vances for Local Improvements; VII. Direct State Taxes; VIII. County Expense:—*Continued*

| LINE No. | 1912 | | 1913 | | 1914 | |
|---|---|---|---|---|---|---|
| | Revenue Expenditures | Corporate Stock Expenditures | Revenue Expenditures | Corporate Stock Expenditures | Revenue Expenditures | Corporate Stock Expenditures |
| 1 | $58,343 57 | .......... | $55,192 99 | .......... | $51,042 74 | .......... |
| 2 | 17,967 15 | .......... | 18,518 32 | .......... | 18,809 71 | .......... |
| 3 | 98,868 13 | .......... | 104,777 13 | .......... | 104,290 81 | .......... |
| 4 | 161,701 06 | .......... | 172,217 84 | .......... | 194,819 52 | .......... |
| 5 | 407,005 14 | .......... | 427,993 31 | .......... | 466,314 53 | .......... |
| 6 | 9,400 00 | .......... | 9,208 77 | .......... | 9,199 69 | .......... |
| 7 | 102,396 12 | .......... | 104,787 35 | .......... | 109,309 33 | .......... |
| 8 | 113,944 87 | .......... | 129,896 16 | .......... | 140,028 28 | .......... |
| 9 | 41,846 42 | .......... | 40,261 44 | .......... | 40,973 03 | .......... |
| 10 | 127,689 95 | .......... | 141,000 60 | .......... | 146,846 34 | .......... |
| 11 | 144,797 25 | .......... | 144,108 25 | .......... | 154,855 75 | .......... |
| 12 | 12,613 83 | .......... | 12,128 06 | .......... | 12,057 13 | .......... |
| 13 | 97,878 01 | .......... | 99,384 24 | .......... | 98,730 49 | .......... |
| 14 | 218,223 69 | .......... | 216,268 06 | .......... | 197,880 05 | .......... |
| 15 | 88,365 26 | .......... | 91,637 78 | .......... | 95,963 53 | .......... |
| 16 | **$1,701,040 45** | .......... | **$1,767,380 30** | .......... | **$1,841,120 93** | .......... |
| 17 | $5,920 50 | .......... | $6,374 61 | .......... | $5,668 71 | .......... |
| 18 | 2,157 27 | .......... | 3,780 61 | .......... | 3,989 95 | .......... |
| 19 | 77,643 53 | .......... | 107,228 67 | .......... | 127,866 34 | .......... |
| 20 | 39,904 23 | .......... | 43,022 73 | .......... | 42,428 26 | .......... |
| 21 | 73,714 73 | .......... | 94,715 94 | .......... | 95,586 38 | .......... |
| 22 | 2,272 65 | .......... | 2,566 43 | .......... | 2,308 06 | .......... |
| 23 | 23,793 60 | .......... | 23,946 59 | .......... | 26,898 03 | .......... |
| 24 | 32,176 02 | .......... | 35,872 22 | .......... | 40,747 17 | .......... |
| 25 | 10,732 04 | .......... | 12,626 86 | .......... | 12,253 88 | .......... |
| 26 | 33,517 90 | .......... | 38,242 52 | .......... | 38,801 57 | .......... |
| 27 | 5,124 00 | .......... | 5,110 00 | .......... | 5,110 00 | .......... |
| 28 | 1,200 00 | .......... | 1,200 00 | .......... | 1,306 00 | .......... |
| 29 | 71,355 14 | .......... | 52,046 22 | .......... | 44,692 01 | .......... |
| 30 | **$379,511 61** | .......... | **$426,733 40** | .......... | **$447,656 36** | .......... |
| 31 | $1,566 41 | .......... | $1,289 18 | .......... | $1,068 39 | .......... |
| 32 | 2,529 45 | .......... | 2,434 39 | .......... | 1,720 69 | .......... |
| 33 | 18,743 30 | .......... | 22,715 45 | .......... | 21,231 32 | .......... |
| 34 | 23,166 68 | .......... | 21,509 51 | .......... | 21,562 55 | .......... |
| 35 | 12,962 68 | .......... | 18,328 55 | .......... | 19,219 73 | .......... |
| 36 | 13,533 17 | .......... | 15,242 51 | .......... | 24,773 75 | .......... |
| 37 | 4,250 14 | .......... | 4,273 57 | .......... | 4,208 78 | .......... |
| 38 | 12,505 00 | .......... | 12,505 00 | .......... | 9,858 00 | .......... |
| 39 | .......... | .......... | 1,460 00 | .......... | 5,969 00 | .......... |
| 40 | 30,241 93 | .......... | 33,073 32 | .......... | 32,259 90 | .......... |
| 41 | **$119,498 76** | .......... | **$132,831 48** | .......... | **$141,872 11** | .......... |

COMPARATIVE SUMMARY STATEMENT SHOWING SEPARATELY THE EXPENDITURES MADE FROM REVENUE AN[D]
TURES FOR I. CITY DEPARTMENTS, OFFICES, COURTS, ETC., GROUPED TO INDICATE THE DIVISION O[F]
OTHER THAN DEBT SERVICE; IV. DEFICIENCIES IN TAXES; V. BOROUGH ASSESSMENTS; VI. A[…]

| | 1910 | | 1911 | | LINE No. |
|---|---|---|---|---|---|
| | Revenue Expenditures | Corporate Stock Expenditures | Revenue Expenditures | Corporate Stock Expenditures | |
| VIII. COUNTY EXPENDITURES—*Con.* | | | | | |
| Bronx County: | | | | | |
| Charitable Institutions | .......... | .......... | .......... | .......... | |
| City Record | .......... | .......... | .......... | .......... | |
| County Clerk | .......... | .......... | .......... | .......... | |
| Courts—County | .......... | .......... | .......... | .......... | |
| Courts—Supreme, First Department | .......... | .......... | .......... | .......... | |
| Courts—Surrogate's | .......... | .......... | .......... | .......... | |
| District Attorney | .......... | .......... | .......... | .......... | |
| Bronx County Law Library | .......... | .......... | .......... | .......... | |
| Commissioner of Jurors | .......... | .......... | .......... | .......... | |
| Miscellaneous | .......... | .......... | .......... | .......... | 1 |
| National Guard and Naval Militia | .......... | .......... | .......... | .......... | 1 |
| Public Administrator | .......... | .......... | .......... | .......... | 1 |
| Register | .......... | .......... | .......... | .......... | 1 |
| Sheriff | .......... | .......... | .......... | .......... | 1 |
| Total | .......... | .......... | .......... | .......... | 1 |
| Total for County Purposes | **$5,367,776 05** | .......... | **$5,653,704 42** | **$19,277 55** | 1 |
| Total for All Purposes | **$169,932,928 30** | **$75,848,106 93** | **$179,520,591 26** | **$89,141,500 35** | 1 |

NEW YORK

FROM CORPORATE STOCK FUNDS FOR THE YEARS 1910 TO 1914, INCLUSIVE, CLASSIFIED TO SHOW EXPENDI-
RESPONSIBILITY FOR EACH GROUP; II. DEBT SERVICE; III. FIXED CHARGES, CONTRIBUTIONS, ETC.,
VANCES FOR LOCAL IMPROVEMENTS; VII. DIRECT STATE TAXES; VIII. COUNTY EXPENSE:—*Continued*

| LINE No. | 1912 | | 1913 | | 1914 | |
|---|---|---|---|---|---|---|
| | Revenue Expenditures | Corporate Stock Expenditures | Revenue Expenditures | Corporate Stock Expenditures | Revenue Expenditures | Corporate Stock Expenditures |
| 1 | .......... | .......... | .......... | .......... | $24,621 52 | .......... |
| 2 | .......... | .......... | .......... | .......... | 11,799 30 | .......... |
| 3 | .......... | .......... | .......... | .......... | 64,743 72 | .......... |
| 4 | .......... | .......... | .......... | .......... | 37,260 01 | .......... |
| 5 | .......... | .......... | .......... | .......... | Included in New York County | .......... |
| 6 | .......... | .......... | .......... | .......... | 35,039 17 | .......... |
| 7 | .......... | .......... | .......... | .......... | 90,188 79 | .......... |
| 8 | .......... | .......... | .......... | .......... | 5,328 38 | .......... |
| 9 | .......... | .......... | $14,501 45 | .......... | 23,864 09 | .......... |
| 10 | .......... | .......... | .......... | .......... | 14,146 38 | .......... |
| 11 | .......... | .......... | .......... | .......... | 29,052 00 | .......... |
| 12 | .......... | .......... | .......... | .......... | 5,708 52 | .......... |
| 13 | .......... | .......... | .......... | .......... | 97,318 11 | .......... |
| 14 | .......... | .......... | .......... | .......... | 98,289 94 | .......... |
| 15 | .......... | .......... | **$14,501 45** | .......... | **$537,359 93** | .......... |
| 16 | **$5,872,391 48** | **$47,589 18** | **$6,192,334 80** | **$6,640 19** | **$6,825,824 53** | .......... |
| 17 | **$188,967,508 50** | **$80,465,240 79** | **$200,830,761 31** | **$104,535,210 50** | **$206,649,100 68** | **$83,565,097 97** |

THE CITY OF

SUMMARY SHOWING SEPARATELY THE TOTAL EXENDITURES MADE FROM REVENUE AND
THE YEARS 1910

| | Refer to Page | Total Expenditures | Personal Service | Supplies | LINE No. |
|---|---|---|---|---|---|
| **1910** | | | | | |
| Revenue Expenditures..................... | 16 | $169,932,928 30 | $81,849,516 69 | $8,362,904 15 | 1 |
| Corporate Stock Expenditures............. | 66 | 75,848,106 93 | 6,502,370 03 | 489,355 41 | 2 |
| Total............................... | | **$245,781,035 23** | **$88,351,886 72** | **$8,852,259 56** | 3 |
| **1911** | | | | | |
| Revenue Expenditures..................... | 16 | $179,520,591 26 | $83,839,695 57 | $8,327,923 74 | 4 |
| Corporate Stock Expenditures............. | 69 | 89,141,500 35 | 6,576,396 11 | 455,331 31 | 5 |
| Total............................... | | **$268,662,091 61** | **$90,416,091 68** | **$8,783,255 05** | 6 |
| **1912** | | | | | |
| Revenue Expenditures..................... | 16 | $188,967,508 50 | $91,689,012 19 | $10,570,748 19 | 7 |
| Corporate Stock Expenditures............. | 72 | 80,465,240 79 | 6,500,330 94 | 591,574 69 | 8 |
| Total............................... | | **$269,432,749 29** | **$98,189,343 13** | **$11,162,322 88** | 9 |
| **1913** | | | | | |
| Revenue Expenditures..................... | 16 | $200,830,761 31 | $95,963,163 78 | $8,849,497 08 | 10 |
| Corporate Stock Expenditures............. | 75 | 104,535,210 50 | 6,386,824 16 | 355,301 40 | 11 |
| Total............................... | | **$305,365,971 81** | **$102,349,987 94** | **$9,204,798 48** | 12 |
| **1914** | | | | | |
| Revenue Expenditures..................... | 16 | $206,649,100 68 | $100,556,308 59 | $8,732,818 12 | 13 |
| Corporate Stock Expenditures............. | 78 | 83,565,097 97 | 4,967,280 98 | 581,512 15 | 14 |
| Total............................... | | **$290,214,198 65** | **$105,523,589 57** | **$9,314,330 27** | 15 |

NEW YORK

FROM CORPORATE STOCK FUNDS, SEGREGATED BY OBJECTS OF EXPENDITURE, FOR TO 1914, INCLUSIVE:

| LINE No. | Purchase of Equipment | Materials | Contract or Open Order Service | Contingencies | Fixed Charges and Contributions | Unclassified |
|---|---|---|---|---|---|---|
| 1 | $1,433,473 58 | $1,554,052 69 | $16,016,779 91 | $719,621 57 | $57,235,559 50 | $2,761,020 21 |
| 2 | 812,964 32 | 102,572 53 | 45,182,069 64 | 25,933 50 | .......... | 22,732,841 50 |
| 3 | **$2,246,437 90** | **$1,656,625 22** | **$61,198,849 55** | **$745,555 07** | **$57,235,559 50** | **$25,493,861 71** |
| 4 | $1,450,030 62 | $1,433,578 04 | $14,146,996 15 | $686,376 82 | $68,509,879 94 | $1,126,110 38 |
| 5 | 1,182,356 96 | 1,983,643 56 | 49,942,088 86 | 42,420 02 | .......... | 28,959,263 53 |
| 6 | **$2,632,387 58** | **$3,417,221 60** | **$64,089,085 01** | **$728,796 84** | **$68,509,879 94** | **$30,085,373 91** |
| 7 | $1,147,265 36 | $87,365 56 | $15,453,496 87 | $798,513 39 | $67,265,855 74 | $1,955,251 20 |
| 8 | 1,455,345 72 | 860,054 07 | 55,214,611 09 | 51,042 34 | .......... | 15,792,281 94 |
| 9 | **$2,602,611 08** | **$947,419 63** | **$70,668,107 96** | **$849,555 73** | **$67,265,855 74** | **$17,747,533 14** |
| 10 | $2,556,694 12 | $1,536,721 85 | $15,190,591 59 | $468,504 43 | $75,527,437 72 | $738,150 74 |
| 11 | 2,023,418 67 | 105,437 45 | 64,187,839 41 | 78,559 12 | .......... | 31,397,830 29 |
| 12 | **$4,580,112 79** | **$1,642,159 30** | **$79,378,431 00** | **$547,063 55** | **$75,527,437 72** | **$32,135,981 03** |
| 13 | $2,410,223 62 | $1,297,368 53 | $17,145,255 74 | $665,844 68 | $74,933,179 50 | $908,101 90 |
| 14 | 2,127,652 76 | 184,779 62 | 55,188,827 18 | 33,175 68 | .......... | 20,481,869 60 |
| 15 | **$4,537,876 38** | **$1,482,148 15** | **$72,334,082 79** | **$699,020 36** | **$74,933,179 50** | **$21,389,971 90** |

Summary of Recapitulation Statements Showing Expenditures from Revenues Separately for Segregated by Objects of Expenditures

| | Refer to Page | Total | Personal Service | Supplies | Line No. |
|---|---|---|---|---|---|
| **1910** | | | | | |
| Budget Appropriations | 17 | $158,463,309 27 | $78,086,603 64 | $7,489,529 66 | 1 |
| Special Revenue Bond Funds | 41 | 7,208,146 57 | 1,861,807 73 | 290,466 29 | 2 |
| Special Accounts | 61 | 4,261,472 46 | 1,901,105 32 | 582,908 20 | 3 |
| Total for 1910, carried to page 15. | | **$169,932,928 30** | **$81,849,516 69** | **$8,362,904 15** | 4 |
| **1911** | | | | | |
| Budget Appropriations | 21 | $170,359,756 23 | $80,387,313 78 | $7,470,976 64 | 5 |
| Special Revenue Bond Funds | 45 | 4,766,895 35 | 1,588,382 79 | 219,157 68 | 6 |
| Special Accounts | 62 | 4,393,939 68 | 1,863,999 00 | 637,789 42 | 7 |
| Total for 1911, carried to page 15. | | **$179,520,591 26** | **$83,839,695 57** | **$8,327,923 74** | 8 |
| **1912** | | | | | |
| Budget Appropriations | 26 | $178,617,795 79 | $87,837,760 35 | *$9,778,642 82 | 9 |
| Special Revenue Bond Funds | 49 | 6,210,975 94 | 2,142,867 38 | 229,722 81 | 10 |
| Special Accounts | 63 | 4,138,736 77 | 1,708,384 46 | 562,382 56 | 11 |
| Total for 1912, carried to page 15. | | **$188,967,508 50** | **$91,689,012 19** | **$10,570,748 19** | 12 |
| **1913** | | | | | |
| Budget Appropriations | 31 | $190,706,070 19 | $91,745,874 30 | $8,016,106 91 | 13 |
| Special Revenue Bond Funds | 53 | 5,969,031 83 | 2,374,358 68 | 359,944 57 | 14 |
| Special Accounts | 64 | 4,155,659 29 | 1,842,930 80 | 473,445 60 | 15 |
| Total for 1913, carried to page 15. | | **$200,830,761 31** | **$95,963,163 78** | **$8,849,497 08** | 16 |
| **1914** | | | | | |
| Budget Appropriations | 36 | $192,457,617 46 | $95,574,568 32 | $7,937,974 31 | 17 |
| Special Revenue Bond Funds | 57 | 10,224,887 88 | 3,246,669 27 | 363,365 83 | 18 |
| Special Accounts | 65 | 3,966,595 34 | 1,735,071 00 | 431,477 98 | 19 |
| Total for 1914, carried to page 15. | | **$206,649,100 68** | **$100,556,308 59** | **$8,732,818 12** | 20 |

* In 1912 the appropriations for Materials and Supplies were not made separately. Therefore the

## NEW YORK

I. Budget Appropriations, II. Special Revenue Bond Funds, and III. Special Accounts; for the Years 1910 to 1914, Inclusive:

| LINE No. | Purchase of Equipment | Materials | Contract or Open Order Service | Contingencies | Fixed Charges and Contributions | Unclassified |
|---|---|---|---|---|---|---|
| 1 | $1,182,153 24 | $1,359,606 72 | $13,820,268 95 | $691,423 74 | $55,833,723 32 | .......... |
| 2 | 182,883 59 | 39,638 86 | 1,886,417 20 | 14,600 75 | 178,410 35 | $2,753,921 80 |
| 3 | 68,436 75 | 154,807 11 | 310,093 76 | 13,597 08 | 1,223,425 83 | 7,098 41 |
| 4 | **$1,433,473 58** | **$1,554,052 69** | **$16,016,779 91** | **$719,621 57** | **$57,235,559 50** | **$2,761,020 21** |
| 5 | $968,764 26 | $1,338,501 90 | $12,808,412 04 | $667,275 89 | $66,718,511 72 | .......... |
| 6 | 416,391 90 | 23,322 10 | 953,690 62 | 4,283 80 | 443,418 99 | $1,118,247 47 |
| 7 | 64,874 46 | 71,754 04 | 384,893 49 | 14,817 13 | 1,347,949 23 | 7,862 91 |
| 8 | **$1,450,030 62** | **$1,433,578 04** | **$14,146,996 15** | **$686,376 82** | **$68,509,879 94** | **$1,126,110 38** |
| 9 | $781,334 60 | *.......... | $14,163,002 19 | $756,409 26 | $65,300,646 57 | .......... |
| 10 | 245,260 77 | $30,346 76 | 981,786 72 | 27,464 63 | 605,670 44 | $1,947,856 43 |
| 11 | 120,669 99 | 57,018 80 | 308,707 96 | 14,639 50 | 1,359,538 73 | 7,394 77 |
| 12 | **$1,147,265 36** | **$87,365 56** | **$15,453,496 87** | **$798,513 39** | **$67,265,855 74** | **$1,955,251 20** |
| 13 | $2,252,357 52 | $1,473,349 06 | $13,888,242 68 | $427,499 40 | $72,902,640 32 | .......... |
| 14 | 190,749 83 | 21,047 52 | 1,034,970 55 | 39,032 14 | 1,218,590 13 | $730,338 41 |
| 15 | 113,586 77 | 42,325 27 | 267,378 36 | 1,972 89 | 1,406,207 27 | 7,812 33 |
| 16 | **$2,556,694 12** | **$1,536,721 85** | **$15,190,591 59** | **$468,504 43** | **$75,527,437 72** | **$738,150 74** |
| 17 | $2,063,063 73 | $1,222,860 63 | $16,454,960 50 | $579,984 64 | $68,624,205 33 | .......... |
| 18 | 238,868 90 | 5,552 24 | 494,619 24 | 83,269 79 | 4,891,930 36 | $900,612 25 |
| 19 | 108,290 99 | 68,955 66 | 195,676 00 | 2,590 25 | 1,417,043 81 | 7,489 65 |
| 20 | **$2,410,223 62** | **$1,297,368 53** | **$17,145,255 74** | **$665,844 68** | **$74,933,179 50** | **$908,101 90** |

Expenditures for Materials for this year are included with Supplies.

RECAPITULATION OF STATEMENT SHOWING EXPENDITURES FROM REVENUE (BUDGET

| | Total | Personal Service | LINE No. |
|---|---|---|---|
| CITY DEPARTMENTS, OFFICES, COURTS, ETC. | | | |
| Mayor and Subordinate Departments, Bureaus, and Offices: | | | |
| Mayor's Office and Departments whose executive heads are appointed by the Mayor and who are removable at his pleasure. | $52,709,937 61 | $37,714,239 44 | 1 |
| Departments whose heads are appointed by the Mayor for a term of office greater than his own, and who are removable only upon charges | 30,514,749 76 | 25,070,020 75 | 2 |
| Boards and Commissions majority of which are appointed by the Mayor and for which no other elected City official shares responsibility | 91,058 40 | 51,585 17 | 3 |
| Total Mayor and Subordinate Departments, Bureaus and Offices | **$83,315,745 77** | **$62,835,845 36** | 4 |
| Comptroller and Finance Department, excluding the Chamberlain's Office | **$1,431,928 58** | **$1,337,681 23** | 5 |
| Borough Presidents and Subordinate Departments: | | | |
| President, Borough of Manhattan | $2,545,110 89 | $1,594,495 91 | 6 |
| President, Borough of The Bronx | 1,115,484 09 | 864,437 22 | 7 |
| President, Borough of Brooklyn | 2,135,403 79 | 1,474,772 61 | 8 |
| President, Borough of Queens | 1,308,608 33 | 909,416 93 | 9 |
| President, Borough of Richmond | 761,720 08 | 501,289 86 | 10 |
| Total, Borough Presidents | **$7,866,327 18** | **$5,344,412 53** | 11 |
| Board of Aldermen, President of Board and City Clerk | **$261,341 97** | **$257,841 97** | 12 |
| Boards, Commissions, etc., whose members are not elected by popular vote and who are not appointed by any elected City official | **$9,423 53** | **$8,610 00** | 13 |
| Boards, Commissions, etc., of mixed responsibility, i.e., ex-officio bodies representing two or more of preceding branches | **$2,262,771 52** | **$670,624 31** | 14 |
| Courts, including Board of Parole and General Interpreters of Brooklyn | **$1,955,151 10** | **$1,923,339 53** | 15 |
| Total, City Departments, Offices, Courts, etc. | **$97,102,689 65** | **$72,378,354 93** | 16 |
| DEBT SERVICE (*See details page 120*) | **$44,743,741 92** | .......... | 17 |
| FIXED CHARGES OTHER THAN DEBT SERVICE, SUBSIDIES, CONTRIBUTIONS, PAYMENTS TO PRIVATE AND STATE INSTITUTIONS, EXPENDITURES NOT ALLOTTED TO DEPARTMENTS | **$7,680,377 57** | **$1,253,603 81** | 18 |
| DEFICIENCIES IN TAXES | **$4,000,000 00** | .......... | 19 |
| Total for City Purposes | **$153,526,809 14** | **$73,631,958 74** | 20 |
| COUNTY EXPENDITURES: | | | |
| New York County | $2,937,465 13 | $2,655,421 18 | 21 |
| Kings County | 1,566,030 27 | 1,434,750 48 | 22 |
| Queens County | 329,777 74 | 280,233 57 | 23 |
| Richmond County | 103,226 99 | 84,239 67 | 24 |
| Total for County Purposes | **$4,936,500 13** | **$4,454,644 90** | 25 |
| Total for All Purposes | **$158,463,309 27** | **$78,086,603 64** | 26 |

NEW YORK

APPROPRIATIONS) FOR THE YEAR 1910, CLASSIFIED BY OBJECTS OF EXPENDITURE:

| LINE No. | Supplies | Purchase of Equipment | Materials | Contract or Open Order Service | Contingencies | Fixed Charges and Contributions |
|---|---|---|---|---|---|---|
| 1 | $4,351,947 86 | $524,218 80 | $860,975 08 | $8,080,092 42 | $351,331 37 | $827,132 64 |
| 2 | 2,357,215 93 | 290,980 19 | 21,500 04 | 2,715,759 25 | 46,795 92 | 12,477 68 |
| 3 | 33,493 34 | .......... | 992 61 | 2,167 03 | 2,820 25 | .......... |
| 4 | **$6,742,657 13** | **$815,198 99** | **$883,467 73** | **$10,798,018 70** | **$400,947 54** | **$839,610 32** |
| 5 | **$38,635 83** | .......... | .......... | **$14,227 61** | **$41,383 91** | .......... |
| 6 | $117,168 12 | $25,790 98 | $43,247 63 | $743,008 63 | $21,399 62 | .......... |
| 7 | 22,485 56 | 6,042 58 | 83,571 47 | 128,791 38 | 10,155 88 | .......... |
| 8 | 123,437 70 | 29,088 00 | 180,299 76 | 308,544 52 | 19,261 20 | .......... |
| 9 | 38,688 61 | 11,456 84 | 36,152 48 | 298,755 56 | 14,137 91 | .......... |
| 10 | 39,088 73 | 15,853 44 | 111,218 84 | 85,115 71 | 9,153 50 | .......... |
| 11 | **$340,868 72** | **$88,231 84** | **$454,490 18** | **$1,564,215 80** | **$74,108 11** | .......... |
| 12 | .......... | .......... | .......... | .......... | **$3,500 00** | .......... |
| 13 | .......... | .......... | .......... | **$452 68** | **$360 85** | .......... |
| 14 | **$88,254 85** | **$135 90** | .......... | **$1,146,555 12** | **$44,170 60** | **$313,030 74** |
| 15 | **$3,020 30** | .......... | .......... | **$7,934 94** | **$20,856 33** | .......... |
| 16 | **$7,213,436 83** | **$903,566 73** | **$1,337,957 91** | **$13,531,404 85** | **$585,327 34** | **$1,152,641 06** |
| 17 | .......... | .......... | .......... | .......... | .......... | ***$44,743,741 92** |
| 18 | **$206,906 28** | **$275,388 88** | **$21,056 92** | **$166,978 12** | **$22,554 86** | **$5,733,888 70** |
| 19 | .......... | .......... | .......... | .......... | .......... | **$4,000,000 00** |
| 20 | **$7,420,343 11** | **$1,178,955 61** | **$1,359,014 83** | **$13,698,382 97** | **$607,882 20** | **$55,630,271 68** |
| 21 | $26,875 26 | $350 50 | $591 89 | $67,101 48 | $46,857 14 | $140,267 68 |
| 22 | 10,765 83 | 986 50 | .......... | 39,269 63 | 23,522 37 | 56,735 46 |
| 23 | 23,035 65 | 1,860 63 | .......... | 10,296 73 | 9,107 11 | 5,244 05 |
| 24 | 8,509 81 | .......... | .......... | 5,218 14 | 4,054 92 | 1,204 45 |
| 25 | **$69,186 55** | **$3,197 63** | **$591 89** | **$121,885 98** | **$83,541 54** | **$203,451 64** |
| 26 | **$7,489,529 66** | **$1,182,153 24** | **$1,359,606 72** | **$13,820,268 95** | **$691,423 74** | **$55,833,723 32** |

*Includes redemption of $5,208,150.00 Special Revenue Bonds issued to defray expenses of 1909.

# THE CITY OF

STATEMENT SHOWING EXPENDITURES FROM REVENUE (BUDGET

| | Total | Personal Service | LINE No. |
|---|---|---|---|
| CITY DEPARTMENTS, OFFICES, COURTS, ETC. | | | |
| Mayor and Subordinate Departments, Bureaus, and Offices: | | | |
| Mayor's Office and Departments whose executive heads are appointed by the Mayor and who are removable at his pleasure: | | | |
| Commissioners of Accounts | $206,139 64 | $195,644 13 | 1 |
| Board of Assessors | 42,525 67 | 40,673 38 | 2 |
| Department of Bridges | 763,369 17 | 595,269 44 | 3 |
| City Chamberlain | 54,273 86 | 52,501 61 | 4 |
| Department of Correction | 1,201,310 09 | 519,074 57 | 5 |
| Department of Docks and Ferries | 2,475,035 40 | 1,478,688 02 | 6 |
| Examining Board of Plumbers | 5,960 48 | 5,685 00 | 7 |
| Fire Department | 7,940,350 15 | 7,199,786 57 | 8 |
| Department of Health | 2,666,045 96 | 1,982,772 43 | 9 |
| Law Department | 770,000 94 | 702,336 19 | 10 |
| Commissioner of Licenses | 51,647 87 | 49,155 34 | 11 |
| Mayoralty—Administration | 53,066 44 | 49,808 69 | 12 |
| Mayoralty—Bureau of Licenses | 34,330 79 | 27,787 16 | 13 |
| Mayoralty—Bureau of Weights and Measures | 35,821 59 | 30,590 69 | 14 |
| Municipal Civil Service Commission | 147,548 61 | 140,463 61 | 15 |
| Municipal Explosives Commission | 3,970 37 | 3,897 81 | 16 |
| Park Board | 25,512 19 | 25,512 19 | 17 |
| Department of Parks—Manhattan and Richmond | 998,342 68 | 735,649 12 | 18 |
| Department of Parks—The Bronx | 412,430 44 | 318,869 89 | 19 |
| Department of Parks—Brooklyn and Queens | 993,801 32 | 626,857 73 | 20 |
| Police Department | 15,055,339 81 | 13,888,661 93 | 21 |
| Department of Public Charities | 2,629,986 86 | 984,900 53 | 22 |
| Department of Street Cleaning | 8,325,857 77 | 5,204,077 84 | 23 |
| Department of Taxes and Assessment | 470,120 45 | 454,766 82 | 24 |
| Tenement House Department | 793,802 75 | 769,587 32 | 25 |
| Department of Water Supply, Gas and Electricity | 6,553,346 31 | 1,631,221 43 | 26 |
| Total | **$52,709,937 61** | **$37,714,239 44** | 27 |
| Departments whose heads are appointed by the Mayor for a term of office greater than his own, and who are removable only upon charges: | | | |
| Bellevue and Allied Hospitals | $1,108,373 05 | $462,993 45 | 28 |
| College of the City of New York | 604,031 45 | 519,308 55 | 29 |
| Department of Education | 28,437,488 00 | 23,760,131 91 | 30 |
| Normal College of the City of New York | 364,857 26 | 327,586 84 | 31 |
| Total | **$30,514,749 76** | **$25,070,020 75** | 32 |
| Boards and Commissions majorities of which are appointed by the Mayor and for which no other elected City official shares responsibility: | | | |
| Art Commission | $7,587 79 | $5,267 03 | 33 |
| Brooklyn Disciplinary Training School for Boys | 54,753 46 | 26,026 27 | 34 |
| Permanent Census Board | 28,717 15 | 20,291 87 | 35 |
| Total | **$91,058 40** | **$51,585 17** | 36 |
| Total, Mayor and Subordinate Departments, Bureaus and Offices | **$83,315,745 77** | **$62,835,845 36** | 37 |
| Comptroller and Finance Department, excluding the Chamberlain's Office: | | | |
| Department of Finance | **$1,431,928 58** | **$1,337,681 23** | 38 |
| Borough Presidents and Subordinate Departments: | | | |
| President, Borough of Manhattan | $2,545,110 89 | $1,594,495 91 | 39 |
| President, Borough of The Bronx | 1,115,484 09 | 864,437 22 | 40 |
| President, Borough of Brooklyn | 2,135,403 79 | 1,474,772 61 | 41 |
| President, Borough of Queens | 1,308,608 33 | 909,416 93 | 42 |
| President, Borough of Richmond | 761,720 08 | 501,289 86 | 43 |
| Total | **$7,866,327 18** | **$5,344,412 53** | 44 |

## NEW YORK

Appropriations) for the Year 1910, Classified by Objects of Expenditure:

| Line No. | Supplies | Purchase of Equipment | Materials | Contract or Open Order Service | Contingencies | Fixed Charges and Contributions |
|---|---|---|---|---|---|---|
| 1 | $1,557 89 | .......... | .......... | $763 28 | $8,174 34 | .......... |
| 2 | 1,083 82 | .......... | .......... | 278 37 | 490 10 | .......... |
| 3 | 29,693 58 | $3,471 63 | $57,500 84 | 73,225 58 | 4,208 10 | .......... |
| 4 | 1,025 25 | .......... | .......... | 469 50 | 277 50 | .......... |
| 5 | 519,417 11 | 7,480 61 | 103,079 30 | 42,649 95 | 4,599 97 | $5,008 58 |
| 6 | 363,590 60 | 512 29 | 180,914 10 | 391,294 52 | 13,400 87 | 46,635 00 |
| 7 | 275 48 | .......... | .......... | .......... | .......... | .......... |
| 8 | 417,996 68 | 102,795 90 | 93,196 88 | 119,921 52 | 6,652 60 | .......... |
| 9 | 434,718 14 | 32,419 32 | 10,759 58 | 113,748 05 | 91,628 44 | .......... |
| 10 | 4,337 76 | .......... | .......... | 6,965 17 | 56,361 82 | .......... |
| 11 | 104 80 | .......... | .......... | 340 26 | 2,047 47 | .......... |
| 12 | .......... | .......... | .......... | 584 51 | 2,673 24 | .......... |
| 13 | .......... | .......... | .......... | 153 75 | 6,389 88 | .......... |
| 14 | 500 00 | .......... | .......... | .......... | 4,730 90 | .......... |
| 15 | 604 19 | .......... | .......... | 945 29 | 5,535 52 | .......... |
| 16 | .......... | .......... | .......... | .......... | 72 56 | .......... |
| 17 | .......... | .......... | .......... | .......... | .......... | .......... |
| 18 | 70,419 35 | 19,845 81 | 94,677 71 | 71,269 77 | 6,480 92 | .......... |
| 19 | 9,209 49 | 6,150 86 | 26,079 69 | 50,688 27 | 1,432 24 | .......... |
| 20 | 71,412 31 | 15,912 98 | 89,138 96 | 184,480 39 | 5,998 95 | .......... |
| 21 | 343,688 07 | 63,082 03 | 11,436 92 | 114,011 66 | 34,459 20 | $600,000 00 |
| 22 | 1,322,898 74 | 19,200 61 | 39,942 86 | 138,937 44 | 7,972 90 | 116,133 78 |
| 23 | 577,971 14 | 232,555 67 | 99,876 51 | 2,207,326 30 | 4,050 31 | .......... |
| 24 | 2,816 31 | .......... | .......... | 709 15 | 11,828 17 | .......... |
| 25 | 4,122 07 | .......... | .......... | 883 03 | 19,210 33 | .......... |
| 26 | 174,505 08 | 20,791 09 | 54,371 73 | 4,560,446 66 | 52,655 04 | 59,355 28 |
| 27 | **$4,351,947 86** | **$524,218 80** | **$860,975 08** | **$8,080,092 42** | **$351,331 37** | **$827,132 64** |
| 28 | $532,298 38 | $22,357 95 | $18,153 82 | $65,781 87 | $6,787 58 | .......... |
| 29 | 55,144 74 | .......... | 3,346 22 | 24,692 91 | 1,539 03 | .......... |
| 30 | 1,744,525 33 | 268,622 24 | .......... | 2,615,717 32 | 36,013 52 | $12,477 68 |
| 31 | 25,247 48 | .......... | .......... | 9,567 15 | 2,455 79 | .......... |
| 32 | **$2,357,215 93** | **$290,980 19** | **$21,500 04** | **$2,715,759 25** | **$46,795 92** | **$12,477 68** |
| 33 | .......... | .......... | .......... | $1,879 11 | $441 65 | .......... |
| 34 | $26,545 21 | .......... | $992 61 | 287 92 | 901 45 | .......... |
| 35 | 6,948 13 | .......... | .......... | .......... | 1,477 15 | .......... |
| 36 | **$33,493 34** | .......... | **$992 61** | **$2,167 03** | **$2,820 25** | .......... |
| 37 | **$6,742,657 13** | **$815,198 99** | **$883,467 73** | **$10,798,018 70** | **$400,947 54** | **$839,610 32** |
| 38 | **$38,635 83** | .......... | .......... | **$14,227 61** | **$41,383 91** | .......... |
| 39 | $117,168 12 | $25,790 98 | $43,247 63 | $743,008 63 | $21,399 62 | .......... |
| 40 | 22,485 56 | 6,042 58 | 83,571 47 | 128,791 38 | 10,155 88 | .......... |
| 41 | 123,437 70 | 29,088 00 | 180,299 76 | 308,544 52 | 19,261 20 | .......... |
| 42 | 38,688 61 | 11,456 84 | 36,152 48 | 298,755 56 | 14,137 91 | .......... |
| 43 | 39,088 73 | 15,853 44 | 111,218 84 | 85,115 71 | 9,153 50 | .......... |
| 44 | **$340,868 72** | **$88,231 84** | **$454,490 18** | **$1,564,215 80** | **$74,108 11** | .......... |

THE CITY OF

STATEMENT SHOWING EXPENDITURES FROM REVENUE (BUDGET

| | Total | Personal Service | LINE No. |
|---|---|---|---|
| CITY DEPARTMENTS, OFFICES, COURTS, ETC.—*Continued* | | | |
| Board of Aldermen, President of Board and City Clerk | **$261,341 97** | **$257,841 97** | 1 |
| Boards, Commissions, etc., whose members are not elected by popular vote and who are not appointed by any elected City Official: | | | |
| Board of Building Examiners | $9,423 53 | $8,610 00 | 2 |
| Total | **$9,423 53** | **$8,610 00** | 3 |
| Boards, Commissions, etc., of mixed responsibility, i.e., ex-officio bodies, representing two or more preceding branches: | | | |
| Armory Board | $105,358 41 | $12,386 00 | 4 |
| Board of City Record, City of New York | 1,064,906 97 | 32,594 48 | 5 |
| Board of Elections | 936,022 18 | 501,907 29 | 6 |
| Board of Estimate and Apportionment | 153,229 71 | 120,686 54 | 7 |
| Commissioners of the Sinking Fund | 3,254 25 | 3,050 00 | 8 |
| Total | **$2,262,771 52** | **$670,624 31** | 9 |
| Courts, including Board of Parole and General Interpreters of Brooklyn: | | | |
| Coroners, Borough of Manhattan | $64,194 29 | $62,170 15 | 10 |
| Coroners, Borough of The Bronx | 28,538 32 | 26,982 96 | 11 |
| Coroners, Borough of Brooklyn | 31,739 87 | 30,590 00 | 12 |
| Coroners, Borough of Queens | 19,154 66 | 17,325 51 | 13 |
| Coroners, Borough of Richmond | 12,151 79 | 11,200 00 | 14 |
| City Court of New York | 233,768 20 | 232,000 00 | 15 |
| City Magistrates' Courts, First Division | 233,045 10 | 228,918 59 | 16 |
| City Magistrates' Courts, Second Division | 238,034 36 | 234,137 10 | 17 |
| Municipal Courts, City of New York | 894,695 56 | 886,793 07 | 18 |
| Court of Special Sessions | 186,661 09 | 180,222 15 | 19 |
| General Interpreters of Brooklyn | 10,200 00 | 10,200 00 | 20 |
| Board of Parole | 2,967 86 | 2,800 00 | 21 |
| Total | **$1,955,151 10** | **$1,923,339 53** | 22 |
| Total City Departments, Offices, Courts, etc | **$97,102,689 65** | **$72,378,354 93** | 23 |
| DEBT SERVICE (*See details page 120*) | **$44,743,741 92** | .......... | 24 |
| FIXED CHARGES, OTHER THAN DEBT SERVICE, SUBSIDIES, CONTRIBUTIONS, PAYMENTS TO PRIVATE AND STATE INSTITUTIONS, EXPENDITURES NOT ALLOTTED TO DEPARTMENTS: | | | |
| American Museum of Natural History | $185,757 00 | $156,500 00 | 25 |
| Charitable Institutions, City | 4,511,647 65 | .......... | 26 |
| Children's Museum, Brooklyn | 11,861 29 | 9,428 86 | 27 |
| Grant's Tomb | 7,000 00 | .......... | 28 |
| Jumel Mansion | 4,129 85 | 3,307 95 | 29 |
| Metropolitan Museum of Art | 200,000 00 | 161,097 75 | 30 |
| Miscellaneous, City | 1,200,097 44 | .......... | 31 |
| Museum of Arts and Sciences | 93,555 59 | 68,366 66 | 32 |
| New York Aquarium | 45,974 86 | 30,202 16 | 33 |
| New York Botanical Garden | 82,936 32 | 64,855 35 | 34 |
| New York Zoological Garden | 167,632 00 | 109,997 20 | 35 |
| Brooklyn Public Library | 418,696 71 | 229,282 72 | 36 |
| New York Public Library | 617,633 60 | 346,638 86 | 37 |
| Queensborough Public Library | 118,463 80 | 64,800 00 | 38 |
| Staten Island Association of Arts and Sciences | 3,991 46 | 3,485 50 | 39 |
| United States Volunteer Life Saving Corps | 11,000 00 | 5,640 80 | 40 |
| Total | **$7,680,377 57** | **$1,253,603 81** | 41 |
| DEFICIENCIES IN TAXES | **$4,000,000 00** | .......... | 42 |
| Total for City Purposes | **$153,526,809 14** | **$73,631,958 74** | 43 |

NEW YORK

APPROPRIATIONS) FOR THE YEAR 1910, CLASSIFIED BY OBJECTS OF EXPENDITURE:—*Continued*

| LINE No. | Supplies | Purchase of Equipment | Materials | Contract or Open Order Service | Contingencies | Fixed Charges and Contributions |
|---|---|---|---|---|---|---|
| 1 | .......... | .......... | .......... | .......... | **$3,500 00** | .......... |
| 2 | .......... | .......... | .......... | $452 68 | $360 85 | .......... |
| 3 | .......... | .......... | .......... | **$452 68** | **$360 85** | .......... |
| 4 | .......... | .......... | .......... | $91,244 55 | $1,727 86 | .......... |
| 5 | $1,030 40 | .......... | .......... | 1,028,047 24 | 3,234 85 | .......... |
| 6 | 87,224 45 | $135 90 | .......... | 27,263 33 | 6,460 47 | $313,030 74 |
| 7 | .......... | .......... | .......... | .......... | 32,543 17 | .......... |
| 8 | .......... | .......... | .......... | .......... | 204 25 | .......... |
| 9 | **$88,254 85** | **$135 90** | .......... | **$1,146,555 12** | **$44,170 60** | **$313,030 74** |
| 10 | $240 24 | .......... | .......... | $776 72 | $1,007 18 | .......... |
| 11 | .......... | .......... | .......... | 951 50 | 603 86 | .......... |
| 12 | .......... | .......... | .......... | 318 08 | 831 79 | .......... |
| 13 | .......... | .......... | .......... | 306 08 | 1,523 07 | .......... |
| 14 | 119 35 | .......... | .......... | 177 16 | 655 28 | .......... |
| 15 | .......... | .......... | .......... | 291 75 | 1,476 45 | .......... |
| 16 | 2,031 74 | .......... | .......... | 1,549 96 | 544 81 | .......... |
| 17 | 300 00 | .......... | .......... | 3,035 47 | 561 79 | .......... |
| 18 | .......... | .......... | .......... | .......... | 7,902 49 | .......... |
| 19 | 328 97 | .......... | .......... | 528 22 | 5,581 75 | .......... |
| 20 | .......... | .......... | .......... | .......... | .......... | .......... |
| 21 | .......... | .......... | .......... | .......... | 167 86 | .......... |
| 22 | **$3,020 30** | .......... | .......... | **$7,934 94** | **$20,856 33** | .......... |
| 23 | **$7,213,436 83** | **$903,566 73** | **$1,337,957 91** | **$13,531,404 85** | **$585,327 34** | **$1,152,641 06** |
| 24 | .......... | .......... | .......... | .......... | .......... | **$44,743,741 92** |
| 25 | $18,669 00 | $850 00 | $6,500 00 | $1,780 00 | $1,458 00 | .......... |
| 26 | .......... | .......... | .......... | .......... | .......... | $4,511,647 65 |
| 27 | 1,019 45 | 272 76 | .......... | 594 35 | 545 87 | .......... |
| 28 | .......... | .......... | .......... | 7,000 00 | .......... | .......... |
| 29 | 591 60 | .......... | .......... | 4 80 | 225 50 | .......... |
| 30 | 17,856 80 | 1,850 00 | 6,685 45 | 600 00 | 11,910 00 | .......... |
| 31 | .......... | .......... | .......... | .......... | .......... | 1,200,097 44 |
| 32 | 10,091 21 | 3,268 18 | 2,990 83 | 3,499 61 | 5,339 10 | .......... |
| 33 | 9,723 60 | .......... | 598 93 | 4,944 16 | 506 01 | .......... |
| 34 | 14,887 82 | 666 48 | 1,249 98 | 783 17 | 493 52 | .......... |
| 35 | 51,845 53 | 383 46 | 3,031 73 | 641 55 | 1,732 53 | .......... |
| 36 | 25,793 00 | 99,125 00 | .......... | 50,990 99 | .......... | 13,505 00 |
| 37 | 48,780 00 | 143,310 00 | .......... | 78,724 74 | .......... | 180 00 |
| 38 | 7,300 00 | 23,927 76 | .......... | 14,764 44 | .......... | 7,671 60 |
| 39 | .......... | .......... | .......... | 505 96 | .......... | .......... |
| 40 | 348 27 | 1,735 24 | .......... | 2,144 35 | 344 33 | 787 01 |
| 41 | **$206,906 28** | **$275,388 88** | **$21,056 92** | **$166,978 12** | **$22,554 86** | **$5,733,888 70** |
| 42 | .......... | .......... | .......... | .......... | .......... | **$4,000,000 00** |
| 43 | **$7,420,343 11** | **$1,178,955 61** | **$1,359,014 83** | **$13,698,382 97** | **$607,882 20** | **$55,630,271 68** |

| | Total | Personal Service | LINE No. |
|---|---|---|---|
| COUNTY EXPENDITURES: | | | |
| New York County: | | | |
| Charitable Institutions | $113,875 22 | .......... | 1 |
| Board of City Record | 34,984 60 | .......... | 2 |
| County Clerk | 140,759 23 | $139,086 23 | 3 |
| District Attorney | 346,854 35 | 317,628 92 | 4 |
| Supreme Court, First Department | 854,074 44 | 831,157 00 | 5 |
| Surrogate's Court | 176,742 30 | 174,403 47 | 6 |
| Commissioner of Jurors | 50,341 57 | 46,122 60 | 7 |
| Miscellaneous | 284,203 06 | 239,235 80 | 8 |
| National Guard and Naval Militia | 185,828 75 | 177,828 75 | 9 |
| Public Administrator | 26,096 50 | 25,330 00 | 10 |
| Commissioner of Records | 70,243 37 | 67,051 35 | 11 |
| Register | 228,490 64 | 222,840 88 | 12 |
| Sheriff | 132,652 83 | 124,507 33 | 13 |
| Court of General Sessions | 292,318 27 | 290,228 85 | 14 |
| Total | **$2,937,465 13** | **$2,655,421 18** | 15 |
| Kings County: | | | |
| Charitable Institutions | $55,735 46 | .......... | 16 |
| Board of City Record | 19,035 52 | .......... | 17 |
| County Clerk | 83,951 43 | $81,628 48 | 18 |
| County Court | 135,531 10 | 133,972 90 | 19 |
| Supreme Court, Second Department | 369,624 57 | 364,746 55 | 20 |
| Surrogate's Court | 88,689 81 | 86,931 93 | 21 |
| District Attorney | 114,004 35 | 102,623 41 | 22 |
| Commissioner of Jurors | 37,335 10 | 35,725 48 | 23 |
| Miscellaneous | 116,925 04 | 104,925 04 | 24 |
| Law Library Supreme Court | 9,191 67 | 8,591 67 | 25 |
| National Guard and Naval Militia | 135,867 50 | 135,867 50 | 26 |
| Commissioner of Records | 98,844 68 | 97,382 88 | 27 |
| Register | 215,692 60 | 203,189 89 | 28 |
| Sheriff | 85,601 44 | 79,164 75 | 29 |
| Total | **$1,566,030 27** | **$1,434,750 48** | 30 |
| Queens County: | | | |
| Charitable Institutions | $5,244 05 | .......... | 31 |
| Board of City Record | 3,648 58 | .......... | 32 |
| County Clerk | 26,209 94 | $21,780 07 | 33 |
| Supreme Court and County Court | 146,779 64 | 141,733 65 | 34 |
| Surrogate's Court | 17,556 55 | 16,519 92 | 35 |
| District Attorney | 28,167 85 | 26,268 98 | 36 |
| Commissioner of Jurors | 11,708 16 | 11,119 70 | 37 |
| Miscellaneous | 6,452 70 | 700 00 | 38 |
| National Guard and Naval Militia | 5,020 00 | 5,020 00 | 39 |
| Public Administrator | 1,200 00 | 1,200 00 | 40 |
| Sheriff | 77,790 27 | 55,891 25 | 41 |
| Total | **$329,777 74** | **$280,233 57** | 42 |
| Richmond County: | | | |
| Charitable Institutions | $1,179 45 | .......... | 43 |
| Board of City Record | 2,712 72 | .......... | 44 |
| County Clerk | 19,464 61 | $19,020 66 | 45 |
| County Court and Surrogate's Court | 18,618 56 | 18,150 00 | 46 |
| Supreme Court | 10,962 51 | 10,962 51 | 47 |
| District Attorney | 12,220 43 | 10,074 60 | 48 |
| Commissioner of Jurors | 4,137 18 | 3,974 60 | 49 |
| Miscellaneous | 10,480 73 | 7,784 50 | 50 |
| Sheriff | 23,450 80 | 14,272 80 | 51 |
| Total | **$103,226 99** | **$84,239 67** | 52 |
| Total for County Purposes | **$4,936,500 13** | **$4,454,644 90** | 53 |
| Total for All Purposes | **$158,463,309 27** | **$78,086,603 64** | 54 |

## NEW YORK

APPROPRIATIONS) FOR THE YEAR 1910, CLASSIFIED BY OBJECTS OF EXPENDITURE:—*Continued*

| LINE No. | Supplies | Purchase of Equipment | Materials | Contract or Open Order Service | Contingencies | Fixed Charges and Contributions |
|---|---|---|---|---|---|---|
| 1 | .......... | .......... | .......... | .......... | .......... | $113,875 22 |
| 2 | .......... | .......... | .......... | $34,984 60 | .......... | .......... |
| 3 | $998 39 | .......... | .......... | 200 00 | $474 61 | .......... |
| 4 | 1,549 18 | .......... | .......... | 2,428 73 | 25,247 52 | .......... |
| 5 | 13,455 37 | .......... | .......... | 8,139 67 | 1,322 40 | .......... |
| 6 | 1,358 18 | .......... | .......... | 535 60 | 445 05 | .......... |
| 7 | 1,937 05 | .......... | .......... | 152 65 | 2,129 27 | .......... |
| 8 | .......... | .......... | .......... | 6,574 80 | 12,000 00 | 26,392 46 |
| 9 | .......... | .......... | .......... | 8,000 00 | .......... | .......... |
| 10 | 282 06 | .......... | .......... | 196 24 | 288 20 | .......... |
| 11 | 1,849 08 | $197 50 | $591 89 | 306 40 | 247 15 | .......... |
| 12 | 1,652 58 | .......... | .......... | 3,524 18 | 473 00 | .......... |
| 13 | 3,793 37 | 153 00 | .......... | 1,112 41 | 3,086 72 | .......... |
| 14 | .......... | .......... | .......... | 946 20 | 1,143 22 | .......... |
| 15 | **$26,875 26** | **$350 50** | **$591 89** | **$67,101 48** | **$46,857 14** | **$140,267 68** |
| 16 | .......... | .......... | .......... | .......... | .......... | $55,735 46 |
| 17 | .......... | .......... | .......... | $19,035 52 | .......... | .......... |
| 18 | .......... | .......... | .......... | 899 65 | $1,423 30 | .......... |
| 19 | $669 99 | .......... | .......... | 888 21 | .......... | .......... |
| 20 | 1,736 54 | $986 50 | .......... | 569 01 | 1,585 97 | .......... |
| 21 | 1,177 94 | .......... | .......... | 152 94 | 427 00 | .......... |
| 22 | 1,392 00 | .......... | .......... | 990 84 | 8,998 10 | .......... |
| 23 | 135 35 | .......... | .......... | 155 18 | 1,319 09 | .......... |
| 24 | .......... | .......... | .......... | 6,000 00 | 5,000 00 | 1,000 00 |
| 25 | .......... | .......... | .......... | .......... | 600 00 | .......... |
| 26 | .......... | .......... | .......... | .......... | .......... | .......... |
| 27 | 979 74 | .......... | .......... | 374 39 | 107 67 | .......... |
| 28 | 1,102 08 | .......... | .......... | 9,509 60 | 1,891 03 | .......... |
| 29 | 3,572 19 | .......... | .......... | 694 29 | 2,170 21 | .......... |
| 30 | **$10,765 83** | **$986 50** | .......... | **$39,269 63** | **$23,522 37** | **$56,735 46** |
| 31 | .......... | .......... | .......... | .......... | .......... | $5,244 05 |
| 32 | .......... | .......... | .......... | $3,648 58 | .......... | .......... |
| 33 | $1,774 00 | $1,688 50 | .......... | 967 37 | .......... | .......... |
| 34 | 369 90 | 172 13 | .......... | 2,472 32 | $2,031 64 | .......... |
| 35 | 559 72 | .......... | .......... | 230 78 | 246 13 | .......... |
| 36 | 196 23 | .......... | .......... | 374 56 | 1,328 08 | .......... |
| 37 | 481 15 | .......... | .......... | 61 31 | 46 00 | .......... |
| 38 | .......... | .......... | .......... | 2,000 00 | 3,752 70 | .......... |
| 39 | .......... | .......... | .......... | .......... | .......... | .......... |
| 40 | .......... | .......... | .......... | .......... | .......... | .......... |
| 41 | 19,654 65 | .......... | .......... | 541 81 | 1,702 56 | .......... |
| 42 | **$23,035 65** | **$1,860 63** | .......... | **$10,296 73** | **$9,107 11** | **$5,244 05** |
| 43 | .......... | .......... | .......... | .......... | .......... | $1,179 45 |
| 44 | .......... | .......... | .......... | $2,712 72 | .......... | .......... |
| 45 | $91 52 | .......... | .......... | 305 85 | $46 58 | .......... |
| 46 | .......... | .......... | .......... | 69 81 | 398 75 | .......... |
| 47 | .......... | .......... | .......... | .......... | .......... | .......... |
| 48 | .......... | .......... | .......... | .......... | 2,145 83 | .......... |
| 49 | 107 60 | .......... | .......... | .......... | 54 98 | .......... |
| 50 | .......... | .......... | .......... | 1,950 00 | 721 23 | 25 00 |
| 51 | 8,310 69 | .......... | .......... | 179 76 | 687 55 | .......... |
| 52 | **$8,509 81** | .......... | .......... | **$5,218 14** | **$4,054 92** | **$1,204 45** |
| 53 | **$69,186 55** | **$3,197 63** | **$591 89** | **$121,885 98** | **$83,541 54** | **$203,451 64** |
| 54 | **$7,489,529 66** | **$1,182,153 24** | **$1,359,606 72** | **$13,820,268 95** | **$691,423 74** | **$55,833,723 32** |

## THE CITY OF

RECAPITULATION OF STATEMENT SHOWING EXPENDITURES FROM REVENUE (BUDGET

| | Total | Personal Service | LINE No. |
|---|---|---|---|
| **CITY DEPARTMENTS, OFFICES, COURTS, ETC.** | | | |
| Mayor and Subordinate Departments, Bureaus, and Offices: | | | |
| Mayor's Office and Departments whose executive heads are appointed by the Mayor and who are removable at his pleasure | $53,287,523 14 | $38,566,275 67 | 1 |
| Departments whose heads are appointed by the Mayor for a term of office greater than his own, and who are removable only upon charges | 31,002,017 71 | 25,976,162 96 | 2 |
| Boards and Commissions majority of which are appointed by the Mayor and for which no other elected City official shares responsibility | 99,545 55 | 64,054 76 | 3 |
| Total Mayor and Subordinate Departments, Bureaus and Offices | **$84,389,086 40** | **$64,606,493 39** | 4 |
| Comptroller and Finance Department, excluding the Chamberlain's Office | **$1,373,170 73** | **$1,285,484 01** | 5 |
| Borough Presidents and Subordinate Departments: | | | |
| President, Borough of Manhattan | $2,370,863 28 | $1,575,294 58 | 6 |
| President, Borough of The Bronx | 1,057,051 71 | 769,040 15 | 7 |
| President, Borough of Brooklyn | 2,022,509 36 | 1,456,636 78 | 8 |
| President, Borough of Queens | 1,306,484 45 | 852,282 02 | 9 |
| President, Borough of Richmond | 736,307 89 | 498,234 88 | 10 |
| Total, Borough Presidents | **$7,493,216 69** | **$5,151,488 41** | 11 |
| Board of Aldermen, President of Board and City Clerk | **$277,969 49** | **$273,230 69** | 12 |
| Boards, Commissions, etc., whose members are not elected by popular vote and who are not appointed by any elected City official | **$9,340 29** | **$8,419 00** | 13 |
| Boards, Commissions, etc., of mixed responsibility, i.e., ex-officio bodies representing two or more of preceding branches | **$2,065,119 81** | **$715,600 54** | 14 |
| Courts, including Board of Parole and General Interpreters of Brooklyn | **$2,269,912 97** | **$2,232,928 22** | 15 |
| Total, City Departments, Offices, Courts, etc. | **$97,877,816 38** | **$74,273,744 26** | 16 |
| DEBT SERVICE *(See details page 120)* | **$49,542,988 56** | .......... | 17 |
| FIXED CHARGES OTHER THAN DEBT SERVICE, SUBSIDIES, CONTRIBUTIONS, PAYMENTS TO PRIVATE AND STATE INSTITUTIONS, EXPENDITURES NOT ALLOTTED TO DEPARTMENTS | **$7,709,561 29** | **$1,319,076 28** | 18 |
| DEFICIENCIES IN TAXES | **$10,000,000 00** | .......... | 19 |
| Total for City Purposes | **$165,130,366 23** | **$75,592,720 54** | 20 |
| COUNTY EXPENDITURES: | | | |
| New York County | $3,224,151 97 | $2,969,790 38 | 21 |
| Kings County | 1,577,782 95 | 1,450,577 55 | 22 |
| Queens County | 324,982 45 | 287,793 77 | 23 |
| Richmond County | 102,472 63 | 86,431 54 | 24 |
| Total for County Purposes | **$5,229,390 00** | **$4,794,593 24** | 25 |
| Total for All Purposes | **$170,359,756 23** | **$80,387,313 78** | 26 |

## NEW YORK

APPROPRIATIONS) FOR THE YEAR 1911, CLASSIFIED BY OBJECTS OF EXPENDITURE:

| LINE No. | Supplies | Purchase of Equipment | Materials | Contract or Open Order Service | Contingencies | Fixed Charges and Contributions |
|---|---|---|---|---|---|---|
| 1 | $4,373,372 62 | $406,291 36 | $745,540 65 | $7,823,678 84 | $369,144 92 | $1,003,219 08 |
| 2 | 2,311,324 03 | 167,101 11 | 20,944 16 | 2,464,694 24 | 45,358 96 | 16,432 25 |
| 3 | 29,327 21 | 454 73 | 740 63 | 1,579 35 | 3,388 87 | .......... |
| 4 | **$6,714,023 86** | **$573,847 20** | **$767,225 44** | **$10,289,952 43** | **$417,892 75** | **$1,019,651 33** |
| 5 | **$22,949 99** | .......... | .......... | **$8,915 00** | **$55,821 73** | .......... |
| 6 | $115,264 86 | $7,253 00 | $94,670 37 | $557,287 79 | $21,092 68 | .......... |
| 7 | 25,131 11 | 12,536 98 | 113,804 60 | 124,028 95 | 12,509 92 | .......... |
| 8 | 113,380 27 | 34,601 33 | 145,565 08 | 255,301 78 | 17,024 12 | .......... |
| 9 | 35,660 65 | 10,370 00 | 103,010 16 | 293,115 07 | 12,046 55 | .......... |
| 10 | 35,490 40 | 9,020 80 | 93,337 92 | 94,179 90 | 6,043 99 | .......... |
| 11 | **$324,927 29** | **$73,782 11** | **$550,388 13** | **$1,323,913 49** | **$68,717 26** | .......... |
| 12 | .......... | .......... | .......... | .......... | **$4,738 80** | .......... |
| 13 | **$93 65** | **$559 50** | .......... | **$109 04** | **$159 10** | .......... |
| 14 | **$112,960 24** | **$30,501 79** | .......... | **$899,189 77** | **$14,818 88** | **$292,048 59** |
| 15 | **$7,223 87** | .......... | .......... | **$9,203 56** | **$20,557 32** | .......... |
| 16 | **$7,182,178 90** | **$678,690 60** | **$1,317,613 57** | **$12,531,183 29** | **$582,705 84** | **$1,311,699 92** |
| 17 | .......... | .......... | .......... | .......... | .......... | ***$49,542,988 56** |
| 18 | **$218,877 00** | **$289,048 53** | **$20,756 73** | **$171,193 57** | **$29,659 19** | **$5,660,949 99** |
| 19 | .......... | .......... | .......... | .......... | .......... | **$10,000,000 00** |
| 20 | **$7,401,055 90** | **$967,739 13** | **$1,338,370 30** | **$12,702,476 86** | **$612,365 03** | **$66,515,638 47** |
| 21 | $29,887 58 | $26 75 | $131 60 | $61,675 28 | $27,838 36 | $134,802 02 |
| 22 | 11,119 40 | 998 38 | .......... | 35,374 07 | 19,601 56 | 60,111 99 |
| 23 | 19,104 22 | .......... | .......... | 8,206 38 | 3,462 67 | 6,415 41 |
| 24 | 9,809 54 | .......... | .......... | 679 45 | 4,008 27 | 1,543 83 |
| 25 | **$69,920 74** | **$1,025 13** | **$131 60** | **$105,935 18** | **$54,910 86** | **$202,873 25** |
| 26 | **$7,470,976 64** | **$968,764 26** | **$1,338,501 90** | **$12,808,412 04** | **$667,275 89** | **$66,718,511 72** |

*Includes redemption of $7,264,625.00 Special Revenue Bonds issued to defray expenses of 1910

STATEMENT SHOWING EXPENDITURES FROM REVENUE (BUDGET

| | Total | Personal Service | LINE No. |
|---|---|---|---|
| CITY DEPARTMENTS, OFFICES, COURTS, ETC. | | | |
| Mayor and Subordinate Departments, Bureaus and Offices: | | | |
| Mayor's Office and Departments whose executive heads are appointed by the Mayor and who are removable at his pleasure: | | | |
| Commissioners of Accounts | $207,716 15 | $197,947 66 | 1 |
| Board of Ambulance Service | 8,792 58 | 8,011 79 | 2 |
| Board of Assessors | 41,693 97 | 40,250 00 | 3 |
| Department of Bridges | 737,656 56 | 639,325 05 | 4 |
| City Chamberlain | 61,382 66 | 59,343 42 | 5 |
| Department of Correction | 1,200,850 71 | 543,799 17 | 6 |
| Department of Docks and Ferries | 2,441,290 63 | 1,614,228 03 | 7 |
| Examining Board of Plumbers | 5,373 50 | 5,120 00 | 8 |
| Fire Department | 8,025,076 53 | 7,428,477 62 | 9 |
| Department of Health | 2,707,961 93 | 2,030,110 64 | 10 |
| Law Department | 781,168 35 | 707,607 06 | 11 |
| Commissioner of Licenses | 50,284 54 | 48,654 66 | 12 |
| Mayoralty—Administration | 53,695 55 | 50,422 22 | 13 |
| Mayoralty—Bureau of Licenses | 74,202 76 | 67,011 25 | 14 |
| Mayoralty—Bureau of Weights and Measures | 62,985 86 | 48,200 83 | 15 |
| Municipal Civil Service Commission | 140,746 44 | 132,837 90 | 16 |
| Municipal Explosives Commission | 5,367 50 | 5,367 50 | 17 |
| Park Board | 25,310 74 | 25,310 74 | 18 |
| Department of Parks—Manhattan and Richmond | 933,217 43 | 708,767 20 | 19 |
| Department of Parks—The Bronx | 410,061 65 | 320,223 21 | 20 |
| Department of Parks—Brooklyn and Queens | 937,420 11 | 611,996 59 | 21 |
| Police Department | 15,446,224 27 | 14,248,038 90 | 22 |
| Department of Public Charities | 3,028,631 25 | 1,062,304 70 | 23 |
| Department of Street Cleaning | 7,703,506 41 | 5,006,580 95 | 24 |
| Department of Taxes and Assessment | 487,212 28 | 477,264 46 | 25 |
| Tenement House Department | 784,637 08 | 761,520 61 | 26 |
| Department of Water Supply, Gas and Electricity | 6,925,055 70 | 1,717,553 51 | 27 |
| Total | **$53,287,523 14** | **$38,566,275 67** | 28 |
| Departments whose heads are appointed by the Mayor for a term of office greater than his own, and who are removable only upon charges: | | | |
| Bellevue and Allied Hospitals | $1,201,505 16 | $511,163 92 | 29 |
| College of the City of New York | 624,088 55 | 557,348 79 | 30 |
| Department of Education | 28,804,474 12 | 24,567,603 61 | 31 |
| Normal College of the City of New York | 371,949 88 | 340,046 64 | 32 |
| Total | **$31,002,017 71** | **$25,976,162 96** | 33 |
| Boards and Commissions majorities of which are appointed by the Mayor and for which no other elected City official shares responsibility: | | | |
| Art Commission | $7,573 00 | $5,381 00 | 34 |
| Brooklyn Disciplinary Training School for Boys | 55,468 16 | 27,147 02 | 35 |
| Permanent Census Board | 36,504 39 | 31,526 74 | 36 |
| Total | **$99,545 55** | **$64,054 76** | 37 |
| Total, Mayor and Subordinate Departments, Bureaus and Offices | **$84,389,086 40** | **$64,606,493 39** | 38 |
| Comptroller and Finance Department, excluding the Chamberlain's Office: | | | |
| Department of Finance | **$1,373,170 73** | **$1,285,484 01** | 39 |
| Borough Presidents and Subordinate Departments: | | | |
| President, Borough of Manhattan | $2,370,863 28 | $1,575,294 58 | 40 |
| President, Borough of The Bronx | 1,057,051 71 | 769,040 15 | 41 |
| President, Borough of Brooklyn | 2,022,509 36 | 1,456,636 78 | 42 |

NEW YORK

APPROPRIATIONS) FOR THE YEAR 1911, CLASSIFIED BY OBJECTS OF EXPENDITURE:

| LINE No. | Supplies | Purchase of Equipment | Materials | Contract or Open Order Service | Contingencies | Fixed Charges and Contributions |
|---|---|---|---|---|---|---|
| 1 | $1,564 68 | .......... | .......... | $755 35 | $7,448 46 | .......... |
| 2 | 226 79 | .......... | .......... | 328 97 | 225 03 | .......... |
| 3 | 622 24 | .......... | .......... | 348 63 | 473 10 | .......... |
| 4 | 21,616 08 | $1,293 69 | $26,431 43 | 45,980 01 | 3,010 30 | .......... |
| 5 | 1,346 00 | .......... | .......... | 393 54 | 299 70 | .......... |
| 6 | 480,500 51 | 7,357 65 | 121,263 02 | 38,499 29 | 4,677 83 | $4,753 24 |
| 7 | 336,052 67 | 428 15 | 130,885 01 | 304,988 34 | 10,548 43 | 44,160 00 |
| 8 | 253 50 | .......... | .......... | .......... | .......... | .......... |
| 9 | 364,684 90 | 31,615 15 | 74,988 27 | 115,797 31 | 9,513 28 | .......... |
| 10 | 444,914 24 | 27,154 32 | 27,451 01 | 100,357 91 | 87,973 81 | .......... |
| 11 | 4,489 50 | .......... | .......... | 7,071 61 | 62,000 18 | .......... |
| 12 | 169 83 | .......... | .......... | 330 55 | 1,129 50 | .......... |
| 13 | .......... | .......... | .......... | 856 03 | 2,417 30 | .......... |
| 14 | .......... | .......... | .......... | 385 09 | 6,806 42 | .......... |
| 15 | 4,901 40 | .......... | .......... | .......... | 9,883 63 | .......... |
| 16 | 396 70 | .......... | .......... | 1,050 00 | 6,461 84 | .......... |
| 17 | .......... | .......... | .......... | .......... | .......... | .......... |
| 18 | .......... | .......... | .......... | .......... | .......... | .......... |
| 19 | 69,385 32 | 13,349 13 | 67,928 24 | 67,125 55 | 6,661 99 | .......... |
| 20 | 10,482 46 | 7,909 42 | 25,141 47 | 45,560 76 | 744 33 | .......... |
| 21 | 68,145 88 | 8,456 10 | 72,953 89 | 170,398 98 | 5,468 67 | .......... |
| 22 | 295,323 94 | 60,297 60 | 10,546 56 | 87,228 92 | 44,788 35 | 700,000 00 |
| 23 | 1,540,567 95 | 41,079 59 | 58,206 21 | 185,445 18 | 12,368 93 | 128,658 69 |
| 24 | 532,762 59 | 189,858 01 | 101,205 06 | 1,868,716 04 | 4,383 76 | .......... |
| 25 | .......... | .......... | .......... | 919 12 | 9,028 70 | .......... |
| 26 | 3,284 90 | .......... | .......... | 899 68 | 18,931 89 | .......... |
| 27 | 191,680 54 | 17,492 55 | 38,540 48 | 4,780,241 98 | 53,899 49 | 125,647 15 |
| 28 | **$4,373,372 62** | **$406,291 36** | **$745,540 65** | **$7,823,678 84** | **$369,144 92** | **$1,003,219 08** |
| 29 | $571,237 76 | $15,682 44 | $17,524 79 | $78,837 36 | $7,058 89 | .......... |
| 30 | 55,141 53 | .......... | 3,419 37 | 6,181 92 | 1,996 94 | .......... |
| 31 | 1,659,574 58 | 151,418 67 | .......... | 2,375,639 90 | 33,805 11 | $16,432 25 |
| 32 | 25,370 16 | .......... | .......... | 4,035 06 | 2,498 02 | .......... |
| 33 | **$2,311,324 03** | **$167,101 11** | **$20,944 16** | **$2,464,694 24** | **$45,358 96** | **$16,432 25** |
| 34 | $62 85 | $454 73 | .......... | $1,131 52 | $542 90 | .......... |
| 35 | 26,773 66 | .......... | $740 63 | 270 37 | 536 48 | .......... |
| 36 | 2,490 70 | .......... | .......... | 177 46 | 2,309 49 | .......... |
| 37 | **$29,327 21** | **$454 73** | **$740 63** | **$1,579 35** | **$3,388 87** | .......... |
| 38 | **$6,714,023 86** | **$573,847 20** | **$767,225 44** | **$10,289,952 43** | **$417,892 75** | **$1,019,651 33** |
| 39 | **$22,949 99** | .......... | .......... | **$8,915 00** | **$55,821 73** | .......... |
| 40 | $115,264 86 | $7,253 00 | $94,670 37 | $557,287 79 | $21,092 68 | .......... |
| 41 | 25,131 11 | 12,536 98 | 113,804 60 | 124,028 95 | 12,509 92 | .......... |
| 42 | 113,380 27 | 34,601 33 | 145,565 08 | 255,301 78 | 17,024 12 | .......... |

STATEMENT SHOWING EXPENDITURES FROM REVENUE (BUDGET

| | Total | Personal Service | LINE No. |
|---|---|---|---|
| CITY DEPARTMENTS, OFFICES, COURTS, ETC.—*Continued* | | | |
| Borough Presidents and Subordinate Departments—*Continued:* | | | |
| President, Borough of Queens | $1,306,484 45 | $852,282 02 | 1 |
| President, Borough of Richmond | 736,307 89 | 498,234 88 | 2 |
| Total Borough Presidents | **$7,493,216 69** | **$5,151,488 41** | 3 |
| Board of Aldermen, President of Board and City Clerk | **$277,969 49** | **$273,230 69** | 4 |
| Boards, Commissions, etc., whose members are not elected by popular vote and who are not appointed by any elected City Official: | | | |
| Board of Building Examiners | $9,340 29 | $8,419 00 | 5 |
| Total | **$9,340 29** | **$8,419 00** | 6 |
| Boards, Commissions, etc., of mixed responsibility, i.e., ex-officio bodies, representing two or more preceding branches: | | | |
| Armory Board | $137,246 78 | $13,086 37 | 7 |
| Board of City Record, City of New York | 828,534 54 | 39,623 55 | 8 |
| Board of Elections | 926,305 38 | 502,718 04 | 9 |
| Board of Estimate and Apportionment | 169,729 06 | 157,122 58 | 10 |
| Board of Revision of Assessments | 104 75 | .......... | 11 |
| Commissioners of the Sinking Fund | 3,199 30 | 3,050 00 | 12 |
| Total | **$2,065,119 81** | **$715,600 54** | 13 |
| Courts, including Board of Parole and General Interpreters of Brooklyn: | | | |
| Coroners, Borough of Manhattan | $64,071 68 | $62,166 00 | 14 |
| Coroners, Borough of The Bronx | 30,241 26 | 28,170 00 | 15 |
| Coroners, Borough of Brooklyn | 34,937 38 | 33,650 00 | 16 |
| Coroners, Borough of Queens | 18,660 55 | 16,783 33 | 17 |
| Coroners, Borough of Richmond | 12,134 37 | 11,245 00 | 18 |
| City Court of New York | 235,537 60 | 233,193 14 | 19 |
| City Magistrates' Courts, First Division | 361,367 93 | 355,987 53 | 20 |
| City Magistrates' Courts, Second Division | 326,443 69 | 321,986 75 | 21 |
| Municipal Courts, City of New York | 897,642 04 | 889,441 37 | 22 |
| Court of Special Sessions | 275,699 27 | 267,304 35 | 23 |
| General Interpreters of Brooklyn | 10,200 00 | 10,200 00 | 24 |
| Board of Parole | 2,977 20 | 2,800 75 | 25 |
| Total | **$2,269,912 97** | **$2,232,928 22** | 26 |
| Total City Departments, Offices, Courts, etc | **$97,877,816 38** | **$74,273,744 26** | 27 |
| DEBT SERVICE (*See details page 120*) | **$49,542,988 56** | .......... | 28 |
| FIXED CHARGES OTHER THAN DEBT SERVICE, SUBSIDIES, CONTRIBUTIONS, PAYMENTS TO PRIVATE AND STATE INSTITUTIONS, EXPENDITURES NOT ALLOTTED TO DEPARTMENTS: | | | |
| American Museum of Natural History | $189,757 00 | $164,000 00 | 29 |
| Botanical Garden and Arboretum | 14,741 31 | 10,000 00 | 30 |
| Charitable Institutions, City | 4,362,050 43 | .......... | 31 |
| Children's Museum, Brooklyn | 11,900 39 | 9,541 88 | 32 |
| Grant's Tomb | 7,000 00 | .......... | 33 |
| Jumel Mansion | 4,487 48 | 3,629 24 | 34 |
| Metropolitan Museum of Art | 200,000 00 | 161,097 75 | 35 |
| Miscellaneous, City | 1,295,685 70 | 3,350 69 | 36 |
| Museum of Arts and Sciences | 93,334 00 | 68,392 25 | 37 |
| New York Aquarium | 47,567 22 | 32,168 16 | 38 |
| New York Botanical Garden | 85,981 40 | 67,860 00 | 39 |
| New York Zoological Garden | 174,579 74 | 113,964 10 | 40 |
| Brooklyn Public Library | 421,156 86 | 236,472 00 | 41 |
| New York Public Library | 646,279 50 | 362,622 07 | 42 |
| Queensborough Public Library | 135,040 26 | 73,680 00 | 43 |

NEW YORK

APPROPRIATIONS) FOR THE YEAR 1911, CLASSIFIED BY OBJECTS OF EXPENDITURE:—*Continued*

| LINE No. | Supplies | Purchase of Equipment | Materials | Contract or Open Order Service | Contingencies | Fixed Charges and Contributions |
|---|---|---|---|---|---|---|
| 1 | $35,660 65 | $10,370 00 | $103,010 16 | $293,115 07 | $12,046 55 | .......... |
| 2 | 35,490 40 | 9,020 80 | 93,337 92 | 94,179 90 | 6,043 99 | .......... |
| 3 | **$324,927 29** | **$73,782 11** | **$550,388 13** | **$1,323,913 49** | **$68,717 26** | .......... |
| 4 | .......... | .......... | .......... | .......... | .......... | **$4,738 80** |
| 5 | $93 65 | $559 50 | .......... | $109 04 | $159 10 | .......... |
| 6 | **$93 65** | **$559 50** | .......... | **$109 04** | **$159 10** | .......... |
| 7 | $13,434 22 | $26,148 51 | .......... | $82,404 87 | $2,172 81 | .......... |
| 8 | 2,099 04 | .......... | .......... | 784,312 05 | 2,499 90 | .......... |
| 9 | 96,836 00 | 988 89 | .......... | 28,704 23 | 5,009 63 | $292,048 59 |
| 10 | 518 16 | 3,262 46 | .......... | 3,768 62 | 5,057 24 | .......... |
| 11 | 2 82 | 101 93 | .......... | .......... | .......... | .......... |
| 12 | 70 00 | .......... | .......... | .......... | 79 30 | .......... |
| 13 | **$112,960 24** | **$30,501 79** | .......... | **$899,189 77** | **$14,818 88** | **$292,048 59** |
| 14 | $399 25 | .......... | .......... | $919 80 | $586 63 | .......... |
| 15 | .......... | .......... | .......... | 766 16 | 1,305 10 | .......... |
| 16 | .......... | .......... | .......... | 287 38 | 1,000 00 | .......... |
| 17 | .......... | .......... | .......... | 306 12 | 1,571 10 | .......... |
| 18 | .......... | .......... | .......... | 168 18 | 721 19 | .......... |
| 19 | .......... | .......... | .......... | 321 77 | 2,022 69 | .......... |
| 20 | 2,312 21 | .......... | .......... | 1,915 15 | 1,153 04 | .......... |
| 21 | 799 55 | .......... | .......... | 2,631 70 | 1,025 69 | .......... |
| 22 | .......... | .......... | .......... | .......... | 8,200 67 | .......... |
| 23 | 3,712 86 | .......... | .......... | 1,887 30 | 2,794 76 | .......... |
| 24 | .......... | .......... | .......... | .......... | .......... | .......... |
| 25 | .......... | .......... | .......... | .......... | 176 45 | .......... |
| 26 | **$7,223 87** | .......... | .......... | **$9,203 56** | **$20,557 32** | .......... |
| 27 | **$7,182,178 90** | **$678,690 60** | **$1,317,013 57** | **$12,531,183 29** | **$582,705 84** | **$1,311,699 92** |
| 28 | .......... | .......... | .......... | .......... | .......... | **$49,542,988 56** |
| 29 | $16,919 00 | $1,150 00 | $4,725 00 | $1,505 00 | $1,458 00 | .......... |
| 30 | 4,297 07 | 199 25 | .......... | 48 70 | 196 29 | .......... |
| 31 | .......... | .......... | .......... | .......... | .......... | $4,362,050 43 |
| 32 | 1,022 53 | 142 45 | .......... | 643 62 | 549 91 | .......... |
| 33 | .......... | .......... | .......... | 7,000 00 | .......... | .......... |
| 34 | 110 73 | 132 00 | 7 70 | 395 00 | 212 81 | .......... |
| 35 | 17,856 80 | 1,850 00 | 6,685 45 | 600 00 | 11,910 00 | .......... |
| 36 | 2,078 50 | 704 22 | .......... | 15,967 47 | 1,201 92 | 1,272,382 90 |
| 37 | 10,426 26 | 2,957 96 | 2,994 65 | 3,215 38 | 5,347 50 | .......... |
| 38 | 9,643 67 | .......... | 745 10 | 4,531 06 | 479 23 | .......... |
| 39 | 14,311 05 | 921 89 | 1,500 00 | 893 46 | 495 00 | .......... |
| 40 | 54,090 60 | 217 22 | 4,098 83 | 602 32 | 1,606 67 | .......... |
| 41 | 26,993 00 | 99,125 00 | .......... | 44,281 86 | .......... | 14,285 00 |
| 42 | 51,380 00 | 153,110 00 | .......... | 78,987 43 | .......... | 180 00 |
| 43 | 9,747 79 | 28,538 54 | .......... | 12,522 27 | .......... | 10,551 66 |

STATEMENT SHOWING EXPENDITURES FROM REVENUE (BUDGET

| | Total | Personal Service | LINE No. |
|---|---|---|---|
| FIXED CHARGES—*Continued:* | | | |
| Staten Island Association of Arts and Sciences | $9,000 00 | $5,774 82 | 1 |
| United States Volunteer Life Saving Corps | 11,000 00 | 6,523 32 | 2 |
| Total | **$7,709,561 29** | **$1,319,076 28** | 3 |
| DEFICIENCIES IN TAXES | **$10,000,000 00** | .......... | 4 |
| Total for City Purposes | **$165,130,366 23** | **$75,592,720 54** | 5 |
| COUNTY EXPENDITURES: | | | |
| New York County: | | | |
| Charitable Institutions | $112,995 01 | .......... | 6 |
| Board of City Record | 38,614 40 | .......... | 7 |
| County Clerk | 138,971 33 | $135,120 60 | 8 |
| Court of General Sessions | 314,139 08 | 311,861 51 | 9 |
| Supreme Court, First Department | 858,978 84 | 849,600 55 | 10 |
| Supreme Court, Maintenance of Appellate Division Court House | 30,613 14 | 18,073 42 | 11 |
| Surrogate's Court | 174,986 84 | 172,735 54 | 12 |
| District Attorney | 388,053 59 | 371,501 88 | 13 |
| Commissioner of Jurors | 52,548 46 | 48,185 27 | 14 |
| Miscellaneous | 372,242 71 | 344,500 00 | 15 |
| National Guard and Naval Militia | 200,132 25 | 192,132 25 | 16 |
| Public Administrator | 26,284 87 | 25,530 00 | 17 |
| Commissioner of Records | 72,461 81 | 69,130 00 | 18 |
| Register | 308,723 52 | 305,341 76 | 19 |
| Sheriff | 134,406 12 | 126,077 60 | 20 |
| Total | **$3,224,151 97** | **$2,969,790 38** | 21 |
| Kings County: | | | |
| Charitable Institutions | $57,911 99 | .......... | 22 |
| Board of City Record | 19,967 45 | .......... | 23 |
| County Clerk | 81,166 72 | $79,343 10 | 24 |
| County Court | 139,765 11 | 138,288 76 | 25 |
| Supreme Court, Second Department | 375,563 95 | 370,577 58 | 26 |
| Surrogate's Court | 88,050 59 | 86,531 56 | 27 |
| District Attorney | 114,183 37 | 105,479 43 | 28 |
| Commissioner of Jurors | 37,615 12 | 35,617 96 | 29 |
| Law Library, Brooklyn | 9,400 00 | 8,800 00 | 30 |
| Miscellaneous | 115,714 95 | 108,884 95 | 31 |
| National Guard and Naval Militia | 141,277 50 | 141,277 50 | 32 |
| Commissioner of Records | 98,706 32 | 96,753 79 | 33 |
| Register | 216,472 89 | 203,589 58 | 34 |
| Sheriff | 81,986 99 | 75,433 34 | 35 |
| Total | **$1,577,782 95** | **$1,450,577 55** | 36 |
| Queens County: | | | |
| Charitable Institutions | $6,415 41 | .......... | 37 |
| Board of City Record | 3,062 83 | .......... | 38 |
| County Clerk | 27,866 39 | $25,008 43 | 39 |
| County Court | 33,139 66 | 31,822 00 | 40 |
| Supreme Court | 69,953 19 | 68,177 16 | 41 |
| Surrogate's Court | 23,348 18 | 22,576 99 | 42 |
| District Attorney | 30,618 76 | 28,958 96 | 43 |
| Commissioner of Jurors | 11,779 12 | 11,121 18 | 44 |
| Miscellaneous | 37,840 53 | 36,919 73 | 45 |
| National Guard and Naval Militia | 5,110 00 | 5,110 00 | 46 |
| Public Administrator | 1,200 00 | 1,200 00 | 47 |
| Sheriff | 74,648 38 | 56,899 32 | 48 |
| Total | **$324,982 45** | **$287,793 77** | 49 |

NEW YORK

Appropriations) for the Year 1911, Classified by Objects of Expenditure:—*Continued*

| LINE No. | Supplies | Purchase of Equipment | Materials | Contract or Open Order Service | Contingencies | Fixed Charges and Contributions |
|---|---|---|---|---|---|---|
| 1 | .......... | .......... | .......... | .......... | $1,725 18 | $1,500 00 |
| 2 | .......... | .......... | .......... | .......... | 4,476 68 | .......... |
| 3 | **$218,877 00** | **$289,048 53** | **$20,756 73** | **$171,193 57** | **$29,659 19** | **$5,660,949 99** |
| 4 | .......... | .......... | .......... | .......... | .......... | **$10,000,000 00** |
| 5 | **$7,401,055 90** | **$967,739 13** | **$1,338,370 30** | **$12,702,476 86** | **$612,365 03** | **$66,515,638 47** |
| 6 | .......... | .......... | .......... | .......... | .......... | $112,995 01 |
| 7 | .......... | .......... | .......... | $38,614 40 | .......... | .......... |
| 8 | $2,434 42 | .......... | .......... | 375 21 | $1,041 10 | .......... |
| 9 | .......... | .......... | .......... | 899 95 | 1,377 62 | .......... |
| 10 | 8,151 01 | .......... | .......... | 1,227 28 | .......... | .......... |
| 11 | 4,819 34 | .......... | .......... | 7,366 30 | 354 08 | .......... |
| 12 | 1,286 75 | .......... | .......... | 506 90 | 457 65 | .......... |
| 13 | 1,550 00 | .......... | .......... | 2,680 09 | 12,321 62 | .......... |
| 14 | 2,076 10 | .......... | .......... | 167 01 | 2,120 08 | .......... |
| 15 | 998 80 | .......... | .......... | .......... | 4,936 90 | 21,807 01 |
| 16 | .......... | .......... | .......... | 8,000 00 | .......... | .......... |
| 17 | 191 20 | .......... | .......... | 199 36 | 364 31 | .......... |
| 18 | 2,500 00 | .......... | $131 60 | 232 00 | 468 21 | .......... |
| 19 | 1,504 54 | .......... | .......... | 130 31 | 1,746 91 | .......... |
| 20 | 4,375 42 | $26 75 | .......... | 1,276 47 | 2,649 88 | .......... |
| 21 | **$29,887 58** | **$26 75** | **$131 60** | **$61,675 28** | **$27,838 36** | **$134,802 02** |
| 22 | .......... | .......... | .......... | .......... | .......... | $57,911 99 |
| 23 | .......... | .......... | .......... | $19,967 45 | .......... | .......... |
| 24 | .......... | .......... | .......... | 634 54 | $1,189 08 | .......... |
| 25 | $642 31 | .......... | .......... | 363 14 | 470 90 | .......... |
| 26 | 1,875 48 | $998 38 | .......... | 840 06 | 1,272 45 | .......... |
| 27 | 994 51 | .......... | .......... | 225 42 | 299 10 | .......... |
| 28 | 279 55 | .......... | .......... | 750 00 | 7,674 39 | .......... |
| 29 | 151 01 | .......... | .......... | 142 74 | 1,703 41 | .......... |
| 30 | .......... | .......... | .......... | .......... | 600 00 | .......... |
| 31 | .......... | .......... | .......... | 1,706 00 | 2,924 00 | 2,200 00 |
| 32 | .......... | .......... | .......... | .......... | .......... | .......... |
| 33 | 1,550 33 | .......... | .......... | 294 34 | 107 86 | .......... |
| 34 | 1,483 86 | .......... | .......... | 9,749 86 | 1,649 59 | .......... |
| 35 | 4,142 35 | .......... | .......... | 700 52 | 1,710 78 | .......... |
| 36 | **$11,119 40** | **$998 38** | .......... | **$35,374 07** | **$19,601 56** | **$60,111 99** |
| 37 | .......... | .......... | .......... | .......... | .......... | $6,415 41 |
| 38 | .......... | .......... | .......... | $3,062 83 | .......... | .......... |
| 39 | .......... | .......... | .......... | 2,857 96 | .......... | .......... |
| 40 | $999 81 | .......... | .......... | 167 85 | $150 00 | .......... |
| 41 | 1,287 14 | .......... | .......... | 288 99 | 199 90 | .......... |
| 42 | 257 10 | .......... | .......... | 239 79 | 274 30 | .......... |
| 43 | 189 75 | .......... | .......... | 365 90 | 1,104 15 | .......... |
| 44 | 495 50 | .......... | .......... | 52 86 | 109 58 | .......... |
| 45 | .......... | .......... | .......... | 640 00 | 280 80 | .......... |
| 46 | .......... | .......... | .......... | .......... | .......... | .......... |
| 47 | .......... | .......... | .......... | .......... | .......... | .......... |
| 48 | 15,874 92 | .......... | .......... | 530 20 | 1,343 94 | .......... |
| 49 | **$19,104 22** | .......... | .......... | **$8,206 38** | **$3,462 67** | **$6,415 41** |

STATEMENT SHOWING EXPENDITURES FROM REVENUE (BUDGET

| | Total | Personal Service | LINE No. |
|---|---|---|---|
| COUNTY EXPENDITURES—*Continued:* | | | |
| Richmond County: | | | |
| Charitable Institutions | $1,518 83 | .......... | 1 |
| Board of City Record | 1,490 24 | .......... | 2 |
| County Clerk | 18,224 12 | $17,900 00 | 3 |
| County Court and Surrogate's Court | 18,336 65 | 17,866 25 | 4 |
| Supreme Court | 12,726 45 | 12,605 47 | 5 |
| District Attorney | 12,344 00 | 11,367 22 | 6 |
| Commissioner of Jurors | 4,172 57 | 3,987 00 | 7 |
| Miscellaneous | 8,352 17 | 7,456 00 | 8 |
| Sheriff | 25,307 60 | 15,249 60 | 9 |
| Total | **$102,472 63** | **$86,431 54** | 10 |
| Total for County Purposes | **$5,229,390 00** | **$4,794,593 24** | 11 |
| Total for All Purposes | **$170,359,756 23** | **$80,387,313 78** | 12 |

NEW YORK

APPROPRIATIONS) FOR THE YEAR 1911, CLASSIFIED BY OBJECTS OF EXPENDITURE:—*Continued*

| LINE No. | Supplies | Purchase of Equipment | Materials | Contract or Open Order Service | Contingencies | Fixed Charges and Contributions |
|---|---|---|---|---|---|---|
| 1 | .......... | .......... | .......... | .......... | .......... | $1,518 83 |
| 2 | .......... | .......... | .......... | .......... | $1,490 24 | .......... |
| 3 | $96 55 | .......... | .......... | $180 09 | 47 48 | .......... |
| 4 | .......... | .......... | .......... | 78 76 | 391 64 | .......... |
| 5 | .......... | .......... | .......... | .......... | 120 98 | .......... |
| 6 | .......... | .......... | .......... | .......... | 976 78 | .......... |
| 7 | 114 00 | .......... | .......... | 57 02 | 14 55 | .......... |
| 8 | .......... | .......... | .......... | 219 20 | 651 97 | 25 00 |
| 9 | 9,598 99 | .......... | .......... | 144 38 | 314 63 | .......... |
| 10 | **$9,809 54** | .......... | .......... | **$679 45** | **$4,008 27** | **$1,543 83** |
| 11 | **$69,920 74** | **$1,025 13** | **$131 60** | **$105,935 18** | **$54,910 86** | **$202,873 25** |
| 12 | **$7,470,976 64** | **$968,764 26** | **$1,338,501 90** | **$12,808,412 04** | **$667,275 89** | **$66,718,511 72** |

RECAPITULATION OF STATEMENT SHOWING EXPENDITURES FROM REVENUE (BUDGET

| | Total | Personal Service | LINE No. |
|---|---|---|---|
| CITY DEPARTMENTS, OFFICES, COURTS, ETC. | | | |
| **Mayor** and Subordinate Departments, Bureaus, and Offices: | | | |
| Mayor's Office and Departments whose executive heads are appointed by the Mayor and who are removable at his pleasure | $56,526,284 33 | $40,345,571 25 | 1 |
| Departments whose heads are appointed by the Mayor for a term of office greater than his own, and who are removable only upon charges | 36,097,760 41 | 30,609,183 00 | 2 |
| Boards and Commissions majority of which are appointed by the Mayor and for which no other elected City official shares responsibility | 117,645 23 | 77,929 36 | 3 |
| Total Mayor and Subordinate Departments, Bureaus and Offices | **$92,741,689 97** | **$71,032,683 61** | 4 |
| Comptroller and Finance Department, excluding the Chamberlain's Office | **$1,460,258 67** | **$1,358,473 69** | 5 |
| Borough Presidents and Subordinate Departments: | | | |
| President, Borough of Manhattan | $2,480,922 46 | $1,577,079 53 | 6 |
| President, Borough of The Bronx | 1,100,892 02 | 784,559 97 | 7 |
| President, Borough of Brooklyn | 2,067,023 33 | 1,485,011 78 | 8 |
| President, Borough of Queens | 1,663,885 13 | 1,052,966 02 | 9 |
| President, Borough of Richmond | 761,792 09 | 523,342 32 | 10 |
| Total, Borough Presidents | **$8,074,515 03** | **$5,422,959 62** | 11 |
| Board of Aldermen, President of Board and City Clerk | **$283,244 05** | **$277,443 58** | 12 |
| Boards, Commissions, etc., whose members are not elected by popular vote and who are not appointed by any elected City official | **$9,108 47** | **$8,679 00** | 13 |
| Boards, Commissions, etc., of mixed responsibility, i. e., ex-officio bodies representing two or more of preceding branches | **$2,489,211 42** | **$870,792 14** | 14 |
| Courts, including Board of Parole and General Interpreters of Brooklyn | **$2,415,213 14** | **$2,361,730 28** | 15 |
| Total, City Departments, Offices, Courts, etc. | **$107,473,240 75** | **$81,332,761 92** | 16 |
| DEBT SERVICE (*See details page 120*) | **$50,218,374 43** | .......... | 17 |
| FIXED CHARGES OTHER THAN DEBT SERVICE, SUBSIDIES, CONTRIBUTIONS, PAYMENTS TO PRIVATE AND STATE INSTITUTIONS, EXPENDITURES NOT ALLOTTED TO DEPARTMENTS | **$7,742,819 27** | **$1,347,006 92** | 18 |
| DEFICIENCIES IN TAXES | **$3,287,366 74** | .......... | 19 |
| Total for City Purposes | **$168,721,801 19** | **$82,679,768 84** | 20 |
| DIRECT STATE TAXES | **$4,301,345 65** | .......... | 21 |
| COUNTY EXPENDITURES: | | | |
| New York County | $3,485,104 38 | $3,228,408 02 | 22 |
| Kings County | 1,669,140 33 | 1,543,892 42 | 23 |
| Queens County | 324,266 51 | 287,469 61 | 24 |
| Richmond County | 116,137 73 | 98,221 46 | 25 |
| Total for County Purposes | **$5,594,648 95** | **$5,157,991 51** | 26 |
| Total for All Purposes | **$178,617,795 79** | **$87,837,760 35** | 27 |

## NEW YORK

APPROPRIATIONS) FOR THE YEAR 1912, CLASSIFIED BY OBJECTS OF EXPENDITURE:

| LINE No. | Supplies | Purchase of Equipment | Materials | Contract or Open Order Service | Contingencies | Fixed Charges and Contributions |
|---|---|---|---|---|---|---|
| 1 | $5,496,086 96 | $487,351 82 | .......... | $8,430,131 23 | $397,556 35 | $1,369,586 72 |
| 2 | 2,633,164 24 | 165,894 36 | .......... | 2,617,694 12 | 54,055 44 | 17,769 25 |
| 3 | 32,254 76 | 1,004 60 | .......... | 1,560 43 | 4,896 08 | .......... |
| 4 | **$8,161,505 96** | **$654,250 78** | .......... | **$11,049,385 78** | **$456,507 87** | **$1,387,355 97** |
| 5 | **$15,494 73** | **$10,490 75** | .......... | **$31,761 90** | **$44,037 60** | .......... |
| 6 | $207,169 16 | $6,636 08 | .......... | $666,549 74 | $23,487 95 | .......... |
| 7 | 142,424 45 | 16,030 26 | .......... | 149,269 16 | 8,608 18 | .......... |
| 8 | 269,995 91 | 23,352 50 | .......... | 273,423 45 | 15,239 69 | .......... |
| 9 | 154,053 27 | 29,706 81 | .......... | 416,281 34 | 10,877 69 | .......... |
| 10 | 129,827 98 | 9,091 57 | .......... | 93,165 94 | 6,364 28 | .......... |
| 11 | **$903,470 77** | **$84,817 22** | .......... | **$1,598,689 63** | **$64,577 79** | .......... |
| 12 | **$1,004 80** | **$60 00** | .......... | **$2,049 29** | **$2,686 38** | .......... |
| 13 | **$98 93** | .......... | .......... | **$93 00** | **$237 54** | .......... |
| 14 | **$182,105 00** | **$5,367 32** | .......... | **$1,033,318 22** | **$53,935 98** | **$343,692 76** |
| 15 | **$23,243 91** | **$393 05** | .......... | **$9,923 46** | **$19,922 44** | .......... |
| 16 | **$9,286,924 10** | **$755,379 12** | .......... | **$13,725,221 28** | **$641,905 60** | **$1,731,048 73** |
| 17 | .......... | .......... | .......... | .......... | .......... | ***$50,218,374 43** |
| 18 | **$438,699 22** | **$17,408 44** | .......... | **$336,982 46** | **$49,299 93** | **$5,553,422 30** |
| 19 | .......... | .......... | .......... | .......... | .......... | **$3,287,366 74** |
| 20 | **$9,725,623 32** | **$772,787 56** | .......... | **$14,062,203 74** | **$691,205 53** | **$60,790,212 20** |
| 21 | .......... | .......... | .......... | .......... | .......... | **$4,301,345 65** |
| 22 | $23,143 71 | $5,933 67 | .......... | $62,363 56 | $36,618 18 | $128,637 24 |
| 23 | 8,925 60 | 1,954 27 | .......... | 21,961 87 | 19,466 60 | 72,939 57 |
| 24 | 11,976 58 | 659 10 | .......... | 11,339 55 | 6,901 17 | 5,920 50 |
| 25 | 8,973 61 | .......... | .......... | 5,133 47 | 2,217 78 | 1,591 41 |
| 26 | **$53,019 50** | **$8,547 04** | .......... | **$100,798 45** | **$65,203 73** | **$209,088 72** |
| 27 | **$9,778,642 82** | **$781,334 60** | .......... | **$14,163,002 19** | **$756,409 26** | **$65,300,646 57** |

*Includes redemption of $5,970,164.92 Special Revenue Bonds issued to defray expenses of 1911

THE CITY OF

STATEMEMT SHOWING EXPENDITURES FROM REVENUE (BUDGET

| | Total | Personal Service | LINE No. |
|---|---|---|---|
| CITY DEPARTMENTS, OFFICES, COURTS, ETC. | | | |
| Mayor and Subordinate Departments, Bureaus and Offices: | | | |
| Mayor's Office and Departments whose executive heads are appointed by the Mayor and who are removable at his pleasure: | | | |
| Commissioners of Accounts | $203,311 19 | $191,740 33 | 1 |
| Board of Ambulance Service | 11,581 09 | 10,874 20 | 2 |
| Board of Assessors | 42,733 68 | 41,450 00 | 3 |
| Department of Bridges | 784,331 04 | 656,816 42 | 4 |
| City Chamberlain | 61,437 60 | 59,452 92 | 5 |
| Department of Correction | 1,276,605 00 | 568,855 24 | 6 |
| Department of Docks and Ferries | 2,718,261 10 | 1,753,988 93 | 7 |
| Examining Board of Plumbers | 5,586 46 | 5,335 00 | 8 |
| Fire Department | 8,407,267 44 | 7,678,993 13 | 9 |
| Department of Health | 3,052,697 53 | 2,226,194 41 | 10 |
| Law Department | 770,031 32 | 662,545 52 | 11 |
| Commissioner of Licenses | 50,498 25 | 48,599 52 | 12 |
| Mayoralty—Administration | 54,738 69 | 51,642 80 | 13 |
| Mayoralty—Bureau of Licenses | 77,002 98 | 68,781 81 | 14 |
| Mayoralty—Bureau of Weights and Measures | 70,550 71 | 57,370 82 | 15 |
| Municipal Civil Service Commission | 175,024 03 | 157,130 38 | 16 |
| Municipal Explosives Commission | 9,623 93 | 9,405 00 | 17 |
| Park Board | 31,646 66 | 31,300 00 | 18 |
| Department of Parks—Manhattan and Richmond | 1,034,747 15 | 783,257 99 | 19 |
| Department of Parks—The Bronx | 426,693 61 | 335,696 17 | 20 |
| Department of Parks—Brooklyn | 875,182 75 | 558,924 58 | 21 |
| Department of Parks—Queens | 149,664 65 | 86,569 87 | 22 |
| Police Department | 16,011,573 34 | 14,638,164 69 | 23 |
| Department of Public Charities | 3,135,649 14 | 1,181,463 93 | 24 |
| Department of Street Cleaning | 8,397,828 46 | 5,250,262 27 | 25 |
| Department of Taxes and Assessment | 582,038 28 | 574,546 34 | 26 |
| Tenement House Department | 776,988 56 | 751,591 06 | 27 |
| Department of Water Supply, Gas and Electricity | 7,332,989 69 | 1,904,617 92 | 28 |
| Total | **56,526,284 33** | **$40,345,571 25** | 29 |
| Departments whose heads are appointed by the Mayor for a term of office greater than his own, and who are removable only upon charges: | | | |
| Bellevue and Allied Hospitals | $1,277,077 66 | $569,636 49 | 30 |
| College of the City of New York | 629,758 37 | 559,163 75 | 31 |
| Department of Education | 33,799,190 74 | 29,120,372 25 | 32 |
| Normal College of the City of New York | 391,733 64 | 360,010 51 | 33 |
| Total | **$36,097,760 41** | **$30,609,183 00** | 34 |
| Boards and Commissions majorities of which are appointed by the Mayor and for which no other elected City official shares responsibility: | | | |
| Art Commission | $7,552 45 | $5,265 00 | 35 |
| Brooklyn Disciplinary Training School for Boys | 56,688 65 | 27,839 48 | 36 |
| Board of Inebriety | 5,909 89 | 3,980 00 | 37 |
| Permanent Census Board | 36,669 65 | 31,439 56 | 38 |
| Public Recreation Commission | 10,824 59 | 9,405 32 | 39 |
| Total | **$117,645 23** | **$77,929 36** | 40 |
| Total, Mayor and Subordinate Departments, Bureaus and Offices | **$92,741,689 97** | **$71,032,683 61** | 41 |
| Comptroller and Finance Department, excluding the Chamberlain's Office: | | | |
| Department of Finance | **$1,460,258 67** | **$1,358,473 69** | 42 |

NEW YORK

Appropriations) for the Year 1912, Classified by Objects of Expenditure:

| LINE No. | Supplies | Purchase of Equipment | Materials | Contract or Open Order Service | Contingencies | Fixed Charges and Contributions |
|---|---|---|---|---|---|---|
| 1 | $312 29 | $424 05 | .......... | $1,550 01 | $9,284 51 | .......... |
| 2 | 404 00 | .......... | .......... | 72 82 | 230 07 | .......... |
| 3 | 620 57 | 133 67 | .......... | 330 59 | 198 85 | .......... |
| 4 | 52,786 98 | 3,873 38 | .......... | 68,135 70 | 2,718 56 | .......... |
| 5 | 282 02 | 114 60 | .......... | 488 46 | 1,099 60 | .......... |
| 6 | 647,981 62 | 7,817 93 | .......... | 42,672 74 | 3,802 36 | $5,475 11 |
| 7 | 542,827 30 | 881 90 | .......... | 232,615 96 | 10,956 93 | 176,990 08 |
| 8 | 157 93 | .......... | .......... | 36 93 | 56 60 | .......... |
| 9 | 507,102 98 | 63,480 26 | .......... | 148,380 73 | 9,310 34 | .......... |
| 10 | 561,059 20 | 41,156 37 | .......... | 125,452 35 | 98,835 20 | .......... |
| 11 | 5,595 50 | .......... | .......... | 6,601 99 | 95,288 31 | .......... |
| 12 | 140 45 | 135 98 | .......... | 333 86 | 1,288 44 | .......... |
| 13 | 575 60 | 221 00 | .......... | 837 38 | 1,461 91 | .......... |
| 14 | 2,505 80 | 84 00 | .......... | 1,380 24 | 4,251 13 | .......... |
| 15 | 4,574 69 | 230 80 | .......... | 5,139 83 | 3,234 57 | .......... |
| 16 | 1,099 30 | 2,218 91 | .......... | 6,972 63 | 7,602 81 | .......... |
| 17 | .......... | 187 98 | .......... | .......... | 30 95 | .......... |
| 18 | 196 76 | 99 90 | .......... | .......... | 50 00 | .......... |
| 19 | 150,024 20 | 7,171 82 | .......... | 87,196 83 | 7,096 31 | .......... |
| 20 | 34,042 91 | 5,618 87 | .......... | 50,274 25 | 1,061 41 | .......... |
| 21 | 144,483 87 | 6,788 55 | .......... | 160,470 26 | 4,515 49 | .......... |
| 22 | 26,868 35 | 15,584 40 | .......... | 18,644 20 | 1,997 83 | .......... |
| 23 | 214,012 10 | 42,923 55 | .......... | 196,803 67 | 46,866 63 | 872,802 70 |
| 24 | 1,632,960 92 | 14,696 97 | .......... | 182,994 24 | 8,901 52 | 114,631 56 |
| 25 | 711,549 86 | 261,635 31 | .......... | 2,166,838 56 | 7,542 46 | .......... |
| 26 | 3,308 52 | .......... | .......... | 1,506 62 | 2,676 80 | .......... |
| 27 | 3,083 29 | 1,406 14 | .......... | 3,437 82 | 17,470 25 | .......... |
| 28 | 247,529 95 | 10,465 48 | .......... | 4,920,962 56 | 49,726 51 | 199,687 27 |
| 29 | **$5,496,086 96** | **$487,351 82** | .......... | **$8,430,131 23** | **$397,556 35** | **$1,369,586 72** |
| 30 | $618,163 65 | $22,290 03 | .......... | $58,390 69 | $8,596 80 | .......... |
| 31 | 56,785 32 | .......... | .......... | 12,168 82 | 1,640 48 | .......... |
| 32 | 1,932,990 97 | 143,604 33 | .......... | 2,543,070 73 | 41,383 21 | $17,769 25 |
| 33 | 25,224 30 | .......... | .......... | 4,063 88 | 2,434 95 | .......... |
| 34 | **$2,633,164 24** | **$165,894 36** | .......... | **$2,617,694 12** | **$54,055 44** | **$17,769 25** |
| 35 | $1,372 73 | .......... | .......... | $291 02 | $623 70 | .......... |
| 36 | 27,408 28 | .......... | .......... | 825 68 | 615 21 | .......... |
| 37 | 428 53 | $754 60 | .......... | 96 00 | 650 76 | .......... |
| 38 | 2,854 91 | .......... | .......... | 179 72 | 2,195 46 | .......... |
| 39 | 190 31 | 250 00 | .......... | 168 01 | 810 95 | .......... |
| 40 | **$32,254 76** | **$1,004 60** | .......... | **$1,560 43** | **$4,896 08** | .......... |
| 41 | **$8,161,505 96** | **$654,250 78** | .......... | **$11,049,385 78** | **$456,507 87** | **$1,387,355 97** |
| 42 | **$15,494 73** | **$10,490 75** | .......... | **$31,761 90** | **$44,037 60** | .......... |

Statement Showing Expenditures from Revenue (Budget Appropriations)

| | Total | Personal Service | Line No. |
|---|---|---|---|
| City Departments, Offices, Courts, Etc.—*Continued* | | | |
| Borough Presidents and Subordinate Departments: | | | |
| President, Borough of Manhattan | $2,480,922 46 | $1,577,079 53 | 1 |
| President, Borough of The Bronx | 1,100,892 02 | 784,559 97 | 2 |
| President, Borough of Brooklyn | 2,067,023 33 | 1,485,011 78 | 3 |
| President, Borough of Queens | 1,663,885 13 | 1,052,966 02 | 4 |
| President, Borough of Richmond | 761,792 09 | 523,342 32 | 5 |
| Total | **$8,074,515 03** | **$5,422,959 62** | 6 |
| Board of Aldermen, President of Board and City Clerk | **$283,244 05** | **$277,443 58** | 7 |
| Boards, Commissions, etc., whose members are not elected by popular vote and who are not appointed by any elected City Official: | | | |
| Board of Building Examiners | $9,108 47 | $8,679 00 | 8 |
| Total | **$9,108 47** | **$8,679 00** | 9 |
| Boards, Commissions, etc., of mixed responsibility, i.e., ex-officio bodies, representing two or more preceding branches: | | | |
| Armory Board | $263,945 10 | $18,364 33 | 10 |
| Board of City Record, City of New York | 865,849 77 | 43,022 77 | 11 |
| Board of Elections | 1,065,784 79 | 571,841 94 | 12 |
| Board of Estimate and Apportionment | 286,618 15 | 234,513 10 | 13 |
| Commissioners of the Sinking Fund | 7,013 61 | 3,050 00 | 14 |
| Total | **$2,489,211 42** | **$870,792 14** | 15 |
| Courts, including Board of Parole and General Interpreters of Brooklyn: | | | |
| Coroners, Borough of Manhattan | $62,675 31 | $61,034 39 | 16 |
| Coroners, Borough of The Bronx | 27,954 84 | 27,054 84 | 17 |
| Coroners, Borough of Brooklyn | 34,578 73 | 33,550 00 | 18 |
| Coroners, Borough of Queens | 19,422 59 | 18,025 00 | 19 |
| Coroners, Borough of Richmond | 12,090 52 | 11,200 00 | 20 |
| City Court of New York | 246,774 69 | 240,916 94 | 21 |
| City Magistrates' Courts, First Division | 377,524 52 | 369,838 19 | 22 |
| City Magistrates' Courts, Second Division | 358,942 04 | 353,290 90 | 23 |
| Municipal Courts, City of New York | 927,241 80 | 908,837 23 | 24 |
| Court of Special Sessions | 334,628 93 | 324,803 48 | 25 |
| General Interpreters of Brooklyn | 9,148 27 | 9,148 27 | 26 |
| Board of Parole | 4,230 90 | 4,031 04 | 27 |
| Total | **$2,415,213 14** | **$2,361,730 28** | 28 |
| Total City Departments, Offices, Courts, etc | **$107,473,240 75** | **$81,332,761 92** | 29 |
| Debt Service (*See details page 120*) | **$50,218,374 43** | .......... | 30 |
| Fixed Charges other than Debt Service, Subsidies, Contributions, Payments to Private and State Institutions, Expenditures not allotted to Departments: | | | |
| American Museum of Natural History | $195,000 00 | $170,023 00 | 31 |
| Botanical Garden and Arboretum | 25,782 40 | 17,135 51 | 32 |
| Charitable Institutions, City | 4,431,326 77 | .......... | 33 |
| Children's Museum, Brooklyn | 12,499 43 | 10,177 52 | 34 |
| Grant's Tomb | 6,817 15 | .......... | 35 |
| Jumel Mansion | 5,437 45 | 3,724 37 | 36 |
| Metropolitan Museum of Art | 200,000 00 | 161,097 75 | 37 |
| Miscellaneous, City | 1,245,312 06 | 3,550 00 | 38 |
| Museum of Arts and Sciences | 97,623 48 | 75,071 20 | 39 |
| New York Aquarium | 46,597 08 | 32,595 63 | 40 |
| New York Botanical Garden | 90,072 46 | 71,890 00 | 41 |
| New York Zoological Garden | 179,272 87 | 116,314 47 | 42 |
| New York Public Library Building | 10,000 00 | .......... | 43 |
| New York Public Library | 616,958 99 | 362,390 00 | 44 |

# NEW YORK

FOR THE YEAR 1912, CLASSIFIED BY OBJECTS OF EXPENDITURE:—*Continued*

| LINE No. | Supplies | Purchase of Equipment | Materials | Contract or Open Order Service | Contingencies | Fixed Charges and Contributions |
|---|---|---|---|---|---|---|
| 1 | $207,169 16 | $6,636 08 | .......... | $666,549 74 | $23,487 95 | .......... |
| 2 | 142,424 45 | 16,030 26 | .......... | 149,269 16 | 8,608 18 | .......... |
| 3 | 269,995 91 | 23,352 50 | .......... | 273,423 45 | 15,239 69 | .......... |
| 4 | 154,053 27 | 29,706 81 | .......... | 416,281 34 | 10,877 69 | .......... |
| 5 | 129,827 98 | 9,091 57 | .......... | 93,165 94 | 6,364 28 | .......... |
| 6 | **$903,470 77** | **$84,817 22** | .......... | **$1,598,689 63** | **$64,577 79** | .......... |
| 7 | **$1,004 80** | **$60 00** | .......... | **$2,049 29** | **$2,686 38** | .......... |
| 8 | $98 93 | .......... | .......... | $93 00 | $237 54 | .......... |
| 9 | **$98 93** | .......... | .......... | **$93 00** | **$237 54** | .......... |
| 10 | $64,365 16 | $3,291 92 | .......... | $176,752 04 | $1,171 65 | .......... |
| 11 | 608 07 | 1,446 70 | .......... | 815,063 39 | 5,708 84 | .......... |
| 12 | 108,132 22 | 628 70 | .......... | 38,389 31 | 3,099 86 | $343,692 76 |
| 13 | 8,999 55 | .......... | .......... | 91 98 | 43,013 52 | .......... |
| 14 | .......... | .......... | .......... | 3,021 50 | 942 11 | .......... |
| 15 | **$182,105 00** | **$5,367 32** | .......... | **$1,033,318 22** | **$53,935 98** | **$343,692 76** |
| 16 | $215 45 | .......... | .......... | $956 54 | $468 93 | .......... |
| 17 | 80 00 | $20 00 | .......... | 700 00 | 100 00 | .......... |
| 18 | 83 95 | 373 05 | .......... | 286 73 | 285 00 | .......... |
| 19 | 94 95 | .......... | .......... | 323 31 | 979 33 | .......... |
| 20 | 117 60 | .......... | .......... | 469 97 | 302 95 | .......... |
| 21 | 3,492 65 | .......... | .......... | 311 57 | 2,053 53 | .......... |
| 22 | 3,331 28 | .......... | .......... | 2,249 11 | 2,105 94 | .......... |
| 23 | 1,476 76 | .......... | .......... | 2,610 79 | 1,563 59 | .......... |
| 24 | 9,986 95 | .......... | .......... | .......... | 8,417 62 | .......... |
| 25 | 4,364 32 | .......... | .......... | 2,015 44 | 3,445 69 | .......... |
| 26 | .......... | .......... | .......... | .......... | .......... | .......... |
| 27 | .......... | .......... | .......... | .......... | 199 86 | .......... |
| 28 | **$23,243 91** | **$393 05** | .......... | **$9,923 46** | **$19,922 44** | .......... |
| 29 | **$9,286,924 10** | **$755,379 12** | .......... | **$13,725,221 28** | **$641,905 60** | **$1,731,048 73** |
| 30 | .......... | .......... | .......... | .......... | .......... | **$50,218,374 43** |
| 31 | $21,419 00 | $1,150 00 | .......... | $950 00 | $1,458 00 | .......... |
| 32 | 5,125 00 | .......... | .......... | 2,448 93 | 1,072 96 | .......... |
| 33 | .......... | .......... | .......... | .......... | .......... | $4,431,326 77 |
| 34 | 1,473 70 | .......... | .......... | 551 45 | 296 76 | .......... |
| 35 | .......... | .......... | .......... | 6,817 15 | .......... | .......... |
| 36 | 287 93 | 120 00 | .......... | 1,096 00 | 209 15 | .......... |
| 37 | 24,542 25 | 1,850 00 | .......... | 600 00 | 11,910 00 | .......... |
| 38 | .......... | .......... | .......... | 148,005 57 | .......... | 1,093,756 49 |
| 39 | 13,961 80 | 2,292 69 | .......... | 3,299 16 | 2,998 63 | .......... |
| 40 | 10,102 27 | 45 00 | .......... | 3,229 42 | 624 76 | .......... |
| 41 | 16,061 36 | 300 00 | .......... | 1,421 10 | 400 00 | .......... |
| 42 | 51,538 66 | 98 75 | .......... | 9,623 60 | 1,697 39 | .......... |
| 43 | 4,000 00 | .......... | .......... | 6,000 00 | .......... | .......... |
| 44 | 155,003 25 | 4,236 92 | .......... | 82,087 29 | 13,061 53 | 180 00 |

STATEMENT SHOWING EXPENDITURES FROM REVENUE (BUDGET

| | Total | Personal Service | LINE No. |
|---|---|---|---|
| FIXED CHARGES—*Continued* | | | |
| Brooklyn Public Library | $413,628 47 | $230,324 84 | 1 |
| Queensborough Public Library | 143,997 99 | 79,813 94 | 2 |
| Staten Island Association of Arts and Sciences | 9,448 44 | 6,383 75 | 3 |
| United States Volunteer Life Saving Corps | 13,044 23 | 6,514 94 | 4 |
| Total | **$7,742,819 27** | **$1,347,006 92** | 5 |
| DEFICIENCIES IN TAXES | **$3,287,366 74** | .......... | 6 |
| Total for City Purposes | **$168,721,801 19** | **$82,679,768 84** | 7 |
| DIRECT STATE TAXES: | $3,211,557 62 | .......... | 8 |
| New York County | 847,328 81 | .......... | 9 |
| Kings County | 200,986 53 | .......... | 10 |
| Queens County | 41,472 69 | .......... | 11 |
| Richmond County | | | |
| | **$4,301,345 65** | .......... | 12 |
| COUNTY EXPENDITURES: | | | |
| New York County: | | | |
| Charitable Institutions | $105,153 59 | .......... | 13 |
| Board of City Record | 39,882 29 | .......... | 14 |
| County Clerk | 184,568 67 | $180,743 94 | 15 |
| Court of General Sessions | 351,687 49 | 348,889 19 | 16 |
| Supreme Court, First Department | 872,614 24 | 866,746 70 | 17 |
| Supreme Court, Maintenance of Appellate Division Court House | 27,374 34 | 18,180 56 | 18 |
| Surrogate's Court | 168,767 23 | 167,011 25 | 19 |
| District Attorney | 417,186 83 | 384,039 68 | 20 |
| Commissioner of Jurors | 52,122 28 | 47,642 75 | 21 |
| Miscellaneous | 431,764 03 | 408,822 38 | 22 |
| National Guard and Naval Militia | 212,527 50 | 204,527 50 | 23 |
| Public Administrator | 25,377 42 | 24,860 00 | 24 |
| Commissioner of Records | 84,491 68 | 80,849 36 | 25 |
| Commissioner of Records, Surrogate's Court | 44,817 93 | 44,243 74 | 26 |
| Register | 317,650 04 | 311,807 63 | 27 |
| Sheriff | 149,118 82 | 140,043 34 | 28 |
| Total | **$3,485,104 38** | **$3,228,408 02** | 29 |
| Kings County: | | | |
| Charitable Institutions | $58,343 57 | .......... | 30 |
| Board of City Record | 17,967 15 | .......... | 31 |
| County Clerk | 92,841 55 | $90,904 28 | 32 |
| County Court | 161,352 86 | 159,913 30 | 33 |
| Supreme Court, Second Department | 406,955 14 | 405,677 26 | 34 |
| Supreme Court Law Library | 9,400 00 | 8,800 00 | 35 |
| Surrogate's Court | 99,138 88 | 97,443 17 | 36 |
| District Attorney | 111,574 17 | 101,443 37 | 37 |
| Commissioner of Jurors | 40,157 20 | 38,163 44 | 38 |
| Miscellaneous | 127,689 95 | 109,149 65 | 39 |
| National Guard and Naval Militia | 144,797 25 | 144,797 25 | 40 |
| Commissioner of Records | 97,878 01 | 96,769 50 | 41 |
| Register | 216,123 69 | 212,981 20 | 42 |
| Sheriff | 84,920 91 | 77,850 00 | 43 |
| Total | **$1,669,140 33** | **$1,543,892 42** | 44 |

NEW YORK

Appropriations) for the Year 1912, Classified by Objects of Expenditure:—*Continued*

| LINE No. | Supplies | Purchase of Equipment | Materials | Contract or Open Order Service | Contingencies | Fixed Charges and Contributions |
|---|---|---|---|---|---|---|
| 1 | $102,611 24 | $4,199 32 | .......... | $53,124 80 | $8,645 86 | $14,722 41 |
| 2 | 29,820 94 | 2,649 83 | .......... | 13,407 12 | 6,369 53 | 11,936 63 |
| 3 | 409 64 | 465 93 | .......... | 618 12 | 71 00 | 1,500 00 |
| 4 | 2,342 18 | .......... | .......... | 3,702 75 | 484 36 | .......... |
| 5 | **$438,699 22** | **$17,408 44** | .......... | **$336,982 46** | **$49,299 93** | **$5,553,422 30** |
| 6 | .......... | .......... | .......... | .......... | .......... | **$3,287,366 74** |
| 7 | **$9,725,623 32** | **$772,787 56** | .......... | **$14,062,203 74** | **$691,205 53** | **$60,790,212 20** |
| 8 | .......... | .......... | .......... | .......... | .......... | $3,211,557 62 |
| 9 | .......... | .......... | .......... | .......... | .......... | 847,328 81 |
| 10 | .......... | .......... | .......... | .......... | .......... | 200,986 53 |
| 11 | .......... | .......... | .......... | .......... | .......... | 41,472 69 |
| 12 | .......... | .......... | .......... | .......... | .......... | **$4,301,345 65** |
| 13 | .......... | .......... | .......... | .......... | .......... | $105,153 59 |
| 14 | .......... | .......... | .......... | $39,882 29 | .......... | .......... |
| 15 | $1,347 68 | $1,139 45 | .......... | 400 00 | $937 60 | .......... |
| 16 | 1,509 10 | .......... | .......... | 989 37 | 299 83 | .......... |
| 17 | .......... | .......... | .......... | 3,783 54 | 84 00 | 2,000 00 |
| 18 | 5,799 81 | 114 26 | .......... | 2,896 48 | 383 23 | .......... |
| 19 | 872 75 | 183 95 | .......... | 217 87 | 481 41 | .......... |
| 20 | 2,041 16 | 1,000 00 | .......... | 2,962 41 | 27,143 58 | .......... |
| 21 | 2,015 39 | 154 00 | .......... | 179 99 | 2,130 15 | .......... |
| 22 | .......... | .......... | .......... | .......... | 1,458 00 | 21,483 65 |
| 23 | .......... | .......... | .......... | 8,000 00 | .......... | .......... |
| 24 | 39 80 | .......... | .......... | 213 54 | 264 08 | .......... |
| 25 | 812 57 | 2,167 72 | .......... | 368 30 | 293 73 | .......... |
| 26 | 530 19 | .......... | .......... | .......... | 44 00 | .......... |
| 27 | 3,947 24 | 1,174 29 | .......... | 356 26 | 364 62 | .......... |
| 28 | 4,228 02 | .......... | .......... | 2,113 51 | 2,733 95 | .......... |
| 29 | **$23,143 71** | **$5,933 67** | .......... | **$62,363 56** | **$36,618 18** | **$128,637 24** |
| 30 | .......... | .......... | .......... | .......... | .......... | $58,343 57 |
| 31 | .......... | .......... | .......... | $17,967 15 | .......... | .......... |
| 32 | $296 82 | $168 05 | .......... | 1,131 27 | $341 13 | .......... |
| 33 | 703 81 | .......... | .......... | 68 21 | 667 54 | .......... |
| 34 | .......... | .......... | .......... | .......... | 1,277 88 | .......... |
| 35 | .......... | .......... | .......... | .......... | 600 00 | .......... |
| 36 | 961 65 | .......... | .......... | 455 82 | 278 24 | .......... |
| 37 | 847 19 | 899 81 | .......... | 750 00 | 7,633 80 | .......... |
| 38 | 298 49 | 200 00 | .......... | 150 87 | 1,344 40 | .......... |
| 39 | .......... | .......... | .......... | .......... | 3,944 30 | 14,596 00 |
| 40 | .......... | .......... | .......... | .......... | .......... | .......... |
| 41 | 641 76 | 89 88 | .......... | 234 07 | 142 80 | .......... |
| 42 | 983 88 | 596 53 | .......... | 562 65 | 999 43 | .......... |
| 43 | 4,192 00 | .......... | .......... | 641 83 | 2,237 08 | .......... |
| 44 | **$8,925 60** | **$1,954 27** | .......... | **$21,961 87** | **$19,466 60** | **$72,939 57** |

STATEMENT SHOWING EXPENDITURES FROM REVENUE (BUDGET

| | Total | Personal Service | LINE No. |
|---|---|---|---|
| COUNTY EXPENDITURES—*Continued* | | | |
| Queens County: | | | |
| Charitable Institutions | $5,920 50 | .......... | 1 |
| Board of City Record | 2,157 27 | .......... | 2 |
| County Clerk | 33,943 89 | $33,492 90 | 3 |
| County Court | 36,021 13 | 34,617 90 | 4 |
| Supreme Court | 67,364 59 | 66,921 61 | 5 |
| Supreme Court Library | 2,272 65 | 1,741 67 | 6 |
| Surrogate's Court | 23,793 60 | 22,941 43 | 7 |
| District Attorney | 31,363 52 | 29,127 72 | 8 |
| Commissioner of Jurors | 10,732 04 | 9,937 12 | 9 |
| Miscellaneous | 33,517 90 | 32,662 00 | 10 |
| National Guard and Naval Militia | 5,124 00 | 5,124 00 | 11 |
| Public Administrator | 1,200 00 | 1,200 00 | 12 |
| Sheriff | 70,855 42 | 49,703 26 | 13 |
| Total | **$324,266 51** | **$287,469 61** | 14 |
| Richmond County: | | | |
| Charitable Institutions | $1,566 41 | .......... | 15 |
| Board of City Record | 2,529 45 | .......... | 16 |
| County Clerk | 17,923 95 | $17,640 55 | 17 |
| County Court and Surrogate's Court | 21,500 00 | 21,100 00 | 18 |
| Supreme Court | 12,962 68 | 12,929 08 | 19 |
| District Attorney | 13,533 17 | 10,950 00 | 20 |
| Commissioner of Jurors | 4,250 14 | 4,050 00 | 21 |
| Miscellaneous | 12,505 00 | 11,705 83 | 22 |
| Sheriff | 29,366 93 | 19,846 00 | 23 |
| Total | **$116,137 73** | **$98,221 46** | 24 |
| Total for County Purposes | **$5,594,648 95** | **$5,157,991 51** | 25 |
| Total for All Purposes | **$178,617,795 79** | **$87,837,760 35** | 26 |

NOTE—In the Budget for 1912, "Materials" were provided for in accounts

NEW YORK

APPROPRIATIONS) FOR THE YEAR 1912, CLASSIFIED BY OBJECTS OF EXPENDITURE:—*Continued*

| LINE No. | Supplies | Purchase of Equipment | Materials | Contract or Open Order Service | Contingencies | Fixed Charges and Contributions |
|---|---|---|---|---|---|---|
| 1 | .......... | .......... | .......... | .......... | .......... | **$5,920 50** |
| 2 | .......... | .......... | .......... | $2,157 27 | .......... | .......... |
| 3 | .......... | .......... | .......... | 450 99 | .......... | .......... |
| 4 | $790 98 | $161 80 | .......... | 178 57 | $271 88 | .......... |
| 5 | .......... | .......... | .......... | 292 98 | 150 00 | .......... |
| 6 | 93 70 | 398 90 | .......... | 21 13 | 17 25 | .......... |
| 7 | 145 00 | 98 40 | .......... | 262 02 | 346 75 | .......... |
| 8 | 199 13 | .......... | .......... | 463 67 | 1,573 00 | .......... |
| 9 | 18 55 | .......... | .......... | 53 91 | 722 46 | .......... |
| 10 | .......... | .......... | .......... | .......... | 855 90 | .......... |
| 11 | .......... | .......... | .......... | .......... | .......... | .......... |
| 12 | .......... | .......... | .......... | .......... | .......... | .......... |
| 13 | 10,729 22 | .......... | .......... | 7,459 01 | 2,963 93 | .......... |
| 14 | **$11,976 58** | **$659 10** | .......... | **$11,339 55** | **$6,901 17** | **$5,920 50** |
| 15 | .......... | .......... | .......... | .......... | .......... | $1,566 41 |
| 16 | .......... | .......... | .......... | $2,529 45 | .......... | .......... |
| 17 | .......... | .......... | .......... | 106 40 | $177 00 | .......... |
| 18 | $191 43 | .......... | .......... | 108 57 | 100 00 | .......... |
| 19 | 33 60 | .......... | .......... | .......... | .......... | .......... |
| 20 | 178 60 | .......... | .......... | 1,557 65 | 846 92 | .......... |
| 21 | 110 00 | .......... | .......... | 70 54 | 19 60 | .......... |
| 22 | .......... | .......... | .......... | .......... | 774 17 | 25 00 |
| 23 | 8,459 98 | .......... | .......... | 760 86 | 300 09 | .......... |
| 24 | **$8,973 61** | .......... | .......... | **$5,133 47** | **$2,217 78** | **$1,591 41** |
| 25 | **$53,019 50** | **$8,547 04** | .......... | **$100,798 45** | **$65,203 73** | **$209,088 72** |
| 26 | **$9,778,642 82** | **$781,334 60** | .......... | **$14,163,002 19** | **$756,409 26** | **$65,300,646 57** |

"Supplies and Materials," which are all included in column headed "Supplies."

THE CITY OF

RECAPITULATION OF STATEMENT SHOWING EXPENDITURES FROM REVENUE (BUDGET

| | Total | Personal Service | LINE No. |
|---|---|---|---|
| CITY DEPARTMENTS, OFFICES, COURTS, ETC. | | | |
| Mayor and Subordinate Departments, Bureaus, and Offices: | | | |
| Mayor's Office and Departments whose executive heads are appointed by the Mayor and who are removable at his pleasure | $58,039,417 07 | $41,740,709 54 | 1 |
| Departments whose heads are appointed by the Mayor for a term of office greater than his own, and who are removable only on charges | 37,884,218 47 | 31,888,897 97 | 2 |
| Boards and Commissions majority of which are appointed by the Mayor and for which no other elected City official shares responsibility | 160,409 34 | 120,066 35 | 3 |
| Total Mayor and Subordinate Departments, Bureaus and Offices | **$96,084,044 88** | **$73,749,673 86** | 4 |
| Comptroller and Finance Department, excluding the Chamberlain's Office | **$1,671,242 42** | **$1,558,315 13** | 5 |
| Borough Presidents and Subordinate Departments: | | | |
| President, Borough of Manhattan | $2,616,527 64 | $1,664,774 86 | 6 |
| President, Borough of The Bronx | 1,165,494 92 | 845,160 62 | 7 |
| President, Borough of Brooklyn | 2,045,404 09 | 1,495,413 90 | 8 |
| President, Borough of Queens | 1,916,028 44 | 1,157,187 86 | 9 |
| President, Borough of Richmond | 823,873 94 | 584,919 08 | 10 |
| Total, Borough Presidents | **$8,567,329 03** | **$5,747,456 32** | 11 |
| Board of Aldermen, President of Board and City Clerk | **$298,780 29** | **$292,991 18** | 12 |
| Boards, Commissions, etc., whose members are not elected by popular vote and who are not appointed by any elected City official | **$26,087 08** | **$24,144 81** | 13 |
| Boards, Commissions, etc., of mixed responsibility, i.e., ex-officio bodies representing two or more of preceding branches | **$2,759,455 93** | **$955,931 49** | 14 |
| Courts, including Board of Parole and General Interpreters of Brooklyn | **$2,493,606 84** | **$2,432,231 11** | 15 |
| Total, City Departments, Offices, Courts, etc. | **$111,900,546 47** | **$84,760,743 90** | 16 |
| DEBT SERVICE (*See details page 120*) | **$54,533,439 05** | .......... | 17 |
| FIXED CHARGES OTHER THAN DEBT SERVICE, SUBSIDIES, CONTRIBUTIONS, PAYMENTS TO PRIVATE AND STATE INSTITUTIONS, EXPENDITURES NOT ALLOTTED TO DEPARTMENTS | **$8,009,872 00** | **$1,440,506 70** | 18 |
| DEFICIENCIES IN TAXES | **$2,300,000 00** | .......... | 19 |
| Total for City Purposes | **$176,743,857 52** | **$86,201,250 60** | 20 |
| DIRECT STATE TAXES | **$7,947,031 96** | .......... | 21 |
| COUNTY EXPENDITURES: | | | |
| New York County | $3,739,348 47 | $3,446,597 35 | 22 |
| Kings County | 1,737,155 22 | 1,608,882 39 | 23 |
| Queens County | 415,694 62 | 383,053 05 | 24 |
| Richmond County | 122,982 40 | 106,090 91 | 25 |
| Total for County Purposes | **$6,015,180 71** | **$5,544,623 70** | 26 |
| Total for All Purposes | **$190,706,070 19** | **$91,745,874 30** | 27 |

## NEW YORK

Appropriations) for the Year 1913, Classified by Objects of Expenditure:

| Line No. | Supplies | Purchase of Equipment | Materials | Contract or Open Order Service | Contingencies | Fixed Charges and Contributions |
|---|---|---|---|---|---|---|
| 1 | $4,504,740 04 | $1,258,089 17 | $752,511 21 | $7,950,513 82 | $124,722 63 | $1,708,130 66 |
| 2 | 2,660,549 59 | 432,212 77 | 27,720 72 | 2,847,752 07 | 20,267 35 | 6,818 00 |
| 3 | 26,322 99 | 5,709 76 | 626 76 | 4,936 31 | 2,254 03 | 493 14 |
| 4 | **$7,191,612 62** | **$1,696,011 70** | **$780,858 69** | **$10,803,202 20** | **$147,244 01** | **$1,715,441 80** |
| 5 | **$13,210 00** | **$9,277 67** | .......... | **$34,293 47** | **$56,146 15** | .......... |
| 6 | $76,556 62 | $32,997 09 | $89,292 49 | $750,985 16 | $1,921 42 | .......... |
| 7 | 22,406 61 | 14,764 65 | 122,547 24 | 159,131 61 | 812 19 | $672 00 |
| 8 | 107,400 99 | 29,599 93 | 146,707 61 | 258,303 31 | 7,978 35 | .......... |
| 9 | 38,259 92 | 55,049 91 | 209,076 71 | 452,406 79 | 4,047 25 | .......... |
| 10 | 36,936 68 | 26,478 58 | 95,644 49 | 71,966 61 | 7,928 50 | .......... |
| 11 | **$281,560 82** | **$158,890 16** | **$663,268 54** | **$1,692,793 48** | **$22,687 71** | **$672 00** |
| 12 | **$3,719 60** | .......... | .......... | **$2,069 51** | .......... | .......... |
| 13 | **$517 00** | **$21 62** | .......... | **$278 66** | **$224 99** | **$900 00** |
| 14 | **$299,776 37** | **$71,086 51** | **$11,074 31** | **$1,038,366 40** | **$113,799 42** | **$269,421 43** |
| 15 | **$11,120 40** | **$25,139 33** | .......... | **$23,950 49** | **$1,165 51** | .......... |
| 16 | **$7,801,516 81** | **$1,960,426 99** | **$1,455,201 54** | **$13,594,954 21** | **$341,267 79** | **$1,986,435 23** |
| 17 | .......... | .......... | .......... | .......... | .......... | ***$54,533,439 05** |
| 18 | **$163,565 30** | **$267,958 70** | **$16,593 57** | **$189,039 89** | **$51,770 87** | **$5,880,436 97** |
| 19 | .......... | .......... | .......... | .......... | .......... | **$2,300,000 00** |
| 20 | **$7,965,082 11** | **$2,228,385 69** | **$1,471,795 11** | **$13,783,994 10** | **$393,038 66** | **$64,700,311 25** |
| 21 | .......... | .......... | .......... | .......... | .......... | **$7,947,031 96** |
| 22 | $27,272 93 | $9,700 27 | $1,054 30 | $66,346 36 | $19,459 52 | $168,917 74 |
| 23 | 10.533 43 | 4,119 60 | 499 65 | 23,819 38 | 10,703 79 | 78,596 98 |
| 24 | 4,352 56 | 8,662 71 | .......... | 10,337 89 | 2,820 20 | 6,468 21 |
| 25 | 8,865 88 | 1,489 25 | .......... | 3,744 95 | 1,477 23 | 1,314 18 |
| 26 | **$51,024 80** | **$23,971 83** | **$1,553 95** | **$104,248 58** | **$34,460 74** | **$255,297 11** |
| 27 | **$8,016,106 91** | **$2,252,357 52** | **$1,473,349 06** | **$13,888,242 68** | **$427,499, 40** | **$72,902,640 32** |

*Includes redemption of $7,038,065.51 Special Revenue Bonds, issued to defray expenses of 1912

STATEMENT SHOWING EXPENDITURES FROM REVENUE (BUDGET

| | Total | Personal Service | Line No. |
|---|---|---|---|
| CITY DEPARTMENTS, OFFICES, COURTS, ETC. | | | |
| Mayor and Subordinate Departments, Bureaus and Offices: | | | |
| Mayor's Office and Departments whose executive heads are appointed by the Mayor and who are removable at his pleasure: | | | |
| Commissioners of Accounts | $195,536 97 | $188,101 41 | 1 |
| Board of Ambulance Service | 76,863 55 | 11,676 66 | 2 |
| Board of Assessors | 41,364 34 | 40,523 39 | 3 |
| Department of Bridges | 878,449 64 | 701,685 39 | 4 |
| City Chamberlain | 62,134 14 | 59,929 20 | 5 |
| Department of Correction | 1,275,620 49 | 594,097 27 | 6 |
| Department of Docks and Ferries | 2,727,669 04 | 1,757,678 30 | 7 |
| Examining Board of Plumbers | 2,307 28 | 1,955 00 | 8 |
| Fire Department | 8,814,057 13 | 8,043,381 86 | 9 |
| Department of Health | 3,254,066 51 | 2,373,473 31 | 10 |
| Law Department | 849,929 23 | 768,665 65 | 11 |
| Commissioner of Licenses | 47,764 59 | 46,048 44 | 12 |
| Mayoralty—Administration | 55,595 28 | 52,520 26 | 13 |
| Mayoralty—Bureau of Licenses | 103,368 04 | 80,492 94 | 14 |
| Mayoralty—Bureau of Weights and Measures | 64,686 35 | 54,337 08 | 15 |
| Municipal Civil Service Commission | 205,143 12 | 186,152 37 | 16 |
| Municipal Explosives Commission | 9,581 25 | 9,405 00 | 17 |
| Park Board | 29,884 36 | 29,488 47 | 18 |
| Department of Parks—Manhattan and Richmond | 1,081,582 41 | 842,919 62 | 19 |
| Department of Parks—The Bronx | 438,911 27 | 345,469 64 | 20 |
| Department of Parks—Brooklyn | 867,234 36 | 578,470 15 | 21 |
| Department of Parks—Queens | 181,847 22 | 116,860 73 | 22 |
| Police Department | 16,719,667 95 | 14,908,259 17 | 23 |
| Department of Public Charities | 3,570,466 26 | 1,341,822 51 | 24 |
| Department of Street Cleaning | 7,686,515 18 | 5,355,129 70 | 25 |
| Department of Taxes and Assessments | 589,068 07 | 578,724 38 | 26 |
| Tenement House Department | 762,036 81 | 736,839 61 | 27 |
| Department of Water Supply, Gas and Electricity | 7,448,066 23 | 1,936,602 03 | 28 |
| Totals | **$58,039,417 07** | **$41,740,709 54** | 29 |
| Departments whose heads are appointed by the Mayor for a term of office greater than his own, and who are removable only upon charges: | | | |
| Bellevue and Allied Hospitals | $1,349,253 14 | $600,353 11 | 30 |
| College of the City of New York | 657,121 19 | 565,446 59 | 31 |
| Department of Education | 35,392,782 17 | 30,275,211 30 | 32 |
| Normal College of the City of New York | 485,061 97 | 447,886 97 | 33 |
| Totals | **$37,884,218 47** | **$31,888,897 97** | 34 |
| Boards and Commissions majorities of which are appointed by the Mayor and for which no other elected City official shares responsibility: | | | |
| Art Commission | $7,551 11 | $5,456 00 | 35 |
| Brooklyn Disciplinary Training School for Boys | 54,267 79 | 27,691 31 | 36 |
| Board of Inebriety | 6,584 83 | 5,294 74 | 37 |
| Permanent Census Board | 73,474 96 | 68,166 76 | 38 |
| Public Recreation Commission | 18,530 65 | 13,457 54 | 39 |
| Totals | **$160,409 34** | **$120,066 35** | 40 |
| Total, Mayor and Subordinate Departments, Bureaus and Offices | **$96,084,044 88** | **$73,749,673 86** | 41 |
| Comptroller and Finance Department, excluding the Chamberlain's Office: | | | |
| Department of Finance | **$1,671,242 42** | **$1,558,315 13** | 42 |

## NEW YORK

APPROPRIATIONS) FOR THE YEAR 1913, CLASSIFIED BY OBJECTS OF EXPENDITURE:

| LINE No. | Supplies | Purchase of Equipment | Materials | Contract or Open Order Service | Contingencies | Fixed Charges and Contributions |
|---|---|---|---|---|---|---|
| 1 | $1,247 06 | $634 97 | .......... | $4,360 53 | $1,193 00 | .......... |
| 2 | 122 73 | 158 55 | .......... | 64,903 41 | 2 20 | .......... |
| 3 | 412 26 | .......... | .......... | 428 69 | .......... | .......... |
| 4 | 19,965 67 | 11,233 89 | $73,541 98 | 72,007 99 | 14 72 | .......... |
| 5 | 1,301 81 | 168 92 | .......... | 613 71 | 120 50 | .......... |
| 6 | 462,462 39 | 40,170 37 | 143,246 62 | 29,850 05 | 100 00 | $5,693 79 |
| 7 | 386,295 43 | 25,910 92 | 118,624 36 | 273,131 03 | .......... | 166,029 00 |
| 8 | 66 94 | 191 20 | .......... | 83 14 | 11 00 | .......... |
| 9 | 385,344 31 | 199,255 96 | 59,348 90 | 120,613 26 | 6,112 84 | .......... |
| 10 | 551,852 07 | 111,590 01 | 32,224 87 | 180,947 17 | 3,979 08 | .......... |
| 11 | 1,430 53 | 3,777 18 | .......... | 17,862 96 | 58,192 91 | .......... |
| 12 | 728 50 | 149 20 | .......... | 788 45 | 50 00 | .......... |
| 13 | 625 00 | 1,035 08 | .......... | 1,014 94 | 400 00 | .......... |
| 14 | 2,483 22 | 15,655 37 | .......... | 4,337 53 | 398 98 | .......... |
| 15 | 984 93 | 2,688 81 | .......... | 6,370 77 | 304 76 | .......... |
| 16 | 7,171 64 | 2,748 74 | .......... | 5,688 33 | 3,382 04 | .......... |
| 17 | 40 25 | 100 00 | .......... | .......... | 36 00 | .......... |
| 18 | 169 91 | 202 73 | .......... | .......... | 23 25 | .......... |
| 19 | 92,787 67 | 17,262 03 | 31,214 10 | 96,112 68 | 1,286 31 | .......... |
| 20 | 14,717 09 | 8,768 52 | 22,139 54 | 47,816 48 | .......... | .......... |
| 21 | 60,065 25 | 19,968 51 | 48,891 08 | 159,652 77 | 186 60 | .......... |
| 22 | 9,670 14 | 8,645 47 | 13,988 12 | 32,662 85 | 19 91 | .......... |
| 23 | 149,041 92 | 94,089 05 | 23,687 71 | 245,773 76 | 34,278 00 | 1,264,538 34 |
| 24 | 1,573,799 80 | 293,286 40 | 77,295 55 | 149,835 52 | 5,721 46 | 128,705 02 |
| 25 | 552,917 39 | 372,374 63 | 74,537 88 | 1,327,242 08 | 4,313 50 | .......... |
| 26 | 2,906 42 | 1,734 89 | .......... | 5,702 38 | .......... | .......... |
| 27 | 9,407 61 | 2,790 90 | .......... | 12,998 69 | .......... | .......... |
| 28 | 216,722 10 | 23,496 87 | 33,770 50 | 5,089,714 65 | 4,595 57 | 143,164 51 |
| 29 | **$4,504,740 04** | **$1,258,089 17** | **$752,511 21** | **$7,950,513 82** | **$124,722 63** | **$1,708,130 66** |
| 30 | $554,928 02 | $111,019 82 | $24,358 81 | $54,350 96 | $4,242 42 | .......... |
| 31 | 39,701 60 | 17,193 07 | 3,229 10 | 30,925 84 | 624 99 | .......... |
| 32 | 2,044,789 54 | 298,900 22 | 132 81 | 2,751,530 36 | 15,399 94 | $6,818 00 |
| 33 | 21,130 43 | 5,099 66 | .......... | 10,944 91 | .......... | .......... |
| 34 | **$2,660,549 59** | **$432,212 77** | **$27,720 72** | **$2,847,752 07** | **$20,267 35** | **$6,818 00** |
| 35 | $596 74 | $378 50 | .......... | $205 64 | $914 23 | .......... |
| 36 | 22,895 81 | 1,453 10 | $626 76 | 1,469 96 | 130 85 | .......... |
| 37 | 204 32 | 97 15 | .......... | 343 57 | 151 91 | $493 14 |
| 38 | 2,142 94 | 1,381 09 | .......... | 1,007 00 | 777 17 | .......... |
| 39 | 483 18 | 2,399 92 | .......... | 1,910 14 | 279 87 | .......... |
| 40 | **$26,322 99** | **$5,709 76** | **$626 76** | **$4,936 31** | **$2,254 03** | **$493 14** |
| 41 | **$7,191,612 62** | **$1,696,011 70** | **$780,858 69** | **$10,803,202 20** | **$147,244 01** | **$1,715,441 80** |
| 42 | **$13,210 00** | **$9,277 67** | .......... | **$34,293 47** | **$56,146 15** | .......... |

STATEMENT SHOWING EXPENDITURES FROM REVENUE (BUDGET

| | Total | Personal Service | LINE No. |
|---|---|---|---|
| CITY DEPARTMENTS, OFFICES, COURTS, ETC.—*Continued.* | | | |
| Borough Presidents and Subordinate Departments: | | | |
| President, Borough of Manhattan | $2,616,527 64 | $1,664,774 86 | 1 |
| President, Borough of The Bronx | 1,165,494 92 | 845,160 62 | 2 |
| President, Borough of Brooklyn | 2,045,404 09 | 1,495,413 90 | 3 |
| President, Borough of Queens | 1,916,028 44 | 1,157,187 86 | 4 |
| President, Borough of Richmond | 823,873 94 | 584,919 08 | 5 |
| Totals | **$8,567,329 03** | **$5,747,456 32** | 6 |
| Board of Aldermen, President of Board and City Clerk | **$298,780 29** | **$292,991 18** | 7 |
| Boards, Commissions, etc., whose members are not elected by popular vote and who are not appointed by any elected City Official: | | | |
| Bronx Parkway Commission | $17,385 05 | $15,795 07 | 8 |
| Board of Building Examiners | 8,702 03 | 8,349 74 | 9 |
| Total | **$26,087 08** | **$24,144 81** | 10 |
| Boards, Commissions, etc., of mixed responsibility, i.e., ex-officio bodies, representing two or more preceding branches: | | | |
| Armory Board | $235,590 77 | $21,396 28 | 11 |
| Board of City Record, City of New York | 920,152 39 | 44,641 27 | 12 |
| Board of Elections | 1,185,124 70 | 599,550 87 | 13 |
| Board of Estimate and Apportionment | 414,760 32 | 287,043 07 | 14 |
| Commissioners of the Sinking Fund | 3,827 75 | 3,300 00 | 15 |
| Total | **$2,759,455 93** | **$955,931 49** | 16 |
| Courts, including Board of Parole and General Interpreters of Brooklyn: | | | |
| Coroners, Borough of Manhattan | $63,073 00 | $61,415 00 | 17 |
| Coroners, Borough of The Bronx | 29,343 26 | 28,200 00 | 18 |
| Coroners, Borough of Brooklyn | 34,847 95 | 33,650 00 | 19 |
| Coroners, Borough of Queens | 19,903 22 | 18,325 00 | 20 |
| Coroners, Borough of Richmond | 12,077 89 | 11,210 00 | 21 |
| City Court of New York | 254,862 24 | 251,631 39 | 22 |
| City Magistrates' Courts, First Division | 397,442 41 | 384,702 72 | 23 |
| City Magistrates' Courts, Second Division | 366,414 66 | 358,134 96 | 24 |
| Municipal Courts, City of New York | 930,515 56 | 912,136 47 | 25 |
| Court of Special Sessions | 367,501 65 | 355,425 57 | 26 |
| General Interpreters of Brooklyn | 9,000 00 | 9,000 00 | 27 |
| Board of Parole | 8,625 00 | 8,400 00 | 28 |
| Total | **$2,493,606 84** | **$2,432,231 11** | 29 |
| Total City Departments, Offices, Courts, etc | **$111,900,546 47** | **$84,760,743 90** | 30 |
| DEBT SERVICE (*See details page 120*) | **$54,533,439 05** | .......... | 31 |
| FIXED CHARGES OTHER THAN DEBT SERVICE, SUBSIDIES, CONTRIBUTIONS, PAYMENTS TO PRIVATE AND STATE INSTITUTIONS, EXPENDITURES NOT ALLOTTED TO DEPARTMENTS: | | | |
| American Museum of Natural History | $200,000 00 | $178,433 57 | 32 |
| Botanical Garden and Arboretum | 29,459 22 | 22,059 89 | 33 |
| Charitable Institutions, City | 4,550,374 28 | .......... | 34 |
| Children's Museum, Brooklyn | 13,121 35 | 10,208 79 | 35 |
| Grant's Tomb | 4,692 64 | .......... | 36 |
| Jumel Mansion | 4,410 96 | 3,615 00 | 37 |
| Metropolitan Museum of Art | 200,000 00 | 174,806 45 | 38 |
| Miscellaneous, City | 1,301,421 12 | .......... | 39 |
| Museum of Arts and Sciences | 102,181 86 | 78,728 76 | 40 |
| New York Aquarium | 47,335 62 | 33,376 64 | 41 |

## NEW YORK

Appropriations) for the Year 1913, Classified by Objects of Expenditure:—*Continued*

| LINE No. | Supplies | Purchase of Equipment | Materials | Contract or Open Order Service | Contingencies | Fixed Charges and Contributions |
|---|---|---|---|---|---|---|
| 1 | $76,556 62 | $32,997 09 | $89,292 49 | $750,985 16 | $1,921 42 | .......... |
| 2 | 22,406 61 | 14,764 65 | 122,547 24 | 159,131 61 | 812 19 | $672 00 |
| 3 | 107,400 99 | 29,599 93 | 146,707 61 | 258,303 31 | 7,978 35 | .......... |
| 4 | 38,259 92 | 55,049 91 | 209,076 71 | 452,406 79 | 4,047 25 | .......... |
| 5 | 36,936 68 | 26,478 58 | 95,644 49 | 71,966 61 | 7,928 50 | .......... |
| 6 | **$281,560 82** | **$158,890 16** | **$663,268 54** | **$1,692,793 48** | **$22,687 71** | **$672 00** |
| 7 | **$3,719 60** | .......... | .......... | **$2,069 51** | .......... | .......... |
| 8 | $299 99 | .......... | .......... | $165 00 | $224 99 | $900 00 |
| 9 | 217 01 | $21 62 | .......... | 113 66 | .......... | .......... |
| 10 | **$517 00** | **$21 62** | .......... | **$278 66** | **$224 99** | **$900 00** |
| 11 | $23,172 47 | $52,205 26 | $11,074 31 | $125,952 58 | $1,789 87 | .......... |
| 12 | 1,098 42 | 2,274 91 | .......... | 871,600 04 | 537 75 | .......... |
| 13 | 271,473 21 | 5,055 43 | .......... | 39,623 76 | .......... | $269,421 43 |
| 14 | 4,032 27 | 11,550 91 | .......... | 1,190 02 | 110,944 05 | .......... |
| 15 | .......... | .......... | .......... | .......... | 527 75 | .......... |
| 16 | **$299,776 37** | **$71,086 51** | **$11,074 31** | **$1,038,366 40** | **$113,799 42** | **$269,421 43** |
| 17 | $433 36 | .......... | .......... | $1,224 64 | .......... | .......... |
| 18 | 254 10 | .......... | .......... | 889 16 | .......... | .......... |
| 19 | 231 47 | $330 00 | .......... | 636 48 | .......... | .......... |
| 20 | 48 20 | 50 00 | .......... | 1,480 02 | .......... | .......... |
| 21 | 116 65 | .......... | .......... | 751 24 | .......... | .......... |
| 22 | 839 20 | 1,873 97 | .......... | 517 68 | .......... | .......... |
| 23 | 2,302 97 | 4,311 77 | .......... | 6,124 95 | .......... | .......... |
| 24 | 2,046 99 | 2,547 68 | .......... | 3,685 03 | .......... | .......... |
| 25 | 2,351 94 | 12,560 97 | .......... | 2,980 20 | $485 98 | .......... |
| 26 | 2,455 52 | 3,464 94 | .......... | 5,476 69 | 678 93 | .......... |
| 27 | .......... | .......... | .......... | .......... | .......... | .......... |
| 28 | 40 00 | .......... | .......... | 184 40 | 60 | .......... |
| 29 | **$11,120 40** | **$25,139 33** | .......... | **$23,950 49** | **$1,165 51** | .......... |
| 30 | **$7,801,516 81** | **$1,960,426 99** | **$1,455,201 54** | **$13,594,954 21** | **$341,267 79** | **$1,986,435 23** |
| 31 | .......... | .......... | .......... | .......... | .......... | **$54,533,439 05** |
| 32 | .......... | .......... | .......... | .......... | $21,566 43 | .......... |
| 33 | $2,351 04 | $2,709 01 | .......... | $2,039 34 | 299 94 | .......... |
| 34 | .......... | .......... | .......... | .......... | .......... | $4,550,374 28 |
| 35 | 808 93 | 303 93 | $199 87 | 1,206 38 | 339 45 | 54 00 |
| 36 | .......... | .......... | .......... | 4,692 64 | .......... | .......... |
| 37 | 209 75 | 72 41 | .......... | 317 50 | 196 30 | .......... |
| 38 | .......... | .......... | .......... | .......... | 25,193 55 | .......... |
| 39 | .......... | .......... | .......... | 3,485 91 | .......... | 1,297,935 21 |
| 40 | 8,861 99 | 3,030 54 | 4,714 08 | 4,999 60 | 1,384 13 | 462 76 |
| 41 | 7,051 52 | 1,088 71 | 491 96 | 5,163 04 | 163 75 | .......... |

STATEMENT SHOWING EXPENDITURES FROM REVENUE (BUDGET

| | Total | Personal Service | LINE No. |
|---|---|---|---|
| FIXED CHARGES—*Continued* | | | |
| New York Botanical Garden | $103,222 19 | $83,773 69 | 1 |
| New York Zoological Garden | 189,570 36 | 122,249 76 | 2 |
| New York Public Library Building | 17,999 37 | .......... | 3 |
| Brooklyn Public Library | 436,494 31 | 246,968 50 | 4 |
| New York Public Library | 633,859 83 | 389,265 50 | 5 |
| Queensborough Public Library | 153,174 71 | 83,062 15 | 6 |
| Staten Island Association of Arts and Sciences | 9,318 74 | 6,840 00 | 7 |
| United States Volunteer Life Saving Corps | 13,235 44 | 7,118 00 | 8 |
| | **$8,009,872 00** | **$1,440,506 70** | 9 |
| DEFICIENCIES IN TAXES | **$2,300,000 00** | .......... | 10 |
| Total for City Purposes | **$176,743,857 52** | **$86,201,250 60** | 11 |
| DIRECT STATE TAXES: | | | |
| New York County | $5,736,005 10 | .......... | 12 |
| Kings County | 1,684,598 71 | .......... | 13 |
| Queens County | 445,609 98 | .......... | 14 |
| Richmond County | 80,818 17 | .......... | 15 |
| Total | **$7,947,031 96** | .......... | 16 |
| COUNTY EXPENDITURES: | | | |
| New York County: | | | |
| Charitable Institutions | $102,928 80 | .......... | 17 |
| Board of City Record | 41,389 61 | .......... | 18 |
| County Clerk | 185,207 91 | $182,318 84 | 19 |
| Court of General Sessions | 363,396 53 | 360,123 06 | 20 |
| Supreme Court, First Department | 973,029 74 | 968,035 32 | 21 |
| Supreme Court, First Department, Maintenance of Appellate Division Court House | 30,812 62 | 19,090 00 | 22 |
| Surrogate's Court | 198,765 76 | 196,422 28 | 23 |
| District Attorney | 451,722 96 | 420,667 39 | 24 |
| Commissioner of Jurors | 52,782 22 | 47,927 41 | 25 |
| Miscellaneous | 471,844 21 | 409,557 24 | 26 |
| National Guard and Naval Militia | 223,931 00 | 215,931 00 | 27 |
| Public Administrator | 26,306 23 | 25,615 00 | 28 |
| Commissioner of Records | 96,519 97 | 93,444 71 | 29 |
| Commissioner of Records, Surrogate's Court | 49,691 25 | 48,520 00 | 30 |
| Register | 314,615 92 | 311,412 19 | 31 |
| Sheriff | 156,403 74 | 147,532 91 | 32 |
| Total | **$3,739,348 47** | **$3,446,597 35** | 33 |
| Kings County: | | | |
| Charitable Institutions | $55,192 99 | .......... | 34 |
| Board of City Record | 18,518 32 | .......... | 35 |
| County Clerk | 99,023 13 | $97,297 17 | 36 |
| County Court | 157,813 59 | 156,472 58 | 37 |
| Supreme Court, Second Department | 423,651 69 | 422,664 68 | 38 |
| Supreme Court Law Library | 9,208 77 | 8,233 87 | 39 |
| Surrogate's Court | 104,787 35 | 103,106 00 | 40 |
| District Attorney | 127,347 14 | 119,747 14 | 41 |
| Commissioner of Jurors | 39,781 69 | 38,190 00 | 42 |
| Miscellaneous | 141,000 60 | 114,423 76 | 43 |
| National Guard and Naval Militia | 144,108 25 | 144,108 25 | 44 |
| Public Administrator | 11,865 00 | 11,019 84 | 45 |
| Commissioner of Records | 99,384 24 | 97,412 89 | 46 |
| Register | 216,268 06 | 214,161 76 | 47 |
| Sheriff | 89,204 40 | 82,044 45 | 48 |
| Total | **$1,737,155 22** | **$1,608,882 39** | 49 |

NEW YORK

APPROPRIATIONS) FOR THE YEAR 1913, CLASSIFIED BY OBJECTS OF EXPENDITURE:—*Continued*

| LINE No. | Supplies | Purchase of Equipment | Materials | Contract or Open Order Service | Contingencies | Fixed Charges and Contributions |
|---|---|---|---|---|---|---|
| 1 | $11,954 16 | $3,301 25 | $1,574 92 | $2,618 17 | .......... | .......... |
| 2 | 51,079 91 | 3,644 42 | 7,502 52 | 4,939 79 | $153 96 | .......... |
| 3 | 2,000 00 | .......... | .......... | 15,999 37 | .......... | .......... |
| 4 | 27,107 88 | 111,889 11 | .......... | 34,326 82 | 199 55 | $16,002 45 |
| 5 | 43,310 66 | 106,899 49 | 1,495 30 | 92,119 51 | 409 37 | 360 00 |
| 6 | 7,624 71 | 31,403 76 | 389 92 | 16,318 46 | 1,367 44 | 13,008 27 |
| 7 | 301 25 | 441 07 | .......... | 206 92 | 29 50 | 1,500 00 |
| 8 | 903 50 | 3,175 00 | 225 00 | 606 44 | 467 50 | 740 00 |
| 9 | **$163,565 30** | **$267,958 70** | **$16,593 57** | **$189,039 89** | **$51,770 87** | **$5,880,436 97** |
| 10 | .......... | .......... | .......... | .......... | .......... | **$2,300,000 00** |
| 11 | **$7,965,082 11** | **$2,228,385 69** | **$1,471,795 11** | **$13,783,994 10** | **$393,038 66** | **$64,700,311 25** |
| 12 | .......... | .......... | .......... | .......... | .......... | $5,736,005 10 |
| 13 | .......... | .......... | .......... | .......... | .......... | 1,684,598 71 |
| 14 | .......... | .......... | .......... | .......... | .......... | 445,609 98 |
| 15 | .......... | .......... | .......... | .......... | .......... | 80,818 17 |
| 16 | .......... | .......... | .......... | .......... | .......... | **$7,947,031 96** |
| 17 | .......... | .......... | .......... | .......... | .......... | $102,928 80 |
| 18 | .......... | .......... | .......... | $41,389 61 | .......... | .......... |
| 19 | $926 19 | $1,148 64 | .......... | 814 24 | .......... | .......... |
| 20 | 1,077 64 | 1,145 45 | .......... | 1,016 98 | $33 40 | .......... |
| 21 | .......... | .......... | .......... | .......... | 110 30 | 4,884 12 |
| 22 | 5,221 17 | 980 96 | .......... | 5,120 49 | 400 00 | .......... |
| 23 | 819 26 | 846 23 | .......... | 653 24 | 24 75 | .......... |
| 24 | 7,808 64 | 2,300 00 | .......... | 3,738 58 | 17,208 35 | .......... |
| 25 | 4,027 53 | 229 08 | .......... | 594 25 | 3 95 | .......... |
| 26 | .......... | .......... | .......... | .......... | 1,182 15 | 61,104 82 |
| 27 | .......... | .......... | .......... | 8,000 00 | .......... | .......... |
| 28 | 209 11 | 177 45 | .......... | 212 76 | 91 91 | .......... |
| 29 | 1,433 42 | 1,116 63 | .......... | 394 70 | 130 51 | .......... |
| 30 | 184 00 | 509 20 | $478 05 | .......... | .......... | .......... |
| 31 | 762 32 | 989 78 | 576 25 | 863 33 | 12 05 | .......... |
| 32 | 4,803 05 | 256 85 | .......... | 3,548 18 | 262 15 | .......... |
| 33 | **$27,272 93** | **$9,700 27** | **$1,054 30** | **$66,346 36** | **$19,459 52** | **$168,917 74** |
| 34 | .......... | .......... | .......... | .......... | .......... | $55,192 99 |
| 35 | .......... | .......... | .......... | $18,518 32 | .......... | .......... |
| 36 | $621 79 | $170 07 | .......... | 934 10 | .......... | .......... |
| 37 | 724 37 | 181 30 | .......... | 261 87 | $173 47 | .......... |
| 38 | 44 00 | .......... | .......... | 465 19 | 477 82 | .......... |
| 39 | .......... | .......... | .......... | .......... | 974 90 | .......... |
| 40 | 684 29 | 552 50 | .......... | 443 06 | 1 50 | .......... |
| 41 | 2,015 00 | 975 00 | .......... | 1,000 00 | 3,610 00 | .......... |
| 42 | 1,318 16 | 75 56 | .......... | 197 97 | .......... | .......... |
| 43 | .......... | .......... | .......... | .......... | 3,172 85 | 23,403 99 |
| 44 | .......... | .......... | .......... | .......... | .......... | .......... |
| 45 | 180 00 | 377 10 | .......... | 288 06 | .......... | .......... |
| 46 | 406 24 | 584 14 | $499 65 | 439 82 | 41 50 | .......... |
| 47 | 437 70 | 1,097 03 | .......... | 474 29 | 97 28 | .......... |
| 48 | 4,101 88 | 106 90 | .......... | 796 70 | 2,154 47 | .......... |
| 49 | **$10,533 43** | **$4,119 60** | **$499 65** | **$23,819 38** | **$10,703 79** | **$78,596 98** |

STATEMENT SHOWING EXPENDITURES FROM REVENUE (BUDGE

| | Total | Personal Service | LINE No |
|---|---|---|---|
| COUNTY EXPENDITURES—*Continued* | | | |
| Queens County: | | | |
| Charitable Institutions | $6,374 61 | .......... | |
| Board of City Record | 3,780 61 | .......... | |
| County Clerk | 104,394 05 | $94,820 69 | |
| County Court | 41,422 73 | 40,072 73 | |
| Supreme Court | 93,572 60 | 93,472 60 | |
| Supreme Court Library | 2,566 43 | 1,800 00 | |
| Surrogate's Court | 23,946 59 | 23,125 10 | |
| District Attorney | 34,597 22 | 32,511 78 | |
| Commissioner of Jurors | 12,043 53 | 11,188 00 | |
| Miscellaneous | 38,242 52 | 36,700 00 | 1 |
| National Guard and Naval Militia | 5,110 00 | 5,110 00 | 1 |
| Public Administrator | 1,200 00 | 1,200 00 | 1 |
| Sheriff | 48,443 73 | 43,052 15 | 1 |
| Total | **$415,694 62** | **$383,053 05** | 1 |
| Richmond County: | | | |
| Charitable Institutions | $1,289 18 | .......... | 1 |
| Board of City Record | 2,434 39 | .......... | 1 |
| County Clerk | 16,800 39 | $16,100 00 | 1 |
| County Court and Surrogate's Court | 21,483 03 | 21,100 00 | 1 |
| Supreme Court | 18,328 55 | 18,263 35 | 1 |
| District Attorney | 14,629 54 | 13,831 90 | 2 |
| Commissioner of Jurors | 4,273 57 | 4,050 00 | 2 |
| Miscellaneous | 12,505 00 | 11,511 66 | 2 |
| National Guard and Naval Militia | 1,460 00 | 1,460 00 | 2 |
| Sheriff | 29,778 75 | 19,774 00 | 2 |
| Total | **$122,982 40** | **$106,090 91** | 2 |
| Total for County Purposes | **$6,015,180 71** | **$5,544,623 70** | 2 |
| Total for All Purposes | **$190,706,070 19** | **$91,745,874 30** | 2 |

NEW YORK

Appropriations) for the Year 1913, Classified by Objects of Expenditure:—*Continued*

| LINE No. | Supplies | Purchase of Equipment | Materials | Contract or Open Order Service | Contingencies | Fixed Charges and Contributions |
|---|---|---|---|---|---|---|
| 1 | .......... | .......... | .......... | .......... | .......... | $6,374 61 |
| 2 | .......... | .......... | .......... | $3,780 61 | .......... | .......... |
| 3 | $1,148 90 | $7,640 71 | .......... | 783 75 | .......... | .......... |
| 4 | 435 21 | 229 80 | .......... | 684 99 | .......... | .......... |
| 5 | 100 00 | .......... | .......... | .......... | .......... | .......... |
| 6 | 10 00 | 505 13 | .......... | 157 70 | .......... | 93 60 |
| 7 | 545 54 | 42 90 | .......... | 233 05 | .......... | .......... |
| 8 | 266 77 | 52 00 | .......... | 488 99 | $1,277 68 | .......... |
| 9 | 741 85 | 7 20 | .......... | 106 48 | .......... | .......... |
| 10 | .......... | .......... | .......... | .......... | 1,542 52 | .......... |
| 11 | .......... | .......... | .......... | .......... | .......... | .......... |
| 12 | .......... | .......... | .......... | .......... | .......... | .......... |
| 13 | 1,104 29 | 184 97 | .......... | 4,102 32 | .......... | .......... |
| 14 | **$4,352 56** | **$8,662 71** | .......... | **$10,337 89** | **$2,820 20** | **$6,468 21** |
| 15 | .......... | .......... | .......... | .......... | .......... | $1,289 18 |
| 16 | .......... | .......... | .......... | $2,434 39 | .......... | .......... |
| 17 | $119 73 | $441 00 | .......... | 139 66 | .......... | .......... |
| 18 | 127 08 | 98 65 | .......... | 144 30 | $13 00 | .......... |
| 19 | .......... | .......... | .......... | .......... | 65 20 | .......... |
| 20 | 98 70 | 74 95 | .......... | 395 04 | 228 95 | .......... |
| 21 | 133 00 | .......... | .......... | 90 57 | .......... | .......... |
| 22 | .......... | .......... | .......... | .......... | 968 34 | 25 00 |
| 23 | .......... | .......... | .......... | .......... | .......... | .......... |
| 24 | 8,387 37 | 874 65 | .......... | 540 99 | 201 74 | .......... |
| 25 | **$8,865 88** | **$1,489 25** | .......... | **$3,744 95** | **$1,477 23** | **$1,314 18** |
| 26 | **$51,024 80** | **$23,971 83** | **$1,553 95** | **$104,248 58** | **$34,460 74** | **$255,297 11** |
| 27 | **$8,016,106 91** | **$2,252,357 52** | **$1,473,349 06** | **$13,888,242 68** | **$427,499 40** | **$72,902,640 32** |

RECAPITULATION OF STATEMENT SHOWING EXPENDITURES FROM REVENUE (BUDGET

| | Total | Personal Service | LINE No. |
|---|---|---|---|
| CITY DEPARTMENTS, OFFICES, COURTS, ETC. | | | |
| Mayor and Subordinate Departments, Bureaus, and Offices: | | | |
| Mayor's Office and Departments whose executive heads are appointed by the Mayor and who are removable at his pleasure | $61,155,797 32 | $42,693,209 21 | 1 |
| Departments whose heads are appointed by the Mayor for a term of office greater than his own, and who are removable only upon charges | 40,449,010 73 | 33,946,097 01 | 2 |
| Boards and Commissions majority of which are appointed by the Mayor and for which no other elected City official shares responsibility | 136,388 91 | 93,405 38 | 3 |
| Total Mayor and Subordinate Departments, Bureaus and Offices | **$101,741,196 96** | **$76,732,711 60** | 4 |
| Comptroller and Finance Department, excluding the Chamberlain's Office | **$1,548,195 08** | **$1,449,870 64** | 5 |
| Borough Presidents and Subordinate Departments: | | | |
| President, Borough of Manhattan | $2,638,731 17 | $1,808,866 71 | 6 |
| President, Borough of The Bronx | 1,171,838 18 | 874,325 74 | 7 |
| President, Borough of Brooklyn | 2,057,200 09 | 1,471,934 33 | 8 |
| President, Borough of Queens | 2,008,276 67 | 1,270,305 24 | 9 |
| President, Borough of Richmond | 692,044 62 | 572,747 94 | 10 |
| Total, Borough Presidents | **$8,568,090 73** | **$5,998,179 96** | 11 |
| Board of Aldermen, President of Board and City Clerk | **$307,778 37** | **$295,757 61** | 12 |
| Boards, Commissions, etc., whose members are not elected by popular vote and who are not appointed by any elected City official | **$30,035 28** | **$24,222 72** | 13 |
| Boards, Commissions, etc., of mixed responsibility, i.e., ex-officio bodies representing two or more of preceding branches | **$2,875,263 12** | **$1,132,046 91** | 14 |
| Courts, including Board of Parole and General Interpreters of Brooklyn | **$2,575,872 14** | **$2,515,986 98** | 15 |
| Total, City Departments, Offices, Courts, etc | **$117,646,431 68** | **$88,148,776 42** | 16 |
| DEBT SERVICE. (*See details page 120*) | **$52,491,846 15** | .......... | 17 |
| FIXED CHARGES OTHER THAN DEBT SERVICE, SUBSIDIES, CONTRIBUTIONS, PAYMENTS TO PRIVATE AND STATE INSTITUTIONS, EXPENDITURES NOT ALLOTTED TO DEPARTMENTS | **$8,374,579 96** | **$1,560,716 00** | 18 |
| DEFICIENCIES IN TAXES | **$2,500,000 00** | .......... | 19 |
| BOROUGH ASSESSMENTS | **$520,015 06** | .......... | 20 |
| Total for City Purposes | **$181,532,872 85** | **$89,709,492 42** | 21 |
| DIRECT STATE TAXES | **$4,576,303 43** | .......... | 22 |
| COUNTY EXPENDITURES: | | | |
| New York County | $3,714,875 09 | $3,440,418 10 | 23 |
| Kings County | 1,795,087 08 | 1,668,097 72 | 24 |
| Queens County | 439,061 53 | 414,638 20 | 25 |
| Richmond County | 130,082 77 | 113,104 18 | 26 |
| Bronx County | 269,334 71 | 228,817 70 | 27 |
| Total for County Purposes | **$6,348,441 18** | **$5,865,075 90** | 28 |
| Total for All Purposes | **$192,457,617 46** | **$95,574,568 32** | 29 |

APPROPRIATIONS) FOR THE YEAR 1914, CLASSIFIED BY OBJECTS OF EXPENDITURE:

| LINE No. | Supplies | Purchase of Equipment | Materials | Contract or Open Order Service | Contingencies | Fixed Charges and Contributions |
|---|---|---|---|---|---|---|
| 1 | $4,464,096 24 | $1,011,773 83 | $613,533 93 | $10,365,015 27 | $125,225 31 | $1,882,943 53 |
| 2 | 2,761,879 75 | 489,266 75 | 26,321 17 | 3,188,576 11 | 31,512 44 | 5,357 50 |
| 3 | 14,909 84 | 3,644 46 | 352 41 | 7,160 31 | 16,623 66 | 292 85 |
| 4 | **$7,240,885 83** | **$1,504,685 04** | **$640,207 51** | **$13,560,751 69** | **$173,361 41** | **$1,888,593 88** |
| 5 | **$13,797 66** | **$9,252 17** | .......... | **$39,036 02** | **$36,238 59** | .......... |
| 6 | $87,788 97 | $72,094 29 | $90,532 15 | $559,341 25 | $20,107 80 | .......... |
| 7 | 19,775 88 | 39,570 71 | 93,937 48 | 143,343 82 | 208 55 | $676 00 |
| 8 | 103,259 94 | 33,508 10 | 154,766 70 | 277,691 61 | 16,039 41 | .......... |
| 9 | 38,211 39 | 58,700 73 | 180,367 14 | 458,601 85 | 2,090 32 | .......... |
| 10 | 28,717 44 | 6,196 67 | 38,837 15 | 44,102 22 | 1,443 20 | .......... |
| 11 | **$277,753 62** | **$210,070 50** | **$558,440 62** | **$1,483,080 75** | **$39,889 28** | **$676 00** |
| 12 | **$4,030 54** | .......... | .......... | **$2,689 43** | **$5,300 79** | .......... |
| 13 | **$724 13** | **$616 66** | .......... | **$2,145 27** | **$409 86** | **$1,916 64** |
| 14 | **$246,882 56** | **$56,652 30** | **$19,939 28** | **$1,005,125 85** | **$100,393 60** | **$314,222 62** |
| 15 | **$15,518 74** | **$21,210 76** | .......... | **$21,940 59** | **$1,215 07** | .......... |
| 16 | **$7,799,593 08** | **$1,802,487 43** | **$1,218,587 41** | **$16,114,769 60** | **$356,808 60** | **$2,205,409 14** |
| 17 | .......... | .......... | .......... | .......... | .......... | ***$52,491,846 15** |
| 18 | **$93,731 65** | **$238,513 62** | **$2,387 81** | **$229,631 23** | **$174,343 37** | **$6,075,256 28** |
| 19 | .......... | .......... | .......... | .......... | .......... | **$2,500,000 00** |
| 20 | .......... | .......... | .......... | .......... | .......... | **$520,015 06** |
| 21 | **$7,893,324 73** | **$2,041,001 05** | **$1,220,975 22** | **$16,344,400 83** | **$531,151 97** | **$63,792,526 63** |
| 22 | .......... | .......... | .......... | .......... | .......... | **$4,576,303 43** |
| 23 | $20,476 49 | $14,701 95 | $1,105 94 | $57,942 30 | $34,635 51 | $145,594 80 |
| 24 | 10,151 64 | 2,942 92 | 779 47 | 27,997 72 | 8,563 72 | 76,553 89 |
| 25 | 3,644 73 | 2,674 78 | .......... | 9,507 75 | 2,833 76 | 5,762 31 |
| 26 | 8,713 77 | 1,487 23 | .......... | 3 156 60 | 2,695 99 | 925 00 |
| 27 | 1,662 95 | 255 80 | .......... | 11,955 30 | 103 69 | 26,539 27 |
| 28 | **$44,649 58** | **$22,062 68** | **$1,885 41** | **$110,559 67** | **$48,832 67** | **$255,375 27** |
| 29 | **$7,937,974 31** | **$2,063,063 73** | **$1,222,860 63** | **$16,454,960 50** | **$579,984 64** | **$68,624,205 33** |

* Includes redemption of $6,319,225.00 Special Revenue Bonds, issued to defray expenses of 1913.

| | Total | Personal Service | LINE No. |
|---|---|---|---|
| CITY DEPARTMENTS, OFFICES, COURTS, ETC. | | | |
| Mayor and Subordinate Departments, Bureaus and Offices: | | | |
| Mayor's Office and Departments whose executive heads are appointed by the Mayor and who are removable at his pleasure: | | | |
| Commissioners of Accounts | $219 940 04 | $209 903 09 | 1 |
| Board of Ambulance Service | 79 910 51 | 9 599 98 | 2 |
| Board of Assessors | 40,150 52 | 39,124 20 | 3 |
| Department of Bridges | 840,956 96 | 694,247 47 | 4 |
| City Chamberlain | 59,568 47 | 56,896 91 | 5 |
| Department of Correction | 1,253,336 57 | 602,477 68 | 6 |
| Department of Docks and Ferries | 2,481,836 59 | 1,633,456 50 | 7 |
| Examining Board of Plumbers | 3,746 67 | 2,890 00 | 8 |
| Fire Department | 9,138,753 30 | 8,450,442 03 | 9 |
| Department of Health | 3,304,130 34 | 2,440,619 98 | 10 |
| Law Department | 827,550 01 | 762,380 96 | 11 |
| Commissioner of Licenses | 28,231 22 | 27,032 78 | 12 |
| Mayoralty—Administration | 62,083 83 | 57,939 18 | 13 |
| Mayoralty—Bureau of Licenses | 137,392 26 | 123,908 22 | 14 |
| Mayoralty—Bureau of Weights and Measures | 76,964 27 | 67,180 58 | 15 |
| Municipal Civil Service Commission | 200,792 38 | 180,800 13 | 16 |
| Municipal Explosives Commission | 8,293 67 | 8,272 92 | 17 |
| Park Board | 29,222 30 | 28,999 97 | 18 |
| Department of Parks—Manhattan and Richmond | 1,072,126 97 | 853,272 69 | 19 |
| Department of Parks—The Bronx | 442,456 78 | 347,978 08 | 20 |
| Department of Parks—Brooklyn | 826,074 43 | 592,489 83 | 21 |
| Department of Parks—Queens | 175,997 63 | 117,926 14 | 22 |
| Police Department | 17,397,035 05 | 15,424,093 87 | 23 |
| Department of Public Charities | 3,643,285 02 | 1,574,124 63 | 24 |
| Department of Street Cleaning | 10,112,883 68 | 5,296,403 16 | 25 |
| Department of Taxes and Assessment | 582,717 69 | 573,876 91 | 26 |
| Tenement House Department | 726,054 19 | 703,745 69 | 27 |
| Department of Water Supply, Gas and Electricity | 7,384,305 97 | 1,813,125 63 | 28 |
| Total | **$61,155,797 32** | **$42,693,209 21** | 29 |
| Departments whose heads are appointed by the Mayor for a term of office greater than his own, and who are removable only upon charges: | | | |
| Bellevue and Allied Hospitals | $1,371,938 09 | $633,951 72 | 30 |
| College of the City of New York | 675,046 00 | 586,704 15 | 31 |
| Department of Education | 37,882,031 68 | 32,250,241 66 | 32 |
| Normal College of the City of New York | 519,994 96 | 475,199 48 | 33 |
| Total | **$40,449,010 73** | **$33,946,097 01** | 34 |
| Boards and Commissions majorities of which are appointed by the Mayor and for which no other elected City official shares responsibility: | | | |
| Art Commission | $7,132 82 | $5,336 67 | 35 |
| Brooklyn Disciplinary Training School for Boys | 29,013 78 | 17,755 97 | 36 |
| Board of Inebriety | 25,101 16 | 7,149 31 | 37 |
| Permanent Census Board | 54,717 04 | 47,957 15 | 38 |
| Public Recreation Commission | 20,424 11 | 15,206 28 | 39 |
| Total | **$136,388 91** | **$93,405 38** | 40 |
| Total, Mayor and Subordinate Departments, Bureaus and Offices | **$101,741,196 96** | **$76,732,711 60** | 41 |
| Comptroller and Finance Department, excluding the Chamberlain's Office: | | | |
| Department of Finance | **$1,548,195 08** | **$1,449,870 64** | 42 |

# NEW YORK

APPROPRIATIONS) FOR THE YEAR 1914, CLASSIFIED BY OBJECTS OF EXPENDITURE:

| LINE No. | Supplies | Purchase of Equipment | Materials | Contract or Open Order Service | Contingencies | Fixed Charges and Contributions |
|---|---|---|---|---|---|---|
| 1 | $2,707 21 | $814 10 | .......... | $5,478 26 | $1,037 38 | .......... |
| 2 | 114 59 | 16 00 | .......... | 70,178 03 | 1 91 | .......... |
| 3 | 202 00 | 115 00 | .......... | 684 32 | 25 00 | .......... |
| 4 | 18,760 68 | 8,043 79 | $63,508 73 | 56,130 44 | 265 85 | .......... |
| 5 | 1,597 18 | 157 00 | .......... | 715 90 | 201 48 | .......... |
| 6 | 483,875 04 | 53,002 93 | 75,032 67 | 33,208 24 | 2,151 20 | $3,588 81 |
| 7 | 343,902 52 | 19,171 45 | 103,226 59 | 209,792 83 | 189 30 | 172,097 40 |
| 8 | 147 33 | 81 00 | .......... | 605 53 | 22 81 | .......... |
| 9 | 371,173 01 | 173,275 41 | 56,776 14 | 79,177 81 | 7,908 90 | .......... |
| 10 | 549,097 03 | 111,127 75 | 23,715 61 | 170,912 65 | 974 78 | 7,682 54 |
| 11 | 1,737 40 | 5,416 35 | .......... | 16,029 21 | 41,986 09 | .......... |
| 12 | 565 32 | 46 45 | .......... | 536 67 | 50 00 | .......... |
| 13 | 1,442 27 | 638 11 | .......... | 1,545 17 | 519 10 | .......... |
| 14 | 5,189 91 | 1,670 09 | .......... | 4,429 58 | 2,194 46 | .......... |
| 15 | 1,651 13 | 922 53 | .......... | 5,836 10 | 1,373 93 | .......... |
| 16 | 5,148 34 | 3,995 48 | .......... | 8,808 95 | 2,039 48 | .......... |
| 17 | .......... | .......... | .......... | .......... | 20 75 | .......... |
| 18 | .......... | .......... | .......... | .......... | 222 33 | .......... |
| 19 | 80,296 13 | 21,292 10 | 38,082 23 | 78,725 19 | 458 63 | .......... |
| 20 | 13,197 91 | 6,024 08 | 26,243 40 | 49,013 31 | .......... | .......... |
| 21 | 48,007 85 | 11,872 62 | 33,961 79 | 139,345 21 | 397 13 | .......... |
| 22 | 10,563 47 | 11,481 28 | 11,893 66 | 23,394 87 | 29 93 | 708 28 |
| 23 | 139,962 46 | 73,189 30 | 22,148 09 | 228,897 79 | 58,743 54 | 1,450,000 00 |
| 24 | 1,583,094 64 | 205,961 58 | 58,502 45 | 108,579 45 | 1,956 72 | 111,065 55 |
| 25 | 545,861 04 | 263,184 19 | 76,931 16 | 3,928,999 83 | 1,504 30 | .......... |
| 26 | 3,442 53 | 514 92 | .......... | 4,706 08 | 177 25 | .......... |
| 27 | 8,511 13 | 2,276 31 | .......... | 11,341 44 | 179 62 | .......... |
| 28 | 243,848 12 | 37,484 01 | 23,511 41 | 5,127,942 41 | 593 44 | 137,800 95 |
| 29 | **$4,464,096 24** | **$1,011,773 83** | **$613,533 93** | **$10,365,015 27** | **$125,225 31** | **$1,882,943 53** |
| 30 | $526,488 34 | $121,025 27 | $22,488 79 | $62,609 19 | $5,374 78 | .......... |
| 31 | 35,770 28 | 16,549 62 | 3,832 38 | 31,615 72 | 573 85 | .......... |
| 32 | 2,186,758 10 | 336,524 69 | .......... | 3,077,585 92 | 25,563 81 | $5,357 50 |
| 33 | 12,863 03 | 15,167 17 | .......... | 16,765 28 | .......... | .......... |
| 34 | **$2,761,879 75** | **$489,266 75** | **$26,321 17** | **$3,188,576 11** | **$31,512 44** | **$5,357 50** |
| 35 | $36 65 | $629 77 | .......... | $223 48 | $906 25 | .......... |
| 36 | 9,908 45 | 261 31 | $352 41 | 721 84 | 13 80 | .......... |
| 37 | 831 08 | 428 00 | .......... | 907 05 | 15,492 87 | $292 85 |
| 38 | 3,744 96 | 1,743 93 | .......... | 1,176 36 | 94 64 | .......... |
| 39 | 388 70 | 581 45 | .......... | 4,131 58 | 116 10 | .......... |
| 40 | **$14,909 84** | **$3,644 46** | **$352 41** | **$7,160 31** | **$16,623 66** | **$292 85** |
| 41 | **$7,240,885 83** | **$1,504,685 04** | **$640,207 51** | **$13,560,751 69** | **$173,361 41** | **$1,888,593 88** |
| 42 | **$13,797 66** | **$9,252 17** | .......... | **$39,036 02** | **$36,238 59** | .......... |

| | Total | Personal Service |
|---|---|---|
| CITY DEPARTMENTS OFFICES, COURTS, ETC.—*Continued.* | | |
| Borough Presidents and Subordinate Departments: | | |
| President, Borough of Manhattan | $2,638,731 17 | $1,808,866 71 |
| President, Borough of The Bronx | 1,171,838 18 | 874,325 74 |
| President, Borough of Brooklyn | 2,057,200 09 | 1,471,934 33 |
| President, Borough of Queens | 2,008,276 67 | 1,270,305 24 |
| President, Borough of Richmond | 692,044 62 | 572,747 94 |
| Total | **$8,568,090 73** | **$5,998,179 96** |
| Board of Aldermen, President of Board and City Clerk | **$307,778 37** | **$295,757 61** |
| Boards, Commissions, etc., whose members are not elected by popular vote and who are not appointed by any elected City Official: | | |
| Bronx Parkway Commission | $20,996 32 | $15,527 72 |
| Board of Building Examiners | 9,038 96 | 8,695 00 |
| Total | **$30,035 28** | **$24,222 72** |
| Boards, Commissions, etc., of mixed responsibility, i.e., ex-officio bodies, representing two or more preceding branches: | | |
| Armory Board | $225,304 98 | $20,954 76 |
| Board of City Record, City of New York | 913,229 69 | 47,137 96 |
| Board of Elections | 1,198,242 87 | 631,966 93 |
| Board of Estimate and Apportionment | 534,835 65 | 428,687 26 |
| Board of Revision of Assessments | 88 00 | .......... |
| Commissioners of the Sinking Fund | 3,561 93 | 3,300 00 |
| Total | **$2,875,263 12** | **$1,132,046 91** |
| Courts, including Board of Parole and General Interpreters of Brooklyn: | | |
| Coroners, Borough of Manhattan | $62,796 00 | $61,224 10 |
| Coroners, Borough of The Bronx | 29,651 68 | 28,129 88 |
| Coroners, Borough of Brooklyn | 31,362 53 | 30,518 27 |
| Coroners, Borough of Queens | 19,951 82 | 18,990 00 |
| Coroners, Borough of Richmond | 12,054 59 | 11,210 00 |
| City Court of New York | 255,754 63 | 252,096 00 |
| City Magistrates' Courts, First Division | 447,489 79 | 430,830 93 |
| City Magistrates' Courts, Second Division | 387,975 52 | 379,782 05 |
| Municipal Courts, City of New York | 929,492 36 | 914,210 79 |
| Court of Special Sessions | 381,898 22 | 371,794 96 |
| General Interpreters of Brooklyn | 8,800 00 | 8,800 00 |
| Board of Parole | 8,645 00 | 8,400 00 |
| Total | **$2,575,872 14** | **$2,515,986 98** |
| Total City Departments, Offices, Courts, etc. | **$117,646,431 68** | **$88,148,776 42** |
| DEBT SERVICE (*See details page 120*) | **$52,491,846 15** | .......... |
| FIXED CHARGES OTHER THAN DEBT SERVICE, SUBSIDIES, CONTRIBUTIONS, PAYMENTS TO PRIVATE AND STATE INSTITUTIONS, EXPENDITURES NOT ALLOTTED TO DEPARTMENTS: | | |
| American Museum of Natural History | $200,000 00 | $172,849 85 |
| Botanical Garden and Arboretum | 37,636 08 | 28,111 67 |
| Charitable Institutions, City | 5,184,610 06 | .......... |
| Children's Museum, Brooklyn | 13,227 21 | 10,679 17 |
| Grant's Tomb | 4,927 27 | .......... |
| Jumel Mansion | 4,163 21 | 3,622 50 |
| Metropolitan Museum of Art | 200,000 00 | 175,590 57 |
| Miscellaneous, City | 865,372 96 | .......... |
| Museum of Arts and Sciences | 106,744 33 | 82,280 98 |

NEW YORK

Appropriations) for the Year 1914, Classified by Objects of Expenditure:—*Continued*

| Line No. | Supplies | Purchase of Equipment | Materials | Contract or Open Order Service | Contingencies | Fixed Charges and Contributions |
|---|---|---|---|---|---|---|
| 1 | $87,788 97 | $72,094 29 | $90,532 15 | $559,341 25 | $20,107 80 | .......... |
| 2 | 19,775 88 | 39,570 71 | 93,937 48 | 143,343 82 | 208 55 | $676 00 |
| 3 | 103,259 94 | 33,508 10 | 154,766 70 | 277,691 61 | 16,039 41 | .......... |
| 4 | 38,211 39 | 58,700 73 | 180,367 14 | 458,601 85 | 2,090 32 | .......... |
| 5 | 28,717 44 | 6,196 67 | 38,837 15 | 44,102 22 | 1,443 20 | .......... |
| 6 | **$277,753 62** | **$210,070 50** | **$558,440 62** | **$1,483,080 75** | **$39,889 28** | **$676 00** |
| 7 | **$4,030 54** | .......... | .......... | **$2,689 43** | **$5,300 79** | .......... |
| 8 | $580 71 | $546 66 | .......... | $2,064 73 | $359 86 | $1,916 64 |
| 9 | 143 42 | 70 00 | .......... | 80 54 | 50 00 | .......... |
| 10 | **$724 13** | **$616 66** | .......... | **$2,145 27** | **$409 86** | **$1,916 64** |
| 11 | $33,155 06 | $45,553 73 | $19,939 28 | $104,268 75 | $1,433 40 | .......... |
| 12 | 902 57 | 874 08 | .......... | 863,388 50 | 926 58 | .......... |
| 13 | 210,654 17 | 1,112 88 | .......... | 35,760 27 | 4,526 00 | $314,222 62 |
| 14 | 2,170 76 | 9,111 61 | .......... | 1,708 33 | 93,157 69 | .......... |
| 15 | .......... | .......... | .......... | .......... | 88 00 | .......... |
| 16 | .......... | .......... | .......... | .......... | 261 93 | .......... |
| 17 | **$246,882 56** | **$56,652 30** | **$19,939 28** | **$1,005,125 85** | **$100,393 60** | **$314,222 62** |
| 18 | $490 80 | .......... | .......... | $1,075 85 | $5 25 | .......... |
| 19 | 350 00 | .......... | .......... | 1,147 37 | 24 43 | .......... |
| 20 | 164 38 | $45 38 | .......... | 587 56 | 46 94 | .......... |
| 21 | .......... | .......... | .......... | 896 87 | 64 95 | .......... |
| 22 | .......... | .......... | .......... | 677 59 | 167 00 | .......... |
| 23 | 667 23 | 2,418 17 | .......... | 572 53 | 70 | .......... |
| 24 | 7,623 60 | 4,476 15 | .......... | 4,296 14 | 262 97 | .......... |
| 25 | 1,338 25 | 2,984 11 | .......... | 3,846 21 | 24 90 | .......... |
| 26 | 2,321 80 | 9,996 17 | .......... | 2,815 67 | 147 93 | .......... |
| 27 | 2,562 68 | 1,290 78 | .......... | 5,824 80 | 125 00 | .......... |
| 28 | .......... | .......... | .......... | .......... | .......... | .......... |
| 29 | .......... | .......... | .......... | 200 00 | 45 00 | .......... |
| 30 | **$15,518 74** | **$21,210 76** | .......... | **$21,940 59** | **$1,215 07** | .......... |
| 31 | **$7,799,593 08** | **$1,802,487 43** | **$1,218,587 41** | **$16,114,769 60** | **$356,808 60** | **$2,205,409 14** |
| 32 | .......... | .......... | .......... | .......... | .......... | **$52,491,846 15** |
| 33 | .......... | .......... | .......... | .......... | $27,150 15 | .......... |
| 34 | $4,990 89 | $2,365 30 | $428 25 | $1,392 72 | 347 25 | .......... |
| 35 | .......... | .......... | .......... | .......... | .......... | $5,184,610 06 |
| 36 | .......... | .......... | .......... | .......... | 2,548 04 | .......... |
| 37 | .......... | .......... | .......... | 4,927 27 | .......... | .......... |
| 38 | 253 37 | .......... | .......... | 93 50 | 193 84 | .......... |
| 39 | .......... | .......... | .......... | .......... | 24,409 43 | .......... |
| 40 | .......... | .......... | .......... | 5,932 57 | .......... | 859,440 39 |
| 41 | .......... | .......... | .......... | .......... | 24,463 35 | .......... |

STATEMENT SHOWING EXPENDITURES FROM REVENUE (BUDGET

| | Total | Personal Service | LINE No. |
|---|---|---|---|
| **FIXED CHARGES**—*Continued.* | | | |
| New York Aquarium | $46,995 53 | $32,841 86 | 1 |
| New York Botanical Garden | 107,163 00 | 90,411 74 | 2 |
| New York Zoological Garden | 200,000 00 | 145,230 24 | 3 |
| New York Public Library Building | 48,500 00 | .......... | 4 |
| Brooklyn Public Library | 437,231 16 | 248,124 50 | 5 |
| New York Public Library | 744,985 85 | 472,351 02 | 6 |
| Queensborough Public Library | 152,028 37 | 85,234 39 | 7 |
| Staten Island Association of Arts and Sciences | 8,639 79 | 6,527 51 | 8 |
| United States Volunteer Life Saving Corps | 12,355 14 | 6,860 00 | 9 |
| Total | **$8,374,579 96** | **$1,560,716 00** | 10 |
| DEFICIENCIES IN TAXES | **$2,500,000 00** | .......... | 11 |
| BOROUGH ASSESSMENTS: | | | |
| Manhattan | $144,448 63 | .......... | 12 |
| Brooklyn | 375,566 43 | .......... | 13 |
| Total Borough Assessments | **$520,015 06** | .......... | 14 |
| Total for City Purposes | **$181,532,872 85** | **$89,709,492 42** | 15 |
| DIRECT STATE TAXES: | | | |
| New York County | $3,308,080 34 | .......... | 16 |
| Kings County | 959,311 91 | .......... | 17 |
| Queens County | 263,332 56 | .......... | 18 |
| Richmond County | 45,578 62 | .......... | 19 |
| Total Direct State Taxes | **$4,576,303 43** | .......... | 20 |
| COUNTY EXPENDITURES: | | | |
| New York County: | | | |
| Charitable Institutions | $78,905 98 | .......... | 21 |
| Board of City Record | 34,203 26 | .......... | 22 |
| County Clerk | 190,013 92 | $186,278 03 | 23 |
| Court of General Sessions | 379,164 45 | 376,044 87 | 24 |
| Supreme Court, First Department | 987,886 13 | 978,960 71 | 25 |
| Supreme Court, First Department, Maintenance Appellate Division Court House | 28,792 71 | 18,295 18 | 26 |
| Surrogate's Court | 193,492 34 | 190,521 02 | 27 |
| District Attorney | 458,096 79 | 420,444 66 | 28 |
| Commissioner of Jurors | 57,151 14 | 52,387 69 | 29 |
| Miscellaneous | 475,295 09 | 411,587 97 | 30 |
| National Guard and Naval Militia | 221,101 00 | 213,101 00 | 31 |
| Public Administrator | 27,261 86 | 26,650 00 | 32 |
| Commissioner of Records | 96,680 42 | 92,961 49 | 33 |
| Commissioner of Records, Surrogate's Court | 47,517 17 | 46,536 13 | 34 |
| Register | 279,280 05 | 275,266 88 | 35 |
| Sheriff | 160,032 78 | 151,382 47 | 36 |
| Total | **$3,714,875 09** | **$3,440,418 10** | 37 |
| Kings County: | | | |
| Charitable Institutions | $51,042 74 | .......... | 38 |
| Board of City Record | 18,809 71 | .......... | 39 |
| County Clerk | 103,930 81 | $103,115 83 | 40 |
| County Court | 172,874 50 | 168,470 50 | 41 |
| Supreme Court, Second Department | 455,484 22 | 454,337 27 | 42 |
| Supreme Court Library | 9,199 69 | 8,200 00 | 43 |
| Surrogate's Court | 108,534 90 | 107,444 75 | 44 |
| District Attorney | 132,581 93 | 122,983 44 | 45 |
| Commissioner of Jurors | 40,973 03 | 38,794 84 | 46 |
| Miscellaneous | 146,846 34 | 120,193 34 | 47 |
| National Guard and Naval Militia | 154,855 75 | 154,855 75 | 48 |

## NEW YORK

Appropriations) for the Year 1914, Classified by Objects of Expenditure:—*Continued*

| LINE No. | Supplies | Purchase of Equipment | Materials | Contract or Open Order Service | Contingencies | Fixed Charges and Contributions |
|---|---|---|---|---|---|---|
| 1 | .......... | .......... | .......... | .......... | **$14,153 67** | .......... |
| 2 | .......... | .......... | .......... | .......... | **16,751 26** | .......... |
| 3 | .......... | .......... | .......... | .......... | **54,769 76** | .......... |
| 4 | $2,000 00 | .......... | .......... | $46,500 00 | .......... | .......... |
| 5 | 27,038 37 | $85,488 43 | .......... | 60,587 70 | 99 42 | $15,892 74 |
| 6 | 50,596 34 | 117,726 97 | $1,299 56 | 94,297 81 | 8,474 15 | 240 00 |
| 7 | 7,673 43 | 29,365 55 | 435 00 | 15,099 86 | 647 05 | 13,573 09 |
| 8 | 264 25 | 77 37 | .......... | 245 66 | 25 00 | 1,500 00 |
| 9 | 915 00 | 3,490 00 | 225 00 | 554 14 | 311 00 | .......... |
| 10 | **$93,731 65** | **$238,513 62** | **$2,387 81** | **$229,631 23** | **$174,343 37** | **$6,075,256 28** |
| 11 | .......... | .......... | .......... | .......... | .......... | **$2,500,000 00** |
| 12 | .......... | .......... | .......... | .......... | .......... | $144,448 63 |
| 13 | .......... | .......... | .......... | .......... | .......... | 375,566 43 |
| 14 | .......... | .......... | .......... | .......... | .......... | **$520,015 06** |
| 15 | **$7,893,324 73** | **$2,041,001 05** | **$1,220,975 22** | **$16,344,400 83** | **$531,151 97** | **$63,792,526 63** |
| 16 | .......... | .......... | .......... | .......... | .......... | $3,308,080 34 |
| 17 | .......... | .......... | .......... | .......... | .......... | 959,311 91 |
| 18 | .......... | .......... | .......... | .......... | .......... | 263,332 56 |
| 19 | .......... | .......... | .......... | .......... | .......... | 45,578 62 |
| 20 | .......... | .......... | .......... | .......... | .......... | **$4,576,303 43** |
| 21 | .......... | .......... | .......... | .......... | .......... | $78,905 98 |
| 22 | .......... | .......... | .......... | $34,203 26 | .......... | .......... |
| 23 | $1,918 66 | $933 35 | .......... | 875 88 | $8 00 | .......... |
| 24 | 879 89 | 1,422 10 | .......... | 789 81 | 27 78 | .......... |
| 25 | .......... | 2,600 00 | .......... | .......... | 48 00 | 6,277 42 |
| 26 | 4,558 52 | 2,211 42 | .......... | 3,327 59 | 400 00 | .......... |
| 27 | 990 00 | 1,440 28 | .......... | 516 04 | 25 00 | .......... |
| 28 | 1,777 75 | 2,582 00 | .......... | 3,000 00 | 30,292 38 | .......... |
| 29 | 3,885 81 | 243 00 | .......... | 630 25 | 4 39 | .......... |
| 30 | .......... | .......... | .......... | .......... | 3,295 72 | 60,411 40 |
| 31 | .......... | .......... | .......... | 8,000 00 | .......... | .......... |
| 32 | 210 68 | 187 45 | .......... | 190 96 | 22 77 | .......... |
| 33 | 494 29 | 759 05 | $21 50 | 2,342 45 | 101 64 | .......... |
| 34 | 192 35 | 366 50 | 422 19 | .......... | .......... | .......... |
| 35 | 677 42 | 1,799 97 | 662 25 | 847 03 | 26 50 | .......... |
| 36 | 4,891 12 | 156 83 | .......... | 3,219 03 | 383 33 | .......... |
| 37 | **$20,476 49** | **$14,701 95** | **$1,105 94** | **$57,942 30** | **$34,635 51** | **$145,594 80** |
| 38 | .......... | .......... | .......... | .......... | .......... | $51,042 74 |
| 39 | .......... | .......... | .......... | $18,809 71 | .......... | .......... |
| 40 | $576 60 | $184 56 | .......... | .......... | $53 82 | .......... |
| 41 | 646 07 | 345 65 | .......... | 1,205 13 | 100 00 | 2,107 15 |
| 42 | .......... | .......... | .......... | 431 51 | 715 44 | .......... |
| 43 | .......... | .......... | .......... | .......... | 999 69 | .......... |
| 44 | 449 37 | 273 42 | .......... | 367 36 | .......... | .......... |
| 45 | 2,498 61 | 824 01 | .......... | 3,234 54 | 3,041 33 | .......... |
| 46 | 1,682 72 | 256 73 | .......... | 233 74 | 5 00 | .......... |
| 47 | .......... | .......... | .......... | .......... | 3,249 00 | 23,404 00 |
| 48 | .......... | .......... | .......... | .......... | .......... | .......... |

Statement Showing Expenditures from Revenue (Budget

| | Total | Personal Service | LINE No. |
|---|---|---|---|
| County Expenditures—*Continued*: | | | |
| Kings County—*Continued:* | | | |
| Public Administrator | $11,954 89 | $11,320 00 | 1 |
| Commissioner of Records | 98,730 49 | 96,931 51 | 2 |
| Register | 197,880 05 | 196,775 11 | 3 |
| Sheriff | 91,388 03 | 84,675 38 | 4 |
| Total | **$1,795,087 08** | **$1,668,097 72** | 5 |
| Queens County: | | | |
| Charitable Institutions | $5,668 71 | .......... | 6 |
| Board of City Record | 3,989 95 | .......... | 7 |
| County Clerk | 124,265 68 | $118,998 89 | 8 |
| County Court | 42,428 26 | 41,800 00 | 9 |
| Supreme Court | 95,586 38 | 95,486 38 | 10 |
| Supreme Court Library | 2,308 06 | 1,992 50 | 11 |
| Surrogate's Court | 24,633 49 | 24,065 32 | 12 |
| District Attorney | 38,017 54 | 35,749 00 | 13 |
| Commissioner of Jurors | 12,253 88 | 11,499 50 | 14 |
| Miscellaneous | 38,801 57 | 36,862 92 | 15 |
| National Guard and Naval Militia | 5,110 00 | 5,110 00 | 16 |
| Public Administrator | 1,306 00 | 1,200 00 | 17 |
| Sheriff | 44,692 01 | 41,873 69 | 18 |
| Total | **$439,061 53** | **$414,638 20** | 19 |
| Richmond County: | | | |
| Charitable Institutions | $1,068 39 | .......... | 20 |
| Board of City Record | 1,720 69 | .......... | 21 |
| County Clerk | 21,071 42 | $20,490 18 | 22 |
| County Court and Surrogate's Court | 21,562 55 | 21,100 00 | 23 |
| Supreme Court | 19,219 73 | 19,165 33 | 24 |
| District Attorney | 14,458 31 | 13,720 99 | 25 |
| Commissioner of Jurors | 4,208 78 | 3,968 68 | 26 |
| Miscellaneous | 9,858 00 | 8,008 50 | 27 |
| National Guard and Naval Militia | 5,969 00 | 5,969 00 | 28 |
| Sheriff | 30,945 90 | 20,681 50 | 29 |
| Total | **$130,082 77** | **$113,104 18** | 30 |
| Bronx County: | | | |
| Charitable Institutions | $24,621 52 | .......... | 31 |
| Board of City Record | 11,799 30 | .......... | 32 |
| County Clerk | 28,945 41 | $28,943 41 | 33 |
| County Court | 10,003 00 | 10,000 00 | 34 |
| Surrogate's Court | 20,937 48 | 20,935 48 | 35 |
| District Attorney | 47,504 17 | 47,500 17 | 36 |
| Commissioner of Jurors | 23,386 09 | 21,232 90 | 37 |
| Miscellaneous | 14,146 38 | 12,223 98 | 38 |
| National Guard and Naval Militia | 29,052 00 | 29,052 00 | 39 |
| Public Administrator | 4,002 60 | 4,000 00 | 40 |
| Register | 26,003 00 | 26,000 00 | 41 |
| Sheriff | 28,933 76 | 28,929 76 | 42 |
| Total | **$269,334 71** | **$228,817 70** | 43 |
| Total for County Purposes | **$6,348,441 18** | **$5,865,075 90** | 44 |
| Total for All Purposes | **$192,457,617 46** | **$95,574,568 32** | 45 |

NEW YORK

APPROPRIATIONS) FOR THE YEAR 1914, CLASSIFIED BY OBJECTS OF EXPENDITURE:—*Continued*

| LINE No. | Supplies | Purchase of Equipment | Materials | Contract or Open Order Service | Contingencies | Fixed Charges and Contributions |
|---|---|---|---|---|---|---|
| 1 | $221 19 | $23 40 | .......... | $381 65 | $8 65 | .......... |
| 2 | 270 77 | 404 05 | $779 47 | 317 93 | 26 76 | .......... |
| 3 | 273 03 | 335 80 | .......... | 450 35 | 45 76 | .......... |
| 4 | 3,533 28 | 295 30 | .......... | 2,565 80 | 318 27 | .......... |
| 5 | **$10,151 64** | **$2,942 92** | **$779 47** | **$27,997 72** | **$8,563 72** | **$76,553 89** |
| 6 | .......... | .......... | .......... | .......... | .......... | $5,668 71 |
| 7 | .......... | .......... | .......... | $3,989 95 | .......... | .......... |
| 8 | $1,802 37 | $1,908 25 | .......... | 1,556 17 | .......... | .......... |
| 9 | 141 64 | 284 65 | .......... | 179 07 | $22 90 | .......... |
| 10 | .......... | .......... | .......... | .......... | 100 00 | .......... |
| 11 | .......... | .......... | .......... | .......... | 221 96 | 93 60 |
| 12 | 220 46 | 167 00 | .......... | 168 71 | 12 00 | .......... |
| 13 | 202 74 | 314 88 | .......... | 1,395 67 | 355 25 | .......... |
| 14 | 616 00 | .......... | .......... | 119 38 | 19 00 | .......... |
| 15 | .......... | .......... | .......... | .......... | 1,938 65 | .......... |
| 16 | .......... | .......... | .......... | .......... | .......... | .......... |
| 17 | .......... | .......... | .......... | .......... | 106 00 | .......... |
| 18 | 661 52 | .......... | .......... | 2,098 80 | 58 00 | .......... |
| 19 | **$3,644 73** | **$2,674 78** | .......... | **$9,507 75** | **$2,833 76** | **$5,762 31** |
| 20 | .......... | .......... | .......... | .......... | $1,068 39 | .......... |
| 21 | .......... | .......... | .......... | $1,720 69 | .......... | .......... |
| 22 | $99 80 | $371 06 | .......... | 100 38 | 10 00 | .......... |
| 23 | 170 29 | 126 90 | .......... | 141 26 | 24 10 | .......... |
| 24 | .......... | .......... | .......... | .......... | 54 40 | .......... |
| 25 | 77 80 | 87 95 | .......... | 499 43 | 72 14 | .......... |
| 26 | .......... | .......... | .......... | .......... | 240 10 | .......... |
| 27 | .......... | .......... | .......... | .......... | 924 50 | $925 00 |
| 28 | .......... | .......... | .......... | .......... | .......... | .......... |
| 29 | 8,365 88 | 901 32 | .......... | 694 84 | 302 36 | .......... |
| 30 | **$8,713 77** | **$1,487 23** | .......... | **$3,156 60** | **$2,695 99** | **$925 00** |
| 31 | .......... | .......... | .......... | .......... | .......... | $24,621 52 |
| 32 | .......... | .......... | .......... | $11,799 30 | .......... | .......... |
| 33 | $1 00 | $1 00 | .......... | .......... | .......... | .......... |
| 34 | 1 00 | .......... | .......... | 1 00 | $1 00 | .......... |
| 35 | 1 00 | 1 00 | .......... | .......... | .......... | .......... |
| 36 | 1 00 | 1 00 | .......... | 1 00 | 1 00 | .......... |
| 37 | 1,655 95 | 249 80 | .......... | 153 00 | 94 44 | .......... |
| 38 | .......... | .......... | .......... | .......... | 4 65 | 1,917 75 |
| 39 | .......... | .......... | .......... | .......... | .......... | .......... |
| 40 | 1 00 | 1 00 | .......... | .......... | 60 | .......... |
| 41 | 1 00 | 1 00 | .......... | .......... | 1 00 | .......... |
| 42 | 1 00 | 1 00 | .......... | 1 00 | 1 00 | .......... |
| 43 | **$1,662 95** | **$255 80** | .......... | **$11,955 30** | **$103 69** | **$26,539 27** |
| 44 | **$44,649 58** | **$22,062 68** | **$1,885 41** | **$110,559 67** | **$48,832 67** | **$255,375 27** |
| 45 | **$7,937,974 31** | **$2,063,063 73** | **$1,222,860 63** | **$16,454,960 50** | **$579,984 64** | **$68,624,205 33** |

THE CITY OF

Recapitulation of Statement Showing Expenditures from Revenue (Special

| | Total | Personal Service | Supplies | Line No. |
|---|---|---|---|---|
| City Departments, Offices, Courts, Etc.: | | | | |
| Mayor and Subordinate Departments, Bureaus and Offices: | | | | |
| Mayor's Office and Departments whose Executive heads are appointed by the Mayor and who are removable at his pleasure........ | $2,389,252 42 | $461,912 70 | $215,827 01 | 1 |
| Departments whose heads are appointed by the Mayor for a term of office greater than his own, and who are removable only on charges. | 148,239 61 | 16,889 19 | 22,149 42 | 2 |
| Boards and Commissions majorities of which are appointed by the Mayor, and for which no other elected City Official shares responsibility | 2,030 17 | .......... | 2,030 17 | 3 |
| Total Mayor and Subordinate Departments, Bureaus and Offices.................. | **$2,539,522 20** | **$478,801 89** | **$240,006 60** | 4 |
| Comptroller and Finance Department, excluding the Chamberlain's Office.................. | **$30,798 39** | **$25,498 29** | .......... | 5 |
| Borough Presidents and Subordinate Departments: | | | | |
| President, Borough of Manhattan............ | $126,550 17 | $3,074 59 | .......... | 6 |
| President, Borough of The Bronx............ | 21,061 47 | 10,316 73 | $12 00 | 7 |
| President, Borough of Brooklyn............ | 18,695 62 | 13,010 55 | .......... | 8 |
| President, Borough of Queens............ | 64,161 97 | 47,433 50 | .......... | 9 |
| President, Borough of Richmond............ | 12,822 31 | 10,145 27 | 60 92 | 10 |
| Total, Borough Presidents.............. | **$243,291 54** | **$83,980 64** | **$72 92** | 11 |
| Board of Aldermen, President of Board and City Clerk.................................. | **$20,473 66** | **$6,906 99** | .......... | 12 |
| Boards, Commissions, etc., whose members are not elected by popular vote, and who are not appointed by any elected City official......... | **$1,217,774 13** | **$1,059,337 35** | **$38,926 80** | 13 |
| Boards, Commissions, etc., of mixed responsibility, i.e., ex-officio bodies representing two or more of preceding branches.................... | **$43,556 83** | **$10,529 55** | **$10,646 83** | 14 |
| Courts, including Board of Parole and General Interpreters of Brooklyn................. | **$106,078 05** | **$101,881 28** | **$476 64** | 15 |
| Total City Departments, Offices, Courts, etc.................................. | **$4,201,494 80** | **$1,766,935 99** | **$290,129 79** | 16 |
| Fixed Charges other than Debt Service, Subsidies, Contributions, Payments to Private and State Institutions, Expenditures not Allotted to Departments................ | **$2,624,300 57** | **$48,315 03** | .......... | 17 |
| Total for City Purposes................ | **$6,825,795 37** | **$1,815,251 02** | **$290,129 79** | 18 |
| County Expenditures: | | | | |
| New York County.......................... | $333,588 42 | $26,777 37 | $336 50 | 19 |
| Kings County.............................. | 28,834 09 | 18,679 89 | .......... | 20 |
| Queens County............................ | 11,684 96 | 266 12 | .......... | 21 |
| Richmond County.......................... | 8,243 73 | 833 33 | .......... | 22 |
| Total for County Purposes.............. | **$382,351 20** | **$46,556 71** | **$336 50** | 23 |
| Total for all Purposes................. | **$7,208,146 57** | **$1,861,807 73** | **$290,466 29** | 24 |

NEW YORK

Revenue Bond Funds) for the Year 1910, Classified by Objects of Expenditure

| Line No. | Purchase of Equipment | Materials | Contract or Open Order Service | Contingencies | Fixed Charges and Contributions | Unclassified |
|---|---|---|---|---|---|---|
| 1 | $136,485 46 | $39,541 36 | $1,454,213 42 | $1,492 31 | $78,246 82 | $1,533 34 |
| 2 | 4,218 93 | .......... | 103,932 07 | .......... | 1,050 00 | .......... |
| 3 | .......... | .......... | .......... | .......... | .......... | .......... |
| 4 | **$140,704 39** | **$39,541 36** | **$1,558,145 49** | **$1,492 31** | **$79,296 82** | **$1,533 34** |
| 5 | **$5,300 10** | .......... | .......... | .......... | .......... | .......... |
| 6 | $8,462 27 | .......... | $115,013 31 | .......... | .......... | .......... |
| 7 | 9,009 04 | .......... | 1,723 70 | .......... | .......... | .......... |
| 8 | 3,313 95 | .......... | 1,086 76 | .......... | $1,284 36 | .......... |
| 9 | .......... | .......... | 13,328 47 | .......... | 3,400 00 | .......... |
| 10 | 51 15 | $97 50 | 2,227 47 | .......... | 240 00 | .......... |
| 11 | **$20,836 41** | **$97 50** | **$133,379 71** | .......... | **$4,924 36** | .......... |
| 12 | .......... | .......... | **$12,766 67** | **$800 00** | .......... | .......... |
| 13 | **$13,827 79** | .......... | **$38,410 32** | .......... | **$60,088 52** | **$7,183 35** |
| 14 | .......... | .......... | **$20,640 45** | .......... | **$1,740 00** | .......... |
| 15 | **$2,120 35** | .......... | **$423 17** | **$476 61** | **$700 00** | .......... |
| 16 | **$182,789 04** | **$39,638 86** | **$1,763,765 81** | **$2,768 92** | **$146,749 70** | **$8,716 69** |
| 17 | .......... | .......... | **$114,787 24** | .......... | **$31,660 65** | **$2,429,537 65** |
| 18 | **$182,789 04** | **$39,638 86** | **$1,878,553 05** | **$2,768 92** | **$178,410 35** | **$2,438,254 34** |
| 19 | $94 55 | .......... | $5,886 05 | $9,259 19 | .......... | $291,234 76 |
| 20 | .......... | .......... | 975 50 | .......... | .......... | 9,178 70 |
| 21 | .......... | .......... | 1,002 60 | 2,572 64 | .......... | 7,843 60 |
| 22 | .......... | .......... | .......... | .......... | .......... | 7,410 40 |
| 23 | **$94 55** | .......... | **$7,864 15** | **$11,831 83** | .......... | **$315,667 46** |
| 24 | **$182,883 59** | **$39,638 86** | **$1,886,417 20** | **$14,600 75** | **$178,410 35** | **$2,753,921 80** |

STATEMENT SHOWING EXPENDITURES FROM REVENUE (SPECIAL REVENUE BOND

| | Total | Personal Service | Supplies | LINE No. |
|---|---|---|---|---|
| CITY DEPARTMENTS, OFFICES, COURTS, ETC. | | | | |
| Mayor and Subordinate Departments, Bureaus and Offices: | | | | |
| Mayor's Office and Departments whose executive heads are appointed by the Mayor and who are removable at his pleasure: | | | | |
| Board of Ambulance Service | $628 39 | $628 39 | .......... | 1 |
| Department of Correction | 3,816 48 | 3,816 48 | .......... | 2 |
| Department of Docks and Ferries | 58,702 38 | .......... | .......... | 3 |
| Examining Board of Plumbers | 960 00 | .......... | .......... | 4 |
| Fire Department | 41,639 43 | 1,467 62 | $1,112 56 | 5 |
| Department of Health | 94,595 40 | 29,192 77 | 23,936 29 | 6 |
| Mayoralty—Bureau of Licenses | 10,653 25 | .......... | .......... | 7 |
| Mayoralty—Bureau of Weights and Measures | 1,737 21 | 1,737 21 | .......... | 8 |
| Municipal Civil Service Commission | 1,731 00 | 1,731 00 | .......... | 9 |
| Department of Parks—Manhattan and Richmond | 58,224 55 | 11,997 67 | .......... | 10 |
| Department of Parks—The Bronx | 998 00 | .......... | .......... | 11 |
| Police Department | 13,916 07 | 12,382 73 | .......... | 12 |
| Department of Public Charities | 289,386 27 | 4,614 59 | 187,543 35 | 13 |
| Department of Street Cleaning | 1,604,244 88 | 348,545 68 | 15 15 | 14 |
| Department of Taxes and Assessments | 40,657 43 | 39,912 10 | 745 33 | 15 |
| Tenement House Department | 10,305 77 | .......... | .......... | 16 |
| Department of Water Supply, Gas and Electricity | 157,055 91 | 5,886 46 | 2,474 33 | 17 |
| Total | **$2,389,252 42** | **$461,912 70** | **$215,827 01** | 18 |
| Departments whose heads are appointed by the Mayor for a term of office greater than his own and who are removable only upon charges: | | | | |
| Bellevue and Allied Hospitals | $59,057 45 | $16,812 09 | $21,917 13 | 19 |
| College of the City of New York | 3,784 76 | .......... | 204 76 | 20 |
| Department of Education | 85,397 40 | 77 10 | 27 53 | 21 |
| Total | **$148,239 61** | **$16,889 19** | **$22,149 42** | 22 |
| Boards and Commissions majorities of which are appointed by the Mayor and for which no other elected city official shares responsibility: | | | | |
| Brooklyn Disciplinary Training School for Boys | $2,030 17 | .......... | $2,030 17 | 23 |
| Total | **$2,030 17** | .......... | **$2,030 17** | 24 |
| Total, Mayor and Subordinate Departments, Bureaus and Offices | **$2,539,522 20** | **$478,801 89** | **$240,006 60** | 25 |
| Comptroller and Finance Department, Excluding the Chamberlain's Office | **$30,798 39** | **$25,498 29** | .......... | 26 |
| Borough Presidents and Subordinate Departments: | | | | |
| President of Manhattan | $126,550 17 | $3,074 59 | .......... | 27 |
| President of The Bronx | 21,061 47 | 10,316 73 | $12 00 | 28 |
| President of Brooklyn | 18,695 62 | 13,010 55 | .......... | 29 |
| President of Queens | 64,161 97 | 47,433 50 | .......... | 30 |
| President of Richmond | 12,822 31 | 10,145 27 | 60 92 | 31 |
| Total | **$243,291 54** | **$83,980 64** | **$72 92** | 32 |
| Board of Aldermen, President of Board and City Clerk | **$20,473 66** | **$6,906 99** | .......... | 33 |

NEW YORK

FUNDS) FOR THE YEAR 1910, CLASSIFIED BY OBJECTS OF EXPENDITURES.

| LINE No. | Purchase of Equipment | Materials | Contract or Open Order Service | Contingencies | Fixed Charges and Contributions | Unclassified |
|---|---|---|---|---|---|---|
| 1 | .......... | .......... | .......... | .......... | .......... | .......... |
| 2 | .......... | .......... | .......... | .......... | .......... | .......... |
| 3 | .......... | .......... | $58,702 38 | .......... | .......... | .......... |
| 4 | .......... | .......... | .......... | .......... | $960 00 | .......... |
| 5 | $37,489 25 | .......... | 50 00 | .......... | 1,520 00 | .......... |
| 6 | 4,500 44 | $979 18 | 35,986 72 | .......... | .......... | .......... |
| 7 | .......... | .......... | 10,653 25 | .......... | .......... | .......... |
| 8 | .......... | .......... | .......... | .......... | .......... | .......... |
| 9 | .......... | .......... | .......... | .......... | .......... | .......... |
| 10 | 3,196 58 | .......... | 43,030 30 | .......... | .......... | .......... |
| 11 | 998 00 | .......... | .......... | .......... | .......... | .......... |
| 12 | .......... | .......... | .......... | .......... | .......... | $1,533 34 |
| 13 | 20,399 42 | 34,408 20 | 29,284 39 | .......... | 13,136 32 | .......... |
| 14 | 53,550 40 | 1,107 50 | 1,201,026 15 | .......... | .......... | .......... |
| 15 | .......... | .......... | .......... | .......... | .......... | .......... |
| 16 | 4,763 27 | .......... | 3,825 00 | .......... | 1,717 50 | .......... |
| 17 | 11,588 10 | 3,046 48 | 71,655 23 | $1,492 31 | 60,913 00 | .......... |
| 18 | **$136,485 46** | **$39,541 36** | **$1,454,213 42** | **$1,492 31** | **$78,246 82** | **$1,533 34** |
| 19 | $3,879 93 | .......... | $15,848 30 | .......... | $600 00 | .......... |
| 20 | 10 00 | .......... | 3,570 00 | .......... | .......... | .......... |
| 21 | 329 00 | .......... | 84,513 77 | .......... | 450 00 | .......... |
| 22 | **$4,218 93** | .......... | **$103,932 07** | .......... | **$1,050 00** | .......... |
| 23 | .......... | .......... | .......... | .......... | .......... | .......... |
| 24 | .......... | .......... | .......... | .......... | .......... | .......... |
| 25 | **$140,704 39** | **$39,541 36** | **$1,558,145 49** | **$1,492 31** | **$79,296 82** | **$1,533 34** |
| 26 | **$5,300 10** | .......... | .......... | .......... | .......... | .......... |
| 27 | $8,462 27 | .......... | $115,013 31 | .......... | .......... | .......... |
| 28 | 9,009 04 | .......... | 1,723 70 | .......... | .......... | .......... |
| 29 | 3,313 95 | .......... | 1,086 76 | .......... | $1,284 36 | .......... |
| 30 | .......... | .......... | 13,328 47 | .......... | 3,400 00 | .......... |
| 31 | 51 15 | $97 50 | 2,227 47 | .......... | 240 00 | .......... |
| 32 | **$20,836 41** | **$97 50** | **$133,379 71** | .......... | **$4,924 36** | .......... |
| 33 | .......... | .......... | **$12,766 67** | **$800 00** | .......... | .......... |

| | Total | Personal Service | Supplies | LINE No. |
|---|---|---|---|---|
| CITY DEPARTMENTS, OFFICES, ETC.—*Continued* | | | | |
| Boards, Commissions, etc., whose members are not elected by popular vote and who are not appointed by any elected city official: | | | | |
| Court House Board | $1,591 73 | $1,322 40 | $269 33 | 1 |
| Public Service Commission | 1,216,182 40 | 1,058,014 95 | 38,657 47 | 2 |
| Total | **$1,217,774 13** | **$1,059,337 35** | **$38,926 80** | 3 |
| Boards, Commissions, etc., of mixed responsibility, i. e., ex-officio bodies representing two or more preceding branches: | | | | |
| Board of City Record, City of New York | $19,689 65 | $3,185 55 | $10,184 45 | 4 |
| Board of Elections | 23,867 18 | 7,344 00 | 462 38 | 5 |
| Total | **$43,556 83** | **$10,529 55** | **$10,646 83** | 6 |
| Courts, including Board of Parole and General Interpreters of Brooklyn: | | | | |
| Coroners, Borough of The Bronx | $1,216 66 | $1,216 66 | .......... | 7 |
| Coroners, Borough of Brooklyn | 1,250 00 | 1,250 00 | .......... | 8 |
| City Magistrates' Courts, First Division | 58,608 15 | 58,220 94 | .......... | 9 |
| City Magistrates' Courts, Second Division | 12,486 07 | 11,653 64 | $350 85 | 10 |
| Court of Special Sessions | 32,517 17 | 29,540 04 | 125 79 | 11 |
| Total | **$106,078 05** | **$101,881 28** | **$476 64** | 12 |
| Total, City Departments, Offices, Courts, etc | **$4,201,494 80** | **$1,766,935 99** | **$290,129 79** | 13 |
| FIXED CHARGES, OTHER THAN DEBT SERVICE, SUBSIDIES, CONTRIBUTIONS, PAYMENTS TO PRIVATE AND STATE INSTITUTIONS, EXPENDITURES, NOT ALLOTTED TO DEPARTMENTS: | | | | |
| Claims | $1,780,056 75 | $48,165 03 | .......... | 14 |
| Miscellaneous, City | 843,515 53 | 150 00 | .......... | 15 |
| New York Public Library | 728 29 | .......... | .......... | 16 |
| Total | **$2,624,300 57** | **$48,315 03** | .......... | 17 |
| Total for City Purposes | **$6,825,795 37** | **$1,815,251 02** | **$290,129 79** | 18 |
| COUNTY EXPENDITURE: | | | | |
| New York County: | | | | |
| County Clerk | $9,829 30 | $9,739 30 | .......... | 19 |
| Surrogate's Court | 120 00 | .......... | .......... | 20 |
| District Attorney | 24,387 90 | 15,128 71 | .......... | 21 |
| Miscellaneous | 291,144 76 | .......... | .......... | 22 |
| Register | 260 00 | 260 00 | .......... | 23 |
| Sheriff | 7,846 46 | 1,649 36 | $336 50 | 24 |
| Total | **$333,588 42** | **$26,777 37** | **$336 50** | 25 |
| Kings County: | | | | |
| County Clerk | $4,710 14 | $4,710 14 | .......... | 26 |
| Supreme Court, Second Department | 2,200 00 | 2,200 00 | .......... | 27 |
| Surrogate's Court | 3,971 43 | 3,971 43 | .......... | 28 |
| District Attorney | 4,225 34 | 3,249 84 | .......... | 29 |
| Miscellaneous | 9,178 70 | .......... | .......... | 30 |
| Register | 4,548 48 | 4,548 48 | .......... | 31 |
| Total | **$28,834 09** | **$18,679 89** | .......... | 32 |

# NEW YORK

FUNDS) FOR THE YEAR 1910, CLASSIFIED BY OBJECTS OF EXPENDITURES:—*Continued*

| LINE No. | Purchase of Equipment | Materials | Contract or Open Order Service | Contingencies | Fixed Charges and Contributions | Unclassified |
|---|---|---|---|---|---|---|
| 1 | .......... | .......... | .......... | .......... | .......... | .......... |
| 2 | $13,827 79 | .......... | $38,410 32 | .......... | $60,088 52 | $7,183 35 |
| 3 | **$13,827 79** | .......... | **$38,410 32** | .......... | **$60,088 52** | **$7,183 35** |
| 4 | .......... | .......... | $6,319 65 | .......... | .......... | .......... |
| 5 | .......... | .......... | 14,320 80 | .......... | $1,740 00 | .......... |
| 6 | .......... | .......... | **$20,640 45** | .......... | **$1,740 00** | .......... |
| 7 | .......... | .......... | .......... | .......... | .......... | .......... |
| 8 | .......... | .......... | .......... | .......... | .......... | .......... |
| 9 | $354 60 | .......... | $32 61 | .......... | .......... | .......... |
| 10 | 416 00 | .......... | 65 58 | .......... | .......... | .......... |
| 11 | 1,349 75 | .......... | 324 98 | $476 61 | $700 00 | .......... |
| 12 | **$2,120 35** | .......... | **$423 17** | **$476 61** | **$700 00** | .......... |
| 13 | **$182,789 04** | **$39,638 86** | **$1,763,765 81** | **$2,768 92** | **$146,749 70** | **$8,716 69** |
| 14 | .......... | .......... | .......... | .......... | .......... | $1,731,891 72 |
| 15 | .......... | .......... | $114,418 24 | .......... | $31,660 65 | 697,286 64 |
| 16 | .......... | .......... | 369 00 | .......... | .......... | 359 29 |
| 17 | .......... | .......... | **$114,787 24** | .......... | **$31,660 65** | **$2,429,537 65** |
| 18 | **$182,789 04** | **$39,638 86** | **$1,878,553 05** | **$2,768 92** | **$178,410 35** | **$2,438,254 34** |
| 19 | .......... | .......... | .......... | .......... | .......... | $90 00 |
| 20 | .......... | .......... | $120 00 | .......... | .......... | .......... |
| 21 | .......... | .......... | .......... | $9,259 19 | .......... | .......... |
| 22 | .......... | .......... | .......... | .......... | .......... | 291,144 76 |
| 23 | .......... | .......... | .......... | .......... | .......... | .......... |
| 24 | $94 55 | .......... | 5,766 05 | .......... | .......... | .......... |
| 25 | **$94 55** | .......... | **$5,886 05** | **$9,259 19** | .......... | **$291,234 76** |
| 26 | .......... | .......... | .......... | .......... | .......... | .......... |
| 27 | .......... | .......... | .......... | .......... | .......... | .......... |
| 28 | .......... | .......... | .......... | .......... | .......... | .......... |
| 29 | .......... | .......... | $975 50 | .......... | .......... | .......... |
| 30 | .......... | .......... | .......... | .......... | .......... | $9,178 70 |
| 31 | .......... | .......... | .......... | .......... | .......... | .......... |
| 32 | .......... | .......... | **$975 50** | .......... | .......... | **$9,178 70** |

Statement Showing Expenditures from Revenue (Special Revenue Bond

| | Total | Personal Service | Supplies | Line No. |
|---|---|---|---|---|
| County Expenditures—*Continued* | | | | |
| Queens County: | | | | |
| County Clerk | $1,002 60 | .......... | .......... | 1 |
| Surrogate's Court | 266 12 | $266 12 | .......... | 2 |
| District Attorney | $2,572 64 | .......... | .......... | 3 |
| Miscellaneous | 7,843 60 | .......... | .......... | 4 |
| Total | **$11,684 96** | **$266 12** | .......... | 5 |
| Richmond County: | | | | |
| County Clerk | $833 33 | $833 33 | .......... | 6 |
| Miscellaneous | 7,410 40 | .......... | .......... | 7 |
| Total | **$8,243 73** | **$833 33** | .......... | 8 |
| Total for County Purposes | **$382,351 20** | **$46,556 71** | **$336 50** | 9 |
| Total for All Purposes | **$7,208,146 57** | **$1,861,807 73** | **$290,466 29** | 10 |

## NEW YORK

FUNDS) FOR THE YEAR 1910, CLASSIFIED BY OBJECTS OF EXPENDITURES:—*Continued*

| LINE No. | Purchase of Equipment | Materials | Contract or Open Order Service | Contingencies | Fixed Charges and Contributions | Unclassified |
|---|---|---|---|---|---|---|
| 1 | .......... | .......... | $1,002 60 | .......... | .......... | .......... |
| 2 | .......... | .......... | .......... | .......... | .......... | .......... |
| 3 | .......... | .......... | .......... | $2,572 64 | .......... | .......... |
| 4 | .......... | .......... | .......... | .......... | .......... | $7,843 60 |
| 5 | .......... | .......... | **$1,002 60** | **$2,572 64** | .......... | **$7,843 60** |
| 6 | .......... | .......... | .......... | .......... | .......... | .......... |
| 7 | .......... | .......... | .......... | .......... | .......... | $7,410 40 |
| 8 | .......... | .......... | .......... | .......... | .......... | **$7,410 40** |
| 9 | **$94 55** | .......... | **$7,864 15** | **$11,831 83** | .......... | **$315,667 46** |
| 10 | **$182,883 59** | **$39,638 86** | **$1,886,417 20** | **$14,600 75** | **$178,410 35** | **$2,753,921 80** |

THE CITY OF

RECAPITULATION OF STATEMENT SHOWING EXPENDITURES FROM REVENUE (SPECIAL

| | Total | Personal Service | Supplies | LINE No. |
|---|---|---|---|---|
| CITY DEPARTMENTS, OFFICES, COURTS, ETC. | | | | |
| Mayor and Subordinate Departments, Bureaus and Offices: | | | | |
| Mayor's Office and Departments whose executive heads are appointed by the Mayor and who are removable at his pleasure.......... | $1,564,410 68 | $477,166 62 | $168,704 25 | 1 |
| Departments whose heads are appointed by the Mayor for a term of office greater than his own, and who are removable only upon charges | 153,089 57 | 17,852 14 | 22,342 62 | 2 |
| Boards and Commissions majority of which are appointed by the Mayor and for which no other elected City official shares responsibility. | 896 28 | 887 19 | 9 09 | 3 |
| Total Mayor and Subordinate Departments, Bureaus and Offices.................. | **$1,718,396 53** | **$495,905 95** | **$191,055 96** | 4 |
| Comptroller and Finance Department, excluding the Chamberlain's Office.................. | **$5,015 17** | .......... | .......... | 5 |
| Borough Presidents and Subordinate Departments: | | | | |
| President, Borough of Manhattan............ | $348,799 00 | .......... | .......... | 6 |
| President, Borough of The Bronx............ | 8,982 82 | $2,703 64 | $21 92 | 7 |
| President, Borough of Brooklyn.............. | 10,706 27 | 6,230 82 | 36 64 | 8 |
| President, Borough of Queens............... | 48,351 15 | 9,989 36 | .......... | 9 |
| President, Borough of Richmond............. | 2,787 48 | 2,470 33 | .......... | 10 |
| Total Borough Presidents............... | **$419,626 72** | **$21,394 15** | **$58 56** | 11 |
| Board of Aldermen, President of Board and City Clerk.................................. | **$48,691 24** | **$4,496 14** | **$2,500 00** | 12 |
| Boards, Commissions, etc., whose members are not elected by popular vote and who are not appointed by any elected City official....... | **$1,101,033 27** | **$884,584 65** | **$12,089 61** | 13 |
| Boards, Commissions, etc., of mixed responsibility, i.e., ex-officio bodies representing two or more of preceding branches.................... | **$12,049 18** | **$9,176 18** | .......... | 14 |
| Courts, including Board of Parole and General Interpreters of Brooklyn................. | **$82,150 10** | **$45,019 25** | **$396 02** | 15 |
| Total City Departments,Offices,Courts, etc. | **$3,386,962 51** | **$1,460,576 32** | **$206,100 15** | 16 |
| DEBT SERVICE.................................. | **$7,500 00** | .......... | .......... | 17 |
| FIXED CHARGES OTHER THAN DEBT SERVICE, SUBSIDIES, CONTRIBUTIONS, PAYMENTS TO PRIVATE AND STATE INSTITUTIONS, EXPENDITURES NOT ALLOTTED TO DEPARTMENTS................ | **$994,424 20** | **$55,540 49** | **$10,167 14** | 18 |
| Total for City Purposes................ | **$4,388,886 41** | **$1,516,116 81** | **$216,267 29** | 19 |
| COUNTY EXPENDITURES: | | | | |
| New York County........................... | $240,370 98 | $18,682 04 | $802 27 | 20 |
| Kings County............................... | 99,212 15 | 35,488 32 | .......... | 21 |
| Queens County.............................. | 31,713 22 | 16,420 64 | 468 81 | 22 |
| Richmond County........................... | 6,712 59 | 1,674 98 | 1,619 31 | 23 |
| Total for County Purposes............ | **$378,008 94** | **$72,265 98** | **$2,890 39** | 24 |
| Total for All Purposes................ | **$4,766,895 35** | **$1,588,382 79** | **$219,157 68** | 25 |

NEW YORK

REVENUE BOND FUNDS) FOR THE YEAR 1911, CLASSIFIED BY OBJECTS OF EXPENDITURE:

| LINE No. | Purchase of Equipment | Materials | Contract or Open Order Service | Contingencies | Fixed Charges and Contributions | Unclassified |
|---|---|---|---|---|---|---|
| 1 | $348,755 89 | $23,156 12 | $339,620 65 | $39 27 | $206,967 88 | .......... |
| 2 | 5,491 82 | .......... | 107,402 99 | .......... | .......... | .......... |
| 3 | .......... | .......... | .......... | .......... | .......... | .......... |
| 4 | **$354,247 71** | **$23,156 12** | **$447,023 64** | **$39 27** | **$206,967 88** | .......... |
| 5 | **$4,525 25** | .......... | **$489 92** | .......... | .......... | .......... |
| 6 | .......... | .......... | $348,799 00 | .......... | .......... | .......... |
| 7 | $45 60 | $116 80 | 6,009 38 | .......... | $85 48 | .......... |
| 8 | 1,831 02 | 49 18 | 2,558 61 | .......... | .......... | .......... |
| 9 | 7,810 59 | .......... | 30,551 20 | .......... | .......... | .......... |
| 10 | .......... | .......... | 317 15 | .......... | .......... | .......... |
| 11 | **$9,687 21** | **$165 98** | **$388,235 34** | .......... | **$85 48** | .......... |
| 12 | .......... | .......... | **$722 18** | **$766 90** | .......... | **$40,206 02** |
| 13 | **$11,932 45** | .......... | **$110,909 29** | .......... | **$70,548 11** | **$10,969 16** |
| 14 | .......... | .......... | **$2,873 00** | .......... | .......... | .......... |
| 15 | **$32,274 21** | .......... | **$2,623 38** | **$612 24** | **$1,225 00** | .......... |
| 16 | **$412,666 83** | **$23,322 10** | **$952,876 75** | **$1,418 41** | **$278,826 47** | **$51,175 18** |
| 17 | .......... | .......... | .......... | .......... | **$7,500 00** | .......... |
| 18 | .......... | .......... | .......... | .......... | **$156,516 02** | **$772,200 55** |
| 19 | **$412,666 83** | **$23,322 10** | **$952,876 75** | **$1,418 41** | **$442,842 49** | **$823,375 73** |
| 20 | $841 96 | .......... | $41 35 | $735 25 | $576 50 | $218,691 61 |
| 21 | 2,706 38 | .......... | 318 95 | 1,810 43 | .......... | 58,825 07 |
| 22 | 176 73 | .......... | 268 22 | 319 71 | .......... | 14,059 11 |
| 23 | .......... | .......... | 122 35 | .......... | .......... | 3,295 95 |
| 24 | **$3,725 07** | .......... | **$813 87** | **$2,865 39** | **$576 50** | **$294,871 74** |
| 25 | **$416,391 90** | **$23,322 10** | **$953,690 62** | **$4,283 80** | **$443,418 99** | **$1,118,247 47** |

STATEMENT SHOWING EXPENDITURES FROM REVENUE (SPECIAL

| | Total | Personal Service | Supplies | LINE No. |
|---|---|---|---|---|
| CITY DEPARTMENTS, OFFICES, COURTS, ETC. | | | | |
| Mayor and Subordinate Departments, Bureaus, and Offices: | | | | |
| Mayor's Office and Departments whose executive heads are appointed by the Mayor and who are removable at his pleasure: | | | | |
| Commissioners of Accounts | $7,682 79 | $4,681 46 | $775 65 | 1 |
| Board of Ambulance Service | 637 56 | 199 46 | .......... | 2 |
| Board of Assessors | 562 50 | 562 50 | .......... | 3 |
| Department of Bridges | 90,596 14 | 62,529 58 | 9,009 91 | 4 |
| Department of Correction | 1,533 52 | 1,533 52 | .......... | 5 |
| Department of Docks and Ferries | 134,545 95 | 4,154 28 | .......... | 6 |
| Fire Department | 97,012 59 | .......... | *5 00 | 7 |
| Department of Health | 17,754 34 | 4,166 30 | 6,235 61 | 8 |
| Law Department | 21,301 40 | 20,289 13 | .......... | 9 |
| Mayoralty—Bureau of Licenses | 8,935 01 | 3,419 56 | 457 91 | 10 |
| Mayoralty—Bureau of Weights and Measures | 2,497 19 | 2,013 34 | 350 22 | 11 |
| Municipal Civil Service Commission | 15,909 22 | 15,909 22 | .......... | 12 |
| Municipal Explosives Commission | 11,100 00 | 11,100 00 | .......... | 13 |
| Department of Parks—Manhattan and Richmond | 64,960 70 | 38,893 32 | 14,009 79 | 14 |
| Department of Parks—The Bronx | 1,650 83 | .......... | .......... | 15 |
| Department of Parks—Brooklyn | 4,364 86 | 4,364 86 | .......... | 16 |
| Department of Parks—Queens | 3,768 44 | 3,768 44 | .......... | 17 |
| Police Department | 208,817 56 | 3,172 63 | .......... | 18 |
| Department of Public Charities | 189,518 94 | 23,739 76 | 136,481 67 | 19 |
| Department of Street Cleaning | 439,054 13 | 98,952 03 | 26 10 | 20 |
| Department of Taxes and Assessments | 100,735 09 | 95,764 37 | 764 52 | 21 |
| Tenement House Department | 5,123 22 | .......... | .......... | 22 |
| Department of Water Supply, Gas and Electricity | 136,348 70 | 77,952 86 | 597 87 | 23 |
| Total | **$1,564,410 68** | **$477,166 62** | **$168,704 25** | 24 |
| Departments whose heads are appointed by the Mayor for a term of office greater than his own and who are removable only upon charges: | | | | |
| Bellevue and Allied Hospitals | $60,032 12 | $14,786 88 | $22,342 62 | 25 |
| College of the City of New York | 698 00 | .......... | .......... | 26 |
| Department of Education | 92,359 45 | 3,065 26 | .......... | 27 |
| Total | **$153,089 57** | **$17,852 14** | **$22,342 62** | 28 |
| Boards and Commissions, majorities of which are appointed by the Mayor and for which no other elected City Official shares responsibility: | | | | |
| Brooklyn Disciplinary Training School for Boys | $9 09 | .......... | $9 09 | 29 |
| Board of Inebriety | 887 19 | $887 19 | .......... | 30 |
| Total | **$896 28** | **$887 19** | **$9 09** | 31 |
| Total Mayor and Subordinate Departments, Bureaus and Offices | **$1,718,396 53** | **$495,905 95** | **$191,055 96** | 32 |
| Comptroller and Finance Department, excluding the Chamberlain's Office | **$5,015 17** | .......... | .......... | 33 |

* Refund

NEW YORK

REVENUE BOND FUNDS) FOR THE YEAR 1911, CLASSIFIED BY OBJECTS OF EXPENDITURE:

| LINE No. | Purchase of Equipment | Materials | Contract or Open Order Service | Contingencies | Fixed Charges and Contributions | Unclassified |
|---|---|---|---|---|---|---|
| 1 | $1,487 02 | .......... | $738 66 | .......... | .......... | .......... |
| 2 | 438 10 | .......... | .......... | .......... | .......... | .......... |
| 3 | .......... | .......... | .......... | .......... | .......... | .......... |
| 4 | 11,892 61 | $750 29 | 6,413 75 | .......... | .......... | .......... |
| 5 | .......... | .......... | .......... | .......... | .......... | .......... |
| 6 | .......... | .......... | 130,391 67 | .......... | .......... | .......... |
| 7 | 93,672 56 | 2,452 00 | 893 03 | .......... | .......... | .......... |
| 8 | 3,860 84 | 46 97 | 3,444 62 | .......... | .......... | .......... |
| 9 | 312 27 | .......... | 700 00 | .......... | .......... | .......... |
| 10 | 4,995 60 | .......... | 61 94 | .......... | .......... | .......... |
| 11 | .......... | .......... | 133 63 | .......... | .......... | .......... |
| 12 | .......... | .......... | .......... | .......... | .......... | .......... |
| 13 | .......... | .......... | .......... | .......... | .......... | .......... |
| 14 | 3,819 09 | 330 00 | 7,908 50 | .......... | .......... | .......... |
| 15 | 1,650 83 | .......... | .......... | .......... | .......... | .......... |
| 16 | .......... | .......... | .......... | .......... | .......... | .......... |
| 17 | .......... | .......... | .......... | .......... | .......... | .......... |
| 18 | .......... | .......... | .......... | .......... | $205,644 93 | .......... |
| 19 | 12,596 42 | 15,859 14 | 841 95 | .......... | .......... | .......... |
| 20 | 203,177 08 | 22 00 | 136,876 92 | .......... | .......... | .......... |
| 21 | .......... | .......... | 4,206 20 | .......... | .......... | .......... |
| 22 | 4,696 97 | .......... | 426 25 | .......... | .......... | .......... |
| 23 | 6,156 50 | 3,695 72 | 4,658 53 | $39 27 | 1,322 95 | .......... |
| 24 | **$348,755 89** | **$23,156 12** | **$339,620 65** | **$39 27** | **$206,967 88** | .......... |
| 25 | $5,148 82 | .......... | $17,753 80 | .......... | .......... | .......... |
| 26 | .......... | .......... | 698 00 | .......... | .......... | .......... |
| 27 | 343 00 | .......... | 88,951 19 | .......... | .......... | .......... |
| 28 | **$5,491 82** | .......... | **$107,402 99** | .......... | .......... | .......... |
| 29 | .......... | .......... | .......... | .......... | .......... | .......... |
| 30 | .......... | .......... | .......... | .......... | .......... | .......... |
| 31 | .......... | .......... | .......... | .......... | .......... | .......... |
| 32 | **$354,247 71** | **$23,156 12** | **$447,023 64** | **$39 27** | **$206,967 88** | .......... |
| 33 | **$4,525 25** | .......... | **$489 92** | .......... | .......... | .......... |

STATEMENT SHOWING EXPENDITURES FROM REVENUE (SPECIAL REVENUE

| | Total | Personal Service | Supplies | LINE No. |
|---|---|---|---|---|
| CITY DEPARTMENTS—*Continued* | | | | |
| Borough Presidents and Subordinate Departments. | | | | |
| President of Manhattan | $348,799 00 | .......... | .......... | 1 |
| President of The Bronx | 8,982 82 | $2,703 64 | $21 92 | 2 |
| President of Brooklyn | 10,706 27 | 6,230 82 | 36 64 | 3 |
| President of Queens | 48,351 15 | 9,989 36 | .......... | 4 |
| President of Richmond | 2,787 48 | 2,470 33 | .......... | 5 |
| Total, Borough Presidents | **$419,626 72** | **$21,394 15** | **$58 56** | 6 |
| Board of Aldermen, President of Board and City Clerk | **$48,691 24** | **$4,496 14** | **$2,500 00** | 7 |
| Boards, Commissions, etc., whose members are not elected by popular vote, and who are not appointed by any elected City Official: | | | | |
| Court House Board | $572 40 | $572 40 | .......... | 8 |
| Public Service Commission | 1,100,460 87 | 884,012 25 | $12,089 61 | 9 |
| Total | **$1,101,033 27** | **$884,584 65** | **$12,089 61** | 10 |
| Boards, Commissions, etc., of mixed responsibility, i.e., ex-officio bodies representing two or more preceding branches: | | | | |
| Armory Board | $4,812 92 | $1,939 92 | .......... | 11 |
| Board of Estimate and Apportionment | 7,236 26 | 7,236 26 | .......... | 12 |
| Total | **$12,049 18** | **$9,176 18** | .......... | 13 |
| Courts, including Board of Parole and General Interpreters of Brooklyn: | | | | |
| Coroners, Borough of Manhattan | $3,082 45 | .......... | .......... | 14 |
| Coroners, Borough of Brooklyn | 1,544 03 | .......... | .......... | 15 |
| City Magistrates' Courts, First Division | 12,475 45 | $6,999 98 | .......... | 16 |
| City Magistrates' Courts, Second Division | 13,102 88 | 9,936 67 | $253 48 | 17 |
| Municipal Courts, City of New York | 10,735 48 | .......... | 12 54 | 18 |
| Court of Special Sessions | 41,209 81 | 28,082 60 | 130 00 | 19 |
| Total | **$82,150 10** | **$45,019 25** | **$396 02** | 20 |
| Total City Departments, Offices, Courts, etc | **$3,386,962 51** | **$1,460,576 32** | **$206,100 15** | 21 |
| DEBT SERVICE | **$7,500 00** | .......... | .......... | 22 |
| FIXED CHARGES OTHER THAN DEBT SERVICE, SUBSIDIES, CONTRIBUTIONS, PAYMENTS TO PRIVATE AND STATE INSTITUTIONS, EXPENDITURES NOT ALLOTTED TO DEPARTMENTS: | | | | |
| Charitable Institutions, City | $487 50 | .......... | .......... | 23 |
| Claims | 287,795 36 | $50,021 31 | .......... | 24 |
| Miscellaneous, City | 690,455 02 | .......... | .......... | 25 |
| New York Public Library | 15,686 32 | 5,519 18 | $10,167 14 | 26 |
| Total | **$994,424 20** | **$55,540 49** | **$10,167 14** | 27 |
| Total for City Purposes | **$4,388,886 41** | **$1,516,116 81** | **$216,267 29** | 28 |

## NEW YORK

BOND FUNDS) FOR THE YEAR 1911, CLASSIFIED BY OBJECTS OF EXPENDITURE:—*Continued*

| LINE No. | Purchase of Equipment | Materials | Contract or Open Order Service | Contingencies | Fixed Charges and Contributions | Unclassified |
|---|---|---|---|---|---|---|
| 1 | .......... | .......... | $348,799 00 | .......... | .......... | .......... |
| 2 | $45 60 | $116 80 | 6,009 38 | .......... | $85 48 | .......... |
| 3 | 1,831 02 | 49 18 | 2,558 61 | .......... | .......... | .......... |
| 4 | 7,810 59 | .......... | 30,551 20 | .......... | .......... | .......... |
| 5 | .......... | .......... | 317 15 | .......... | .......... | .......... |
| 6 | **$9,687 21** | **$165 98** | **$388,235 34** | .......... | **$85 48** | .......... |
| 7 | .......... | .......... | **$722 18** | **$766 90** | .......... | **$40,206 02** |
| 8 | .......... | .......... | .......... | .......... | .......... | .......... |
| 9 | $11,932 45 | .......... | $110,909 29 | .......... | $70,548 11 | $10,969 16 |
| 10 | **$11,932 45** | .......... | **$110,909 29** | .......... | **$70,548 11** | **$10,969 16** |
| 11 | .......... | .......... | $2,873 00 | .......... | .......... | .......... |
| 12 | .......... | .......... | .......... | .......... | .......... | .......... |
| 13 | .......... | .......... | **$2,873 00** | .......... | .......... | .......... |
| 14 | $3,082 45 | .......... | .......... | .......... | .......... | .......... |
| 15 | 820 63 | .......... | $723 40 | .......... | .......... | .......... |
| 16 | 5,320 06 | .......... | 155 41 | .......... | .......... | .......... |
| 17 | 2,843 76 | .......... | 68 97 | .......... | .......... | .......... |
| 18 | 9,254 76 | .......... | 1,468 18 | .......... | .......... | .......... |
| 19 | 10,952 55 | .......... | 207 42 | $612 24 | $1,225 00 | .......... |
| 20 | **$32,274 21** | .......... | **$2,623 38** | **$612 24** | **$1,225 00** | .......... |
| 21 | **$412,666 83** | **$23,322 10** | **$952,876 75** | **$1,418 41** | **$278,826 47** | **$51,175 18** |
| 22 | .......... | .......... | .......... | .......... | **$7,500 00** | .......... |
| 23 | .......... | .......... | .......... | .......... | $487 50 | .......... |
| 24 | .......... | .......... | .......... | .......... | .......... | $237,774 05 |
| 25 | .......... | .......... | .......... | .......... | 156,028 52 | 534,426 50 |
| 26 | .......... | .......... | .......... | .......... | .......... | .......... |
| 27 | .......... | .......... | .......... | .......... | **$156,516 02** | **$772,200 55** |
| 28 | **$412,666 83** | **$23,322 10** | **$952,876 75** | **$1,418 41** | **$442,842 49** | **$823,375 73** |

STATEMENT SHOWING EXPENDITURES FROM REVENUE (SPECIAL REVENUE

| | Total | Personal Service | Supplies | LINE No. |
|---|---|---|---|---|
| COUNTY EXPENDITURES: | | | | |
| New York County: | | | | |
| County Clerk | $1,586 45 | $851 20 | .......... | 1 |
| Surrogate's Court | 800 28 | .......... | $800 28 | 2 |
| District Attorney | 21,054 86 | 16,252 01 | .......... | 3 |
| Miscellaneous | 215,348 57 | .......... | .......... | 4 |
| Register | 1,578 83 | 1,578 83 | .......... | 5 |
| Sheriff | 1 99 | .......... | 1 99 | 6 |
| Total | **$240,370 98** | **$18,682 04** | **$802 27** | 7 |
| Kings County: | | | | |
| County Clerk | $8,504 08 | $8,504 08 | .......... | 8 |
| County Court | 5,591 88 | 3,000 00 | .......... | 9 |
| Supreme Court, Second Department | 291 63 | 291 63 | .......... | 10 |
| Surrogate's Court | 3,373 33 | 3,373 33 | .......... | 11 |
| District Attorney | 17,489 71 | 15,182 83 | .......... | 12 |
| Miscellaneous | 58,825 07 | .......... | .......... | 13 |
| Sheriff | 5,136 45 | 5,136 45 | .......... | 14 |
| Total | **$99,212 15** | **$35,488 32** | .......... | 15 |
| Queens County: | | | | |
| County Clerk | $9,219 63 | $9,046 31 | .......... | 16 |
| District Attorney | 7,701 18 | 6,641 03 | $468 81 | 17 |
| Miscellaneous | 14,059 11 | .......... | .......... | 18 |
| Sheriff | 733 30 | 733 30 | .......... | 19 |
| Total | **$31,713 22** | **$16,420 64** | **$468 81** | 20 |
| Richmond County: | | | | |
| County Clerk | $561 95 | $561 95 | .......... | 21 |
| County Court and Surrogate's Court | 62 50 | 62 50 | .......... | 22 |
| District Attorney | 313 86 | 313 86 | .......... | 23 |
| Miscellaneous | 3,295 95 | .......... | .......... | 24 |
| Sheriff | 2,478 33 | 736 67 | $1,619 31 | 25 |
| Total | **$6,712 59** | **$1,674 98** | **$1,619 31** | 26 |
| Total for County Purposes | **$378,008 94** | **$72,265 98** | **$2,890 39** | 27 |
| Total for All Purposes | **$4,766,895 35** | **$1,588,382 79** | **$219,157 68** | 28 |

## NEW YORK

BOND FUNDS) FOR THE YEAR 1911, CLASSIFIED BY OBJECTS OF EXPENDITURE:—*Continued*

| LINE No. | Purchase of Equipment | Materials | Contract or Open Order Service | Contingencies | Fixed Charges and Contributions | Unclassified |
|---|---|---|---|---|---|---|
| 1 | .......... | .......... | .......... | $735 25 | .......... | .......... |
| 2 | .......... | .......... | .......... | .......... | .......... | .......... |
| 3 | $841 96 | .......... | $41 35 | .......... | $576 50 | $3,343 04 |
| 4 | .......... | .......... | .......... | .......... | .......... | 215,348 57 |
| 5 | .......... | .......... | .......... | .......... | .......... | .......... |
| 6 | .......... | .......... | .......... | .......... | .......... | .......... |
| 7 | **$841 96** | .......... | **$41 35** | **$735 25** | **$576 50** | **$218,691 61** |
| 8 | .......... | .......... | .......... | .......... | .......... | .......... |
| 9 | $2,591 88 | .......... | .......... | .......... | .......... | .......... |
| 10 | .......... | .......... | .......... | .......... | .......... | .......... |
| 11 | .......... | .......... | .......... | .......... | .......... | .......... |
| 12 | 114 50 | .......... | $381 95 | $1,810 43 | .......... | .......... |
| 13 | .......... | .......... | .......... | .......... | .......... | $58,825 07 |
| 14 | .......... | .......... | .......... | .......... | .......... | .......... |
| 15 | **$2,706 38** | .......... | **$381 95** | **$1,810 43** | .......... | **$58,825 07** |
| 16 | $173 32 | .......... | .......... | .......... | .......... | .......... |
| 17 | 3 41 | .......... | $268 22 | $319 71 | .......... | .......... |
| 18 | .......... | .......... | .......... | .......... | .......... | $14,059 11 |
| 19 | .......... | .......... | .......... | .......... | .......... | .......... |
| 20 | **$176 73** | .......... | **$268 22** | **$319 71** | .......... | **$14,059 11** |
| 21 | .......... | .......... | .......... | .......... | .......... | .......... |
| 22 | .......... | .......... | .......... | .......... | .......... | .......... |
| 23 | .......... | .......... | .......... | .......... | .......... | .......... |
| 24 | .......... | .......... | .......... | .......... | .......... | $3,295 95 |
| 25 | .......... | .......... | $122 35 | .......... | .......... | .......... |
| 26 | .......... | .......... | **$122 35** | .......... | .......... | **$3,295 95** |
| 27 | **$3,725 07** | .......... | **$813 87** | **$2,865 39** | **$576 50** | **$294,871 74** |
| 28 | **$416,391 90** | **$23,322 10** | **$953,690 62** | **$4,283 80** | **$443,418 99** | **$1,118,247 47** |

THE CITY OF

RECAPITULATION OF STATEMENT SHOWING EXPENDITURES FROM REVENUE (SPECIAL

| | Total | Personal Service | Supplies | LINE No. |
|---|---|---|---|---|
| CITY DEPARTMENTS, OFFICES, COURTS, ETC. | | | | |
| Mayor and Subordinate Departments, Bureaus and Offices: | | | | |
| Mayor's Office and Departments whose executive heads are appointed by the Mayor and who are removable at his pleasure......... | $1,592,714 13 | $542,820 16 | $98,767 01 | 1 |
| Departments whose heads are appointed by the Mayor for a term of office greater than his own, and who are removable only on charges. | 117,541 88 | 7,766 65 | 73,380 72 | 2 |
| Boards and Commissions, majority of which are appointed by the Mayor and for which no other elected City official shares responsibility. | 3,015 92 | 75 00 | 854 39 | 3 |
| Total Mayor and Subordinate Departments, Bureaus and Offices............ | **$1,713,271 93** | **$550,661 81** | **$173,002 12** | 4 |
| Borough Presidents and Subordinate Departments: | | | | |
| President, Borough of Manhattan............. | $152,022 81 | .......... | $48 60 | 5 |
| President, Borough of The Bronx............. | 16,415 98 | $7,659 11 | 73 50 | 6 |
| President, Borough of Brooklyn.............. | 69,559 69 | 2,947 36 | 3,119 44 | 7 |
| President, Borough of Queens................ | 73,762 27 | 13,951 97 | 323 55 | 8 |
| President, Borough of Richmond.............. | 7,963 32 | 2,788 56 | 868 55 | 9 |
| Total, Borough Presidents............... | **$319,724 07** | **$27,347 00** | **$4,433 64** | 10 |
| Board of Aldermen, President of Board and City Clerk.................................. | **$114,124 70** | **$26,457 01** | .......... | 11 |
| Boards, Commissions, etc., whose members are not elected by popular vote and who are not appointed by any elected City official...... | **$1,362,093 32** | **$1,129,636 71** | **$49,244 52** | 12 |
| Boards, Commissions, etc., of mixed responsibility, i.e., ex-officio bodies representing two or more of preceding branches.................... | **$360,806 71** | **$121,851 00** | .......... | 13 |
| Courts, including Board of Parole and General Interpreters of Brooklyn.................. | **$13,837 85** | **$3,760 00** | **$294 87** | 14 |
| Total City Departments, Offices, Courts, etc.................................. | **$3,883,858 58** | **$1,859,713 53** | **$226,975 15** | 15 |
| FIXED CHARGES OTHER THAN DEBT SERVICE, SUBSIDIES, CONTRIBUTIONS, PAYMENTS TO PRIVATE AND STATE INSTITUTIONS, EXPENDITURES NOT ALLOTTED TO DEPARTMENTS................. | **$2,102,559 71** | **$124,367 94** | **$746 29** | 16 |
| Total for City Purposes................ | **$5,986,418 29** | **$1,984,081 47** | **$227,721 44** | 17 |
| COUNTY EXPENDITURES: | | | | |
| New York County.......................... | $134,051 40 | $118,083 94 | $495 65 | 18 |
| Kings County............................. | 31,900 12 | 26,295 20 | 911 72 | 19 |
| Queens County............................ | 55,245 10 | 11,045 74 | 594 00 | 20 |
| Richmond County.......................... | 3,361 03 | 3,361 03 | .......... | 21 |
| Total for County Purposes.............. | **$224,557 65** | **$158,785 91** | **$2,001 37** | 22 |
| Total for All Purposes................. | **$6,210,975 94** | **$2,142,867 38** | **$229,722 81** | 23 |

## NEW YORK

REVENUE BOND FUNDS) FOR THE YEAR 1912, CLASSIFIED BY OBJECTS OF EXPENDITURE:

| LINE No. | Purchase of Equipment | Materials | Contract or Open Order Service | Contingencies | Fixed Charges and Contributions | Unclassified |
|---|---|---|---|---|---|---|
| 1 | $192,950 71 | $19,527 12 | $220,747 75 | $8,719 96 | $506,485 39 | $2,696 03 |
| 2 | 10,067 06 | .......... | 26,327 45 | .......... | .......... | .......... |
| 3 | 256 07 | .......... | 373 34 | .......... | .......... | 1,457 12 |
| 4 | **$203,273 84** | **$19,527 12** | **$247,448 54** | **$8,719 96** | **$506,485 39** | **$4,153 15** |
| 5 | $1,143 87 | $9,386 06 | $141,444 28 | .......... | .......... | .......... |
| 6 | 204 79 | 567 40 | 7,861 18 | .......... | $50 00 | .......... |
| 7 | 6,510 62 | 156 41 | 48,785 29 | .......... | .......... | $8,040 57 |
| 8 | 3,053 03 | 709 77 | 55,723 95 | .......... | .......... | .......... |
| 9 | 701 21 | .......... | 3,605 00 | .......... | .......... | .......... |
| 10 | **$11,613 52** | **$10,819 64** | **$257,419 70** | .......... | **$50 00** | **$8,040 57** |
| 11 | .......... | .......... | **$75,668 69** | **$250 00** | .......... | **$11,749 00** |
| 12 | **$11,071 64** | .......... | **$90,375 99** | .......... | **$72,729 85** | **$9,034 61** |
| 13 | **$748 00** | .......... | **$236,067 71** | **$2,140 00** | .......... | .......... |
| 14 | **$9,434 68** | .......... | **$348 30** | .......... | .......... | .......... |
| 15 | **$236,141 68** | **$30,346 76** | **$907,328 93** | **$11,109 96** | **$579,265 24** | **$32,977 33** |
| 16 | **$1,063 87** | .......... | **$35,097 31** | .......... | **$26,405 20** | **$1,914,879 10** |
| 17 | **$237,205 55** | **$30,346 76** | **$942,426 24** | **$11,109 96** | **$605,670 44** | **$1,947,856 43** |
| 18 | .......... | .......... | $1,041 48 | $14,430 33 | .......... | .......... |
| 19 | $2,357 22 | .......... | 411 64 | 1,924 34 | .......... | .......... |
| 20 | 5,698 00 | .......... | 37,907 36 | .......... | .......... | .......... |
| 21 | .......... | .......... | .......... | .......... | .......... | .......... |
| 22 | **$8,055 22** | .......... | **$39,360 48** | **$16,354 67** | .......... | .......... |
| 23 | **$245,260 77** | **$30,346 76** | **$981,786 72** | **$27,464 63** | **$605,670 44** | **$1,947,856 43** |

STATEMENT SHOWING EXPENDITURES FROM REVENUE (SPECIAL REVENUE BOND

| | Total | Personal Service | Supplies | LINE No. |
|---|---|---|---|---|
| CITY DEPARTMENTS, OFFICES, COURTS, ETC. | | | | |
| Mayor and Subordinate Departments, Bureaus and Offices: | | | | |
| Mayor's Office and Departments whose executive heads are appointed by the Mayor, and who are removable at his pleasure: | | | | |
| Commissioners of Accounts | $11,353 27 | $6,103 03 | $1,485 97 | 1 |
| Board of Assessors | 150 00 | 150 00 | .......... | 2 |
| Department of Bridges | 253,218 82 | 213,480 92 | 12,758 67 | 3 |
| Department of Correction | 7,974 42 | 7,974 42 | .......... | 4 |
| Department of Docks and Ferries | 17,410 00 | .......... | .......... | 5 |
| Fire Department | 266,471 07 | .......... | .......... | 6 |
| Department of Health | 7,004 46 | 10,464 02 | 13,782 62 | 7 |
| Law Department | 34,081 03 | 33,339 44 | 62 00 | 8 |
| Mayoralty—Bureau of Licenses | 5,090 05 | 2,332 48 | 351 62 | 9 |
| Mayoralty—Bureau of Weights and Measures | 1,607 89 | 627 63 | 116 15 | 10 |
| Municipal Civil Service Commission | 14,959 06 | 10,773 69 | .......... | 11 |
| Municipal Explosives Commission | 255 00 | 255 00 | .......... | 12 |
| Department of Parks—Manhattan and Richmond | 97,924 28 | 48,759 64 | 9,188 85 | 13 |
| Department of Parks—The Bronx | 26,140 97 | .......... | .......... | 14 |
| Department of Parks—Queens | 3,753 75 | 2,803 75 | .......... | 15 |
| Police Department | 439,073 88 | 61,189 09 | .......... | 16 |
| Department of Public Charities | 83,379 91 | 56,818 77 | 10,362 71 | 17 |
| Department of Street Cleaning | 201,517 77 | 36,982 23 | 48,001 96 | 18 |
| Department of Taxes and Assessments | 54,961 59 | 45,976 97 | 2,711 46 | 19 |
| Department of Water Supply, Gas and Electricity | 66,366 91 | 4,789 08 | *55 00* | 20 |
| Total | **$1,592,714 13** | **$542,820 16** | **$98,767 01** | 21 |
| Departments whose heads are appointed by the Mayor for a term of office greater than his own, and who are removable only on charges: | | | | |
| Bellevue and Allied Hospitals | $22,270 90 | $7,677 51 | .......... | 22 |
| College of the City of New York | 605 35 | .......... | .......... | 23 |
| Department of Education | 94,665 63 | 89 14 | $73,380 72 | 24 |
| Total | **$117,541 88** | **$7,766 65** | **$73,380 72** | 25 |
| Boards and Commissions, majorities of which are appointed by the Mayor and for which no other elected City official shares responsibility: | | | | |
| Committee on Congestion of Population | $1,457 12 | .......... | .......... | 26 |
| Board of Inebriety | 84 36 | .......... | .......... | 27 |
| Public Recreation Commission | 1,474 44 | $75 00 | $854 39 | 28 |
| Total | **$3,015 92** | **$75 00** | **$854 39** | 29 |
| Total, Mayor and Subordinate Departments, Bureaus and Offices | **$1,713,271 93** | **$550,661 81** | **$173,002 12** | 30 |
| Borough Presidents and Subordinate Departments: | | | | |
| President, Borough of Manhattan | $152,022 81 | .......... | $48 60 | 31 |
| President, Borough of The Bronx | 16,415 98 | $7,659 11 | 73 50 | 32 |
| President, Borough of Brooklyn | 69,559 69 | 2,947 36 | 3,119 44 | 33 |
| President, Borough of Queens | 73,762 27 | 13,951 97 | 323 55 | 34 |
| President, Borough of Richmond | 7,963 32 | 2,788 56 | 868 55 | 35 |
| Total | **$319,724 07** | **$27,347 00** | **$4,433 64** | 36 |
| Board of Aldermen, President of Board and City Clerk | **$114,124 70** | **$26,457 01** | .......... | 37 |

NEW YORK

FUNDS), FOR THE YEAR 1912, CLASSIFIED BY OBJECTS OF EXPENDITURE:

| LINE No. | Purchase of Equipment | Materials | Contract or Open Order Service | Contingencies | Fixed Charges and Contributions | Unclassified |
|---|---|---|---|---|---|---|
| 1 | $3,696 71 | .......... | $67 56 | .......... | .......... | .......... |
| 2 | .......... | .......... | .......... | .......... | .......... | .......... |
| 3 | 15,659 18 | $8,550 58 | 2,769 47 | .......... | .......... | .......... |
| 4 | .......... | .......... | .......... | .......... | .......... | .......... |
| 5 | .......... | .......... | 17,410 00 | .......... | .......... | .......... |
| 6 | 137,763 50 | .......... | 106 97 | .......... | $128,600 60 | .......... |
| 7 | 8,541 05 | .......... | 28,268 39 | $2,485 16 | .......... | .......... |
| 8 | 12 35 | .......... | 667 24 | .......... | .......... | .......... |
| 9 | 147.83 | .......... | 855 71 | 1,402 41 | .......... | .......... |
| 10 | 864 11 | .......... | .......... | .......... | .......... | .......... |
| 11 | .......... | 32 35 | 1,267 00 | 2,886 02 | .......... | .......... |
| 12 | .......... | .......... | .......... | .......... | .......... | .......... |
| 13 | 2,900 57 | 1,571 08 | 32,808 11 | .......... | .......... | $2,696 03 |
| 14 | 2,000 00 | .......... | 24,140 97 | .......... | .......... | .......... |
| 15 | 950 00 | .......... | .......... | .......... | .......... | .......... |
| 16 | .......... | .......... | .......... | .......... | 377,884 79 | .......... |
| 17 | 10,254 21 | 1,615 00 | 3,329 22 | 1,000 00 | .......... | .......... |
| 18 | 6,433 00 | .......... | 110,120 58 | .......... | .......... | .......... |
| 19 | 2,823 76 | .......... | 3,449 40 | .......... | .......... | .......... |
| 20 | 904 44 | 7,758 11 | 52,023 91 | 946 37 | .......... | .......... |
| 21 | **$192,950 71** | **$19,527 12** | **$220,747 75** | **$8,719 96** | **$506,485 39** | **$2,696 03** |
| 22 | $9,768 06 | .......... | $4,825 33 | .......... | .......... | .......... |
| 23 | .......... | .......... | 605 35 | .......... | .......... | .......... |
| 24 | 299 00 | .......... | 20,896 77 | .......... | .......... | .......... |
| 25 | **$10,067 06** | .......... | **$26,327 45** | .......... | .......... | .......... |
| 26 | .......... | .......... | .......... | .......... | .......... | $1,457 12 |
| 27 | $54 17 | .......... | $30 19 | .......... | .......... | .......... |
| 28 | 201 90 | .......... | 343 15 | .......... | .......... | .......... |
| 29 | **$256 07** | .......... | **$373 34** | .......... | .......... | **$1,457 12** |
| 30 | **$203,273 84** | **$19,527 12** | **$247,448 54** | **$8,719 96** | **$506,485 39** | **$4,153 15** |
| 31 | $1,143 87 | $9,386 06 | $141,444 28 | .......... | .......... | .......... |
| 32 | 204 79 | 567 40 | 7,861 18 | .......... | $50 00 | .......... |
| 33 | 6,510 62 | 156 41 | 48,785 29 | .......... | .......... | $8,040 57 |
| 34 | 3,053 03 | 709 77 | 55,723 95 | .......... | .......... | .......... |
| 35 | 701 21 | .......... | 3,605 00 | .......... | .......... | .......... |
| 36 | **$11,613 52** | **$10,819 64** | **$257,419 70** | .......... | **$50 00** | **$8,040 57** |
| 37 | .......... | .......... | **$75,668 69** | **$250 00** | .......... | **$11,749 00** |

THE CITY OF

STATEMENT SHOWING EXPENDITURES FROM REVENUE (SPECIAL REVENUE

| | Total | Personal Service | Supplies | LINE No. |
|---|---|---|---|---|
| CITY DEPARTMENTS—*Continued* | | | | |
| Boards, Commissions, etc., whose members are not elected by popular vote and who are not appointed by any elected City official: | | | | |
| Commission on Lunacy | $3,590 30 | $3,590 30 | .......... | 1 |
| Public Service Commission | 1,358,503 02 | 1,126,046 41 | $49,244 52 | 2 |
| Total | **$1,362,093 32** | **$1,129,636 71** | **$49,244 52** | 3 |
| Boards, Commissions, etc., of mixed responsibility, i.e., ex-officio bodies representing two or more preceding branches: | | | | |
| Armory Board | $30,763 50 | $9,336 50 | .......... | 4 |
| Board of Elections | 330,043 21 | 112,514 50 | .......... | 5 |
| Total | **$360,806 71** | **$121,851 00** | .......... | 6 |
| Courts, including Board of Parole and General Interpreters of Brooklyn: | | | | |
| Coroners, Borough of The Bronx | $2,030 60 | $130 00 | $294 87 | 7 |
| City Magistrates' Courts, First Division | 4,425 32 | 3,500 00 | .......... | 8 |
| City Magistrates' Courts, Second Division | 1,620 02 | 130 00 | .......... | 9 |
| Court of Special Sessions | 5,761 91 | .......... | .......... | 10 |
| Total | **$13,837 85** | **$3,760 00** | **$294 87** | 11 |
| Total City Departments, Offices, Courts, etc | **$3,883,858 58** | **$1,859,713 53** | **$226,975 15** | 12 |
| FIXED CHARGES OTHER THAN DEBT SERVICE, SUBSIDIES, CONTRIBUTIONS, PAYMENTS TO PRIVATE AND STATE INSTITUTIONS, EXPENDITURES NOT ALLOTTED TO DEPARTMENTS: | | | | |
| Claims | $1,582,360 56 | $95,213 67 | .......... | 13 |
| Miscellaneous, City | 518,348 43 | 29,154 27 | .......... | 14 |
| Miscellaneous, Inactive Accounts | 1,850 72 | .......... | $746 29 | 15 |
| Total | **$2,102,559 71** | **$124,367 94** | **$746 29** | 16 |
| Total for City Purposes | **$5,986,418 29** | **$1,984,081 47** | **$227,721 44** | 17 |
| COUNTY EXPENDITURES: | | | | |
| New York County: | | | | |
| Court of General Sessions | $214 42 | $214 42 | .......... | 18 |
| Supreme Court, First Department | 46,254 18 | 46,238 53 | $15 65 | 19 |
| Surrogates' Court | 15,580 87 | 15,441 97 | .......... | 20 |
| District Attorney | 33,350 07 | 18,919 74 | .......... | 21 |
| Miscellaneous | 17,307 15 | 17,307 15 | .......... | 22 |
| Commissioner of Records | 12,031 67 | 11,551 67 | 480 00 | 23 |
| Sheriff | 9,313 04 | 8,410 46 | .......... | 24 |
| Total | **$134,051 40** | **$118,083 94** | **$495 65** | 25 |
| Kings County: | | | | |
| County Clerk | $6,026 58 | $6,026 58 | .......... | 26 |
| Court, County | 348 20 | .......... | $348 20 | 27 |
| Court, Supreme, Second Department | 50 00 | 50 00 | .......... | 28 |
| Court, Surrogate's | 3,257 24 | 3,257 24 | .......... | 29 |
| District Attorney | 2,370 70 | 170 00 | 60 40 | 30 |
| Commissioner of Jurors | 1,689 22 | .......... | 156 03 | 31 |
| Public Administrator | 12,613 83 | 11,247 03 | 347 09 | 32 |
| Register | 2,100 00 | 2,100 00 | .......... | 33 |
| Sheriff | 3,444 35 | 3,444 35 | .......... | 34 |
| Total | **$31,900 12** | **$26,295 20** | **$911 72** | 35 |

NEW YORK

Bond Funds) for the Year 1912, Classified by Objects of Expenditure:—*Continued*

| LINE No. | Purchase of Equipment | Materials | Contract or Open Order Service | Contingencies | Fixed Charges and Contributions | Unclassified |
|---|---|---|---|---|---|---|
| 1 | .......... | .......... | .......... | .......... | .......... | .......... |
| 2 | $11,071 64 | .......... | $90,375 99 | .......... | $72,729 85 | $9,034 61 |
| 3 | **$11,071 64** | .......... | **$90,375 99** | .......... | **$72,729 85** | **$9,034 61** |
| 4 | .......... | .......... | $21,427 00 | .......... | .......... | .......... |
| 5 | $748 00 | .......... | 214,640 71 | $2,140 00 | .......... | .......... |
| 6 | **$748 00** | .......... | **$236,067 71** | **$2,140 00** | .......... | .......... |
| 7 | $1,279 43 | .......... | $326 30 | .......... | .......... | .......... |
| 8 | 925 32 | .......... | .......... | .......... | .......... | .......... |
| 9 | 1,490 02 | .......... | .......... | .......... | .......... | .......... |
| 10 | 5,739 91 | .......... | 22 00 | .......... | .......... | .......... |
| 11 | **$9,434 68** | .......... | **$348 30** | .......... | .......... | .......... |
| 12 | **$236,141 68** | **$30,346 76** | **$907,328 93** | **$11,109 96** | **$579,265 24** | **$32,977 33** |
| 13 | .......... | .......... | $28,676 50 | .......... | $357 07 | $1,458,113 32 |
| 14 | $854 25 | .......... | 5,526 00 | .......... | 26,048 13 | 456,765 78 |
| 15 | 209 62 | .......... | 894 81 | .......... | .......... | .......... |
| 16 | **$1,063 87** | .......... | **$35,097 31** | .......... | **$26,405 20** | **$1,914,879 10** |
| 17 | **$237,205 55** | **$30,346 76** | **$942,426 24** | **$11,109 96** | **$605,670 44** | **$1,947,856 43** |
| 18 | .......... | .......... | .......... | .......... | .......... | .......... |
| 19 | .......... | .......... | .......... | .......... | .......... | .......... |
| 20 | .......... | .......... | $138 90 | .......... | .......... | .......... |
| 21 | .......... | .......... | .......... | $14,430 33 | .......... | .......... |
| 22 | .......... | .......... | .......... | .......... | .......... | .......... |
| 23 | .......... | .......... | .......... | .......... | .......... | .......... |
| 24 | .......... | .......... | 902 58 | .......... | .......... | .......... |
| 25 | .......... | .......... | **$1,041 48** | **$14,430 33** | .......... | .......... |
| 26 | .......... | .......... | .......... | .......... | .......... | .......... |
| 27 | .......... | .......... | .......... | .......... | .......... | .......... |
| 28 | .......... | .......... | .......... | .......... | .......... | .......... |
| 29 | .......... | .......... | .......... | .......... | .......... | .......... |
| 30 | .......... | .......... | $219 96 | $1,920 34 | .......... | .......... |
| 31 | $1,533 19 | .......... | .......... | .......... | .......... | .......... |
| 32 | 824 03 | .......... | 191 68 | 4 00 | .......... | .......... |
| 33 | .......... | .......... | .......... | .......... | .......... | .......... |
| 34 | .......... | .......... | .......... | .......... | .......... | .......... |
| 35 | **$2,357 22** | .......... | **$411 64** | **$1,924 34** | .......... | .......... |

STATEMENT SHOWING EXPENDITURES FROM REVENUE (SPECIAL REVENUE

| | Total | Personal Service | Supplies | LINE No. |
|---|---|---|---|---|
| COUNTY EXPENDITURES—*Continued* | | | | |
| Queens County: | | | | |
| County Clerk | $43,699 64 | .......... | $594 00 | 1 |
| Court, County | 3,883 10 | $3,883 10 | .......... | 2 |
| Court, Supreme, Second Department | 6,350 14 | 6,350 14 | .......... | 3 |
| District Attorney | 812 50 | 812 50 | .......... | 4 |
| Sheriff | 499 72 | .......... | .......... | 5 |
| Total | **$55,245 10** | **$11,045 74** | **$594 00** | 6 |
| Richmond County: | | | | |
| County Clerk | $819 35 | $819 35 | .......... | 7 |
| Court, County | 1,666 68 | 1,666 68 | .......... | 8 |
| Sheriff | 875 00 | 875 00 | .......... | 9 |
| Total | **$3,361 03** | **$3,361 03** | .......... | 10 |
| Total for County Purposes | **$224,557 65** | **$158,785 91** | **$2,001 37** | 11 |
| Total for All Purposes | **$6,210,975 94** | **$2,142,867 38** | **$229,722 81** | 12 |

NEW YORK

BOND FUNDS) THE YEAR 1912, CLASSIFIED BY OBJECTS OF EXPENDITURE:—*Continued*

| LINE No. | Purchase of Equipment | Materials | Contract or Open Order Service | Contingencies | Fixed Charges and Contributions | Unclassified |
|---|---|---|---|---|---|---|
| 1 | $5,698 00 | .......... | $37,407 64 | .......... | .......... | .......... |
| 2 | .......... | .......... | .......... | .......... | .......... | .......... |
| 3 | .......... | .......... | .......... | .......... | .......... | .......... |
| 4 | .......... | .......... | .......... | .......... | .......... | .......... |
| 5 | .......... | .......... | 499 72 | .......... | .......... | .......... |
| 6 | **$5,698 00** | .......... | **$37,907 36** | .......... | .......... | .......... |
| 7 | .......... | .......... | .......... | .......... | .......... | .......... |
| 8 | .......... | .......... | .......... | .......... | .......... | .......... |
| 9 | .......... | .......... | .......... | .......... | .......... | .......... |
| 10 | .......... | .......... | .......... | .......... | .......... | .......... |
| 11 | **$8,055 22** | .......... | **$39,360 48** | **$16,354 67** | .......... | .......... |
| 12 | **$245,260 77** | **$30,346 76** | **$981,786 72** | **$27,464 63** | **$605,670 44** | **$1,947,856 43** |

THE CITY OF

Recapitulation of Statement Showing Expenditures from Revenue (Special

| | Total | Personal Service | Supplies | Line No. |
|---|---|---|---|---|
| City Departments, Offices, Courts, Etc.: | | | | |
| Mayor and Subordinate Departments, Bureaus and Offices: | | | | |
| Mayor's Office and Departments whose Executive heads are appointed by the Mayor and who are removable at his pleasure.......... | $1,039,544 06 | $263,922 33 | $190,720 05 | 1 |
| Departments whose heads are appointed by the Mayor for a term of office greater than his own, and who are removable only on charges. | 138,852 75 | 30,992 46 | 69,913 57 | 2 |
| Boards and Commissions, majorities of which are appointed by the Mayor and for which no other elected City official shares responsibility | 5,852 01 | 756 81 | 967 00 | 3 |
| Total Mayor and Subordinate Departments, Bureaus and Offices............ | **$1,184,248 82** | **$295,671 60** | **$261,600 62** | 4 |
| Borough Presidents and Subordinate Departments: | | | | |
| President, Borough of Manhattan............ | $143,446 95 | $8,853 29 | $7,764 76 | 5 |
| President, Borough of The Bronx............ | 40,147 05 | 493 31 | .......... | 6 |
| President, Borough of Brooklyn............ | 24,642 59 | 4,915 24 | 756 29 | 7 |
| President, Borough of Queens............ | 51,827 23 | 24,666 06 | 606 23 | 8 |
| President, Borough of Richmond............ | 12,361 50 | 3,918 21 | 638 19 | 9 |
| Total Borough Presidents.............. | **$272,425 32** | **$42,846 11** | **$9,765 47** | 10 |
| Board of Aldermen, President of Board and City Clerk.................................. | **$46,970 68** | **$24,901 37** | **$967 08** | 11 |
| Boards, Commissions, etc., whose members are not elected by popular vote and who are not appointed by any elected City official...... | **$1,864,282 12** | **$1,635,316 09** | **$77,768 25** | 12 |
| Boards, Commissions, etc., of mixed responsibility, i.e., ex-officio bodies representing two or more of preceding branches.................. | **$16,172 04** | **$16,375 50** | **$28 50** | 13 |
| Courts, including Board of Parole and General Interpreters of Brooklyn.................. | **$29,396 97** | **$25,409 53** | **$1,396 97** | 14 |
| Total City Departments, Offices, Courts, etc.............................. | **$3,413,495 95** | **$2,040,520 20** | **$351,526 89** | 15 |
| Fixed Charges other than Debt Service, Subsidies, Contributions, Payments to Private and State Institutions, Expenditures not Allotted to Departments................ | **$2,429,887 64** | **$271,078 53** | **$1,218 65** | 16 |
| Total for City Purposes................ | **$5,843,383 59** | **$2,311,598 73** | **$352,745 54** | 17 |
| County Expenditures: | | | | |
| New York County.............................. | $60,033 85 | $13,764 85 | $3,809 61 | 18 |
| Kings County.............................. | 30,225 08 | 24,090 97 | 9 00 | 19 |
| Queens County.............................. | 11,038 78 | 9,519 29 | .......... | 20 |
| Richmond County.............................. | 9,849 08 | 5,982 56 | 3,294 57 | 21 |
| Bronx County.............................. | 14,501 45 | 9,402 28 | 85 85 | 22 |
| Total for County Purposes.............. | **$125,648 24** | **$62,759 95** | **$7,199 03** | 23 |
| Total for All Purposes.................. | **$5,969,031 83** | **$2,374,358 68** | **$359,944 57** | 24 |

## NEW YORK

REVENUE BOND FUNDS) FOR THE YEAR 1913, CLASSIFIED BY OBJECTS OF EXPENDITURE

| LINE No. | Purchase of Equipment | Materials | Contract or Open Order Service | Contingencies | Fixed Charges and Contributions | Unclassified |
|---|---|---|---|---|---|---|
| 1 | $115,819 93 | $9,464 43 | $188,446 41 | $5,907 88 | $206,247 56 | $59,015 47 |
| 2 | 8,187 69 | .......... | 29,258 23 | 394 76 | .......... | 106 04 |
| 3 | 1,572 53 | .......... | 2,440 33 | 115 34 | .......... | .......... |
| 4 | **$125,580 15** | **$9,464 43** | **$220,144 97** | **$6,417 98** | **$206,247 56** | **$59,121 51** |
| 5 | $3,907 61 | .......... | $122,921 29 | .......... | .......... | .......... |
| 6 | 2,472 90 | .......... | 37,180 84 | .......... | .......... | .......... |
| 7 | 4,057 18 | $3,492 24 | 9,229 19 | .......... | .......... | $2,192 45 |
| 8 | 11,639 43 | 8,021 14 | 6,894 37 | .......... | .......... | .......... |
| 9 | 5,351 10 | .......... | 2,439 00 | .......... | $15 00 | .......... |
| 10 | **$27,428 22** | **$11,513 38** | **$178,664 69** | .......... | **$15 00** | **$2,192 45** |
| 11 | .......... | .......... | **$10,840 87** | **$869 11** | **$764 50** | **$8,627 75** |
| 12 | **$24,120 35** | .......... | **$35,211 38** | .......... | **$79,743 56** | **$12,122 49** |
| 13 | .......... | .......... | **$239 81** | **$7 85** | .......... | .......... |
| 14 | **$1,065 60** | .......... | **$1,125 27** | **$399 60** | .......... | .......... |
| 15 | **$178,194 32** | **$20,977 81** | **$445,747 37** | **$7,694 54** | **$286,770 62** | **$82,064 20** |
| 16 | **$4,978 32** | **$69 71** | **$547,975 80** | **$24,952 35** | **$931,340 07** | **$648,274 21** |
| 17 | **$183,172 64** | **$21,047 52** | **$993,723 17** | **$32,646 89** | **$1,218,110 69** | **$730,338 41** |
| 18 | $3,905 77 | .......... | $34,578 61 | $3,975 01 | .......... | .......... |
| 19 | 479 75 | .......... | 4,116 09 | 1,529 27 | .......... | .......... |
| 20 | .......... | .......... | 970 49 | 549 00 | .......... | .......... |
| 21 | .......... | .......... | 243 28 | 328 67 | .......... | .......... |
| 22 | 3,191 67 | .......... | 1,338 91 | 3 30 | $479 44 | .......... |
| 23 | **$7,577 19** | .......... | **$41,247 38** | **$6,385 25** | **$479 44** | .......... |
| 24 | **$190,749 83** | **$21,047 52** | **$1,034,970 55** | **$39,032 14** | **$1,218,590 13** | **$730,338 41** |

STATEMENT SHOWING EXPENDITURES FROM REVENUE (SPECIAL REVENUE BOND

| | Total | Personal Service | Supplies | LINE No. |
|---|---|---|---|---|
| CITY DEPARTMENTS, OFFICES, COURTS, ETC.: | | | | |
| Mayor and Subordinate Departments, Bureaus and Offices: | | | | |
| Mayor's Office and Departments, whose executive heads are appointed by the Mayor, and who are removable at his pleasure: | | | | |
| Commissioners of Accounts | $440 85 | .......... | $125 69 | 1 |
| Department of Bridges | 39,690 82 | $15,166 18 | 14,465 99 | 2 |
| Department of Correction | 38,230 63 | 9,838 37 | 26,720 99 | 3 |
| Department of Docks and Ferries | 15,209 41 | 9,985 00 | 3,622 85 | 4 |
| Examining Board of Plumbers | 3,043 30 | 2,461 50 | 97 47 | 5 |
| Fire Department | 236,625 20 | 1,150 00 | .......... | 6 |
| Department of Health | 27,816 68 | 671 40 | 119 71 | 7 |
| Law Department | 12,149 67 | 6,000 00 | 7 25 | 8 |
| Commissioner of Licenses | 2,827 69 | 2,827 69 | .......... | 9 |
| Mayoralty—Bureau of Licenses | 12,396 31 | 9,393 74 | .......... | 10 |
| Municipal Civil Service Commission | 6,572 85 | 6,140 10 | .......... | 11 |
| Municipal Explosives Commission | 4,935 00 | 4,935 00 | .......... | 12 |
| Department of Parks—Manhattan and Richmond | 43,742 51 | 199 50 | .......... | 13 |
| Department of Parks—The Bronx | 25,983 87 | .......... | 5,999 26 | 14 |
| Department of Parks—Queens | 715 00 | 715 00 | .......... | 15 |
| Police Department | 61,386 60 | 5,386 60 | .......... | 16 |
| Department of Public Charities | 148,622 91 | 25,468 46 | 87,780 13 | 17 |
| Department of Street Cleaning | 249,584 40 | 116,383 00 | 51,074 85 | 18 |
| Department of Taxes and Assessments | 43,850 69 | 42,188 38 | 705 86 | 19 |
| Department of Water Supply, Gas and Electricity | 65,719 67 | 5,012 41 | .......... | 20 |
| Total | **$1,039,544 06** | **$263,922 33** | **$190,720 05** | 21 |
| Departments, whose heads are appointed by the Mayor for a term of office greater than his own and who are removable only upon charges: | | | | |
| Bellevue and Allied Hospitals | $103,777 15 | $4,721 96 | $69,084 47 | 22 |
| College of the City of New York | 200 00 | .......... | .......... | 23 |
| Department of Education | 25,093 92 | 17,188 44 | 232 43 | 24 |
| Normal College of the City of New York | 9,781 68 | 9,082 06 | 596 67 | 25 |
| Total | **$138,852 75** | **$30,992 46** | **$69,913 57** | 26 |
| Boards and Commissions, majorities of which are appointed by the Mayor and for which no other elected official shares responsibility: | | | | |
| Board of Inebriety | $5,068 90 | $756 81 | $380 29 | 27 |
| Public Recreation Commission | 783 11 | .......... | 586 71 | 28 |
| Total | **$5,852 01** | **$756 81** | **$967 00** | 29 |
| Total Mayor and Subordinate Departments, Bureaus and Offices | **$1,184,248 82** | **$295,671 60** | **$261,600 62** | 30 |
| Borough Presidents and Subordinate Departments: | | | | |
| President of Manhattan | $143,446 95 | $8,853 29 | $7,764 76 | 31 |
| President of The Bronx | 40,147 05 | 493 31 | .......... | 32 |
| President of Brooklyn | 24,642 59 | 4,915 24 | 756 29 | 33 |
| President of Queens | 51,827 23 | 24,666 06 | 606 23 | 34 |
| President of Richmond | 12,361 50 | 3,918 21 | 638 19 | 35 |
| Total | **$272,425 32** | **$42,846 11** | **$9,765 47** | 36 |
| Board of Aldermen, President of Board and City Clerk | **$46,970 68** | **$24,901 37** | **$967 08** | 37 |

## NEW YORK

Funds) for the Year 1913, Classified by Objects of Expenditure

| LINE No. | Purchase of Equipment | Materials | Contract or Open Order Service | Contingencies | Fixed Charges and Contributions | Unclassified |
|---|---|---|---|---|---|---|
| 1 | $229 10 | .......... | $65 31 | $20 75 | .......... | .......... |
| 2 | 1,351 02 | $4,994 27 | 3,284 61 | 428 75 | .......... | .......... |
| 3 | 801 90 | 869 37 | .......... | .......... | .......... | .......... |
| 4 | 354 00 | 1,247 56 | .......... | .......... | .......... | .......... |
| 5 | 12 08 | .......... | 328 74 | 143 51 | .......... | .......... |
| 6 | 85,733 50 | .......... | .......... | .......... | $149,741 70 | .......... |
| 7 | 6,897 36 | 41 13 | 20,080 05 | 7 03 | .......... | .......... |
| 8 | 5,677 90 | .......... | 464 52 | .......... | .......... | .......... |
| 9 | .......... | .......... | .......... | .......... | .......... | .......... |
| 10 | 1,382 30 | .......... | 1,188 10 | 432 17 | .......... | .......... |
| 11 | 32 75 | .......... | 400 00 | .......... | .......... | .......... |
| 12 | .......... | .......... | .......... | .......... | .......... | .......... |
| 13 | .......... | 2,280 83 | 34,427 84 | .......... | .......... | $6,834 34 |
| 14 | .......... | .......... | 19,984 61 | .......... | .......... | .......... |
| 15 | .......... | .......... | .......... | .......... | .......... | .......... |
| 16 | .......... | .......... | .......... | .......... | 56,000 00 | .......... |
| 17 | 6,280 62 | .......... | 5,484 54 | 4,669 54 | 505 86 | 18,433 76 |
| 18 | *100 00* | .......... | 82,226 55 | .......... | .......... | .......... |
| 19 | 824 45 | .......... | 132 00 | .......... | .......... | .......... |
| 20 | 6,342 95 | 31 27 | 20,379 54 | 206 13 | .......... | 33,747 37 |
| 21 | **$115,819 93** | **$9,464 43** | **$188,446 41** | **$5,907 88** | **$206,247 56** | **$59,015 47** |
| 22 | $6,819 93 | .......... | $23,150 79 | .......... | .......... | .......... |
| 23 | .......... | .......... | 200 00 | .......... | .......... | .......... |
| 24 | 1,367 76 | .......... | 5,804 49 | $394 76 | .......... | $106 04 |
| 25 | .......... | .......... | 102 95 | .......... | .......... | .......... |
| 26 | **$8,187 69** | .......... | **$29,258 23** | **$394 76** | .......... | **$106 04** |
| 27 | $1,402 63 | .......... | $2,413 83 | $115 34 | .......... | .......... |
| 28 | 169 90 | .......... | 26 50 | .......... | .......... | .......... |
| 29 | **$1,572 53** | .......... | **$2,440 33** | **$115 34** | .......... | .......... |
| 30 | **$125,580 15** | **$9,464 43** | **$220,144 97** | **$6,417 98** | **$206,247 56** | **$59,121 51** |
| 31 | $3,907 61 | .......... | $122,921 29 | .......... | .......... | .......... |
| 32 | 2,472 90 | .......... | 37,180 84 | .......... | .......... | .......... |
| 33 | 4,057 18 | $3,492 24 | 9,229 19 | .......... | .......... | $2,192 45 |
| 34 | 11,639 43 | 8,021 14 | 6,894 37 | .......... | .......... | .......... |
| 35 | 5,351 10 | .......... | 2,439 00 | .......... | $15 00 | .......... |
| 36 | **$27,428 22** | **$11,513 38** | **$178,664 69** | .......... | **$15 00** | **$2,192 45** |
| 37 | .......... | .......... | **$10,840 87** | **$869 11** | **$764 50** | **$8,627 75** |

STATEMENT SHOWING EXPENDITURES FROM REVENUE (SPECIAL REVENUE

| | Total | Personal Service | Supplies | LINE No. |
|---|---|---|---|---|
| CITY DEPARTMENTS, ETC.—*Continued* | | | | |
| Boards, Commissions, etc., whose members are not elected by popular vote, and who are not appointed by any elected City official: | | | | |
| Commissioner of Lunacy | $1,120 80 | $1,120 80 | .......... | 1 |
| Public Service Commission | 1,863,161 32 | 1,634,195 29 | $77,768 25 | 2 |
| Total | **$1,864,282 12** | **$1,635,316 09** | **$77,768 25** | 3 |
| Boards, Commissions, etc., of mixed responsibility, i.e., ex-officio bodies representing two or more preceding branches: | | | | |
| Armory Board | $14,492 69 | $14,758 00 | .......... | 4 |
| Board of Elections | 1,679 35 | 1,617 50 | $28 50 | 5 |
| Total | **$16,172 04** | **$16,375 50** | **$28 50** | 6 |
| Courts, including Board of Parole and General Interpreters of Brooklyn: | | | | |
| Coroners—Borough of Manhattan | $410 00 | $410 00 | .......... | 7 |
| Coroners—Borough of The Bronx | 1,215 93 | .......... | $232 68 | 8 |
| Coroners—Borough of Brooklyn | 475 76 | 225 00 | 9 40 | 9 |
| City Magistrates' Courts, First Division | 16,890 18 | 15,362 03 | 1,196 89 | 10 |
| City Magistrates' Courts, Second Division | 4,496 96 | 3,462 36 | .......... | 11 |
| Court of Special Sessions | 5,908 14 | 5,950 14 | *42 00* | 12 |
| Total | **$29,396 97** | **$25,409 53** | **$1,396 97** | 13 |
| Total City Departments, Offices, Courts, etc. | **$3,413,495 95** | **$2,040,520 20** | **$351,526 89** | 14 |
| FIXED CHARGES, OTHER THAN DEBT SERVICE, SUBSIDIES, CONTRIBUTIONS, PAYMENTS TO PRIVATE AND STATE INSTITUTIONS, EXPENDITURES NOT ALLOTTED TO DEPARTMENTS: | | | | |
| Claims | $1,780,061 72 | $87,632 74 | $1,168 15 | 15 |
| Miscellaneous, City | 643,042 25 | 183,445 79 | 50 50 | 16 |
| New York Public Library | 4,583 67 | .......... | .......... | 17 |
| Queensboro Public Library | 2,200 00 | .......... | .......... | 18 |
| Total | **$2,429,887 64** | **$271,078 53** | **$1,218 65** | 19 |
| Total for City Purposes | **$5,843,383 59** | **$2,311,598 73** | **$352,745 54** | 20 |
| COUNTY EXPENDITURES: | | | | |
| New York County: | | | | |
| Court of General Sessions | $15,599 78 | $5,596 70 | .......... | 21 |
| Supreme Court, First Department | 3,560 01 | 58 32 | .......... | 22 |
| Surrogates' Court, New York County | 4,910 26 | 3,160 35 | $41 20 | 23 |
| District Attorney | 18,154 07 | 2,251 23 | .......... | 24 |
| Miscellaneous | 11,118 66 | .......... | .......... | 25 |
| Public Administrator | 477 83 | 477 83 | .......... | 26 |
| Commissioner of Records | 3,780 65 | .......... | 3,768 41 | 27 |
| Sheriff | 2,432 59 | 2,220 42 | .......... | 28 |
| Total | **$60,033 85** | **$13,764 85** | **$3,809 61** | 29 |
| Kings County: | | | | |
| County Clerk | $5,754 00 | $5,754 00 | .......... | 30 |
| County Court | 14,404 25 | 12,495 35 | .......... | 31 |
| Supreme Court, Second Department | 4,341 62 | 4,341 62 | .......... | 32 |
| District Attorney | 2,549 02 | .......... | .......... | 33 |
| Commissioner of Jurors | 479 75 | .......... | .......... | 34 |
| Public Administrator | 263 06 | .......... | $9 00 | 35 |
| Sheriff | 2,433 38 | 1,500 00 | .......... | 36 |
| Total | **$30,225 08** | **$24,090 97** | **$9 00** | 37 |

*Refund

## NEW YORK

BOND FUNDS) FOR THE YEAR 1913, CLASSIFIED BY OBJECTS OF EXPENDITURE:—*Continued*

| LINE No. | Purchase of Equipment | Materials | Contract or Open Order Service | Contingencies | Fixed Charges and Contributions | Unclassified |
|---|---|---|---|---|---|---|
| 1 | .......... | .......... | .......... | .......... | .......... | .......... |
| 2 | $24,120 35 | .......... | $35,211 38 | .......... | $79,743 56 | $12,122 49 |
| 3 | **$24,120 35** | .......... | **$35,211 38** | .......... | **$79,743 56** | **$12,122 49** |
| 4 | .......... | .......... | **$265 31* | .......... | .......... | .......... |
| 5 | .......... | .......... | 25 50 | $7 85 | .......... | .......... |
| 6 | .......... | .......... | *$239 81* | **$7 85** | .......... | .......... |
| 7 | .......... | .......... | .......... | .......... | .......... | .......... |
| 8 | $31 00 | .......... | $783 65 | $168 60 | .......... | .......... |
| 9 | .......... | .......... | 10 36 | 231 00 | .......... | .......... |
| 10 | .......... | .......... | 331 26 | .......... | .......... | .......... |
| 11 | 1,034 60 | .......... | .......... | .......... | .......... | .......... |
| 12 | .......... | .......... | .......... | .......... | .......... | .......... |
| 13 | **$1,065 60** | .......... | **$1,125 27** | **$399 60** | .......... | .......... |
| 14 | **$178,194 32** | **$20,977 81** | **$445,747 37** | **$7,694 54** | **$286,770 62** | **$82,064 20** |
| 15 | .......... | $69 71 | $538,443 75 | $114 75 | $883,371 61 | $269,261 01 |
| 16 | $4,381 35 | .......... | 3,345 35 | 24,837 60 | 47,968 46 | 379,013 20 |
| 17 | 394 97 | .......... | 4,188 70 | .......... | .......... | .......... |
| 18 | 202 00 | .......... | 1,998 00 | .......... | .......... | .......... |
| 19 | **$4,978 32** | **$69 71** | **$547,975 80** | **$24,952 35** | **$931,340 07** | **$648,274 21** |
| 20 | **$183,172 64** | **$21,047 52** | **$993,723 17** | **$32,646 89** | **$1,218,110 69** | **$730,338 41** |
| 21 | .......... | .......... | $10,003 08 | .......... | .......... | .......... |
| 22 | $2,776 19 | .......... | 722 50 | $3 00 | .......... | .......... |
| 23 | 1,129 58 | .......... | 579 13 | .......... | .......... | .......... |
| 24 | .......... | .......... | 11,943 07 | 3,959 77 | .......... | .......... |
| 25 | .......... | .......... | 11,118 66 | .......... | .......... | .......... |
| 26 | .......... | .......... | .......... | .......... | .......... | .......... |
| 27 | .......... | .......... | .......... | 12 24 | .......... | .......... |
| 28 | .......... | .......... | 212 17 | .......... | .......... | .......... |
| 29 | **$3,905 77** | .......... | **$34,578 61** | **$3,975 01** | .......... | .......... |
| 30 | .......... | .......... | .......... | .......... | .......... | .......... |
| 31 | .......... | .......... | $1,908 90 | .......... | .......... | .......... |
| 32 | .......... | .......... | .......... | .......... | .......... | .......... |
| 33 | .......... | .......... | 1,019 75 | $1,529 27 | .......... | .......... |
| 34 | $479 75 | .......... | .......... | .......... | .......... | .......... |
| 35 | .......... | .......... | 254 06 | .......... | .......... | .......... |
| 36 | .......... | .......... | 933 38 | .......... | .......... | .......... |
| 37 | **$479 75** | .......... | **$4,116 09** | **$1,529 27** | .......... | .......... |

STATEMENT SHOWING EXPENDITURES FROM REVENUE (SPECIAL REVENUE

| | Total | Personal Service | Supplies | LINE No. |
|---|---|---|---|---|
| COUNTY EXPENDITURES—*Continued* | | | | |
| Queens County: | | | | |
| County Clerk | $2,834 62 | $2,817 62 | .......... | 1 |
| County Court | 1,600 00 | 1,600 00 | .......... | 2 |
| Supreme Court, Queens County | 1,143 34 | 1,143 34 | .......... | 3 |
| District Attorney | 1,275 00 | 1,275 00 | .......... | 4 |
| Commissioner of Jurors | 583 33 | 583 33 | .......... | 5 |
| Sheriff | 3,602 49 | 2,100 00 | .......... | 6 |
| Total | **$11,038 78** | **$9,519 29** | .......... | 7 |
| Richmond County: | | | | |
| County Clerk | $5,915 06 | $5,915 06 | .......... | 8 |
| County Court and Surrogate's Court | 26 48 | .......... | .......... | 9 |
| District Attorney | 612 97 | 67 50 | .......... | 10 |
| Sheriff | 3,294 57 | .......... | $3,294 57 | 11 |
| Total | **$9,849 08** | **$5,982 56** | **$3,294 57** | 12 |
| Bronx County: | | | | |
| Commissioner of Jurors | **$14,501 45** | **$9,402 28** | **$85 85** | 13 |
| Total for County Purposes | **$125,648 24** | **$62,759 95** | **$7,199 03** | 14 |
| Total for All Purposes | **$5,969,031 83** | **$2,374,358 68** | **$359,944 57** | 15 |

## NEW YORK

BOND FUNDS) FOR THE YEAR 1913, CLASSIFIED BY OBJECTS OF EXPENDITURE:—*Continued*

| LINE No. | Purchase of Equipment | Materials | Contract or Open Order Service | Contingencies | Fixed Charges and Contributions | Unclassified |
|---|---|---|---|---|---|---|
| 1 | .......... | .......... | .......... | $17 00 | .......... | .......... |
| 2 | .......... | .......... | .......... | .......... | .......... | .......... |
| 3 | .......... | .......... | .......... | .......... | .......... | .......... |
| 4 | .......... | .......... | .......... | .......... | .......... | .......... |
| 5 | .......... | .......... | .......... | .......... | .......... | .......... |
| 6 | .......... | .......... | $970 49 | 532 00 | .......... | .......... |
| 7 | .......... | .......... | **$970 49** | **$549 00** | .......... | .......... |
| 8 | .......... | .......... | .......... | .......... | .......... | .......... |
| 9 | .......... | .......... | $20 28 | $6 20 | .......... | .......... |
| 10 | .......... | .......... | 223 00 | 322 47 | .......... | .......... |
| 11 | .......... | .......... | .......... | .......... | .......... | .......... |
| 12 | .......... | .......... | **$243 28** | **$328 67** | .......... | .......... |
| 13 | **$3,191 67** | .......... | **$1,338 91** | **$3 30** | **$479 44** | .......... |
| 14 | **$7,577 19** | .......... | **$41,247 38** | **$6,385 25** | **$479 44** | .......... |
| 15 | **$190,749 83** | **$21,047 52** | **$1,034,970 55** | **$39,032 14** | **$1,218,590 13** | **$730,338 41** |

RECAPITULATION OF STATEMENT SHOWING EXPENDITURES FROM REVENUES (SPECIAL REVENUE

| | Total | Personal Service | Supplies | LINE No. |
|---|---|---|---|---|
| CITY DEPARTMENTS, OFFICES, COURTS, ETC.: | | | | |
| Mayor and Subordinate Departments, Bureaus and Offices: | | | | |
| Mayor's Office and Departments whose executive heads are appointed by the Mayor and who are removable at his pleasure | $689,314 70 | $72,601 31 | $98,342 56 | 1 |
| Departments whose heads are appointed by the Mayor for a term of office greater than his own, and who are removable only on charges | 75,775 86 | 6,398 64 | 57,991 40 | 2 |
| Boards and Commissions, majority of which are appointed by the Mayor and for which no other elected City official shares responsibility | 592 83 | 587 33 | 5 50 | 3 |
| Total Mayor and Subordinate Departments, Bureaus and Offices | **$765,683 39** | **$79,587 28** | **$156,339 46** | 4 |
| Borough Presidents and Subordinate Departments: | | | | |
| President, Borough of Manhattan | $114,932 93 | $25,567 35 | $4,932 43 | 5 |
| President, Borough of The Bronx | 32,303 17 | 4,917 10 | 1,912 36 | 6 |
| President, Borough of Brooklyn | 29,740 91 | 5,733 76 | 2,605 00 | 7 |
| President, Borough of Queens | 53,877 47 | 5 00 | 499 00 | 8 |
| President, Borough of Richmond | 24,827 96 | .......... | .......... | 9 |
| Total Borough Presidents | **$255,682 44** | **$36,223 21** | **$9,948 79** | 10 |
| Board of Aldermen, President of Board and City Clerk | **$49,667 74** | **$8,090 70** | **$10 753 90** | 11 |
| Boards, Commissions, etc., whose members are not elected by popular vote and who are not appointed by any elected City official | **$2,946,956 73** | **$2,488,070 71** | **$171 778 08** | 12 |
| Boards, Commissions, etc., of mixed responsibility, i.e., ex-officio bodies representing two or more of preceding branches | **$315,163 29** | **$305 396 65** | **$664 31** | 13 |
| Courts, including Board of Parole and General Interpreters of Brooklyn | **$10,185 69** | **$270 00** | **$287 73** | 14 |
| Total City Departments, Offices, Courts, etc | **$4,343,339 28** | **$2,917,638 55** | **$349,772 27** | 15 |
| FIXED CHARGES OTHER THAN DEBT SERVICE, SUBSIDIES, CONTRIBUTIONS, PAYMENTS TO PRIVATE AND STATE INSTITUTIONS, EXPENDITURES NOT ALLOTTED TO DEPARTMENTS | **$5 450,207 07** | **$37,858 60** | .......... | 16 |
| Total for City Purposes | **$9,793,546 35** | **$2,955,497 15** | **$349,772 27** | 17 |
| COUNTY EXPENDITURES: | | | | |
| New York County | $96,898 29 | $31,244 57 | .......... | 18 |
| Kings County | 46,033 85 | 36,236 91 | $82 02 | 19 |
| Queens County | 8,594 83 | 1,506 22 | 396 76 | 20 |
| Richmond County | 11,789 34 | 6,085 80 | .......... | 21 |
| Bronx County | 268,025 22 | 216,098 62 | 13,114 78 | 22 |
| Total for County Purposes | **$431,341 53** | **$291,172 12** | **$13,593 56** | 23 |
| Total for All Purposes | **$10,224,887 88** | **$3,246,669 27** | **$363,365 83** | 24 |

NEW YORK

BOND FUNDS) FOR THE YEAR 1914, CLASSIFIED BY OBJECTS OF EXPENDITURE:

| LINE No. | Purchase of Equipment | Materials | Contract or Open Order Service | Contingencies | Fixed Charges and Contributions | Unclassified |
|---|---|---|---|---|---|---|
| 1 | $72,385 55 | $3,635 30 | $160,755 23 | $1,740 34 | $279,854 41 | .......... |
| 2 | 4,954 47 | .......... | 6,342 43 | 88 92 | .......... | .......... |
| 3 | .......... | .......... | .......... | .......... | .......... | .......... |
| 4 | **$77,340 02** | **$3,635 30** | **$167,097 66** | **$1,829 26** | **$279,854 41** | .......... |
| 5 | $4,018 31 | $246 28 | $80,168 56 | .......... | .......... | .......... |
| 6 | 16,899 80 | 413 28 | 8,160 63 | .......... | .......... | .......... |
| 7 | 352 91 | 1,047 82 | 20,001 42 | .......... | .......... | .......... |
| 8 | 1,555 28 | 209 56 | 51,608 63 | .......... | .......... | .......... |
| 9 | 47 50 | .......... | 24,780 46 | .......... | .......... | .......... |
| 10 | **$22,873 80** | **$1,916 94** | **$184,719 70** | .......... | .......... | .......... |
| 11 | **$7,943 35** | .......... | **$22,879 79** | .......... | .......... | .......... |
| 12 | **$86,703 14** | .......... | **$32,712 09** | .......... | **$146,947 99** | **$20,744 72** |
| 13 | **$489 65** | .......... | **$8,362 68** | .......... | **$250 00** | .......... |
| 14 | **$6,433 19** | .......... | **$2,647 63** | **$547 14** | .......... | .......... |
| 15 | **$201,783 15** | **$5,552 24** | **$418,419 55** | **$2,376 40** | **$427,052 40** | **$20,744 72** |
| 16 | **$7,427 48** | .......... | **$60,597 62** | .......... | **$4,464,455 84** | **$879,867 53** |
| 17 | **$209,210 63** | **$5,552 24** | **$479,017 17** | **$2,376 40** | **$4,891,508 24** | **$900,612 25** |
| 18 | $59 70 | .......... | $4,923 33 | $60,670 69 | .......... | .......... |
| 19 | 4,370 26 | .......... | 459 96 | 4,782 20 | $102 50 | .......... |
| 20 | 1,572 00 | .......... | 3,548 79 | 1,571 06 | .......... | .......... |
| 21 | 420 63 | .......... | .......... | 5,282 91 | .......... | .......... |
| 22 | 23,235 68 | .......... | 6,669 99 | 8,586 53 | 319 62 | .......... |
| 23 | **$29,658 27** | .......... | **$15,602 07** | **$80,893 39** | **$422 12** | .......... |
| 24 | **$238,868 90** | **$5,552 24** | **$494,619 24** | **$83,269 79** | **$4,891,930 36** | **$900,612 25** |

STATEMENT SHOWING EXPENDITURES FROM REVENUE (SPECIAL REVENUE

| | Total | Personal Service | Supplies | LINE No. |
|---|---|---|---|---|
| CITY DEPARTMENTS, OFFICES, COURTS, ETC. | | | | |
| Mayor and Subordinate Departments, Bureaus and Offices: | | | | |
| Mayor's Office and Departments, whose executive heads are appointed by the Mayor, and who are removable at his pleasure: | | | | |
| Department of Bridges | $27,283 59 | $10,189 60 | $8,547 00 | 1 |
| Department of Correction | 65,654 45 | .......... | 65,654 45 | 2 |
| Department of Docks and Ferries | 28,990 83 | .......... | 3,858 88 | 3 |
| Examining Board of Plumbers | 161 75 | 150 00 | 11 75 | 4 |
| Fire Department | 257,588 38 | 1,297 19 | .......... | 5 |
| Department of Health | 19,778 98 | .......... | 4 04 | 6 |
| Law Department | 27,649 95 | .......... | .......... | 7 |
| Mayoralty—Bureau of Licenses | 420 35 | 223 45 | .......... | 8 |
| Municipal Explosives Commission | 672 50 | 672 50 | .......... | 9 |
| Department of Parks–Boroughs of Manhattan and Richmond | 11,243 53 | .......... | .......... | 10 |
| Department of Parks—Borough of The Bronx | 27,129 41 | 1,900 00 | 757 30 | 11 |
| Department of Parks—Borough of Queens | 8,400 04 | 8,400 04 | .......... | 12 |
| Police Department | 42,792 72 | 736 29 | 6,468 90 | 13 |
| Department of Public Charities | 39,695 94 | 1,842 32 | 948 05 | 14 |
| Department of Street Cleaning | 19,279 65 | .......... | .......... | 15 |
| Department of Taxes and Assessments | 52,723 81 | 42,294 35 | 880 87 | 16 |
| Tenement House Department | 1,046 38 | .......... | .......... | 17 |
| Department of Water Supply, Gas and Electricity | 58,802 44 | 4,895 57 | 11,211 32 | 18 |
| Total | **$689,314 70** | **$72,601 31** | **$98,342 56** | 19 |
| Departments whose heads are appointed by the Mayor for a term of office greater than his own, and who are removable only upon charges: | | | | |
| Bellevue and Allied Hospitals | $65,673 93 | $3,740 44 | $57,844 57 | 20 |
| Department of Education | 10,101 93 | 2,658 20 | 146 83 | 21 |
| Total | **$75,775 86** | **$6,398 64** | **$57,991 40** | 22 |
| Boards and Commissions, majorities of which are appointed by the Mayor and for which no other elected City official shares responsibility: | | | | |
| Board of Inebriety | $587 33 | $587 33 | .......... | 23 |
| Public Recreation Commission | 5 50 | .......... | $5 50 | 24 |
| Total | **$592 83** | **$587 33** | **$5 50** | 25 |
| Total Mayor and Subordinate Departments, Bureaus and Offices | **$765,683 39** | **$79,587 28** | **$156,339 46** | 26 |
| Borough Presidents and Subordinate Departments: | | | | |
| President, Borough of Manhattan | $114,932 93 | $25,567 35 | $4,932 43 | 27 |
| President, Borough of The Bronx | 32,303 17 | 4,917 10 | 1,912 36 | 28 |
| President, Borough of Brooklyn | 29,740 91 | 5,733 76 | 2,605 00 | 29 |
| President, Borough of Queens | 53,877 47 | 5 00 | 499 00 | 30 |
| President, Borough of Richmond | 24,827 96 | .......... | .......... | 31 |
| Total | **$255,682 44** | **$36,223 21** | **$9,948 79** | 32 |
| Board of Aldermen, President of Board and City Clerk | **$49,667 74** | **$8,090 70** | **$10,753 90** | 33 |

## NEW YORK

Bond Funds), for the Year 1914, Classified by Objects of Expenditure:

| LINE No. | Purchase of Equipment | Materials | Contract or Open Order Service | Contingencies | Fixed Charges and Contributions | Unclassified |
|---|---|---|---|---|---|---|
| 1 | $6,837 60 | .......... | .......... | $1,709 39 | .......... | .......... |
| 2 | .......... | .......... | .......... | .......... | .......... | .......... |
| 3 | 3,155 27 | $1,354 59 | $20,622 19 | .......... | .......... | .......... |
| 4 | .......... | .......... | .......... | .......... | .......... | .......... |
| 5 | 43,914 00 | .......... | 5,002 25 | .......... | $207,374 94 | .......... |
| 6 | 2,644 44 | .......... | 17,130 50 | .......... | .......... | .......... |
| 7 | 311 00 | .......... | 27,308 00 | 30 95 | .......... | .......... |
| 8 | .......... | .......... | 196 90 | .......... | .......... | .......... |
| 9 | .......... | .......... | .......... | .......... | .......... | .......... |
| 10 | 3,579 05 | .......... | 7,664 48 | .......... | .......... | .......... |
| 11 | 552 00 | 2,267 18 | 21,652 93 | .......... | .......... | .......... |
| 12 | .......... | .......... | .......... | .......... | .......... | .......... |
| 13 | .......... | .......... | .......... | .......... | 35,587 53 | .......... |
| 14 | .......... | 13 63 | .......... | .......... | 36,891 94 | .......... |
| 15 | 8,550 00 | .......... | 10,729 65 | .......... | .......... | .......... |
| 16 | 1,772 90 | .......... | 7,775 69 | .......... | .......... | .......... |
| 17 | 346 38 | .......... | 700 00 | .......... | .......... | .......... |
| 18 | 722 91 | .......... | 41,972 64 | .......... | .......... | .......... |
| 19 | **$72,385 55** | **$3,635 30** | **$160,755 23** | **$1,740 34** | **$279,854 41** | .......... |
| 20 | $4,000 00 | .......... | .......... | $88 92 | .......... | .......... |
| 21 | 954 47 | .......... | $6,342 43 | .......... | .......... | .......... |
| 22 | **$4,954 47** | .......... | **$6,342 43** | **$88 92** | .......... | .......... |
| 23 | .......... | .......... | .......... | .......... | .......... | .......... |
| 24 | .......... | .......... | .......... | .......... | .......... | .......... |
| 25 | .......... | .......... | .......... | .......... | .......... | .......... |
| 26 | **$77,340 02** | **$3,635 30** | **$167,097 66** | **$1,829 26** | **$279,854 41** | .......... |
| 27 | $4,018 31 | $246 28 | $80,168 56 | .......... | .......... | .......... |
| 28 | 16,899 80 | 413 28 | 8,160 63 | .......... | .......... | .......... |
| 29 | 352 91 | 1,047 82 | 20,001 42 | .......... | .......... | .......... |
| 30 | 1,555 28 | 209 56 | 51,608 63 | .......... | .......... | .......... |
| 31 | 47 50 | .......... | 24,780 46 | .......... | .......... | .......... |
| 32 | **$22,873 80** | **$1,916 94** | **$184,719 70** | .......... | .......... | .......... |
| 33 | **$7,943 35** | .......... | **$22,879 79** | .......... | .......... | .......... |

STATEMENT SHOWING EXPENDITURES FROM REVENUE (SPECIAL REVENUE

| | Total | Personal Service | Supplies | LINE No. |
|---|---|---|---|---|
| CITY DEPARTMENTS, ETC.—*Continued* | | | | |
| Boards, Commissions, etc., whose members are not elected by popular vote and who are not appointed by any elected City official: | | | | |
| Bronx Parkway Commission | $21,035 70 | $14,328 06 | $1,530 34 | 1 |
| Public Service Commission | 2,925,921 03 | 2,473,742 65 | 170,247 74 | 2 |
| Total | **$2,946,956 73** | **$2,488,070 71** | **$171,778 08** | 3 |
| Boards, Commissions, etc., of mixed responsibility, i.e., ex-officio bodies representing two or more preceding branches: | | | | |
| Armory Board | $18,972 81 | $18,707 50 | .......... | 4 |
| Board of City Record, City of New York | 2,416 47 | .......... | $654 31 | 5 |
| Board of Elections | 293,774 01 | 286,689 15 | 10 00 | 6 |
| Total | **$315,163 29** | **$305,396 65** | **$664 31** | 7 |
| Courts, including Board of Parole and General Interpreters of Brooklyn: | | | | |
| Coroners, Borough of The Bronx | $664 21 | $270 00 | $18 56 | 8 |
| Coroners, Borough of Manhattan | 684 32 | .......... | .......... | 9 |
| Courts, City Magistrates, 1st Division | 2,242 35 | .......... | 269 17 | 10 |
| Courts, City Magistrates, 2nd Division | 269 00 | .......... | .......... | 11 |
| Court of Special Sessions | 6,325 81 | .......... | .......... | 12 |
| Total | **$10,185 69** | **$270 00** | **$287 73** | 13 |
| Total City Departments, Offices, Courts, etc | **$4,343,339 28** | **$2,917,638 55** | **$349,772 27** | 14 |
| FIXED CHARGES, OTHER THAN DEBT SERVICE, SUBSIDIES, CONTRIBUTIONS, PAYMENTS TO PRIVATE AND STATE INSTITUTIONS, EXPENDITURES NOT ALLOTTED TO DEPARTMENTS: | | | | |
| Claims | $4,392,750 73 | $37,858 60 | .......... | 15 |
| Miscellaneous, City | 1,048,051 94 | .......... | .......... | 16 |
| New York Public Library | 2,433 33 | .......... | .......... | 17 |
| Brooklyn Public Library | 6,971 07 | .......... | .......... | 18 |
| Total | **$5,450,207 07** | **$37,858 60** | .......... | 19 |
| Total for City Purposes | **$9,793,546 35** | **$2,955,497 15** | **$349,772 27** | 20 |
| COUNTY EXPENDITURES: | | | | |
| New York County: | | | | |
| County Clerk | $3,722 16 | $3,722 16 | .......... | 21 |
| Court, General Sessions | 25,560 45 | 20,637 12 | .......... | 22 |
| Court, Supreme Court—First Department | 2,643 53 | 2,637 53 | .......... | 23 |
| Court, Surrogates' | 191 20 | 137 50 | .......... | 24 |
| District Attorney | 64,750 95 | 4,080 26 | .......... | 25 |
| Commissioner of Jurors | 30 00 | 30 00 | .......... | 26 |
| Total | **$96,898 29** | **$31,244 57** | .......... | 27 |
| Kings County: | | | | |
| County Clerk | $360 00 | $360 00 | .......... | 28 |
| Court, County | 21,945 02 | 21,799 12 | .......... | 29 |
| Court, Supreme Court—Second Department | 10,830 31 | 8,966 69 | .......... | 30 |
| Court, Surrogate's | 774 43 | .......... | .......... | 31 |
| District Attorney | 7,446 35 | 4,527 77 | .......... | 32 |
| Public Administrator | 102 24 | .......... | $82 02 | 33 |
| Sheriff | 4,575 50 | 583 33 | .......... | 34 |
| Total | **$46,033 85** | **$36,236 91** | **$82 02** | 35 |

NEW YORK

BOND FUNDS) FOR THE YEAR 1914, CLASSIFIED BY OBJECTS OF EXPENDITURE:—*Continued*

| LINE No. | Purchase of Equipment | Materials | Contract or Open Order Service | Contingencies | Fixed Charges and Contributions | Unclassified |
|---|---|---|---|---|---|---|
| 1 | $1,062 30 | .......... | $4,115 00 | .......... | .......... | .......... |
| 2 | 85,640 84 | .......... | 28,597 09 | .......... | $146,947 99 | $20,744 72 |
| 3 | **$86,703 14** | .......... | **$32,712 09** | .......... | **$146,947 99** | **$20,744 72** |
| 4 | .......... | .......... | $265 31 | .......... | .......... | .......... |
| 5 | .......... | .......... | 1,762 16 | .......... | .......... | .......... |
| 6 | $489 65 | .......... | 6,335 21 | .......... | $250 00 | .......... |
| 7 | **$489 65** | .......... | **$8,362 68** | .......... | **$250 00** | .......... |
| 8 | $21 25 | .......... | $317 10 | $37 30 | .......... | .......... |
| 9 | .......... | .......... | 684 32 | .......... | .......... | .......... |
| 10 | 1,325 50 | .......... | 647 68 | .......... | .......... | .......... |
| 11 | 269 00 | .......... | .......... | .......... | .......... | .......... |
| 12 | 4,817 44 | .......... | 998 53 | 509 84 | .......... | .......... |
| 13 | **$6,433 19** | .......... | **$2,647 63** | **$547 14** | .......... | .......... |
| 14 | **$201,783 15** | **$5,552 24** | **$418,419 55** | **$2,376 40** | **$427,052 40** | **$20,744 72** |
| 15 | .......... | .......... | $55,242 20 | .......... | $4,156,484 38 | $143,165 55 |
| 16 | $7,427 48 | .......... | 5,355 42 | .......... | 298,567 06 | 736,701 98 |
| 17 | .......... | .......... | .......... | .......... | 2,433 33 | .......... |
| 18 | .......... | .......... | .......... | .......... | 6,971 07 | .......... |
| 19 | **$7,427 48** | .......... | **$60,597 62** | .......... | **$4,464,455 84** | **$879,867 53** |
| 20 | **$209,210 63** | **$5,552 24** | **$479,017 17** | **$2,376 40** | **$4,891,508 24** | **$900,612 25** |
| 21 | .......... | .......... | .......... | .......... | .......... | .......... |
| 22 | .......... | .......... | $4,923 33 | .......... | .......... | .......... |
| 23 | $6 00 | .......... | .......... | .......... | .......... | .......... |
| 24 | 53 70 | .......... | .......... | .......... | .......... | .......... |
| 25 | .......... | .......... | .......... | $60,670 69 | .......... | .......... |
| 26 | .......... | .......... | .......... | .......... | .......... | .......... |
| 27 | **$59 70** | .......... | **$4,923 33** | **$60,670 69** | .......... | .......... |
| 28 | .......... | .......... | .......... | .......... | .......... | .......... |
| 29 | .......... | .......... | $145 90 | .......... | .......... | .......... |
| 30 | .......... | .......... | .......... | $1,863 62 | .......... | .......... |
| 31 | $774 43 | .......... | .......... | .......... | .......... | .......... |
| 32 | .......... | .......... | .......... | 2,918 58 | .......... | .......... |
| 33 | .......... | .......... | 20 22 | .......... | .......... | .......... |
| 34 | 3,595 83 | .......... | 293 84 | .......... | $102 50 | .......... |
| 35 | **$4,370 26** | .......... | **$459 96** | **$4,782 20** | **$102 50** | .......... |

STATEMENT SHOWING EXPENDITURES FROM REVENUE (SPECIAL REVENUE

| | Total | Personal Service | Supplies | LINE No. |
|---|---|---|---|---|
| COUNTY EXPENDITURES—*Continued* | | | | |
| Queens County: | | | | |
| County Clerk | $3,600 66 | $1,094 26 | $396 76 | 1 |
| Court, Surrogate's | 2,264 54 | .......... | .......... | 2 |
| District Attorney | 2,729 63 | 411 96 | .......... | 3 |
| Total | **$8,594 83** | **$1,506 22** | **$396 76** | 4 |
| Richmond County: | | | | |
| County Clerk | $159 90 | $159 90 | .......... | 5 |
| District Attorney | 10,315 44 | 4,611 90 | .......... | 6 |
| Sheriff | 1,314 00 | 1,314 00 | .......... | 7 |
| Total | **$11,789 34** | **$6,085 80** | .......... | 8 |
| Bronx County: | | | | |
| County Clerk | $35,798 31 | $32,150 43 | $453 72 | 9 |
| Court, County | 27,257 01 | 23,446 35 | 692 30 | 10 |
| Court, Surrogate's | 14,101 69 | 12,266 13 | 635 00 | 11 |
| District Attorney | 42,684 62 | 30,224 01 | 1,102 53 | 12 |
| Commissioner of Jurors | 478 00 | .......... | 3 62 | 13 |
| Law Library | 5,328 38 | 449 16 | .......... | 14 |
| Public Administrator | 1,705 92 | 699 20 | 173 75 | 15 |
| Register | 71,315 11 | 59,803 66 | 4,008 03 | 16 |
| Sheriff | 69,356 18 | 57,059 68 | 6,045 83 | 17 |
| Total | **$268,025 22** | **$216,098 62** | **$13,114 78** | 18 |
| Total for County Purposes | **$431,341 53** | **$291,172 12** | **$13,593 56** | 19 |
| Total for All Purposes | **$10,224,887 88** | **$3,246,669 27** | **$363,365 83** | 20 |

NEW YORK

BOND FUNDS) FOR THE YEAR 1914, CLASSIFIED BY OBJECTS OF EXPENDITURE:—*Continued*

| LINE No. | Purchase of Equipment | Materials | Contract or Open Order Service | Contingencies | Fixed Charges and Contributions | Unclassified |
|---|---|---|---|---|---|---|
| 1 | $1,572 00 | .......... | $537 64 | .......... | .......... | .......... |
| 2 | .......... | .......... | 2,264 54 | .......... | .......... | .......... |
| 3 | .......... | .......... | 746 61 | $1,571 06 | .......... | .......... |
| 4 | **$1,572 00** | .......... | **$3,548 79** | **$1,571 06** | .......... | .......... |
| 5 | .......... | .......... | .......... | .......... | .......... | .......... |
| 6 | $420 63 | .......... | .......... | $5,282 91 | .......... | .......... |
| 7 | .......... | .......... | .......... | .......... | .......... | .......... |
| 8 | **$420 63** | .......... | .......... | **$5,282 91** | .......... | .......... |
| 9 | $1,924 00 | .......... | $1,058 62 | $211 54 | .......... | .......... |
| 10 | 2,652 82 | .......... | 303 97 | 161 57 | .......... | .......... |
| 11 | 1,144 56 | .......... | .......... | 56 00 | .......... | .......... |
| 12 | 2,567 55 | .......... | 1,643 45 | 7,147 08 | .......... | .......... |
| 13 | 111 37 | .......... | 40 04 | 3 35 | $319 62 | .......... |
| 14 | 4,879 22 | .......... | .......... | .......... | .......... | .......... |
| 15 | 795 88 | .......... | 23 95 | 13 14 | .......... | .......... |
| 16 | 6,700 00 | .......... | 543 57 | 259 85 | .......... | .......... |
| 17 | 2,460 28 | .......... | 3,056 39 | 734 00 | .......... | .......... |
| 18 | **$23,235 68** | .......... | **$6,669 99** | **$8,586 53** | **$319 62** | .......... |
| 19 | **$29,658 27** | .......... | **$15,602 07** | **$80,893 39** | **$422 12** | .......... |
| 20 | **$238,868 90** | **$5,552 24** | **$494,619 24** | **$83,269 79** | **$4,891,930 36** | **$900,612 25** |

STATEMENT SHOWING EXPENDITURES FROM REVENUE (SPECIAL ACCOUNTS) FOR

| | Total | Personal Service | Supplies | LINE No. |
|---|---|---|---|---|
| CITY DEPARTMENTS, OFFICES, COURTS, ETC.: | | | | |
| Mayor and Subordinate Departments, Bureaus and Offices, | | | | |
| Mayor's Office and Departments whose executive heads are appointed by the Mayor and who are removable at his pleasure: | | | | |
| Department of Bridges | $769,314 43 | $609,183 90 | $40,419 29 | 1 |
| Department of Correction | 49,248 47 | 257 59 | 793 62 | 2 |
| Department of Health | 44,334 69 | 23,185 20 | 13,130 51 | 3 |
| Department of Parks, Manhattan and Richmond | 1,239 50 | .......... | .......... | 4 |
| Department of Parks, Brooklyn | 723 50 | 723 50 | .......... | 5 |
| Department of Water Supply, Gas and Electricity | 1,957,504 19 | 1,188,023 07 | 412,318 33 | 6 |
| Total | **$2,822,364 78** | **$1,821,373 26** | **$466,661 75** | 7 |
| Departments whose heads are appointed by the Mayor for a term of office greater than his own and who are removable only on charges: | | | | |
| Department of Education | **$153,258 28** | **$1,114 15** | **$116,239 37** | 8 |
| Total Mayor and Subordinate Departments, Bureaus and Offices | **$2,975,623 06** | **$1,822,487 41** | **$582,901 12** | 9 |
| Comptroller and Department of Finance excluding the City Chamberlain's Office: | | | | |
| Wallabout Market (Special Fund) | **$17,857 60** | **$1,004 49** | **$7 08** | 10 |
| Borough Presidents and Subordinate Departments: | | | | |
| President, Borough of The Bronx | $122 00 | .......... | .......... | 11 |
| President, Borough of Brooklyn | 2,503 85 | $1,764 08 | .......... | 12 |
| President, Borough of Queens | 254 65 | 254 65 | .......... | 13 |
| President, Borough of Richmond | 25 00 | 25 00 | .......... | 14 |
| Total Borough Presidents | **$2,905 50** | **$2,043 73** | .......... | 15 |
| Total City Departments, Offices, Courts, etc. | **$2,996,386 16** | **$1,825,535 63** | **$582,908 20** | 16 |
| FIXED CHARGES OTHER THAN DEBT SERVICE, SUBSIDIES, CONTRIBUTIONS, PAYMENTS TO PRIVATE AND STATE INSTITUTIONS, EXPENDITURES NOT ALLOTTED TO DEPARTMENTS: | | | | |
| Excise Taxes, City of New York | **$1,216,161 58** | **$26,644 97** | .......... | 17 |
| Total for City Purposes | **$4,212,547 74** | **$1,852,180 60** | **$582,908 20** | 18 |
| COUNTY EXPENDITURES: | | | | |
| New York County: | | | | |
| Sheriff | **$48,924 72** | **$48,924 72** | .......... | 19 |
| Total for All Purposes | **$4,261,472 46** | **$1,901,105 32** | **$582,908 20** | 20 |

NEW YORK

THE YEAR 1910, CLASSIFIED BY OBJECTS OF EXPENDITURE:

| LINE No. | Purchase of Equipment | Materials | Contract or Open Order Service | Contingencies | Fixed Charges and Contributions | Unclassified |
|---|---|---|---|---|---|---|
| 1 | $21,621 63 | $80,441 59 | $15,833 52 | $1,814 50 | .......... | .......... |
| 2 | 923 75 | 17,666 65 | 29,606 86 | .......... | .......... | .......... |
| 3 | 6,779 16 | 31 58 | 1,181 80 | 26 44 | .......... | .......... |
| 4 | 1,239 50 | .......... | .......... | .......... | .......... | .......... |
| 5 | .......... | .......... | .......... | .......... | .......... | .......... |
| 6 | 21,624 53 | 51,168 79 | 231,645 70 | 11,756 14 | $40,967 63 | .......... |
| 7 | **$52,188 57** | **$149,308 61** | **$278,267 88** | **$13,597 08** | **$40,967 63** | .......... |
| 8 | **$16,248 18** | **$5,498 50** | **$14,118 08** | .......... | **$40 00** | .......... |
| 9 | **$68,436 75** | **$154,807 11** | **$292,385 96** | **$13,597 08** | **$41,007 63** | .......... |
| 10 | .......... | .......... | **$16,846 03** | .......... | .......... | .......... |
| 11 | .......... | .......... | $122 00 | .......... | .......... | .......... |
| 12 | .......... | .......... | 739 77 | .......... | .......... | .......... |
| 13 | .......... | .......... | .......... | .......... | .......... | .......... |
| 14 | .......... | .......... | .......... | .......... | .......... | .......... |
| 15 | .......... | .......... | **$861 77** | .......... | .......... | .......... |
| 16 | **$68,436 75** | **$154,807 11** | **$310,093 76** | **$13,597 08** | **$41,007 63** | .......... |
| 17 | .......... | .......... | .......... | .......... | **$1,182,418 20** | **$7,098 41** |
| 18 | **$68,436 75** | **$154,807 11** | **$310,093 76** | **$13,597 08** | **$1,223,425 83** | **$7,098 41** |
| 19 | .......... | .......... | .......... | .......... | .......... | .......... |
| 20 | **$68,436 75** | **$154,807 11** | **$310,093 76** | **$13,597 08** | **$1,223,425 83** | **$7,098 41** |

STATEMENT SHOWING EXPENDITURES FROM REVENUE (SPECIAL ACCOUNTS

| | Total | Personal Service | Supplies |
|---|---|---|---|
| CITY DEPARTMENTS, OFFICES, COURTS, ETC.: | | | |
| Mayor and Subordinate Departments, Bureaus and Offices, | | | |
| Mayor's Office and Departments whose executive heads are appointed by the Mayor and who are removable at his pleasure: | | | |
| Department of Bridges | $596,326 73 | $516,558 47 | $21,588 81 |
| Department of Correction | 16,711 68 | .......... | .......... |
| Department of Health | 54,305 91 | 28,055 86 | 19,920 83 |
| Department of Parks, Manhattan and Richmond | 1,757 40 | .......... | .......... |
| Department of Parks, Brooklyn | 826 25 | 807 25 | .......... |
| Department of Water Supply, Gas and Electricity | 2,170,521 25 | 1,236,398 16 | 509,287 44 |
| Total | **$2,840,449 22** | **$1,781,819 74** | **$550,797 08** |
| Departments whose heads are appointed by the Mayor for a term of office greater than his own, and who are removable only on charges | | | |
| Department of Education | **$147,252 42** | .......... | **$86,992 34** |
| Total Mayor and Subordinate Departments, Bureaus and Offices | **$2,987,701 64** | **$1,781,819 74** | **$637,789 42** |
| Comptroller and Finance Department, excluding the Chamberlain's Office: | | | |
| Wallabout Market (Special Fund) | **$1,396 80** | **$1,396 80** | .......... |
| Borough Presidents and Subordinate Departments: | | | |
| President, Borough of Manhattan | $4,875 00 | .......... | .......... |
| President, Borough of The Bronx | 462 70 | .......... | .......... |
| President, Borough of Brooklyn | 4,991 98 | $3,178 93 | .......... |
| President, Borough of Queens | 1,240 19 | 1,240 19 | .......... |
| President, Borough of Richmond | 3,317 18 | 3,317 18 | .......... |
| Total Borough Presidents | **$14,887 05** | **$7,736 30** | .......... |
| Total City Departments, Offices, Courts, etc. | **$3,003,985 49** | **$1,790,952 84** | **$637,789 42** |
| FIXED CHARGES OTHER THAN DEBT SERVICE, SUBSIDIES, CONTRIBUTIONS, PAYMENTS TO PRIVATE AND STATE INSTITUTIONS, EXPENDITURES NOT ALLOTTED TO DEPARTMENTS: | | | |
| Excise Taxes, City of New York | **$1,343,648 71** | **$26,740 68** | .......... |
| Total for City Purposes | **$4,347,634 20** | **$1,817,693 52** | **$637,789 42** |
| COUNTY EXPENDITURES: | | | |
| New York County | | | |
| Sheriff | **$46,305 48** | **$46,305 48** | .......... |
| Total for All Purposes | **$4,393,939 68** | **$1,863,999 00** | **$637,789 42** |

## NEW YORK

FOR THE YEAR 1911, CLASSIFIED BY OBJECTS OF EXPENDITURE:

| LINE No. | Purchase of Equipment | Materials | Contract or Open Order Service | Contingencies | Fixed Charges and Contributions | Unclassified |
|---|---|---|---|---|---|---|
| 1 | $2,312 92 | $41,921 26 | $13,422 03 | $523 24 | .......... | .......... |
| 2 | .......... | 443 75 | 16,267 93 | .......... | .......... | .......... |
| 3 | 4,533 46 | 201 23 | 1,594 53 | .......... | .......... | .......... |
| 4 | 1,757 40 | .......... | .......... | .......... | .......... | .......... |
| 5 | .......... | 19 00 | .......... | .......... | .......... | .......... |
| 6 | 5,560 96 | 26,626 76 | 339,449 93 | 14,293 89 | $38,904 11 | .......... |
| 7 | **$14,164 74** | **$69,212 00** | **$370,734 42** | **$14,817 13** | **$38,904 11** | .......... |
| 8 | **$50,709 72** | **$2,542 04** | **$7,008 32** | .......... | .......... | .......... |
| 9 | **$64,874 46** | **$71,754 04** | **$377,742 74** | **$14,817 13** | **$38,904 11** | .......... |
| 10 | .......... | .......... | .......... | .......... | .......... | .......... |
| 11 | .......... | .......... | $4,875 00 | .......... | .......... | .......... |
| 12 | .......... | .......... | 462 70 | .......... | .......... | .......... |
| 13 | .......... | .......... | 1,813 05 | .......... | .......... | .......... |
| 14 | .......... | .......... | .......... | .......... | .......... | .......... |
| 15 | .......... | .......... | .......... | .......... | .......... | .......... |
| 16 | .......... | .......... | **$7,150 75** | .......... | .......... | .......... |
| 17 | **$64,874 46** | **$71,754 04** | **$384,893 49** | **$14,817 13** | **$38,904 11** | .......... |
| 18 | .......... | .......... | .......... | .......... | **$1,309,045 12** | **$7,862 91** |
| 19 | **$64,874 46** | **$71,754 04** | **$384,893 49** | **$14,817 13** | **$1,347,949 23** | **$7,862 91** |
| 20 | .......... | .......... | .......... | .......... | .......... | .......... |
| 21 | **$64,874 46** | **$71,754 04** | **$384,893 49** | **$14,817 13** | **$1,347,949 23** | **$7,862 91** |

STATEMENT SHOWING EXPENDITURES FROM REVENUE (SPECIAL ACCOUNTS)

| | Total | Personal Service | Supplies | LINE No. |
|---|---|---|---|---|
| CITY DEPARTMENTS, OFFICES, COURTS, ETC. | | | | |
| Mayor and Subordinate Departments, Bureaus and Offices: | | | | |
| Mayor's Office and Departments whose executive heads are appointed by the Mayor and who are removable at his pleasure:........ | | | | |
| Department of Bridges.................... | $408,621 51 | $346,730 76 | $5,299 40 | 1 |
| Department of Correction.................. | 12,468 52 | .......... | 388 12 | 2 |
| Department of Health...................... | 13,540 16 | 273 34 | 8,120 15 | 3 |
| Department of Parks—Manhattan and Richmond............................... | 1,478 27 | .......... | 575 00 | 4 |
| Department of Parks—Brooklyn............ | 1,831 43 | 848 75 | .......... | 5 |
| Department of Water Supply, Gas and Electricity.............................. | 2,036,931 47 | 1,250,786 59 | 425,599 54 | 6 |
| Department of Water Supply, Gas and Electricity—Water Meter Fund............ | 8,866 45 | .......... | .......... | 7 |
| Total.................................. | **$2,483,737 81** | **$1,598,639 44** | **$439,982 21** | 8 |
| Departments whose heads are appointed by the Mayor for a term of office greater than his own and who are removable only upon charges: | | | | |
| Department of Education.................. | **$245,908 85** | **$23,412 80** | **$122,399 35** | 9 |
| Total Mayor and Subordinate Departments, Bureaus and Offices............. | **$2,729,646 66** | **$1,622,052 24** | **$562,381 56** | 10 |
| Comptroller and Finance Department, excluding the Chamberlain's Office: | | | | |
| Wallabout Market (Special Fund)............ | **$4,977 26** | **$230 34** | .......... | 11 |
| Borough Presidents and Subordinate Departments: | | | | |
| President, Borough of Manhattan............. | $3,233 47 | .......... | .......... | 12 |
| President, Borough of The Bronx............. | 351 00 | .......... | .......... | 13 |
| President, Borough of Brooklyn.............. | 3,448 34 | $2,774 22 | .......... | 14 |
| President, Borough of Queens................ | 2,361 28 | 2,016 78 | $1 00 | 15 |
| President, Borough of Richmond.............. | 1,130 76 | 1,130 76 | .......... | 16 |
| Total Borough Presidents................ | **$10,524 85** | **$5,921 76** | **$1 00** | 17 |
| Total City Departments, Offices, Courts, etc. | **$2,745,148 77** | **$1,628,204 34** | **$562,382 56** | 18 |
| FIXED CHARGES OTHER THAN DEBT SERVICE, SUBSIDIES, CONTRIBUTIONS, PAYMENTS TO PRIVATE AND STATE INSTITUTIONS, EXPENDITURES NOT ALLOTTED TO DEPARTMENTS: | | | | |
| Excise Taxes—City of New York........... | **$1,340,403 12** | **$26,995 24** | .......... | 19 |
| Total for City Purposes.................. | **$4,085,551 89** | **$1,655,199 58** | **$562,382 56** | 20 |
| COUNTY EXPENDITURES: | | | | |
| New York County— | | | | |
| Sheriff.................................. | **$53,184 88** | **$53,184 88** | .......... | 21 |
| Total for All Purposes.................. | **$4,138,736 77** | **$1,708,384 46** | **$562,382 56** | 22 |

NEW YORK

FOR THE YEAR 1912, CLASSIFIED BY OBJECTS OF EXPENDITURES.

| LINE No. | Purchase of Equipment | Materials | Contract or Open Order Service | Contingencies | Fixed Charges and Contributions | Unclassified |
|---|---|---|---|---|---|---|
| 1 | $3,321 89 | $36,328 03 | $16,843 53 | $97 90 | .......... | .......... |
| 2 | .......... | 511 49 | 11,568 91 | .......... | .......... | .......... |
| 3 | 3,096 48 | 159 33 | 1,873 46 | 17 40 | .......... | .......... |
| 4 | 875 27 | .......... | 20 95 | 7 05 | .......... | .......... |
| 5 | .......... | 9 68 | 973 00 | .......... | .......... | .......... |
| 6 | 27,915 79 | 19,005 56 | 245,581 22 | 14,517 15 | $53,525 62 | .......... |
| 7 | .......... | .......... | 8 866 45 | .......... | .......... | .......... |
| 8 | **$35,209 43** | **$56,014 09** | **$285,727 52** | **$14,639 50** | **$53,525 62** | .......... |
| 9 | **$85,460 56** | **$1,004 71** | **$13,631 43** | .......... | .......... | .......... |
| 10 | **$120,669 99** | **$57,018 80** | **$299,358 95** | **$14,639 50** | **$53,525 62** | .......... |
| 11 | .......... | .......... | **$4,746 92** | .......... | .......... | .......... |
| 12 | .......... | .......... | $3 233 47 | .......... | .......... | .......... |
| 13 | .......... | .......... | 351 00 | .......... | .......... | .......... |
| 14 | .......... | .......... | 674 12 | .......... | .......... | .......... |
| 15 | .......... | .......... | 343 50 | .......... | .......... | .......... |
| 16 | .......... | .......... | .......... | .......... | .......... | .......... |
| 17 | .......... | .......... | **$4,602 09** | .......... | .......... | .......... |
| 18 | **$120,669 99** | **$57,018 96** | **$308,707 96** | **$14,639 50** | **$53,525 62** | .......... |
| 19 | .......... | .......... | .......... | .......... | **$1,306,013 11** | **$7,394 77** |
| 20 | **$120,669 99** | **$57,018 80** | **$308,707 96** | **$14,639 50** | **$1,359,538 73** | **$7,394 77** |
| 21 | .......... | .......... | .......... | .......... | .......... | .......... |
| 22 | **$120,669 99** | **$57,018 80** | **$308,707 96** | **$14,639 50** | **$1,359,538 73** | **$7,394 77** |

Statement Showing Expenditures from Revenue (Special Accounts),

| | Total | Personal Service | Supplies | Line No. |
|---|---|---|---|---|
| City Departments, Offices, Courts, Etc. | | | | |
| Mayor and Subordinate Departments, Bureaus and Offices: | | | | |
| Mayor's Office and Departments whose executive heads are appointed by the Mayor, and who are removable at his pleasure: | | | | |
| Department of Bridges | $450,408 79 | $419,706 87 | $31 50 | 1 |
| Department of Correction | 44,961 50 | .......... | 3,388 34 | 2 |
| Department of Health | 16,199 09 | 8,423 22 | 3,596 04 | 3 |
| Department of Parks—Manhattan and Richmond | 1,199 79 | .......... | 35 00 | 4 |
| Department of Water Supply, Gas and Electricity | 1,927,788 91 | 1,244,403 58 | 398,460 13 | 5 |
| Department of Water Supply, Gas and Electricity, Water Meter Fund | 12,553 21 | .......... | .......... | 6 |
| Total | **$2,453,111 29** | **$1,672,533 67** | **$405,511 01** | 7 |
| Departments whose heads are appointed by the Mayor for a term of office greater than his own, and who are removable only upon charges: | | | | |
| Department of Education | **$252,517 90** | **$87,100 54** | **$67,934 59** | 8 |
| Total, Mayor and Subordinate Departments, Bureaus and Offices | **$2,705,629 19** | **$1,759,634 21** | **$473,445 60** | 9 |
| Comptroller and Finance Department, excluding the Chamberlain's Office: | | | | |
| Wallabout Market (Special Fund) | **$1,489 72** | **$78 32** | .......... | 10 |
| Borough Presidents and Subordinate Departments. | | | | |
| President, Borough of Manhattan | $2,032 61 | .......... | .......... | 11 |
| President, Borough of The Bronx | 270 00 | .......... | .......... | 12 |
| President, Borough of Brooklyn | 1,934 73 | $1,240 09 | .......... | 13 |
| President, Borough of Queens | 2,145 30 | 1,893 27 | .......... | 14 |
| President, Borough of Richmond | 1,643 25 | 1,643 25 | .......... | 15 |
| Total, Borough Presidents | **$8,025 89** | **$4,776 61** | .......... | 16 |
| Total City Departments, Offices, Courts, etc. | **$2,715,144 80** | **$1,764,489 14** | **$473,445 60** | 17 |
| Fixed Charges other than Debt Service, Subsidies, Contributions, Payments to Private and State Institutions, Expenditures not Alloted to Departments: | | | | |
| Excise Taxes, City of New York | **$1,389,008 64** | **$26,935 81** | .......... | 18 |
| Total for City Purposes | **$4,104,153 44** | **$1,791,424 95** | **$473,445 60** | 19 |
| County Expenditures: | | | | |
| New York County— | | | | |
| Sheriff | **$51,505 85** | **$51,505 85** | .......... | 20 |
| Total for All Purposes | **$4,155,659 29** | **$1,842,930 80** | **$473,445 60** | 21 |

NEW YORK

FOR THE YEAR 1913, CLASSIFIED BY OBJECTS OF EXPENDITURE:

| LINE No. | Purchase of Equipment | Materials | Contract or Open Order Service | Contingencies | Fixed Charges and Contributions | Unclassified |
|---|---|---|---|---|---|---|
| 1 | $907 45 | $1,745 74 | $28,000 33 | $16 90 | .......... | .......... |
| 2 | 2,915 84 | 13,086 17 | 25,571 15 | .......... | .......... | .......... |
| 3 | 3,072 58 | 527 62 | 462 08 | 117 55 | .......... | .......... |
| 4 | 1,108 15 | .......... | 49 80 | 6 84 | .......... | .......... |
| 5 | 15,312 26 | 25,904 92 | 190.227 04 | 1,534 21 | $51,946 77 | .......... |
| 6 | .......... | .......... | 12,553 21 | .......... | .......... | .......... |
| 7 | **$23,316 28** | **$41,264 45** | **$256,863 61** | **$1,675 50** | **$51,946 77** | .......... |
| 8 | **$90,270 49** | **$1,060 82** | **$5,854 07** | **$297 39** | .......... | .......... |
| 9 | **$113,586 77** | **$42,325 27** | **$262,717 68** | **$1,972 89** | **$51,946 77** | .......... |
| 10 | .......... | .......... | **$1,411 40** | .......... | .......... | .......... |
| 11 | .......... | .......... | $2,032 61 | .......... | .......... | .......... |
| 12 | .......... | .......... | 270 00 | .......... | .......... | .......... |
| 13 | .......... | .......... | 694 64 | .......... | .......... | .......... |
| 14 | .......... | .......... | 252 03 | .......... | .......... | .......... |
| 15 | .......... | .......... | .......... | .......... | .......... | .......... |
| 16 | .......... | .......... | **$3,249 28** | .......... | .......... | .......... |
| 17 | **$113,586 77** | **$42,325 27** | **$267,378 36** | **$1,972 89** | **$51,946 77** | .......... |
| 18 | .......... | .......... | .......... | .......... | **$1,354,260 50** | **$7,812 33** |
| 19 | **$113,586 77** | **$42,325 27** | **$267,378 36** | **$1,972 89** | **$1,406,207 27** | **$7,812 33** |
| 20 | .......... | .......... | .......... | .......... | .......... | .......... |
| 21 | **$113,586 77** | **$42,325 27** | **$267,378 36** | **$1,972 89** | **$1,406,207 27** | **$7,812 33** |

STATEMENT SHOWING EXPENDITURES FROM REVENUE (SPECIAL ACCOUNTS)

| | Total | Personal Service | Supplies | LINE No. |
|---|---|---|---|---|
| CITY DEPARTMENTS, OFFICES, COURTS, ETC. | | | | |
| Mayor and Subordinate Departments, Bureaus and Offices: | | | | |
| Mayor's Office and Departments whose executive heads are appointed by the Mayor and who are removable at his pleasure: | | | | |
| Department of Bridges | $405,743 33 | $403,805 92 | .......... | 1 |
| Departments of Correction | 59,186 55 | .......... | $6,446 42 | 2 |
| Department of Health | 2,245 92 | .......... | 201 10 | 3 |
| Department of Parks—Manhattan and Richmond | 401 74 | .......... | 103 00 | 4 |
| Department of Parks—Brooklyn | 198 75 | 198 75 | .......... | 5 |
| Department of Water Supply, Gas and Electricity | 1,867,031 95 | 1,220,161 48 | 379,744 23 | 6 |
| Department of Water Supply, Gas and Electricity—Water Meter Fund | 9,358 74 | .......... | .......... | 7 |
| Total | **$2,344,166 98** | **$1,624,166 15** | **$386,494 75** | 8 |
| Departments whose heads are appointed by the Mayor for a term of office greater than his own and who are removable only upon charges: | | | | |
| Department of Education | **$181,651 92** | **$32,681 63** | **$44,983 23** | 9 |
| Total, Mayor and Subordinate Departments, Bureaus and Offices | **$2,525,818 90** | **$1,656,847 78** | **$431,477 98** | 10 |
| Comptroller and Finance Department, excluding the Chamberlain's Office: | | | | |
| Wallabout Market (Special Fund) | **$60 00** | .......... | .......... | 11 |
| Borough Presidents and Subordinate Departments: | | | | |
| President, Borough of Manhattan | $646 20 | .......... | .......... | 12 |
| President, Borough of The Bronx | 75 00 | .......... | .......... | 13 |
| President, Borough of Brooklyn | 1,404 45 | $855 12 | .......... | 14 |
| President, Borough of Queens | 2,467 18 | 2,330 66 | .......... | 15 |
| President, Borough of Richmond | 2,389 21 | 1,109 59 | .......... | 16 |
| Total, Borough Presidents | **$6,982 04** | **$4,295 37** | .......... | 17 |
| Boards, Commissions, etc., of mixed responsibility, i.e., ex-officio bodies representing two or more preceding branches: | | | | |
| Board of Estimate and Apportionment | **$4,369 05** | .......... | .......... | 18 |
| Total, City Departments, Offices, Courts, etc. | **$2,537,229 99** | **$1,661,143 15** | **$431,477 98** | 19 |
| FIXED CHARGES, OTHER THAN DEBT SERVICE, SUBSIDIES, CONTRIBUTIONS, PAYMENTS TO PRIVATE AND STATE INSTITUTIONS, EXPENDITURES NOT ALLOTTED TO DEPARTMENTS: | | | | |
| Excise Taxes, City of New York | **$1,383,323 53** | **$27,886 03** | .......... | 20 |
| Total for City Purposes | **$3,920,553 52** | **$1,689,029 18** | **$431,477 98** | 21 |
| COUNTY EXPENDITURES: | | | | |
| New York County: | | | | |
| Sheriff | **$46,041 82** | **$46,041 82** | .......... | 22 |
| Total for All Purposes | **$3,966,595 34** | **$1,735,071 00** | **$431,477 98** | 23 |

## NEW YORK

FOR THE YEAR 1914, CLASSIFIED BY OBJECTS OF EXPENDITURE

| LINE No. | Purchase of Equipment | Materials | Contract or Open Order Service | Contingencies | Fixed Charges and Contributions | Unclassified |
|---|---|---|---|---|---|---|
| 1 | .......... | .......... | $1,937 41 | .......... | .......... | .......... |
| 2 | $1,789 31 | $33,060 39 | 17,877 78 | $12 65 | .......... | .......... |
| 3 | 1,127 36 | 243 75 | 673 71 | .......... | .......... | .......... |
| 4 | 275 57 | .......... | .......... | 23 17 | .......... | .......... |
| 5 | .......... | .......... | .......... | .......... | .......... | .......... |
| 6 | 18,075 98 | 30,103 64 | 153,960 68 | 259 03 | $64,726 91 | .......... |
| 7 | .......... | .......... | 9,358 74 | .......... | .......... | .......... |
| 8 | **$21,268 22** | **$63,407 78** | **$183,808 32** | **$294 85** | **$64,726 91** | .......... |
| 9 | **$87,022 77** | **$5,547 88** | **$9,121 01** | **$2,295 40** | .......... | .......... |
| 10 | **$108,290 99** | **$68,955 66** | **$192,929 33** | **$2,590 25** | **$64,726 91** | .......... |
| 11 | .......... | .......... | **$60 00** | .......... | .......... | .......... |
| 12 | .......... | .......... | $646 20 | .......... | .......... | .......... |
| 13 | .......... | .......... | 75 00 | .......... | .......... | .......... |
| 14 | .......... | .......... | 549 33 | .......... | .......... | .......... |
| 15 | .......... | .......... | 136 52 | .......... | .......... | .......... |
| 16 | .......... | .......... | 1,279 62 | .......... | .......... | .......... |
| 17 | .......... | .......... | **$2,686 67** | .......... | .......... | .......... |
| 18 | .......... | .......... | .......... | .......... | **$4,369 05** | .......... |
| 19 | **$108,290 99** | **$68,955 66** | **$195,676 00** | **$2,590 25** | **$69,095 96** | .......... |
| 20 | .......... | .......... | .......... | .......... | **$1,347,947 85** | **$7,489 65** |
| 21 | **$108,290 99** | **$68,955 66** | **$195,676 00** | **$2,590 25** | **$1,417,043 81** | **$7,489 65** |
| 22 | .......... | .......... | .......... | .......... | .......... | .......... |
| 23 | **$108,290 99** | **$68,955 66** | **$195,676 00** | **$2,590 25** | **$1,417,043 81** | **$7,489 65** |

Recapitulation of Statement Showing Expenditures from Corporate

| | Total | Personal Service | Supplies | Line No. |
|---|---|---|---|---|
| City Departments, Offices, Courts, Etc. | | | | |
| Mayor and Subordinate Departments, Bureaus and Offices: | | | | |
| Mayor's Office and Departments whose executive heads are appointed by the Mayor and who are removable at his pleasure | $21,863,484 28 | $2,602,947 88 | $121,051 52 | 1 |
| Departments whose heads are appointed by the Mayor for a term of office greater than his own, and who are removable only upon charges | 24,121,573 60 | 2,272,334 47 | 366,723 59 | 2 |
| Total Mayor and Subordinate Departments, Bureaus and Offices | **$45,985,057 88** | **$4,875,282 35** | **$487,775 11** | 3 |
| Borough Presidents and Subordinate Departments: | | | | |
| President, Borough of Manhattan | $2,088,119 36 | $147,103 26 | .......... | 4 |
| President, Borough of The Bronx | 842,186 69 | 172,315 59 | $12 33 | 5 |
| President, Borough of Brooklyn | 1,637,870 66 | 121,601 20 | .......... | 6 |
| President, Borough of Queens | 392,699 26 | 210,906 95 | .......... | 7 |
| President, Borough of Richmond | 438,076 45 | 163,780 91 | .......... | 8 |
| Total Borough Presidents | **$5,398,952 42** | **$815,707 91** | **$12 33** | 9 |
| Boards, Commissions, etc., whose members are not elected by popular vote and who are not appointed by any elected City official | **$6,472,707 67** | **$33,591 49** | **$61 66** | 10 |
| Boards, Commissions, etc., of mixed responsibility, i.e., ex-officio bodies representing two or more of preceding branches | **$531,122 80** | .......... | .......... | 11 |
| Total City Departments, Offices, Courts, etc. | **$58,387,840 77** | **$5,724,581 75** | **$487,849 10** | 12 |
| Fixed Charges other than Debt Service, Subsidies, Contributions, Payments to Private and State Institutions, Expenditures not Allotted to Departments | **$1,374,958 15** | **$6,341 43** | .......... | 13 |
| Advances for Local Improvements | **$16,085,308 01** | **$771,446 85** | **$1,506 31** | 14 |
| Total for City Purposes | **$75,848,106 93** | **$6,502,370 03** | **$489,355 41** | 15 |
| Total for All Purposes | **$75,848,106 93** | **$6,502,370 03** | **$489,355 41** | 16 |

## NEW YORK

STOCK FUNDS FOR THE YEAR 1910, CLASSIFIED BY OBJECTS OF EXPENDITURE.

| LINE No. | Purchase of Equipment | Materials | Contract or Open Order Service | Contingencies | Fixed Charges and Contributions | Unclassified |
|---|---|---|---|---|---|---|
| 1 | $170,767 76 | $100,986 16 | $11,435,979 06 | $13,522 91 | .......... | $7,418,228 99 |
| 2 | 562,503 81 | 383 15 | 16,957,070 79 | 1,320 18 | .......... | 3,961,237 61 |
| 3 | **$733,271 57** | **$101,369 31** | **$28,393,049 85** | **$14,843 09** | .......... | **$11,379,466 60** |
| 4 | $37,521 77 | .......... | $1,900,191 63 | .......... | .......... | $3,302 70 |
| 5 | 268 25 | $1,203 22 | 658,386 05 | $7 50 | .......... | 9,993 75 |
| 6 | .......... | .......... | 1,510,311 58 | .......... | .......... | 5,957 88 |
| 7 | 33,315 40 | .......... | 127,097 54 | .......... | .......... | 21,379 37 |
| 8 | 770 00 | .......... | 255,680 47 | .......... | .......... | 17,845 07 |
| 9 | **$71,875 42** | **$1,203 22** | **$4,451,667 27** | **$7 50** | .......... | **$58,478 77** |
| 10 | **$704 59** | .......... | **$6,194,135 60** | **$8,523 45** | .......... | **$235,690 88** |
| 11 | **$2,316 36** | .......... | **$485,198 94** | .......... | .......... | **$43,607 50** |
| 12 | **$808,167 94** | **$102,572 53** | **$39,524,051 66** | **$23,374 04** | .......... | **$11,717,243 75** |
| 13 | **$1,027 53** | .......... | **$1,351,334 66** | **$759 46** | .......... | **$15,495 07** |
| 14 | **$3,768 85** | .......... | **$4,306,683 32** | **$1,800 00** | .......... | **$11,000,102 68** |
| 15 | **$812,964 32** | **$102,572 53** | **$45,182,069 64** | **$25,933 50** | .......... | **$22,732,841 50** |
| 16 | **$812,964 32** | **$102,572 53** | **$45,182,069 64** | **$25,933 50** | .......... | **$22,732,841 50** |

STATEMENT SHOWING EXPENDITURES FROM CORPORATE STOCK

| | Total | Personal Service | Supplies | LINE No. |
|---|---|---|---|---|
| CITY DEPARTMENTS, OFFICES, COURTS, ETC.: | | | | |
| Mayor and Subordinate Departments, Bureaus and Offices: | | | | |
| Mayor's Office and Departments whose executive heads are appointed by the Mayor and who are removable at his pleasure: | | | | |
| Brooklyn Grade Crossing Commission | $200,000 00 | .......... | .......... | 1 |
| Change of Grade Damage Commission | 36,835 71 | $18,089 79 | $134 42 | 2 |
| Commission for the Improvement and Development of Jamaica Bay | 40,793 10 | 38,560 46 | .......... | 3 |
| Department of Bridges | 8,321,922 76 | 286,104 51 | 20,431 97 | 4 |
| Department of Corrections | 309,381 09 | .......... | .......... | 5 |
| Department of Docks and Ferries | 5,500,681 80 | 1,256,961 64 | 77,523 02 | 6 |
| Department of Health | 206,916 44 | 51,571 36 | 3,614 00 | 7 |
| Department of Parks—Brooklyn and Queens | 184,579 73 | 57,627 53 | .......... | 8 |
| Department of Parks—The Bronx | 405,815 51 | 99,582 48 | 3,372 52 | 9 |
| Department of Parks—Manhattan and Richmond | 540,099 77 | 153,896 04 | 5,754 04 | 10 |
| Department of Police | 245,312 92 | .......... | .......... | 11 |
| Department of Public Charities | 1,240,027 74 | 148 98 | 5,312 51 | 12 |
| Department of Street Cleaning | 37,889 02 | .......... | .......... | 13 |
| Department of Water Supply, Gas and Electricity | 4,170,185 83 | 593,570 53 | 4,111 41 | 14 |
| Fire Department | 383,126 69 | 17,425 76 | .......... | 15 |
| Metropolitan Sewerage Commission | 39,916 17 | 29,408 80 | 797 63 | 16 |
| Total | **$21,863,484 28** | **$2,602,947 88** | **$121,051 52** | 17 |
| Departments whose heads are appointed by the Mayor for a term of office greater than his own, and who are removable only on charges: | | | | |
| Aqueduct Commission | $1,316,228 48 | $149,174 99 | $2,111 85 | 18 |
| Bellevue and Allied Hospitals | 739,523 23 | 6,189 67 | .......... | 19 |
| Board of Water Supply | 19,392,417 49 | 1,943,982 09 | 364,445 89 | 20 |
| Department of Education | 2,642,643 83 | 167,152 84 | .......... | 21 |
| College of the City of New York | 23,661 50 | 243 33 | 165 85 | 22 |
| Normal College | 7,099 07 | 5,591 55 | .......... | 23 |
| Total | **$24,121,573 60** | **$2,272,334 47** | **$366,723 59** | 24 |
| Total, Mayor and Subordinate Departments, Bureaus and Offices | **$45,985,057 88** | **$4,875,282 35** | **$487,775 11** | 25 |
| Borough Presidents and Subordinate Departments: | | | | |
| President, Borough of Manhattan | $2,088,119 36 | $147,103 26 | .......... | 26 |
| President, Borough of The Bronx | 842,186 69 | 172,315 59 | $12 33 | 27 |
| President, Borough of Brooklyn | 1,637,870 66 | 121,601 20 | .......... | 28 |
| President, Borough of Queens | 392,699 26 | 210,906 95 | .......... | 29 |
| President, Borough of Richmond | 438,076 45 | 163,780 91 | .......... | 30 |
| Total | **$5,398,952 42** | **$815,707 91** | **$12 33** | 31 |
| Boards, Commissions, etc., whose members are not elected by popular vote and who are not appointed by any elected City official: | | | | |
| Commissioners of Estimate and Appraisal | $21,220 24 | $17,328 72 | $39 87 | 32 |
| Public Service Commission | 6,450,073 03 | 16,262 77 | 21 79 | 33 |
| Water Pollution Commission | 1,414 40 | .......... | .......... | 34 |
| Total | **$6,472,707 67** | **$33,591 49** | **$61 66** | 35 |

## NEW YORK

Funds for the Year 1910, Classified by Objects of Expenditure:

| Line No. | Purchase of Equipment | Materials | Contract or Open Order Service | Contingencies | Fixed Charges and Contributions | Unclassified |
|---|---|---|---|---|---|---|
| 1 | .......... | .......... | .......... | .......... | .......... | $200,000 00 |
| 2 | $115 84 | .......... | .......... | $2 07 | .......... | 18,493 59 |
| 3 | 9 50 | $6 53 | .......... | 1,375 41 | .......... | 841 20 |
| 4 | 4,195 64 | 5,266 89 | $3,381,692 72 | 244 52 | .......... | 4,623,986 51 |
| 5 | 915 30 | .......... | 308,465 79 | .......... | .......... | .......... |
| 6 | 4,777 71 | 508 46 | 1,937,711 75 | 9,524 00 | .......... | 2,213,675 22 |
| 7 | 5,191 05 | 25,409 04 | 120,615 99 | .......... | .......... | 515 00 |
| 8 | .......... | .......... | 126,952 20 | .......... | .......... | .......... |
| 9 | 667 00 | 32,125 35 | 270,068 16 | .......... | .......... | .......... |
| 10 | 44,613 34 | 33,379 33 | 302,152 26 | 162 45 | .......... | 142 31 |
| 11 | 9,978 59 | .......... | 235,334 33 | .......... | .......... | .......... |
| 12 | 21,598 92 | .......... | 1,177,891 33 | .......... | .......... | 35,076 00 |
| 13 | .......... | .......... | 37,889 02 | .......... | .......... | .......... |
| 14 | 2,327 41 | 4,290 56 | 3,264,772 02 | 2,125 67 | .......... | 298,988 23 |
| 15 | 75,774 87 | .......... | 268,966 85 | .......... | .......... | 20,959 21 |
| 16 | 602 59 | .......... | 3,466 64 | 88 79 | .......... | 5,551 72 |
| 17 | **$170,767 76** | **$100,986 16** | **$11,435,979 06** | **$13,522 91** | .......... | **$7,418,228 99** |
| 18 | $413 01 | $383 15 | $631,597 45 | $1,320 18 | .......... | $531,227 85 |
| 19 | 5,803 42 | .......... | 727,530 14 | .......... | .......... | .......... |
| 20 | 108,559 10 | .......... | 14,008,616 10 | .......... | .......... | 2,966,814 31 |
| 21 | 447,415 08 | .......... | 1,574,349 94 | .......... | .......... | 453,725 97 |
| 22 | 313 20 | .......... | 14,977 16 | .......... | .......... | 7,961 96 |
| 23 | .......... | .......... | .......... | .......... | .......... | 1,507 52 |
| 24 | **$562,503 81** | **$383 15** | **$16,957,070 79** | **$1,320 18** | .......... | **$3,961,237 61** |
| 25 | **$733,271 57** | **$101,369 31** | **$28,393,049 85** | **$14,843 09** | .......... | **$11,379,466 60** |
| 26 | $37,521 77 | .......... | $1,900,191 63 | .......... | .......... | $3,302 70 |
| 27 | 268 25 | $1,203 22 | 658,386 05 | $7 50 | .......... | 9,993 75 |
| 28 | .......... | .......... | 1,510,311 58 | .......... | .......... | 5,957 88 |
| 29 | 33,315 40 | .......... | 127,097 54 | .......... | .......... | 21,379 37 |
| 30 | 770 00 | .......... | 255,680 47 | .......... | .......... | 17,845 07 |
| 31 | **$71,875 42** | **$1,203 22** | **$4,451,667 27** | **$7 50** | .......... | **$58,478 77** |
| 32 | $704 59 | .......... | $12 75 | $27 97 | .......... | $3,106 34 |
| 33 | .......... | .......... | 6,192,708 45 | 8,495 48 | .......... | 232,584 54 |
| 34 | .......... | .......... | 1,414 40 | .......... | .......... | .......... |
| 35 | **$704 59** | .......... | **$6,194,135 60** | **$8,523 45** | .......... | **$235,690 88** |

STATEMENT SHOWING EXPENDITURES FROM CORPORATE STOCK FUNDS

| | Total | Personal Service | Supplies | LINE No. |
|---|---|---|---|---|
| CITY DEPARTMENTS, OFFICES, ETC.—*Continued* | | | | |
| Boards, Commissions, etc., of mixed responsibility, i.e., ex-officio bodies representing two or more preceding branches: | | | | |
| Armory Board | **$531,122 80** | .......... | .......... | 1 |
| Total City Departments, Offices, Courts, etc. | **$58,387,840 77** | **$5,724,581 75** | **$487,849 10** | 2 |
| FIXED CHARGES OTHER THAN DEBT SERVICE, SUBSIDIES, CONTRIBUTIONS, PAYMENTS TO PRIVATE AND STATE INSTITUTIONS, EXPENDITURES NOT ALLOTTED TO DEPARTMENTS: | | | | |
| Brooklyn Public Library | $218 98 | .......... | .......... | 3 |
| Miscellaneous, City | 27,465 73 | $3,701 12 | .......... | 4 |
| New York Public Library | 1,347,248 44 | 2,640 31 | .......... | 5 |
| Queensboro Public Library | 25 00 | .......... | .......... | 6 |
| Total | **$1,374,958 15** | **$6,341 43** | .......... | 7 |
| ADVANCES FOR LOCAL IMPROVEMENTS: | | | | |
| Fund for Street and Park Openings | $8,530,644 12 | $292,959 71 | $1,506 31 | 8 |
| Street Improvement Fund | 7,554,663 89 | 478,487 14 | .......... | 9 |
| Total | **$16,085,308 01** | **$771,446 85** | **$1,506 31** | 10 |
| Total for City Purposes | **$75,848,106 93** | **$6,502,370 03** | **$489,355 41** | 11 |
| Total for All Purposes | **$75,848,106 93** | **$6,502,370 03** | **$489,355 41** | 12 |

NEW YORK

FOR THE YEAR 1910, CLASSIFIED BY OBJECTS OF EXPENDITURE:—*Continued*

| LINE No. | Purchase of Equipment | Materials | Contract or Open Order Service | Contingencies | Fixed Charges and Contributions | Unclassified |
|---|---|---|---|---|---|---|
| 1 | **$2,316 36** | .......... | **$485,198 94** | .......... | .......... | **$43,607 50** |
| 2 | **$808,167 94** | **$102,572 53** | **$39,524,051 66** | **$23,374 04** | .......... | **$11,717,243 75** |
| 3 | $208 98 | .......... | .......... | .......... | .......... | $10 00 |
| 4 | .......... | .......... | $7,693 83 | $759 46 | .......... | 15,311 32 |
| 5 | 818 55 | .......... | 1,343,640 83 | .......... | .......... | 148 75 |
| 6 | .......... | .......... | .......... | .......... | .......... | 25 00 |
| 7 | **$1,027 53** | .......... | **$1,351,334 66** | **$759 46** | .......... | **$15,495 07** |
| 8 | $3,768 85 | .......... | $62,359 07 | $1,800 00 | .......... | $8,168,250 18 |
| 9 | .......... | .......... | 4,244,324 25 | .......... | .......... | 2,831,852 50 |
| 10 | **$3,768 85** | .......... | **$4,306,683 32** | **$1,800 00** | .......... | **$11,000,102 68** |
| 11 | **$812,964 32** | **$102,572 53** | **$45,182,069 64** | **$25,933 50** | .......... | **$22,732,841 50** |
| 12 | **$812,964 32** | **$102,572 53** | **$45,182,069 64** | **$25,933 50** | .......... | **$22,732,841 50** |

RECAPITULATION OF STATEMENT SHOWING EXPENDITURES FROM CORPORATE STOCK

| | Total | Personal Service | Supplies | LINE No. |
|---|---|---|---|---|
| CITY DEPARTMENTS, OFFICES, COURTS, ETC.: | | | | |
| Mayor and Subordinate Departments, Bureaus and Offices: | | | | |
| Mayor's Office and Departments whose executive heads are appointed by the Mayor and who are removable at his pleasure | $26,929,637 45 | $2,502,543 60 | $102,196 00 | 1 |
| Departments whose heads are appointed by the Mayor for a term of office greater than his own, and who are removable only on charges: | 32,103,501 14 | 2,396,285 54 | 340,148 21 | 2 |
| Total Mayor and Subordinate Departments, Bureaus and Offices | **$59,033,138 59** | **$4,898,829 14** | **$442,344 21** | 3 |
| Borough Presidents and Subordinate Departments: | | | | |
| President, Borough of Manhattan | $2,478,662 38 | $177,540 41 | .......... | 4 |
| President, Borough of The Bronx | 441,070 25 | 129,874 50 | $1,299 88 | 5 |
| President, Borough of Brooklyn | 1,550,396 18 | 114,729 46 | 1,566 49 | 6 |
| President, Borough of Queens | 343,530 67 | 153,284 70 | 3,356 76 | 7 |
| President, Borough of Richmond | 414,648 86 | 156,788 32 | 3,602 19 | 8 |
| Total Borough Presidents | **$5,228,308 34** | **$732,217 39** | **$9,825 32** | 9 |
| Boards, Commissions, etc., whose members are not elected by popular vote and who are not appointed by any elected City official | **$10,493,672 21** | **$113,896 76** | **$74 78** | 10 |
| Boards, Commissions, etc., of mixed responsibility, i.e., ex-officio bodies representing two or more of preceding branches | **$337,476 23** | .......... | .......... | 11 |
| Total City Departments, Offices, Courts, etc. | **$75,092,595 37** | **$5,744,943 29** | **$452,244 31** | 12 |
| FIXED CHARGES OTHER THAN DEBT SERVICE, SUBSIDIES, CONTRIBUTIONS, PAYMENTS TO PRIVATE AND STATE INSTITUTIONS, EXPENDITURES NOT ALLOTTED TO DEPARTMENTS | **$934,015 76** | **$9,489 78** | .......... | 13 |
| ADVANCES FOR LOCAL IMPROVEMENTS | **$13,095,611 67** | **$821,963 04** | **$3,087 00** | 14 |
| Total for City Purposes | **$89,122,222 80** | **$6,576,396 11** | **$455,331 31** | 15 |
| COUNTY EXPENDITURES: | | | | |
| New York County | **$19,277 55** | .......... | .......... | 16 |
| Total for All Purposes | **$89,141,500 35** | **$6,576,396 11** | **$455,331 31** | 17 |

NEW YORK

Funds for the Year 1911, Classified by Objects of Expenditure:

| Line No. | Purchase of Equipment | Materials | Contract or Open Order Service | Contingencies | Fixed Charges and Contributions | Unclassified |
|---|---|---|---|---|---|---|
| 1 | $321,163 48 | $1,963,604 69 | $7,119,077 55 | $33,176 15 | .......... | $14,887,875 98 |
| 2 | 745,372 27 | .......... | 22,822,995 12 | .......... | .......... | 5,798,700 00 |
| 3 | $1,066,535 75 | $1,963,604 69 | $29,942,072 67 | $33,176 15 | .......... | $20,686,575 98 |
| 4 | $21,115 39 | $18,341 72 | $2,261,664 86 | .......... | .......... | .......... |
| 5 | 1,755 26 | 506 96 | 307,200 48 | $419 17 | .......... | $14 00 |
| 6 | 21,116 00 | 168 08 | 1,410,736 10 | 869 05 | .......... | 1,211 00 |
| 7 | 2,454 97 | .......... | 162,810 75 | 1,976 24 | .......... | 19,647 25 |
| 8 | 2,237 29 | 869 71 | 245,813 42 | 3,644 93 | .......... | 1,693 00 |
| 9 | $48,678 91 | $19,886 47 | $4,388,225 61 | $6,909 39 | .......... | $22,565 25 |
| 10 | $698 61 | .......... | $8,445,288 01 | $179 38 | .......... | $1,933,534 67 |
| 11 | $17,348 10 | .......... | $312,602 54 | .......... | .......... | $7,525 59 |
| 12 | $1,133,261 37 | $1,983,491 16 | $43,088,188 83 | $40,264 92 | .......... | $22,650,201 49 |
| 13 | .......... | .......... | $664,974 40 | $155 10 | .......... | $259,396 48 |
| 14 | $31,071 90 | $152 40 | $6,188,925 63 | $2,000 00 | .......... | $6,048,411 70 |
| 15 | $1,164,333 27 | $1,983,643 56 | $49,942,088 86 | $42,420 02 | .......... | $28,958,009 67 |
| 16 | $18,023 69 | .......... | .......... | .......... | .......... | $1,253 86 |
| 17 | $1,182,356 96 | $1,983,643 56 | $49,942,088 86 | $42,420 02 | .......... | $28,959,263 53 |

STATEMENT OF EXPENDITURES FROM CORPORATE STOCK FUNDS

| | Total | Personal Service | Supplies | LINE No. |
|---|---|---|---|---|
| CITY DEPARTMENTS, OFFICES, COURTS, ETC.: | | | | |
| Mayor and Subordinate Departments, Bureaus and Offices: | | | | |
| Mayor's Office and Departments whose executive heads are appointed by the Mayor and who are removable at his pleasure: | | | | |
| Brooklyn Grade Crossing Commission........ | $330,000 00 | .......... | .......... | 1 |
| Change of Grade Damage Commission...... | 798,203 96 | $23,764 28 | $472 03 | 2 |
| Commission for the Improvement and Development of Jamaica Bay.................. | 460 00 | 310 00 | .......... | 3 |
| Department of Bridges.................... | 14,556,363 27 | 283,930 20 | 2,321 76 | 4 |
| Department of Corrections................. | 115,125 77 | .......... | .......... | 5 |
| Department of Docks and Ferries........... | 2,511,074 09 | 1,191,398 29 | 49,185 62 | 6 |
| Department of Health..................... | 179,475 53 | 38,431 59 | 3,651 58 | 7 |
| Department of Parks, Brooklyn and Queens. | 316,332 17 | 12,332 02 | 429 05 | 8 |
| Department of Parks, The Bronx........... | 272,275 52 | 84,142 76 | .......... | 9 |
| Department of Parks, Manhattan and Richmond................................ | 714,393 52 | 110,715 61 | 2,347 24 | 10 |
| Department of Police...................... | 500,161 93 | 3,280 35 | 9,118 90 | 11 |
| Department of Public Charities............ | 1,025,922 23 | 846 25 | .......... | 12 |
| Department of Street Cleaning............. | 79,353 68 | .......... | .......... | 13 |
| Department of Water Supply, Gas and Electricity............................ | 5,208,744 60 | 693,818 39 | 30,198 91 | 14 |
| Fire Department.......................... | 279,930 46 | 24,170 55 | .......... | 15 |
| Metropolitan Sewerage Commission......... | 41,820 72 | 35,403 31 | 4,470 91 | 16 |
| Total................................ | **$26,929,637 45** | **$2,502,543 60** | **$102,196 00** | 17 |
| Departments whose heads are appointed by the Mayor for a term of office greater than his own, and who are removable only on charges: | | | | |
| Aqueduct Commissions..................... | $1,109,534 04 | $86,254 97 | .......... | 18 |
| Bellevue and Allied Hospitals.............. | 528,675 53 | 3,892 00 | .......... | 19 |
| Board of Water Supply..................... | 25,948,565 93 | 2,062,619 31 | $340,148 21 | 20 |
| Department of Education.................. | 4,428,892 54 | 228,203 29 | .......... | 21 |
| College of the City of New York............ | 57,278 60 | .......... | .......... | 22 |
| Normal College........................... | 30,554 50 | 15,315 97 | .......... | 23 |
| Total................................ | **$32,103,501 14** | **$2,396,285 54** | **$340,148 21** | 24 |
| Total Mayor and Subordinate Departments, Bureaus and Offices............. | **$59,033,138 59** | **$4,898,829 14** | **$442,344 21** | 25 |
| Borough Presidents and Subordinate Departments. | | | | |
| President, Borough of Manhattan........... | $2,478,662 38 | $177,540 41 | .......... | 26 |
| President, Borough of The Bronx........... | 441,070 25 | 129,874 50 | $1,299 88 | 27 |
| President, Borough of Brooklyn............ | 1,550,396 18 | 114,729 46 | 1,566 49 | 28 |
| President, Borough of Queens.............. | 343,530 67 | 153,284 70 | 3,356 76 | 29 |
| President, Borough of Richmond............ | 414,648 86 | 156,788 32 | 3,602 19 | 30 |
| Total................................ | **$5,228,308 34** | **$732,217 39** | **$9,825 32** | 31 |
| Boards, Commissions, etc., whose members are not elected by popular vote, and who are not appointed by any elected City official: | | | | |
| Bronx Parkway Commission............... | $5,408 91 | $5,026 85 | .......... | 32 |
| Commissioners of Estimate and Appraisal... | 16,523 16 | 12,418 32 | $65 78 | 33 |
| Public Service Commission................ | 10,471,740 14 | 96,451 59 | 9 00 | 34 |
| Total................................ | **$10,493,672 21** | **$113,896 76** | **$74 78** | 35 |

## NEW YORK

FOR THE YEAR 1911, CLASSIFIED BY OBJECTS OF EXPENDITURE:

| LINE No. | Purchase of Equipment | Materials | Contract or Open Order Service | Contingencies | Fixed Charges and Contributions | Unclassified |
|---|---|---|---|---|---|---|
| 1 | .......... | .......... | .......... | .......... | .......... | $330,000 00 |
| 2 | .......... | .......... | .......... | $79 20 | .......... | 773,888 45 |
| 3 | .......... | .......... | .......... | .......... | .......... | 150 00 |
| 4 | $765 16 | $487 03 | $3,637,620 48 | 1,700 39 | .......... | 10,629,538 25 |
| 5 | 454 00 | .......... | 114,671 77 | .......... | .......... | .......... |
| 6 | 31,470 03 | 119,433 82 | 356,342 44 | 9,997 98 | .......... | 753,245 91 |
| 7 | 2,818 80 | 12,779 54 | 121,573 42 | 18 60 | .......... | 202 00 |
| 8 | 18 70 | .......... | 303,552 40 | .......... | .......... | .......... |
| 9 | 10,882 37 | 10,533 31 | 166,717 08 | .......... | .......... | .......... |
| 10 | 14,091 42 | 42,366 93 | 544,460 51 | 249 81 | .......... | 162 00 |
| 11 | .......... | .......... | 91,268 83 | .......... | .......... | 396,493 85 |
| 12 | 40,084 40 | .......... | 984,481 89 | .......... | .......... | 509 69 |
| 13 | .......... | .......... | 79,353 68 | .......... | .......... | .......... |
| 14 | 158,600 10 | 1,772,125 56 | 621,131 81 | 20,558 42 | .......... | 1,912,311 41 |
| 15 | 61,978 50 | 5,878 50 | 97,903 24 | 571 75 | .......... | 89,427 92 |
| 16 | .......... | .......... | .......... | .......... | .......... | 1,946 50 |
| 17 | **$321,163 48** | **$1,963,604 69** | **$7,119,077 55** | **$33,176 15** | .......... | **$14,887,875 98** |
| 18 | .......... | .......... | $554,249 64 | .......... | .......... | $469,029 43 |
| 19 | $18,549 49 | .......... | 506,234 04 | .......... | .......... | .......... |
| 20 | 63,478 53 | .......... | 18,596,411 87 | .......... | .......... | 4,885,908 01 |
| 21 | 663,344 25 | .......... | 3,093,637 44 | .......... | .......... | 443,707 56 |
| 22 | .......... | .......... | 57,278 60 | .......... | .......... | .......... |
| 23 | .......... | .......... | 15,183 53 | .......... | .......... | 55 00 |
| 24 | **$745,372 27** | .......... | **$22,822,995 12** | .......... | .......... | **$5,798,700 00** |
| 25 | **$1,066,535 75** | **$1,963,604 69** | **$29,942,072 67** | **$33,176 15** | .......... | **$20,686,575 98** |
| 26 | $21,115 39 | $18,341 72 | $2,261,664 86 | .......... | .......... | .......... |
| 27 | 1,755 26 | 506 96 | 307,200 48 | $419 17 | .......... | $14 00 |
| 28 | 21,116 00 | 168 08 | 1,410,736 10 | 869 05 | .......... | 1,211 00 |
| 29 | 2,454 97 | .......... | 162,810 75 | 1,976 24 | .......... | 19,647 25 |
| 30 | 2,237 29 | 869 71 | 245,813 42 | 3,644 93 | .......... | 1,693 00 |
| 31 | **$48,678 91** | **$19,886 47** | **$4,388,225 61** | **$6,909 39** | .......... | **$22,565 25** |
| 32 | $101 63 | .......... | .......... | $108 03 | .......... | $172 40 |
| 33 | 235 50 | .......... | .......... | 44 65 | .......... | 3,758 91 |
| 34 | 361 48 | .......... | $8,445,288 01 | 26 70 | .......... | 1,929,603 36 |
| 35 | **$698 61** | .......... | **$8,445,288 01** | **$179 38** | .......... | **$1,933,534 67** |

STATEMENT SHOWING EXPENDITURES FROM CORPORATE STOCK FUNDS

| | Total | Personal Service | Supplies | LINE No |
|---|---|---|---|---|
| CITY DEPARTMENTS, OFFICES, ETC.—*Continued* | | | | |
| Boards, Commissions, etc., of mixed responsibility, i.e., ex-officio bodies representing two or more of preceding branches: | | | | |
| Armory Board | **$337,476 23** | .......... | .......... | 1 |
| Total City Departments, Offices, Courts, etc. | **$75,092,595 37** | **$5,744,943 29** | **$452,244 31** | 2 |
| FIXED CHARGES OTHER THAN DEBT SERVICE, SUBSIDIES, CONTRIBUTIONS, PAYMENTS TO PRIVATE AND STATE INSTITUTIONS, EXPENDITURES NOT ALLOTTED TO DEPARTMENTS: | | | | |
| Brooklyn Public Library | $560 00 | .......... | .......... | 3 |
| Miscellaneous, City | 230,226 55 | $4,840 76 | .......... | 4 |
| New York Public Library | 703,229 21 | 4,649 02 | .......... | 5 |
| Total | **$934,015 76** | **$9,489 78** | .......... | 6 |
| ADVANCES FOR LOCAL IMPROVEMENTS: | | | | |
| Fund for Street and Park Openings | $6,300,963 84 | $296,763 98 | $2,239 55 | 7 |
| Street Improvement Fund | 6,794,647 83 | 525,199 06 | 847 45 | 8 |
| Total | **$13,095,611 67** | **$821,963 04** | **$3,087 00** | 9 |
| Total for City Purposes | **$89,122,222 80** | **$6,576,396 11** | **$455,331 31** | 10 |
| COUNTY EXPENDITURES: | | | | |
| New York County: | | | | |
| Clerk, New York County | **$19,277 55** | .......... | .......... | 11 |
| Total for All Purposes | **$89,141,500 35** | **$6,576,396 11** | **$455,331 31** | 12 |

NEW YORK

FOR THE YEAR 1911, CLASSIFIED BY OBJECTS OF EXPENDITURE:—*Continued*

| LINE No. | Purchase of Equipment | Materials | Contract or Open Order Service | Contingencies | Fixed Charges and Contributions | Unclassified |
|---|---|---|---|---|---|---|
| 1 | **$17,348 10** | .......... | **$312,602 54** | .......... | .......... | **$7,525 59** |
| 2 | **$1,133,261 37** | **$1,983,491 16** | **$43,088,188 83** | **$40,264 92** | .......... | **$22,650,201 49** |
| 3 | .......... | .......... | .......... | .......... | .......... | $560 00 |
| 4 | .......... | .......... | $729 94 | .......... | .......... | 224,655 85 |
| 5 | .......... | .......... | 664,244 46 | $155 10 | .......... | 34,180 63 |
| 6 | .......... | .......... | **$664,974 40** | **$155 10** | .......... | **$259,296 48** |
| 7 | $3,498 25 | .......... | $58,942 13 | $2,000 00 | .......... | $5,937,519 93 |
| 8 | 27,573 65 | $152 40 | 6,129,983 50 | .......... | .......... | 110,891 77 |
| 9 | **$31,071 90** | **$152 40** | **$6,188,925 63** | **$2,000 00** | .......... | **$6,048,411 70** |
| 10 | **$1,164,333 27** | **$1,983,643 56** | **$49,942,088 86** | **$42,420 02** | .......... | **$28,958,009 67** |
| 11 | **$18,023 69** | .......... | .......... | .......... | .......... | **$1,253 86** |
| 12 | **$1,182,356 96** | **$1,983,643 56** | **$49,942,088 86** | **$42,420 02** | .......... | **$28,959,263 53** |

RECAPITULATION OF STATEMENT SHOWING EXPENDITURES FROM CORPORATE

| | Total | Personal Service | Supplies | LINE No. |
|---|---|---|---|---|
| CITY DEPARTMENTS, OFFICES, COURTS, ETC.: | | | | |
| Mayor and Subordinate Departments, Bureaus and Offices: | | | | |
| Mayor's Office and Departments whose executive heads are appointed by the Mayor and who are removable at his pleasure.......... | $15,436,366 03 | $2,384,135 58 | $264,529 30 | 1 |
| Departments whose heads are appointed by the Mayor for a term of office greater than his own, and who are removable only on charges.. | 29,344,649 22 | 2,328,123 67 | 304,052 26 | 2 |
| Boards and Commissions majority of which are appointed by the Mayor and for which no other City Official shares responsibility...... | 71,542 41 | .......... | .......... | 3 |
| Total Mayor and Subordinate Departments, Bureaus and Offices............. | **$44,852,557 66** | **$4,712,259 25** | **$568,581 56** | 4 |
| Borough Presidents and Subordinate Departments: | | | | |
| President, Borough of Manhattan............. | $3,342,702 32 | $275,362 70 | .......... | 5 |
| President, Borough of The Bronx............. | 913,877 60 | 126,282 12 | $1,214 95 | 6 |
| President, Borough of Brooklyn.............. | 2,152,297 77 | 118,365 77 | 1,179 09 | 7 |
| President, Borough of Queens................ | 484,596 28 | 175,520 10 | 5,801 67 | 8 |
| President, Borough of Richmond.............. | 604,009 89 | 134,347 62 | 4,007 95 | 9 |
| Total Borough Presidents................ | **$7,497,483 86** | **$829,878 31** | **$12,203 66** | 10 |
| Boards, Commissions, etc., whose members are not elected by popular vote and who are not appointed by any elected City official......... | **$11,974,288 08** | **$81,235 12** | **$3,729 59** | 11 |
| Boards, Commissions, etc., of mixed responsibility, i.e. ex-officio bodies representing two or more of preceding branches.............. | **$428,971 91** | .......... | .......... | 12 |
| Total City Departments, Offices, Courts, etc.......................... | **$64,753,301 51** | **$5,623,372 68** | **$584,514 81** | 13 |
| FIXED CHARGES OTHER THAN DEBT SERVICE, SUBSIDIES, CONTRIBUTIONS, PAYMENTS TO PRIVATE AND STATE INSTITUTIONS, EXPENDITURES NOT ALLOTTED TO DEPARTMENTS................. | **$463,838 88** | **$636 30** | .......... | 14 |
| ADVANCES FOR LOCAL IMPROVEMENTS............ | **$15,200,511 22** | **$876,321 96** | **$7,059 88** | 15 |
| Total for City Purposes................. | **$80,417,651 61** | **$6,500,330 94** | **$591,574 69** | 16 |
| COUNTY EXPENDITURES: | | | | |
| New York County | **$47,589 18** | .......... | .......... | 17 |
| Total for All Purposes.................. | **$80,465,240 79** | **$6,500,330 94** | **$591,574 69** | 18 |

## NEW YORK

STOCK FUNDS FOR THE YEAR 1912, CLASSIFIED BY OBJECTS OF EXPENDITURE:

| LINE No. | Purchase of Equipment | Materials | Contract or Open Order Service | Contingencies | Fixed Charges and Contributions | Unclassified |
|---|---|---|---|---|---|---|
| 1 | $478,314 87 | $836,103 23 | $8,548,993 35 | $40,028 34 | .......... | $2,884,261 36 |
| 2 | 886,985 80 | 996 00 | 22,934,844 03 | .......... | .......... | 2,889,647 46 |
| 3 | .......... | .......... | .......... | .......... | .......... | 71,542 41 |
| 4 | **$1,365,300 67** | **$837,099 23** | **$31,483,837 38** | **$40,028 34** | .......... | **$5,845,451 23** |
| 5 | $13,909 26 | .......... | $2,995,803 59 | $19 81 | .......... | $57,606 96 |
| 6 | 695 91 | .......... | 784,675 60 | 456 85 | .......... | 552 17 |
| 7 | 186 66 | $60 60 | 1,949,588 15 | 588 75 | .......... | 82,328 75 |
| 8 | 2,689 42 | .......... | 291,896 83 | 2,672 74 | .......... | 6,015 52 |
| 9 | 1,598 50 | 76 25 | 454,308 58 | 3,200 80 | .......... | 6,470 19 |
| 10 | **$19,079 75** | **$136 85** | **$6,476,272 75** | **$6,938 95** | .......... | **$152,973 59** |
| 11 | **$8,602 28** | **$19,112 61** | **$9,987,748 62** | **$868 05** | .......... | **$1,872,991 81** |
| 12 | **$11,184 64** | .......... | **$417,530 63** | **$38 00** | .......... | **$218 64** |
| 13 | **$1,404,167 34** | **$856,348 69** | **$48,365,389 38** | **$47,873 34** | .......... | **$7,871,635 27** |
| 14 | .......... | .......... | **$141,499 37** | **$369 00** | .......... | **$321,334 21** |
| 15 | **$3,589 20** | **$3,705 38** | **$6,707,722 34** | **$2,800 00** | .......... | **$7,599,312 46** |
| 16 | **$1,407,756 54** | **$860,054 07** | **$55,214,611 09** | **$51,042 34** | .......... | **$15,792,281 94** |
| 17 | **$47,589 18** | .......... | .......... | .......... | .......... | .......... |
| 18 | **$1,455,345 72** | **$860,054 07** | **$55,214,611 09** | **$51,042 34** | .......... | **$15,792,281 94** |

# THE CITY OF

STATEMENT SHOWING EXPENDITURES FROM CORPORATE STOCK

| | Total | Personal Service | Supplies | LINE No. |
|---|---|---|---|---|
| CITY DEPARTMENTS, OFFICES, COURTS, ETC.: | | | | |
| Mayor and Subordinate Departments, Bureaus and Offices: | | | | |
| Mayor's Office and Departments whose executive heads are appointed by the Mayor, and who are removable at his pleasure: | | | | |
| Change of Grade Damage Commission...... | $410,846 42 | $14,423 96 | $438 93 | 1 |
| Department of Bridges.................... | 4,196,300 73 | 309,132 00 | 4,486 12 | 2 |
| Department of Corrections................. | 4,641 12 | .......... | .......... | 3 |
| Department of Docks and Ferries........... | 1,889,059 32 | 1,083,392 52 | 213,608 08 | 4 |
| Department of Health...................... | 401,110 72 | 37,609 44 | 4,510 62 | 5 |
| Department of Parks, Brooklyn and Queens. | 587,482 84 | 65,178 11 | .......... | 6 |
| Department of Parks, The Bronx........... | 239,511 06 | 75,471 37 | 29 35 | 7 |
| Department of Parks, Manhattan and Richmond.................................. | 912,889 23 | 67,151 86 | 921 73 | 8 |
| Department of Parks, Queens.............. | 18,814 03 | 1,964 03 | .......... | 9 |
| Department of Police...................... | 233,174 29 | 150 00 | .......... | 10 |
| Department of Public Charities............ | 1,741,366 59 | 3,582 39 | .......... | 11 |
| Department of Street Cleaning............. | 16,378 42 | 710 00 | .......... | 12 |
| Department of Water Supply, Gas and Electricity.................................. | 3,888,819 23 | 655,401 12 | 23,472 68 | 13 |
| Fire Department.......................... | 849,250 49 | 39,321 89 | 10,950 46 | 14 |
| Metropolitan Sewerage Commission......... | 46,721 54 | 30,646 89 | 6,111 33 | 15 |
| Total.................................. | **$15,436,366 03** | **$2,384,135 58** | **$264,529 30** | 16 |
| Departments, whose heads are appointed by the Mayor for a term of office greater than his own, and who are removable only on charges: | | | | |
| Aqueduct Commission...................... | $11,600 67 | $7,789 25 | $9 95 | 17 |
| Bellevue and Allied Hospitals.............. | 677,453 01 | 2,999 88 | .......... | 18 |
| Board of Water Supply..................... | 23,583,976 10 | 2,054,016 51 | 304,042 31 | 19 |
| Department of Education.................. | 4,787,473 13 | 258,324 97 | .......... | 20 |
| Normal College........................... | 284,146 31 | 4,993 06 | .......... | 21 |
| Total.................................. | **$29,344,649 22** | **$2,328,123 67** | **$304,052 26** | 22 |
| Boards and Commissions, majority of which are appointed by the Mayor, and for which no other elected City official shares responsibility: | | | | |
| Brooklyn Disciplinary Training School for Boys.................................. | $42 41 | .......... | .......... | 23 |
| Board of Inebriety........................ | 71,500 00 | .......... | .......... | 24 |
| Total.................................. | **$71,542 41** | .......... | .......... | 25 |
| Total, Mayor and Subordinate Departments, Bureaus and Offices............. | **$44,852,557 66** | **$4,712,259 25** | **$568,581 56** | 26 |
| Borough Presidents and Subordinate Departments: | | | | |
| President, Borough of Manhattan........... | $3,342,702 32 | $275,362 70 | .......... | 27 |
| President, Borough of The Bronx........... | 913,877 60 | 126,282 12 | $1,214 95 | 28 |
| President, Borough of Brooklyn............ | 2,152,297 77 | 118,365 77 | 1,179 09 | 29 |
| President, Borough of Queens.............. | 484,596 28 | 175,520 10 | 5,801 67 | 30 |
| President, Borough of Richmond............ | 604,009 89 | 134,347 62 | 4,007 95 | 31 |
| Total.................................. | **$7,497,483 86** | **$829,878 31** | **$12,203 66** | 32 |
| Boards, Commissions, etc., whose members are not elected by popular vote and who are not appointed by any elected city official: | | | | |
| Bronx Parkway Commission................ | $31,206 80 | $13,105 20 | $856 71 | 33 |
| Commissioners of Estimate and Appraisal.... | 15,472 56 | 11,855 95 | 92 75 | 34 |
| Court House Board........................ | 32,247 62 | 15,708 43 | 2,209 43 | 35 |
| Public Service Commission................. | 11,895,361 10 | 40,565 54 | 570 70 | 36 |
| Total.................................. | **$11,974,288 08** | **$81,235 12** | **$3,729 59** | 37 |

## NEW YORK

FUNDS FOR THE YEAR 1912, CLASSIFIED BY OBJECTS OF EXPENDITURE:

| LINE No. | Purchase of Equipment | Materials | Contract or Open Order Service | Contingencies | Fixed Charges and Contributions | Unclassified |
|---|---|---|---|---|---|---|
| 1 | .......... | .......... | .......... | .......... | .......... | $395,983 53 |
| 2 | $4,465 38 | $96,281 54 | $2,115,031 60 | $917 48 | .......... | 1,665,986 61 |
| 3 | .......... | 56 12 | 4,585 00 | .......... | .......... | .......... |
| 4 | 151,046 29 | 58,152 65 | 252,889 69 | 3,703 73 | .......... | 126,266 36 |
| 5 | 933 91 | 18,381 29 | 339,675 46 | .......... | .......... | .......... |
| 6 | 9,011 50 | 12,157 22 | 501,136 01 | .......... | .......... | .......... |
| 7 | 1,450 11 | 35,103 27 | 127,456 96 | .......... | .......... | .......... |
| 8 | 28,171 47 | 27,832 99 | 787,214 14 | 1,273 04 | .......... | 324 00 |
| 9 | .......... | 897 00 | 15,953 00 | .......... | .......... | .......... |
| 10 | 18,437 87 | .......... | 111,264 95 | .......... | .......... | 103,321 47 |
| 11 | 48,059 14 | .......... | 1,621,418 93 | .......... | .......... | 68,306 13 |
| 12 | .......... | .......... | 15,668 42 | .......... | .......... | .......... |
| 13 | 90,518 52 | 581,548 42 | 2,007,347 79 | 33,702 10 | .......... | 496,828 60 |
| 14 | 125,441 85 | 5,692 73 | 649,124 94 | 52 45 | .......... | 18,666 17 |
| 15 | 778 83 | .......... | 226 46 | 379 54 | .......... | 8,578 49 |
| 16 | **$478,314 87** | **$836,103 23** | **$8,548,993 35** | **$40,028 34** | .......... | **$2,884,261 36** |
| 17 | .......... | .......... | $163 47 | .......... | .......... | $3,638 00 |
| 18 | $85,945 21 | $996 00 | 586,825 81 | .......... | .......... | 686 11 |
| 19 | 39,921 73 | .......... | 19,202,180 78 | .......... | .......... | 1,983,814 77 |
| 20 | 761,118 86 | .......... | 2,866,520 72 | .......... | .......... | 901,508 58 |
| 21 | .......... | .......... | 279,153 25 | .......... | .......... | .......... |
| 22 | **$886,985 80** | **$996 00** | **$22,934,844 03** | .......... | .......... | **$2,889,647 46** |
| 23 | .......... | .......... | .......... | .......... | .......... | $42 41 |
| 24 | .......... | .......... | .......... | .......... | .......... | 71,500 00 |
| 25 | .......... | .......... | .......... | .......... | .......... | **$71,542 41** |
| 26 | **$1,365,300 67** | **$837,099 23** | **$31,483,837 38** | **$40,028 34** | .......... | **$5,845,451 23** |
| 27 | $13,909 26 | .......... | $2,995,803 59 | $19 81 | .......... | $57,606 96 |
| 28 | 695 91 | .......... | 784,675 60 | 456 85 | .......... | 552 17 |
| 29 | 186 66 | $60 60 | 1,949,588 15 | 588 75 | .......... | 82,328 75 |
| 30 | 2,689 42 | .......... | 291,896 83 | 2,672 74 | .......... | 6,015 52 |
| 31 | 1,598 50 | 76 25 | 454,308 58 | 3,200 80 | .......... | 6,470 19 |
| 32 | **$19,079 75** | **$136 85** | **$6,476,272 75** | **$6,938 95** | .......... | **$152,973 59** |
| 33 | $8,479 35 | .......... | $5,569 03 | $118 09 | .......... | $3,078 42 |
| 34 | .......... | .......... | .......... | 18 55 | .......... | 3,505 31 |
| 35 | 106 93 | .......... | 139 37 | 693 49 | .......... | 13,389 97 |
| 36 | 16 00 | $19,112 61 | 9,982,040 22 | 37 92 | .......... | 1,853,018 11 |
| 37 | **$8,602 28** | **$19,112 61** | **$9,987,748 62** | **$868 05** | .......... | **$1,872,991 81** |

Statement Showing Expenditures from Corporate Stock

| | Total | Personal Service | Supplies | Line No. |
|---|---|---|---|---|
| City Departments, Offices, Etc.—*Continued* | | | | |
| Boards, Commissions, etc., of mixed responsibility, i.e., ex-officio bodies representing two or more of preceding branches: | | | | |
| Armory Board | **$428,971 91** | .......... | .......... | 1 |
| Total City Departments, Offices, Courts, etc. | **$64,753,301 51** | **$5,623,372 68** | **$584,514 81** | 2 |
| Fixed Charges other than Debt Service, Subsidies, Contributions, Payments to Private and State Institutions, Expenditures not Allotted to Departments: | | | | |
| Brooklyn Public Library | $34,186 07 | .......... | .......... | 3 |
| Miscellaneous, City | 205,191 74 | $636 30 | .......... | 4 |
| New York Public Library | 224,461 07 | .......... | .......... | 5 |
| Total | **$463,838 88** | **$636 30** | .......... | 6 |
| Advances for Local Improvements: | | | | |
| Fund for Street and Park Openings | $7,916,073 05 | $318,804 41 | $3,391 08 | 7 |
| Street Improvement Fund | 7,284,438 17 | 557,517 55 | 3,668 80 | 8 |
| Total | **$15,200,511 22** | **$876,321 96** | **$7,059 88** | 9 |
| Total for City Purposes | **$80,417,651 61** | **$6,500,330 94** | **$591,574 69** | 10 |
| County Expenditures: | | | | |
| New York County: | | | | |
| Clerk, New York County | **$47,589 18** | .......... | .......... | 11 |
| Total for All Purposes | **$80,465,240 79** | **$6,500,330 94** | **$591,574 69** | 12 |

NEW YORK

FUNDS FOR THE YEAR 1912, CLASSIFIED BY OBJECTS OF EXPENDITURE:—*Continued*

| LINE No. | Purchase of Equipment | Materials | Contract or Open Order Service | Contingencies | Fixed Charges and Contributions | Unclassified |
|---|---|---|---|---|---|---|
| 1 | **$11,184 64** | .......... | **$417,530 63** | **$38 00** | .......... | **$218 64** |
| 2 | **$1,404,167 34** | **$856,348 69** | **$48,365,389 38** | **$47,873 34** | .......... | **$7,871,635 27** |
| 3 | .......... | .......... | .......... | .......... | .......... | $34,186 07 |
| 4 | .......... | .......... | $3,038 30 | $369 00 | .......... | 201,148 14 |
| 5 | .......... | .......... | 138,461 07 | .......... | .......... | 86,000 00 |
| 6 | .......... | .......... | **$141,499 37** | **$369 00** | .......... | **$321,334 21** |
| 7 | $2,784 15 | .......... | $52,529 12 | $2,800 00 | .......... | $7,535,764 29 |
| 8 | 805 05 | $3,705 38 | 6,655,193 22 | .......... | .......... | 63,548 17 |
| 9 | **$3,589 20** | **$3,705 38** | **$6,707,722 34** | **$2,800 00** | .......... | **$7,599,312 46** |
| 10 | **$1,407,756 54** | **$860,054 07** | **$55,214,611 09** | **$51,042 34** | .......... | **$15,792,281 94** |
| 11 | **$47,589 18** | .......... | .......... | .......... | .......... | .......... |
| 12 | **$1,455,345 72** | **$860,054 07** | **$55,214,611 09** | **$51,042 34** | .......... | **$15,792,281 94** |

RECAPITULATION OF STATEMENT SHOWING EXPENDITURES FROM CORPORATE

| | Total | Personal Service | Supplies | LINE No. |
|---|---|---|---|---|
| CITY DEPARTMENTS, OFFICES, COURTS, ETC.: | | | | |
| Mayor and Subordinate Departments, Bureaus and Offices: | | | | |
| Mayor's Office and Departments whose executive heads are appointed by the Mayor and who are removable at his pleasure......... | $22,819,261 95 | $2,358,730 03 | $34,818 42 | 1 |
| Departments whose heads are appointed by the Mayor for a term of office greater than his own, and who are removable only on charges. | 27,590,048 17 | 2,096,370 66 | 305,211 46 | 2 |
| Boards and Commissions majority of which are appointed by the Mayor and for which no other elected City official shares responsibility | 3,525 00 | .......... | .......... | 3 |
| Total Mayor and Subordinate Departments, Bureaus and Offices............ | **$50,412,835 12** | **$4,455,100 68** | **$340,029 88** | 4 |
| Borough Presidents and Subordinate Departments: | | | | |
| President, Borough of Manhattan............. | $3,108,160 60 | $167,201 36 | $58 14 | 5 |
| President, Borough of The Bronx............. | 974,954 31 | 90,505 86 | 945 71 | 6 |
| President, Borough of Brooklyn.............. | 2,117,246 09 | 143,960 51 | 1,133 51 | 7 |
| President, Borough of Queens................ | 673,638 84 | 120,227 83 | 3,837 54 | 8 |
| President, Borough of Richmond.............. | 779,036 92 | 84,867 68 | 1,302 47 | 9 |
| Total Borough Presidents................ | **$7,653,036 76** | **$606,763 24** | **$7,277 37** | 10 |
| Boards, Commissions, etc., whose members are not elected by popular vote and who are not appointed by any elected City official...... | **$27,451,950 39** | **$31,438 41** | **$2,280 00** | 11 |
| Boards, Commissions, etc., of mixed responsibility, i.e., ex-officio bodies representing two or more of preceding branches..................... | **$570,620 05** | .......... | **$994 50** | 12 |
| Total City Departments, Office, Courts, etc. | **$86,088,442 32** | **$5,093,302 33** | **$350,581 75** | 13 |
| FIXED CHARGES OTHER THAN DEBT SERVICE, SUBSIDIES, CONTRIBUTIONS, PAYMENTS TO PRIVATE AND STATE INSTITUTIONS, EXPENDITURES NOT ALLOTTED TO DEPARTMENTS................. | **$563,072 77** | .......... | **$70 00** | 14 |
| ADVANCES FOR LOCAL IMPROVEMENTS............ | **$17,877,055 22** | **$1,293,521 83** | **$4,649 65** | 15 |
| Total for City Purposes................. | **$104,528,570 31** | **$6,386,824 16** | **$355,301 40** | 16 |
| COUNTY EXPENDITURES: | | | | |
| New York County: | **$6,640 19** | .......... | .......... | 17 |
| Total for All Purposes.................. | **$104,535,210 50** | **$6,386,824 16** | **$355,301 40** | 18 |

## NEW YORK

Stock Funds for the Year 1913, Classified by Objects of Expenditure

| LINE No. | Purchase of Equipment | Materials | Contract or Open Order Service | Contingencies | Fixed Charges and Contributions | Unclassified |
|---|---|---|---|---|---|---|
| 1 | $694,412 55 | $101,842 25 | $11,796,502 71 | $75,071 15 | .......... | $7,757,884 85 |
| 2 | 1,220,720 20 | 14 95 | 21,530,532 76 | .......... | .......... | 2,437,198 14 |
| 3 | .......... | .......... | .......... | .......... | .......... | 3,525 00 |
| 4 | **$1,915,132 75** | **$101,857 20** | **$33,327,035 47** | **$75,071 15** | .......... | **$10,198,607 99** |
| 5 | $5,621 76 | $78 00 | $2,912,330 71 | .......... | .......... | $22,870 63 |
| 6 | 1,557 57 | 57 50 | 877,994 20 | $380 76 | .......... | 3,512 71 |
| 7 | 721 06 | .......... | 1,716,756 21 | .......... | .......... | 254,674 80 |
| 8 | 3,506 61 | 162 85 | 543,708 76 | .......... | .......... | 2,195 25 |
| 9 | 7,225 94 | 1,177 77 | 451,857 43 | 707 21 | .......... | 231,898 42 |
| 10 | **$18,632 94** | **$1,476 12** | **$6,502,647 31** | **$1,087 97** | .......... | **$515,151 81** |
| 11 | **$2,150 11** | **$403 18** | **$15,105,959 67** | .......... | .......... | **$12,309,719 02** |
| 12 | **$58,286 86** | .......... | **$511,338 69** | .......... | .......... | .......... |
| 13 | **$1,994,202 66** | **$103,736 50** | **$55,446,981 14** | **$76,159 12** | .......... | **$23,023,478 82** |
| 14 | **$20,078 10** | .......... | **$142,866 11** | .......... | .......... | **$400,058 56** |
| 15 | **$2,497 72** | **$1,700 95** | **$8,597,992 16** | **$2,400 00** | .......... | **$7,974,292 91** |
| 16 | **$2,016,778 48** | **$105,437 45** | **$64,187,839 41** | **$78,559 12** | .......... | **$31,397,830 29** |
| 17 | **$6,640 19** | .......... | .......... | .......... | .......... | .......... |
| 18 | **$2,023,418 67** | **$105,437 45** | **$64,187,839 41** | **$78,559 12** | .......... | **$31,397,830 29** |

Statement of Expenditures from Corporate Stock Funds

| | Total | Personal Service | Supplies | LINE No. |
|---|---|---|---|---|
| City Departments, Offices, Courts, Etc.: | | | | |
| Mayor and Subordinate Departments, Bureaus and Offices: | | | | |
| Mayor's Office and Departments whose executive heads are appointed by the Mayor and who are removable at his pleasure: | | | | |
| Brooklyn Grade Crossing Commission | $262,500 00 | .......... | .......... | 1 |
| Change of Grade Damage Commission | 173,132 49 | $17,399 96 | $18 50 | 2 |
| Department of Bridges | 4,318,872 71 | 342,083 69 | 2,788 63 | 3 |
| Department of Correction | 148,201 61 | .......... | .......... | 4 |
| Department of Docks and Ferries | 9,074,543 46 | 1,137,286 13 | 17,441 08 | 5 |
| Department of Health | 277,226 55 | 30,221 15 | 752 65 | 6 |
| Department of Parks, Brooklyn and Queens | 699,466 01 | 43,862 05 | 220 65 | 7 |
| Department of Parks, The Bronx | 142,994 87 | 37,287 65 | 2,353 21 | 8 |
| Department of Parks, Manhattan and Richmond | 981,874 86 | 44,625 44 | 3,161 81 | 9 |
| Department of Parks, Queens | 14,862 40 | 6,928 23 | 160 00 | 10 |
| Department of Police | 479,886 23 | .......... | 59 29 | 11 |
| Department of Public Charities | 1,887,563 94 | 996 83 | 386 72 | 12 |
| Department of Street Cleaning | 28,224 36 | .......... | .......... | 13 |
| Department of Water Supply, Gas and Electricity | 2,582,159 29 | 622,413 52 | 5,192 99 | 14 |
| Fire Department | 1,704,330 65 | 54,592 39 | 1,847 27 | 15 |
| Metropolitan Sewerage Commission | 43,422 52 | 21,032 98 | 435 62 | 16 |
| Total | **$22,819,261 95** | **$2,358,730 02** | **$34,818 42** | 17 |
| Departments whose heads are appointed by the Mayor for a term of office greater than his own and who are removable only on charges: | | | | |
| Aqueduct Commission | $51,225 10 | .......... | .......... | 18 |
| Bellevue and Allied Hospitals | 1,246,337 30 | $2,468 10 | .......... | 19 |
| Board of Water Supply | 21,352,421 87 | 1,827,882 72 | $301,865 85 | 20 |
| Department of Education | 4,731,385 07 | 262,897 09 | .......... | 21 |
| College of the City of New York | 33,742 23 | .......... | 620 86 | 22 |
| Normal College | 174,936 60 | 3,122 75 | 2,724 75 | 23 |
| Total | **$27,590,048 17** | **$2,096,370 66** | **$305,211 46** | 24 |
| Boards and Commissions, majority of which are appointed by the Mayor and for which no other City official shares responsibility: | | | | |
| Board of Inebriety | **$3,525 55** | .......... | .......... | 25 |
| Total, Mayor and Subordinate Departments, Bureaus and Offices | **$50,412,835 12** | **$4,455,100 68** | **$340,029 88** | 26 |
| Borough Presidents and Subordinate Departments: | | | | |
| President, Borough of Manhattan | $3,108,160 60 | $167,201 36 | $58 14 | 27 |
| President, Borough of The Bronx | 974,954 31 | 90,505 86 | 945 71 | 28 |
| President, Borough of Brooklyn | 2,117,246 09 | 143,960 51 | 1,133 51 | 29 |
| President, Borough of Queens | 673,638 84 | 120,227 83 | 3,837 54 | 30 |
| President, Borough of Richmond | 779,036 92 | 84,867 68 | 1,302 47 | 31 |
| Total | **$7,653,036 76** | **$606,763 24** | **$7,277 37** | 32 |

## NEW YORK

FOR THE YEAR 1913, CLASSIFIED BY OBJECTS OF EXPENDITURE

| LINE No. | Purchase of Equipment | Materials | Contract or Open Order Service | Contingencies | Fixed Charges and Contributions | Unclassified |
|---|---|---|---|---|---|---|
| 1 | .......... | .......... | .......... | .......... | .......... | $262,500 00 |
| 2 | .......... | .......... | .......... | .......... | .......... | 155,714 03 |
| 3 | $4,094 59 | $7,701 48 | $3,854,151 92 | $10,315 46 | .......... | 97,736 94 |
| 4 | .......... | .......... | 94,018 11 | .......... | .......... | 54,183 50 |
| 5 | 7,273 99 | 14,416 76 | 882.917 09 | .......... | .......... | 7,015,208 41 |
| 6 | 5,224 50 | 5,916 91 | 235,111 34 | .......... | .......... | .......... |
| 7 | 361 80 | 2,926 02 | 649,948 62 | .......... | .......... | 2,146 87 |
| 8 | 2,959 68 | 8,763 28 | 91,631 05 | .......... | .......... | .......... |
| 9 | 18,180 06 | 24,078 88 | 840,029 57 | .......... | .......... | 51,799 10 |
| 10 | .......... | .......... | 6,824 17 | .......... | .......... | 950 00 |
| 11 | 7,452 63 | .......... | 472,289 31 | .......... | .......... | 85 00 |
| 12 | 79,183 98 | 407 50 | 1,724,106 48 | 50,612 45 | .......... | 31,869 98 |
| 13 | .......... | .......... | 28,224 36 | .......... | .......... | .......... |
| 14 | 15,375 05 | 27,137 71 | 1,848,780 68 | 14,143 24 | .......... | 49,116 10 |
| 15 | 553,637 11 | 10,493 71 | 1,065,070 53 | .......... | .......... | 18,689 64 |
| 16 | 669 16 | .......... | 3,399 48 | .......... | .......... | 17,885 28 |
| 17 | **$694,412 55** | **$101,842 25** | **$11,796,502 71** | **$75,071 15** | .......... | **$7,757,884 85** |
| 18 | .......... | .......... | .......... | .......... | .......... | $51,225 10 |
| 19 | $4,980 46 | .......... | $1,238,276 24 | .......... | .......... | 612 50 |
| 20 | 15,729 10 | .......... | 17,225,758 79 | .......... | .......... | 1,981,185 41 |
| 21 | 1,198,476 23 | .......... | 2,865,928 29 | .......... | .......... | 404,083 46 |
| 22 | 1,534 41 | $14 95 | 31,480 34 | .......... | .......... | 91 67 |
| 23 | .......... | .......... | 169,089 10 | .......... | .......... | .......... |
| 24 | **$1,220,720 20** | **$14 95** | **$21,530,532 76** | .......... | .......... | **$2,437,198 14** |
| 25 | .......... | .......... | .......... | .......... | .......... | **$3,525 00** |
| 26 | **$1,915,132 75** | **$101,857 20** | **$33,327,035 47** | **$75,071 15** | .......... | **$10,198,607 99** |
| 27 | $5,621 76 | $78 00 | $2,912,330 71 | .......... | .......... | $22,870 63 |
| 28 | 1,557 57 | 57 50 | 877,994 20 | $380 76 | .......... | 3,512 71 |
| 29 | 721 06 | .......... | 1,716,756 21 | .......... | .......... | 254,674 80 |
| 30 | 3,506 61 | 162 85 | 543,708 76 | .......... | .......... | 2,195 25 |
| 31 | 7,225 94 | 1,177 77 | 451,857 43 | 707 21 | .......... | 231,898 42 |
| 32 | **$18,632 94** | **$1,476 12** | **$6,502,647 31** | **$1,087 97** | .......... | **$515,151 81** |

STATEMENT SHOWING EXPENDITURES FROM CORPORATE STOCK

| | Total | Personal Service | Supplies | LINE No. |
|---|---|---|---|---|
| CITY DEPARTMENTS, ETC.—*Continued.* | | | | |
| Boards, Commissions, etc., whose members are not elected by popular vote and who are not appointed by any elected City official: | | | | |
| Bronx Parkway Commission | $779,233 07 | $15,826 90 | $1,024 14 | 1 |
| Court House Board | 6,485,390 98 | 12,160 20 | 1,246 86 | 2 |
| Public Service Commission | 20,187,326 34 | 3,451 31 | 9 00 | 3 |
| Total | **$27,451,950 39** | **$31,438 41** | **$2,280 00** | 4 |
| Boards, Commissions, etc., of mixed responsibility, i. e., ex-officio bodies representing two or more of preceding branches: | | | | |
| Armory Board | **$570,620 05** | .......... | **$994 50** | 5 |
| Total City Departments, Offices, Courts, etc. | **$86,088,442 32** | **$5,093,302 33** | **$350,581 75** | 6 |
| FIXED CHARGES OTHER THAN DEBT SERVICE, SUBSIDIES, CONTRIBUTIONS, PAYMENTS TO PRIVATE AND STATE INSTITUTIONS, EXPENDITURES NOT ALLOTTED TO DEPARTMENTS: | | | | |
| Brooklyn Public Library | $115,997 82 | .......... | .......... | 7 |
| Miscellaneous, City | 401,062 51 | .......... | .......... | 8 |
| New York Public Library | 46,012 44 | .......... | $70 00 | 9 |
| Total | **$563,072 77** | .......... | **$70 00** | 10 |
| ADVANCES FOR LOCAL IMPROVEMENTS: | | | | |
| Fund for Street and Park Openings | $8,286,777 28 | $299,292 55 | $3,687 95 | 11 |
| Street Improvement Fund | 9,590,277 94 | 994,229 28 | 961 70 | 12 |
| Total | **$17,877,055 22** | **$1,293,521 83** | **$4,649 65** | 13 |
| Total for City Purposes | **$104,528,570 31** | **$6,386,824 16** | **$355,301 40** | 14 |
| COUNTY EXPENDITURES: | | | | |
| New York County: | | | | |
| Clerk, New York County | **$6,640 19** | .......... | .......... | 15 |
| Total for All Purposes | **$104,535,210 50** | **$6,386,824 16** | **$355,301 40** | 16 |

## NEW YORK

FUNDS, FOR THE YEAR 1913, CLASSIFIED BY OBJECTS OF EXPENDITURE:—*Continued*

| LINE No. | Purchase of Equipment | Materials | Contract or Open Order Service | Contingencies | Fixed Charges and Contributions | Unclassified |
|---|---|---|---|---|---|---|
| 1 | $1,662 09 | $403 18 | $160 05 | .......... | .......... | $760,156 71 |
| 2 | 454 28 | .......... | .......... | .......... | .......... | 6,471,529 64 |
| 3 | 33 74 | .......... | 15,105,799 62 | .......... | .......... | 5,078,032 67 |
| 4 | **$2,150 11** | **$403 18** | **$15,105,959 67** | .......... | .......... | **$12,309,719 02** |
| 5 | **$58,286 86** | .......... | **$511,338 69** | .......... | .......... | .......... |
| 6 | **$1,994,202 66** | **$103,736 50** | **$55,446,981 14** | **$76,159 12** | .......... | **$23,023,478 82** |
| 7 | $1,072 53 | .......... | $112,383 41 | .......... | .......... | $2,541 88 |
| 8 | .......... | .......... | 4,007 30 | .......... | .......... | 397,055 21 |
| 9 | 19,005 57 | .......... | 26,475 40 | .......... | .......... | 461 47 |
| 10 | **$20,078 10** | .......... | **$142,866 11** | .......... | .......... | **$400,058 56** |
| 11 | $1,246 00 | .......... | $50,297 27 | $2,400 00 | .......... | $7,929,853 51 |
| 12 | 1,251 72 | $1,700 95 | 8,547,694 89 | .......... | .......... | 44,439 40 |
| 13 | **$2,497 72** | **$1,700 95** | **$8,597,992 16** | **$2,400 00** | .......... | **$7,974,292 91** |
| 14 | **$2,016,778 48** | **$105,437 45** | **$64,187,839 41** | **$78,559 12** | .......... | **$31,397,830 29** |
| 15 | **$6,640 19** | .......... | .......... | .......... | .......... | .......... |
| 16 | **$2,023,418 67** | **$105,437 45** | **$64,187,839 41** | **$78,559 12** | .......... | **$31,397,830 29** |

Recapitulation of Statement Showing Expenditures from Corporate Stock

| | Total | Personal Service | Supplies | Line No. |
|---|---|---|---|---|
| City Departments, Offices, Courts, Etc. | | | | |
| Mayor and Subordinate Departments, Bureaus and Offices: | | | | |
| Mayor's Office and Departments whose executive heads are appointed by the Mayor and heads who are removable at his pleasure..... | $10,764,182 54 | $1,973,520 06 | $350,652 43 | 1 |
| Departments whose heads are appointed by the Mayor for a term of office greater than his own and who are removable only on charges.. | 20,391,400 84 | 1,652,184 94 | 220,901 23 | 2 |
| Total Mayor and Subordinate Departments, Bureaus and Offices............. | **$31,155,583 38** | **$3,625,705 00** | **$571,553 66** | 3 |
| Borough Presidents and Subordinate Departments: | | | | |
| President, Borough of Manhattan........... | $2,255,201 20 | $151,211 18 | $2,040 85 | 4 |
| President, Borough of The Bronx........... | 633,170 73 | 33,701 97 | .......... | 5 |
| President, Borough of Brooklyn............ | 1,102,652 22 | 72,245 00 | 998 93 | 6 |
| President, Borough of Queens.............. | 507,891 81 | 41,179 96 | 1,680 06 | 7 |
| President, Borough of Richmond............ | 339,375 68 | 35,938 70 | 286 68 | 8 |
| Total Borough Presidents............... | **$4,838,291 64** | **$334,276 81** | **$5,006 52** | 9 |
| Boards, Commissions, etc., whose members are not elected by popular vote and who are not appointed by any elected City official....... | **$24,814,274 61** | **$37,460 91** | **$2,306 69** | 10 |
| Boards, Commissions, etc., of mixed responsibility, i.e., ex-officio bodies representing two or more of preceding branches................ | **$514,203 36** | .......... | **$372 75** | 11 |
| Total City Departments, Offices, Courts, etc. | **$61,322,352 99** | **$3,997,442 72** | **$579,239 62** | 12 |
| Fixed Charges other than Debt Service, Subsidies, Contributions, Payments to Private and State Institutions, Expenditures not Allotted to Departments.................. | **$1,463,227 44** | **$1,650 00** | .......... | 13 |
| Advances for Local Improvements............ | **$20,779,517 54** | **$968,188 26** | **$2,272 53** | 14 |
| Total for City Purposes.................. | **$83,565,097 97** | **$4,967,280 98** | **$581,512 15** | 15 |
| Total for All Purposes.................. | **$83,565,097 97** | **$4,967,280 98** | **$581,512 15** | 16 |

NEW YORK

FUNDS, FOR THE YEAR 1914, CLASSIFIED BY OBJECTS OF EXPENDITURE:

| LINE No. | Purchase of Equipment | Materials | Contract or Open Order Service | Contingencies | Fixed Charges and Contributions | Unclassified |
|---|---|---|---|---|---|---|
| 1 | $596,711 07 | $183,582 29 | $7,144,373 03 | $21,629 62 | .......... | $493,714 04 |
| 2 | 1,463,352 95 | 150 00 | 16,012,916 78 | .......... | .......... | 1,041,894 94 |
| 3 | **$2,060,064 02** | **$183,732 29** | **$23,157,289 81** | **$21,629 62** | .......... | **$1,535,608 98** |
| 4 | $15,592 91 | $659 19 | $1,832,933 83 | .......... | .......... | $252,763 24 |
| 5 | 63 45 | .......... | 599,405 31 | .......... | .......... | .......... |
| 6 | .......... | .......... | 1,026,168 69 | $29 50 | .......... | 3,210 10 |
| 7 | 1,820 55 | 47 24 | 462,227 25 | .......... | .......... | 936 75 |
| 8 | 299 56 | 198 20 | 296,421 66 | 279 56 | .......... | 5,951 32 |
| 9 | **$17,776 47** | **$904 63** | **$4,217,156 74** | **$309 06** | .......... | **$262,861 41** |
| 10 | **$2,028 68** | **$17 10** | **$19,863,450 15** | **$3,312 12** | .......... | **$4,905,698 96** |
| 11 | **$12,118 10** | .......... | **$501,712 51** | .......... | .......... | .......... |
| 12 | **$2,091,987 27** | **$184,654 02** | **$47,739,609 21** | **$25,250 80** | .......... | **$6,704,169 35** |
| 13 | **$29,921 90** | .......... | **$456,058 91** | **$255 13** | .......... | **$975,341 50** |
| 14 | **$5,743 59** | **$125 60** | **$6,993,159 06** | **$7,669 75** | .......... | **$12,802,358 75** |
| 15 | **$2,127,652 76** | **$184,779 62** | **$55,188,827 18** | **$33,175 68** | .......... | **$20,481,869 60** |
| 16 | **$2,127,652 76** | **$184,779 62** | **$55,188,827 18** | **$33,175 68** | .......... | **$20,481,869 60** |

# THE CITY OF

STATEMENT SHOWING EXPENDITURES FROM CORPORATE STOCK FUNDS

| | Total | Personal Service | Supplies | LINE No. |
|---|---|---|---|---|
| CITY DEPARTMENTS, OFFICES, COURTS, ETC. | | | | |
| Mayor and Subordinate Departments, Bureaus and Offices: | | | | |
| Mayor's Office and Departments whose executive heads are appointed by the Mayor and who are removable at his pleasure: | | | | |
| Brooklyn Grade Crossing Commission | $365,000 00 | .......... | .......... | 1 |
| Change of Grade Damage Commission | 7,156 63 | $6,351 29 | .......... | 2 |
| Department of Bridges | 2,636,742 84 | 239,965 41 | $5,015 16 | 3 |
| Department of Correction | 41,241 20 | .......... | 360 83 | 4 |
| Department of Docks and Ferries | 2,009,343 98 | 1,075,940 05 | 57,427 19 | 5 |
| Department of Health | 258,891 52 | 35,207 53 | 6,385 06 | 6 |
| Department of Parks—Brooklyn | 404,424 12 | 15,991 77 | 1,980 25 | 7 |
| Department of Parks—The Bronx | 43,703 79 | 8,355 88 | 7,410 36 | 8 |
| Department of Parks—Manhattan and Richmond | 390,900 22 | 60,360 83 | 9,572 55 | 9 |
| Department of Parks—Queens | 8,052 11 | 4,051 95 | 387 00 | 10 |
| Department of Police | 218,651 47 | .......... | .......... | 11 |
| Department of Public Charities | 968,135 23 | 1,709 00 | 1,380 92 | 12 |
| Department of Street Cleaning | 26,672 07 | 1,436 51 | .......... | 13 |
| Department of Water Supply, Gas and Electricity | 2,383,102 24 | 447,169 57 | 242,928 93 | 14 |
| Fire Department | 977,167 99 | 59,771 57 | 17,660 85 | 15 |
| Metropolitan Sewerage Commission | 24,997 13 | 17,208 70 | 143 33 | 16 |
| Total | **$10,764,182 54** | **$1,973,520 06** | **$350,652 43** | 17 |
| Departments whose heads are appointed by the Mayor for a term of office greater than his own and who are removable only on charges: | | | | |
| Bellevue and Allied Hospitals | $720,361 00 | $2,280 65 | $99 00 | 18 |
| Board of Water Supply | 14,107,495 59 | 1,416,004 78 | 220,058 00 | 19 |
| Department of Education | 5,437,237 30 | 231,977 68 | .......... | 20 |
| College of the City of New York | 25,163 00 | .......... | 112 75 | 21 |
| Normal College | 101,143 95 | 1,921 83 | 631 48 | 22 |
| Total | **$20,391,400 84** | **$1,652,184 94** | **$220,901 23** | 23 |
| Total Mayor and Subordinate Departments, Bureaus and Offices | **$31,155,583 38** | **$3,625,705 00** | **$571,553 66** | 24 |
| Borough Presidents and Subordinate Departments: | | | | |
| President, Borough of Manhattan | $2,255,201 20 | $151,211 18 | $2,040 85 | 25 |
| President, Borough of The Bronx | 633,170 73 | 33,701 97 | .......... | 26 |
| President, Borough of Brooklyn | 1,102,652 22 | 72,245 00 | 998 93 | 27 |
| President, Borough of Queens | 507,891 81 | 41,179 96 | 1,680 06 | 28 |
| President, Borough of Richmond | 339,375 68 | 35,938 70 | 286 68 | 29 |
| Total | **$4,838,291 64** | **$334,276 81** | **$5,006 52** | 30 |
| Boards, Commissions, etc., whose members are not elected by popular vote and who are not appointed by any elected City official: | | | | |
| Bronx Parkway Commission | $1,117,071 85 | $10,828 24 | $1,193 78 | 31 |
| Court House Board | 183,440 09 | 26,632 67 | 1,112 91 | 32 |
| Public Service Commission | 23,513,762 67 | .......... | .......... | 33 |
| Total | **$24,814,274 61** | **$37,460 91** | **$2,306 69** | 34 |
| Boards, Commissions, etc. of mixed responsibility, i.e., ex-officio bodies representing two or more of preceding branches: | | | | |
| Armory Board | **$514,203 36** | .......... | **$372 75** | 35 |
| Total City Departments, Offices, Courts, etc. | **$61,322,352 99** | **$3,997,442 72** | **$579,239 62** | 36 |

NEW YORK

FOR THE YEAR 1914, CLASSIFIED BY OBJECTS OF EXPENDITURE:

| LINE No. | Purchase of Equipment | Materials | Contract or Open Order Service | Contingencies | Fixed Charges and Contributions | Unclassified |
|---|---|---|---|---|---|---|
| 1 | .......... | .......... | .......... | .......... | .......... | $365,000 00 |
| 2 | .......... | .......... | $118 25 | $37 09 | .......... | 650 00 |
| 3 | $4,536 95 | $3,135 88 | 2,381,437 82 | 565 10 | .......... | 2,086 52 |
| 4 | .......... | 392 24 | 40,063 06 | 2 87 | .......... | 422 20 |
| 5 | 215,370 35 | 163,911 39 | 477,214 24 | 5,684 34 | .......... | 13,796 42 |
| 6 | 4,268 30 | 5,000 68 | 207,786 69 | 243 26 | .......... | .......... |
| 7 | 2,629 55 | 785 00 | 382,868 58 | 168 97 | .......... | .......... |
| 8 | 1,285 94 | 1,089 88 | 25 561 73 | .......... | .......... | .......... |
| 9 | 14,320 35 | 6,305 61 | 297,605 19 | 2,735 69 | .......... | .......... |
| 10 | .......... | .......... | 3,613 16 | .......... | .......... | .......... |
| 11 | 5,588 56 | .......... | 186,780 28 | .......... | .......... | 26,282 63 |
| 12 | 79,298 06 | 1,859 19 | 883,858 13 | .......... | .......... | 29 93 |
| 13 | .......... | 592 59 | 24,642 97 | .......... | .......... | .......... |
| 14 | 9,573 78 | 477 08 | 1,587,640 92 | 11,828 03 | .......... | 83,483 93 |
| 15 | 258,451 02 | 32 75 | 640,072 92 | 183 14 | .......... | 995 74 |
| 16 | 1,388 21 | .......... | 5,109 09 | 181 13 | .......... | 966 67 |
| 17 | **$596,711 07** | **$183,582 29** | **$7,144,373 03** | **$21,629 62** | .......... | **$493,714 04** |
| 18 | $7,448 87 | .......... | $665,532 48 | .......... | .......... | $45,000 00 |
| 19 | 24,089 51 | .......... | 11,688,156 63 | .......... | .......... | 759.186 67 |
| 20 | 1,416,150 27 | .......... | 3,551,401 08 | .......... | .......... | 237,708 27 |
| 21 | 4,073 30 | .......... | 20,976 95 | .......... | .......... | .......... |
| 22 | 11,591 00 | $150 00 | 86,849 64 | .......... | .......... | .......... |
| 23 | **$1,463,352 95** | **$150 00** | **$16,012,916 78** | .......... | .......... | **$1,041,894 94** |
| 24 | **$2,060,064 02** | **$183,732 29** | **$23,157,289 81** | **$21,629 62** | .......... | **$1,535,608 98** |
| 25 | $15,592 91 | $659 19 | $1,832,933 83 | .......... | .......... | $252,763 24 |
| 26 | 63 45 | .......... | 599,405 31 | .......... | .......... | .......... |
| 27 | .......... | .......... | 1,026,168 69 | $29 50 | .......... | 3,210 10 |
| 28 | 1,820 55 | 47 24 | 462,227 25 | .......... | .......... | 936 75 |
| 29 | 299 56 | 198 20 | 296,421 66 | 279 56 | .......... | 5,951 32 |
| 30 | **$17,776 47** | **$904 63** | **$4,217,156 74** | **$309 06** | .......... | **$262,861 41** |
| 31 | $1,576 36 | $17 10 | $1,043 77 | $583 35 | .......... | $1,101,829 25 |
| 32 | 452 32 | .......... | 103,367 27 | 2,420 67 | .......... | 49,454 25 |
| 33 | .......... | .......... | 19,759,039 11 | 308 10 | .......... | 3,754,415 46 |
| 34 | **$2,028 68** | **$17 10** | **$19,863,450 15** | **$3,312 12** | .......... | **$4,905,698 96** |
| 35 | **$12,118 10** | .......... | **$501,712 51** | .......... | .......... | .......... |
| 36 | **$2,091,987 27** | **$184,654 02** | **$47,739,609 21** | **$25,250 80** | .......... | **$6,704,169 35** |

Statement Showing Expenditures from Corporate Stock Funds

| | Total | Personal Service | Supplies | Line No. |
|---|---|---|---|---|
| Fixed Charges other than Debt Service, Subsidies, Contributions, Payments to Private and State Institutions, Expenditures not Allotted to Departments: | | | | |
| Brooklyn Public Library | $24,506 22 | .......... | .......... | 1 |
| Miscellaneous, City | 1,400,516 04 | $1,650 00 | .......... | 2 |
| New York Public Library | 38,205 18 | .......... | .......... | 3 |
| Total | **$1,463,227 44** | **$1,650 00** | .......... | 4 |
| Advances for Local Improvements: | | | | |
| Fund for Street and Park Openings | $4,855,640 93 | $247,945 18 | $1,742 00 | 5 |
| Street Improvement Fund | 15,923,876 61 | 720,243 08 | 530 53 | 6 |
| Total | **$20,779,517 54** | **$968,188 26** | **$2,272 53** | 7 |
| Total for City Purposes | **$83,565,097 97** | **$4,967,280 98** | **$581,512 15** | 8 |
| Total for All Purposes | **$83,565,097 97** | **$4,967,280 98** | **$581,512 15** | 9 |

NEW YORK

FOR THE YEAR 1914, CLASSIFIED BY OBJECTS OF EXPENDITURE:—*Continued*

| LINE No. | Purchase of Equipment | Materials | Contract or Open Order Service | Contingencies | Fixed Charges and Contributions | Unclassified |
|---|---|---|---|---|---|---|
| 1 | $13,927 47 | .......... | .......... | .......... | .......... | $10,578 75 |
| 2 | .......... | .......... | $433,848 16 | $255 13 | .......... | 964,762 75 |
| 3 | 15,994 43 | .......... | 22,210 75 | .......... | .......... | .......... |
| 4 | **$29,921 90** | .......... | **$456,058 91** | **$255 13** | .......... | **$975,341 50** |
| 5 | $3,992 73 | .......... | $4,921 97 | $2,955 70 | .......... | $4,594,083 35 |
| 6 | 1,750 86 | $125 60 | 6,988,237 09 | 4,714 05 | .......... | 8,208,275 40 |
| 7 | **$5,743 59** | **$125 60** | **$6,993,159 06** | **$7,669 75** | .......... | **$12,802,358 75** |
| 8 | **$2,127,652 76** | **$184,779 62** | **$55,188,827 18** | **$33,175 68** | .......... | **$20,481,869 60** |
| 9 | **$2,127,652 76** | **$184,779 62** | **$55,188,827 18** | **$33,175 68** | .......... | **$20,481,869 60** |

THE CITY OF

COMPARATIVE STATEMENTS SHOWING SEPARATELY THE EXPENDITURES
YEARS 1910 TO 1914, INCLUSIVE, CLASSIFIED BY

| | Total | Personal Service | Supplies | LINE No. |
|---|---|---|---|---|
| **COMMISSIONERS OF ACCOUNTS** | | | | |
| **1910** | | | | |
| Revenue Expenditures | $206,139 64 | $195,644 13 | $1,557 89 | 1 |
| Corporate Stock Expenditures | .......... | .......... | .......... | 2 |
| Total for 1910 | **$206,139 64** | **$195,644 13** | **$1,557 89** | 3 |
| **1911** | | | | |
| Revenue Expenditures | $215,398 94 | $202,629 12 | $2,340 33 | 4 |
| Corporate Stock Expenditures | .......... | .......... | .......... | 5 |
| Total for 1911 | **$215,398 94** | **$202,629 12** | **$2,340 33** | 6 |
| **1912** | | | | |
| Revenue Expenditures | $214,664 46 | $197,843 36 | $1,798 26 | 7 |
| Corporate Stock Expenditures | .......... | .......... | .......... | 8 |
| Total for 1912 | **$214,664 46** | **$197,843 36** | **$1,798 26** | 9 |
| **1913** | | | | |
| Revenue Expenditures | $195,977 82 | $188,101 41 | $1,372 75 | 10 |
| Corporate Stock Expenditures | .......... | .......... | .......... | 11 |
| Total for 1913 | **$195,977 82** | **$188,101 41** | **$1,372 75** | 12 |
| **1914** | | | | |
| Revenue Expenditures | $219,940 04 | $209,903 09 | $2,707 21 | 13 |
| Corporate Stock Expenditures | .......... | .......... | .......... | 14 |
| Total for 1914 | **$219,940 04** | **$209,903 09** | **$2,707 21** | 15 |
| **BOARD OF AMBULANCE SERVICE** | | | | |
| **1910** | | | | |
| Revenue Expenditures | $628 39 | $628 39 | .......... | 16 |
| Corporate Stock Expenditures | .......... | .......... | .......... | 17 |
| Total for 1910 | **$628 39** | **$628 39** | .......... | 18 |
| **1911** | | | | |
| Revenue Expenditures | $9,430 14 | $8,211 25 | $226 79 | 19 |
| Corporate Stock Expenditures | .......... | .......... | .......... | 20 |
| Total for 1911 | **$9,430 14** | **$8,211 25** | **$226 79** | 21 |
| **1912** | | | | |
| Revenue Expenditures | $11,581 09 | $10,874 20 | $404 00 | 22 |
| Corporate Stock Expenditures | .......... | .......... | .......... | 23 |
| Total for 1912 | **$11,581 09** | **$10,874 20** | **$404 00** | 24 |
| **1913** | | | | |
| Revenue Expenditures | $76,863 55 | $11,676 66 | $122 73 | 25 |
| Corporate Stock Expenditures | .......... | .......... | .......... | 26 |
| Total for 1913 | **$76,863 55** | **$11,676 66** | **$122 73** | 27 |
| **1914** | | | | |
| Revenue Expenditures | $79,910 51 | $9,599 98 | $114 59 | 28 |
| Corporate Stock Expenditures | .......... | .......... | .......... | 29 |
| Total for 1914 | **$79,910 51** | **$9,599 98** | **$114 59** | 30 |

## NEW YORK

MADE FROM REVENUE AND FROM CORPORATE STOCK FUNDS FOR THE DEPARTMENTS, ACCORDING TO OBJECTS OF EXPENDITURE:

| LINE No. | Purchase of Equipment | Materials | Contract or Open Order Service | Contingencies | Fixed Charges and Contributions | Unclassified |
|---|---|---|---|---|---|---|
| 1 | .......... | .......... | $763 28 | $8,174 34 | .......... | .......... |
| 2 | .......... | .......... | .......... | .......... | .......... | .......... |
| 3 | .......... | .......... | **$763 28** | **$8,174 34** | .......... | .......... |
| 4 | $1,487 02 | .......... | $1,494 01 | $7,448 46 | .......... | .......... |
| 5 | .......... | .......... | .......... | .......... | .......... | .......... |
| 6 | **$1,487 02** | .......... | **$1,494 01** | **$7,448 46** | .......... | .......... |
| 7 | $4,120 76 | .......... | $1,617 57 | $9,284 51 | .......... | .......... |
| 8 | .......... | .......... | .......... | .......... | .......... | .......... |
| 9 | **$4,120 76** | .......... | **$1,617 57** | **$9,284 51** | .......... | .......... |
| 10 | $864 07 | .......... | $4,425 84 | $1,213 75 | .......... | .......... |
| 11 | .......... | .......... | .......... | .......... | .......... | .......... |
| 12 | **$864 07** | .......... | **$4,425 84** | **$1,213 75** | .......... | .......... |
| 13 | $814 10 | .......... | $5,478 26 | $1,037 38 | .......... | .......... |
| 14 | .......... | .......... | .......... | .......... | .......... | .......... |
| 15 | **$814 10** | .......... | **$5,478 26** | **$1,037 38** | .......... | .......... |
| 16 | .......... | .......... | .......... | .......... | .......... | .......... |
| 17 | .......... | .......... | .......... | .......... | .......... | .......... |
| 18 | .......... | .......... | .......... | .......... | .......... | .......... |
| 19 | $438 10 | .......... | $328 97 | $225 03 | .......... | .......... |
| 20 | .......... | .......... | .......... | .......... | .......... | .......... |
| 21 | **$438 10** | .......... | **$328 97** | **$225 03** | .......... | .......... |
| 22 | .......... | .......... | $72 82 | $230 07 | .......... | .......... |
| 23 | .......... | .......... | .......... | .......... | .......... | .......... |
| 24 | .......... | .......... | **$72 82** | **$230 07** | .......... | .......... |
| 25 | $158 55 | .......... | $64,903 41 | $2 20 | .......... | .......... |
| 26 | .......... | .......... | .......... | .......... | .......... | .......... |
| 27 | **$158 55** | .......... | **$64,903 41** | **$2 20** | .......... | .......... |
| 28 | $16 00 | .......... | $70,178 03 | $1 91 | .......... | .......... |
| 29 | .......... | .......... | .......... | .......... | .......... | .......... |
| 30 | **$16 00** | .......... | **$70,178 03** | **$1 91** | .......... | .......... |

COMPARATIVE STATEMENTS SHOWING SEPARATELY THE EXPENDITURES
YEARS 1910 TO 1914, INCLUSIVE, CLASSIFIED BY

| | Total | Personal Service | Supplies | LINE No. |
|---|---|---|---|---|
| **BOARD OF ASSESSORS** | | | | |
| **1910** | | | | |
| Revenue Expenditures | $42,525 67 | $40,673 38 | $1,083 82 | 1 |
| Corporate Stock Expenditures | .......... | .......... | .......... | 2 |
| Total for 1910 | **$42,525 67** | **$40,673 38** | **$1,083 82** | 3 |
| **1911** | | | | |
| Revenue Expenditures | $42,256 47 | $40,812 50 | $622 24 | 4 |
| Corporate Stock Expenditures | .......... | .......... | .......... | 5 |
| Total for 1911 | **$43,256 47** | **$40,812 50** | **$622 24** | 6 |
| **1912** | | | | |
| Revenue Expenditures | $42,883 68 | $41,600 00 | $620 57 | 7 |
| Corporate Stock Expenditures | .......... | .......... | .......... | 8 |
| Total for 1912 | **$42,883 68** | **$41,600 00** | **$620 57** | 9 |
| **1913** | | | | |
| Revenue Expenditures | $41,364 34 | $40,523 39 | $412 26 | 10 |
| Corporate Stock Expenditures | .......... | .......... | .......... | 11 |
| Total for 1913 | **$41,364 34** | **$40,523 39** | **$412 26** | 12 |
| **1914** | | | | |
| Revenue Expenditures | $40,150 52 | $39,124 20 | $202 00 | 13 |
| Corporate Stock Expenditures | .......... | .......... | .......... | 14 |
| Total for 1914 | **$40,150 52** | **$39,124 20** | **$202 00** | 15 |
| **DEPARTMENT OF BRIDGES** | | | | |
| **1910** | | | | |
| Revenue Expenditures | $1,532,683 60 | $1,204,453 34 | $70,112 87 | 16 |
| Corporate Stock Expenditures | 8,321,922 76 | 286,104 51 | 20,431 97 | 17 |
| Total for 1910 | **$9,854,606 36** | **$1,490,557 85** | **$90,544 84** | 18 |
| **1911** | | | | |
| Revenue Expenditures | $1,424,579 43 | $1,218,413 10 | $52,214 80 | 19 |
| Corporate Stock Expenditures | 14,556,363 27 | 283,930 20 | 2,321 76 | 20 |
| Total for 1911 | **$15,980,942 70** | **$1,502,343 30** | **$54,536 56** | 21 |
| **1912** | | | | |
| Revenue Expenditures | $1,446,171 37 | $1,217,028 10 | $70,845 05 | 22 |
| Corporate Stock Expenditures | 4,196,300 73 | 309,132 00 | 4,486 12 | 23 |
| Total for 1912 | **$5,642,472 10** | **$1,526,160 10** | **$75,331 17** | 24 |
| **1913** | | | | |
| Revenue Expenditures | $1,368,549 25 | $1,136,558 44 | $34,463 16 | 25 |
| Corporate Stock Expenditures | 4,318,872 71 | 342,083 69 | 2,788 63 | 26 |
| Total for 1913 | **$5,687,421 96** | **$1,478,642 13** | **$37,251 79** | 27 |
| **1914** | | | | |
| Revenue Expenditures | $1,273,983 88 | $1,108,242 99 | $27,307 68 | 28 |
| Corporate Stock Expenditures | 2,636,742 84 | 239,965 41 | 5,015 16 | 29 |
| Total for 1914 | **$3,910,726 72** | **$1,348,208 40** | **$32,322 84** | 30 |

# NEW YORK

MADE FROM REVENUE AND FROM CORPORATE STOCK FUNDS FOR THE DEPARTMENTS, ACCORDING TO OBJECTS OF EXPENDITURE:

| LINE No. | Purchase of Equipment | Materials | Contract or Open Order Service | Contingencies | Fixed Charges and Contributions | Unclassified |
|---|---|---|---|---|---|---|
| 1 | .......... | .......... | $278 37 | $490 10 | .......... | .......... |
| 2 | .......... | .......... | .......... | .......... | .......... | .......... |
| 3 | .......... | .......... | **$278 37** | **$490 10** | .......... | .......... |
| 4 | .......... | .......... | $348 63 | $473 10 | .......... | .......... |
| 5 | .......... | .......... | .......... | .......... | .......... | .......... |
| 6 | .......... | .......... | **$348 63** | **$473 10** | .......... | .......... |
| 7 | $133 67 | .......... | $330 59 | $198 85 | .......... | .......... |
| 8 | .......... | .......... | .......... | .......... | .......... | .......... |
| 9 | **$133 67** | .......... | **$330 59** | **$198 85** | .......... | .......... |
| 10 | .......... | .......... | $428 69 | .......... | .......... | .......... |
| 11 | .......... | .......... | .......... | .......... | .......... | .......... |
| 12 | .......... | .......... | **$428 69** | .......... | .......... | .......... |
| 13 | $115 00 | .......... | $684 32 | $25 00 | .......... | .......... |
| 14 | .......... | .......... | .......... | .......... | .......... | .......... |
| 15 | **$115 00** | .......... | **$684 32** | **$25 00** | .......... | .......... |
| 16 | $25,093 26 | $137,942 43 | $89,059 10 | $6,022 60 | .......... | .......... |
| 17 | 4,195 64 | 5,266 89 | 3,381,692 72 | 244 52 | .......... | $4,623,986 51 |
| 18 | **$29,288 90** | **$143,209 32** | **$3,470,751 82** | **$6,267 12** | .......... | **$4,623,986 51** |
| 19 | $15,499 22 | $69,102 98 | $65,815 79 | $3,533 54 | .......... | .......... |
| 20 | 765 16 | 487 03 | 3,637,620 48 | 1,700 39 | .......... | $10,629,538 25 |
| 21 | **$16,264 38** | **$69,590 01** | **$3,703,436 27** | **$5,233 93** | .......... | **$10,629,538 25** |
| 22 | $22,854 45 | $44,878 61 | $87,748 70 | $2,816 46 | .......... | .......... |
| 23 | 4,465 38 | 96,281 54 | 2,115,031 60 | 917 48 | .......... | $1,665,986 61 |
| 24 | **$27,319 83** | **$141,160 15** | **$2,202,780 30** | **$3,733 94** | .......... | **$1,665,986 61** |
| 25 | $13,492 36 | $80,281 99 | $103,292 93 | $460 37 | .......... | .......... |
| 26 | 4,094 59 | 7,701 48 | 3,854,151 92 | 10,315 46 | .......... | $97,736 94 |
| 27 | **$17,586 95** | **$87,983 47** | **$3,957,444 85** | **$10,775 83** | .......... | **$97,736 94** |
| 28 | $14,881 39 | $63,508 73 | $58,067 85 | $1,975 24 | .......... | .......... |
| 29 | 4,536 95 | 3,135 88 | 2,381,437 82 | 565 10 | .......... | $2,086 52 |
| 30 | **$19,418 34** | **$66,644 61** | **$2,439,505 67** | **$2,540 34** | .......... | **$2,086 52** |

COMPARATIVE STATEMENTS SHOWING SEPARATELY THE EXPENDITURES
YEARS 1910 TO 1914, INCLUSIVE, CLASSIFIED BY

| | Total | Personal Service | Supplies | LINE No. |
|---|---|---|---|---|
| **BROOKLYN GRADE CROSSING COMMISSION** | | | | |
| **1910** | | | | |
| Revenue Expenditures........................ | .......... | .......... | .......... | 1 |
| Corporate Stock Expenditures................. | $200,000 00 | .......... | .......... | 2 |
| Total for 1910........................... | **$200,000 00** | .......... | .......... | 3 |
| **1911** | | | | |
| Revenue Expenditures........................ | .......... | .......... | .......... | 4 |
| Corporate Stock Expenditures................. | $330,000 00 | .......... | .......... | 5 |
| Total for 1911........................... | **$330,000 00** | .......... | .......... | 6 |
| **1912** | | | | |
| Revenue Expenditures........................ | .......... | .......... | .......... | 7 |
| Corporate Stock Expenditures................. | .......... | .......... | .......... | 8 |
| Total for 1912........................... | .......... | .......... | .......... | 9 |
| **1913** | | | | |
| Revenue Expenditures........................ | .......... | .......... | .......... | 10 |
| Corporate Stock Expenditures................. | $262,500 00 | .......... | .......... | 11 |
| Total for 1913........................... | **$262,500 00** | .......... | .......... | 12 |
| **1914** | | | | |
| Revenue Expenditures........................ | .......... | .......... | .......... | 13 |
| Corporate Stock Expenditures................. | $365,000 00 | .......... | .......... | 14 |
| Total for 1914........................... | **$365,000 00** | .......... | .......... | 15 |
| **CITY CHAMBERLAIN** | | | | |
| **1910** | | | | |
| Revenue Expenditures........................ | $54,273 86 | $52,501 61 | $1,025 25 | 16 |
| Corporate Stock Expenditures................. | .......... | .......... | .......... | 17 |
| Total for 1910........................... | **$54,273 86** | **$52,501 61** | **$1,025 25** | 18 |
| **1911** | | | | |
| Revenue Expenditures........................ | $61,382 66 | $59,343 42 | $1,346 00 | 19 |
| Corporate Stock Expenditures................. | .......... | .......... | .......... | 20 |
| Total for 1911........................... | **$61,382 66** | **$59,343 42** | **$1,346 00** | 21 |
| **1912** | | | | |
| Revenue Expenditures........................ | $61,437 60 | $59,452 92 | $282 02 | 22 |
| Corporate Stock Expenditures................. | .......... | .......... | .......... | 23 |
| Total for 1912........................... | **$61,437 60** | **$59,452 92** | **$282 02** | 24 |
| **1913** | | | | |
| Revenue Expenditures........................ | $62,134 14 | $59,929 20 | $1,301 81 | 25 |
| Corporate Stock Expenditures................. | .......... | .......... | .......... | 26 |
| Total for 1913........................... | **$62,134 14** | **$59,929 20** | **$1,301 81** | 27 |
| **1914** | | | | |
| Revenue Expenditures........................ | $59,568 47 | $56,896 91 | $1,597 18 | 28 |
| Corporate Stock Expenditures................. | .......... | .......... | .......... | 29 |
| Total for 1914........................... | **$59,568 47** | **$56,896 91** | **$1,597 18** | 30 |

NEW YORK

MADE FROM REVENUE AND FROM CORPORATE STOCK FUNDS FOR THE DEPARTMENTS, ACCORDING TO OBJECTS OF EXPENDITURE:

| LINE No. | Purchase of Equipment | Materials | Contract or Open Order Service | Contingencies | Fixed Charges and Contributions | Unclassified |
|---|---|---|---|---|---|---|
| 1 | .......... | .......... | .......... | .......... | .......... | .......... |
| 2 | .......... | .......... | .......... | .......... | .......... | $200,000 00 |
| 3 | .......... | .......... | .......... | .......... | .......... | **$200,000 00** |
| 4 | .......... | .......... | .......... | .......... | .......... | .......... |
| 5 | .......... | .......... | .......... | .......... | .......... | $330,000 00 |
| 6 | .......... | .......... | .......... | .......... | .......... | **$330,000 00** |
| 7 | .......... | .......... | .......... | .......... | .......... | .......... |
| 8 | .......... | .......... | .......... | .......... | .......... | .......... |
| 9 | .......... | .......... | .......... | .......... | .......... | .......... |
| 10 | .......... | .......... | .......... | .......... | .......... | .......... |
| 11 | .......... | .......... | .......... | .......... | .......... | $262,500 00 |
| 12 | .......... | .......... | .......... | .......... | .......... | **$262,500 00** |
| 13 | .......... | .......... | .......... | .......... | .......... | .......... |
| 14 | .......... | .......... | .......... | .......... | .......... | $365,000 00 |
| 15 | .......... | .......... | .......... | .......... | .......... | **$365,000 00** |
| 16 | .......... | .......... | $469 50 | $277 50 | .......... | .......... |
| 17 | .......... | .......... | .......... | .......... | .......... | .......... |
| 18 | .......... | .......... | **$469 50** | **$277 50** | .......... | .......... |
| 19 | | .......... | $393 54 | $299 70 | .......... | .......... |
| 20 | .......... | .......... | .......... | .......... | .......... | .......... |
| 21 | .......... | .......... | **$393 54** | **$299 70** | .......... | .......... |
| 22 | $114 60 | .......... | $488 46 | $1,099 60 | .......... | .......... |
| 23 | .......... | .......... | .......... | .......... | .......... | .......... |
| 24 | **$114 60** | .......... | **$488 46** | **$1,099 60** | .......... | .......... |
| 25 | $168 92 | .......... | $613 71 | $120 50 | .......... | .......... |
| 26 | .......... | .......... | .......... | .......... | .......... | .......... |
| 27 | **$168 92** | .......... | **$613 71** | **$120 50** | .......... | .......... |
| 28 | $157 00 | .......... | $715 90 | $201 48 | .......... | .......... |
| 29 | .......... | .......... | .......... | .......... | .......... | .......... |
| 30 | **$157 00** | .......... | **$715 90** | **$201 48** | .......... | .......... |

COMPARATIVE STATEMENTS SHOWING SEPARATELY THE EXPENDITURES
YEARS 1910 TO 1914, INCLUSIVE, CLASSIFIED BY

| | Total | Personal Service | Supplies | LINE No. |
|---|---|---|---|---|
| **CHANGE OF GRADE DAMAGE COMMISSION** | | | | |
| **1910** | | | | |
| Revenue Expenditures | .......... | .......... | .......... | 1 |
| Corporate Stock Expenditures | $36,835 71 | $18,089 79 | $134 42 | 2 |
| Total for 1910 | **$36,835 71** | **$18,089 79** | **$134 42** | 3 |
| **1911** | | | | |
| Revenue Expenditures | .......... | .......... | .......... | 4 |
| Corporate Stock Expenditures | $798,203 96 | $23,764 28 | $472 03 | 5 |
| Total for 1911 | **$798,203 96** | **$23,764 28** | **$472 03** | 6 |
| **1912** | | | | |
| Revenue Expenditures | .......... | .......... | .......... | 7 |
| Corporate Stock Expenditures | $410,846 42 | $14,423 96 | $438 93 | 8 |
| Total for 1912 | **$410,846 42** | **$14,423 96** | **$438 93** | 9 |
| **1913** | | | | |
| Revenue Expenditures | .......... | .......... | .......... | 10 |
| Corporate Stock Expenditures | $173,132 49 | $17,399 96 | $18 50 | 11 |
| Total for 1913 | **$173,132 49** | **$17,399 96** | **$18 50** | 12 |
| **1914** | | | | |
| Revenue Expenditures | .......... | .......... | .......... | 13 |
| Corporate Stock Expenditures | $7,156 63 | $6,351 29 | .......... | 14 |
| Total for 1914 | **$7,156 63** | **$6,351 29** | .......... | 15 |
| **DEPARTMENT OF CORRECTION** | | | | |
| **1910** | | | | |
| Revenue Expenditures | $1,254,375 04 | $523,148 64 | $520,210 73 | 16 |
| Corporate Stock Expenditures | 309,381 09 | .......... | .......... | 17 |
| Total for 1910 | **$1,563,756 13** | **$523,148 64** | **$520,210 73** | 18 |
| **1911** | | | | |
| Revenue Expenditures | $1,219,095 91 | $545,332 69 | $480,500 51 | 19 |
| Corporate Stock Expenditures | 115,125 77 | .......... | .......... | 20 |
| Total for 1911 | **$1,334,221 68** | **$545,332 69** | **$480,500 51** | 21 |
| **1912** | | | | |
| Revenue Expenditures | $1,297,047 94 | $576,829 66 | $648,369 74 | 22 |
| Corporate Stock Expenditures | 4,641 12 | .......... | .......... | 23 |
| Total for 1912 | **$1,301,689 06** | **$576,829 66** | **$648,369 74** | 24 |
| **1913** | | | | |
| Revenue Expenditures | $1,358,812 62 | $603,935 64 | $492,571 72 | 25 |
| Corporate Stock Expenditures | 148,201 61 | .......... | .......... | 26 |
| Total for 1913 | **$1,507,014 23** | **$603,935 64** | **$492,571 72** | 27 |
| **1914** | | | | |
| Revenue Expenditures | $1,378,177 57 | $602,477 68 | $555,975 91 | 28 |
| Corporate Stock Expenditures | 41,241 20 | .......... | 360 83 | 29 |
| Total for 1914 | **$1,419,418 77** | **$602,477 68** | **$556,336 74** | 30 |

NEW YORK

Made from Revenue and from Corporate Stock Funds for the Departments, According to Objects of Expenditure:

| LINE No. | Purchase of Equipment | Materials | Contract or Open Order Service | Contingencies | Fixed Charges and Contributions | Unclassified |
|---|---|---|---|---|---|---|
| 1 | .......... | .......... | .......... | .......... | .......... | .......... |
| 2 | $115 84 | .......... | .......... | $2 07 | .......... | $18,493 59 |
| 3 | **$115 84** | .......... | .......... | **$2 07** | .......... | **$18,493 59** |
| 4 | .......... | .......... | .......... | .......... | .......... | .......... |
| 5 | .......... | .......... | .......... | $79 20 | .......... | $773,888 45 |
| 6 | .......... | .......... | .......... | **$79 20** | .......... | **$773,888 45** |
| 7 | .......... | .......... | .......... | .......... | .......... | .......... |
| 8 | .......... | .......... | .......... | .......... | .......... | $395,983 53 |
| 9 | .......... | .......... | .......... | .......... | .......... | **$395,983 53** |
| 10 | .......... | .......... | .......... | .......... | .......... | .......... |
| 11 | .......... | .......... | .......... | .......... | .......... | $155,714 03 |
| 12 | .......... | .......... | .......... | .......... | .......... | **$155,714 03** |
| 13 | .......... | .......... | .......... | .......... | .......... | .......... |
| 14 | .......... | .......... | $118 25 | $37 09 | .......... | $650 00 |
| 15 | .......... | .......... | **$118 25** | **$37 09** | .......... | **$650 00** |
| 16 | $8,404 36 | $120,745 95 | $72,256 81 | $4,599 97 | $5,008 58 | .......... |
| 17 | 915 30 | .......... | 308,465 79 | .......... | .......... | .......... |
| 18 | **$9,319 66** | **$120,745 95** | **$380,722 60** | **$4,599 97** | **$5,008 58** | .......... |
| 19 | $7,357 65 | $121,706 77 | $54,767 22 | $4,677 83 | $4,753 24 | .......... |
| 20 | 454 00 | .......... | 114,671 77 | .......... | .......... | .......... |
| 21 | **$7,811 65** | **$121,706 77** | **$169,438 99** | **$4,677 83** | **$4,753 24** | .......... |
| 22 | $8,329 42 | $11,568 91 | $42,672 74 | $3,802 36 | $5,475 11 | .......... |
| 23 | .......... | 56 12 | 4,585 00 | .......... | .......... | .......... |
| 24 | **$8,329 42** | **$11,625 03** | **$47,257 74** | **$3,802 36** | **$5,475 11** | .......... |
| 25 | $43,888 11 | $157,202 16 | $55,421 20 | $100 00 | $5,693 79 | .......... |
| 26 | .......... | .......... | 94,018 11 | .......... | .......... | $54,183 50 |
| 27 | **$43,888 11** | **$157,202 16** | **$149,439 31** | **$100 00** | **$5,693 79** | **$54,183 50** |
| 28 | $54,792 24 | $108,093 06 | $51,086 02 | $2,163 85 | $3,588 81 | .......... |
| 29 | .......... | 392 24 | 40,063 06 | 2 87 | .......... | $422 20 |
| 30 | **$54,792 24** | **$108,485 30** | **$91,149 08** | **$2,166 72** | **$3,588 81** | **$422 20** |

Comparative Statements Showing Separately the Expenditures
Years 1910 to 1914, Inclusive, Classified by

| | Total | Personal Service | Supplies | Line No. |
|---|---|---|---|---|
| **DEPARTMENT OF DOCKS AND FERRIES** | | | | |
| **1910** | | | | |
| Revenue Expenditures | $2,533,737 78 | $1,478,688 02 | $363,590 60 | 1 |
| Corporate Stock Expenditures | 5,500,681 80 | 1,256,961 64 | 77,523 02 | 2 |
| Total for 1910 | **$8,034,419 58** | **$2,735,649 66** | **$441,113 62** | 3 |
| **1911** | | | | |
| Revenue Expenditures | $2,575,836 58 | $1,618,382 31 | $336,052 67 | 4 |
| Corporate Stock Expenditures | 2,511,074 09 | 1,191,398 29 | 49,185 62 | 5 |
| Total for 1911 | **$5,086,910 67** | **$2,809,780 60** | **$385,238 29** | 6 |
| **1912** | | | | |
| Revenue Expenditures | $2,735,671 10 | $1,753,988 93 | $542,827 30 | 7 |
| Corporate Stock Expenditures | 1,889,059 32 | 1,083,392 52 | 213,608 08 | 8 |
| Total for 1912 | **$4,624,730 42** | **$2,837,381 45** | **$756,435 38** | 9 |
| **1913** | | | | |
| Revenue Expenditures | $2,742,878 45 | $1,767,663 30 | $389,918 28 | 10 |
| Corporate Stock Expenditures | 9,074,543 46 | 1,137,286 13 | 17,441 08 | 11 |
| Total for 1913 | **$11,817,421 91** | **$2,904,949 43** | **$407,359 36** | 12 |
| **1914** | | | | |
| Revenue Expenditures | $2,510,827 42 | $1,633,456 50 | $347,761 40 | 13 |
| Corporate Stock Expenditures | 2,009.343 98 | 1,075,940 05 | 57,427 19 | 14 |
| Total for 1914 | **$4,520,171 40** | **$2,709,396 55** | **$405,188 59** | 15 |
| **EXAMINING BOARD OF PLUMBERS** | | | | |
| **1910** | | | | |
| Revenue Expenditures | $6,920 48 | $5,685 00 | $275 48 | 16 |
| Corporate Stock Expenditures | .......... | .......... | .......... | 17 |
| Total for 1910 | **$6,920 48** | **$5,685 00** | **$275 48** | 18 |
| **1911** | | | | |
| Revenue Expenditures | $5,373 50 | $5,120 00 | $253 50 | 19 |
| Corporate Stock Expenditures | .......... | .......... | .......... | 20 |
| Total for 1911 | **$5,373 50** | **$5,120 00** | **$253 50** | 21 |
| **1912** | | | | |
| Revenue Expenditures | $5,586 46 | $5,335 00 | $157 93 | 22 |
| Corporate Stock Expenditures | .......... | .......... | .......... | 23 |
| Total for 1912 | **$5,586 46** | **$5,335 00** | **$157 93** | 24 |
| **1913** | | | | |
| Revenue Expenditures | $5,350 58 | $4,416 50 | $164 41 | 25 |
| Corporate Stock Expenditures | .......... | .......... | .......... | 26 |
| Total for 1913 | **$5,350 58** | **$4,416 50** | **$164 41** | 27 |
| **1914** | | | | |
| Revenue Expenditures | $3,908 42 | $3,040 00 | $159 08 | 28 |
| Corporate Stock Expenditures | .......... | .......... | .......... | 29 |
| Total for 1914 | **$3,908 42** | **$3,040 00** | **$159 08** | 30 |

## NEW YORK

MADE FROM REVENUE AND FROM CORPORATE STOCK FUNDS FOR THE DEPARTMENTS, ACCORDING TO OBJECTS OF EXPENDITURE:

| LINE No. | Purchase of Equipment | Materials | Contract or Open Order Service | Contingencies | Fixed Charges and Contributions | Unclassified |
|---|---|---|---|---|---|---|
| 1 | $512 29 | $180,914 10 | $449,996 90 | $13,400 87 | $46,635 00 | .......... |
| 2 | 4,777 71 | 508 46 | 1,937,711 75 | 9,524 00 | .......... | $2,213,675 22 |
| 3 | **$5,290 00** | **$181,422 56** | **$2,387,708 65** | **$22,924 87** | **$46,635 00** | **$2,213,675 22** |
| 4 | $428 15 | $130,885 01 | $435,380 01 | $10,548 43 | $44,160 00 | .......... |
| 5 | 31,470 03 | 119,433 82 | 356,342 44 | 9,997 98 | .......... | $753,245 91 |
| 6 | **$31,898 18** | **$250,318 83** | **$791,722 45** | **$20,546 41** | **$44,160 00** | **$753,245 91** |
| 7 | $881 90 | .......... | $250,025 96 | $10,956 93 | $176,990 08 | .......... |
| 8 | 151,046 29 | $58,152 65 | 252,889 69 | 3,703 73 | .......... | $126,266 36 |
| 9 | **$151,928 19** | **$58,152 65** | **$502,915 65** | **$14,660 66** | **$176,990 08** | **$126,266 36** |
| 10 | $26,264 92 | $119,871 92 | $273,131 03 | .......... | $166,029 00 | .......... |
| 11 | 7,273 99 | 14,416 76 | 882,917 09 | .......... | .......... | $7,015,208 41 |
| 12 | **$33,538 91** | **$134,288 68** | **$1,156,048 12** | .......... | **$166,029 00** | **$7,015,208 41** |
| 13 | $22,326 72 | $104,581 08 | $230,415 02 | $189 30 | $172,097 40 | .......... |
| 14 | 215,370 35 | 163,911 39 | 477,214 24 | 5,684 34 | .......... | $13,796 42 |
| 15 | **$237,697 07** | **$268,492 47** | **$707,629 26** | **$5,873 64** | **$172,097 40** | **$13,796 42** |
| 16 | .......... | .......... | .......... | .......... | $960 00 | .......... |
| 17 | .......... | .......... | .......... | .......... | .......... | .......... |
| 18 | .......... | .......... | .......... | .......... | **$960 00** | .......... |
| 19 | .......... | .......... | .......... | .......... | .......... | .......... |
| 20 | .......... | .......... | .......... | .......... | .......... | .......... |
| 21 | .......... | .......... | .......... | .......... | .......... | .......... |
| 22 | .......... | .......... | $36 93 | $56 60 | .......... | .......... |
| 23 | .......... | .......... | .......... | .......... | .......... | .......... |
| 24 | .......... | .......... | **$36 93** | **$56 60** | .......... | .......... |
| 25 | $203 28 | .......... | $411 88 | $154 51 | .......... | .......... |
| 26 | .......... | .......... | .......... | .......... | .......... | .......... |
| 27 | **$203 28** | .......... | **$411 88** | **$154 51** | .......... | .......... |
| 28 | $81 00 | .......... | $605 53 | $22 81 | .......... | .......... |
| 29 | .......... | .......... | .......... | .......... | .......... | .......... |
| 30 | **$81 00** | .......... | **$605 53** | **$22 81** | .......... | .......... |

Comparative Statements Showing Separately the Expenditures
Years 1910 to 1914, Inclusive, Classified by

| | Total | Personal Service | Supplies | LINE No. |
|---|---|---|---|---|
| **FIRE DEPARTMENT** | | | | |
| **1910** | | | | |
| Revenue Expenditures | $7,981,989 58 | $7,201,254 19 | $419,109 24 | 1 |
| Corporate Stock Expenditures | 383,126 69 | 17,425 76 | .......... | 2 |
| Total for 1910 | **$8,365,116 27** | **$7,218,679 95** | **$419,109 24** | 3 |
| **1911** | | | | |
| Revenue Expenditures | $8,122,089 12 | $7,428,477 62 | $364,679 90 | 4 |
| Corporate Stock Expenditures | 279,930 46 | 24,170 55 | .......... | 5 |
| Total for 1911 | **$8,402,019 58** | **$7,452,648 17** | **$364,679 90** | 6 |
| **1912** | | | | |
| Revenue Expenditures | $8,673,738 51 | $7,678,993 13 | $507,102 98 | 7 |
| Corporate Stock Expenditures | 849,250 49 | 39,321 89 | 10,950 46 | 8 |
| Total for 1912 | **$9,522,989 00** | **$7,718,315 02** | **$518,053 44** | 9 |
| **1913** | | | | |
| Revenue Expenditures | $9,050,682 33 | $8,044,531 86 | $385,344 31 | 10 |
| Corporate Stock Expenditures | 1,704,330 65 | 54,592 39 | 1,847 27 | 11 |
| Total for 1913 | **$10,755,012 98** | **$8,099,124 25** | **$387,191 58** | 12 |
| **1914** | | | | |
| Revenue Expenditures | $9,396,341 68 | $8,451,739 22 | $371,173 01 | 13 |
| Corporate Stock Expenditures | 977,167 99 | 59,771 57 | 17,660 85 | 14 |
| Total for 1914 | **$10,373,509 67** | **$8,511,510 79** | **$388,833 86** | 15 |
| **DEPARTMENT OF HEALTH** | | | | |
| **1910** | | | | |
| Revenue Expenditures | $2,804,976 05 | $2,035,150 40 | $471,784 94 | 16 |
| Corporate Stock Expenditures | 206,916 44 | 51,571 36 | 3,614 00 | 17 |
| Total for 1910 | **$3,011,892 49** | **$2,086,721 76** | **$475,398 94** | 18 |
| **1911** | | | | |
| Revenue Expenditures | $2,780,022 18 | $2,062,332 80 | $471,070 68 | 19 |
| Corporate Stock Expenditures | 179,475 53 | 38,431 59 | 3,651 58 | 20 |
| Total for 1911 | **$2,959,497 71** | **$2,100,764 39** | **$474,722 26** | 21 |
| **1912** | | | | |
| Revenue Expenditures | $3,073,242 15 | $2,236,931 77 | $582,961 97 | 22 |
| Corporate Stock Expenditures | 401,110 72 | 37,609 44 | 4,510 62 | 23 |
| Total for 1912 | **$3,474,352 87** | **$2,274,541 21** | **$587,472 59** | 24 |
| **1913** | | | | |
| Revenue Expenditures | $3,298,082 28 | $2,382,567 93 | $555,567 82 | 25 |
| Corporate Stock Expenditures | 277,226 55 | 30,221 15 | 752 65 | 26 |
| Total for 1913 | **$3,575,308 83** | **$2,412,789 08** | **$55[illegible],320 47** | 27 |
| **1914** | | | | |
| Revenue Expenditures | $3,326,155 24 | $2,440,619 98 | $549,302 17 | 28 |
| Corporate Stock Expenditures | 258,891 52 | 35,207 53 | 6,385 06 | 29 |
| Total for 1914 | **$3,585,046 76** | **$2,475,827 51** | **$555,687 23** | 30 |

NEW YORK

MADE FROM REVENUE AND FROM CORPORATE STOCK FUNDS FOR THE DEPARTMENTS, ACCORDING TO OBJECTS OF EXPENDITURE:

| LINE No. | Purchase of Equipment | Materials | Contract or Open Order Service | Contingencies | Fixed Charges and Contributions | Unclassified |
|---|---|---|---|---|---|---|
| 1 | $140,285 15 | $93,196 88 | $119,971 52 | $6,652 60 | $1,520 00 | .......... |
| 2 | 75,774 87 | .......... | 268,966 85 | .......... | .......... | $20,959 21 |
| 3 | **$216,060 02** | **$93,196 88** | **$388,938 37** | **$6,652 60** | **$1,520 00** | **$20,959 21** |
| 4 | $125,287 71 | $77,440 27 | $116,690 34 | $9,513 28 | .......... | .......... |
| 5 | 61,978 50 | 5,878 50 | 97,903 24 | 571 75 | .......... | $89,427 92 |
| 6 | **$187,266 21** | **83,318 77** | **$214,593 58** | **$10,085 03** | .......... | **$89,427 92** |
| 7 | $201,243 76 | .......... | $148,487 70 | $9,310 34 | $128,600 60 | .......... |
| 8 | 125,441 85 | $5,692 73 | 649,124 94 | 52 45 | .......... | $18,666 17 |
| 9 | **$326,685 61** | **$5,692 73** | **$797,612 64** | **$9,362 79** | **$128,600 60** | **$18,666 17** |
| 10 | $284,989 46 | $59,348 90 | $120,613 26 | $6,112 84 | $149,741 70 | .......... |
| 11 | 553,637 11 | 10,493 71 | 1,065,070 53 | .......... | .......... | $18,689 64 |
| 12 | **$838,626 57** | **$69,842 61** | **1,185,683 79** | **$6,112 84** | **$149,741 70** | **$18,689 64** |
| 13 | $217,189 41 | $56,776 14 | $84,180 06 | $7,908 90 | $207,374 94 | .......... |
| 14 | 258,451 02 | 32 75 | 640,072 92 | 183 14 | .......... | $995 74 |
| 15 | **$475,640 43** | **$56,808 89** | **$724,252 98** | **$8,092 04** | **$207,374 94** | **$995 74** |
| 16 | $43,698 92 | $11,770 34 | $150,916 57 | $91,654 88 | .......... | .......... |
| 17 | 5,191 05 | 25,409 04 | 120,615 99 | .......... | .......... | $515 00 |
| 18 | **$48,889 97** | **$37,179 38** | **$271,532 56** | **$91,654 88** | .......... | **$515 00** |
| 10 | $35,548 62 | $17,699 21 | $105,397 06 | $87,973 81 | .......... | .......... |
| 20 | 2,818 80 | 12,779 54 | 121,573 42 | 18 60 | .......... | $202 00 |
| 21 | **$38,367 42** | **$30,478 75** | **$226,970 48** | **$87,992 41** | .......... | **$202 00** |
| 22 | $52,793 90 | $159 33 | $99,057 42 | $101,337 76 | .......... | .......... |
| 23 | 933 91 | 18,381 29 | 339,675 46 | .......... | .......... | .......... |
| 24 | **$53,727 81** | **$18,540 62** | **$438,732 88** | **$101,337 76** | .......... | .......... |
| 25 | $121,559 95 | $32,793 62 | $201,489 30 | $4,103 66 | .......... | .......... |
| 26 | 5,224 50 | 5,916 91 | 235,111 34 | .......... | .......... | .......... |
| 27 | **$126,784 45** | **$38,710 53** | **$436,600 64** | **$4,103 66** | .......... | ........ |
| 28 | $114,899 55 | $23,959 36 | $188,716 86 | $974 78 | $7,682 54 | .......... |
| 29 | 4,268.30 | 5,000 68 | 207,786 69 | 243 26 | .......... | .......... |
| 30 | **$119,167 85** | **$28,960 04** | **$396,503 55** | **$1,218 04** | **$7,682 54** | .......... |

COMPARATIVE STATEMENTS SHOWING SEPARATELY THE EXPENDITURES
YEARS 1910 TO 1914, INCLUSIVE, CLASSIFIED BY

| | Total | Personal Service | Supplies | LINE No. |
|---|---|---|---|---|
| **COMMISSION FOR THE IMPROVEMENT AND DEVELOPMENT OF JAMAICA BAY** | | | | |
| **1910** | | | | |
| Revenue Expenditures | .......... | .......... | .......... | 1 |
| Corporate Stock Expenditures | $40,793 10 | $38,560 46 | .......... | 2 |
| Total for 1910 | **$40,793 10** | **$38,560 46** | .......... | 3 |
| **1911** | | | | |
| Revenue Expenditures | .......... | .......... | .......... | 4 |
| Corporate Stock Expenditures | $460 00 | $310 00 | .......... | 5 |
| Total for 1911 | **$460 00** | **$310 00** | .......... | 6 |
| **1912** | | | | |
| Revenue Expenditures | .......... | .......... | .......... | 7 |
| Corporate Stock Expenditures | .......... | .......... | .......... | 8 |
| Total for 1912 | .......... | .......... | .......... | 9 |
| **1913** | | | | |
| Revenue Expenditures | .......... | .......... | .......... | 10 |
| Corporate Stock Expenditures | .......... | .......... | .......... | 11 |
| Total for 1913 | .......... | .......... | .......... | 12 |
| **1914** | | | | |
| Revenue Expenditures | .......... | .......... | .......... | 13 |
| Corporate Stock Expenditures | .......... | .......... | .......... | 14 |
| Total for 1914 | .......... | .......... | .......... | 15 |
| **LAW DEPARTMENT** | | | | |
| **1910** | | | | |
| Revenue Expenditures | $770,000 94 | $702,336 19 | $4,337 76 | 16 |
| Corporate Stock Expenditures | .......... | .......... | .......... | 17 |
| Total for 1910 | **$770,000 94** | **$702,336 19** | **$4,337 76** | 18 |
| **1911** | | | | |
| Revenue Expenditures | $802,469 75 | $727,896 19 | $4,489 50 | 19 |
| Corporate Stock Expenditures | .......... | .......... | .......... | 20 |
| Total for 1911 | **$802,469 75** | **$727,896 19** | **$4,489 50** | 21 |
| **1912** | | | | |
| Revenue Expenditures | $804,112 35 | $695,884 96 | $5,657 50 | 22 |
| Corporate Stock Expenditures | .......... | .......... | .......... | 23 |
| Total for 1912 | **$804,112 35** | **$695,884 96** | **$5,657 50** | 24 |
| **1913** | | | | |
| Revenue Expenditures | $862,078 90 | $774,665 65 | $1,437 78 | 25 |
| Corporate Stock Expenditures | .......... | .......... | .......... | 26 |
| Total for 1913 | **$862,078 90** | **$774,665 65** | **$1,437 78** | 27 |
| **1914** | | | | |
| Revenue Expenditures | $855,199 96 | $762,380 96 | $1,737 40 | 28 |
| Corporate Stock Expenditures | .......... | .......... | .......... | 29 |
| Total for 1914 | **$855,199 96** | **$762,380 96** | **$1,737 40** | 30 |

# NEW YORK

MADE FROM REVENUE AND FROM CORPORATE STOCK FUNDS FOR THE DEPARTMENTS, ACCORDING TO OBJECTS OF EXPENDITURE:

| LINE No. | Purchase of Equipment | Materials | Contract or Open Order Service | Contingencies | Fixed Charges and Contributions | Unclassified |
|---|---|---|---|---|---|---|
| 1 | ... | ... | ... | ... | ... | ... |
| 2 | $9 50 | $6 53 | ... | $1,375 41 | ... | $841 20 |
| 3 | **$9 50** | **$6 53** | ... | **$1,375 41** | ... | **$841 20** |
| 4 | ... | ... | ... | ... | ... | ... |
| 5 | ... | ... | ... | ... | ... | $150 00 |
| 6 | ... | ... | ... | ... | ... | **$150 00** |
| 7 | ... | ... | ... | ... | ... | ... |
| 8 | ... | ... | ... | ... | ... | ... |
| 9 | ... | ... | ... | ... | ... | ... |
| 10 | ... | ... | ... | ... | ... | ... |
| 11 | ... | ... | ... | ... | ... | ... |
| 12 | ... | ... | ... | ... | ... | ... |
| 13 | ... | ... | ... | ... | ... | ... |
| 14 | ... | ... | ... | ... | ... | ... |
| 15 | ... | ... | ... | ... | ... | ... |
| 16 | ... | ... | $6,965 17 | $56,361 82 | ... | ... |
| 17 | ... | ... | ... | ... | ... | ... |
| 18 | ... | ... | **$6,965 17** | **$56,361 82** | ... | ... |
| 19 | $312 27 | ... | $7,771 61 | $62,000 18 | ... | ... |
| 20 | ... | ... | ... | ... | ... | ... |
| 21 | **$312 27** | ... | **$7,771 61** | **$62,000 18** | ... | ... |
| 22 | $12 35 | ... | $7,269 23 | $95,288 31 | ... | ... |
| 23 | ... | ... | ... | ... | ... | ... |
| 24 | **$12 35** | ... | **$7,269 23** | **$95,288 31** | ... | ... |
| 25 | $9,455 08 | ... | $18,327 48 | $58,192 91 | ... | ... |
| 26 | ... | ... | ... | ... | ... | ... |
| 27 | **$9,455 08** | ... | **$18,327 48** | **$58,192 91** | ... | ... |
| 28 | $5,727 35 | ... | $43,337 21 | $42,017 04 | ... | ... |
| 29 | ... | ... | ... | ... | ... | ... |
| 30 | **$5,727 35** | ... | **$43,337 21** | **$42,017 04** | ... | ... |

COMPARATIVE STATEMENTS SHOWING SEPARATELY THE EXPENDITURES
YEARS 1910 TO 1914, INCLUSIVE, CLASSIFIED BY

| | Total | Personal Service | Supplies | LINE No. |
|---|---|---|---|---|
| **COMMISSIONER OF LICENSES** | | | | |
| **1910** | | | | |
| Revenue Expenditures | $51,647 87 | $49,155 34 | $104 80 | 1 |
| Corporate Stock Expenditures | .......... | .......... | .......... | 2 |
| Total for 1910 | **$51,647 87** | **$49,155 34** | **$104 80** | 3 |
| **1911** | | | | |
| Revenue Expenditures | $50,284 54 | $48,654 66 | $169 83 | 4 |
| Corporate Stock Expenditures | .......... | .......... | .......... | 5 |
| Total for 1911 | **$50,284 54** | **$48,654 66** | **$169 83** | 6 |
| **1912** | | | | |
| Revenue Expenditures | $50,498 25 | $48,599 52 | $140 45 | 7 |
| Corporate Stock Expenditures | .......... | .......... | .......... | 8 |
| Total for 1912 | **$50,498 25** | **$48,599 52** | **$140 45** | 9 |
| **1913** | | | | |
| Revenue Expenditures | $50,592 28 | $48,876 13 | $728 50 | 10 |
| Corporate Stock Expenditures | .......... | .......... | .......... | 11 |
| Total for 1913 | **$50,592 28** | **$48,876 13** | **$728 50** | 12 |
| **1914** | | | | |
| Revenue Expenditures | $28,231 22 | $27,032 78 | $565 32 | 13 |
| Corporate Stock Expenditures | .......... | .......... | .......... | 14 |
| Total for 1914 | **$28,231 22** | **$27,032 78** | **$565 32** | 15 |
| **MAYORALTY—ADMINISTRATION** | | | | |
| **1910** | | | | |
| Revenue Expenditures | $53,066 44 | $49,808 69 | .......... | 16 |
| Corporate Stock Expenditures | .......... | .......... | .......... | 17 |
| Total for 1910 | **$53,066 44** | **$49,808 69** | .......... | 18 |
| **1911** | | | | |
| Revenue Expenditures | $53,695 55 | $50,422 22 | .......... | 19 |
| Corporate Stock Expenditures | .......... | .......... | .......... | 20 |
| Total for 1911 | **$53,695 55** | **$50,422 22** | .......... | 21 |
| **1912** | | | | |
| Revenue Expenditures | $54,738 69 | $51,642 80 | $575 60 | 22 |
| Corporate Stock Expenditures | .......... | .......... | .......... | 23 |
| Total for 1912 | **$54,738 69** | **$51,642 80** | **$575 60** | 24 |
| **1913** | | | | |
| Revenue Expenditures | $55,595 28 | $52,520 26 | $625 00 | 25 |
| Corporate Stock Expenditures | .......... | .......... | .......... | 26 |
| Total for 1913 | **$55,595 28** | **$52,520 26** | **$625 00** | 27 |
| **1914** | | | | |
| Revenue Expenditures | $62,083 83 | $57,939 18 | $1,442 27 | 28 |
| Corporate Stock Expenditures | .......... | .......... | .......... | 29 |
| Total for 1914 | **$62,083 83** | **$57,939 18** | **$1,442 27** | 30 |

NEW YORK

MADE FROM REVENUE AND FROM CORPORATE STOCK FUNDS FOR THE DEPARTMENTS, ACCORDING TO OBJECTS OF EXPENDITURE:

| LINE No. | Purchase of Equipment | Materials | Contract or Open Order Service | Contingencies | Fixed Charges and Contributions | Unclassified |
|---|---|---|---|---|---|---|
| 1 | .......... | .......... | $340 26 | $2,047 47 | .......... | .......... |
| 2 | .......... | .......... | .......... | .......... | .......... | .......... |
| 3 | .......... | .......... | **$340 26** | **$2,047 47** | .......... | .......... |
| 4 | .......... | .......... | $330 55 | $1,129 50 | .......... | .......... |
| 5 | .......... | .......... | .......... | .......... | .......... | .......... |
| 6 | .......... | .......... | **$330 55** | **$1,129 50** | .......... | .......... |
| 7 | $135 98 | .......... | $333 86 | $1,288 44 | .......... | .......... |
| 8 | .......... | .......... | .......... | .......... | .......... | .......... |
| 9 | **$135 98** | .......... | **$333 86** | **$1,288 44** | .......... | .......... |
| 10 | $149 20 | .......... | $788 45 | $50 00 | .......... | .......... |
| 11 | .......... | .......... | .......... | .......... | .......... | .......... |
| 12 | **$149 20** | .......... | **$788 45** | **$50 00** | .......... | .......... |
| 13 | $46 45 | .......... | $536 67 | $50 00 | .......... | .......... |
| 14 | .......... | .......... | .......... | .......... | .......... | .......... |
| 15 | **$46 45** | .......... | **$536 67** | **$50 00** | .......... | .......... |
| 16 | .......... | .......... | $584 51 | $2,073 24 | .......... | .......... |
| 17 | .......... | .......... | .......... | .......... | .......... | .......... |
| 18 | .......... | .......... | **$584 51** | **$2,673 24** | .......... | .......... |
| 19 | .......... | .......... | $856 03 | $2,417 30 | .......... | .......... |
| 20 | .......... | .......... | .......... | .......... | .......... | .......... |
| 21 | .......... | .......... | **$856 03** | **$2,417 30** | .......... | .......... |
| 22 | $221 00 | .......... | $837 38 | $1,461 91 | .......... | .......... |
| 23 | .......... | .......... | .......... | .......... | .......... | .......... |
| 24 | **$221 00** | .......... | **$837 38** | **$1,461 91** | .......... | .......... |
| 25 | $1,035 08 | .......... | $1,014 94 | $400 00 | .......... | .......... |
| 26 | .......... | .......... | .......... | .......... | .......... | .......... |
| 27 | **$1,035 08** | .......... | **$1,014 94** | **$400 00** | .......... | .......... |
| 28 | $638 11 | .......... | $1,545 17 | $519 10 | .......... | .......... |
| 29 | .......... | .......... | .......... | .......... | .......... | .......... |
| 30 | **$638 11** | .......... | **$1,545 17** | **$519 10** | .......... | .......... |

COMPARATIVE STATEMENTS SHOWING SEPARATELY THE EXPENDITURES
YEARS 1910 TO 1914, INCLUSIVE, CLASSIFIED BY

| | Total | Personal Service | Supplies | LINE No. |
|---|---|---|---|---|
| **MAYORALTY-BUREAU OF LICENSES** | | | | |
| **1910** | | | | |
| Revenue Expenditures | $44,984 04 | $27,787 16 | .......... | 1 |
| Corporate Stock Expenditures | .......... | .......... | .......... | 2 |
| Total for 1910 | **$44,984 04** | **$27,787 16** | .......... | 3 |
| **1911** | | | | |
| Revenue Expenditures | $83,137 77 | $70,430 81 | $457 91 | 4 |
| Corporate Stock Expenditures | .......... | .......... | .......... | 5 |
| Total for 1911 | **$83,137 77** | **$70,430 81** | **$457 91** | 6 |
| **1912** | | | | |
| Revenue Expenditures | $82,093 03 | $71,114 29 | $2,857 42 | 7 |
| Corporate Stock Expenditures | .......... | .......... | .......... | 8 |
| Total for 1912 | **$82,093 03** | **$71,114 29** | **$2,857 42** | 9 |
| **1913** | | | | |
| Revenue Expenditures | $115,764 35 | $89,886 68 | $2,483 22 | 10 |
| Corporate Stock Expenditures | .......... | .......... | .......... | 11 |
| Total for 1913 | **$115,764 35** | **$89,886 68** | **$2,483 22** | 12 |
| **1914** | | | | |
| Revenue Expenditures | $137,812 61 | $124,131 67 | $5,189 91 | 13 |
| Corporate Stock Expenditures | .......... | .......... | .......... | 14 |
| Total for 1914 | **$137,812 61** | **$124,131 67** | **$5,189 91** | 15 |
| **MAYORALTY-BUREAU OF WEIGHTS AND MEASURES** | | | | |
| **1910** | | | | |
| Revenue Expenditures | $37,558 80 | $32,327 90 | $500 00 | 16 |
| Corporate Stock Expenditures | .......... | .......... | .......... | 17 |
| Total for 1910 | **$37,558 80** | **$32,327 90** | **$500 00** | 18 |
| **1911** | | | | |
| Revenue Expenditures | $65,483 05 | $50,214 17 | $5,251 62 | 19 |
| Corporate Stock Expenditures | .......... | .......... | .......... | 20 |
| Total for 1911 | **$65,483 05** | **$50,214 17** | **$5,251 62** | 21 |
| **1912** | | | | |
| Revenue Expenditures | $72,158 60 | $57,998 45 | $4,690 84 | 22 |
| Corporate Stock Expenditures | .......... | .......... | .......... | 23 |
| Total for 1912 | **$72,158 60** | **$57,998 45** | **$4,690 84** | 24 |
| **1913** | | | | |
| Revenue Expenditures | $64,686 35 | $54,337 08 | $984 93 | 25 |
| Corporate Stock Expenditures | .......... | .......... | .......... | 26 |
| Total for 1913 | **$64,686 35** | **$54,337 08** | **$984 93** | 27 |
| **1914** | | | | |
| Revenue Expenditures | $76,964 27 | $67,180 58 | $1,651 13 | 28 |
| Corporate Stock Expenditures | .......... | .......... | .......... | 29 |
| Total for 1914 | **$76,964 27** | **$67,180 58** | **$1,651 13** | 30 |

NEW YORK

MADE FROM REVENUE AND FROM CORPORATE STOCK FUNDS FOR THE DEPARTMENTS, ACCORDING TO OBJECTS OF EXPENDITURE:

| LINE No. | Purchase of Equipment | Materials | Contract or Open Order Service | Contingencies | Fixed Charges and Contributions | Unclassified |
|---|---|---|---|---|---|---|
| 1 | .......... | .......... | $10,807 00 | $6,389 88 | .......... | .......... |
| 2 | .......... | .......... | .......... | .......... | .......... | .......... |
| 3 | .......... | .......... | **$10,807 00** | **$6,389 88** | .......... | .......... |
| 4 | $4,995 60 | .......... | $447 03 | $6,806 42 | .......... | .......... |
| 5 | .......... | .......... | .......... | .......... | .......... | .......... |
| 6 | **$4,995 60** | .......... | **$447 03** | **$6,806 42** | .......... | .......... |
| 7 | $231 83 | .......... | $2,235 95 | $5,653 54 | .......... | .......... |
| 8 | .......... | .......... | .......... | .......... | .......... | .......... |
| 9 | **$231 83** | .......... | **$2,235 95** | **$5,653 54** | .......... | .......... |
| 10 | $17,037 67 | .......... | $5,525 63 | $831 15 | .......... | .......... |
| 11 | .......... | .......... | .......... | .......... | .......... | .......... |
| 12 | **$17,037 67** | .......... | **$5,525 63** | **$831 15** | .......... | .......... |
| 13 | $1,670 09 | .......... | $4,626 48 | $2,194 46 | .......... | .......... |
| 14 | .......... | .......... | .......... | .......... | .......... | .......... |
| 15 | **$1,670 09** | .......... | **$4,626 48** | **$2,194 46** | .......... | .......... |
| 16 | .......... | .......... | .......... | $4,730 90 | .......... | .......... |
| 17 | .......... | .......... | .......... | .......... | .......... | .......... |
| 18 | .......... | .......... | .......... | **$4,730 90** | .......... | .......... |
| 19 | .......... | .......... | $133 63 | $9,883 63 | .......... | .......... |
| 20 | .......... | .......... | .......... | .......... | .......... | .......... |
| 21 | .......... | .......... | **$133 63** | **$9,883 63** | .......... | .......... |
| 22 | $1,094 91 | .......... | $5,139 83 | $3,234 57 | .......... | .......... |
| 23 | .......... | .......... | .......... | .......... | .......... | .......... |
| 24 | **$1,094 91** | .......... | **$5,139 83** | **$3,234 57** | .......... | .......... |
| 25 | $2,688 81 | .......... | $6,370 77 | $304 76 | .......... | .......... |
| 26 | .......... | .......... | .......... | .......... | .......... | .......... |
| 27 | **$2,688 81** | .......... | **$6,370 77** | **$304 76** | .......... | .......... |
| 28 | $922 53 | .......... | $5,836 10 | $1,373 93 | .......... | .......... |
| 29 | .......... | .......... | .......... | .......... | .......... | .......... |
| 30 | **$922 53** | .......... | **$5,836 10** | **$1,373 93** | .......... | .......... |

Comparative Statements Showing Separately the Expenditures
Years 1910 to 1914, Inclusive, Classified by

| | Total | Personal Service | Supplies | Line No. |
|---|---|---|---|---|
| **METROPOLITAN SEWERAGE COMMISSION** | | | | |
| **1910** | | | | |
| Revenue Expenditures | .......... | .......... | .......... | 1 |
| Corporate Stock Expenditures | $39,916 17 | $29,408 80 | $797 63 | 2 |
| Total for 1910 | **$39,916 17** | **$29,408 80** | **$797 63** | 3 |
| **1911** | | | | |
| Revenue Expenditures | .......... | .......... | .......... | 4 |
| Corporate Stock Expenditures | $41,820 72 | $35,403 31 | $4,470 91 | 5 |
| Total for 1911 | **$41,820 72** | **$35,403 31** | **$4,470 91** | 6 |
| **1912** | | | | |
| Revenue Expenditures | .......... | .......... | .......... | 7 |
| Corporate Stock Expenditures | $46,721 54 | $30,646 89 | $6,111 33 | 8 |
| Total for 1912 | **$46,721 54** | **$30,646 89** | **$6,111 33** | 9 |
| **1913** | | | | |
| Revenue Expenditures | .......... | .......... | .......... | 10 |
| Corporate Stock Expenditures | $43,422 52 | $21,032 98 | $435 62 | 11 |
| Total for 1913 | **$43,422 52** | **$21,032 98** | **$435 62** | 12 |
| **1914** | | | | |
| Revenue Expenditures | .......... | .......... | .......... | 13 |
| Corporate Stock Expenditures | $24,997 13 | $17,208 70 | $143 33 | 14 |
| Total for 1914 | **$24,997 13** | **$17,208 70** | **$143 33** | 15 |
| **MUNICIPAL CIVIL SERVICE COMMISSION** | | | | |
| **1910** | | | | |
| Revenue Expenditures | $149,279 61 | $142,194 61 | $604 19 | 16 |
| Corporate Stock Expenditures | .......... | .......... | .......... | 17 |
| Total for 1910 | **$149,279 61** | **$142,194 61** | **$604 19** | 18 |
| **1911** | | | | |
| Revenue Expenditures | $156,655 66 | $148,747 12 | $396 70 | 19 |
| Corporate Stock Expenditures | .......... | .......... | .......... | 20 |
| Total for 1911 | **$156,655 66** | **$148,747 12** | **$396 70** | 21 |
| **1912** | | | | |
| Revenue Expenditures | $189,983 09 | $167,904 07 | $1,099 30 | 22 |
| Corporate Stock Expenditures | .......... | .......... | .......... | 23 |
| Total for 1912 | **$189,983 09** | **$167,904 07** | **$1,099 30** | 24 |
| **1913** | | | | |
| Revenue Expenditures | $211,715 97 | $192,292 47 | $7,171 64 | 25 |
| Corporate Stock Expenditures | .......... | .......... | .......... | 26 |
| Total for 1913 | **$211,715 97** | **$192,292 47** | **$7,171 64** | 27 |
| **1914** | | | | |
| Revenue Expenditures | $200,792 38 | $180,800 13 | $5,148 34 | 28 |
| Corporate Stock Expenditures | .......... | .......... | .......... | 29 |
| Total for 1914 | **$200,792 38** | **$180,800 13** | **$5,148 34** | 30 |

NEW YORK

MADE FROM REVENUE AND FROM CORPORATE STOCK FUNDS FOR THE DEPARTMENTS, ACCORDING TO OBJECTS OF EXPENDITURE:

| LINE No. | Purchase of Equipment | Materials | Contract or Open Order Service | Contingencies | Fixed Charges and Contributions | Unclassified |
|---|---|---|---|---|---|---|
| 1 | .......... | .......... | .......... | .......... | .......... | .......... |
| 2 | $602 59 | .......... | $3,466 64 | $88 79 | .......... | $5,551 72 |
| 3 | **$602 59** | .......... | **$3,466 64** | **$88 79** | .......... | **$5,551 72** |
| 4 | .......... | .......... | .......... | .......... | .......... | .......... |
| 5 | .......... | .......... | .......... | .......... | .......... | $1,946 50 |
| 6 | .......... | .......... | .......... | .......... | .......... | **$1,946 50** |
| 7 | .......... | .......... | .......... | .......... | .......... | .......... |
| 8 | $778 83 | .......... | $226 46 | $379 54 | .......... | $8,578 49 |
| 9 | **$778 83** | .......... | **$226 46** | **$379 54** | .......... | **$8,578 49** |
| 10 | .......... | .......... | .......... | .......... | .......... | .......... |
| 11 | $669 16 | .......... | $3,399 48 | .......... | .......... | $17,885 28 |
| 12 | **$669 16** | .......... | **$3,399 48** | .......... | .......... | **$17,885 28** |
| 13 | .......... | .......... | .......... | .......... | .......... | .......... |
| 14 | $1,388 21 | .......... | $5,109 09 | $181 13 | .......... | $966 67 |
| 15 | **$1,388 21** | .......... | **$5,109 09** | **$181 13** | .......... | **$966 67** |
| 16 | .......... | .......... | $945 29 | $5,535 52 | .......... | .......... |
| 17 | .......... | .......... | .......... | .......... | .......... | .......... |
| 18 | .......... | .......... | **$945 29** | **$5,535 52** | .......... | .......... |
| 19 | .......... | .......... | $1,050 00 | $6,461 84 | .......... | .......... |
| 20 | .......... | .......... | .......... | .......... | .......... | .......... |
| 21 | .......... | .......... | **$1,050 00** | **$6,461 84** | .......... | .......... |
| 22 | $2,218 91 | $32 35 | $8,239 63 | $10,488 83 | .......... | .......... |
| 23 | .......... | .......... | .......... | .......... | .......... | .......... |
| 24 | **$2,218 91** | **$32 35** | **$8,239 63** | **$10,488 83** | .......... | .......... |
| 25 | $2,781 49 | .......... | $6,088 33 | $3,382 04 | .......... | .......... |
| 26 | .......... | .......... | .......... | .......... | .......... | .......... |
| 27 | **$2,781 49** | .......... | **$6,088 33** | **$3,382 04** | .......... | .......... |
| 28 | $3,995 48 | .......... | $8,808 95 | $2,039 48 | .......... | .......... |
| 29 | .......... | .......... | .......... | .......... | .......... | .......... |
| 30 | **$3,995 48** | .......... | **$8,808 95** | **$2,039 48** | .......... | .......... |

COMPARATIVE STATEMENTS SHOWING SEPARATELY THE EXPENDITURES
YEARS 1910 TO 1914, INCLUSIVE, CLASSIFIED BY

| | Total | Personal Service | Supplies | LINE No. |
|---|---|---|---|---|
| **MUNICIPAL EXPLOSIVES COMMISSION** | | | | |
| **1910** | | | | |
| Revenue Expenditures | $3,970 37 | $3,897 81 | .......... | 1 |
| Corporate Stock Expenditures | .......... | .......... | .......... | 2 |
| Total for 1910 | **$3,970 37** | **$3,897 81** | .......... | 3 |
| **1911** | | | | |
| Revenue Expenditures | $16,467 50 | $16,467 50 | .......... | 4 |
| Corporate Stock Expenditures | .......... | .......... | .......... | 5 |
| Total for 1911 | **$16,467 50** | **$16,467 50** | .......... | 6 |
| **1912** | | | | |
| Revenue Expenditures | $9,878 93 | $9,660 00 | .......... | 7 |
| Corporate Stock Expenditures | .......... | .......... | .......... | 8 |
| Total for 1912 | **$9,878 93** | **$9,660 00** | .......... | 9 |
| **1913** | | | | |
| Revenue Expenditures | $14,516 25 | $14,340 00 | $40 25 | 10 |
| Corporate Stock Expenditures | .......... | .......... | .......... | 11 |
| Total for 1913 | **$14,516 25** | **$14,340 00** | **$40 25** | 12 |
| **1914** | | | | |
| Revenue Expenditures | $8,966 17 | $8,945 42 | .......... | 13 |
| Corporate Stock Expenditures | .......... | .......... | .......... | 14 |
| Total for 1914 | **$8,966 17** | **$8,945 42** | .......... | 15 |
| **PARK BOARD** | | | | |
| **1910** | | | | |
| Revenue Expenditures | $25,512 19 | $25,512 19 | .......... | 16 |
| Corporate Stock Expenditures | .......... | .......... | .......... | 17 |
| Total for 1910 | **$25,512 19** | **$25,512 19** | .......... | 18 |
| **1911** | | | | |
| Revenue Expenditures | $25,310 74 | $25,310 74 | .......... | 19 |
| Corporate Stock Expenditures | .......... | .......... | .......... | 20 |
| Total for 1911 | **$25,310 74** | **$25,310 74** | .......... | 21 |
| **1912** | | | | |
| Revenue Expenditures | $31,646 66 | $31,300 00 | $196 76 | 22 |
| Corporate Stock Expenditures | .......... | .......... | .......... | 23 |
| Total for 1912 | **$31,646 66** | **$31,300 00** | **$196 76** | 24 |
| **1913** | | | | |
| Revenue Expenditures | $29,884 36 | $29,488 47 | $169 91 | 25 |
| Corporate Stock Expenditures | .......... | .......... | .......... | 26 |
| Total for 1913 | **$29,884 36** | **$29,488 47** | **$169 91** | 27 |
| **1914** | | | | |
| Revenue Expenditures | $29,222 30 | $28,999 97 | .......... | 28 |
| Corporate Stock Expenditures | .......... | .......... | .......... | 29 |
| Total for 1914 | **$29,222 30** | **$28,999 97** | .......... | 30 |

## NEW YORK

MADE FROM REVENUE AND FROM CORPORATE STOCK FUNDS FOR THE DEPARTMENTS, ACCORDING TO OBJECTS OF EXPENDITURE:

| LINE No. | Purchase of Equipment | Materials | Contract or Open Order Service | Contingencies | Fixed Charges and Contributions | Unclassified |
|---|---|---|---|---|---|---|
| 1 | .......... | .......... | .......... | $72 56 | .......... | .......... |
| 2 | .......... | .......... | .......... | .......... | .......... | .......... |
| 3 | .......... | .......... | .......... | **$72 56** | .......... | .......... |
| 4 | .......... | .......... | .......... | .......... | .......... | .......... |
| 5 | .......... | .......... | .......... | .......... | .......... | .......... |
| 6 | .......... | .......... | .......... | .......... | .......... | .......... |
| 7 | $187 98 | .......... | .......... | $30 95 | .......... | .......... |
| 8 | .......... | .......... | .......... | .......... | .......... | .......... |
| 9 | **$187 98** | .......... | .......... | **$30 95** | .......... | .......... |
| 10 | $100 00 | .......... | .......... | $36 00 | .......... | .......... |
| 11 | .......... | .......... | .......... | .......... | .......... | .......... |
| 12 | **$100 00** | .......... | .......... | **$36 00** | .......... | .......... |
| 13 | .......... | .......... | .......... | $20 75 | .......... | .......... |
| 14 | .......... | .......... | .......... | .......... | .......... | .......... |
| 15 | .......... | .......... | .......... | **$20 75** | .......... | .......... |
| 16 | .......... | .......... | .......... | .......... | .......... | .......... |
| 17 | .......... | .......... | .......... | .......... | .......... | .......... |
| 18 | .......... | .......... | .......... | .......... | .......... | .......... |
| 19 | .......... | .......... | .......... | .......... | .......... | .......... |
| 20 | .......... | .......... | .......... | .......... | .......... | .......... |
| 21 | .......... | .......... | .......... | .......... | .......... | .......... |
| 22 | $99 90 | .......... | .......... | $50 00 | .......... | .......... |
| 23 | .......... | .......... | .......... | .......... | .......... | .......... |
| 24 | **$99 90** | .......... | .......... | **$50 00** | .......... | .......... |
| 25 | $202 73 | .......... | .......... | $23 25 | .......... | .......... |
| 26 | .......... | .......... | .......... | .......... | .......... | .......... |
| 27 | **$202 73** | .......... | .......... | **$23 25** | .......... | .......... |
| 28 | .......... | .......... | .......... | $222 33 | .......... | .......... |
| 29 | .......... | .......... | .......... | .......... | .......... | .......... |
| 30 | .......... | .......... | .......... | **$222 33** | .......... | .......... |

COMPARATIVE STATEMENTS SHOWING SEPARATELY THE EXPENDITURES
YEARS 1910 TO 1914, INCLUSIVE, CLASSIFIED BY

| | Total | Personal Service | Supplies | LINE No. |
|---|---|---|---|---|
| **DEPARTMENT OF PARKS, MANHATTAN AND RICHMOND** | | | | |
| **1910** | | | | |
| Revenue Expenditures | $1,057,806 73 | $747,646 79 | $70,419 35 | 1 |
| Corporate Stock Expenditures | 540,099 77 | 153,896 04 | 5,754 04 | 2 |
| Total for 1910 | **$1,597,906 50** | **$901,542 83** | **$76,173 39** | 3 |
| **1911** | | | | |
| Revenue Expenditures | $999,935 53 | $747,660 52 | $83,395 11 | 4 |
| Corporate Stock Expenditures | 714,393 52 | 110,715 61 | 2,347 24 | 5 |
| Total for 1911 | **$1,714,329 05** | **$858,376 13** | **$85,742 35** | 6 |
| **1912** | | | | |
| Revenue Expenditures | $1,134,149 70 | $832,017 63 | $159,788 05 | 7 |
| Corporate Stock Expenditures | 912,889 23 | 67,151 86 | 921 73 | 8 |
| Total for 1912 | **$2,047,038 93** | **$899,169 49** | **$160,709 78** | 9 |
| **1913** | | | | |
| Revenue Expenditures | $1,126,524 71 | $843,119 12 | $92,822 67 | 10 |
| Corporate Stock Expenditures | 981,874 86 | 44,625 44 | 3,161 81 | 11 |
| Total for 1913 | **$2,108,399 57** | **$887,744 56** | **$95,984 48** | 12 |
| **1914** | | | | |
| Revenue Expenditures | $1,083,772 24 | $853,272 69 | $80,399 13 | 13 |
| Corporate Stock Expenditures | 390,900 22 | 60,360 83 | 9,572 55 | 14 |
| Total for 1914 | **$1,474,672 46** | **$913,633 52** | **$89,971 68** | 15 |
| **DEPARTMENT OF PARKS, THE BRONX** | | | | |
| **1910** | | | | |
| Revenue Expenditures | $413,428 44 | $318,869 89 | $9,209 49 | 16 |
| Corporate Stock Expenditures | 405,815 51 | 99,582 48 | 3,372 52 | 17 |
| Total for 1910 | **$819,243 95** | **$418,452 37** | **$12,582 01** | 18 |
| **1911** | | | | |
| Revenue Expenditures | $411,712 48 | $320,223 21 | $10,482 46 | 19 |
| Corporate Stock Expenditures | 272,275 52 | 84,142 76 | .......... | 20 |
| Total for 1911 | **$683,988 00** | **$404,365 97** | **$10,482 46** | 21 |
| **1912** | | | | |
| Revenue Expenditures | $452,834 58 | $335,696 17 | $34,042 91 | 22 |
| Corporate Stock Expenditures | 239,511 06 | 75,471 37 | 29 35 | 23 |
| Total for 1912 | **$692,345 64** | **$411,167 54** | **$34,072 26** | 24 |
| **1913** | | | | |
| Revenue Expenditures | $464,895 14 | $345,469 64 | $20,716 35 | 25 |
| Corporate Stock Expenditures | 142,994 87 | 37,287 65 | 2,353 21 | 26 |
| Total for 1913 | **$607,890 01** | **$382,757 29** | **$23,069 56** | 27 |
| **1914** | | | | |
| Revenue Expenditures | $469,586 19 | $349,878 08 | $13,955 21 | 28 |
| Corporate Stock Expenditures | 43,703 79 | 8,355 88 | 7,410 36 | 29 |
| Total for 1914 | **$513,289 98** | **$358,233 96** | **$21,365 57** | 30 |

NEW YORK

MADE FROM REVENUE AND FROM CORPORATE STOCK FUNDS FOR THE DEPARTMENTS, ACCORDING TO OBJECTS OF EXPENDITURE:

| LINE No. | Purchase of Equipment | Materials | Contract or Open Order Service | Contingencies | Fixed Charges and Contributions | Unclassified |
|---|---|---|---|---|---|---|
| 1 | $24,281 89 | $94,677 71 | $114,300 07 | $6,480 92 | .......... | .......... |
| 2 | 44,613 34 | 33,379 33 | 302,152 26 | 162 45 | .......... | $142 31 |
| 3 | **$68,895 23** | **$128,057 04** | **$416,452 33** | **$6,643 37** | .......... | **$142 31** |
| 4 | $18,925 62 | $68,258 24 | $75,034 05 | $6,661 99 | .......... | .......... |
| 5 | 14,091 42 | 42,366 93 | 544,460 51 | 249 81 | .......... | $162 00 |
| 6 | **$33,017 04** | **$110,625 17** | **$619,494 56** | **$6,911 80** | .......... | **$162 00** |
| 7 | $10,947 66 | $1,571 08 | $120,025 89 | $7,103 36 | .......... | $2,696 03 |
| 8 | 28,171 47 | 27,832 99 | 787,214 14 | 1,273 04 | .......... | 324 00 |
| 9 | **$39,119 13** | **$29,404 07** | **$907,240 03** | **$8,376 40** | .......... | **$3,020 03** |
| 10 | $18,370 18 | $33,494 93 | $130,590 32 | $1,293 15 | .......... | $6,834 34 |
| 11 | 18,180 06 | 24,078 88 | 840,029 57 | .......... | .......... | 51,799 10 |
| 12 | **$36,550 24** | **$57,573 81** | **$970,619 89** | **$1,293 15** | .......... | **$58,633 44** |
| 13 | $25,146 72 | $38,082 23 | $86,389 67 | $481 80 | .......... | .......... |
| 14 | 14,320 35 | 6,305 61 | 297,605 19 | 2,735 69 | .......... | .......... |
| 15 | **$39,467 07** | **$44,387 84** | **$383,994 86** | **$3,217 49** | .......... | .......... |
| 16 | $7,148 86 | $26,079 69 | $50,688 27 | $1,432 24 | .......... | .......... |
| 17 | 667 00 | 32,125 35 | 270,068 16 | .......... | .......... | .......... |
| 18 | **$7,815 86** | **$58,205 04** | **$320,756 43** | **$1,432 24** | .......... | .......... |
| 19 | $9,560 25 | $25,141 47 | $45,560 76 | $744 33 | .......... | .......... |
| 20 | 10,882 37 | 10,533 31 | 166,717 08 | .......... | .......... | .......... |
| 21 | **$20,442 62** | **$35,674 78** | **$212,277 84** | **$744 33** | .......... | .......... |
| 22 | $7,618 87 | .......... | $74,415 22 | $1,061 41 | .......... | .......... |
| 23 | 1,450 11 | $35,103 27 | 127,456 96 | .......... | .......... | .......... |
| 24 | **$9,068 98** | **$35,103 27** | **$201,872 18** | **$1,061 41** | .......... | .......... |
| 25 | $8,768 52 | $22,139 54 | $67,801 09 | .......... | .......... | .......... |
| 26 | 2,959 68 | 8,763 28 | 91,631 05 | .......... | .......... | .......... |
| 27 | **$11,728 20** | **$30,902 82** | **$159,432 14** | .......... | .......... | .......... |
| 28 | $6,576 08 | $28,510 58 | $70,666 24 | .......... | .......... | .......... |
| 29 | 1,285 94 | 1,089 88 | 25,561 73 | .......... | .......... | .......... |
| 30 | **$7,862 02** | **$29,600 46** | **$96,227 97** | .......... | .......... | .......... |

COMPARATIVE STATEMENTS SHOWING SEPARATELY THE EXPENDITURES
YEARS 1910 TO 1914, INCLUSIVE, CLASSIFIED BY

| | Total | Personal Service | Supplies | LINE No. |
|---|---|---|---|---|
| **DEPARTMENT OF PARKS, BROOKLYN (Years 1910 and 1911 include "Queens")** | | | | |
| **1910** | | | | |
| Revenue Expenditures | $994,524 82 | $627,581 23 | $71,412 31 | 1 |
| Corporate Stock Expenditures | .184,579 73 | 57,627 53 | .......... | 2 |
| Total for 1910 | **$1,179,104 55** | **$685,208 76** | **$71,412 31** | 3 |
| **1911** | | | | |
| Revenue Expenditures | $942,611 22 | $617,168 70 | $68,145 88 | 4 |
| Corporate Stock Expenditures | 316,332 17 | 12,332 02 | 429 05 | 5 |
| Total for 1911 | **$1,258,943 39** | **$629,500 72** | **$68,574 93** | 6 |
| **1912** | | | | |
| Revenue Expenditures | $877,014 18 | $559,773 33 | $144,483 87 | 7 |
| Corporate Stock Expenditures | 587,482 84 | 65,178 11 | .......... | 8 |
| Total for 1912 | **$1,464,497 02** | **$624,951 44** | **$144,483 87** | 9 |
| **1913** | | | | |
| Revenue Expenditures | $867,234 36 | $578,470 15 | $60,065 25 | 10 |
| Corporate Stock Expenditures | 699,466 01 | 43,862 05 | 220 65 | 11 |
| Total for 1913 | **$1,566,700 37** | **$622,332 20** | **$60,285 90** | 12 |
| **1914** | | | | |
| Revenue Expenditures | $826,273 18 | $592,688 58 | $48,007 85 | 13 |
| Corporate Stock Expenditures | 404,424 12 | 15,991 77 | 1,980 25 | 14 |
| Total for 1914 | **$1,230,697 30** | **$608,680 35** | **$49,988 10** | 15 |
| **DEPARTMENT OF PARKS, BOROUGH OF QUEENS** | | | | |
| **1910** | | | | |
| Revenue Expenditures | .......... | .......... | .......... | 16 |
| Corporate Stock Expenditures | .......... | .......... | .......... | 17 |
| Total for 1910 | .......... | .......... | .......... | 18 |
| **1911** | | | | |
| Revenue Expenditures | $3,768 44 | $3,768 44 | .......... | 19 |
| Corporate Stock Expenditures | .......... | .......... | .......... | 20 |
| Total for 1911 | **$3,768 44** | **$3,768 44** | .......... | 21 |
| **1912** | | | | |
| Revenue Expenditures | $153,418 40 | $89,373 62 | $26,868 35 | 22 |
| Corporate Stock Expenditures | 18,814 03 | 1,964 03 | .......... | 23 |
| Total for 1912 | **$172,232 43** | **$91,337 65** | **$26,868 35** | 24 |
| **1913** | | | | |
| Revenue Expenditures | $182,562 22 | $117,575 73 | $9,670 14 | 25 |
| Corporate Stock Expenditures | 14,862 40 | 6,928 23 | 160 00 | 26 |
| Total for 1913 | **$197,424 62** | **$124,503 96** | **$9,830 14** | 27 |
| **1914** | | | | |
| Revenue Expenditures | $184,397 67 | $126,326 18 | $10,563 47 | 28 |
| Corporate Stock Expenditures | 8,052 11 | 4,051 95 | 387 00 | 29 |
| Total for 1914 | **$192,449 78** | **$130,378 13** | **$10,950 47** | 30 |

NEW YORK

MADE FROM REVENUE AND FROM CORPORATE STOCK FUNDS FOR THE DEPARTMENTS, ACCORDING TO OBJECTS OF EXPENDITURE:

| LINE No. | Purchase of Equipment | Materials | Contract or Open Order Service | Contingencies | Fixed Charges and Contributions | Unclassified |
|---|---|---|---|---|---|---|
| 1 | $15,912 98 | $89,138 96 | $184,480 39 | $5,998 95 | .......... | .......... |
| 2 | .......... | .......... | 126,952 20 | .......... | .......... | .......... |
| 3 | **$15,912 98** | **$89,138 96** | **$311,432 59** | **$5,998 95** | .......... | .......... |
| 4 | $8,456 10 | $72,972 89 | $170,398 98 | $5,468 67 | .......... | .......... |
| 5 | 18 70 | .......... | 303,552 40 | .......... | .......... | .......... |
| 6 | **$8,474 80** | **$72,972 89** | **$473,951 38** | **$5,468 67** | .......... | .......... |
| 7 | $6,788 55 | $9 68 | $160,470 26 | $5,488 49 | .......... | .......... |
| 8 | 9,011 50 | 12,157 22 | 501,136 01 | .......... | .......... | .......... |
| 9 | **$15,800 05** | **$12,166 90** | **$661,606 27** | **$5,488 49** | .......... | .......... |
| 10 | $19,968 51 | $48,891 08 | $159,652 77 | $186 60 | .......... | .......... |
| 11 | 361 80 | 2,926 02 | 649,948 62 | .......... | .......... | $2,146 87 |
| 12 | **$20,330 31** | **$51,817 10** | **$809,601 39** | **$186 60** | .......... | **$2,146 87** |
| 13 | $11,872 62 | $33,961 79 | $139,345 21 | $397 13 | .......... | .......... |
| 14 | 2,629 55 | 785 00 | 382,868 58 | 168 97 | .......... | .......... |
| 15 | **$14,502 17** | **$34,746 79** | **$522,213 79** | **$566 10** | .......... | .......... |
| 16 | .......... | .......... | .......... | .......... | .......... | .......... |
| 17 | .......... | .......... | .......... | .......... | .......... | .......... |
| 18 | .......... | .......... | .......... | .......... | .......... | .......... |
| 19 | .......... | .......... | .......... | .......... | .......... | .......... |
| 20 | .......... | .......... | .......... | .......... | .......... | .......... |
| 21 | .......... | .......... | .......... | .......... | .......... | .......... |
| 22 | $16,534 40 | .......... | $18,644 20 | $1,997 83 | .......... | .......... |
| 23 | .......... | $897 00 | 15,953 00 | .......... | .......... | .......... |
| 24 | **$16,534 40** | **$897 00** | **$34,597 20** | **$1,997 83** | .......... | .......... |
| 25 | $8,645 47 | $13,988 12 | $32,662 85 | $19 91 | .......... | .......... |
| 26 | .......... | .......... | 6,824 17 | .......... | .......... | $950 00 |
| 27 | **$8,645 47** | **$13,988 12** | **$39,487 02** | **$19 91** | .......... | **$950.00** |
| 28 | $11,481 28 | $11,893 66 | $23,394 87 | $29 93 | $708 28 | .......... |
| 29 | .......... | .......... | 3,613 16 | .......... | .......... | .......... |
| 30 | **$11,481 28** | **$11,893 66** | **$27,008 03** | **$29 93** | **$708 28** | .......... |

COMPARATIVE STATEMENTS SHOWING SEPARATELY THE EXPENDITURES
YEARS 1910 TO 1914, INCLUSIVE, CLASSIFIED BY

| | Total | Personal Service | Supplies | LINE No. |
|---|---|---|---|---|
| **POLICE DEPARTMENT** | | | | |
| **1910** | | | | |
| Revenue Expenditures | $15,069,255 88 | $13,901,044 66 | $343,688 07 | 1 |
| Corporate Stock Expenditures | 245,312 92 | .......... | .......... | 2 |
| Total for 1910 | **$15,314,568 80** | **$13,901,044 66** | **$343,688 07** | 3 |
| **1911** | | | | |
| Revenue Expenditures | $15,655,041 83 | $14,251,211 53 | $295,323 94 | 4 |
| Corporate Stock Expenditures | 500,161 93 | 3,280 35 | 9,118 90 | 5 |
| Total for 1911 | **$16,155,203 76** | **$14,254,491 88** | **$304,442 84** | 6 |
| **1912** | | | | |
| Revenue Expenditures | $16,450,647 22 | $14,699,353 78 | $214,012 10 | 7 |
| Corporate Stock Expenditures | 233,174 29 | 150 00 | .......... | 8 |
| Total for 1912 | **$16,683,821 51** | **$14,699,503 78** | **$214,012 10** | 9 |
| **1913** | | | | |
| Revenue Expenditures | $16,781,054 55 | $14,913,645 77 | $149,041 92 | 10 |
| Corporate Stock Expenditures | 479,886 23 | .......... | 59 29 | 11 |
| Total for 1913 | **$17,260,940 78** | **$14,913,645 77** | **$149,101 21** | 12 |
| **1914** | | | | |
| Revenue Expenditures | $17,439,827 77 | $15,424,830 16 | $146,431 36 | 13 |
| Corporate Stock Expenditures | 218,651 47 | .......... | .......... | 14 |
| Total for 1914 | **$17,658,479 24** | **$15,424,830 16** | **$146,431 36** | 15 |
| **DEPARTMENT OF PUBLIC CHARITIES** | | | | |
| **1910** | | | | |
| Revenue Expenditures | $2,919,373 13 | $989,515 12 | $1,510,442 09 | 16 |
| Corporate Stock Expenditures | 1,240,027 74 | 148 98 | 5,312 51 | 17 |
| Total for 1910 | **$4,159,400 87** | **$989,664 10** | **$1,515,754 60** | 18 |
| **1911** | | | | |
| Revenue Expenditures | $3,218,150 19 | $1,086,044 46 | $1,677,049 62 | 19 |
| Corporate Stock Expenditures | 1,025,922 23 | 846 25 | .......... | 20 |
| Total for 1911 | **$4,244,072 42** | **$1,086,890 71** | **$1,677,049 62** | 21 |
| **1912** | | | | |
| Revenue Expenditures | $3,219,029 05 | $1,238,282 70 | $1,643,323 63 | 22 |
| Corporate Stock Expenditures | 1,741,366 59 | 3,582 39 | .......... | 23 |
| Total for 1912 | **$4,960,395 64** | **$1,241,865 09** | **$1,643,323 63** | 24 |
| **1913** | | | | |
| Revenue Expenditures | $3,719,089 17 | $1,367,290 97 | $1,661,579 93 | 25 |
| Corporate Stock Expenditures | 1,887,563 94 | 996 83 | 386 72 | 26 |
| Total for 1913 | **$5,606,653 11** | **$1,368,287 80** | **$1,661,966 65** | 27 |
| **1914** | | | | |
| Revenue Expenditures | $3,682,980 96 | $1,575,966 95 | $1,584,042 69 | 28 |
| Corporate Stock Expenditures | 968,135 23 | 1,709 00 | 1,380 92 | 29 |
| Total for 1914 | **$4,651,116 19** | **$1,577,675 95** | **$1,585,423 61** | 30 |

## NEW YORK

MADE FROM REVENUE AND FROM CORPORATE STOCK FUNDS FOR THE DEPARTMENTS, ACCORDING TO OBJECTS OF EXPENDITURE:

| LINE No. | Purchase of Equipment | Materials | Contract or Open Order Service | Contingencies | Fixed Charges and Contributions | Unclassified |
|---|---|---|---|---|---|---|
| 1 | $63,082 03 | $11,436 92 | $114,011 66 | $34,459 20 | $600,000 00 | $1,533 34 |
| 2 | 9,978 59 | .......... | 235,334 33 | .......... | .......... | .......... |
| 3 | **$73,060 62** | **$11,436 92** | **$349,345 99** | **$34,459 20** | **$600,000 00** | **$1,533 34** |
| 4 | $60,297 60 | $10,546 56 | $87,228 92 | $44,788 35 | $905,644 93 | .......... |
| 5 | .......... | .......... | 91,268 83 | .......... | .......... | $396,493 85 |
| 6 | **$60,297 60** | **$10,546 56** | **$178,497 75** | **$44,788 35** | **$905,644 93** | **$396,493 85** |
| 7 | $42,923 55 | .......... | $196,803 67 | $46,866 63 | $1,250,687 49 | .......... |
| 8 | 18,437 87 | .......... | 111,264 95 | .......... | .......... | $103,321 47 |
| 9 | **$61,361 42** | .......... | **$308,068 62** | **$46,866 63** | **$1,250,687 49** | **$103,321 47** |
| 10 | $94,089 05 | $23,687 71 | $245,773 76 | $34,278 00 | $1,320,538 34 | .......... |
| 11 | 7,452 63 | .......... | 472,289 31 | .......... | .......... | $85 00 |
| 12 | **$101,541 68** | **$23,687 71** | **$718,063 07** | **$34,278 00** | **$1,320,538 34** | **$85 00** |
| 13 | $73,189 30 | $22,148 09 | $228,897 79 | $58,743 54 | $1,485 587 53 | .......... |
| 14 | 5,588 56 | .......... | 186,780 28 | .......... | .......... | $26,282 63 |
| 15 | **$78,777 86** | **$22,148 09** | **$415,678 07** | **$58,743 54** | **$1,485,587 53** | **$26,282 63** |
| 16 | $39,600 03 | $74,351 06 | $168,221 83 | $7,972 90 | $129,270 10 | .......... |
| 17 | 21,598 92 | .......... | 1,177,891 33 | .......... | .......... | $35,076 00 |
| 18 | **$61,198 95** | **$74,351 06** | **$1,346,113 16** | **$7,972 90** | **$129,270 10** | **$35,076 00** |
| 19 | $53,676 01 | $74,065 35 | $186,287 13 | $12,368 93 | $128,658 69 | .......... |
| 20 | 40,084 40 | .......... | 984,481 89 | .......... | .......... | $509 69 |
| 21 | **$93,760 41** | **$74,065 35** | **$1,170,769 02** | **$12,368 93** | **$128,658 69** | **$509 69** |
| 22 | $24,951 18 | $1,615 00 | $186,323 46 | $9,901 52 | $114,631 56 | .......... |
| 23 | 48,059 14 | .......... | 1,621,418 93 | .......... | .......... | $68,306 13 |
| 24 | **$73,010 32** | **$1,615 00** | **$1,807,742 39** | **$9,901 52** | **$114,631 56** | **$68,306 13** |
| 25 | $299,567 02 | $77,295 55 | $155,320 06 | $10,391 00 | $129,210 88 | $18,433 76 |
| 26 | 79,183 98 | 407 50 | 1,724,106 48 | 50,612 45 | .......... | 31,869 98 |
| 27 | **$378,751 00** | **$77,703 05** | **$1,879,426 54** | **$61,003 45** | **$129,210 88** | **$50,303 74** |
| 28 | $205,961 58 | $58,516 08 | $108,579 45 | $1,956 72 | $147,957 49 | .......... |
| 29 | 79,298 06 | 1,859 19 | 883,858 13 | .......... | .......... | $29 93 |
| 30 | **285,259 64** | **$60,375 27** | **$992,437 58** | **$1,956 72** | **$147,957 49** | **$29 93** |

COMPARATIVE STATEMENTS SHOWING SEPARATELY THE EXPENDITURES
YEARS 1910 TO 1914, INCLUSIVE, CLASSIFIED BY

| | Total | Personal Service | Supplies | LINE No. |
|---|---|---|---|---|
| **DEPARTMENT OF STREET CLEANING** | | | | |
| **1910** | | | | |
| Revenue Expenditures | $9,930,102 65 | $5,552,623 52 | $577,986 29 | 1 |
| Corporate Stock Expenditures | 37,889 02 | .......... | .......... | 2 |
| Total for 1910 | **$9,967,991 67** | **$5,552,623 52** | **$577,986 29** | 3 |
| **1911** | | | | |
| Revenue Expenditures | $8,142,560 54 | $5,105,532 98 | $532,788 69 | 4 |
| Corporate Stock Expenditures | 79,353 68 | .......... | .......... | 5 |
| Total for 1911 | **$8,221,914 22** | **$5,105,532 98** | **$532,788 69** | 6 |
| **1912** | | | | |
| Revenue Expenditures | $8,599,366 23 | $5,287,244 50 | $759,551 82 | 7 |
| Corporate Stock Expenditures | 16,378 42 | 710 00 | .......... | 8 |
| Total for 1912 | **$8,615,744 65** | **$5,287,954 50** | **$759,551 82** | 9 |
| **1913** | | | | |
| Revenue Expenditures | $7,936,099 58 | $5,471,512 70 | $603,992 24 | 10 |
| Corporate Stock Expenditures | 28,224 36 | .......... | .......... | 11 |
| Total for 1913 | **$7,964,323 94** | **$5,471,512 70** | **$603,992 24** | 12 |
| **1914** | | | | |
| Revenue Expenditures | $10,132,163 33 | $5,296,403 16 | $545,861 04 | 13 |
| Corporate Stock Expenditures | 26,672 07 | 1,436 51 | .......... | 14 |
| Total for 1914 | **$10,158,835 40** | **$5,297,839 67** | **$545,861 04** | 15 |
| **DEPARTMENT OF TAXES AND ASSESSMENTS** | | | | |
| **1910** | | | | |
| Revenue Expenditures | $510,777 88 | $494,678 92 | $3,561 64 | 16 |
| Corporate Stock Expenditures | .......... | .......... | .......... | 17 |
| Total for 1910 | **$510,777 88** | **$494,678 92** | **$3,561 64** | 18 |
| **1911** | | | | |
| Revenue Expenditures | $587,947 37 | $573,028 83 | $764 52 | 19 |
| Corporate Stock Expenditures | .......... | .......... | .......... | 20 |
| Total for 1911 | **$587,947 37** | **$573,028 83** | **$764 52** | 21 |
| **1912** | | | | |
| Revenue Expenditures | $636,999 87 | $620,523 31 | $6,019 98 | 22 |
| Corporate Stock Expenditures | .......... | .......... | .......... | 23 |
| Total for 1912 | **$636,999 87** | **$620,523 31** | **$6,019 98** | 24 |
| **1913** | | | | |
| Revenue Expenditures | $632,918 76 | $620,912 76 | $3,612 28 | 25 |
| Corporate Stock Expenditures | .......... | .......... | .......... | 26 |
| Total for 1913 | **$632,918 76** | **$620,912 76** | **$3,612 28** | 27 |
| **1914** | | | | |
| Revenue Expenditures | $635,441 50 | $616,171 26 | $4,323 40 | 28 |
| Corporate Stock Expenditures | .......... | .......... | .......... | 29 |
| Total for 1914 | **$635,441 50** | **$616,171 26** | **$4,323 40** | 30 |

## NEW YORK

MADE FROM REVENUE AND FROM CORPORATE STOCK FUNDS FOR THE DEPARTMENTS, ACCORDING TO OBJECTS OF EXPENDITURE:

| LINE No. | Purchase of Equipment | Materials | Contract or Open Order Service | Contingencies | Fixed Charges and Contributions | Unclassified |
|---|---|---|---|---|---|---|
| 1 | $286,106 07 | $100,984 01 | $3,408,352 45 | $4,050 31 | .......... | .......... |
| 2 | .......... | .......... | 37,889 02 | .......... | .......... | .......... |
| 3 | **$286,106 07** | **$100,984 01** | **$3,446,241 47** | **$4,050 31** | .......... | .......... |
| 4 | $393,035 09 | $101,227 06 | $2,005,592 96 | $4,383 76 | .......... | .......... |
| 5 | .......... | .......... | 79,353 68 | .......... | .......... | .......... |
| 6 | **$393,035 09** | **$101,227 06** | **$2,084,946 64** | **$4,383 76** | .......... | .......... |
| 7 | $268,068 31 | .......... | $2,276,959 14 | $7,542 46 | .......... | .......... |
| 8 | .......... | .......... | 15,668 42 | .......... | .......... | .......... |
| 9 | **$268,068 31** | .......... | **$2,292,627 56** | **7,542 46** | .......... | .......... |
| 10 | $372,274 63 | $74,537 88 | $1,409,468 63 | $4,313 50 | .......... | .......... |
| 11 | .......... | .......... | 28,224 36 | .......... | .......... | .......... |
| 12 | **$372,274 63** | **$74,537 88** | **$1,437,692 99** | **$4,313 50** | .......... | .......... |
| 13 | $271,734 19 | $76,931 16 | $3,939,729 48 | $1,504 30 | .......... | .......... |
| 14 | .......... | 592 59 | 24,642 97 | .......... | .......... | .......... |
| 15 | **$271,734 19** | **$77,523 75** | **$3,964,372 45** | **$1,504 30** | .......... | .......... |
| 16 | .......... | .......... | $709 15 | $11,828 17 | .......... | .......... |
| 17 | .......... | .......... | .......... | .......... | .......... | .......... |
| 18 | .......... | .......... | **$709 15** | **$11,828 17** | .......... | .......... |
| 19 | .......... | .......... | $5,125 32 | $9,028 70 | .......... | .......... |
| 20 | .......... | .......... | .......... | .......... | .......... | .......... |
| 21 | .......... | .......... | **$5,125 32** | **$9,028 70** | .......... | .......... |
| 22 | $2,823 76 | .......... | $4,956 02 | $2,676 80 | .......... | .......... |
| 23 | .......... | .......... | .......... | .......... | .......... | .......... |
| 24 | **$2,823 76** | .......... | **$4,956 02** | **$2,676 80** | .......... | .......... |
| 25 | $2,559 34 | .......... | $5,834 38 | .......... | .......... | .......... |
| 26 | .......... | .......... | .......... | .......... | .......... | .......... |
| 27 | **$2,559 34** | .......... | **$5,834 38** | .......... | .......... | .......... |
| 28 | $2,287 82 | .......... | $12,481 77 | $177 25 | .......... | .......... |
| 29 | .......... | .......... | .......... | .......... | .......... | .......... |
| 30 | **$2,287 82** | .......... | **$12,481 77** | **$177 25** | .......... | .......... |

COMPARATIVE STATEMENTS SHOWING SEPARATELY THE EXPENDITURES
YEARS 1910 TO 1914, INCLUSIVE, CLASSIFIED BY

| | Total | Personal Service | Supplies | LINE No. |
|---|---|---|---|---|
| **TENEMENT HOUSE DEPARTMENT** | | | | |
| **1910** | | | | |
| Revenue Expenditures | $804,108 52 | $769,587 32 | $4,122 07 | 1 |
| Corporate Stock Expenditures | .......... | .......... | .......... | 2 |
| Total for 1910 | **$804,108 52** | **$769,587 32** | **$4,122 07** | 3 |
| **1911** | | | | |
| Revenue Expenditures | $789,760 30 | $761,520 61 | $3,284 90 | 4 |
| Corporate Stock Expenditures | .......... | .......... | .......... | 5 |
| Total for 1911 | **$789,760 30** | **$761,520 61** | **$3,284 90** | 6 |
| **1912** | | | | |
| Revenue Expenditures | $776,988 56 | $751,591 06 | $3,083 29 | 7 |
| Corporate Stock Expenditures | .......... | .......... | .......... | 8 |
| Total for 1912 | **$776,988 56** | **$751,591 06** | **$3,083 29** | 9 |
| **1913** | | | | |
| Revenue Expenditures | $762,036 81 | $736,839 61 | $9,407 61 | 10 |
| Corporate Stock Expenditures | .......... | .......... | .......... | 11 |
| Total for 1913 | **$762,036 81** | **$736,839 61** | **$9,407 61** | 12 |
| **1914** | | | | |
| Revenue Expenditures | $727,100 57 | $703,745 69 | $8,511 13 | 13 |
| Corporate Stock Expenditures | .......... | .......... | .......... | 14 |
| Total for 1914 | **$727,100 57** | **$703,745 69** | **$8,511 13** | 15 |
| **DEPARTMENT OF WATER SUPPLY, GAS AND ELECTRICITY** | | | | |
| **1910** | | | | |
| Revenue Expenditures | $8,667,906 41 | $2,825,130 96 | $589,297 74 | 16 |
| Corporate Stock Expenditures | 4,170,185 83 | 593,570 53 | 4,111 41 | 17 |
| Total for 1910 | **$12,838,092 24** | **$3,418,701 49** | **$593,409 15** | 18 |
| **1911** | | | | |
| Revenue Expenditures | $9,231,925 65 | $3,031,904 53 | $701,565 85 | 19 |
| Corporate Stock Expenditures | 5,208,744 60 | 693,818 39 | 30,198 91 | 20 |
| Total for 1911 | **$14,440,670 25** | **$3,725,722 92** | **$731,764 76** | 21 |
| **1912** | | | | |
| Revenue Expenditures | $9,436,288 07 | $3,160,193 59 | $673,074 49 | 22 |
| Corporate Stock Expenditures | 3,888,819 23 | 655,401 12 | 23,472 68 | 23 |
| Total for 1912 | **$13,325,107 30** | **$3,815,594 71** | **$696,547 17** | 24 |
| **1913** | | | | |
| Revenue Expenditures | $9,441,574 81 | $3,186,018 02 | $615,182 23 | 25 |
| Corporate Stock Expenditures | 2,582,159 29 | 622,413 52 | 5,192 99 | 26 |
| Total for 1913 | **$12,023,734 10** | **$3,808,431 54** | **$620,375 22** | 27 |
| **1914** | | | | |
| Revenue Expenditures | $9,310,140 36 | $3,038,182 68 | $634,803 67 | 28 |
| Corporate Stock Expenditures | 2,383,102 24 | 447,169 57 | 242,928 93 | 29 |
| Total for 1914 | **$11,693,242 60** | **$3,485,352 25** | **$877,732 60** | 30 |

# NEW YORK

Made from Revenue and from Corporate Stock Funds for the Departments, According to Objects of Expenditure:

| Line No. | Purchase of Equipment | Materials | Contract or Open Order Service | Contingencies | Fixed Charges and Contributions | Unclassified |
|---|---|---|---|---|---|---|
| 1 | $4,763 27 | .......... | $4,708 03 | $19,210 33 | $1,717 50 | .......... |
| 2 | .......... | .......... | .......... | .......... | .......... | .......... |
| 3 | **$4,763 27** | .......... | **$4,708 03** | **$19,210 33** | **$1,717 50** | ........ |
| 4 | $4,696 97 | .......... | $1,325 93 | $18,931 89 | .......... | .......... |
| 5 | .......... | .......... | .......... | ............ | .......... | .......... |
| 6 | **$4,696 97** | .......... | **$1,325 93** | **$18,931 89** | .......... | .......... |
| 7 | $1,406 14 | .......... | $3,437 82 | $17,470 25 | .......... | .......... |
| 8 | .......... | .......... | .......... | .......... | .......... | .......... |
| 9 | **$1,406 14** | .......... | **$3,437 82** | **$17,470 25** | .......... | .......... |
| 10 | $2,790 90 | .......... | $12,998 69 | .......... | .......... | .......... |
| 11 | .......... | .......... | .......... | .......... | .......... | .......... |
| 12 | **$2,790 90** | .......... | **$12,998 69** | .......... | .......... | .......... |
| 13 | $2,622 69 | .......... | $12,041 44 | $179 62 | .......... | .......... |
| 14 | .......... | .......... | .......... | .......... | .......... | .......... |
| 15 | **$2,622 69** | .......... | **$12,041 44** | **$179 62** | .......... | .......... |
| 16 | $54,003 72 | $108,587 00 | $4,863,747 59 | $65,903 49 | $161,235 91 | .......... |
| 17 | 2,327 41 | 4,290 56 | 3,264,772 02 | 2,125 67 | .......... | $298,988 23 |
| 18 | **$56,331 13** | **$112,877 56** | **$8,128,519 61** | **$68,029 16** | **$161,235 91** | **$298,988 23** |
| 19 | $29,210 01 | $68,862 96 | $5,166,275 44 | $68,232 65 | $165,874 21 | .......... |
| 20 | 158,600 10 | 1,772,125 56 | 621,131 81 | 20,558 42 | .......... | $1,912,311 41 |
| 21 | **$187,810 11** | **$1,840,988 52** | **$5,787,407 25** | **$88,791 07** | **$165,874 21** | **$1,912,311 41** |
| 22 | $39,285 71 | $26,763 67 | $5,218,567 69 | $65,190 03 | $253,212 89 | .......... |
| 23 | 90,518 52 | 581,548 42 | 2,007,347 79 | 33,702 10 | .......... | $496,828 60 |
| 24 | **$129,804 23** | **$608,312 09** | **$7,225,915 48** | **$98,892 13** | **$253,212 89** | **$496,828 60** |
| 25 | $45,152 08 | $59,706 69 | $5,300,321 23 | $6,335 91 | $195,111 28 | $33,747 37 |
| 26 | 15,375 05 | 27,137 71 | 1,848,780 68 | 14,143 24 | .......... | $49,116 10 |
| 27 | **$60,527 13** | **$86,844 40** | **$7,149,101 91** | **$20,479 15** | **$195,111 28** | **$82,863 47** |
| 28 | $56,282 90 | $53,615 05 | $5,323,875 73 | $852 47 | $202,527 86 | .......... |
| 29 | 9,573 78 | 477 08 | 1,587,640 92 | 11,828 03 | ........ | $83,483 93 |
| 30 | **$65,856 68** | **$54,092 13** | **$6,911,516 65** | **$12,680 50** | **$202,527 86** | **$83,483 93** |

COMPARATIVE STATEMENTS SHOWING SEPARATELY THE EXPENDITURES
YEARS 1910 TO 1914, INCLUSIVE, CLASSIFIED BY

| | Total | Personal Service | Supplies | LINE No. |
|---|---|---|---|---|
| **WATER METER FUND** | | | | |
| **1910** | | | | |
| Revenue Expenditures | ... | ... | ... | 1 |
| Corporate Stock Expenditures | ... | ... | ... | 2 |
| Total for 1910 | ... | ... | ... | 3 |
| **1911** | | | | |
| Revenue Expenditures | ... | ... | ... | 4 |
| Corporate Stock Expenditures | ... | ... | ... | 5 |
| Total for 1911 | ... | ... | ... | 6 |
| **1912** | | | | |
| Revenue Expenditures | $8,866 45 | ... | ... | 7 |
| Corporate Stock Expenditures | ... | ... | ... | 8 |
| Total for 1912 | **$8,866 45** | ... | ... | 9 |
| **1913** | | | | |
| Revenue Expenditures | $12,553 21 | ... | ... | 10 |
| Corporate Stock Expenditures | ... | ... | ... | 11 |
| Total for 1913 | **$12,553 21** | ... | ... | 12 |
| **1914** | | | | |
| Revenue Expenditures | $9,358 74 | ... | ... | 13 |
| Corporate Stock Expenditures | ... | ... | ... | 14 |
| Total for 1914 | **$9,358 74** | ... | ... | 15 |
| **AQUEDUCT COMMISSION** | | | | |
| **1910** | | | | |
| Revenue Expenditures | ... | ... | ... | 16 |
| Corporate Stock Expenditures | $1,316,228 48 | $149,174 99 | $2,111 85 | 17 |
| Total for 1910 | **$1,316,228 48** | **$149,174 99** | **$2,111 85** | 18 |
| **1911** | | | | |
| Revenue Expenditures | ... | ... | ... | 19 |
| Corporate Stock Expenditures | $1,109,534 04 | $86,254 97 | ... | 20 |
| Total for 1911 | **$1,109,534 04** | **$86,254 97** | ... | 21 |
| **1912** | | | | |
| Revenue Expenditures | ... | ... | ... | 22 |
| Corporate Stock Expenditures | $11,600 67 | $7,789 25 | $9 95 | 23 |
| Total for 1912 | **$11,600 67** | **$7,789 25** | **$9 95** | 24 |
| **1913** | | | | |
| Revenue Expenditures | ... | ... | ... | 25 |
| Corporate Stock Expenditures | $51,225 10 | ... | ... | 26 |
| Total for 1913 | **$51,225 10** | ... | ... | 27 |
| **1914** | | | | |
| Revenue Expenditures | ... | ... | ... | 28 |
| Corporate Stock Expenditures | ... | ... | ... | 29 |
| Total for 1914 | ... | ... | ... | 30 |

NEW YORK

MADE FROM REVENUE AND FROM CORPORATE STOCK FUNDS FOR THE DEPARTMENTS, ACCORDING TO OBJECTS OF EXPENDITURE:

| LINE No. | Purchase of Equipment | Materials | Contract or Open Order Service | Contingencies | Fixed Charges and Contributions | Unclassified |
|---|---|---|---|---|---|---|
| 1 | .......... | .......... | .......... | .......... | .......... | .......... |
| 2 | .......... | .......... | .......... | .......... | .......... | .......... |
| 3 | .......... | .......... | .......... | .......... | .......... | .......... |
| 4 | .......... | .......... | .......... | .......... | .......... | .......... |
| 5 | .......... | .......... | .......... | .......... | .......... | .......... |
| 6 | .......... | .......... | .......... | .......... | .......... | .......... |
| 7 | .......... | .......... | $8,866 45 | .......... | .......... | .......... |
| 8 | .......... | .......... | .......... | .......... | .......... | .......... |
| 9 | .......... | .......... | **$8,866 45** | .......... | .......... | .......... |
| 10 | .......... | .......... | $12,553 21 | .......... | .......... | .......... |
| 11 | .......... | .......... | .......... | .......... | .......... | .......... |
| 12 | .......... | .......... | **$12,553 21** | .......... | .......... | .......... |
| 13 | .......... | .......... | $9,358 74 | .......... | .......... | .......... |
| 14 | .......... | .......... | .......... | .......... | .......... | .......... |
| 15 | .......... | .......... | **$9,358 74** | .......... | .......... | .......... |
| 16 | .......... | .......... | .......... | .......... | .......... | .......... |
| 17 | $413 01 | $383 15 | $631,597 45 | $1,320 18 | .......... | $531,227 85 |
| 18 | **$413 01** | **$383 15** | **$631,597 45** | **$1,320 18** | .......... | **$531,227 85** |
| 19 | .......... | .......... | .......... | .......... | .......... | .......... |
| 20 | .......... | .......... | $554,249 04 | .......... | .......... | $469,029 43 |
| 21 | .......... | .......... | **$554,249 64** | .......... | .......... | **$469,029 43** |
| 22 | .......... | .......... | .......... | .......... | .......... | .......... |
| 23 | .......... | .......... | $163 47 | .......... | .......... | $3,638 00 |
| 24 | .......... | .......... | **$163 47** | .......... | .......... | **$3,638 00** |
| 25 | .......... | .......... | .......... | .......... | .......... | .......... |
| 26 | .......... | .......... | .......... | .......... | .......... | $51,225 10 |
| 27 | .......... | .......... | .......... | .......... | .......... | **$51,225 10** |
| 28 | .......... | .......... | .......... | .......... | .......... | .......... |
| 29 | .......... | .......... | .......... | .......... | .......... | .......... |
| 30 | .......... | .......... | .......... | .......... | .......... | .......... |

Comparative Statements Showing Separately the Expenditures
Years 1910 to 1914, Inclusive, Classified by

| | Total | Personal Service | Supplies | Line No. |
|---|---|---|---|---|
| **BELLEVUE AND ALLIED HOSPITALS** | | | | |
| **1910** | | | | |
| Revenue Expenditures | $1,167,430 50 | $479,805 54 | $554,215 51 | 1 |
| Corporate Stock Expenditures | 739,523 23 | 6,189 67 | .......... | 2 |
| Total for 1910 | **$1,906,953 73** | **$485,995 21** | **$554,215 51** | 3 |
| **1911** | | | | |
| Revenue Expenditures | $1,261,537 28 | $525,950 80 | $593,580 38 | 4 |
| Corporate Stock Expenditures | 528,675 53 | 3,892 00 | .......... | 5 |
| Total for 1911 | **$1,790,212 81** | **$529,842 80** | **$593,580 38** | 6 |
| **1912** | | | | |
| Revenue Expenditures | $1,299,348 56 | $577,314 00 | $618,163 65 | 7 |
| Corporate Stock Expenditures | 677,453 01 | 2,999 88 | .......... | 8 |
| Total for 1912 | **$1,976,801 57** | **$580,313 88** | **$618,163 65** | 9 |
| **1913** | | | | |
| Revenue Expenditures | $1,453,030 29 | $605,075 07 | $624,012 49 | 10 |
| Corporate Stock Expenditures | 1,246,337 30 | 2,468 10 | .......... | 11 |
| Total for 1913 | **$2,699,367 59** | **$607,543 17** | **$624,012 49** | 12 |
| **1914** | | | | |
| Revenue Expenditures | $1,437,612 02 | $637,692 16 | $584,332 91 | 13 |
| Corporate Stock Expenditures | 720,361 00 | 2,280 65 | 99 00 | 14 |
| Total for 1914 | **$2,157,973 02** | **$639,972 81** | **$584,431 91** | 15 |
| **COLLEGE OF THE CITY OF NEW YORK** | | | | |
| **1910** | | | | |
| Revenue Expenditures | $607,816 21 | $519,308 55 | $55,349 50 | 16 |
| Corporate Stock Expenditures | 23,661 50 | 243 33 | 165 85 | 17 |
| Total for 1910 | **$631,477 71** | **$519,551 88** | **$55,515 35** | 18 |
| **1911** | | | | |
| Revenue Expenditures | $624,786 55 | $557,348 79 | $55,141 53 | 19 |
| Corporate Stock Expenditures | 57,278 60 | .......... | .......... | 20 |
| Total for 1911 | **$682,065 15** | **$557,348 79** | **$55,141 53** | 21 |
| **1912** | | | | |
| Revenue Expenditures | $630,363 72 | $559,163 75 | $56,785 32 | 22 |
| Corporate Stock Expenditures | .......... | .......... | .......... | 23 |
| Total for 1912 | **$630,363 72** | **$559,163 75** | **$56,785 32** | 24 |
| **1913** | | | | |
| Revenue Expenditures | $657,321 19 | $565,446 59 | $39,701 60 | 25 |
| Corporate Stock Expenditures | 33,742 23 | .......... | 620 86 | 26 |
| Total for 1913 | **$691,063 42** | **$565,446 59** | **$40,322 46** | 27 |
| **1914** | | | | |
| Revenue Expenditures | $675,046 00 | $586,704 15 | $35,770 28 | 28 |
| Corporate Stock Expenditures | 25,163 00 | .......... | 112 75 | 29 |
| Total for 1914 | **$700,209 00** | **$586,704 15** | **$35,883 03** | 30 |

NEW YORK

MADE FROM REVENUE AND FROM CORPORATE STOCK FUNDS FOR THE DEPARTMENTS, ACCORDING TO OBJECTS OF EXPENDITURE:

| LINE No. | Purchase of Equipment | Materials | Contract or Open Order Service | Contingencies | Fixed Charges and Contributions | Unclassified |
|---|---|---|---|---|---|---|
| 1 | $26,237 88 | $18,153 82 | $81,630 17 | $6,787 58 | $600 00 | .......... |
| 2 | 5,803 42 | .......... | 727,530 14 | .......... | .......... | .......... |
| 3 | **$32,041 30** | **$18,153 82** | **$809,160 31** | **$6,787 58** | **$600 00** | .......... |
| 4 | $20,831 26 | $17,524 79 | $96,591 16 | $7,058 89 | .......... | .......... |
| 5 | 18,549 49 | .......... | 506,234 04 | .......... | .......... | .......... |
| 6 | **$39,380 75** | **$17,524 79** | **$602,825 20** | **$7,058 89** | .......... | .......... |
| 7 | $32,058 09 | .......... | $63,216 02 | $8,596 80 | .......... | .......... |
| 8 | 85,945 21 | $996 00 | 586,825 81 | .......... | .......... | $686 11 |
| 9 | **$118,003 30** | **$996 00** | **$650,041 83** | **$8,596 80** | .......... | **$686 11** |
| 10 | $117,839 75 | $24,358 81 | $77,501 75 | $4,242 42 | .......... | .......... |
| 11 | 4,980 46 | .......... | 1,238,276 24 | .......... | .......... | $612 50 |
| 12 | **$122,820 21** | **$24,358 81** | **$1,315,777 99** | **$4,242 42** | .......... | **$612 50** |
| 13 | $125,025 27 | $22,488 79 | $62,609 19 | $5,463 70 | .......... | .......... |
| 14 | 7,448 87 | .......... | 665,532 48 | .......... | .......... | $45,000 00 |
| 15 | **$132,474 14** | **$22,488 79** | **$728,141 67** | **$5,463 70** | .......... | **$45,000 00** |
| 16 | $10 00 | $3,346 22 | $28,262 91 | $1,539 03 | .......... | .......... |
| 17 | 313 20 | .......... | 14,977 16 | .......... | .......... | $7,961 96 |
| 18 | **$323 20** | **$3,346 22** | **$43,240 07** | **$1,539 03** | .......... | **$7,961 96** |
| 19 | .......... | $3,419 37 | $6,879 92 | $1,996 94 | .......... | .......... |
| 20 | .......... | .......... | 57,278 60 | .......... | .......... | .......... |
| 21 | .......... | **$3,419 37** | **$64,158 52** | **$1,996 94** | .......... | .......... |
| 22 | .......... | .......... | $12,774 17 | $1,640 48 | .......... | .......... |
| 23 | .......... | .......... | .......... | .......... | .......... | .......... |
| 24 | .......... | .......... | **$12,774 17** | **$1,640 48** | .......... | .......... |
| 25 | $17,193 07 | $3,229 10 | $31,125 84 | $624 99 | .......... | .......... |
| 26 | 1,534 41 | 14 95 | 31,480 34 | .......... | .......... | $91 67 |
| 27 | **$18,727 48** | **$3,244 05** | **$62,606 18** | **$624 99** | .......... | **$91 67** |
| 28 | $16,549 62 | $3,832 38 | $31,615 72 | $573 85 | .......... | .......... |
| 29 | 4,073 30 | .......... | 20,976 95 | .......... | .......... | .......... |
| 30 | **$20,622 92** | **$3,832 38** | **$52,592 67** | **$573 85** | .......... | .......... |

COMPARATIVE STATEMENTS SHOWING SEPARATELY THE EXPENDITURES
YEARS 1910 TO 1914, INCLUSIVE, CLASSIFIED BY

| | Total | Personal Service | Supplies | LINE No. |
|---|---|---|---|---|
| **DEPARTMENT OF EDUCATION** | | | | |
| **1910** | | | | |
| Revenue Expenditures | $28,676,143 68 | $23,761,323 16 | $1,860,792 23 | 1 |
| Corporate Stock Expenditures | 2,642,643 83 | 167,152 84 | .......... | 2 |
| Total for 1910 | **$31,318,787 51** | **$23,928,476 00** | **$1,860,792 23** | 3 |
| **1911** | | | | |
| Revenue Expenditures | $29,044,085 99 | $24,570,668 87 | $1,746,566 92 | 4 |
| Corporate Stock Expenditures | 4,428,892 54 | 228,203 29 | .......... | 5 |
| Total for 1911 | **$33,472,978 53** | **$24,798,872 16** | **$1,746,566 92** | 6 |
| **1912** | | | | |
| Revenue Expenditures | $34,139,765 22 | $29,143,874 19 | $2,128,771 04 | 7 |
| Corporate Stock Expenditures | 4,787,473 13 | 258,324 97 | .......... | 8 |
| Total for 1912 | **$38,927,238 35** | **$29,402,199 16** | **$2,128,771 04** | 9 |
| **1913** | | | | |
| Revenue Expenditures | $35,670,393 99 | $30,379,500 28 | $2,112,956 56 | 10 |
| Corporate Stock Expenditures | 4,731,385 07 | 262,897 09 | .......... | 11 |
| Total for 1913 | **$40,401,779 06** | **$30,642,397 37** | **$2,112,956 56** | 12 |
| **1914** | | | | |
| Revenue Expenditures | $38,073,785 53 | $32,285,581 49 | $2,231,888 16 | 13 |
| Corporate Stock Expenditures | *5,437,237 30 | 231,977 68 | .......... | 14 |
| Total for 1914 | **$43,511,022 83** | **$32,517,559 17** | **$2,231,888 16** | 15 |
| **NORMAL COLLEGE OF THE CITY OF NEW YORK** | | | | |
| **1910** | | | | |
| Revenue Expenditures | $364,857 26 | $327,586 84 | $25,247 48 | 16 |
| Corporate Stock Expenditures | 7,099 07 | 5,591 55 | .......... | 17 |
| Total for 1910 | **$371,956 33** | **$333,178 39** | **$25,247 48** | 18 |
| **1911** | | | | |
| Revenue Expenditures | $371,949 88 | $340,046 64 | $25,370 16 | 19 |
| Corporate Stock Expenditures | 30,554 50 | 15,315 97 | .......... | 20 |
| Total for 1911 | **$402,504 38** | **$355,362 61** | **$25,370 16** | 21 |
| **1912** | | | | |
| Revenue Expenditures | $391,733 64 | $360,010 51 | $25,224 30 | 22 |
| Corporate Stock Expenditures | 284,146 31 | 4,993 06 | .......... | 23 |
| Total for 1912 | **$675,879 95** | **$365,003 57** | **$25,224 30** | 24 |
| **1913** | | | | |
| Revenue Expenditures | $494,843 65 | $456,969 03 | $21,727 10 | 25 |
| Corporate Stock Expenditures | 174,936 60 | 3,122 75 | 2,724 75 | 26 |
| Total for 1913 | **$669,780 25** | **$460,091 78** | **$24,451 85** | 27 |
| **1914** | | | | |
| Revenue Expenditures | $519,994 96 | $475,199 48 | $12,863 03 | 28 |
| Corporate Stock Expenditures | 101,143 95 | 1,921 83 | 631 48 | 29 |
| Total for 1914 | **$621,138 91** | **$477,121 31** | **$13,494 51** | 30 |

NEW YORK

MADE FROM REVENUE AND FROM CORPORATE STOCK FUNDS FOR THE DEPARTMENTS, ACCORDING TO OBJECTS OF EXPENDITURE:

| LINE No. | Purchase of Equipment | Materials | Contract or Open Order Service | Contingencies | Fixed Charges and Contributions | Unclassified |
|---|---|---|---|---|---|---|
| 1 | $285,199 42 | $5,498 50 | $2,714,349 17 | $36,013 52 | $12,967 68 | .......... |
| 2 | 447,415 08 | .......... | 1,574,349 94 | .......... | .......... | $453,725 97 |
| 3 | **$732,614 50** | **$5,498 50** | **$4,288,699 11** | **$36,013 52** | **$12,967 68** | **$453,725 97** |
| 4 | $202,471 39 | $2,542 04 | $2,471,599 41 | $33,805 11 | $16,432 25 | .......... |
| 5 | 663,344 25 | .......... | 3,093,637 44 | .......... | .......... | $443,707 56 |
| 6 | **$865,815 64** | **$2,542 04** | **$5,565,236 85** | **$33,805 11** | **$16,432 25** | **$443,707 56** |
| 7 | $229,363 89 | $1,004 71 | $2,577,598 93 | $41,383 21 | $17,769 25 | .......... |
| 8 | 761,118 86 | .......... | 2,866,520 72 | .......... | .......... | $901,508 58 |
| 9 | **$990,482 75** | **$1,004 71** | **$5,444,119 65** | **$41,383 21** | **$17,769 25** | **$901,508 58** |
| 10 | $390,538 47 | $1,193 63 | $2,763,188 92 | $16,092 09 | $6,818 00 | $106 04 |
| 11 | 1,198,476 23 | .......... | 2,865,928 29 | .......... | .......... | 404,083 46 |
| 12 | **$1,589,014 70** | **$1,193 63** | **$5,629,117 21** | **$16,092 09** | **$6,818 00** | **$404,189 50** |
| 13 | $424,501 93 | .......... | $3,089,476 23 | $34,684 82 | $7,652 90 | .......... |
| 14 | 1,416,150 27 | .......... | 3,551,401 08 | .......... | .......... | $237,708 27 |
| 15 | **$1,840,652 20** | .......... | **$6,640,877 31** | **$34,684 82** | **$7,652 90** | **$237,708 27** |
| 16 | .......... | .......... | $9,567 15 | $2,455 79 | .......... | .......... |
| 17 | .......... | .......... | .......... | .......... | .......... | $1,507 52 |
| 18 | .......... | .......... | **$9,567 15** | **$2,455 79** | .......... | **$1,507 52** |
| 19 | .......... | .......... | $4,035 06 | $2,498 02 | .......... | .......... |
| 20 | .......... | .......... | 15,183 53 | .......... | .......... | $55.00 |
| 21 | .......... | .......... | **$19,218 59** | **$2,498 02** | .......... | **$55 00** |
| 22 | .......... | .......... | $4,063 88 | $2,434 95 | .......... | .......... |
| 23 | .......... | .......... | 279,153 25 | .......... | .......... | .......... |
| 24 | .......... | .......... | **$283,217 13** | **$2,434 95** | .......... | .......... |
| 25 | $5,099 66 | .......... | $11,047 86 | .......... | .......... | .......... |
| 26 | .......... | .......... | 169,089 10 | .......... | .......... | .......... |
| 27 | **$5,099 66** | .......... | **$180,136 96** | .......... | .......... | ........ |
| 28 | $15,167 17 | .......... | $16,765 28 | .......... | .......... | .......... |
| 29 | 11,591 00 | $150 00 | 86,849 64 | .......... | .......... | .......... |
| 30 | **$26,758 17** | **$150 00** | **$103,614 92** | .......... | .......... | .......... |

COMPARATIVE STATEMENTS SHOWING SEPARATELY THE EXPENDITURES
YEARS 1910 TO 1914, INCLUSIVE, CLASSIFIED BY

| | Total | Personal Service | Supplies | LINE No. |
|---|---|---|---|---|
| **BOARD OF WATER SUPPLY** | | | | |
| **1910** | | | | |
| Revenue Expenditures | .......... | .......... | .......... | 1 |
| Corporate Stock Expenditures | $19,392,417 49 | $1,943,982 09 | $364,445 89 | 2 |
| Total for 1910 | **$19,392,417 49** | **$1,943,982 09** | **$364,445 89** | 3 |
| **1911** | | | | |
| Revenue Expenditures | .......... | .......... | .......... | 4 |
| Corporate Stock Expenditures | $25,948,565 93 | $2,062,619 31 | $340,148 21 | 5 |
| Total for 1911 | **$25,948,565 93** | **$2,062,619 31** | **$340,148 21** | 6 |
| **1912** | | | | |
| Revenue Expenditures | .......... | .......... | .......... | 7 |
| Corporate Stock Expenditures | $23,583,976 10 | $2,054,016 51 | $304,042 31 | 8 |
| Total for 1912 | **$23,583,976 10** | **$2,054,016 51** | **$304,042 31** | 9 |
| **1913** | | | | |
| Revenue Expenditures | .......... | .......... | .......... | 10 |
| Corporate Stock Expenditures | $21,352,421 87 | $1,827,882 72 | $301,865 85 | 11 |
| Total for 1913 | **$21,352,421 87** | **$1,827,882 72** | **$301,865 85** | 12 |
| **1914** | | | | |
| Revenue Expenditures | .......... | .......... | .......... | 13 |
| Corporate Stock Expenditures | $14,107,495 59 | $1,416,004 78 | $220,058 00 | 14 |
| Total for 1914 | **$14,107,495 59** | **$1,416,004 78** | **$220,058 00** | 15 |
| **ART COMMISSION** | | | | |
| **1910** | | | | |
| Revenue Expenditures | $7,587 79 | $5,267 03 | .......... | 16 |
| Corporate Stock Expenditures | .......... | .......... | .......... | 17 |
| Total for 1910 | **$7,587 79** | **$5,267 03** | .......... | 18 |
| **1911** | | | | |
| Revenue Expenditures | $7,573 00 | $5,381 00 | $62 85 | 19 |
| Corporate Stock Expenditures | .......... | .......... | .......... | 20 |
| Total for 1911 | **$7,573 00** | **$5,381 00** | **$62 85** | 21 |
| **1912** | | | | |
| Revenue Expenditures | $7,552 45 | $5,265 00 | $1,372 73 | 22 |
| Corporate Stock Expenditures | .......... | .......... | .......... | 23 |
| Total for 1912 | **$7,552 45** | **$5,265 00** | **$1,372 73** | 24 |
| **1913** | | | | |
| Revenue Expenditures | $7,551 11 | $5,456 00 | $596 74 | 25 |
| Corporate Stock Expenditures | .......... | .......... | .......... | 26 |
| Total for 1913 | **$7,551 11** | **$5,456 00** | **$596 74** | 27 |
| **1914** | | | | |
| Revenue Expenditures | $7,132 82 | $5,336 67 | $36 65 | 28 |
| Corporate Stock Expenditures | .......... | .......... | .......... | 29 |
| Total for 1914 | **$7,132 82** | **$5,336 67** | **$36 65** | 30 |

NEW YORK

MADE FROM REVENUE AND FROM CORPORATE STOCK FUNDS FOR THE DEPARTMENTS, ACCORDING TO OBJECTS OF EXPENDITURE:

| LINE No. | Purchase of Equipment | Materials | Contract or Open Order Service | Contingencies | Fixed Charges and Contributions | Unclassified |
|---|---|---|---|---|---|---|
| 1 | .......... | .......... | .......... | .......... | .......... | .......... |
| 2 | $108,559 10 | .......... | $14,008,616 10 | .......... | .......... | $2,966,814 31 |
| 3 | **$108,559 10** | .......... | **$14,008,616 10** | .......... | .......... | **$2,966,814 31** |
| 4 | .......... | .......... | .......... | .......... | .......... | .......... |
| 5 | $63,478 53 | .......... | $18,596,411 87 | .......... | .......... | $4,885,908 01 |
| 6 | **$63,478 53** | .......... | **$18,596,411 87** | .......... | .......... | **$4,885,908 01** |
| 7 | .......... | .......... | .......... | .......... | .......... | .......... |
| 8 | $39,921 73 | .......... | $19,202,180 78 | .......... | .......... | $1,983,814 77 |
| 9 | **$39,921 73** | .......... | **$19,202,180 78** | .......... | .......... | **$1,983,814 77** |
| 10 | .......... | .......... | .......... | .......... | .......... | .......... |
| 11 | $15,729 10 | .......... | $17,225,758 79 | .......... | .......... | $1,981,185 41 |
| 12 | **$15,729 10** | .......... | **$17,225,758 79** | .......... | .......... | **$1,981,185 41** |
| 13 | .......... | .......... | .......... | .......... | .......... | .......... |
| 14 | $24,089 51 | .......... | $11,688,156 63 | .......... | .......... | $759,186 67 |
| 15 | **$24,089 51** | .......... | **$11,688,156 63** | .......... | .......... | **$759,186 67** |
| 16 | .......... | .......... | $1,879 11 | $441 65 | .......... | .......... |
| 17 | .......... | .......... | .......... | .......... | .......... | .......... |
| 18 | .......... | .......... | **$1,879 11** | **$441 65** | .......... | .......... |
| 19 | $454 73 | .......... | $1,131 52 | $542 90 | .......... | .......... |
| 20 | .......... | .......... | .......... | .......... | .......... | .......... |
| 21 | **$454 73** | .......... | **$1,131 52** | **$542 90** | .......... | .......... |
| 22 | .......... | .......... | $291 02 | $623 70 | .......... | .......... |
| 23 | .......... | .......... | .......... | .......... | .......... | .......... |
| 24 | .......... | .......... | **$291 02** | **$623 70** | .......... | .......... |
| 25 | $378 50 | .......... | $205 64 | $914 23 | .......... | .......... |
| 26 | .......... | .......... | .......... | .......... | .......... | .......... |
| 27 | **$378 50** | .......... | **$205 64** | **$914 23** | .......... | .......... |
| 28 | $629 77 | .......... | $223 48 | $906 25 | .......... | .......... |
| 29 | .......... | .......... | .......... | .......... | .......... | .......... |
| 30 | **$629 77** | .......... | **$223 48** | **$906 25** | .......... | .......... |

Comparative Statements Showing Separately the Expenditures
Years 1910 to 1914, Inclusive, Classified by

| | Total | Personal Service | Supplies | Line No. |
|---|---|---|---|---|
| **BROOKLYN DISCIPLINARY TRAINING SCHOOL FOR BOYS** | | | | |
| **1910** | | | | |
| Revenue Expenditures | $56,783 63 | $26,026 27 | $28,575 38 | 1 |
| Corporate Stock Expenditures | .......... | .......... | .......... | 2 |
| Total for 1910 | **$56,783 63** | **$26,026 27** | **$28,575 38** | 3 |
| **1911** | | | | |
| Revenue Expenditures | $55,477 25 | $27,147 02 | $26,782 75 | 4 |
| Corporate Stock Expenditures | .......... | .......... | .......... | 5 |
| Total for 1911 | **$55,477 25** | **$27,147 02** | **$26,782 75** | 6 |
| **1912** | | | | |
| Revenue Expenditures | $56,688 65 | $27,839 48 | $27,408 28 | 7 |
| Corporate Stock Expenditures | 42 41 | .......... | .......... | 8 |
| Total for 1912 | **$56,731 06** | **$27,839 48** | **$27,408 28** | 9 |
| **1913** | | | | |
| Revenue Expenditures | $54,267 79 | $27,691 31 | $22,895 81 | 10 |
| Corporate Stock Expenditures | .......... | .......... | .......... | 11 |
| Total for 1913 | **$54,267 79** | **$27,691 31** | **$22,895 81** | 12 |
| **1914** | | | | |
| Revenue Expenditures | $29,013 78 | $17,755 97 | $9,908 45 | 13 |
| Corporate Stock Expenditures | .......... | .......... | .......... | 14 |
| Total for 1914 | **$29,013 78** | **$17,755 97** | **$9,908 45** | 15 |
| **COMMITTEE ON CONGESTION OF POPULATION** | | | | |
| **1910** | | | | |
| Revenue Expenditures | .......... | .......... | .......... | 16 |
| Corporate Stock Expenditures | .......... | .......... | .......... | 17 |
| Total for 1910 | .......... | .......... | .......... | 18 |
| **1911** | | | | |
| Revenue Expenditures | .......... | .......... | .......... | 19 |
| Corporate Stock Expenditures | .......... | .......... | .......... | 20 |
| Total for 1911 | .......... | .......... | .......... | 21 |
| **1912** | | | | |
| Revenue Expenditures | $1,457 12 | .......... | .......... | 22 |
| Corporate Stock Expenditures | .......... | .......... | .......... | 23 |
| Total for 1912 | **$1,457 12** | .......... | .......... | 24 |
| **1913** | | | | |
| Revenue Expenditures | .......... | .......... | .......... | 25 |
| Corporate Stock Expenditures | .......... | .......... | .......... | 26 |
| Total for 1913 | .......... | .......... | .......... | 27 |
| **1914** | | | | |
| Revenue Expenditures | .......... | .......... | .......... | 28 |
| Corporate Stock Expenditures | .......... | .......... | .......... | 29 |
| Total for 1914 | .......... | .......... | .......... | 30 |

NEW YORK

MADE FROM REVENUE AND FROM CORPORATE STOCK FUNDS FOR THE DEPARTMENTS, ACCORDING TO OBJECTS OF EXPENDITURE:

| LINE No. | Purchase of Equipment | Materials | Contract or Open Order Service | Contingencies | Fixed Charges and Contributions | Unclassified |
|---|---|---|---|---|---|---|
| 1 | .......... | $992 61 | $287 92 | $901 45 | .......... | .......... |
| 2 | .......... | .......... | .......... | .......... | .......... | .......... |
| 3 | .......... | **$992 61** | **$287 92** | **$901 45** | .......... | .......... |
| 4 | .......... | $740 63 | $270 37 | $536 48 | .......... | .......... |
| 5 | .......... | .......... | .......... | .......... | .......... | .......... |
| 6 | .......... | **$740 63** | **$270 37** | **536 48** | .......... | .......... |
| 7 | .......... | .......... | $825 68 | $615 21 | .......... | .......... |
| 8 | .......... | .......... | .......... | .......... | .......... | $42 41 |
| 9 | .......... | .......... | **$825 68** | **$615 21** | .......... | **$42 41** |
| 10 | $1,453 10 | $626 76 | $1,469 96 | $130 85 | .......... | .......... |
| 11 | .......... | .......... | .......... | .......... | .......... | .......... |
| 12 | **$1,453 10** | **$626 76** | **$1,469 96** | **$130 85** | .......... | .......... |
| 13 | $261 31 | $352 41 | $721 84 | $13 80 | .......... | .......... |
| 14 | .......... | .......... | .......... | .......... | .......... | .......... |
| 15 | **$261 31** | **$352 41** | **$721 84** | **$13 80** | .......... | .......... |
| 16 | .......... | .......... | .......... | .......... | .......... | .......... |
| 17 | .......... | .......... | .......... | .......... | .......... | .......... |
| 18 | .......... | .......... | .......... | .......... | .......... | .......... |
| 19 | .......... | .......... | .......... | .......... | .......... | .......... |
| 20 | .......... | .......... | .......... | .......... | .......... | .......... |
| 21 | .......... | .......... | .......... | .......... | .......... | .......... |
| 22 | .......... | .......... | .......... | .......... | .......... | $1,457 12 |
| 23 | .......... | .......... | .......... | .......... | .......... | .......... |
| 24 | .......... | .......... | .......... | .......... | .......... | **$1,457 12** |
| 25 | .......... | .......... | .......... | .......... | .......... | .......... |
| 26 | .......... | .......... | .......... | .......... | .......... | .......... |
| 27 | .......... | .......... | .......... | .......... | .......... | .......... |
| 28 | .......... | .......... | .......... | .......... | .......... | .......... |
| 29 | .......... | .......... | .......... | .......... | .......... | .......... |
| 30 | .......... | .......... | .......... | .......... | .......... | .......... |

COMPARATIVE STATEMENTS SHOWING SEPARATELY THE EXPENDITURES
YEARS 1910 TO 1914, INCLUSIVE, CLASSIFIED BY

| | Total | Personal Service | Supplies | LINE No. |
|---|---|---|---|---|
| **BOARD OF INEBRIETY** | | | | |
| **1910** | | | | |
| Revenue Expenditures | .......... | .......... | .......... | 1 |
| Corporate Stock Expenditures | .......... | .......... | .......... | 2 |
| Total for 1910 | .......... | .......... | .......... | 3 |
| **1911** | | | | |
| Revenue Expenditures | $887 19 | $887 19 | .......... | 4 |
| Corporate Stock Expenditures | .......... | .......... | .......... | 5 |
| Total for 1911 | **$887 19** | **$887 19** | .......... | 6 |
| **1912** | | | | |
| Revenue Expenditures | $5,994 25 | $3,980 00 | $428 53 | 7 |
| Corporate Stock Expenditures | 71,500 00 | .......... | .......... | 8 |
| Total for 1912 | **$77,494 25** | **$3,980 00** | **$428 53** | 9 |
| **1913** | | | | |
| Revenue Expenditures | $11,653 73 | $6,051 55 | $584 61 | 10 |
| Corporate Stock Expenditures | 3,525 00 | .......... | .......... | 11 |
| Total for 1913 | **$15,178 73** | **$6,051 55** | **$584 61** | 12 |
| **1914** | | | | |
| Revenue Expenditures | $25,688 49 | $7,736 64 | $831 08 | 13 |
| Corporate Stock Expenditures | .......... | .......... | .......... | 14 |
| Total for 1914 | **$25,688 49** | **$7,736 64** | **$831 08** | 15 |
| **PERMANENT CENSUS BOARD** | | | | |
| **1910** | | | | |
| Revenue Expenditures | $28,717 15 | $20,291 87 | $6,948 13 | 16 |
| Corporate Stock Expenditures | .......... | .......... | .......... | 17 |
| Total for 1910 | **$28,717 15** | **$20,291 87** | **$6,948 13** | 18 |
| **1911** | | | | |
| Revenue Expenditures | $36,504 39 | $31,526 74 | $2,490 70 | 19 |
| Corporate Stock Expenditures | .......... | .......... | .......... | 20 |
| Total for 1911 | **$36,504 39** | **$31,526 74** | **$2,490 70** | 21 |
| **1912** | | | | |
| Revenue Expenditures | $36,669 65 | $31,439 56 | $2,854 91 | 22 |
| Corporate Stock Expenditures | .......... | .......... | .......... | 23 |
| Total for 1912 | **$36,669 65** | **$31,439 56** | **$2,854 91** | 24 |
| **1913** | | | | |
| Revenue Expenditures | $73,474 96 | $68,166 76 | $2,142 94 | 25 |
| Corporate Stock Expenditures | .......... | .......... | .......... | 26 |
| Total for 1913 | **$73,474 96** | **$68,166 76** | **$2,142 94** | 27 |
| **1914** | | | | |
| Revenue Expenditures | $54,717 04 | $47,957 15 | $3,744 96 | 28 |
| Corporate Stock Expenditures | .......... | .......... | .......... | 29 |
| Total for 1914 | **$54,717 04** | **$47,957 15** | **$3,744 96** | 30 |

NEW YORK

MADE FROM REVENUE AND FROM CORPORATE STOCK FUNDS FOR THE DEPARTMENTS, ACCORDING TO OBJECTS OF EXPENDITURE:

| LINE No. | Purchase of Equipment | Materials | Contract or Open Order Service | Contingencies | Fixed Charges and Contributions | Unclassified |
|---|---|---|---|---|---|---|
| 1 | .......... | .......... | .......... | .......... | .......... | .......... |
| 2 | .......... | .......... | .......... | .......... | .......... | .......... |
| 3 | .......... | .......... | .......... | .......... | .......... | .......... |
| 4 | .......... | .......... | .......... | .......... | .......... | .......... |
| 5 | .......... | .......... | .......... | .......... | .......... | .......... |
| 6 | .......... | .......... | .......... | .......... | .......... | .......... |
| 7 | $808 77 | .......... | $126 19 | $650 76 | .......... | .......... |
| 8 | .......... | .......... | .......... | .......... | .......... | $71,500 00 |
| 9 | **$808 77** | .......... | **$126 19** | **$650 76** | .......... | **$71,500 00** |
| 10 | $1,499 78 | .......... | $2,757 40 | $267 25 | $493 14 | .......... |
| 11 | .......... | .......... | .......... | .......... | .......... | $3,525 00 |
| 12 | **$1,499 78** | .......... | **$2,757 40** | **$267 25** | **$493 14** | **$3,525 00** |
| 13 | $428 00 | .......... | $907 05 | $15,492 87 | $292 85 | .......... |
| 14 | .......... | .......... | .......... | .......... | .......... | .......... |
| 15 | **$428 00** | .......... | **$907 05** | **$15,492 87** | **$292 85** | .......... |
| 16 | .......... | .......... | .......... | $1,477 15 | .......... | .......... |
| 17 | .......... | .......... | .......... | .......... | .......... | .......... |
| 18 | .......... | .......... | .......... | **$1,477 15** | .......... | .......... |
| 19 | .......... | .......... | $177 46 | $2,309 49 | .......... | .......... |
| 20 | .......... | .......... | .......... | .......... | .......... | .......... |
| 21 | .......... | .......... | **$177 46** | **$2,309 49** | .......... | .......... |
| 22 | .......... | .......... | $179 72 | $2,195 46 | .......... | .......... |
| 23 | .......... | .......... | .......... | .......... | .......... | .......... |
| 24 | .......... | .......... | **$179 72** | **$2,195 46** | .......... | .......... |
| 25 | $1,381 09 | .......... | $1,007 00 | $777 17 | .......... | .......... |
| 26 | .......... | .......... | .......... | .......... | .......... | .......... |
| 27 | **$1,381 09** | .......... | **$1,007 00** | **$777 17** | .......... | .......... |
| 28 | $1,743 93 | .......... | $1,176 36 | $94 64 | .......... | .......... |
| 29 | .......... | .......... | .......... | .......... | .......... | .......... |
| 30 | **$1,743 93** | .......... | **$1,176 36** | **$94 64** | .......... | .......... |

COMPARATIVE STATEMENTS SHOWING SEPARATELY THE EXPENDITURES
YEARS 1910 TO 1914, INCLUSIVE, CLASSIFIED BY

| | Total | Personal Service | Supplies | LINE No. |
|---|---|---|---|---|
| **PUBLIC RECREATION COMMISSION** | | | | |
| **1910** | | | | |
| Revenue Expenditures | .......... | .......... | .......... | 1 |
| Corporate Stock Expenditures | .......... | .......... | .......... | 2 |
| Total for 1910 | .......... | .......... | .......... | 3 |
| **1911** | | | | |
| Revenue Expenditures | .......... | .......... | .......... | 4 |
| Corporate Stock Expenditures | .......... | .......... | .......... | 5 |
| Total for 1911 | .......... | .......... | .......... | 6 |
| **1912** | | | | |
| Revenue Expenditures | $12,299 03 | $9,480 32 | $1,044 70 | 7 |
| Corporate Stock Expenditures | .......... | .......... | .......... | 8 |
| Total for 1912 | **$12,299 03** | **$9,480 32** | **$1,044 70** | 9 |
| **1913** | | | | |
| Revenue Expenditures | $19,313 76 | $13,457 54 | $1,069 89 | 10 |
| Corporate Stock Expenditures | .......... | .......... | .......... | 11 |
| Total for 1913 | **$19,313 76** | **$13,457 54** | **$1,069 89** | 12 |
| **1914** | | | | |
| Revenue Expenditures | $20,429 61 | $15,206 28 | $394 20 | 13 |
| Corporate Stock Expenditures | .......... | .......... | .......... | 14 |
| Total for 1914 | **$20,429 61** | **$15,206 28** | **$394 20** | 15 |
| **DEPARTMENT OF FINANCE** | | | | |
| **1910** | | | | |
| Revenue Expenditures | $1,462,726 97 | $1,363,179 52 | $38,635 83 | 16 |
| Corporate Stock Expenditures | .......... | .......... | .......... | 17 |
| Total for 1910 | **$1,462,726 97** | **$1,363,179 52** | **$38,635 83** | 18 |
| **1911** | | | | |
| Revenue Expenditures | $1,378,185 90 | $1,285,484 01 | $22,949 99 | 19 |
| Corporate Stock Expenditures | .......... | .......... | .......... | 20 |
| Total for 1911 | **$1,378,185 90** | **$1,285,484 01** | **$22,949,99** | 21 |
| **1912** | | | | |
| Revenue Expenditures | $1,460,258 67 | $1,358,473 69 | $15,494 73 | 22 |
| Corporate Stock Expenditures | .......... | .......... | .......... | 23 |
| Total for 1912 | **$1,460,258 67** | **$1,358,473 69** | **$15,494 73** | 24 |
| **1913** | | | | |
| Revenue Expenditures | $1,671,242 42 | $1,558,315 13 | $13,210 00 | 25 |
| Corporate Stock Expenditures | .......... | .......... | .......... | 26 |
| Total for 1913 | **$1,671,242 42** | **$1,558,315 13** | **$13,210 00** | 27 |
| **1914** | | | | |
| Revenue Expenditures | $1,548,195 08 | $1,449,870 64 | $13,797 66 | 28 |
| Corporate Stock Expenditures | .......... | .......... | .......... | 29 |
| Total for 1914 | **$1,548,195 08** | **$1,449,870 64** | **$13,797 66** | 30 |

NEW YORK

MADE FROM REVENUE AND FROM CORPORATE STOCK FUNDS FOR THE DEPARTMENTS, ACCORDING TO OBJECTS OF EXPENDITURE:

| LINE No. | Purchase of Equipment | Materials | Contract or Open Order Service | Contingencies | Fixed Charges and Contributions | Unclassified |
|---|---|---|---|---|---|---|
| 1 | .......... | .......... | .......... | .......... | .......... | .......... |
| 2 | .......... | .......... | .......... | .......... | .......... | .......... |
| 3 | .......... | .......... | .......... | .......... | .......... | .......... |
| 4 | .......... | .......... | .......... | .......... | .......... | .......... |
| 5 | .......... | .......... | .......... | .......... | .......... | .......... |
| 6 | .......... | .......... | .......... | .......... | .......... | .......... |
| 7 | $451 90 | .......... | $511 16 | $810 95 | .......... | .......... |
| 8 | .......... | .......... | .......... | .......... | .......... | .......... |
| 9 | **$451 90** | .......... | **$511 16** | **$810 95** | .......... | .......... |
| 10 | $2,569 82 | .......... | $1,936 64 | $279 87 | .......... | .......... |
| 11 | .......... | .......... | .......... | .......... | .......... | .......... |
| 12 | **$2,569 82** | .......... | **$1,936 64** | **$279 87** | .......... | .......... |
| 13 | $581 45 | .......... | $4,131 58 | $116 10 | .......... | .......... |
| 14 | .......... | .......... | .......... | .......... | .......... | .......... |
| 15 | **$581 45** | .......... | **$4,131 58** | **$116 10** | .......... | .......... |
| 16 | $5,300 10 | .......... | $14,227 61 | $41,383 91 | .......... | .......... |
| 17 | .......... | .......... | .......... | .......... | .......... | .......... |
| 18 | **$5,300 10** | .......... | **$14,227 61** | **$41,383 91** | .......... | .......... |
| 19 | $4,525 25 | .......... | $9,404 92 | $55,821 73 | .......... | .......... |
| 20 | .......... | .......... | .......... | .......... | .......... | .......... |
| 21 | **$4,525 25** | .......... | **$9,404 92** | **$55,821 73** | .......... | .......... |
| 22 | $10,490 75 | .......... | $31,761 90 | $44,037 60 | .......... | .......... |
| 23 | .......... | .......... | .......... | .......... | .......... | .......... |
| 24 | **$10,490 75** | .......... | **$31,761 90** | **$44,037 60** | .......... | .......... |
| 25 | $9,277 67 | .......... | $34,293 47 | $56,146 15 | .......... | .......... |
| 26 | .......... | .......... | .......... | .......... | .......... | .......... |
| 27 | **$9,277 67** | .......... | **$34,293 47** | **$56,146 15** | .......... | .......... |
| 28 | $9,252 17 | .......... | $39,036 02 | $36,238 59 | .......... | .......... |
| 29 | .......... | .......... | .......... | .......... | .......... | .......... |
| 30 | **$9,252 17** | .......... | **$39,036 02** | **$36,238 59** | .......... | .......... |

Comparative Statements Showing Separately the Expenditures
Years 1910 to 1914, Inclusive, Classified by

| | Total | Personal Service | Supplies | Line No. |
|---|---|---|---|---|
| **WALLABOUT MARKET SPECIAL FUND** | | | | |
| **1910** | | | | |
| Revenue Expenditures | $17,857 60 | $1,004 49 | $7 08 | 1 |
| Corporate Stock Expenditures | .......... | .......... | .......... | 2 |
| Total for 1910 | **$17,857 60** | **$1,004 49** | **$7 08** | 3 |
| **1911** | | | | |
| Revenue Expenditures | $1,396 80 | $1,396 80 | .......... | 4 |
| Corporate Stock Expenditures | .......... | .......... | .......... | 5 |
| Total for 1911 | **$1,396 80** | **$1,396 80** | .......... | 6 |
| **1912** | | | | |
| Revenue Expenditures | $4,977 26 | $230 34 | .......... | 7 |
| Corporate Stock Expenditures | .......... | .......... | .......... | 8 |
| Total for 1912 | **$4,977 26** | **$230 34** | .......... | 9 |
| **1913** | | | | |
| Revenue Expenditures | $1,489 72 | $78 32 | .......... | 10 |
| Corporate Stock Expenditures | .......... | .......... | .......... | 11 |
| Total for 1913 | **$1,489 72** | **$78 32** | .......... | 12 |
| **1914** | | | | |
| Revenue Expenditures | $60 00 | .......... | .......... | 13 |
| Corporate Stock Expenditures | .......... | .......... | .......... | 14 |
| Total for 1914 | **$60 00** | .......... | .......... | 15 |
| **PRESIDENT, BOROUGH OF MANHATTAN** | | | | |
| **1910** | | | | |
| Revenue Expenditures | $2,671,661 06 | $1,597,570 50 | $117,168 12 | 16 |
| Corporate Stock Expenditures | 2,088,119 36 | 147,103 26 | .......... | 17 |
| Total for 1910 | **$4,759,780 42** | **$1,744,673 76** | **$117,168 12** | 18 |
| **1911** | | | | |
| Revenue Expenditures | $2,724,537 28 | $1,575,294 58 | $115,264 86 | 19 |
| Corporate Stock Expenditures | 2,478,662 38 | 177,540 41 | .......... | 20 |
| Total for 1911 | **$5,203,199 66** | **$1,752,834 99** | **$115,264 86** | 21 |
| **1912** | | | | |
| Revenue Expenditures | $2,636,178 74 | $1,577,079 53 | $207,217 76 | 22 |
| Corporate Stock Expenditures | 3,342,702 32 | 275,362 70 | .......... | 23 |
| Total for 1912 | **$5,978,881 06** | **$1,852,442 23** | **$207,217 76** | 24 |
| **1913** | | | | |
| Revenue Expenditures | $2,762,007 20 | $1,673,628 15 | $84,321 38 | 25 |
| Corporate Stock Expenditures | 3,108,160 60 | 167,201 36 | 58 14 | 26 |
| Total for 1913 | **$5,870,167 80** | **$1,840,829 51** | **$84,379 52** | 27 |
| **1914** | | | | |
| Revenue Expenditures | $2,754,310 30 | $1,834,434 06 | $92,721 40 | 28 |
| Corporate Stock Expenditures | 2,255,201 20 | 151,211 18 | 2,040 85 | 29 |
| Total for 1914 | **$5,009,511 50** | **$1,985,645 24** | **$94,762 25** | 30 |

## NEW YORK

MADE FROM REVENUE AND FROM CORPORATE STOCK FUNDS FOR THE DEPARTMENTS, ACCORDING TO OBJECTS OF EXPENDITURE:

| LINE No. | Purchase of Equipment | Materials | Contract or Open Order Service | Contingencies | Fixed Charges and Contributions | Unclassified |
|---|---|---|---|---|---|---|
| 1 | .......... | .......... | $16,846 03 | .......... | .......... | .......... |
| 2 | .......... | .......... | .......... | .......... | .......... | .......... |
| 3 | .......... | .......... | **$16,846 03** | .......... | .......... | .......... |
| 4 | .......... | .......... | .......... | .......... | .......... | .......... |
| 5 | .......... | .......... | .......... | .......... | .......... | .......... |
| 6 | .......... | .......... | .......... | .......... | .......... | .......... |
| 7 | .......... | .......... | $4,746 92 | .......... | .......... | .......... |
| 8 | .......... | .......... | .......... | .......... | .......... | .......... |
| 9 | .......... | .......... | **$4,746 92** | .......... | .......... | .......... |
| 10 | .......... | .......... | $1,411 40 | .......... | .......... | .......... |
| 11 | .......... | .......... | .......... | .......... | .......... | .......... |
| 12 | .......... | .......... | **$1,411 40** | .......... | .......... | .......... |
| 13 | .......... | .......... | $60 00 | .......... | .......... | .......... |
| 14 | .......... | .......... | .......... | .......... | .......... | .......... |
| 15 | .......... | .......... | **$60 00** | .......... | .......... | .......... |
| 16 | $34,253 25 | $43,247 63 | $858,021 94 | $21,399 62 | .......... | .......... |
| 17 | 37,521 77 | .......... | 1,900,191 63 | .......... | .......... | $3,302 70 |
| 18 | **$71,775 02** | **$43,247 63** | **$2,758,213 57** | **$21,399 62** | .......... | **$3,302 70** |
| 19 | $7,253 00 | $94,670 37 | $910,961 79 | $21,092 68 | .......... | .......... |
| 20 | 21,115 39 | 18,341 72 | 2,261,664 86 | .......... | .......... | .......... |
| 21 | **$28,368 39** | **$113,012 09** | **$3,172,626 65** | **$21,092 68** | .......... | .......... |
| 22 | $7,779 95 | $9,386 06 | $811,227 49 | $23,487 95 | .......... | .......... |
| 23 | 13,909 26 | .......... | 2,995,803 59 | 19 81 | .......... | $57,606 96 |
| 24 | **$21,689 21** | **$9,386 06** | **$3,807,031 08** | **$23,507 76** | .......... | **$57,606 96** |
| 25 | $36,904 70 | $89,292 49 | $875,939 06 | $1,921 42 | .......... | .......... |
| 26 | 5,621 76 | 78 00 | 2,912,330 71 | .......... | .......... | $22,870 63 |
| 27 | **$42,526 46** | **$89,370 49** | **$3,788,269 77** | **$1,921 42** | .......... | **$22,870 63** |
| 28 | $76,112 60 | $90,778 43 | $640,156 01 | $20,107 80 | .......... | .......... |
| 29 | 15,592 91 | 659 19 | 1,832,933 83 | .......... | .......... | $252,763 24 |
| 30 | **$91,705 51** | **$91,437 62** | **$2,473,089 84** | **$20,107 80** | .......... | **$252,763 24** |

COMPARATIVE STATEMENTS SHOWING SEPARATELY THE EXPENDITURES
YEARS 1910 TO 1914, INCLUSIVE, CLASSIFIED BY

| | Total | Personal Service | Supplies | LINE No. |
|---|---|---|---|---|
| **PRESIDENT, BOROUGH OF THE BRONX** | | | | |
| **1910** | | | | |
| Revenue Expenditures | $1,136,667 56 | $874,753 95 | $22,497 56 | 1 |
| Corporate Stock Expenditures | 842,186 69 | 172,315 59 | 12 33 | 2 |
| Total for 1910 | **$1,978,854 25** | **$1,047,069 54** | **$22,509 89** | 3 |
| **1911** | | | | |
| Revenue Expenditures | $1,066,497 23 | $771,743 79 | $25,153 03 | 4 |
| Corporate Stock Expenditures | 441,070 25 | 129,874 50 | 1,299 88 | 5 |
| Total for 1911 | **$1,507,567 48** | **$901,618 29** | **$26,452 91** | 6 |
| **1912** | | | | |
| Revenue Expenditures | $1,117,659 00 | $792,219 08 | $142,497 95 | 7 |
| Corporate Stock Expenditures | 913,877 60 | 126,282 12 | 1,214 95 | 8 |
| Total for 1912 | **$2,031,536 60** | **$918,501 20** | **$143,712 90** | 9 |
| **1913** | | | | |
| Revenue Expenditures | $1,205,911 97 | $845,653 93 | $22,406 61 | 10 |
| Corporate Stock Expenditures | 974,954 31 | 90,505 86 | 945 71 | 11 |
| Total for 1913 | **$2,180,866 28** | **$936,159 79** | **$23,352 32** | 12 |
| **1914** | | | | |
| Revenue Expenditures | $1,204,216 35 | $879,242 84 | $21,688 24 | 13 |
| Corporate Stock Expenditures | 633,170 73 | 33,701 97 | .......... | 14 |
| Total for 1914 | **$1,837,387 08** | **$912,944 81** | **$21,688 24** | 15 |
| **PRESIDENT, BOROUGH OF BROOKLYN** | | | | |
| **1910** | | | | |
| Revenue Expenditures | $2,156,603 26 | $1,489,547 24 | $123,437 70 | 16 |
| Corporate Stock Expenditures | 1,637,870 66 | 121,601 20 | .......... | 17 |
| Total for 1910 | **$3,794,473 92** | **$1,611,148 44** | **$123,437 70** | 18 |
| **1911** | | | | |
| Revenue Expenditures | $2,038,207 61 | $1,466,046 53 | $113,416 91 | 19 |
| Corporate Stock Expenditures | 1,550,396 18 | 114,729 46 | 1,566 49 | 20 |
| Total for 1911 | **$3,588,603 79** | **$1,580,775 99** | **$114,983 40** | 21 |
| **1912** | | | | |
| Revenue Expenditures | $2,140,031 36 | $1,490,733 36 | $273,115 35 | 22 |
| Corporate Stock Expenditures | 2,152,297 77 | 118,365 77 | 1,179 09 | 23 |
| Total for 1912 | **$4,292,329 13** | **$1,609,099 13** | **$274,294 44** | 24 |
| **1913** | | | | |
| Revenue Expenditures | $2,071,981 41 | $1,501,569 23 | $108,157 28 | 25 |
| Corporate Stock Expenditures | 2,117,246 09 | 143,960 51 | 1,133 51 | 26 |
| Total for 1913 | **$4,189,227 50** | **$1,645,529 74** | **$109,290 79** | 27 |
| **1914** | | | | |
| Revenue Expenditures | $2,088,345 45 | $1,478,523 21 | $105,864 94 | 28 |
| Corporate Stock Expenditures | 1,102,652 22 | 72,245 00 | 998 93 | 29 |
| Total for 1914 | **$3,190,997 67** | **$1,550,768 21** | **$106,863 87** | 30 |

NEW YORK

MADE FROM REVENUE AND FROM CORPORATE STOCK FUNDS FOR THE DEPARTMENTS, ACCORDING TO OBJECTS OF EXPENDITURE:

| LINE No. | Purchase of Equipment | Materials | Contract or Open Order Service | Contingencies | Fixed Charges and Contributions | Unclassified |
|---|---|---|---|---|---|---|
| 1 | $15,051 62 | $83,571 47 | $130,637 08 | $10,155 88 | .......... | .......... |
| 2 | 268 25 | 1,203 22 | 658,386 05 | 7 50 | .......... | $9,993 75 |
| 3 | **$15,319 87** | **$84,774 69** | **$789,023 13** | **$10,163 38** | .......... | **$9,993 75** |
| 4 | $12,582 58 | $113,921 40 | $130,501 03 | $12,509 92 | $85 48 | .......... |
| 5 | 1,755 26 | 506 96 | 307,200 48 | 419 17 | .......... | $14 00 |
| 6 | **$14,337 84** | **$114,428 36** | **$437,701 51** | **$12,929 09** | **$85 48** | **$14 00** |
| 7 | $16,235 05 | $567 40 | $157,481 34 | $8,608 18 | $50 00 | .......... |
| 8 | 695 91 | .......... | 784,675 60 | 456 85 | .......... | $552 17 |
| 9 | **$16,930 96** | **$567 40** | **$942,156 94** | **$9,065 03** | **$50 00** | **$552 17** |
| 10 | $17,237 55 | $122,547 24 | $196,582 45 | $812 19 | $672 00 | .......... |
| 11 | 1,557 57 | 57 50 | 877,994 20 | 380 76 | .......... | $3,512 71 |
| 12 | **$18,795 12** | **122,604 74** | **$1,074,576 65** | **$1,192 95** | **$672 00** | **$3,512 71** |
| 13 | $56,470 51 | $94,350 76 | $151,579 45 | $208 55 | $676 00 | .......... |
| 14 | 63 45 | .......... | 599,405 31 | .......... | .......... | .......... |
| 15 | **$56,533 96** | **$94,350 76** | **$750,984 76** | **$208 55** | **$676 00** | .......... |
| 16 | $32,401 95 | $180,299 76 | $310,371 05 | $19,261 20 | $1,284 36 | .......... |
| 17 | .......... | .......... | 1,510,311 58 | .......... | .......... | $5,957 88 |
| 18 | **$32,401 95** | **$180,299 76** | **$1,820,682 63** | **$19,261 20** | **$1,284 36** | **$5,957 88** |
| 19 | $36,432 35 | $145,614 26 | $259,673 44 | $17,024 12 | .......... | .......... |
| 20 | 21,116 00 | 168 08 | 1,410,736 10 | 869 05 | .......... | $1,211 00 |
| 21 | **$57,548 35** | **$145,782 34** | **$1,670,409 54** | **$17,893 17** | .......... | **$1,211 00** |
| 22 | $29,863 12 | $156 41 | $322,882 86 | $15,239 69 | .......... | $8,040 57 |
| 23 | 186 66 | 60 60 | 1,949,588 15 | 588 75 | .......... | 82,328 75 |
| 24 | **$30,049 78** | **$217 01** | **$2,272,471 01** | **$15,828 44** | .......... | **$90,369 32** |
| 25 | $33,657 11 | $150,199 85 | $268,227 14 | $7,978 35 | .......... | $2,192 45 |
| 26 | 721 06 | .......... | 1,716,756 21 | .......... | .......... | 254,674 80 |
| 27 | **$34,378 17** | **$150,199 85** | **$1,984,983 35** | **$7,978 35** | .......... | **$256,867 25** |
| 28 | $33,861 01 | $155,814 52 | $298,242 36 | $16,039 41 | .......... | .......... |
| 29 | .......... | .......... | 1,026,168 69 | 29 50 | .......... | $3,210 10 |
| 30 | **$33,861 01** | **$155,814 52** | **$1,324,411 05** | **$16,068 91** | .......... | **$3,210 10** |

COMPARATIVE STATEMENTS SHOWING SEPARATELY THE EXPENDITURES
YEARS 1910 TO 1914, INCLUSIVE, CLASSIFIED BY

| | Total | Personal Service | Supplies | LINE No. |
|---|---|---|---|---|
| **PRESIDENT, BOROUGH OF QUEENS** | | | | |
| **1910** | | | | |
| Revenue Expenditures | $1,373,024 95 | $957,105 08 | $38,688 61 | 1 |
| Corporate Stock Expenditures | 392,699 26 | 210,906 95 | .......... | 2 |
| Total for 1910 | **$1,765,724 21** | **$1,168,012 03** | **$38,688 61** | 3 |
| **1911** | | | | |
| Revenue Expenditures | $1,356,075 79 | $863,511 57 | $35,660 65 | 4 |
| Corporate Stock Expenditures | 343,530 67 | 153,284 70 | 3,356 76 | 5 |
| Total for 1911 | **$1,699,606 46** | **$1,016,796 27** | **$39,017 41** | 6 |
| **1912** | | | | |
| Revenue Expenditures | $1,740,008 68 | $1,068,934 77 | $154,377 82 | 7 |
| Corporate Stock Expenditures | 484,596 28 | 175,520 10 | 5,801 67 | 8 |
| Total for 1912 | **$2,224,604 96** | **$1,244,454 87** | **$160,179 49** | 9 |
| **1913** | | | | |
| Revenue Expenditures | $1,970,000 97 | $1,183,747 19 | $38,866 15 | 10 |
| Corporate Stock Expenditures | 673,638 84 | 120,227 83 | 3,837 54 | 11 |
| Total for 1913 | **$2,643,639 81** | **$1,303,975 02** | **$42,703 69** | 12 |
| **1914** | | | | |
| Revenue Expenditures | $2,064,621 32 | $1,272,640 90 | $38,710 39 | 13 |
| Corporate Stock Expenditures | 507,891 81 | 41,179 96 | 1,680 06 | 14 |
| Total for 1914 | **$2,572,513 13** | **$1,313,820 86** | **$40,390 45** | 15 |
| **PRESIDENT, BOROUGH OF RICHMOND** | | | | |
| **1910** | | | | |
| Revenue Expenditures | $774,567 39 | $511,460 13 | $39,149 65 | 16 |
| Corporate Stock Expenditures | 438,076 45 | 163,780 91 | .......... | 17 |
| Total for 1910 | **$1,212,643 84** | **$675,241 04** | **$39,149 65** | 18 |
| **1911** | | | | |
| Revenue Expenditures | $742,412 55 | $504,022 39 | $35,490 40 | 19 |
| Corporate Stock Expenditures | 414,648 86 | 156,788 32 | 3,602 19 | 20 |
| Total for 1911 | **$1,157,061 41** | **$660,810 71** | **$39,092 59** | 21 |
| **1912** | | | | |
| Revenue Expenditures | $770,886 17 | $527,261 64 | $130,696 53 | 22 |
| Corporate Stock Expenditures | 604,009 89 | 134,347 62 | 4,007 95 | 23 |
| Total for 1912 | **$1,374,896 06** | **$6 1,609 26** | **$134,704 48** | 24 |
| **1913** | | | | |
| Revenue Expenditures | $837,878 69 | $590,480 54 | $37,574 87 | 25 |
| Corporate Stock Expenditures | 779,036 92 | 84,867 68 | 1,302 47 | 26 |
| Total for 1913 | **$1,616,915 61** | **$675,348 22** | **$38,877 34** | 27 |
| **1914** | | | | |
| Revenue Expenditures | $719,261 79 | $573,857 53 | $28,717 44 | 28 |
| Corporate Stock Expenditures | 339,375 68 | 35,938 70 | 2,286 68 | 29 |
| Total for 1914 | **$1,058,637 47** | **$609,796 23** | **$29,004 12** | 30 |

# NEW YORK

MADE FROM REVENUE AND FROM CORPORATE STOCK FUNDS FOR THE DEPARTMENTS, ACCORDING TO OBJECTS OF EXPENDITURE:

| LINE No. | Purchase of Equipment | Materials | Contract or Open Order Service | Contingencies | Fixed Charges and Contributions | Unclassified |
|---|---|---|---|---|---|---|
| 1 | $11,456 84 | $36,152 48 | $312,084 03 | $14,137 91 | $3,400 00 | .......... |
| 2 | 33,315 40 | .......... | 127,097 54 | .......... | .......... | $21,379 37 |
| 3 | **$44,772 24** | **$36,152 48** | **$439,181 57** | **$14,137 91** | **$3,400 00** | **$21,379 37** |
| 4 | $18,180 59 | $103,010 16 | $323,666 27 | $12,046 55 | .......... | .......... |
| 5 | 2,454 97 | .......... | 162,810 75 | 1,976 24 | .......... | $19,647 25 |
| 6 | **$20,635 56** | **$ 03,010 16** | **$486,477 02** | **$14,022 79** | .......... | **$19,647 25** |
| 7 | $32,759 84 | $709 77 | $472,348 79 | $10,877 69 | .......... | .......... |
| 8 | 2,689 42 | .......... | 291,896 83 | 2,672 74 | .......... | $6,015 52 |
| 9 | **$35,449 26** | **$709 77** | **$764,245 62** | **$13,550 43** | .......... | **$6,015 52** |
| 10 | $66,689 34 | $217,097 85 | $459,553 19 | $4,047 25 | .......... | .......... |
| 11 | 3,506 61 | 162 85 | 543,708 76 | .......... | .......... | $2,195 25 |
| 12 | **$70,195 95** | **$217,260 70** | **$1,003,261 95** | **$4,047 25** | .......... | **$2,195 25** |
| 13 | $60,256 01 | $180,576 70 | $510,347 00 | $2,090 32 | .......... | .......... |
| 14 | 1,820 55 | 47 24 | 462,227 25 | .......... | .......... | $936 75 |
| 15 | **$62,076 56** | **$180,6 3 94** | **$972,574 25** | **$2,090 32** | .......... | **$936 75** |
| 16 | $15,904 59 | $111,316 34 | $87,343 18 | $9,153 50 | $240 00 | .......... |
| 17 | 770 00 | .......... | 255,680 47 | .......... | .......... | $17,845 07 |
| 18 | **$16,674 59** | **$111,316 34** | **$343,023 65** | **$9,153 50** | **$240 00** | **$17,845 07** |
| 19 | $9,020 80 | $93,337 92 | $94,497 05 | $6,043 99 | .......... | .......... |
| 20 | 2,237 29 | 869 71 | 245,813 42 | 3,644 93 | .......... | $1,693 00 |
| 21 | **$11,258 09** | **$94,207 63** | **$340,310 47** | **$9,688 92** | .......... | **$1,693 00** |
| 22 | $9,792 78 | .......... | $96,770 94 | $6,364 28 | .......... | .......... |
| 23 | 1,598 50 | 76 25 | 454,308 58 | 3,200 80 | .......... | $6,470 19 |
| 24 | **$11,391 28** | **$76 25** | **$551,079 52** | **$9,565 08** | .......... | **$6,470 19** |
| 25 | $31,829 68 | $95,644 49 | $74,405 61 | $7,928 50 | $15.00 | .......... |
| 26 | 7,225 94 | 1,177 77 | 451,857 43 | 707 21 | .......... | $231,898 42 |
| 27 | **$39,055 62** | **$96,822 26** | **$526,263 04** | **$8,635 71** | **$15 00** | **$231,898, 42** |
| 28 | $6,244 17 | $38,837 15 | $70,162 30 | $1,443 20 | .......... | .......... |
| 29 | 299 56 | 198 20 | 296,421 66 | 279 56 | .......... | $5,951 32 |
| 30 | **$6,543 73** | **$39,035 35** | **$366,583 96** | **$1,722 76** | .......... | **$5,951 32** |

COMPARATIVE STATEMENTS SHOWING SEPARATELY THE EXPENDITURES
YEARS 1910 TO 1914, INCLUSIVE, CLASSIFIED BY

| | Total | Personal Service | Supplies | LINE No. |
|---|---|---|---|---|
| **BOARD OF ALDERMEN, PRESIDENT OF BOARD AND CITY CLERK** | | | | |
| **1910** | | | | |
| Revenue Expenditures | $281,815 63 | $264,748 96 | .......... | 1 |
| Corporate Stock Expenditures | .......... | .......... | .......... | 2 |
| Total for 1910 | **$281,815 63** | **$264,748 96** | .......... | 3 |
| **1911** | | | | |
| Revenue Expenditures | $326,660 73 | $277,726 83 | $2,500 00 | 4 |
| Corporate Stock Expenditures | .......... | .......... | .......... | 5 |
| Total for 1911 | **$326,660 73** | **$277,726 83** | **$2,500 00** | 6 |
| **1912** | | | | |
| Revenue Expenditures | $397,368 75 | $303,900 59 | $1,004 80 | 7 |
| Corporate Stock Expenditures | .......... | .......... | .......... | 8 |
| Total for 1912 | **$397,368 75** | **$303,900 59** | **$1,004 80** | 9 |
| **1913** | | | | |
| Revenue Expenditures | $345,750 97 | $317,892 55 | $4,686 68 | 10 |
| Corporate Stock Expenditures | .......... | .......... | .......... | 11 |
| Total for 1913 | **$345,750 97** | **$317,892 55** | **$4,686 68** | 12 |
| **1914** | | | | |
| Revenue Expenditures | $357,446 11 | $303,848 31 | $14,784 44 | 13 |
| Corporate Stock Expenditures | .......... | .......... | .......... | 14 |
| Total for 1914 | **$357,446 11** | **$303,848 31** | **$14,784 44** | 15 |
| **BRONX PARKWAY COMMISSION** | | | | |
| **1910** | | | | |
| Revenue Expenditures | .......... | .......... | .......... | 16 |
| Corporate Stock Expenditures | .......... | .......... | .......... | 17 |
| Total for 1910 | .......... | .......... | .......... | 18 |
| **1911** | | | | |
| Revenue Expenditures | .......... | .......... | .......... | 19 |
| Corporate Stock Expenditures | $5,408 91 | $5,026 85 | .......... | 20 |
| Total for 1911 | **$5,408 91** | **$5,026 85** | .......... | 21 |
| **1912** | | | | |
| Revenue Expenditures | .......... | .......... | .......... | 22 |
| Corporate Stock Expenditures | $31,206 80 | $13,105 20 | $856 71 | 23 |
| Total for 1912 | **$31,206 80** | **$13,105 20** | **$856 71** | 24 |
| **1913** | | | | |
| Revenue Expenditures | $17,385 05 | $15,795 07 | $299 99 | 25 |
| Corporate Stock Expenditures | 779,233 07 | 15,826 90 | 1,024 14 | 26 |
| Total for 1913 | **$796,618 12** | **$31,621 97** | **$1,324 13** | 27 |
| **1914** | | | | |
| Revenue Expenditures | $42,032 02 | $29,855 78 | $2,111 05 | 28 |
| Corporate Stock Expenditures | 1,117,071 85 | 10,828 24 | 1,193 78 | 29 |
| Total for 1914 | **$1,159,103 87** | **$40,684 02** | **$3,304 83** | 30 |

## NEW YORK

MADE FROM REVENUE AND FROM CORPORATE STOCK FUNDS FOR THE DEPARTMENTS, ACCORDING TO OBJECTS OF EXPENDITURE:

| LINE No. | Purchase of Equipment | Materials | Contract or Open Order Service | Contingencies | Fixed Charges and Contributions | Unclassified |
|---|---|---|---|---|---|---|
| 1 | .......... | .......... | $12,766 67 | $4,300 00 | .......... | .......... |
| 2 | .......... | .......... | .......... | .......... | .......... | .......... |
| 3 | .......... | .......... | **$12,766 67** | **$4,300 00** | .......... | .......... |
| 4 | .......... | .......... | $722 18 | $5,505 70 | .......... | $40,206 02 |
| 5 | .......... | .......... | .......... | .......... | .......... | .......... |
| 6 | .......... | .......... | **$722 18** | **$5,505 70** | .......... | **$40,206 02** |
| 7 | $60 00 | .......... | $77,717 98 | $2,936 38 | .......... | $11,749 00 |
| 8 | .......... | .......... | .......... | .......... | .......... | .......... |
| 9 | **$60 00** | .......... | **$77,717 98** | **$2,936 38** | .......... | **$11,749 00** |
| 10 | .......... | .......... | $12,910 38 | $869 11 | $764 50 | $8,627 75 |
| 11 | .......... | .......... | .......... | .......... | .......... | .......... |
| 12 | .......... | .......... | **$12,910 38** | **$869 11** | **$764 50** | **$8,627 75** |
| 13 | $7,943 35 | .......... | $25,569 22 | $5,300 79 | .......... | .......... |
| 14 | .......... | .......... | .......... | .......... | .......... | .......... |
| 15 | **$7,943 35** | .......... | **$25,569 22** | **$5,300 79** | .......... | .......... |
| 16 | .......... | .......... | .......... | .......... | .......... | .......... |
| 17 | .......... | .......... | .......... | .......... | .......... | .......... |
| 18 | .......... | .......... | .......... | .......... | .......... | .......... |
| 19 | .......... | .......... | .......... | .......... | .......... | .......... |
| 20 | $101 63 | .......... | .......... | $108 03 | .......... | $172 40 |
| 21 | **$101 63** | .......... | .......... | **$108 03** | .......... | **$172 40** |
| 22 | .......... | .......... | .......... | .......... | .......... | .......... |
| 23 | $8,479 35 | .......... | $5,569 03 | $118 09 | .......... | $3,078 42 |
| 24 | **$8,479 35** | .......... | **$5,569 03** | **$118 09** | .......... | **$3,078 42** |
| 25 | .......... | .......... | $165 00 | $224 99 | $900 00 | .......... |
| 26 | $1,662 09 | $403 18 | 160 05 | .......... | .......... | $760,156 71 |
| 27 | **$1,662 09** | **$403 18** | **$325 05** | **$224 99** | **$900 00** | **$760,156 71** |
| 28 | $1,608 96 | .......... | $6,179 73 | $359 86 | $1,916 64 | .......... |
| 29 | 1,576 36 | $17 10 | 1,043 77 | 583 35 | .......... | $1,101,829 25 |
| 30 | **$3,185 32** | **$17 10** | **$7,223 50** | **$943 21** | **$1,916 64** | **$1,101,829 25** |

COMPARATIVE STATEMENTS SHOWING SEPARATELY THE EXPENDITURES
YEARS 1910 TO 1914, INCLUSIVE, CLASSIFIED BY

| | Total | Personal Service | Supplies | LINE No. |
|---|---|---|---|---|
| **BOARD OF BUILDING EXAMINERS** | | | | |
| **1910** | | | | |
| Revenue Expenditures | $9,423 53 | $8,610 00 | .......... | 1 |
| Corporate Stock Expenditures | .......... | .......... | .......... | 2 |
| Total for 1910 | **$9,423 53** | **$8,610 00** | .......... | 3 |
| **1911** | | | | |
| Revenue Expenditures | $9,340 29 | $8,419 00 | $93 65 | 4 |
| Corporate Stock Expenditures | .......... | .......... | .......... | 5 |
| Total for 1911 | **$9,340 29** | **$8,419 00** | **$93 65** | 6 |
| **1912** | | | | |
| Revenue Expenditures | $9,108 47 | $8,679 00 | $98 93 | 7 |
| Corporate Stock Expenditures | .......... | .......... | .......... | 8 |
| Total for 1912 | **$9,108 47** | **$8,679 00** | **$98 93** | 9 |
| **1913** | | | | |
| Revenue Expenditures | $8,702 03 | $8,349 74 | $217 01 | 10 |
| Corporate Stock Expenditures | .......... | .......... | .......... | 11 |
| Total for 1913 | **$8,702 03** | **$8,349 74** | **$217 01** | 12 |
| **1914** | | | | |
| Revenue Expenditures | $9,038 96 | $8,695 00 | $143 42 | 13 |
| Corporate Stock Expenditures | .......... | .......... | .......... | 14 |
| Total for 1914 | **$9,038 96** | **$8,695 00** | **$143 42** | 15 |
| **COURT HOUSE BOARD** | | | | |
| **1910** | | | | |
| Revenue Expenditures | $1,591 73 | $1,322 40 | $269 33 | 16 |
| Corporate Stock Expenditures | .......... | .......... | .......... | 17 |
| Total for 1910 | **$1,591 73** | **$1,322 40** | **$269 33** | 18 |
| **1911** | | | | |
| Revenue Expenditures | $572 40 | $572 40 | .......... | 19 |
| Corporate Stock Expenditures | .......... | .......... | .......... | 20 |
| Total for 1911 | **$572 40** | **$572 40** | .......... | 21 |
| **1912** | | | | |
| Revenue Expenditures | .......... | .......... | .......... | 22 |
| Corporate Stock Expenditures | $32,247 62 | $15,708 43 | $2,209 43 | 23 |
| Total for 1912 | **$32,247 62** | **$15,708 43** | **$2,209 43** | 24 |
| **1913** | | | | |
| Revenue Expenditures | .......... | .......... | .......... | 25 |
| Corporate Stock Expenditures | $6,485,390 98 | $12,160 20 | $1,246 86 | 26 |
| Total for 1913 | **$6,485,390 98** | **$12,160 20** | **$1,246 86** | 27 |
| **1914** | | | | |
| Revenue Expenditures | .......... | .......... | .......... | 28 |
| Corporate Stock Expenditures | $183,440 09 | $26,632 67 | $1,112 91 | 29 |
| Total for 1914 | **$183,440 09** | **$26,632 67** | **$1,112 91** | 30 |

NEW YORK

MADE FROM REVENUE AND FROM CORPORATE STOCK FUNDS FOR THE DEPARTMENTS, ACCORDING TO OBJECTS OF EXPENDITURE:

| LINE No. | Purchase of Equipment | Materials | Contract or Open Order Service | Contingencies | Fixed Charges and Contributions | Unclassified |
|---|---|---|---|---|---|---|
| 1 | .......... | .......... | $452 68 | $360 85 | .......... | .......... |
| 2 | .......... | .......... | .......... | .......... | .......... | .......... |
| 3 | .......... | .......... | **$452 68** | **$360 85** | .......... | .......... |
| 4 | $559 50 | .......... | $109 04 | $159 10 | .......... | .......... |
| 5 | .......... | .......... | .......... | .......... | .......... | .......... |
| 6 | **$559 50** | .......... | **$109 04** | **$159 10** | .......... | .......... |
| 7 | .......... | .......... | $93 00 | $237 54 | .......... | .......... |
| 8 | .......... | .......... | .......... | .......... | .......... | .......... |
| 9 | .......... | .......... | **$93 00** | **$237 54** | .......... | .......... |
| 10 | $21 62 | .......... | $113 66 | .......... | .......... | .......... |
| 11 | .......... | .......... | .......... | .......... | .......... | .......... |
| 12 | **$21 62** | .......... | **$113 66** | .......... | .......... | .......... |
| 13 | $70 00 | .......... | $80 54 | $50 00 | .......... | .......... |
| 14 | .......... | .......... | .......... | .......... | .......... | .......... |
| 15 | **$70 00** | .......... | **$80 54** | **$50 00** | .......... | .......... |
| 16 | .......... | .......... | .......... | .......... | .......... | .......... |
| 17 | .......... | .......... | .......... | .......... | .......... | .......... |
| 18 | .......... | .......... | .......... | .......... | .......... | .......... |
| 19 | .......... | .......... | .......... | .......... | .......... | .......... |
| 20 | .......... | .......... | .......... | .......... | .......... | .......... |
| 21 | .......... | .......... | .......... | .......... | .......... | .......... |
| 22 | .......... | .......... | .......... | .......... | .......... | .......... |
| 23 | $106 93 | .......... | $139 37 | $693 49 | .......... | $13,389 97 |
| 24 | **$106 93** | .......... | **$139 37** | **$693 49** | .......... | **$13,389 97** |
| 25 | .......... | .......... | .......... | .......... | .......... | .......... |
| 26 | $454 28 | .......... | .......... | .......... | .......... | $6,471,529 64 |
| 27 | **$454 28** | .......... | .......... | .......... | .......... | **$6,471 529 64** |
| 28 | .......... | .......... | .......... | .......... | .......... | .......... |
| 29 | $452 32 | .......... | $103,367 27 | $2,420 67 | .......... | $49,454 25 |
| 30 | **$452 32** | .......... | **$103,367 27** | **$2,420 67** | .......... | **$49,454 25** |

COMPARATIVE STATEMENTS SHOWING SEPARATELY THE EXPENDITURES
YEARS 1910 TO 1914, INCLUSIVE, CLASSIFIED BY

| | Total | Personal Service | Supplies | LINE No. |
|---|---|---|---|---|
| **COMMISSIONERS OF ESTIMATE AND APPRAISAL** | | | | |
| **1910** | | | | |
| Revenue Expenditures.......... | .......... | .......... | .......... | 1 |
| Corporate Stock Expenditures.......... | $21,220 24 | $17,328 72 | $39 87 | 2 |
| Total for 1910.......... | **$21,220 24** | **$17,328 72** | **$39 87** | 3 |
| **1911** | | | | |
| Revenue Expenditures.......... | .......... | .......... | .......... | 4 |
| Corporate Stock Expenditures.......... | $16,523 16 | $12,418 32 | $65 78 | 5 |
| Total for 1911.......... | **$16,523 16** | **$12,418 32** | **$65 78** | 6 |
| **1912** | | | | |
| Revenue Expenditures.......... | .......... | .......... | .......... | 7 |
| Corporate Stock Expenditures.......... | $15,472 56 | $11,855 95 | $92 75 | 8 |
| Total for 1912.......... | **$15,472 56** | **$11,855 95** | **$92 75** | 9 |
| **1913** | | | | |
| Revenue Expenditures.......... | .......... | .......... | .......... | 10 |
| Corporate Stock Expenditures.......... | .......... | .......... | .......... | 11 |
| Total for 1913.......... | .......... | .......... | .......... | 12 |
| **1914** | | | | |
| Revenue Expenditures.......... | .......... | .......... | .......... | 13 |
| Corporate Stock Expenditures.......... | .......... | .......... | .......... | 14 |
| Total for 1914.......... | .......... | .......... | .......... | 15 |
| **COMMISSION ON LUNACY** | | | | |
| **1910** | | | | |
| Revenue Expenditures.......... | .......... | .......... | .......... | 16 |
| Corporate Stock Expenditures.......... | .......... | .......... | .......... | 17 |
| Total for 1910.......... | .......... | .......... | .......... | 18 |
| **1911** | | | | |
| Revenue Expenditures.......... | .......... | .......... | .......... | 19 |
| Corporate Stock Expenditures.......... | .......... | .......... | .......... | 20 |
| Total for 1911.......... | .......... | .......... | .......... | 21 |
| **1912** | | | | |
| Revenue Expenditures.......... | $3,590 30 | $3,590 30 | .......... | 22 |
| Corporate Stock Expenditures.......... | .......... | .......... | .......... | 23 |
| Total for 1912.......... | **$3,590 30** | **$3,590 30** | .......... | 24 |
| **1913** | | | | |
| Revenue Expenditures.......... | $1,120 80 | $1,120 80 | .......... | 25 |
| Corporate Stock Expenditures.......... | .......... | .......... | .......... | 26 |
| Total for 1913.......... | **$1,120 80** | **$1,120 80** | .......... | 27 |
| **1914** | | | | |
| Revenue Expenditures.......... | .......... | .......... | .......... | 28 |
| Corporate Stock Expenditures.......... | .......... | .......... | .......... | 29 |
| Total for 1914.......... | .......... | .......... | .......... | 30 |

NEW YORK

Made from Revenue and from Corporate Stock Funds for the Departments, According to Objects of Expenditure:

| LINE No. | Purchase of Equipment | Materials | Contract or Open Order Service | Contingencies | Fixed Charges and Contributions | Unclassified |
|---|---|---|---|---|---|---|
| 1 | .......... | .......... | .......... | .......... | .......... | .......... |
| 2 | $704 59 | .......... | $12 75 | $27 97 | .......... | $3,106 34 |
| 3 | **$704 59** | .......... | **$12 75** | **$27 97** | .......... | **$3,106 34** |
| 4 | .......... | .......... | .......... | .......... | .......... | .......... |
| 5 | $235 50 | .......... | .......... | $44 65 | .......... | $3,758 91 |
| 6 | **$235 50** | .......... | .......... | **$44 65** | .......... | **$3,758 91** |
| 7 | .......... | .......... | .......... | .......... | .......... | .......... |
| 8 | .......... | .......... | .......... | $18.55 | .......... | $3,505 31 |
| 9 | .......... | .......... | .......... | **$18 55** | .......... | **$3,505 31** |
| 10 | .......... | .......... | .......... | .......... | .......... | .......... |
| 11 | .......... | .......... | .......... | .......... | .......... | .......... |
| 12 | .......... | .......... | .......... | .......... | .......... | .......... |
| 13 | .......... | .......... | .......... | .......... | .......... | .......... |
| 14 | .......... | .......... | .......... | .......... | .......... | .......... |
| 15 | .......... | .......... | .......... | .......... | .......... | .......... |
| 16 | .......... | .......... | .......... | .......... | .......... | .......... |
| 17 | .......... | .......... | .......... | .......... | .......... | .......... |
| 18 | .......... | .......... | .......... | .......... | .......... | .......... |
| 19 | .......... | .......... | .......... | .......... | .......... | .......... |
| 20 | .......... | .......... | .......... | .......... | .......... | .......... |
| 21 | .......... | .......... | .......... | .......... | .......... | .......... |
| 22 | .......... | .......... | .......... | .......... | .......... | .......... |
| 23 | .......... | .......... | .......... | .......... | .......... | .......... |
| 24 | .......... | .......... | .......... | .......... | .......... | .......... |
| 25 | .......... | .......... | .......... | .......... | .......... | .......... |
| 26 | .......... | .......... | .......... | .......... | .......... | .......... |
| 27 | .......... | .......... | .......... | .......... | .......... | .......... |
| 28 | .......... | .......... | .......... | .......... | .......... | .......... |
| 29 | .......... | .......... | .......... | .......... | .......... | .......... |
| 30 | .......... | .......... | .......... | .......... | .......... | .......... |

Comparative Statements Showing Separately the Expenditur[e]
Years 1910 to 1914, Inclusive, Classified b[y]

| | Total | Personal Service | Supplies |
|---|---|---|---|
| **PUBLIC SERVICE COMMISSION** | | | |
| **1910** | | | |
| Revenue Expenditures | $1,216,182 40 | $1,058,014 95 | $38,657 47 |
| Corporate Stock Expenditures | 6,450,073 03 | 16,262 77 | 21 79 |
| Total for 1910 | **$7,666,255 43** | **$1,074,277 72** | **$38,679 26** |
| **1911** | | | |
| Revenue Expenditures | $1,100,460 87 | $884,012 25 | $12,089 61 |
| Corporate Stock Expenditures | 10,471,740 14 | 96,451 59 | 9 00 |
| Total for 1911 | **$11,572,201 01** | **$980,463 84** | **$12,098 61** |
| **1912** | | | |
| Revenue Expenditures | $1,358,503 02 | $1,126,046 41 | $49,244 52 |
| Corporate Stock Expenditures | 11,895,361 10 | 40,565 54 | 570 70 |
| Total for 1912 | **$13,253,864 12** | **$1,166,611 95** | **$49,815 22** |
| **1913** | | | |
| Revenue Expenditures | $1,863,161 32 | $1,634,195 29 | $77,768 25 |
| Corporate Stock Expenditures | 20,187,326 34 | 3,451 31 | 9 00 |
| Total for 1913 | **$22,050,487 66** | **$1,637,646 60** | **$77,777 25** |
| **1914** | | | |
| Revenue Expenditures | $2,925,921 03 | $2,473,742 65 | $170,247 74 |
| Corporate Stock Expenditures | 23,513,762 67 | .......... | .......... |
| Total for 1914 | **$26,439,683 70** | **$2,473,742 65** | **$170,247 74** |
| **WATER POLLUTION COMMISSION** | | | |
| **1910** | | | |
| Revenue Expenditures | .......... | .......... | .......... |
| Corporate Stock Expenditures | $1,414 40 | .......... | .......... |
| Total for 1910 | **$1,414 40** | .......... | .......... |
| **1911** | | | |
| Revenue Expenditures | .......... | .......... | .......... |
| Corporate Stock Expenditures | .......... | .......... | .......... |
| Total for 1911 | .......... | .......... | .......... |
| **1912** | | | |
| Revenue Expenditures | .......... | .......... | .......... |
| Corporate Stock Expenditures | .......... | .......... | .......... |
| Total for 1912 | .......... | .......... | .......... |
| **1913** | | | |
| Revenue Expenditures | .......... | .......... | .......... |
| Corporate Stock Expenditures | .......... | .......... | .......... |
| Total for 1913 | .......... | .......... | .......... |
| **1914** | | | |
| Revenue Expenditures | .......... | .......... | .......... |
| Corporate Stock Expenditures | .......... | .......... | .......... |
| Total for 1914 | .......... | .......... | .......... |

NEW YORK

MADE FROM REVENUE AND FROM CORPORATE STOCK FUNDS FOR THE DEPARTMENTS, ACCORDING TO OBJECTS OF EXPENDITURE:

| LINE No. | Purchase of Equipment | Materials | Contract or Open Order Service | Contingencies | Fixed Charges and Contributions | Unclassified |
|---|---|---|---|---|---|---|
| 1 | $13,827 79 | .......... | $38,410 32 | .......... | $60,088 52 | $7,183 35 |
| 2 | .......... | .......... | 6,192,708 45 | $8,495 48 | .......... | 232,584 54 |
| 3 | **$13,827 79** | .......... | **$6,231,118 77** | **$8,495 48** | **$60,088 52** | **$239,767 89** |
| 4 | $11,932 45 | .......... | $110,909 29 | .......... | $70,548 11 | $10,969 16 |
| 5 | 361 48 | .......... | 8,445,288 01 | $26 70 | .......... | 1,929,603 36 |
| 6 | **$12,293 93** | .......... | **$8,556,197 30** | **$26 70** | **$70,548 11** | **$1,940,572 52** |
| 7 | $11,071 64 | .......... | $90,375 99 | .......... | $72,729 85 | $9,034 61 |
| 8 | 16 00 | $19,112 61 | 9,982,040 22 | $37 92 | .......... | 1,853,018 11 |
| 9 | **$11,087 64** | **$19,112 61** | **$10,072,416 21** | **$37 92** | **$72,729 85** | **$1,862,052 72** |
| 10 | $24,120 35 | .......... | $35,211 38 | .......... | $79,743 56 | $12,122 49 |
| 11 | 33 74 | .......... | 15,105,799 62 | .......... | .......... | 5,078,032 67 |
| 12 | **$24,154 09** | .......... | **$15,141,011 00** | .......... | **$79,743 56** | **$5,090,155 16** |
| 13 | $85,640 84 | .......... | $28,597 09 | .......... | $146,947 99 | $20,744 72 |
| 14 | .......... | .......... | 19,759,039 11 | $308 10 | .......... | 3,754,415 46 |
| 15 | **$85,640 84** | .......... | **$19,787,636 20** | **$308 10** | **$146,947 99** | **$3,775,160 18** |
| 16 | .......... | .......... | .......... | .......... | .......... | .......... |
| 17 | .......... | .......... | $1,414 40 | .......... | .......... | .......... |
| 18 | .......... | .......... | **$1,414 40** | .......... | .......... | .......... |
| 19 | .......... | .......... | .......... | .......... | .......... | .......... |
| 20 | .......... | .......... | .......... | .......... | .......... | .......... |
| 21 | .......... | .......... | .......... | .......... | .......... | .......... |
| 22 | .......... | .......... | .......... | .......... | .......... | .......... |
| 23 | .......... | .......... | .......... | .......... | .......... | .......... |
| 24 | .......... | .......... | .......... | .......... | .......... | .......... |
| 25 | .......... | .......... | .......... | .......... | .......... | .......... |
| 26 | .......... | .......... | .......... | .......... | .......... | .......... |
| 27 | .......... | .......... | .......... | .......... | .......... | .......... |
| 28 | .......... | .......... | .......... | .......... | .......... | .......... |
| 29 | .......... | .......... | .......... | .......... | .......... | .......... |
| 30 | .......... | .......... | .......... | .......... | .......... | .......... |

COMPARATIVE STATEMENTS SHOWING SEPARATELY THE EXPENDITURES
YEARS 1910 TO 1914, INCLUSIVE, CLASSIFIED BY

| | Total | Personal Service | Supplies | LINE No. |
|---|---|---|---|---|
| **ARMORY BOARD** | | | | |
| **1910** | | | | |
| Revenue Expenditures | $105,358 41 | $12,386 00 | .......... | 1 |
| Corporate Stock Expenditures | 531,122 80 | .......... | .......... | 2 |
| Total for 1910 | **$636,481 21** | **$12,386 00** | .......... | 3 |
| **1911** | | | | |
| Revenue Expenditures | $142,059 70 | $15,026 29 | $13,434 22 | 4 |
| Corporate Stock Expenditures | 337,476 23 | .......... | .......... | 5 |
| Total for 1911 | **$479,535 93** | **$15,026 29** | **$13,434 22** | 6 |
| **1912** | | | | |
| Revenue Expenditures | $294,708 60 | $27,700 83 | $64,365 16 | 7 |
| Corporate Stock Expenditures | 428,971 91 | .......... | .......... | 8 |
| Total for 1912 | **$723,680 51** | **$27,700 83** | **$64,365 16** | 9 |
| **1913** | | | | |
| Revenue Expenditures | $250,083 46 | $36,154 28 | $23,172 47 | 10 |
| Corporate Stock Expenditures | 570,620 05 | .......... | 994 50 | 11 |
| Total for 1913 | **$820,703 51** | **$36,154 28** | **$24,166 97** | 12 |
| **1914** | | | | |
| Revenue Expenditures | $244,277 79 | $39,662 26 | $33,155 06 | 13 |
| Corporate Stock Expenditures | 514,203 36 | .......... | 372 75 | 14 |
| Total for 1914 | **$758,481 15** | **$39,662 26** | **$33,527 81** | 15 |
| **BOARD OF CITY RECORD, CITY OF NEW YORK** | | | | |
| **1910** | | | | |
| Revenue Expenditures | $1,084,596 62 | $35,780 03 | $11,214 85 | 16 |
| Corporate Stock Expenditures | .......... | .......... | .......... | 17 |
| Total for 1910 | **$1,084,596 62** | **$35,780 03** | **$11,214 85** | 18 |
| **1911** | | | | |
| Revenue Expenditures | $828,534 54 | $39,623 55 | $2,099 04 | 19 |
| Corporate Stock Expenditures | .......... | .......... | .......... | 20 |
| Total for 1911 | **$828,534 54** | **$39,623 55** | **$2,099 04** | 21 |
| **1912** | | | | |
| Revenue Expenditures | $865,849 77 | $43,022 77 | $608 07 | 22 |
| Corporate Stock Expenditures | .......... | .......... | .......... | 23 |
| Total for 1912 | **$865,849 77** | **$43,022 77** | **$608 07** | 24 |
| **1913** | | | | |
| Revenue Expenditures | $920,152 39 | $44,641 27 | $1,098 42 | 25 |
| Corporate Stock Expenditures | .......... | .......... | .......... | 26 |
| Total for 1913 | **$920,152 39** | **$44,641 27** | **$1,098 42** | 27 |
| **1914** | | | | |
| Revenue Expenditures | $915,646 16 | $47,137 96 | $1,556 88 | 28 |
| Corporate Stock Expenditures | .......... | .......... | .......... | 29 |
| Total for 1914 | **$915,646 16** | **$47,137 96** | **$1,556 88** | 30 |

## NEW YORK

Made from Revenue and from Corporate Stock Funds for the Departments, According to Objects of Expenditure:

| Line No. | Purchase of Equipment | Materials | Contract or Open Order Service | Contingencies | Fixed Charges and Contributions | Unclassified |
|---|---|---|---|---|---|---|
| 1 | .......... | .......... | $91,244 55 | $1,727 86 | .......... | .......... |
| 2 | $2,316 36 | .......... | 485,198 94 | .......... | .......... | $43,607 50 |
| 3 | **$2,316 36** | .......... | **$576,443 49** | **$1,727 86** | .......... | **$43,607 50** |
| 4 | $26,148 51 | .......... | $85,277 87 | $2,172 81 | .......... | .......... |
| 5 | 17,348 10 | .......... | 312,602 54 | .......... | .......... | $7,525 59 |
| 6 | **$43,496 61** | .......... | **$397,880 41** | **$2,172 81** | .......... | **$7,525 59** |
| 7 | $3,291 92 | .......... | $198,179 04 | $1,171 65 | .......... | .......... |
| 8 | 11,184 64 | .......... | 417,530 63 | 38 00 | .......... | $218 64 |
| 9 | **$14,476 56** | .......... | **$615,709 67** | **$1,209 65** | .......... | **$218 64** |
| 10 | $52,205 26 | $11,074 31 | $125,687 27 | $1,789 87 | .......... | .......... |
| 11 | 58,286 86 | .......... | 511,338 69 | .......... | .......... | .......... |
| 12 | **$110,492 12** | **$11,074 31** | **$637,025 96** | **$1,789 87** | .......... | .......... |
| 13 | $45,553 73 | $19,939 28 | $104,534 06 | $1,433 40 | .......... | .......... |
| 14 | 12,118 10 | .......... | 501,712 51 | .......... | .......... | .......... |
| 15 | **$57,671 83** | **$19,939 28** | **$606,246 57** | **$1,433 40** | .......... | .......... |
| 16 | .......... | .......... | $1,034,366 89 | $3,234 85 | .......... | .......... |
| 17 | .......... | .......... | .......... | .......... | .......... | .......... |
| 18 | .......... | .......... | **$1,034,366 89** | **$3,234 85** | .......... | .......... |
| 19 | .......... | .......... | $784,312 05 | $2,499 90 | .......... | .......... |
| 20 | .......... | .......... | .......... | .......... | .......... | .......... |
| 21 | .......... | .......... | **$784,312 05** | **$2,499 90** | .......... | .......... |
| 22 | $1,446 70 | .......... | $815,063 39 | $5,708 84 | .......... | .......... |
| 23 | .......... | .......... | .......... | .......... | .......... | .......... |
| 24 | **$1,446 70** | .......... | **$815,063 39** | **$5,708 84** | .......... | .......... |
| 25 | $2,274 91 | .......... | $871,600 04 | $537 75 | .......... | .......... |
| 26 | .......... | .......... | .......... | .......... | .......... | .......... |
| 27 | **$2,274 91** | .......... | **$871,600 04** | **$537 75** | .......... | .......... |
| 28 | $874 08 | .......... | $865,150 66 | $926 58 | .......... | .......... |
| 29 | .......... | .......... | .......... | .......... | .......... | .......... |
| 30 | **$874 08** | .......... | **$865,150 66** | **$926 58** | .......... | .......... |

COMPARATIVE STATEMENTS SHOWING SEPARATELY THE EXPENDITURES
YEARS 1910 TO 1914, INCLUSIVE, CLASSIFIED BY

| | Total | Personal Service | Supplies | LINE No. |
|---|---|---|---|---|
| **BOARD OF ELECTIONS** | | | | |
| **1910** | | | | |
| Revenue Expenditures | $959,889 36 | $509,251 29 | $87,686 83 | 1 |
| Corporate Stock Expenditures | .......... | .......... | .......... | 2 |
| Total for 1910 | **$959,889 36** | **$509,251 29** | **$87,686 83** | 3 |
| **1911** | | | | |
| Revenue Expenditures | $926,305 38 | $502,718 04 | $96,836 00 | 4 |
| Corporate Stock Expenditures | .......... | .......... | .......... | 5 |
| Total for 1911 | **$926,305 38** | **$502,718 04** | **$96,836 00** | 6 |
| **1912** | | | | |
| Revenue Expenditures | $1,395,828 00 | $684,356 44 | $108,132 22 | 7 |
| Corporate Stock Expenditures | .......... | .......... | .......... | 8 |
| Total for 1912 | **$1,395,828 00** | **$684,356 44** | **$108,132 22** | 9 |
| **1913** | | | | |
| Revenue Expenditures | $1,186,804 05 | $601,168 37 | $271,501 71 | 10 |
| Corporate Stock Expenditures | .......... | .......... | .......... | 11 |
| Total for 1913 | **$1,186,804 05** | **$601,168 37** | **$271,501 71** | 12 |
| **1914** | | | | |
| Revenue Expenditures | $1,492,016 88 | $918,656 08 | $210,664 17 | 13 |
| Corporate Stock Expenditures | .......... | .......... | .......... | 14 |
| Total for 1914 | **$1,492,016 88** | **$918,656 08** | **$210,664 17** | 15 |
| **BOARD OF ESTIMATE AND APPORTIONMENT** | | | | |
| **1910** | | | | |
| Revenue Expenditures | $153,229 71 | $120,686 54 | .......... | 16 |
| Corporate Stock Expenditures | .......... | .......... | .......... | 17 |
| Total for 1910 | **$153,229 71** | **$120,686 54** | .......... | 18 |
| **1911** | | | | |
| Revenue Expenditures | $176,965 32 | $164,358 84 | $518 16 | 19 |
| Corporate Stock Expenditures | .......... | .......... | .......... | 20 |
| Total for 1911 | **$176,965 32** | **$164,358 84** | **$518 16** | 21 |
| **1912** | | | | |
| Revenue Expenditures | $286,618 15 | $234,513 10 | $8,999 55 | 22 |
| Corporate Stock Expenditures | .......... | .......... | .......... | 23 |
| Total for 1912 | **$286,618 15** | **$234,513 10** | **$8,999 55** | 24 |
| **1913** | | | | |
| Revenue Expenditures | $414,760 32 | $287,043 07 | $4,032 27 | 25 |
| Corporate Stock Expenditures | .......... | .......... | .......... | 26 |
| Total for 1913 | **$414,760 32** | **$287,043 07** | **$4,032 27** | 27 |
| **1914** | | | | |
| Revenue Expenditures | $539,204 70 | $428,687 26 | $2,170 76 | 28 |
| Corporate Stock Expenditures | .......... | .......... | .......... | 29 |
| Total for 1914 | **$539,204 70** | **$428,687 26** | **$2,170 76** | 30 |

# NEW YORK

MADE FROM REVENUE AND FROM CORPORATE STOCK FUNDS FOR THE DEPARTMENTS, ACCORDING TO OBJECTS OF EXPENDITURE:

| LINE No. | Purchase of Equipment | Materials | Contract or Open Order Service | Contingencies | Fixed Charges and Contributions | Unclassified |
|---|---|---|---|---|---|---|
| 1 | $135 90 | .......... | $41,584 13 | $6,460 47 | $314,770 74 | .......... |
| 2 | .......... | .......... | .......... | .......... | .......... | .......... |
| 3 | **$135 90** | .......... | **$41,584 13** | **$6,460 47** | **$314,770 74** | .......... |
| 4 | $988 89 | .......... | $28,704 23 | $5,009 63 | $292,048 59 | .......... |
| 5 | .......... | .......... | .......... | .......... | .......... | .......... |
| 6 | **$988 89** | .......... | **$28,704 23** | **$5,009 63** | **$292,048 59** | .......... |
| 7 | $1,376 70 | .......... | $253,030 02 | $5,239 86 | $343,692 76 | .......... |
| 8 | .......... | .......... | .......... | .......... | .......... | .......... |
| 9 | **$1,376 70** | .......... | **$253,030 02** | **$5,239 86** | **$343,692 76** | .......... |
| 10 | $5,055 43 | .......... | $39,649 26 | $7 85 | $269,421 43 | .......... |
| 11 | .......... | .......... | .......... | .......... | .......... | .......... |
| 12 | **$5,055 43** | .......... | **$39,649 26** | **$7 85** | **$269,421 43** | .......... |
| 13 | $1,602 53 | .......... | $42,095 48 | $4,526 00 | $314,472 62 | .......... |
| 14 | .......... | .......... | .......... | .......... | .......... | .......... |
| 15 | **$1,602 53** | .......... | **$42,095 48** | **$4,526 00** | **$314,472 62** | .......... |
| 16 | .......... | .......... | .......... | $32,543 17 | .......... | .......... |
| 17 | .......... | .......... | .......... | .......... | .......... | .......... |
| 18 | .......... | .......... | .......... | **$32,543 17** | .......... | .......... |
| 19 | $3,262 46 | .......... | $3,768 62 | $5,057 24 | .......... | .......... |
| 20 | .......... | .......... | .......... | .......... | .......... | .......... |
| 21 | **$3,262 46** | .......... | **$3,768 62** | **$5,057 24** | .......... | .......... |
| 22 | .......... | .......... | $91 98 | $43,013 52 | .......... | .......... |
| 23 | .......... | .......... | .......... | .......... | .......... | .......... |
| 24 | .......... | .......... | **$91 98** | **$43,013 52** | .......... | .......... |
| 25 | $11,550 91 | .......... | $1,190 02 | $110,944 05 | .......... | .......... |
| 26 | .......... | .......... | .......... | .......... | .......... | .......... |
| 27 | **$11,550 91** | .......... | **$1,190 02** | **$110,944 05** | .......... | .......... |
| 28 | $9,111 61 | .......... | $1,708 33 | $93,157 69 | $4,369 05 | .......... |
| 29 | .......... | .......... | .......... | .......... | .......... | .......... |
| 30 | **$9,111 61** | .......... | **$1,708 33** | **$93,157 69** | **$4,369 05** | .......... |

Comparative Statements Showing Separately the Expenditures
Years 1910 to 1914, Inclusive, Classified by

| | Total | Personal Service | Supplies | Line No. |
|---|---|---|---|---|
| **BOARD OF REVISION OF ASSESSMENTS** | | | | |
| **1910** | | | | |
| Revenue Expenditures | .......... | .......... | .......... | 1 |
| Corporate Stock Expenditures | .......... | .......... | .......... | 2 |
| Total for 1910 | .......... | .......... | .......... | 3 |
| **1911** | | | | |
| Revenue Expenditures | $104 75 | .......... | $2 82 | 4 |
| Corporate Stock Expenditures | .......... | .......... | .......... | 5 |
| Total for 1911 | **$104 75** | .......... | **$2 82** | 6 |
| **1912** | | | | |
| Revenue Expenditures | .......... | .......... | .......... | 7 |
| Corporate Stock Expenditures | .......... | .......... | .......... | 8 |
| Total for 1912 | .......... | .......... | .......... | 9 |
| **1913** | | | | |
| Revenue Expenditures | .......... | .......... | .......... | 10 |
| Corporate Stock Expenditures | .......... | .......... | .......... | 11 |
| Total for 1913 | .......... | .......... | .......... | 12 |
| **1914** | | | | |
| Revenue Expenditures | $88 00 | .......... | .......... | 13 |
| Corporate Stock Expenditures | .......... | .......... | .......... | 14 |
| Total for 1914 | **$88 00** | .......... | .......... | 15 |
| **COMMISSIONERS OF THE SINKING FUND** | | | | |
| **1910** | | | | |
| Revenue Expenditures | $3,254 25 | $3,050 00 | .......... | 16 |
| Corporate Stock Expenditures | .......... | .......... | .......... | 17 |
| Total for 1910 | **$3,254 25** | **$3,050 00** | .......... | 18 |
| **1911** | | | | |
| Revenue Expenditures | $3,199 30 | $3,050 00 | $70 00 | 19 |
| Corporate Stock Expenditures | .......... | .......... | .......... | 20 |
| Total for 1911 | **$3,199 30** | **$3,050 00** | **$70 00** | 21 |
| **1912** | | | | |
| Revenue Expenditures | $7,013 61 | $3,050 00 | .......... | 22 |
| Corporate Stock Expenditures | .......... | .......... | .......... | 23 |
| Total for 1912 | **$7,013 61** | **$3,050 00** | .......... | 24 |
| **1913** | | | | |
| Revenue Expenditures | $3,827 75 | $3,300 00 | .......... | 25 |
| Corporate Stock Expenditures | .......... | .......... | .......... | 26 |
| Total for 1913 | **$3,827 75** | **$3,300 00** | .......... | 27 |
| **1914** | | | | |
| Revenue Expenditures | $3,561 93 | $3,300 00 | .......... | 28 |
| Corporate Stock Expenditures | .......... | .......... | .......... | 29 |
| Total for 1914 | **$3,561 93** | **$3,300 00** | .......... | 30 |

NEW YORK

MADE FROM REVENUE AND FROM CORPORATE STOCK FUNDS FOR THE DEPARTMENTS, ACCORDING TO OBJECTS OF EXPENDITURE:

| LINE No. | Purchase of Equipment | Materials | Contract or Open Order Service | Contingencies | Fixed Charges and Contributions | Unclassified |
|---|---|---|---|---|---|---|
| 1 | | | | | | |
| 2 | | | | | | |
| 3 | | | | | | |
| 4 | $101 93 | | | | | |
| 5 | | | | | | |
| 6 | **$101 93** | | | | | |
| 7 | | | | | | |
| 8 | | | | | | |
| 9 | | | | | | |
| 10 | | | | | | |
| 11 | | | | | | |
| 12 | | | | | | |
| 13 | | | | $88 00 | | |
| 14 | | | | | | |
| 15 | | | | **$88 00** | | |
| 16 | | | | $204 25 | | |
| 17 | | | | | | |
| 18 | | | | **$204 25** | | |
| 19 | | | | $79 30 | | |
| 20 | | | | | | |
| 21 | | | | **$79 30** | | |
| 22 | | | $3,021 50 | $942 11 | | |
| 23 | | | | | | |
| 24 | | | **$3,021 50** | **942 11** | | |
| 25 | | | | $527 75 | | |
| 26 | | | | | | |
| 27 | | | | **$527 75** | | |
| 28 | | | | $261 93 | | |
| 29 | | | | | | |
| 30 | | | | **$261 93** | | |

COMPARATIVE STATEMENTS SHOWING SEPARATELY THE EXPENDITURES
YEARS 1910 TO 1914, INCLUSIVE, CLASSIFIED BY

| | Total | Personal Service | Supplies | LINE No. |
|---|---|---|---|---|
| **CORONERS—BOROUGH OF MANHATTAN** | | | | |
| **1910** | | | | |
| Revenue Expenditures........................ | $64,194 29 | $62,170 15 | $240 24 | 1 |
| Corporate Stock Expenditures.................. | .......... | .......... | .......... | 2 |
| Total for 1910.............................. | **$64,194 29** | **$62,170 15** | **$240 24** | 3 |
| **1911** | | | | |
| Revenue Expenditures........................ | $67,154 13 | $62,166 00 | $399 25 | 4 |
| Corporate Stock Expenditures.................. | .......... | .......... | .......... | 5 |
| Total for 1911.............................. | **$67,154 13** | **$62,166 00** | **$399 25** | 6 |
| **1912** | | | | |
| Revenue Expenditures........................ | $62,675 31 | $61,034 39 | $215 45 | 7 |
| Corporate Stock Expenditures.................. | .......... | .......... | .......... | 8 |
| Total for 1912.............................. | **$62,675 31** | **$61,034 39** | **$215 45** | 9 |
| **1913** | | | | |
| Revenue Expenditures........................ | $63,483 00 | $61,825 00 | $433 36 | 10 |
| Corporate Stock Expenditures.................. | .......... | .......... | .......... | 11 |
| Total for 1913.............................. | **$63,483 00** | **$61,825 00** | **$433 36** | 12 |
| **1914** | | | | |
| Revenue Expenditures........................ | $63,480 32 | $61,224 10 | $490 80 | 13 |
| Corporate Stock Expenditures.................. | .......... | .......... | .......... | 14 |
| Total for 1914.............................. | **$63,480 32** | **$61,224 10** | **$490 80** | 15 |
| **CORONERS—THE BRONX** | | | | |
| **1910** | | | | |
| Revenue Expenditures........................ | $29,754 98 | $28,199 62 | .......... | 16 |
| Corporate Stock Expenditures.................. | .......... | .......... | .......... | 17 |
| Total for 1910.............................. | **$29,754 98** | **$28,199 62** | .......... | 18 |
| **1911** | | | | |
| Revenue Expenditures........................ | $30,241 26 | $28,170 00 | .......... | 19 |
| Corporate Stock Expenditures.................. | .......... | .......... | .......... | 20 |
| Total for 1911.............................. | **$30,241 26** | **$28,170 00** | .......... | 21 |
| **1912** | | | | |
| Revenue Expenditures........................ | $29,985 44 | $27,184 84 | $374 87 | 22 |
| Corporate Stock Expenditures.................. | .......... | .......... | .......... | 23 |
| Total for 1912.............................. | **$29,985 44** | **$27,184 84** | **$374 87** | 24 |
| **1913** | | | | |
| Revenue Expenditures........................ | $30,559 19 | $28,200 00 | $486 78 | 25 |
| Corporate Stock Expenditures.................. | .......... | .......... | .......... | 26 |
| Total for 1913.............................. | **$30,559 19** | **$28,200 00** | **$486 78** | 27 |
| **1914** | | | | |
| Revenue Expenditures........................ | $30,315 89 | $28,399 88 | $368 56 | 28 |
| Corporate Stock Expenditures.................. | .......... | .......... | .......... | 29 |
| Total for 1914.............................. | **$30,315 89** | **$28,399 88** | **$368 56** | 30 |

NEW YORK

Made from Revenue and from Corporate Stock Funds for the Departments, According to Objects of Expenditure:

| LINE No. | Purchase of Equipment | Materials | Contract or Open Order Service | Contingencies | Fixed Charges and Contributions | Unclassified |
|---|---|---|---|---|---|---|
| 1 | .......... | .......... | $776 72 | $1,007 18 | .......... | .......... |
| 2 | .......... | .......... | .......... | .......... | .......... | .......... |
| 3 | .......... | .......... | **$776 72** | **$1,007 18** | .......... | .......... |
| 4 | $3,082 45 | .......... | $919 80 | $586 63 | .......... | .......... |
| 5 | .......... | .......... | .......... | .......... | .......... | .......... |
| 6 | **$3,082 45** | .......... | **$919 80** | **$586 63** | .......... | .......... |
| 7 | .......... | .......... | $956 54 | $468 93 | .......... | .......... |
| 8 | .......... | .......... | .......... | .......... | .......... | .......... |
| 9 | .......... | .......... | **$956 54** | **$468 93** | .......... | .......... |
| 10 | .......... | .......... | $1,224 64 | .......... | .......... | .......... |
| 11 | .......... | .......... | .......... | .......... | .......... | .......... |
| 12 | .......... | .......... | **$1,224 64** | .......... | .......... | .......... |
| 13 | .......... | .......... | $1,760 17 | $5 25 | .......... | .......... |
| 14 | .......... | .......... | .......... | .......... | .......... | .......... |
| 15 | .......... | .......... | **$1,760 17** | **$5 25** | .......... | .......... |
| 16 | .......... | .......... | $951 50 | $603 86 | .......... | .......... |
| 17 | .......... | .......... | .......... | .......... | .......... | .......... |
| 18 | .......... | .......... | **$951 50** | **$603 86** | .......... | .......... |
| 19 | .......... | .......... | $766 16 | $1,305 10 | .......... | .......... |
| 20 | .......... | .......... | .......... | .......... | .......... | .......... |
| 21 | .......... | .......... | **$766 16** | **$1,305 10** | .......... | .......... |
| 22 | $1,299 43 | .......... | $1,026 30 | $100 00 | .......... | .......... |
| 23 | .......... | .......... | .......... | .......... | .......... | .......... |
| 24 | **$1,299 43** | .......... | **$1,026 30** | **$100 00** | .......... | .......... |
| 25 | $31 00 | .......... | $1,672 81 | $168 60 | .......... | .......... |
| 26 | .......... | .......... | .......... | .......... | .......... | .......... |
| 27 | **$31 00** | .......... | **$1,672 81** | **$168 60** | .......... | .......... |
| 28 | $21 25 | .......... | $1,464 47 | $61 73 | .......... | .......... |
| 29 | .......... | .......... | .......... | .......... | .......... | .......... |
| 30 | **$21 25** | .......... | **$1,464 47** | **$61 73** | .......... | .......... |

Comparative Statements Showing Separately the Expenditures
Years 1910 to 1914, Inclusive, Classified by

| | Total | Personal Service | Supplies | Line No. |
|---|---|---|---|---|
| **CORONERS—BROOKLYN** | | | | |
| **1910** | | | | |
| Revenue Expenditures | $32,989 87 | $31,840 00 | .......... | 1 |
| Corporate Stock Expenditures | .......... | .......... | .......... | 2 |
| Total for 1910 | **$32,989 87** | **$31,840 00** | .......... | 3 |
| **1911** | | | | |
| Revenue Expenditures | $36,481 41 | $33,650 00 | .......... | 4 |
| Corporate Stock Expenditures | .......... | .......... | .......... | 5 |
| Total for 1911 | **$36,481 41** | **$33,650 00** | .......... | 6 |
| **1912** | | | | |
| Revenue Expenditures | $34,578 73 | $33,550 00 | $83 95 | 7 |
| Corporate Stock Expenditures | .......... | .......... | .......... | 8 |
| Total for 1912 | **$34,578 73** | **$33,550 00** | **$83 95** | 9 |
| **1913** | | | | |
| Revenue Expenditures | $35,323 71 | $33,875 00 | $240 87 | 10 |
| Corporate Stock Expenditures | .......... | .......... | .......... | 11 |
| Total for 1913 | **$35,323 71** | **$33,875 00** | **$240 87** | 12 |
| **1914** | | | | |
| Revenue Expenditures | $31,362 53 | $30,518 27 | $164 38 | 13 |
| Corporate Stock Expenditures | .......... | .......... | .......... | 14 |
| Total for 1914 | **$31,362 53** | **$30,518 27** | **$164 38** | 15 |
| **CORONERS—QUEENS** | | | | |
| **1910** | | | | |
| Revenue Expenditures | $19,154 66 | $17,325 51 | .......... | 16 |
| Corporate Stock Expenditures | .......... | .......... | .......... | 17 |
| Total for 1910 | **$19,154 66** | **$17,325 51** | .......... | 18 |
| **1911** | | | | |
| Revenue Expenditures | $18,660 55 | $16,783 33 | .......... | 19 |
| Corporate Stock Expenditures | .......... | .......... | .......... | 20 |
| Total for 1911 | **$18,660 55** | **$16,783 33** | .......... | 21 |
| **1912** | | | | |
| Revenue Expenditures | $19,422 59 | $18,025 00 | $94 95 | 22 |
| Corporate Stock Expenditures | .......... | .......... | .......... | 23 |
| Total for 1912 | **$19,422 59** | **$18,025 00** | **$94 95** | 24 |
| **1913** | | | | |
| Revenue Expenditures | $19,903 22 | $18,325 00 | $48 20 | 25 |
| Corporate Stock Expenditures | .......... | .......... | .......... | 26 |
| Total for 1913 | **$19,903 22** | **$18,325 00** | **$48 20** | 27 |
| **1914** | | | | |
| Revenue Expenditures | $19,951 82 | $18,990 00 | .......... | 28 |
| Corporate Stock Expenditures | .......... | .......... | .......... | 29 |
| Total for 1914 | **$19,951 82** | **$18,990 00** | .......... | 30 |

# NEW YORK

MADE FROM REVENUE AND FROM CORPORATE STOCK FUNDS FOR THE DEPARTMENTS, ACCORDING TO OBJECTS OF EXPENDITURE:

| LINE No. | Purchase of Equipment | Materials | Contract or Open Order Service | Contingencies | Fixed Charges and Contributions | Unclassified |
|---|---|---|---|---|---|---|
| 1 | .......... | .......... | $318 08 | $831 79 | .......... | .......... |
| 2 | .......... | .......... | .......... | .......... | .......... | .......... |
| 3 | .......... | .......... | **$318 08** | **$831 79** | .......... | .......... |
| 4 | $820 63 | .......... | $1,010 78 | $1,000 00 | .......... | .......... |
| 5 | .......... | .......... | .......... | .......... | .......... | .......... |
| 6 | **$820 63** | .......... | **$1,010 78** | **$1,000 00** | .......... | .......... |
| 7 | $373 05 | .......... | $286 73 | $285 00 | .......... | .......... |
| 8 | .......... | .......... | .......... | .......... | .......... | .......... |
| 9 | **$373 05** | .......... | **$286 73** | **$285 00** | .......... | .......... |
| 10 | $330 00 | .......... | $646 84 | $231 00 | .......... | .......... |
| 11 | .......... | .......... | .......... | .......... | .......... | .......... |
| 12 | **$330 00** | .......... | **$646 84** | **$231 00** | .......... | .......... |
| 13 | $45 38 | .......... | $587 56 | $46 94 | .......... | .......... |
| 14 | .......... | .......... | .......... | .......... | .......... | .......... |
| 15 | **$45 38** | .......... | **$587 56** | **$46 94** | .......... | .......... |
| 16 | .......... | .......... | $306 08 | $1,523 07 | .......... | .......... |
| 17 | .......... | .......... | .......... | .......... | .......... | .......... |
| 18 | .......... | .......... | **$306 08** | **$1,523 07** | .......... | .......... |
| 19 | .......... | .......... | $306 12 | $1,571 10 | .......... | .......... |
| 20 | .......... | .......... | .......... | .......... | .......... | .......... |
| 21 | .......... | .......... | **$306 12** | **$1,571 10** | .......... | .......... |
| 22 | .......... | .......... | $323 31 | $979 33 | .......... | .......... |
| 23 | .......... | .......... | .......... | .......... | .......... | .......... |
| 24 | .......... | .......... | **$323 31** | **$979 33** | .......... | .......... |
| 25 | $50 00 | .......... | $1,480 02 | .......... | .......... | .......... |
| 26 | .......... | .......... | .......... | .......... | .......... | .......... |
| 27 | **$50 00** | .......... | **$1,480 02** | .......... | .......... | .......... |
| 28 | .......... | .......... | $896 87 | $64 95 | .......... | .......... |
| 29 | .......... | .......... | .......... | .......... | .......... | .......... |
| 30 | .......... | .......... | **$896 87** | **$64 95** | .......... | .......... |

COMPARATIVE STATEMENTS SHOWING SEPARATELY THE EXPENDITURES
YEARS 1910 TO 1914, INCLUSIVE, CLASSIFIED BY

| | Total | Personal Service | Supplies | LINE No. |
|---|---|---|---|---|
| **CORONERS—RICHMOND** | | | | |
| **1910** | | | | |
| Revenue Expenditures | $12,151 79 | $11,200 00 | $119 35 | 1 |
| Corporate Stock Expenditures | .......... | .......... | .......... | 2 |
| Total for 1910 | **$12,151 79** | **$11,200 00** | **$119 35** | 3 |
| **1911** | | | | |
| Revenue Expenditures | $12,134 37 | $11,245 00 | .......... | 4 |
| Corporate Stock Expenditures | .......... | .......... | .......... | 5 |
| Total for 1911 | **$12,134 37** | **$11,245 00** | .......... | 6 |
| **1912** | | | | |
| Revenue Expenditures | $12,090 52 | $11,200 00 | $117 60 | 7 |
| Corporate Stock Expenditures | .......... | .......... | .......... | 8 |
| Total for 1912 | **$12,090 52** | **$11,200 00** | **$117 60** | 9 |
| **1913** | | | | |
| Revenue Expenditures | $12,077 89 | $11,210 00 | $116 65 | 10 |
| Corporate Stock Expenditures | .......... | .......... | .......... | 11 |
| Total for 1913 | **$12,077 89** | **$11,210 00** | **$116 65** | 12 |
| **1914** | | | | |
| Revenue Expenditures | $12,054 59 | $11,210 00 | .......... | 13 |
| Corporate Stock Expenditures | .......... | .......... | .......... | 14 |
| Total for 1914 | **$12,054 59** | **$11,210 00** | .......... | 15 |
| **THE CITY COURT OF NEW YORK** | | | | |
| **1910** | | | | |
| Revenue Expenditures | $233,768 20 | $232,000 00 | .......... | 16 |
| Corporate Stock Expenditures | .......... | .......... | .......... | 17 |
| Total for 1910 | **$233,768 20** | **$232,000 00** | .......... | 18 |
| **1911** | | | | |
| Revenue Expenditures | $235,537 60 | $233,193 14 | .......... | 19 |
| Corporate Stock Expenditures | .......... | .......... | .......... | 20 |
| Total for 1911 | **$235,537 60** | **$233,193 14** | .......... | 21 |
| **1912** | | | | |
| Revenue Expenditures | $246,774 69 | $240,916 94 | $3,492 65 | 22 |
| Corporate Stock Expenditures | .......... | .......... | .......... | 23 |
| Total for 1912 | **$246,774 69** | **$240,916 94** | **$3,492 65** | 24 |
| **1913** | | | | |
| Revenue Expenditures | $254,862 24 | $251,631 39 | $839 20 | 25 |
| Corporate Stock Expenditures | .......... | .......... | .......... | 26 |
| Total for 1913 | **$254,862 24** | **$251,631 39** | **$839 20** | 27 |
| **1914** | | | | |
| Revenue Expenditures | $255,754 63 | $252,096 00 | $667 23 | 28 |
| Corporate Stock Expenditures | .......... | .......... | .......... | 29 |
| Total for 1914 | **$255,754 63** | **$252,096 00** | **$667 23** | 30 |

NEW YORK

MADE FROM REVENUE AND FROM CORPORATE STOCK FUNDS FOR THE DEPARTMENTS, ACCORDING TO OBJECTS OF EXPENDITURE:

| LINE No. | Purchase of Equipment | Materials | Contract or Open Order Service | Contingencies | Fixed Charges and Contributions | Unclassified |
|---|---|---|---|---|---|---|
| 1 | .......... | .......... | $177 16 | $655 28 | .......... | .......... |
| 2 | .......... | .......... | .......... | .......... | .......... | .......... |
| 3 | .......... | .......... | **$177 16** | **$655 28** | .......... | .......... |
| 4 | .......... | .......... | $168 18 | $721 19 | .......... | .......... |
| 5 | .......... | .......... | .......... | .......... | .......... | .......... |
| 6 | .......... | .......... | **$168 18** | **$721 19** | .......... | .......... |
| 7 | .......... | .......... | $469 97 | $302 95 | .......... | .......... |
| 8 | .......... | .......... | .......... | .......... | .......... | .......... |
| 9 | .......... | .......... | **$469 97** | **$302 95** | .......... | .......... |
| 10 | .......... | .......... | $751 24 | .......... | .......... | .......... |
| 11 | .......... | .......... | .......... | .......... | .......... | .......... |
| 12 | .......... | .......... | $751 24 | .......... | .......... | .......... |
| 13 | .......... | .......... | $677 59 | $167 00 | .......... | .......... |
| 14 | .......... | .......... | .......... | .......... | .......... | .......... |
| 15 | .......... | .......... | **$677 59** | **$167 00** | .......... | .......... |
| 16 | .......... | .......... | $291 75 | $1,476 45 | .......... | .......... |
| 17 | .......... | .......... | .......... | .......... | .......... | .......... |
| 18 | .......... | .......... | **$291 75** | **$1,476 45** | .......... | .......... |
| 19 | .......... | .......... | $321 77 | $2,022 09 | .......... | .......... |
| 20 | .......... | .......... | .......... | .......... | .......... | .......... |
| 21 | .......... | .......... | **$321 77** | **$2,022 69** | .......... | .......... |
| 22 | .......... | .......... | $311 57 | $2,053 53 | .......... | .......... |
| 23 | .......... | .......... | .......... | .......... | .......... | .......... |
| 24 | .......... | .......... | **$311 57** | **$2,053 53** | .......... | .......... |
| 25 | $1,873 97 | .......... | $517 68 | .......... | .......... | .......... |
| 26 | .......... | .......... | .......... | .......... | .......... | .......... |
| 27 | **$1,873 97** | .......... | **$517 68** | .......... | .......... | .......... |
| 28 | $2,418 17 | .......... | $572 53 | .70 | .......... | .......... |
| 29 | .......... | .......... | .......... | .......... | .......... | .......... |
| 30 | **$2,418 17** | .......... | **$572 53** | .70 | .......... | .......... |

COMPARATIVE STATEMENTS SHOWING SEPARATELY THE EXPENDITURES
YEARS 1910 TO 1914, INCLUSIVE, CLASSIFIED BY

| | Total | Personal Service | Supplies | LINE No. |
|---|---|---|---|---|
| **CITY MAGISTRATES' COURT, FIRST DIVISION** | | | | |
| **1910** | | | | |
| Revenue Expenditures | $291,653 25 | $287,139 53 | $2,031 74 | 1 |
| Corporate Stock Expenditures | .......... | .......... | .......... | 2 |
| Total for 1910 | **$291,653 25** | **$287,139 53** | **$2,031 74** | 3 |
| **1911** | | | | |
| Revenue Expenditures | $373,843 38 | $362,987 51 | $2,312 21 | 4 |
| Corporate Stock Expenditures | .......... | .......... | .......... | 5 |
| Total for 1911 | **$373,843 38** | **$362,987 51** | **$2,312 21** | 6 |
| **1912** | | | | |
| Revenue Expenditures | $381,949 84 | $373,338 19 | $3,331 28 | 7 |
| Corporate Stock Expenditures | .......... | .......... | .......... | 8 |
| Total for 1912 | **$381,949 84** | **$373,338 19** | **$3,331 28** | 9 |
| **1913** | | | | |
| Revenue Expenditures | $414,332 59 | $400,064 75 | $3,499 86 | 10 |
| Corporate Stock Expenditures | .......... | .......... | .......... | 11 |
| Total for 1913 | **$414,332 59** | **$400,064 75** | **$3,499 86** | 12 |
| **1914** | | | | |
| Revenue Expenditures | $449,732 14 | $430,830 93 | $7,892 77 | 13 |
| Corporate Stock Expenditures | .......... | .......... | .......... | 14 |
| Total for 1914 | **$449,732 14** | **$430,830 93** | **$7,892 77** | 15 |
| **CITY MAGISTRATES' COURT, SECOND DIVISION** | | | | |
| **1910** | | | | |
| Revenue Expenditures | $250,520 43 | $245,790 74 | $650 85 | 16 |
| Corporate Stock Expenditures | .......... | .......... | .......... | 17 |
| Total for 1910 | **$250,520 43** | **$245,790 74** | **$650 85** | 18 |
| **1911** | | | | |
| Revenue Expenditures | $339,546 57 | $331,923 42 | $1,053 03 | 19 |
| Corporate Stock Expenditures | .......... | .......... | .......... | 20 |
| Total for 1911 | **$339,546 57** | **$331,923 42** | **$1,053 03** | 21 |
| **1912** | | | | |
| Revenue Expenditures | $360,562 06 | $353,420 90 | $1,476 76 | 22 |
| Corporate Stock Expenditures | .......... | .......... | .......... | 23 |
| Total for 1912 | **$360,562 06** | **$353,420 90** | **$1,476 76** | 24 |
| **1913** | | | | |
| Revenue Expenditures | $370,911 62 | $361,597 32 | $2,046 99 | 25 |
| Corporate Stock Expenditures | .......... | .......... | .......... | 26 |
| Total for 1913 | **$370,911 62** | **$361,597 32** | **$2,046 99** | 27 |
| **1914** | | | | |
| Revenue Expenditures | $388,244 52 | $379,782 05 | $1,338 25 | 28 |
| Corporate Stock Expenditures | .......... | .......... | .......... | 29 |
| Total for 1914 | **$388,244 52** | **$379,782 05** | **$1,338 25** | 30 |

NEW YORK

MADE FROM REVENUE AND FROM CORPORATE STOCK FUNDS FOR THE DEPARTMENTS, ACCORDING TO OBJECTS OF EXPENDITURE:

| LINE No. | Purchase of Equipment | Materials | Contract or Open Order Service | Contingencies | Fixed Charges and Contributions | Unclassified |
|---|---|---|---|---|---|---|
| 1 | $354 60 | .......... | $1,582 57 | $544 81 | .......... | .......... |
| 2 | .......... | .......... | .......... | .......... | .......... | .......... |
| 3 | **$354 60** | .......... | **$1,582 57** | **$544 81** | .......... | .......... |
| 4 | $5,320 06 | .......... | $2,070 56 | $1,153 04 | .......... | .......... |
| 5 | .......... | .......... | .......... | .......... | .......... | .......... |
| 6 | **$5,320 06** | .......... | **$2,070 56** | **$1,153 04** | .......... | .......... |
| 7 | $925 32 | .......... | $2,249 11 | $2,105 94 | .......... | .......... |
| 8 | .......... | .......... | .......... | .......... | .......... | .......... |
| 9 | **$925 32** | .......... | **$2,249 11** | **$2,105 94** | .......... | .......... |
| 10 | $4,311 77 | .......... | $6,456 21 | .......... | .......... | .......... |
| 11 | .......... | .......... | .......... | .......... | .......... | .......... |
| 12 | **$4,311 77** | .......... | **$6,456 21** | .......... | .......... | .......... |
| 13 | $5,801 65 | .......... | $4,943 82 | $262 97 | .......... | .......... |
| 14 | .......... | .......... | .......... | .......... | .......... | .......... |
| 15 | **$5,801 65** | .......... | **$4,943 82** | **$262 97** | .......... | .......... |
| 16 | $416 00 | .......... | $3,101 05 | $561 79 | .......... | .......... |
| 17 | .......... | .......... | .......... | .......... | .......... | .......... |
| 18 | **$416 00** | .......... | **$3,101 05** | **$561 79** | .......... | .......... |
| 19 | $2,843 76 | .......... | $2,700 67 | $1,025 69 | .......... | .......... |
| 20 | .......... | .......... | .......... | .......... | .......... | .......... |
| 21 | **$2,843 76** | .......... | **$2,700 67** | **$1,025 69** | .......... | .......... |
| 22 | $1,490 02 | .......... | $2,610 79 | $1,563 59 | .......... | .......... |
| 23 | .......... | .......... | .......... | .......... | .......... | .......... |
| 24 | **$1,490 02** | .......... | **$2,610 79** | **$1,563 59** | .......... | .......... |
| 25 | $3,582 28 | .......... | $3,685 03 | .......... | .......... | .......... |
| 26 | .......... | .......... | .......... | .......... | .......... | .......... |
| 27 | **$3,582 28** | .......... | **$3,685 03** | .......... | .......... | .......... |
| 28 | $3,253 11 | .......... | $3,846 21 | $24 90 | .......... | .......... |
| 29 | .......... | .......... | .......... | .......... | .......... | .......... |
| 30 | **$3,253 11** | .......... | **$3,846 21** | **$24 90** | .......... | .......... |

COMPARATIVE STATEMENTS SHOWING SEPARATELY THE EXPENDITURE
YEARS 1910 TO 1914, INCLUSIVE, CLASSIFIED B

| | Total | Personal Service | Supplies | LINE No |
|---|---|---|---|---|
| **MUNICIPAL COURTS, CITY OF NEW YORK** | | | | |
| **1910** | | | | |
| Revenue Expenditures | $894,695 56 | $886,793 07 | .......... | |
| Corporate Stock Expenditures | .......... | .......... | .......... | |
| Total for 1910 | **$894,695 56** | **$886,793 07** | .......... | |
| **1911** | | | | |
| Revenue Expenditures | $908,377 52 | $889,441 37 | $12 54 | |
| Corporate Stock Expenditures | .......... | .......... | .......... | |
| Total for 1911 | **$908,377 52** | **$889,441 37** | **$12 54** | |
| **1912** | | | | |
| Revenue Expenditures | $927,241 80 | $908,837 23 | $9,986 95 | |
| Corporate Stock Expenditures | .......... | .......... | .......... | |
| Total for 1912 | **$927,241 80** | **$908,837 23** | **$9,986 95** | |
| **1913** | | | | |
| Revenue Expenditures | $930,515 56 | $912,136 47 | $2,351 94 | 1 |
| Corporate Stock Expenditures | .......... | .......... | .......... | 1 |
| Total for 1913 | **$930,515 56** | **$912,136 47** | **$2,351 94** | 1 |
| **1914** | | | | |
| Revenue Expenditures | $929,492 36 | $914,210 79 | $2,321 80 | 1 |
| Corporate Stock Expenditures | .......... | .......... | .......... | 1 |
| Total for 1914 | **$929,492 36** | **$914,210 79** | **$2,321 80** | 1 |
| **COURT OF SPECIAL SESSIONS** | | | | |
| **1910** | | | | |
| Revenue Expenditures | $219,178 26 | $209,762 19 | $454 76 | 1 |
| Corporate Stock Expenditures | .......... | .......... | .......... | 1 |
| Total for 1910 | **$219,178 26** | **$209,762 19** | **$454 76** | 1 |
| **1911** | | | | |
| Revenue Expenditures | $316,909 08 | $295,386 95 | $3,842 86 | 1 |
| Corporate Stock Expenditures | .......... | .......... | .......... | 2 |
| Total for 1911 | **$316,909 08** | **$295,386 95** | **$3,842 86** | 2 |
| **1912** | | | | |
| Revenue Expenditures | $340,390 84 | $324,803 48 | $4,364 32 | 2 |
| Corporate Stock Expenditures | .......... | .......... | .......... | 2 |
| Total for 1912 | **$340,390 84** | **$324,803 48** | **$4,364 32** | 2 |
| **1913** | | | | |
| Revenue Expenditures | $373,409 79 | $361,375 71 | $2,413 52 | 2 |
| Corporate Stock Expenditures | .......... | .......... | .......... | 2 |
| Total for 1913 | **$373,409 79** | **$361,375 71** | **$2,413 52** | 2 |
| **1914** | | | | |
| Revenue Expenditures | $388,224 03 | $371,794 96 | $2,562 68 | 2 |
| Corporate Stock Expenditures | .......... | .......... | .......... | 2 |
| Total for 1914 | **$388,224 03** | **$371,794 96** | **$2,562 68** | 3 |

# NEW YORK

MADE FROM REVENUE AND FROM CORPORATE STOCK FUNDS FOR THE DEPARTMENTS, ACCORDING TO OBJECTS OF EXPENDITURE:

| Line No. | Purchase of Equipment | Materials | Contract or Open Order Service | Contingencies | Fixed Charges and Contributions | Unclassified |
|---|---|---|---|---|---|---|
| 1 | .......... | .......... | .......... | $7,902 49 | .......... | .......... |
| 2 | .......... | .......... | .......... | .......... | .......... | .......... |
| 3 | .......... | .......... | .......... | **$7,902 49** | .......... | .......... |
| 4 | $9,254 76 | .......... | $1,468 18 | $8,200 67 | .......... | .......... |
| 5 | .......... | .......... | .......... | .......... | .......... | .......... |
| 6 | **$9,254 76** | .......... | **$1,468 18** | **$8,200 67** | .......... | .......... |
| | .......... | .......... | .......... | $8,417 62 | .......... | .......... |
| | .......... | .......... | .......... | .......... | .......... | .......... |
| | .......... | .......... | .......... | **$8,417 62** | .......... | .......... |
| | $12,560 97 | .......... | $2,980 20 | $485 98 | .......... | .......... |
| | .......... | .......... | .......... | .......... | .......... | .......... |
| | **$12,560 97** | .......... | **$2,980 20** | **$485 98** | .......... | .......... |
| | $9,996 17 | .......... | $2,815 67 | $147 93 | .......... | .......... |
| | .......... | .......... | .......... | .......... | .......... | .......... |
| | **$9,996 17** | .......... | **$2,815 67** | **$147 93** | .......... | .......... |
| | $1,349 75 | .......... | $853 20 | $6,058 36 | $700 00 | .......... |
| | .......... | .......... | .......... | .......... | .......... | .......... |
| | **$1,349 75** | .......... | **$853 20** | **$6,058 36** | **$700 00** | .......... |
| | $10,952 55 | .......... | $2,094 72 | $3,407 00 | $1,225 00 | .......... |
| | .......... | .......... | .......... | .......... | .......... | .......... |
| | **$10,952 55** | .......... | **$2,094 72** | **$3,407 00** | **$1,225 00** | .......... |
| | $5,739 91 | .......... | $2,037 44 | $3,445 69 | .......... | .......... |
| | .......... | .......... | .......... | .......... | .......... | .......... |
| | **$5,739 91** | .......... | **$2,037 44** | **$3,445 69** | .......... | .......... |
| | $3,464 94 | .......... | $5,476 69 | $678 93 | .......... | .......... |
| | .......... | .......... | .......... | .......... | .......... | .......... |
| | **$3,464 94** | .......... | **$5,476 69** | **$678 93** | .......... | .......... |
| | $6,108 22 | .......... | $6,823 33 | $934 84 | .......... | .......... |
| | .......... | .......... | .......... | .......... | .......... | .......... |
| | **$6,108 22** | .......... | **$6,823 33** | **$934 84** | .......... | .......... |

COMPARATIVE STATEMENTS SHOWING SEPARATELY THE EXPENDITURES
YEARS 1910 TO 1914, INCLUSIVE, CLASSIFIED BY

| | Total | Personal Service | Supplies | LINE No. |
|---|---|---|---|---|
| **GENERAL INTERPRETERS, BROOKLYN** | | | | |
| **1910** | | | | |
| Revenue Expenditures | $10,200 00 | $10,200 00 | .......... | 1 |
| Corporate Stock Expenditures | .......... | .......... | .......... | 2 |
| Total for 1910 | **$10,200 00** | **$10,200 00** | .......... | 3 |
| **1911** | | | | |
| Revenue Expenditures | $10,200 00 | $10,200 00 | .......... | 4 |
| Corporate Stock Expenditures | .......... | .......... | .......... | 5 |
| Total for 1911 | **$10,200 00** | **$10,200 00** | .......... | 6 |
| **1912** | | | | |
| Revenue Expenditures | $9,148 27 | $9,148 27 | .......... | 7 |
| Corporate Stock Expenditures | .......... | .......... | .......... | 8 |
| Total for 1912 | **$9,148 27** | **$9,148 27** | .......... | 9 |
| **1913** | | | | |
| Revenue Expenditures | $9,000 00 | $9,000 00 | .......... | 10 |
| Corporate Stock Expenditures | .......... | .......... | .......... | 11 |
| Total for 1913 | **$9,000 00** | **$9,000 00** | .......... | 12 |
| **1914** | | | | |
| Revenue Expenditures | $8,800 00 | $8,800 00 | .......... | 13 |
| Corporate Stock Expenditures | .......... | .......... | .......... | 14 |
| Total for 1914 | **$8,800 00** | **$8,800 00** | .......... | 15 |
| **BOARD OF PAROLE** | | | | |
| **1910** | | | | |
| Revenue Expenditures | $2,967 86 | $2,800 00 | .......... | 16 |
| Corporate Stock Expenditures | .......... | .......... | .......... | 17 |
| Total for 1910 | **$2,967 86** | **$2,800 00** | .......... | 18 |
| **1911** | | | | |
| Revenue Expenditures | $2,977 20 | $2,800 75 | .......... | 19 |
| Corporate Stock Expenditures | .......... | .......... | .......... | 20 |
| Total for 1911 | **$2,977 20** | **$2,800 75** | .......... | 21 |
| **1912** | | | | |
| Revenue Expenditures | $4,230 90 | $4,031 04 | .......... | 22 |
| Corporate Stock Expenditures | .......... | .......... | .......... | 23 |
| Total for 1912 | **$4,230 90** | **$4,031 04** | .......... | 24 |
| **1913** | | | | |
| Revenue Expenditures | $8,625 00 | $8,400 00 | $40 00 | 25 |
| Corporate Stock Expenditures | .......... | .......... | .......... | 26 |
| Total for 1913 | **$8,625 00** | **$8,400 00** | **$40 00** | 27 |
| **1914** | | | | |
| Revenue Expenditures | $8,645 00 | $8,400 00 | .......... | 28 |
| Corporate Stock Expenditures | .......... | .......... | .......... | 29 |
| Total for 1914 | **$8,645 00** | **$8,400 00** | .......... | 30 |

NEW YORK

MADE FROM REVENUE AND FROM CORPORATE STOCK FUNDS FOR THE DEPARTMENTS, ACCORDING TO OBJECTS OF EXPENDITURE:

| LINE No. | Purchase of Equipment | Materials | Contract or Open Order Service | Contingencies | Fixed Charges and Contributions | Unclassified |
|---|---|---|---|---|---|---|
| 1 | .......... | .......... | .......... | .......... | .......... | .......... |
| 2 | .......... | .......... | .......... | .......... | .......... | .......... |
| 3 | .......... | .......... | .......... | .......... | .......... | .......... |
| 4 | .......... | .......... | .......... | .......... | .......... | .......... |
| 5 | .......... | .......... | .......... | .......... | .......... | .......... |
| 6 | .......... | .......... | .......... | .......... | .......... | .......... |
| 7 | .......... | .......... | .......... | .......... | .......... | .......... |
| 8 | .......... | .......... | .......... | .......... | .......... | .......... |
| 9 | .......... | .......... | .......... | .......... | .......... | .......... |
| 10 | .......... | .......... | .......... | .......... | .......... | .......... |
| 11 | .......... | .......... | .......... | .......... | .......... | .......... |
| 12 | .......... | .......... | .......... | .......... | .......... | .......... |
| 13 | .......... | .......... | .......... | .......... | .......... | .......... |
| 14 | .......... | .......... | .......... | .......... | .......... | .......... |
| 15 | .......... | .......... | .......... | .......... | .......... | .......... |
| 16 | .......... | .......... | .......... | $167 86 | .......... | .......... |
| 17 | .......... | .......... | .......... | .......... | .......... | .......... |
| 18 | .......... | .......... | .......... | **$167 86** | .......... | .......... |
| 19 | .......... | .......... | .......... | $176 45 | .......... | .......... |
| 20 | .......... | .......... | .......... | .......... | .......... | .......... |
| 21 | .......... | .......... | .......... | **$176 45** | .......... | .......... |
| 22 | .......... | .......... | .......... | $199 86 | .......... | .......... |
| 23 | .......... | .......... | .......... | .......... | .......... | .......... |
| 24 | .......... | .......... | .......... | **$199 86** | .......... | .......... |
| 25 | .......... | .......... | $184 40 | $ 60 | .......... | .......... |
| 26 | .......... | .......... | .......... | .......... | .......... | .......... |
| 27 | .......... | .......... | **$184 40** | **$ 60** | .......... | .......... |
| 28 | .......... | .......... | $200 00 | $45 00 | .......... | .......... |
| 29 | .......... | .......... | .......... | .......... | .......... | .......... |
| 30 | .......... | .......... | **$200 00** | **$45 00** | .......... | .......... |

Comparative Statements Showing Separately the Expenditures
Years 1910 to 1914, Inclusive, Classified by

Fixed Charges

| | 1910 | Line No. |
|---|---|---|
| **DEBT SERVICE** | | |
| Revenue Expenditures | | |
| * Interest on City Debt | $30,770,656 89 | 1 |
| † Redemption of City Debt, including Sinking Fund Instalments | 8,764,935 03 | 2 |
| Redemption of Special Revenue Bonds | 5,208,150 00 | 3 |
| Total | **$44,743,741 92** | 4 |

| | Total | Personal Service | Supplies | Line No. |
|---|---|---|---|---|
| **AMERICAN MUSEUM OF NATURAL HISTORY** | | | | |
| **1910** | | | | |
| Revenue Expenditures | $185,757 00 | $156,500 00 | $18,669 00 | 5 |
| Corporate Stock Expenditures | .......... | .......... | .......... | 6 |
| Total for 1910 | **$185,757 00** | **$156,500 00** | **$18,669 00** | 7 |
| **1911** | | | | |
| Revenue Expenditures | $189,757 00 | $164,000 00 | $16,919 00 | 8 |
| Corporate Stock Expenditures | .......... | .......... | .......... | 9 |
| Total for 1911 | **$189,757 00** | **$164,000 00** | **$16,919 00** | 10 |
| **1912** | | | | |
| Revenue Expenditures | $195,000 00 | $170,023 00 | $21,419 00 | 11 |
| Corporate Stock Expenditures | .......... | .......... | .......... | 12 |
| Total for 1912 | **$195,000 00** | **$170,023 00** | **$21,419 00** | 13 |
| **1913** | | | | |
| Revenue Expenditures | $200,000 00 | $178,433 57 | .......... | 14 |
| Corporate Stock Expenditures | .......... | .......... | .......... | 15 |
| Total for 1913 | **$200,000 00** | **$178,433 57** | .......... | 16 |
| **1914** | | | | |
| Revenue Expenditures | $200,000 00 | $172,849 85 | .......... | 17 |
| Corporate Stock Expenditures | .......... | .......... | .......... | 18 |
| Total for 1914 | **$200,000 00** | **$172,849 85** | .......... | 19 |

* Exclusive of Interest on City Debt paid from Sinking Fund.
† Exclusive of Redemption from Sinking Fund.

NEW YORK

MADE FROM REVENUE AND FROM CORPORATE STOCK FUNDS FOR THE DEPARTMENTS, ACCORDING TO OBJECTS OF EXPENDITURE:

and Contributions

| LINE No. | 1911 | 1912 | 1913 | 1914 |
|---|---|---|---|---|
| 1 | $33,172,303 66 | $34,477,682 19 | $37,698,934 38 | $37,329,765 08 |
| 2 | 9,113,559 90 | 9,770,527 32 | 9,796,439 16 | 8,842,856 07 |
| 3 | 7,264,625 00 | 5,970,164 92 | 7,038,065 51 | 6,319,225 00 |
| 4 | **$49,550,488 56** | **$50,218,374 43** | **$54,533,439 05** | **$52,491,846 15** |

| LINE No. | Purchase of Equipment | Materials | Contract or Open Order Service | Contingencies | Fixed Charges and Contributions | Unclassified |
|---|---|---|---|---|---|---|
| 5 | $850 00 | $6,500 00 | $1,780 00 | $1,458 00 | .......... | .......... |
| 6 | .......... | .......... | .......... | .......... | .......... | .......... |
| 7 | **$850 00** | **$6,500 00** | **$1,780 00** | **$1,458 00** | .......... | .......... |
| 8 | $1,150 00 | $4,725 00 | $1,505 00 | $1,458 00 | .......... | .......... |
| 9 | .......... | .......... | .......... | .......... | .......... | .......... |
| 10 | **$1,150 00** | **$4,725 00** | **$1,505 00** | **$1,458 00** | .......... | .......... |
| 11 | $1,150 00 | .......... | $950 00 | $1,458 00 | .......... | .......... |
| 12 | .......... | .......... | .......... | .......... | .......... | .......... |
| 13 | **$1,150 00** | .......... | **$950 00** | **$1,458 00** | .......... | .......... |
| 14 | .......... | .......... | .......... | $21,566 43 | .......... | .......... |
| 15 | .......... | .......... | .......... | .......... | .......... | .......... |
| 16 | .......... | .......... | .......... | **$21,566 43** | .......... | .......... |
| 17 | .......... | .......... | .......... | $27,150 15 | .......... | .......... |
| 18 | .......... | .......... | .......... | .......... | .......... | .......... |
| 19 | .......... | .......... | .......... | **$27,150 15** | .......... | .......... |

COMPARATIVE STATEMENTS SHOWING SEPARATELY THE EXPENDITURES
YEARS 1910 TO 1914, INCLUSIVE, CLASSIFIED BY

| | Total | Personal Service | Supplies | LINE No. |
|---|---|---|---|---|
| **BOTANICAL GARDEN AND ARBORETUM** | | | | |
| **1910** | | | | |
| Revenue Expenditures | .......... | .......... | .......... | 1 |
| Corporate Stock Expenditures | .......... | .......... | .......... | 2 |
| Total for 1910 | .......... | .......... | .......... | 3 |
| **1911** | | | | |
| Revenue Expenditures | $14,741 31 | $10,000 00 | $4,297 07 | 4 |
| Corporate Stock Expenditures | .......... | .......... | .......... | 5 |
| Total for 1911 | **$14,741 31** | **$10,000 00** | **$4,297 07** | 6 |
| **1912** | | | | |
| Revenue Expenditures | $25,782 40 | $17,135 51 | $5,125 00 | 7 |
| Corporate Stock Expenditures | .......... | .......... | .......... | 8 |
| Total for 1912 | **$25,782 40** | **$17,135 51** | **$5,125 00** | 9 |
| **1913** | | | | |
| Revenue Expenditures | $29,459 22 | $22,059 89 | $2,351 04 | 10 |
| Corporate Stock Expenditures | .......... | .......... | .......... | 11 |
| Total for 1913 | **$29,459 22** | **$22,059 89** | **$2,351 04** | 12 |
| **1914** | | | | |
| Revenue Expenditures | $37,636 08 | $28,111 67 | $4,990 89 | 13 |
| Corporate Stock Expenditures | .......... | .......... | .......... | 14 |
| Total for 1914 | **$37,636 08** | **$28,111 67** | **$4,990 89** | 15 |
| **CHARITABLE INSTITUTIONS—CITY** | | | | |
| **1910** | | | | |
| Revenue Expenditures | $4,511,647 65 | .......... | .......... | 16 |
| Corporate Stock Expenditures | .......... | .......... | .......... | 17 |
| Total for 1910 | **$4,511,647 65** | .......... | .......... | 18 |
| **1911** | | | | |
| Revenue Expenditures | $4,362,537 93 | .......... | .......... | 19 |
| Corporate Stock Expenditures | .......... | .......... | .......... | 20 |
| Total for 1911 | **$4,362,537 93** | .......... | .......... | 21 |
| **1912** | | | | |
| Revenue Expenditures | $4,431,326 77 | .......... | .......... | 22 |
| Corporate Stock Expenditures | .......... | .......... | .......... | 23 |
| Total for 1912 | **$4,431,326 77** | .......... | .......... | 24 |
| **1913** | | | | |
| Revenue Expenditures | $4,550,374 28 | .......... | .......... | 25 |
| Corporate Stock Expenditures | .......... | .......... | .......... | 26 |
| Total for 1913 | **$4,550,374 28** | .......... | .......... | 27 |
| **1914** | | | | |
| Revenue Expenditures | $5,184,610 06 | .......... | .......... | 28 |
| Corporate Stock Expenditures | .......... | .......... | .......... | 29 |
| Total for 1914 | **$5,184,610 06** | .......... | .......... | 30 |

NEW YORK

MADE FROM REVENUE AND FROM CORPORATE STOCK FUNDS FOR THE DEPARTMENTS, ACCORDING TO OBJECTS OF EXPENDITURE:

| LINE No. | Purchase of Equipment | Materials | Contract or Open Order Service | Contingencies | Fixed Charges and Contributions | Unclassified |
|---|---|---|---|---|---|---|
| 1 | .......... | .......... | .......... | .......... | .......... | .......... |
| 2 | .......... | .......... | .......... | .......... | .......... | .......... |
| 3 | .......... | .......... | .......... | .......... | .......... | .......... |
| 4 | $199 25 | .......... | $48 70 | $196 29 | .......... | .......... |
| 5 | .......... | .......... | .......... | .......... | .......... | .......... |
| 6 | **$199 25** | .......... | **$48 70** | **$196 29** | .......... | .......... |
| 7 | .......... | .......... | $2,448 93 | $1,072 96 | .......... | .......... |
| 8 | .......... | .......... | .......... | .......... | .......... | .......... |
| 9 | .......... | .......... | **$2,448 93** | **$1,072 96** | .......... | .......... |
| 10 | $2,709 01 | .......... | $2,039 34 | $299 94 | .......... | .......... |
| 11 | .......... | .......... | .......... | .......... | .......... | .......... |
| 12 | **$2,709 01** | .......... | **$2,039 34** | **$299 94** | .......... | .......... |
| 13 | $2,365 30 | $428 25 | $1,392 72 | $347 25 | .......... | .......... |
| 14 | .......... | .......... | .......... | .......... | .......... | .......... |
| 15 | **$2,365 30** | **$428 25** | **$1,392 72** | **$347 25** | .......... | .......... |
| 16 | .......... | .......... | .......... | .......... | $4,511,647 65 | .......... |
| 17 | .......... | .......... | .......... | .......... | .......... | .......... |
| 18 | .......... | .......... | .......... | .......... | **$4,511,647 65** | .......... |
| 19 | .......... | .......... | .......... | .......... | $4,362,537 93 | .......... |
| 20 | .......... | .......... | .......... | .......... | .......... | .......... |
| 21 | .......... | .......... | .......... | .......... | **$4,362,537 93** | .......... |
| 22 | .......... | .......... | .......... | .......... | $4,431,326 77 | .......... |
| 23 | .......... | .......... | .......... | .......... | .......... | .......... |
| 24 | .......... | .......... | .......... | .......... | **$4,431,326 77** | .......... |
| 25 | .......... | .......... | .......... | .......... | $4,550,374 28 | .......... |
| 26 | .......... | .......... | .......... | .......... | .......... | .......... |
| 27 | .......... | .......... | .......... | .......... | **$4,550,374 28** | .......... |
| 28 | .......... | .......... | .......... | .......... | $5,184,610 06 | .......... |
| 29 | .......... | .......... | .......... | .......... | .......... | .......... |
| 30 | .......... | .......... | .......... | .......... | **$5,184,610 06** | .......... |

COMPARATIVE STATEMENTS SHOWING SEPARATELY THE EXPENDITURES
YEARS 1910 TO 1914, INCLUSIVE, CLASSIFIED BY

| | Total | Personal Service | Supplies | LINE No. |
|---|---|---|---|---|
| **CHILDREN'S MUSEUM—BROOKLYN** | | | | |
| **1910** | | | | |
| Revenue Expenditures | $11,861 29 | $9,428 86 | $1,019 45 | 1 |
| Corporate Stock Expenditures | .......... | .......... | .......... | 2 |
| Total for 1910 | **$11,861 29** | **$9,428 86** | **$1,019 45** | 3 |
| **1911** | | | | |
| Revenue Expenditures | $11,900 39 | $9,541 88 | $1,022 53 | 4 |
| Corporate Stock Expenditures | .......... | .......... | .......... | 5 |
| Total for 1911 | **$11,900 39** | **$9,541 88** | **$1,022 53** | 6 |
| **1912** | | | | |
| Revenue Expenditures | $12,499 43 | $10,177 52 | $1,473 70 | 7 |
| Corporate Stock Expenditures | .......... | .......... | .......... | 8 |
| Total for 1912 | **$12,499 43** | **$10,177 52** | **$1,473 70** | 9 |
| **1913** | | | | |
| Revenue Expenditures | $13,121 35 | $10,208 79 | $808 93 | 10 |
| Corporate Stock Expenditures | .......... | .......... | .......... | 11 |
| Total for 1913 | **$13,121 35** | **$10,208 79** | **$808 93** | 12 |
| **1914** | | | | |
| Revenue Expenditures | $13,227 21 | $10,679 17 | .......... | 13 |
| Corporate Stock Expenditures | .......... | .......... | .......... | 14 |
| Total for 1914 | **$13,227 21** | **$10,679 17** | .......... | 15 |
| **CLAIMS** | | | | |
| **1910** | | | | |
| Revenue Expenditures | $1,780,056 75 | $48,165 03 | .......... | 16 |
| Corporate Stock Expenditures | .......... | .......... | .......... | 17 |
| Total for 1910 | **$1,780,056 75** | **$48,165 03** | .......... | 18 |
| **1911** | | | | |
| Revenue Expenditures | $287,795 36 | $50,021 31 | .......... | 19 |
| Corporate Stock Expenditures | .......... | .......... | .......... | 20 |
| Total for 1911 | **$287,795 36** | **$50,021 31** | .......... | 21 |
| **1912** | | | | |
| Revenue Expenditures | $1,582,360 56 | $95,213 67 | .......... | 22 |
| Corporate Stock Expenditures | .......... | .......... | .......... | 23 |
| Total for 1912 | **$1,582,360 56** | **$95,213 67** | .......... | 24 |
| **1913** | | | | |
| Revenue Expenditures | $1,780,061 72 | $87,632 74 | $1,168 15 | 25 |
| Corporate Stock Expenditures | .......... | .......... | .......... | 26 |
| Total for 1913 | **$1,780,061 72** | **$87,632 74** | **$1,168 15** | 27 |
| **1914** | | | | |
| Revenue Expenditures | $4,392,750 73 | $37,858 60 | .......... | 28 |
| Corporate Stock Expenditures | .......... | .......... | .......... | 29 |
| Total for 1914 | **$4,392,750 73** | **$37,858 60** | .......... | 30 |

## NEW YORK

MADE FROM REVENUE AND FROM CORPORATE STOCK FUNDS FOR THE DEPARTMENTS, ACCORDING TO OBJECTS OF EXPENDITURE:

| LINE No. | Purchase of Equipment | Materials | Contract or Open Order Service | Contingencies | Fixed Charges and Contributions | Unclassified |
|---|---|---|---|---|---|---|
| 1 | $272 76 | .......... | $594 35 | $545 87 | .......... | .......... |
| 2 | .......... | .......... | .......... | .......... | .......... | .......... |
| 3 | **$272 76** | .......... | **$594 35** | **$545 87** | .......... | .......... |
| 4 | $142 45 | .......... | $643 62 | $549 91 | .......... | .......... |
| 5 | .......... | .......... | .......... | .......... | .......... | .......... |
| 6 | **$142 45** | .......... | **$643 62** | **$549 91** | .......... | .......... |
| 7 | .......... | .......... | $551 45 | $296 76 | .......... | .......... |
| 8 | .......... | .......... | .......... | .......... | .......... | .......... |
| 9 | .......... | .......... | **$551 45** | **$296 76** | .......... | .......... |
| 10 | $303 93 | $199 87 | $1,206 38 | $339 45 | $54 00 | .......... |
| 11 | .......... | .......... | .......... | .......... | .......... | .......... |
| 12 | **$303 93** | **$199 87** | **$1,206 38** | **$339 45** | **$54 00** | .......... |
| 13 | .......... | .......... | .......... | $2,548 04 | .......... | .......... |
| 14 | .......... | .......... | .......... | .......... | .......... | .......... |
| 15 | .......... | .......... | .......... | **$2,548 04** | .......... | .......... |
| 16 | .......... | .......... | .......... | .......... | .......... | $1,731,891 72 |
| 17 | .......... | .......... | .......... | .......... | .......... | .......... |
| 18 | .......... | .......... | .......... | .......... | .......... | **$1,731,891 72** |
| 19 | .......... | .......... | .......... | .......... | .......... | $237,774 05 |
| 20 | .......... | .......... | .......... | .......... | .......... | .......... |
| 21 | .......... | .......... | .......... | .......... | .......... | **$237,774 05** |
| 22 | .......... | .......... | $28,676 50 | .......... | $357 07 | $1,458,113 32 |
| 23 | .......... | .......... | .......... | .......... | .......... | .......... |
| 24 | .......... | .......... | **$28,676 50** | .......... | **$357 07** | **$1,458,113 32** |
| 25 | .......... | $69 71 | $538,443 75 | $114 75 | $883,371 61 | $269,261 01 |
| 26 | .......... | .......... | .......... | .......... | .......... | .......... |
| 27 | .......... | **$69 71** | **$538,443 75** | **$114 75** | **$883,371 61** | **$269,261 01** |
| 28 | .......... | .......... | $55,242 20 | .......... | $4,156,484 38 | $143,165 55 |
| 29 | .......... | .......... | .......... | .......... | .......... | .......... |
| 30 | .......... | .......... | **$55,242 20** | .......... | **$4,156,484 38** | **$143,165 55** |

THE CITY OF

COMPARATIVE STATEMENTS SHOWING SEPARATELY THE EXPENDITURES
YEARS 1910 TO 1914, INCLUSIVE, CLASSIFIED BY

| | Total | Personal Service | Supplies | LINE No. |
|---|---|---|---|---|
| **EXCISE TAXES—SPECIAL ACCOUNT** | | | | |
| **1910** | | | | |
| Revenue Expenditures | $1,216,161 58 | $26,644 97 | .......... | 1 |
| Corporate Stock Expenditures | .......... | .......... | .......... | 2 |
| Total for 1910 | **$1,216,161 58** | **$26,644 97** | .......... | 3 |
| **1911** | | | | |
| Revenue Expenditures | $1,343,648 71 | $26,740 68 | .......... | 4 |
| Corporate Stock Expenditures | .......... | .......... | .......... | 5 |
| Total for 1911 | **$1,343,648 71** | **$26,740 68** | .......... | 6 |
| **1912** | | | | |
| Revenue Expenditures | $1,340,403 12 | $26,995 24 | .......... | 7 |
| Corporate Stock Expenditures | .......... | .......... | .......... | 8 |
| Total for 1912 | **$1,340,403 12** | **$26,995 24** | .......... | 9 |
| **1913** | | | | |
| Revenue Expenditures | $1,389,008 64 | $26,935 81 | .......... | 10 |
| Corporate Stock Expenditures | .......... | .......... | .......... | 11 |
| Total for 1913 | **$1,389,008 64** | **$26,935 81** | .......... | 12 |
| **1914** | | | | |
| Revenue Expenditures | $1,383,323 53 | $27,886 03 | .......... | 13 |
| Corporate Stock Expenditures | .......... | .......... | .......... | 14 |
| Total for 1914 | **$1,383,323 53** | **$27,886 03** | .......... | 15 |
| **GRANT'S TOMB** | | | | |
| **1910** | | | | |
| Revenue Expenditures | $7,000 00 | .......... | .......... | 16 |
| Corporate Stock Expenditures | .......... | .......... | .......... | 17 |
| Total for 1910 | **$7,000 00** | .......... | .......... | 18 |
| **1911** | | | | |
| Revenue Expenditures | $7,000 00 | .......... | .......... | 19 |
| Corporate Stock Expenditures | .......... | .......... | .......... | 20 |
| Total for 1911 | **$7,000 00** | .......... | .......... | 21 |
| **1912** | | | | |
| Revenue Expenditures | $6,817 15 | .......... | .......... | 22 |
| Corporate Stock Expenditures | .......... | .......... | .......... | 23 |
| Total for 1912 | **$6,817 15** | .......... | .......... | 24 |
| **1913** | | | | |
| Revenue Expenditures | $4,692 64 | .......... | .......... | 25 |
| Corporate Stock Expenditures | .......... | .......... | .......... | 26 |
| Total for 1913 | **$4,692 64** | .......... | .......... | 27 |
| **1914** | | | | |
| Revenue Expenditures | $4,927 27 | .......... | .......... | 28 |
| Corporate Stock Expenditures | .......... | .......... | .......... | 29 |
| Total for 1914 | **$4,927 27** | .......... | .......... | 30 |

NEW YORK

MADE FROM REVENUE AND FROM CORPORATE STOCK FUNDS FOR THE DEPARTMENTS, ACCORDING TO OBJECTS OF EXPENDITURE:

| LINE No. | Purchase of Equipment | Materials | Contract or Open Order Service | Contingencies | Fixed Charges and Contributions (Pensions) | Unclassified |
|---|---|---|---|---|---|---|
| 1 | ........ | ........ | ........ | ........ | $1,182,418 20 | $7,098 41 |
| 2 | ........ | ........ | ........ | ........ | ........ | ........ |
| 3 | ........ | ........ | ........ | ........ | **$1,182,418 20** | **$7,098 41** |
| 4 | ........ | ........ | ........ | ........ | $1,309,045 12 | $7,862 91 |
| 5 | ........ | ........ | ........ | ........ | ........ | ........ |
| 6 | ........ | ........ | ........ | ........ | **$1,309,045 12** | **$7,862 91** |
| 7 | ........ | ........ | ........ | ........ | $1,306,013 11 | $7,394 77 |
| 8 | ........ | ........ | ........ | ........ | ........ | ........ |
| 9 | ........ | ........ | ........ | ........ | **$1,306,013 11** | **$7,394 77** |
| 10 | ........ | ........ | ........ | ........ | $1,354,260 50 | $7,812 33 |
| 11 | ........ | ........ | ........ | ........ | ........ | ........ |
| 12 | ........ | ........ | ........ | ........ | **$1,354,260 50** | **$7,812 33** |
| 13 | ........ | ........ | ........ | ........ | $1,347,947 85 | $7,489 65 |
| 14 | ........ | ........ | ........ | ........ | ........ | ........ |
| 15 | ........ | ........ | ........ | ........ | **$1,347,947 85** | **$7,489 65** |
| 16 | ........ | ........ | $7,000 00 | ........ | ........ | ........ |
| 17 | ........ | ........ | ........ | ........ | ........ | ........ |
| 18 | ........ | ........ | **$7,000 00** | ........ | ........ | ........ |
| 19 | ........ | ........ | $7,000 00 | ........ | ........ | ........ |
| 20 | ........ | ........ | ........ | ........ | ........ | ........ |
| 21 | ........ | ........ | **$7,000 00** | ........ | ........ | ........ |
| 22 | ........ | ........ | $6,817 15 | ........ | ........ | ........ |
| 23 | ........ | ........ | ........ | ........ | ........ | ........ |
| 24 | ........ | ........ | **$6,817 15** | ........ | ........ | ........ |
| 25 | ........ | ........ | $4,692 64 | ........ | ........ | ........ |
| 26 | ........ | ........ | ........ | ........ | ........ | ........ |
| 27 | ........ | ........ | **$4,692 64** | ........ | ........ | ........ |
| 28 | ........ | ........ | $4,927 27 | ........ | ........ | ........ |
| 29 | ........ | ........ | ........ | ........ | ........ | ........ |
| 30 | ........ | ........ | **$4,927 27** | ........ | ........ | ........ |

Comparative Statements Showing Separately the Expenditures
Years 1910 to 1914, Inclusive, Classified by

| | Total | Personal Service | Supplies | Line No. |
|---|---|---|---|---|
| **JUMEL MANSION** | | | | |
| **1910** | | | | |
| Revenue Expenditures | $4,129 85 | $3,307 95 | $591 60 | 1 |
| Corporate Stock Expenditures | .......... | .......... | .......... | 2 |
| Total for 1910 | **$4,129 85** | **$3,307 95** | **$591 60** | 3 |
| **1911** | | | | |
| Revenue Expenditures | $4,487 48 | $3,629 24 | $110 73 | 4 |
| Corporate Stock Expenditures | .......... | .......... | .......... | 5 |
| Total for 1911 | **$4,487 48** | **$3,629 24** | **$110 73** | 6 |
| **1912** | | | | |
| Revenue Expenditures | $5,437 45 | $3,724 37 | $287 93 | 7 |
| Corporate Stock Expenditures | .......... | .......... | .......... | 8 |
| Total for 1912 | $5,437 45 | $3,724 37 | $287 93 | 9 |
| **1913** | | | | |
| Revenue Expenditures | $4,410 96 | $3,615 00 | $209 75 | 10 |
| Corporate Stock Expenditures | .......... | .......... | .......... | 11 |
| Total for 1913 | **$4,410 96** | **$3,615 00** | **$209 75** | 12 |
| **1914** | | | | |
| Revenue Expenditures | $4,163 21 | $3,622 50 | $253 37 | 13 |
| Corporate Stock Expenditures | .......... | .......... | .......... | 14 |
| Total for 1914 | **$4,163 21** | **$3,622 50** | **$253 37** | 15 |
| **METROPOLITAN MUSEUM OF ART** | | | | |
| **1910** | | | | |
| Revenue Expenditures | $200,000 00 | $161,097 75 | $17,856 80 | 16 |
| Corporate Stock Expenditures | .......... | .......... | .......... | 17 |
| Total for 1910 | **$200,000 00** | **$161,097 75** | **$17,856 80** | 18 |
| **1911** | | | | |
| Revenue Expenditures | $200,000 00 | $161,097 75 | $17,856 80 | 19 |
| Corporate Stock Expenditures | .......... | .......... | .......... | 20 |
| Total for 1911 | **$200,000 00** | **$161,097 75** | **$17,856 80** | 21 |
| **1912** | | | | |
| Revenue Expenditures | $200,000 00 | $161,097 75 | $24,542 25 | 22 |
| Corporate Stock Expenditures | .......... | .......... | .......... | 23 |
| Total for 1912 | **$200,000 00** | **$161,097 75** | **$24,542 25** | 24 |
| **1913** | | | | |
| Revenue Expenditures | $200,000 00 | $174,806 45 | .......... | 25 |
| Corporate Stock Expenditures | .......... | .......... | .......... | 26 |
| Total for 1913 | **$200,000 00** | **$174,806 45** | .......... | 27 |
| **1914** | | | | |
| Revenue Expenditures | $200,000 00 | $175,590 57 | .......... | 28 |
| Corporate Stock Expenditures | .......... | .......... | .......... | 29 |
| Total for 1914 | **$200,000 00** | **$175,590 57** | .......... | 30 |

NEW YORK

MADE FROM REVENUE AND FROM CORPORATE STOCK FUNDS FOR THE DEPARTMENTS, ACCORDING TO OBJECTS OF EXPENDITURE:

| LINE No. | Purchase of Equipment | Materials | Contract or Open Order Service | Contingencies | Fixed Charges and Contributions | Unclassified |
|---|---|---|---|---|---|---|
| 1 | .......... | .......... | $4 80 | $225 50 | .......... | .......... |
| 2 | .......... | .......... | .......... | .......... | .......... | .......... |
| 3 | .......... | .......... | **$4 80** | **$225 50** | .......... | .......... |
| 4 | $132 00 | $7 70 | $395 00 | $212 81 | .......... | .......... |
| 5 | .......... | .......... | .......... | .......... | .......... | .......... |
| 6 | **$132 00** | **$7 70** | **$395 00** | **$212 81** | .......... | .......... |
| 7 | $120 00 | .......... | $1,096 00 | $209 15 | .......... | .......... |
| 8 | .......... | .......... | .......... | .......... | .......... | .......... |
| 9 | $120 00 | .......... | $1,096 00 | $209 15 | .......... | .......... |
| 10 | $72 41 | .......... | $317 50 | $196 30 | .......... | .......... |
| 11 | .......... | .......... | .......... | .......... | .......... | .......... |
| 12 | **$72 41** | .......... | **$317 50** | **$196 30** | .......... | .......... |
| 13 | .......... | .......... | $93 50 | $193 84 | .......... | .......... |
| 14 | .......... | .......... | .......... | .......... | .......... | .......... |
| 15 | .......... | .......... | **$93 50** | **$193 84** | .......... | .......... |
| 16 | $1,850 00 | $6,685 45 | $600 00 | $11,910 00 | .......... | .......... |
| 17 | .......... | .......... | .......... | .......... | .......... | .......... |
| 18 | **$1,850 00** | **$6,685 45** | **$600 00** | **$11,910 00** | .......... | .......... |
| 19 | $1,850 00 | $6,685 45 | $600 00 | $11,910 00 | .......... | .......... |
| 20 | .......... | .......... | .......... | .......... | .......... | .......... |
| 21 | **$1,850 00** | **$6,685 45** | **$600 00** | **$11,910 00** | .......... | .......... |
| 22 | $1,850 00 | .......... | $600 00 | $11,910 00 | .......... | .......... |
| 23 | .......... | .......... | .......... | .......... | .......... | .......... |
| 24 | **$1,850 00** | .......... | **$600 00** | **$11,910 00** | .......... | .......... |
| 25 | .......... | .......... | .......... | $25,193 55 | .......... | .......... |
| 26 | .......... | .......... | .......... | .......... | .......... | .......... |
| 27 | .......... | .......... | .......... | **$25,193 55** | .......... | .......... |
| 28 | .......... | .......... | .......... | $24,409 43 | .......... | .......... |
| 29 | .......... | .......... | .......... | .......... | .......... | .......... |
| 30 | .......... | .......... | .......... | **$24,409 43** | .......... | .......... |

Comparative Statements Showing Separately the Expenditures
Years 1910 to 1914, Inclusive, Classified by

| | Total | Personal Service | Supplies | Line No. |
|---|---|---|---|---|
| **MISCELLANEOUS—CITY** | | | | |
| **1910** | | | | |
| Revenue Expenditures | $2,043,612 97 | $150 00 | .......... | 1 |
| Corporate Stock Expenditures | 27,465 73 | 3,701 12 | .......... | 2 |
| Total for 1910 | **$2,071,078 70** | **$3,851 12** | .......... | 3 |
| **1911** | | | | |
| Revenue Expenditures | $1,986,140 72 | $3,350 69 | $2,078 50 | 4 |
| Corporate Stock Expenditures | 230,226 55 | 4,840 76 | .......... | 5 |
| Total for 1911 | **$2,216,367 27** | **$8,191 45** | **$2,078 50** | 6 |
| **1912** | | | | |
| Revenue Expenditures | $1,763,660 49 | $32,704 27 | .......... | 7 |
| Corporate Stock Expenditures | 205,191 74 | 636 30 | .......... | 8 |
| Total for 1912 | **$1,968,852 23** | **$33,340 57** | .......... | 9 |
| **1913** | | | | |
| Revenue Expenditures | $1,944,463 37 | $183,445 79 | $50 50 | 10 |
| Corporate Stock Expenditures | 401,062 51 | .......... | .......... | 11 |
| Total for 1913 | **$2,345,525 88** | **$183,445 79** | **$50 50** | 12 |
| **1914** | | | | |
| Revenue Expenditures | $1,913,424 90 | .......... | .......... | 13 |
| Corporate Stock Expenditures | 1,400,516 04 | $1,650 00 | .......... | 14 |
| Total for 1914 | **$3,313,940 94** | **$1,650 00** | .......... | 15 |
| **INACTIVE ACCOUNTS—MISCELLANEOUS** | | | | |
| **1910** | | | | |
| Revenue Expenditures | .......... | .......... | .......... | 16 |
| Corporate Stock Expenditures | .......... | .......... | .......... | 17 |
| Total for 1910 | .......... | .......... | .......... | 18 |
| **1911** | | | | |
| Revenue Expenditures | .......... | .......... | .......... | 19 |
| Corporate Stock Expenditures | .......... | .......... | .......... | 20 |
| Total for 1911 | .......... | .......... | .......... | 21 |
| **1912** | | | | |
| Revenue Expenditures | $1,850 72 | .......... | $746 29 | 22 |
| Corporate Stock Expenditures | .......... | .......... | .......... | 23 |
| Total for 1912 | **$1,850 72** | .......... | **$746 29** | 24 |
| **1913** | | | | |
| Revenue Expenditures | .......... | .......... | .......... | 25 |
| Corporate Stock Expenditures | .......... | .......... | .......... | 26 |
| Total for 1913 | .......... | .......... | .......... | 27 |
| **1914** | | | | |
| Revenue Expenditures | .......... | .......... | .......... | 28 |
| Corporate Stock Expenditures | .......... | .......... | .......... | 29 |
| Total for 1914 | .......... | .......... | .......... | 30 |

NEW YORK

MADE FROM REVENUE AND FROM CORPORATE STOCK FUNDS FOR THE DEPARTMENTS, ACCORDING TO OBJECTS OF EXPENDITURE:

| LINE No. | Purchase of Equipment | Materials | Contract or Open Order Service | Contingencies | Fixed Charges and Contributions | Unclassified |
|---|---|---|---|---|---|---|
| 1 | .......... | .......... | $114,418 24 | .......... | $1,231,758 09 | $697,286 64 |
| 2 | .......... | .......... | 7,693 83 | $759 46 | .......... | 15,311 32 |
| 3 | .......... | .......... | **$122,112 07** | **$759 46** | **$1,231,758 09** | **$712,597 96** |
| 4 | $704 22 | .......... | $15,967 47 | $1,201 92 | $1,428,411 42 | $534,426 50 |
| 5 | .......... | .......... | 729 94 | .......... | .......... | 224,655 85 |
| 6 | **$704 22** | .......... | **$16,697 41** | **$1,201 92** | **$1,428,411 42** | **$759,082 35** |
| 7 | $854 25 | .......... | $153,531 57 | .......... | $1,119,804 62 | $456,765 78 |
| 8 | .......... | .......... | 3,038 30 | $369 00 | .......... | 201,148 14 |
| 9 | **$854 25** | .......... | **$156,569 87** | **$369 00** | **$1,119,804 62** | **$657,913 92** |
| 10 | $4,381 35 | .......... | $6,831 26 | $24,837 60 | $1,345,903 67 | $379,013 20 |
| 11 | .......... | .......... | 4,007 30 | .......... | .......... | 397,055 21 |
| 12 | **$4,381 35** | .......... | **$10,838 56** | **$24,837 60** | **$1,345,903 67** | **$776,068 41** |
| 13 | $7,427 48 | .......... | $11,287 99 | .......... | $1,158,007 45 | $736,701 98 |
| 14 | .......... | .......... | 433,848 16 | $255 13 | .......... | 964,762 75 |
| 15 | **$7,427 48** | .......... | **$445,136 15** | **$255 13** | **$1,158,007 45** | **$1,701,464 73** |
| 16 | .......... | .......... | .......... | .......... | .......... | .......... |
| 17 | .......... | .......... | .......... | .......... | .......... | .......... |
| 18 | .......... | .......... | .......... | .......... | .......... | .......... |
| 19 | .......... | .......... | .......... | .......... | .......... | .......... |
| 20 | .......... | .......... | .......... | .......... | .......... | .......... |
| 21 | .......... | .......... | .......... | .......... | .......... | .......... |
| 22 | $209 62 | .......... | $894 81 | .......... | .......... | .......... |
| 23 | .......... | .......... | .......... | .......... | .......... | .......... |
| 24 | **$209 62** | .......... | **$894 81** | .......... | .......... | .......... |
| 25 | .......... | .......... | .......... | .......... | .......... | .......... |
| 26 | .......... | .......... | .......... | .......... | .......... | .......... |
| 27 | .......... | .......... | .......... | .......... | .......... | .......... |
| 28 | .......... | .......... | .......... | .......... | .......... | .......... |
| 29 | .......... | .......... | .......... | .......... | .......... | .......... |
| 30 | .......... | .......... | .......... | .......... | .......... | .......... |

Comparative Statements Showing Separately the Expenditures Years 1910 to 1914, Inclusive, Classified by

| | Total | Personal Service | Supplies | Line No. |
|---|---|---|---|---|
| **MUSEUM OF ARTS AND SCIENCES** | | | | |
| **1910** | | | | |
| Revenue Expenditures | $93,555 59 | $68,366 66 | $10,091 21 | 1 |
| Corporate Stock Expenditures | .......... | .......... | .......... | 2 |
| Total for 1910 | **$93,555 59** | **$68,366 66** | **$10,091 21** | 3 |
| **1911** | | | | |
| Revenue Expenditures | $93,334 00 | $68,392 25 | $10,426 26 | 4 |
| Corporate Stock Expenditures | .......... | .......... | .......... | 5 |
| Total for 1911 | **$93,334 00** | **$68,392 25** | **$10,426 26** | 6 |
| **1912** | | | | |
| Revenue Expenditures | $97,623 48 | $75,071 20 | $13,961 80 | 7 |
| Corporate Stock Expenditures | .......... | .......... | .......... | 8 |
| Total for 1912 | **$97,623 48** | **$75,071 20** | **$13,961 80** | 9 |
| **1913** | | | | |
| Revenue Expenditures | $102,181 86 | $78,728 76 | $8,861 99 | 10 |
| Corporate Stock Expenditures | .......... | .......... | .......... | 11 |
| Total for 1913 | **$102,181 86** | **$78,728 76** | **$8,861 99** | 12 |
| **1914** | | | | |
| Revenue Expenditures | $106,744 33 | $82,280 98 | .......... | 13 |
| Corporate Stock Expenditures | .......... | .......... | .......... | 14 |
| Total for 1914 | **$106,744 33** | **$82,280 98** | .......... | 15 |
| **NEW YORK AQUARIUM** | | | | |
| **1910** | | | | |
| Revenue Expenditures | $45,974 86 | $30,202 16 | $9,723 60 | 16 |
| Corporate Stock Expenditures | .......... | .......... | .......... | 17 |
| Total for 1910 | **$45,974 86** | **$30,202 16** | **$9,723 60** | 18 |
| **1911** | | | | |
| Revenue Expenditures | $47,567 22 | $32,168 16 | $9,643 67 | 19 |
| Corporate Stock Expenditures | .......... | .......... | .......... | 20 |
| Total for 1911 | **$47,567 22** | **$32,168 16** | **$9,643 67** | 21 |
| **1912** | | | | |
| Revenue Expenditures | $46,597 08 | $32,595 63 | $10,102 27 | 22 |
| Corporate Stock Expenditures | .......... | .......... | .......... | 23 |
| Total for 1912 | **$46,597 08** | **$32,595 63** | **$10,102 27** | 24 |
| **1913** | | | | |
| Revenue Expenditures | $47,335 62 | $33,376 64 | $7,051 52 | 25 |
| Corporate Stock Expenditures | .......... | .......... | .......... | 26 |
| Total for 1913 | **$47,335 62** | **$33,376 64** | **$7,051 52** | 27 |
| **1914** | | | | |
| Revenue Expenditures | $46,995 53 | $32,841 86 | .......... | 28 |
| Corporate Stock Expenditures | .......... | .......... | .......... | 29 |
| Total for 1914 | **$46,995 53** | **$32,841 86** | .......... | 30 |

## NEW YORK

MADE FROM REVENUE AND FROM CORPORATE STOCK FUNDS FOR THE DEPARTMENTS, ACCORDING TO OBJECTS OF EXPENDITURE:

| LINE No. | Purchase of Equipment | Materials | Contract or Open Order Service | Contingencies | Fixed Charges and Contributions | Unclassified |
|---|---|---|---|---|---|---|
| 1 | $3,268 18 | $2,990 83 | $3,499 61 | $5,339 10 | .......... | .......... |
| 2 | .......... | .......... | .......... | .......... | .......... | .......... |
| 3 | **$3,268 18** | **$2,990 83** | **$3,499 61** | **$5,339 10** | .......... | .......... |
| 4 | $2,957 96 | $2,994 65 | $3,215 38 | $5,347 50 | .......... | .......... |
| 5 | .......... | .......... | .......... | .......... | .......... | .......... |
| 6 | **$2,957 96** | **$2,994 65** | **$3,215 38** | **$5,347 50** | .......... | .......... |
| 7 | $2,292 69 | .......... | $3,299 16 | $2,998 63 | .......... | .......... |
| 8 | .......... | .......... | .......... | .......... | .......... | .......... |
| 9 | **$2,292 69** | .......... | **$3,299 16** | **$2,998 63** | .......... | .......... |
| 10 | $3,030 54 | $4,714 08 | $4,999 60 | $1,384 13 | $462 76 | .......... |
| 11 | .......... | .......... | .......... | .......... | .......... | .......... |
| 12 | **$3,030 54** | **$4,714 08** | **$4,999 60** | **$1,384 13** | **$462 76** | .......... |
| 13 | .......... | .......... | .......... | $24,463 35 | .......... | .......... |
| 14 | .......... | .......... | .......... | .......... | .......... | .......... |
| 15 | .......... | .......... | .......... | **$24,463 35** | .......... | .......... |
| 16 | .......... | $598 93 | $4,944 16 | $506 01 | .......... | .......... |
| 17 | .......... | .......... | .......... | .......... | .......... | .......... |
| 18 | .......... | **$598 93** | **$4,944 16** | **$506 01** | .......... | .......... |
| 19 | .......... | $745 10 | $4,531 06 | $479 23 | .......... | .......... |
| 20 | .......... | .......... | .......... | .......... | .......... | .......... |
| 21 | .......... | **$745 10** | **$4,531 06** | **$479 23** | .......... | .......... |
| 22 | $45 00 | .......... | $3,229 42 | $624 76 | .......... | .......... |
| 23 | .......... | .......... | .......... | .......... | .......... | .......... |
| 24 | **$45 00** | .......... | **$3,229 42** | **$624 76** | .......... | .......... |
| 25 | $1,088 71 | $491 96 | $5,163 04 | $163 75 | .......... | .......... |
| 26 | .......... | .......... | .......... | .......... | .......... | .......... |
| 27 | **$1,088 71** | **$491 96** | **$5,163 04** | **$163 75** | .......... | .......... |
| 28 | .......... | .......... | .......... | $14,153 67 | .......... | .......... |
| 29 | .......... | .......... | .......... | .......... | .......... | .......... |
| 30 | .......... | .......... | .......... | **$14,153 67** | .......... | .......... |

COMPARATIVE STATEMENTS SHOWING SEPARATELY THE EXPENDITURES
YEARS 1910 TO 1914, INCLUSIVE, CLASSIFIED BY

| | Total | Personal Service | Supplies | LINE No. |
|---|---|---|---|---|
| **NEW YORK BOTANICAL GARDEN** | | | | |
| **1910** | | | | |
| Revenue Expenditures | $82,936 32 | $64,855 35 | $14,887 82 | 1 |
| Corporate Stock Expenditures | .......... | .......... | .......... | 2 |
| Total for 1910 | **$82,936 32** | **$64,855 35** | **$14,887 82** | 3 |
| **1911** | | | | |
| Revenue Expenditures | $85,981 40 | $67,860 00 | $14,311 05 | 4 |
| Corporate Stock Expenditures | .......... | .......... | .......... | 5 |
| Total for 1911 | **$85,981 40** | **$67,860 00** | **$14,311 05** | 6 |
| **1912** | | | | |
| Revenue Expenditures | $90,072 46 | $71,890 00 | $16,061 36 | 7 |
| Corporate Stock Expenditures | .......... | .......... | .......... | 8 |
| Total for 1912 | **$90,072 46** | **$71,890 00** | **$16,061 36** | 9 |
| **1913** | | | | |
| Revenue Expenditures | $103,222 19 | $83,773 69 | $11,954 16 | 10 |
| Corporate Stock Expenditures | .......... | .......... | .......... | 11 |
| Total for 1913 | **$103,222 19** | **$83,773 69** | **$11,954 16** | 12 |
| **1914** | | | | |
| Revenue Expenditures | $107,163 00 | $90,411 74 | .......... | 13 |
| Corporate Stock Expenditures | .......... | .......... | .......... | 14 |
| Total for 1914 | **$107,163 00** | **$90,411 74** | .......... | 15 |
| **NEW YORK ZOOLOGICAL GARDEN** | | | | |
| **1910** | | | | |
| Revenue Expenditures | $167,632 00 | $109,997 20 | $51,845 53 | 16 |
| Corporate Stock Expenditures | .......... | .......... | .......... | 17 |
| Total for 1910 | **$167,632 00** | **$109,997 20** | **$51,845 53** | 18 |
| **1911** | | | | |
| Revenue Expenditures | $174,579 74 | $113,964 10 | $54,090 60 | 19 |
| Corporate Stock Expenditures | .......... | .......... | .......... | 20 |
| Total for 1911 | **$174,579 74** | **$113,964 10** | **$54,090 60** | 21 |
| **1912** | | | | |
| Revenue Expenditures | $179,272 87 | $116,314 47 | $51,538 66 | 22 |
| Corporate Stock Expenditures | .......... | .......... | .......... | 23 |
| Total for 1912 | **$179,272 87** | **$116,314 47** | **$51,538 66** | 24 |
| **1913** | | | | |
| Revenue Expenditures | $189,570 36 | $122,249 76 | $51,079 91 | 25 |
| Corporate Stock Expenditures | .......... | .......... | .......... | 26 |
| Total for 1913 | **$189,570 36** | **$122,249 76** | **$51,079 91** | 27 |
| **1914** | | | | |
| Revenue Expenditures | $200,000 00 | $145,230 24 | .......... | 28 |
| Corporate Stock Expenditures | .......... | .......... | .......... | 29 |
| Total for 1914 | **$200,000 00** | **$145,230 24** | .......... | 30 |

NEW YORK

Made from Revenue and from Corporate Stock Funds for the Departments, According to Objects of Expenditure:

| Line No. | Purchase of Equipment | Materials | Contract or Open Order Service | Contingencies | Fixed Charges and Contributions | Unclassified |
|---|---|---|---|---|---|---|
| 1 | $666 48 | $1,249 98 | $783 17 | $493 52 | .......... | .......... |
| 2 | .......... | .......... | .......... | .......... | .......... | .......... |
| 3 | **$666 48** | **$1,249 98** | **$783 17** | **$493 52** | .......... | .......... |
| 4 | $921 89 | $1,500 00 | $893 46 | $495 00 | .......... | .......... |
| 5 | .......... | .......... | .......... | .......... | .......... | .......... |
| 6 | **$921 89** | **$1,500 00** | **$893 46** | **$495 00** | .......... | .......... |
| 7 | $300 00 | .......... | $1,421 10 | $400 00 | .......... | .......... |
| 8 | .......... | .......... | .......... | .......... | .......... | .......... |
| 9 | **$300 00** | .......... | **$1,421 10** | **$400 00** | .......... | .......... |
| 10 | $3,301 25 | $1,574 92 | $2,618 17 | .......... | .......... | .......... |
| 11 | .......... | .......... | .......... | .......... | .......... | .......... |
| 12 | **$3,301 25** | **$1,574 92** | **$2,618 17** | .......... | .......... | .......... |
| 13 | .......... | .......... | .......... | $16,751 26 | .......... | .......... |
| 14 | .......... | .......... | .......... | .......... | .......... | .......... |
| 15 | .......... | .......... | .......... | **$16,751 26** | .......... | .......... |
| 16 | $383 46 | $3,031 73 | $641 55 | $1,732 53 | .......... | .......... |
| 17 | .......... | .......... | .......... | .......... | .......... | .......... |
| 18 | **$383 46** | **$3,031 73** | **$641 55** | **$1,732 53** | .......... | .......... |
| 19 | $217 22 | $4,098 83 | $602 32 | $1,606 67 | .......... | .......... |
| 20 | .......... | .......... | .......... | .......... | .......... | .......... |
| 21 | **$217 22** | **$4,098 83** | **$602 32** | **$1,606 67** | .......... | .......... |
| 22 | $98 75 | .......... | $9,623 60 | $1,697 39 | .......... | .......... |
| 23 | .......... | .......... | .......... | .......... | .......... | .......... |
| 24 | **$98 75** | .......... | **$9,623 60** | **$1,697 39** | .......... | .......... |
| 25 | $3,644 42 | $7,502 52 | $4,939 79 | $153 96 | .......... | .......... |
| 26 | .......... | .......... | .......... | .......... | .......... | .......... |
| 27 | **$3,644 42** | **$7,502 52** | **$4,939 79** | **$153 96** | .......... | .......... |
| 28 | .......... | .......... | .......... | $54,769 76 | .......... | .......... |
| 29 | .......... | .......... | .......... | .......... | .......... | .......... |
| 30 | .......... | .......... | .......... | **$54,769 76** | .......... | .......... |

COMPARATIVE STATEMENTS SHOWING SEPARATELY THE EXPENDITURES-
YEARS 1910 TO 1914, INCLUSIVE, CLASSIFIED BY

| | Total | Personal Service | Supplies | LINE No. |
|---|---|---|---|---|
| **NEW YORK PUBLIC LIBRARY BUILDING** | | | | |
| **1910** | | | | |
| Revenue Expenditures | .......... | .......... | .......... | 1 |
| Corporate Stock Expenditures | .......... | .......... | .......... | 2 |
| Total for 1910 | .......... | .......... | .......... | 3 |
| **1911** | | | | |
| Revenue Expenditures | .......... | .......... | .......... | 4 |
| Corporate Stock Expenditures | .......... | .......... | .......... | 5 |
| Total for 1911 | .......... | .......... | .......... | 6 |
| **1912** | | | | |
| Revenue Expenditures | $10,000 00 | .......... | $4,000 00 | 7 |
| Corporate Stock Expenditures | .......... | .......... | .......... | 8 |
| Total for 1912 | **$10,000 00** | .......... | **$4,000 00** | 9 |
| **1913** | | | | |
| Revenue Expenditures | $17,999 37 | .......... | $2,000 00 | 10 |
| Corporate Stock Expenditures | .......... | .......... | .......... | 11 |
| Total for 1913 | **$17,999 37** | .......... | **$2,000 00** | 12 |
| **1914** | | | | |
| Revenue Expenditures | $48,500 00 | .......... | $2,000 00 | 13 |
| Corporate Stock Expenditures | .......... | .......... | .......... | 14 |
| Total for 1914 | **$48,500 00** | .......... | **$2,000 00** | 15 |
| **BROOKLYN PUBLIC LIBRARY** | | | | |
| **1910** | | | | |
| Revenue Expenditures | $418,696 71 | $229,282 72 | $25,793 00 | 16 |
| Corporate Stock Expenditures | 218 98 | .......... | .......... | 17 |
| Total for 1910 | **$418,915 69** | **$229,282 72** | **$25,793 00** | 18 |
| **1911** | | | | |
| Revenue Expenditures | $421,156 86 | $236,472 00 | $26,993 00 | 19 |
| Corporate Stock Expenditures | 560 00 | .......... | .......... | 20 |
| Total for 1911 | **$421,716 86** | **$236,472 00** | **$26,993 00** | 21 |
| **1912** | | | | |
| Revenue Expenditures | $413,628 47 | $230,324 84 | $102,611 24 | 22 |
| Corporate Stock Expenditures | 34,186 07 | .......... | .......... | 23 |
| Total for 1912 | **$447,814 54** | **$230,324 84** | **$102,611 24** | 24 |
| **1913** | | | | |
| Revenue Expenditures | $436,494 31 | $246,968 50 | $27,107 88 | 25 |
| Corporate Stock Expenditures | 115,997 82 | .......... | .......... | 26 |
| Total for 1913 | **$552,492 13** | **$246,968 50** | **$27,107 88** | 27 |
| **1914** | | | | |
| Revenue Expenditures | $444,202 23 | $248,124 50 | $27,038 37 | 28 |
| Corporate Stock Expenditures | 24,506 22 | .......... | .......... | 29 |
| Total for 1914 | **$468,708 45** | **$248,124 50** | **$27,038 37** | 30 |

NEW YORK

MADE FROM REVENUE AND FROM CORPORATE STOCK FUNDS FOR THE DEPARTMENTS, ACCORDING TO OBJECTS OF EXPENDITURE:

| LINE No. | Purchase of Equipment | Materials | Contract or Open Order Service | Contingencies | Fixed Charges and Contributions | Unclassified |
|---|---|---|---|---|---|---|
| 1 | .......... | .......... | .......... | .......... | .......... | .......... |
| 2 | .......... | .......... | .......... | .......... | .......... | .......... |
| 3 | .......... | .......... | .......... | .......... | .......... | .......... |
| 4 | .......... | .......... | .......... | .......... | .......... | .......... |
| 5 | .......... | .......... | .......... | .......... | .......... | .......... |
| 6 | .......... | .......... | .......... | .......... | .......... | .......... |
| 7 | .......... | .......... | $6,000 00 | .......... | .......... | .......... |
| 8 | .......... | .......... | .......... | .......... | .......... | .......... |
| 9 | .......... | .......... | **$6,000 00** | .......... | .......... | .......... |
| 10 | .......... | .......... | $15,999 37 | .......... | .......... | .......... |
| 11 | .......... | .......... | .......... | .......... | .......... | .......... |
| 12 | .......... | .......... | **$15,999 37** | .......... | .......... | .......... |
| 13 | .......... | .......... | $46,500 00 | .......... | .......... | .......... |
| 14 | .......... | .......... | .......... | .......... | .......... | .......... |
| 15 | .......... | .......... | **$46,500 00** | .......... | .......... | .......... |
| 16 | $99,125 00 | .......... | $50,990 99 | .......... | $13,505 00 | .......... |
| 17 | 208 98 | .......... | .......... | .......... | .......... | $10 00 |
| 18 | **$99,333 98** | .......... | **$50,990 99** | .......... | **$13,505 00** | **$10 00** |
| 19 | $99,125 00 | .......... | $44,281 86 | .......... | $14,285 00 | .......... |
| 20 | .......... | .......... | .......... | .......... | .......... | $560 00 |
| 21 | **$99,125 00** | .......... | **$44,281 86** | .......... | **$14,285 00** | **$560 00** |
| 22 | $4,199 32 | .......... | $53,124 80 | $8,645 86 | $14,722 41 | .......... |
| 23 | .......... | .......... | .......... | .......... | .......... | $34,186 07 |
| 24 | **$4,199 32** | .......... | **$53,124 80** | **$8,645 86** | **$14,722 41** | **$34,186 07** |
| 25 | $111,889 11 | .......... | $34,326 82 | $199 55 | $16,002 45 | .......... |
| 26 | 1,072 53 | .......... | 112,383 41 | .......... | .......... | $2,541 88 |
| 27 | **$112,961 64** | .......... | **$146,710 23** | **$199 55** | **$16,002 45** | **$2,541 88** |
| 28 | $85,488 43 | .......... | $60,587 70 | $99 42 | $22,863 81 | .......... |
| 29 | 13,927 47 | .......... | .......... | .......... | .......... | $10,578 75 |
| 30 | **$99,415 90** | .......... | **$60,587 70** | **$99 42** | **$22,863 81** | **$10,578 75** |

COMPARATIVE STATEMENTS SHOWING SEPARATELY THE EXPENDITURES
YEARS 1910 TO 1914, INCLUSIVE, CLASSIFIED BY

| | Total | Personal Service | Supplies | LINE No. |
|---|---|---|---|---|
| **NEW YORK PUBLIC LIBRARY** | | | | |
| **1910** | | | | |
| Revenue Expenditures | $618,361 89 | $346,638 86 | $48,780 00 | 1 |
| Corporate Stock Expenditures | 1,347,248 44 | 2,640 31 | .......... | 2 |
| Total for 1910 | **$1,965,610 33** | **$349,279 17** | **$48,780 00** | 3 |
| **1911** | | | | |
| Revenue Expenditures | $661,965 82 | $368,141 25 | $61,547 14 | 4 |
| Corporate Stock Expenditures | 703,229 21 | 4,649 02 | .......... | 5 |
| Total for 1911 | **$1,365,195 03** | **$372,790 27** | **$61,547 14** | 6 |
| **1912** | | | | |
| Revenue Expenditures | $616,958 99 | $362,390 00 | $155,003 25 | 7 |
| Corporate Stock Expenditures | 224,461 07 | .......... | .......... | 8 |
| Total for 1912 | **$841,420 06** | **$362,390 00** | **$155,003 25** | 9 |
| **1913** | | | | |
| Revenue Expenditures | $638,443 50 | $389,265 50 | $43,310 66 | 10 |
| Corporate Stock Expenditures | 46,012 44 | .......... | 70 00 | 11 |
| Total for 1913 | **$684,455 94** | **$389,265 50** | **$43,380 66** | 12 |
| **1914** | | | | |
| Revenue Expenditures | $747,419 18 | $472,351 02 | $50,596 34 | 13 |
| Corporate Stock Expenditures | 38,205 18 | .......... | .......... | 14 |
| Total for 1914 | **$785,624 36** | **$472,351 02** | **$50,596 34** | 15 |
| **QUEENS BOROUGH PUBLIC LIBRARY** | | | | |
| **1910** | | | | |
| Revenue Expenditures | $118,463 80 | $64,800 00 | $7,300 00 | 16 |
| Corporate Stock Expenditures | 25 00 | .......... | .......... | 17 |
| Total for 1910 | **$118,488 80** | **$64,800 00** | **$7,300 00** | 18 |
| **1911** | | | | |
| Revenue Expenditures | $135,040 26 | $73,680 00 | $9,747 79 | 19 |
| Corporate Stock Expenditures | .......... | .......... | .......... | 20 |
| Total for 1911 | **$135,040 26** | **$73,680 00** | **$9,747 79** | 21 |
| **1912** | | | | |
| Revenue Expenditures | $143,997 99 | $79,813 94 | $29,820 94 | 22 |
| Corporate Stock Expenditures | .......... | .......... | .......... | 23 |
| Total for 1912 | **$143,997 99** | **$79,813 94** | **$29,820 94** | 24 |
| **1913** | | | | |
| Revenue Expenditures | $155,374 71 | $83,062 15 | $7,624 71 | 25 |
| Corporate Stock Expenditures | .......... | .......... | .......... | 26 |
| Total for 1913 | **$155,374 71** | **$83,062 15** | **$7,624 71** | 27 |
| **1914** | | | | |
| Revenue Expenditures | $152,028 37 | $85,234 39 | $7,673 43 | 28 |
| Corporate Stock Expenditures | .......... | .......... | .......... | 29 |
| Total for 1914 | **$152,028 37** | **$85,234 39** | **$7,673 43** | 30 |

NEW YORK

MADE FROM REVENUE AND FROM CORPORATE STOCK FUNDS FOR THE DEPARTMENTS, ACCORDING TO OBJECTS OF EXPENDITURE:

| LINE No. | Purchase of Equipment | Materials | Contract or Open Order Service | Contingencies | Fixed Charges and Contributions | Unclassified |
|---|---|---|---|---|---|---|
| 1 | $143,310 00 | .......... | $79,093 74 | .......... | $180 00 | $359 29 |
| 2 | 818 55 | .......... | 1,343,640 83 | .......... | .......... | 148 75 |
| 3 | **$144,128 55** | .......... | **$1,422,734 57** | .......... | **$180 00** | **$508 04** |
| 4 | $153,110 00 | .......... | $78,987 43 | .......... | $180 00 | .......... |
| 5 | .......... | .......... | 664,244 46 | $155 10 | .......... | $34,180 63 |
| 6 | **$153,110 00** | .......... | **$743,231 89** | **$155 10** | **$180 00** | **$34,180 63** |
| 7 | $4,236 92 | .......... | $82 087 29 | $13,061 53 | $180 00 | .......... |
| 8 | .......... | .......... | 138,461 07 | .......... | .......... | $86,000 00 |
| 9 | **$4,236 92** | .......... | **$220,548 36** | **$13,061 53** | **$180 00** | **$86,000 00** |
| 10 | $107,294 46 | $1,495 30 | $96,308 21 | $409 37 | $360 00 | .......... |
| 11 | 19,005 57 | .......... | 26,475 40 | .......... | .......... | $461 47 |
| 12 | **$126,300 03** | **$1,495 30** | **$122,783 61** | **$409 37** | **$360 00** | **$461 47** |
| 13 | $117,726 97 | $1,299 56 | $94,297 81 | $8,474 15 | $2,673 33 | .......... |
| 14 | 15,994 43 | .......... | 22,210 75 | .......... | .......... | .......... |
| 15 | **$133,721 40** | **$1,299 56** | **$116,508 56** | **$8,474 15** | **$2,673 33** | .......... |
| 16 | $23,927 76 | .......... | $14,764 44 | .......... | $7,671 60 | .......... |
| 17 | .......... | .......... | .......... | .......... | .......... | $25 00 |
| 18 | **$23,927 76** | .......... | **$14,764 44** | .......... | **$7,671 60** | **$25 00** |
| 19 | $28,538 54 | .......... | $12,522 27 | .......... | $10,551 66 | .......... |
| 20 | .......... | .......... | .......... | .......... | .......... | .......... |
| 21 | **$28,538 54** | .......... | **$12,522 27** | .......... | **$10,551 66** | .......... |
| 22 | $2,649 83 | .......... | $13,407 12 | $6,369 53 | $11,936 63 | .......... |
| 23 | .......... | .......... | .......... | .......... | .......... | .......... |
| 24 | $2,649 83 | .......... | **$13,407 12** | **$6,369 53** | **$11,936 63** | .......... |
| 25 | $31,605 76 | $389 92 | $18,316 46 | $1,367 44 | $13,008 27 | .......... |
| 26 | .......... | .......... | .......... | .......... | .......... | .......... |
| 27 | **$31,605 76** | **$389 92** | **$18,316 46** | **$1,367 44** | **$13,008 27** | .......... |
| 28 | $29,365 55 | $435 00 | $15,099 86 | $647 05 | $13,573 09 | .......... |
| 29 | .......... | .......... | .......... | .......... | .......... | .......... |
| 30 | **$29,365 55** | **$435 00** | **$15,099 86** | **$647 05** | **$13,573 09** | .......... |

Comparative Statements Showing Separately the Expenditures
Years 1910 to 1914, Inclusive, Classified by

| | Total | Personal Service | Supplies | Line No. |
|---|---|---|---|---|
| **STATEN ISLAND ASSOCIATION OF ARTS AND SCIENCES** | | | | |
| **1910** | | | | |
| Revenue Expenditures | $3,991 46 | $3,485 50 | .......... | 1 |
| Corporate Stock Expenditures | .......... | .......... | .......... | 2 |
| Total for 1910 | **$3,991 46** | **$3,485 50** | .......... | 3 |
| **1911** | | | | |
| Revenue Expenditures | $9,000 00 | $5,774 82 | .......... | 4 |
| Corporate Stock Expenditures | .......... | .......... | .......... | 5 |
| Total for 1911 | **$9,000 00** | **$5,774 82** | .......... | 6 |
| **1912** | | | | |
| Revenue Expenditures | $9,448 44 | $6,383 75 | $409 64 | 7 |
| Corporate Stock Expenditures | .......... | .......... | .......... | 8 |
| Total for 1912 | **$9,448 44** | **$6,383 75** | **$409 64** | 9 |
| **1913** | | | | |
| Revenue Expenditures | $9,318 74 | $6,840 00 | $301 25 | 10 |
| Corporate Stock Expenditures | .......... | .......... | .......... | 11 |
| Total for 1913 | **$9,318 74** | **$6,840 00** | **$301 25** | 12 |
| **1914** | | | | |
| Revenue Expenditures | $8,639 79 | $6,527 51 | $264 25 | 13 |
| Corporate Stock Expenditures | .......... | .......... | .......... | 14 |
| Total for 1914 | **$8,639 79** | **$6,527 51** | **$264 25** | 15 |
| **UNITED STATES VOLUNTEER LIFE SAVING CORPS** | | | | |
| **1910** | | | | |
| Revenue Expenditures | $11,000 00 | $5,640 80 | $348 27 | 16 |
| Corporate Stock Expenditures | .......... | .......... | .......... | 17 |
| Total for 1910 | **$11,000 00** | **$5,640 80** | **$348 27** | 18 |
| **1911** | | | | |
| Revenue Expenditures | $11,000 00 | $6,523 32 | .......... | 19 |
| Corporate Stock Expenditures | .......... | .......... | .......... | 20 |
| Total for 1911 | **$11,000 00** | **$6,523 32** | .......... | 21 |
| **1912** | | | | |
| Revenue Expenditures | $13,044 23 | $6,514 94 | $2,342 18 | 22 |
| Corporate Stock Expenditures | .......... | .......... | .......... | 23 |
| Total for 1912 | **$13,044 23** | **$6,514 94** | **$2,342 18** | 24 |
| **1913** | | | | |
| Revenue Expenditures | $13,235 44 | $7,118 00 | $903 50 | 25 |
| Corporate Stock Expenditures | .......... | .......... | .......... | 26 |
| Total for 1913 | **$13,235 44** | **$7,118 00** | **$903 50** | 27 |
| **1914** | | | | |
| Revenue Expenditures | $12,355 14 | $6,860 00 | $915 00 | 28 |
| Corporate Stock Expenditures | .......... | .......... | .......... | 29 |
| Total for 1914 | **$12,355 14** | **$6,860 00** | **$915 00** | 30 |

NEW YORK

MADE FROM REVENUE AND FROM CORPORATE STOCK FUNDS FOR THE DEPARTMENTS, ACCORDING TO OBJECTS OF EXPENDITURE:

| LINE No. | Purchase of Equipment | Materials | Contract or Open Order Service | Contingencies | Fixed Charges and Contributions | Unclassified |
|---|---|---|---|---|---|---|
| 1 | .......... | .......... | $505 96 | .......... | .......... | .......... |
| 2 | .......... | .......... | .......... | .......... | .......... | .......... |
| 3 | .......... | .......... | **$505 96** | .......... | .......... | .......... |
| 4 | .......... | .......... | .......... | $1,725 18 | $1,500 00 | .......... |
| 5 | .......... | .......... | .......... | .......... | .......... | .......... |
| 6 | .......... | .......... | .......... | **$1,725 18** | **$1,500 00** | .......... |
| 7 | $465 93 | .......... | $618 12 | $71 00 | $1,500 00 | .......... |
| 8 | .......... | .......... | .......... | .......... | .......... | .......... |
| 9 | **$465 93** | .......... | **$618 12** | **$71 00** | **$1,500 00** | .......... |
| 10 | $441 07 | .......... | $206 92 | $29 50 | $1,500 00 | .......... |
| 11 | .......... | .......... | .......... | .......... | .......... | .......... |
| 12 | **$441 07** | .......... | **$206 92** | **$29 50** | **$1,500 00** | .......... |
| 13 | $77 37 | .......... | $245 66 | $25 00 | $1,500 00 | .......... |
| 14 | .......... | .......... | .......... | .......... | .......... | .......... |
| 15 | **$77 37** | .......... | **$245 66** | **$25 00** | **$1,500 00** | .......... |
| 16 | $1,735 24 | .......... | $2,144 35 | $344 33 | $787 01 | .......... |
| 17 | .......... | .......... | .......... | .......... | .......... | .......... |
| 18 | **$1,735 24** | .......... | **$2,144 35** | **$344 33** | **$787 01** | .......... |
| 19 | .......... | .......... | .......... | $4,476 68 | .......... | .......... |
| 20 | .......... | .......... | .......... | .......... | .......... | .......... |
| 21 | .......... | .......... | .......... | **$4,476 68** | .......... | .......... |
| 22 | .......... | .......... | $3,702 75 | $484 36 | .......... | .......... |
| 23 | .......... | .......... | .......... | .......... | .......... | .......... |
| 24 | .......... | .......... | **$3,702 75** | **$484 36** | .......... | .......... |
| 25 | $3,175 00 | $225 00 | $606 44 | $467 50 | $740 00 | .......... |
| 26 | .......... | .......... | .......... | .......... | .......... | .......... |
| 27 | **$3,175 00** | **$225 00** | **$606 44** | **$467 50** | **$740 00** | .......... |
| 28 | $3,490 00 | $225 00 | $554 14 | $311 00 | .......... | .......... |
| 29 | .......... | .......... | .......... | .......... | .......... | .......... |
| 30 | **$3,490 00** | **$225 00** | **$554 14** | **$311 00** | .......... | .......... |

COMPARATIVE STATEMENTS SHOWING SEPARATELY THE EXPENDITURES
YEARS 1910 TO 1914, INCLUSIVE, CLASSIFIED BY

| | Total | Personal Service | Supplies | LINE No. |
|---|---|---|---|---|
| **DEFICIENCES IN TAXES** | | | | |
| **1910** | | | | |
| Revenue Expenditures | $4,000,000 00 | .......... | .......... | 1 |
| Corporate Stock Expenditures | .......... | .......... | .......... | 2 |
| Total for 1910 | **$4,000,000 00** | .......... | .......... | 3 |
| **1911** | | | | |
| Revenue Expenditures | $10,000,000 00 | .......... | .......... | 4 |
| Corporate Stock Expenditures | .......... | .......... | .......... | 5 |
| Total for 1911 | **$10,000,000 00** | .......... | .......... | 6 |
| **1912** | | | | |
| Revenue Expenditures | $3,287,366 74 | .......... | .......... | 7 |
| Corporate Stock Expenditures | .......... | .......... | .......... | 8 |
| Total for 1912 | **$3,287,366 74** | .......... | .......... | 9 |
| **1913** | | | | |
| Revenue Expenditures | $2,300,000 00 | .......... | .......... | 10 |
| Corporate Stock Expenditures | .......... | .......... | .......... | 11 |
| Total for 1913 | **$2,300,000 00** | .......... | .......... | 12 |
| **1914** | | | | |
| Revenue Expenditures | $2,500,000 00 | .......... | .......... | 13 |
| Corporate Stock Expenditures | .......... | .......... | .......... | 14 |
| Total for 1914 | **$2,500,000 00** | .......... | .......... | 15 |
| **BOROUGH ASSESSMENTS** | | | | |
| **1910** | | | | |
| Revenue Expenditures | .......... | .......... | .......... | 16 |
| Corporate Stock Expenditures | .......... | .......... | .......... | 17 |
| Total for 1910 | .......... | .......... | .......... | 18 |
| **1911** | | | | |
| Revenue Expenditures | .......... | .......... | .......... | 19 |
| Corporate Stock Expenditures | .......... | .......... | .......... | 20 |
| Total for 1911 | .......... | .......... | .......... | 21 |
| **1912** | | | | |
| Revenue Expenditures | .......... | .......... | .......... | 22 |
| Corporate Stock Expenditures | .......... | .......... | .......... | 23 |
| Total for 1912 | .......... | .......... | .......... | 24 |
| **1913** | | | | |
| Revenue Expenditures | .......... | .......... | .......... | 25 |
| Corporate Stock Expenditures | .......... | .......... | .......... | 26 |
| Total for 1913 | .......... | .......... | .......... | 27 |
| **1914** | | | | |
| Revenue Expenditures | $144,448 63 | .......... | .......... | 28 |
| Corporate Stock Expenditures | 375,566 43 | .......... | .......... | 29 |
| Total for 1914 | **$520,015 06** | .......... | .......... | 30 |

## NEW YORK

Made from Revenue and from Corporate Stock Funds for the Departments, According to Objects of Expenditure:

| LINE No. | Purchase of Equipment | Materials | Contract or Open Order Service | Contingencies | Fixed Charges and Contributions | Unclassified |
|---|---|---|---|---|---|---|
| 1 | .......... | .......... | .......... | .......... | $4,000,000 00 | .......... |
| 2 | .......... | .......... | .......... | .......... | .......... | .......... |
| 3 | .......... | .......... | .......... | .......... | **$4,000,000 00** | .......... |
| 4 | .......... | .......... | .......... | .......... | $10,000,000 00 | .......... |
| 5 | .......... | .......... | .......... | .......... | .......... | .......... |
| 6 | .......... | .......... | .......... | .......... | **$10,000,000 00** | .......... |
| 7 | .......... | .......... | .......... | .......... | $3,287,366 74 | .......... |
| 8 | .......... | .......... | .......... | .......... | .......... | .......... |
| 9 | .......... | .......... | .......... | .......... | **$3,287,366 74** | .......... |
| 10 | .......... | .......... | .......... | .......... | $2,300,000 00 | .......... |
| 11 | .......... | .......... | .......... | .......... | .......... | .......... |
| 12 | .......... | .......... | .......... | .......... | **$2,300,000 00** | .......... |
| 13 | .......... | .......... | .......... | .......... | $2,500,000 00 | .......... |
| 14 | .......... | .......... | .......... | .......... | .......... | .......... |
| 15 | .......... | .......... | .......... | .......... | **$2,500,000 00** | .......... |
| 16 | .......... | .......... | .......... | .......... | .......... | .......... |
| 17 | .......... | .......... | .......... | .......... | .......... | .......... |
| 18 | .......... | .......... | .......... | .......... | .......... | .......... |
| 19 | .......... | .......... | .......... | .......... | .......... | .......... |
| 20 | .......... | .......... | .......... | .......... | .......... | .......... |
| 21 | .......... | .......... | .......... | .......... | .......... | .......... |
| 22 | .......... | .......... | .......... | .......... | .......... | .......... |
| 23 | .......... | .......... | .......... | .......... | .......... | .......... |
| 24 | .......... | .......... | .......... | .......... | .......... | .......... |
| 25 | .......... | .......... | .......... | .......... | .......... | .......... |
| 26 | .......... | .......... | .......... | .......... | .......... | .......... |
| 27 | .......... | .......... | .......... | .......... | .......... | .......... |
| 28 | .......... | .......... | .......... | .......... | $144,448 63 | .......... |
| 29 | .......... | .......... | .......... | .......... | 375,566 43 | .......... |
| 30 | .......... | .......... | .......... | .......... | **$520,015 06** | .......... |

COMPARATIVE STATEMENTS SHOWING SEPARATELY THE EXPENDITURES YEARS 1910 TO 1914, INCLUSIVE, CLASSIFIED BY

| | Total | Personal Service | Supplies | LINE No. |
|---|---|---|---|---|
| **ADVANCES FOR LOCAL IMPROVEMENTS—FUND FOR STREET AND PARK OPENINGS** | | | | |
| **1910** | | | | |
| Revenue Expenditures | .......... | .......... | .......... | 1 |
| Corporate Stock Expenditures | $8,530,644 12 | $292,959 71 | $1,506 31 | 2 |
| Total for 1910 | **$8,530,644 12** | **$292,959 71** | **$1,506 31** | 3 |
| **1911** | | | | |
| Revenue Expenditures | .......... | .......... | .......... | 4 |
| Corporate Stock Expenditures | $6,300,963 84 | $296,763 98 | $2,239 55 | 5 |
| Total for 1911 | **$6,300,963 84** | **$296,763 98** | **$2,239 55** | 6 |
| **1912** | | | | |
| Revenue Expenditures | .......... | .......... | .......... | 7 |
| Corporate Stock Expenditures | $7,916,073 05 | $318,804 41 | $3,391 08 | 8 |
| Total for 1912 | **$7,916,073 05** | **$318,804 41** | **$3,391 08** | 9 |
| **1913** | | | | |
| Revenue Expenditures | .......... | .......... | .......... | 10 |
| Corporate Stock Expenditures | $8,286,777 28 | $299,292 55 | $3,687 95 | 11 |
| Total for 1913 | **$8,286,777 28** | **$299,292 55** | **$3,687 95** | 12 |
| **1914** | | | | |
| Revenue Expenditures | .......... | .......... | .......... | 13 |
| Corporate Stock Expenditures | $4,855,640 93 | $247,945 18 | $1,742 00 | 14 |
| Total for 1914 | **$4,855,640 93** | **$237,945 18** | **$1,742 00** | 15 |
| **ADVANCES FOR LOCAL IMPROVEMENTS—STREET IMPROVEMENT FUND** | | | | |
| **1910** | | | | |
| Revenue Expenditures | .......... | .......... | .......... | 16 |
| Corporate Stock Expenditures | $7,554,663 89 | $478,487 14 | .......... | 17 |
| Total for 1910 | **$7,554,663 89** | **$478,487 14** | .......... | 18 |
| **1911** | | | | |
| Revenue Expenditures | .......... | .......... | .......... | 19 |
| Corporate Stock Expenditures | $6,794,647 83 | $525,199 06 | $847 45 | 20 |
| Total for 1911 | **$6,794,647 83** | **$525,199 06** | **$847 45** | 21 |
| **1912** | | | | |
| Revenue Expenditures | .......... | .......... | .......... | 22 |
| Corporate Stock Expenditures | $7,284,438 17 | $557,517 55 | $3,668 80 | 23 |
| Total for 1912 | **$7,284,438 17** | **$557,517 55** | **$3,668 80** | 24 |
| **1913** | | | | |
| Revenue Expenditures | .......... | .......... | .......... | 25 |
| Corporate Stock Expenditures | $9,590,277 94 | $994,229 28 | $961 70 | 26 |
| Total for 1913 | **$9,590,277 94** | **$994,229 28** | **$961 70** | 27 |
| **1914** | | | | |
| Revenue Expenditures | .......... | .......... | .......... | 28 |
| Corporate Stock Expenditures | $15,923,876 61 | $720,243 08 | $530 53 | 29 |
| Total for 1914 | **$15,923,876 61** | **$720,243 08** | **$530 53** | 30 |

NEW YORK

Made from Revenue and from Corporate Stock Funds for the Departments, According to Objects of Expenditure:

| Line No. | Purchase of Equipment | Materials | Contract or Open Order Service | Contingencies | Fixed Charges and Contributions | Unclassified |
|---|---|---|---|---|---|---|
| 1 | .......... | .......... | .......... | .......... | .......... | .......... |
| 2 | $3,768 85 | .......... | $62,359 07 | $1,800 00 | .......... | $8,168,250 18 |
| 3 | **$3,768 85** | .......... | **$62,359 07** | **$1,800 00** | .......... | **$8,168,250 18** |
| 4 | .......... | .......... | .......... | .......... | .......... | .......... |
| 5 | $3,398 25 | .......... | $58,942 13 | $2,000 00 | .......... | $5,937,519 93 |
| 6 | **$3,498 25** | .......... | **$58,942 13** | **$2,000 00** | .......... | **$9,937,519 93** |
| 7 | .......... | .......... | .......... | .......... | .......... | .......... |
| 8 | $2,784 15 | .......... | $52,529 12 | $2,800 00 | .......... | $7,535,764 29 |
| 9 | **$2,784 15** | .......... | **$52,529 12** | **$2,800 00** | .......... | **$7,535,764 29** |
| 10 | .......... | .......... | .......... | .......... | .......... | .......... |
| 11 | $1,246 00 | .......... | $50,297 27 | $2,400 00 | .......... | $7,929,853 51 |
| 12 | **$1,246 00** | .......... | **$50,297 27** | **$2,400 00** | .......... | **$7,929,853 51** |
| 13 | .......... | .......... | .......... | .......... | .......... | .......... |
| 14 | $3,992 73 | .......... | $4,921 97 | $2,955 70 | .......... | $4,594,083 35 |
| 15 | **$3,992 73** | .......... | **$4,921 97** | **$2,955 70** | .......... | **$4,594,083 35** |
| 16 | .......... | .......... | .......... | .......... | .......... | .......... |
| 17 | .......... | .......... | $4,244,324 25 | .......... | .......... | $2,831,852 50 |
| 18 | .......... | ........ | **$4,244,324 25** | .......... | .......... | **$2,831,852 50** |
| 19 | .......... | .......... | .......... | .......... | .......... | .......... |
| 20 | $27,573 65 | $152 40 | $6,129,983 50 | .......... | .......... | $110,891 77 |
| 21 | **$27,573 65** | **$152 40** | **$6,129,983 50** | .......... | .... | **$110,891 77** |
| 22 | .......... | .......... | .......... | .......... | .......... | .......... |
| 23 | $805 05 | $3,705 38 | $6,655,193 22 | .......... | .......... | $63,548 17 |
| 24 | **$805 05** | **$3,705 38** | **$6,655,193 22** | .......... | .......... | **$63,548 17** |
| 25 | .......... | .......... | .......... | .......... | .......... | .......... |
| 26 | $1,251 72 | $1,700 95 | $8,547,694 89 | .......... | .......... | $44,439 40 |
| 27 | **$1,251 72** | **$1,700 95** | **$8,547,694 89** | .......... | .......... | **$44,439 40** |
| 28 | .......... | .......... | .......... | .......... | .......... | .......... |
| 29 | $1,750 86 | $125 00 | $6,988,237 09 | $4,714 05 | .......... | $8,208,275 40 |
| 30 | **$1,750 86** | **$125 00** | **$6,988,237 09** | **$4,714 05** | .......... | **$8,208,275 40** |

Comparative Statements Showing Separately the Expenditures
Years 1910 to 1914, Inclusive, Classified by

| | Total | Personal Service | Supplies | Line No. |
|---|---|---|---|---|
| **DIRECT STATE TAX** | | | | |
| **1912** | | | | |
| Tax Levy: | | | | |
| New York County | $3,211,557 62 | .......... | .......... | 1 |
| Kings County | 847,328 81 | .......... | .......... | 2 |
| Queens County | 200,986 53 | .......... | .......... | 3 |
| Richmond County | 41,472 69 | .......... | .......... | 4 |
| Total for 1912 | **$4,301,345 65** | .......... | .......... | 5 |
| **1913** | | | | |
| Tax Levy: | | | | |
| New York County | $5,736,005 10 | .......... | .......... | 6 |
| Kings County | 1,684,598 71 | .......... | .......... | 7 |
| Queens County | 445,609 98 | .......... | .......... | 8 |
| Richmond County | 80,818 17 | .......... | .......... | 9 |
| Total for 1913 | **$7,947,031 96** | .......... | .......... | 10 |
| **1914** | | | | |
| Tax Levy: | | | | |
| New York County | $3,308,080 34 | .......... | .......... | 11 |
| Kings County | 959,311 91 | .......... | .......... | 12 |
| Queens County | 263,332 56 | .......... | .......... | 13 |
| Richmond County | 45,578 62 | .......... | .......... | 14 |
| Total for 1914 | **$4,576,303 43** | .......... | .......... | 15 |
| **CHARITABLE INSTITUTIONS—NEW YORK COUNTY** | | | | |
| **1910** | | | | |
| Revenue Expenditures | $113,875 22 | .......... | .......... | 16 |
| Corporate Stock Expenditures | .......... | .......... | .......... | 17 |
| Total for 1910 | **$113,875 22** | .......... | .......... | 18 |
| **1911** | | | | |
| Revenue Expenditures | $112,995 01 | .......... | .......... | 19 |
| Corporate Stock Expenditures | .......... | .......... | .......... | 20 |
| Total for 1911 | **$112,995 01** | .......... | .......... | 21 |
| **1912** | | | | |
| Revenue Expenditures | $105,153 59 | .......... | .......... | 22 |
| Corporate Stock Expenditures | .......... | .......... | .......... | 23 |
| Total for 1912 | **$105,153 59** | .......... | .......... | 24 |
| **1913** | | | | |
| Revenue Expenditures | $102,928 80 | .......... | .......... | 25 |
| Corporate Stock Expenditures | .......... | .......... | .......... | 26 |
| Total for 1913 | **$102,928 80** | .......... | .......... | 27 |
| **1914** | | | | |
| Revenue Expenditures | $78,905 98 | .......... | .......... | 28 |
| Corporate Stock Expenditures | .......... | .......... | .......... | 29 |
| Total for 1914 | **$78,905 98** | .......... | .......... | 30 |

NEW YORK

Made from Revenue and from Corporate Stock Funds for the Departments, According to Objects of Expenditure:

| Line No. | Purchase of Equipment | Materials | Contract or Open Order Service | Contingencies | Fixed Charges and Contributions | Unclassified |
|---|---|---|---|---|---|---|
| 1 | .......... | .......... | .......... | .......... | $3,211,557 62 | .......... |
| 2 | .......... | .......... | .......... | .......... | 847,328 81 | .......... |
| 3 | .......... | .......... | .......... | .......... | 200,986 53 | .......... |
| 4 | .......... | .......... | .......... | .......... | 41,472 69 | .......... |
| 5 | .......... | .......... | .......... | .......... | **$4,301,345 65** | .......... |
| 6 | .......... | .......... | .......... | .......... | $5,736,005 10 | .......... |
| 7 | .......... | .......... | .......... | .......... | 1,684,598 71 | .......... |
| 8 | .......... | .......... | .......... | .......... | 445,609 98 | .......... |
| 9 | .......... | .......... | .......... | .......... | 80,818 17 | .......... |
| 10 | .......... | .......... | .......... | .......... | **$7,947,031 96** | .......... |
| 11 | .......... | .......... | .......... | .......... | $3,308,080 34 | .......... |
| 12 | .......... | .......... | .......... | .......... | 959,311 91 | .......... |
| 13 | .......... | .......... | .......... | .......... | 263,332 56 | .......... |
| 14 | .......... | .......... | .......... | .......... | 45,578 62 | .......... |
| 15 | .......... | .......... | .......... | .......... | **$4,576,303 43** | .......... |
| 16 | .......... | .......... | .......... | .......... | $113,875 22 | .......... |
| 17 | .......... | .......... | .......... | .......... | .......... | .......... |
| 18 | .......... | .......... | .......... | .......... | **$113,875 22** | .......... |
| 19 | .......... | .......... | .......... | .......... | $112,995 01 | .......... |
| 20 | .......... | .......... | .......... | .......... | .......... | .......... |
| 21 | .......... | .......... | .......... | .......... | **$112,995 01** | .......... |
| 22 | .......... | .......... | .......... | .......... | $105,153 59 | .......... |
| 23 | .......... | .......... | .......... | .......... | .......... | .......... |
| 24 | .......... | .......... | .......... | .......... | **$105,153 59** | .......... |
| 25 | .......... | .......... | .......... | .......... | $102,928 80 | .......... |
| 26 | .......... | .......... | .......... | .......... | .......... | .......... |
| 27 | .......... | .......... | .......... | .......... | **$102,928 80** | .......... |
| 28 | .......... | .......... | .......... | .......... | $78,905 98 | .......... |
| 29 | .......... | .......... | .......... | .......... | .......... | .......... |
| 30 | .......... | .......... | .......... | .......... | **$78,905 98** | .......... |

COMPARATIVE STATEMENTS SHOWING SEPARATELY THE EXPENDITURES
YEARS 1910 TO 1914, INCLUSIVE, CLASSIFIED BY

| | Total | Personal Service | Supplies | LINE No. |
|---|---|---|---|---|
| **BOARD OF CITY RECORD—NEW YORK COUNTY** | | | | |
| **1910** | | | | |
| Revenue Expenditures | $34,984 60 | .......... | .......... | 1 |
| Corporate Stock Expenditures | .......... | .......... | .......... | 2 |
| Total for 1910 | **$34,984 60** | .......... | .......... | 3 |
| **1911** | | | | |
| Revenue Expenditures | $38,614 40 | .......... | .......... | 4 |
| Corporate Stock Expenditures | .......... | .......... | .......... | 5 |
| Total for 1911 | **$38,614 40** | .......... | .......... | 6 |
| **1912** | | | | |
| Revenue Expenditures | $39,882 29 | .......... | .......... | 7 |
| Corporate Stock Expenditures | .......... | .......... | .......... | 8 |
| Total for 1912 | **$39,882 29** | .......... | .......... | 9 |
| **1913** | | | | |
| Revenue Expenditures | $41,389 61 | .......... | .......... | 10 |
| Corporate Stock Expenditures | .......... | .......... | .......... | 11 |
| Total for 1913 | **$41,389 61** | .......... | .......... | 12 |
| **1914** | | | | |
| Revenue Expenditures | $34,203 26 | .......... | .......... | 13 |
| Corporate Stock Expenditures | .......... | .......... | .......... | 14 |
| Total for 1914 | **$34,203 26** | .......... | .......... | 15 |
| **COUNTY CLERK—NEW YORK COUNTY** | | | | |
| **1910** | | | | |
| Revenue Expenditures | $150,558 53 | $148,825 53 | $998 39 | 16 |
| Corporate Stock Expenditures | .......... | .......... | .......... | 17 |
| Total for 1910 | **$150,588 53** | **$148,825 53** | **$998 39** | 18 |
| **1911** | | | | |
| Revenue Expenditures | $140,557 78 | $135,971 80 | $2,434 42 | 19 |
| Corporate Stock Expenditures | 19,277 55 | .......... | .......... | 20 |
| Total for 1911 | **$159,835 33** | **$135,971 80** | **$2,434 42** | 21 |
| **1912** | | | | |
| Revenue Expenditures | $184,568 67 | $180,743 94 | $1,347 68 | 22 |
| Corporate Stock Expenditures | 47,589 18 | .......... | .......... | 23 |
| Total for 1912 | **$232,157 85** | **$180,743 94** | **$1,347 68** | 24 |
| **1913** | | | | |
| Revenue Expenditures | $185,207 91 | $182,318 84 | $926 19 | 25 |
| Corporate Stock Expenditures | 6,640 19 | .......... | .......... | 26 |
| Total for 1913 | **$191,848 10** | **$182,318 84** | **$926 19** | 27 |
| **1914** | | | | |
| Revenue Expenditures | $193,736 08 | $190,000 19 | $1,918 66 | 28 |
| Corporate Stock Expenditures | .......... | .......... | .......... | 29 |
| Total for 1914 | **$193,736 08** | **$190,000 19** | **$1,918 66** | 30 |

# NEW YORK

Made from Revenue and from Corporate Stock Funds for the Departments, According to Objects of Expenditure:

| LINE No. | Purchase of Equipment | Materials | Contract or Open Order Service | Contingencies | Fixed Charges and Contributions | Unclassified |
|---|---|---|---|---|---|---|
| 1 | .......... | .......... | $34,984 60 | .......... | .......... | .......... |
| 2 | .......... | .......... | .......... | .......... | .......... | .......... |
| 3 | .......... | .......... | **$34,984 60** | .......... | .......... | .......... |
| 4 | .......... | .......... | $38,614 40 | .......... | .......... | .......... |
| 5 | .......... | .......... | .......... | .......... | .......... | .......... |
| 6 | .......... | .......... | **$38,614 40** | .......... | .......... | .......... |
| 7 | .......... | .......... | $39,882 29 | .......... | .......... | .......... |
| 8 | .......... | .......... | .......... | .......... | .......... | .......... |
| 9 | .......... | .......... | **$39,882 29** | .......... | .......... | .......... |
| 10 | .......... | .......... | $41,389 61 | .......... | .......... | .......... |
| 11 | .......... | .......... | .......... | .......... | .......... | .......... |
| 12 | .......... | .......... | **$41,389 61** | .......... | .......... | .......... |
| 13 | .......... | .......... | $34,203 26 | .......... | .......... | .......... |
| 14 | .......... | .......... | .......... | .......... | .......... | .......... |
| 15 | .......... | .......... | **$34,203 26** | .......... | .......... | .......... |
| 16 | .......... | .......... | $200 00 | $474 61 | .......... | $90 00 |
| 17 | .......... | .......... | .......... | .......... | .......... | .......... |
| 18 | .......... | .......... | **$200 00** | **$474 61** | .......... | **$90 00** |
| 19 | .......... | .......... | $375 21 | $1,776 35 | .......... | .......... |
| 20 | $18,023 69 | .......... | .......... | .......... | .......... | $1,253 86 |
| 21 | **$18,023 69** | .......... | **$375 21** | **$1,776 35** | .......... | **$1,253 86** |
| 22 | $1,139 45 | .......... | $400 00 | $937 60 | .......... | .......... |
| 23 | 47,589 18 | .......... | .......... | .......... | .......... | .......... |
| 24 | **$48,728 63** | .......... | **$400 00** | **$937 60** | .......... | .......... |
| 25 | $1,148 64 | .......... | $814 24 | .......... | .......... | .......... |
| 26 | 6,640 19 | .......... | .......... | .......... | .......... | .......... |
| 27 | **$7,788 83** | .......... | **$814 24** | .......... | .......... | .......... |
| 28 | $933 35 | .......... | $875 88 | $8 00 | .......... | .......... |
| 29 | .......... | .......... | .......... | .......... | .......... | .......... |
| 30 | **$933 35** | .......... | **$875 88** | **$8 00** | .......... | .......... |

Comparative Statements Showing Separately the Expenditures
Years 1910 to 1914, Inclusive, Classified by

| | Total | Personal Service | Supplies | Line No. |
|---|---|---|---|---|
| **COURT OF GENERAL SESSIONS, NEW YORK COUNTY** | | | | |
| **1910** | | | | |
| Revenue Expenditures | $292,318 27 | $290,228 85 | .......... | 1 |
| Corporate Stock Expenditures | .......... | .......... | .......... | 2 |
| Total for 1910 | **$292,318 27** | **$290,228 85** | .......... | 3 |
| **1911** | | | | |
| Revenue Expenditures | $314,139 08 | $311,861 51 | .......... | 4 |
| Corporate Stock Expenditures | .......... | .......... | .......... | 5 |
| Total for 1911 | **$314,139 08** | **$311,861 51** | .......... | 6 |
| **1912** | | | | |
| Revenue Expenditures | $351,901 91 | $349 103 61 | $1,509 10 | 7 |
| Corporate Stock Expenditures | .......... | .......... | .......... | 8 |
| Total for 1912 | **$351,901 91** | **$349,103 61** | **$1,509 10** | 9 |
| **1913** | | | | |
| Revenue Expenditures | $378,996 31 | 365,719 76 | $1,077 64 | 10 |
| Corporate Stock Expenditures | .......... | .......... | .......... | 11 |
| Total for 1913 | **$378,996 31** | **$365,719 76** | **$1,077 64** | 12 |
| **1914** | | | | |
| Revenue Expenditures | $404,724 90 | $396,681 99 | $879 89 | 13 |
| Corporate Stock Expenditures | .......... | .......... | .......... | 14 |
| Total for 1914 | **$404,724 90** | **$396,681 99** | **$879 89** | 15 |
| **SUPREME COURT, FIRST DEPARTMENT (NEW YORK COUNTY)** | | | | |
| **1910** | | | | |
| Revenue Expenditures | $823,294 42 | $813,599 98 | $7,699 96 | 16 |
| Corporate Stock Expenditures | .......... | .......... | .......... | 17 |
| Total for 1910 | **$823,294 42** | **$813,599 98** | **$7,699 96** | 18 |
| **1911** | | | | |
| Revenue Expenditures | $858,978 84 | $849,600 55 | $8,151 01 | 19 |
| Corporate Stock Expenditures | .......... | .......... | .......... | 20 |
| Total for 1911 | **$858,978 84** | **$849,600 55** | **$8,151 01** | 21 |
| **1912** | | | | |
| Revenue Expenditures | $918,868 42 | $912,985 23 | $15 65 | 22 |
| Corporate Stock Expenditures | .......... | .......... | .......... | 23 |
| Total for 1912 | **$918,868 42** | **$912,985 23** | **$15 65** | 24 |
| **1913** | | | | |
| Revenue Expenditures | $976,589 75 | $968,093 64 | .......... | 25 |
| Corporate Stock Expenditures | .......... | .......... | .......... | 26 |
| Total for 1913 | **$976,589 75** | **$968,093 64** | .......... | 27 |
| **1914** | | | | |
| Revenue Expenditures | $990,529 66 | $981,598 24 | .......... | 28 |
| Corporate Stock Expenditures | .......... | .......... | .......... | 29 |
| Total for 1914 | **$990,529 66** | **$981,598 24** | .......... | 30 |

## NEW YORK

MADE FROM REVENUE AND FROM CORPORATE STOCK FUNDS FOR THE DEPARTMENTS, ACCORDING TO OBJECTS OF EXPENDITURE:

| LINE No. | Purchase of Equipment | Materials | Contract or Open Order Service | Contingencies | Fixed Charges and Contributions | Unclassified |
|---|---|---|---|---|---|---|
| 1 | .......... | .......... | $946 20 | $1,143 22 | .......... | .......... |
| 2 | .......... | .......... | .......... | .......... | .......... | .......... |
| 3 | .......... | .......... | **$946 20** | **$1,143 22** | .......... | .......... |
| 4 | .......... | .......... | $899 95 | $1,377 62 | .......... | .......... |
| 5 | .......... | .......... | .......... | .......... | .......... | .......... |
| 6 | .......... | .......... | **$899 95** | **$1,377 62** | .......... | .......... |
| 7 | .......... | .......... | $989 37 | $299 83 | .......... | .......... |
| 8 | .......... | .......... | .......... | .......... | .......... | .......... |
| 9 | .......... | .......... | **$989 37** | **$299 83** | .......... | .......... |
| 10 | $1,145 45 | .......... | $11,020 06 | $33 40 | .......... | .......... |
| 11 | .......... | .......... | .......... | .......... | .......... | .......... |
| 12 | **$1,145 45** | .......... | **$11,020 06** | **$33 40** | .......... | .......... |
| 13 | $1,422 10 | .......... | $5,713 14 | $27 78 | .......... | .......... |
| 14 | .......... | .......... | .......... | .......... | .......... | .......... |
| 15 | **$1,422 10** | .......... | **$5,713 14** | **$27 78** | .......... | .......... |
| 16 | .......... | .......... | $1,138 68 | $855 80 | .......... | .......... |
| 17 | .......... | .......... | .......... | .......... | .......... | .......... |
| 18 | .......... | .......... | **$1,138 68** | **$855 80** | .......... | .......... |
| 19 | .......... | .......... | $1,227 28 | .......... | .......... | .......... |
| 20 | .......... | .......... | .......... | .......... | .......... | .......... |
| 21 | .......... | .......... | **$1,227 28** | .......... | .......... | .......... |
| 22 | .......... | .......... | $3,783 54 | $84 00 | $2,000 00 | .......... |
| 23 | .......... | .......... | .......... | .......... | .......... | .......... |
| 24 | .......... | .......... | **$3,783 54** | **$84 00** | **$2,000 00** | .......... |
| 25 | $2,776 19 | .......... | $722 50 | $113 30 | $4,884 12 | .......... |
| 26 | .......... | .......... | .......... | .......... | .......... | .......... |
| 27 | **$2,776 19** | .......... | **$722 50** | **$113 30** | **$4,884 12** | .......... |
| 28 | $2,606 00 | .......... | .......... | $48 00 | $6,277 42 | .......... |
| 29 | .......... | .......... | .......... | .......... | .......... | .......... |
| 30 | **$2,606 00** | .......... | .......... | **$48 00** | **$6,277 42** | .......... |

Comparative Statements Showing Separately the Expenditures
Years 1910 to 1914, Inclusive, Classified by

| | Total | Personal Service | Supplies | Line No. |
|---|---|---|---|---|
| **SUPREME COURT, FIRST DEPARTMENT, MAINTENANCE OF APPELLATE DIVISION COURT HOUSE** | | | | |
| **1910** | | | | |
| Revenue Expenditures | $30,780 02 | $17,557 02 | $5,755 41 | 1 |
| Corporate Stock Expenditures | .......... | .......... | .......... | 2 |
| Total for 1910 | **$30,780 02** | **$17,557 02** | **$5,755 41** | 3 |
| **1911** | | | | |
| Revenue Expenditures | $30,613 14 | $18,073 42 | $4,819 34 | 4 |
| Corporate Stock Expenditures | .......... | .......... | .......... | 5 |
| Total for 1911 | **$30,613 14** | **$18,073 42** | **$4,819 34** | 6 |
| **1912** | | | | |
| Revenue Expenditures | $27,374 34 | $18,180 56 | $5,799 81 | 7 |
| Corporate Stock Expenditures | .......... | .......... | .......... | 8 |
| Total for 1912 | **$27,374 34** | **$18,180 56** | **$5,799 81** | 9 |
| **1913** | | | | |
| Revenue Expenditures | $30,812 62 | $19,090 00 | $5,221 17 | 10 |
| Corporate Stock Expenditures | .......... | .......... | .......... | 11 |
| Total for 1913 | **$30,812 62** | **$19,090 00** | **$5,221 17** | 12 |
| **1914** | | | | |
| Revenue Expenditures | $28,792 71 | $18,295 18 | $4,558 52 | 13 |
| Corporate Stock Expenditures | .......... | .......... | .......... | 14 |
| Total for 1914 | **$28,792 71** | **$18,295 18** | **$4,558 52** | 15 |
| **SURROGATES' COURT, NEW YORK COUNTY** | | | | |
| **1910** | | | | |
| Revenue Expenditures | $176,862 30 | $174,403 47 | $1,358 18 | 16 |
| Corporate Stock Expenditures | .......... | .......... | .......... | 17 |
| Total for 1910 | **$176,862 30** | **$174,403 47** | **$1,358 18** | 18 |
| **1911** | | | | |
| Revenue Expenditures | $175,787 12 | $172,735 54 | $2,087 03 | 19 |
| Corporate Stock Expenditures | .......... | .......... | .......... | 20 |
| Total for 1911 | **$175,787 12** | **$172,735 54** | **$2,087 03** | 21 |
| **1912** | | | | |
| Revenue Expenditures | $184,348 10 | $182,453 22 | $872 75 | 22 |
| Corporate Stock Expenditures | .......... | .......... | .......... | 23 |
| Total for 1912 | **$184,348 10** | **$182,453 22** | **$872 75** | 24 |
| **1913** | | | | |
| Revenue Expenditures | $203,676 02 | $199,582 63 | $860 46 | 25 |
| Corporate Stock Expenditures | .......... | .......... | .......... | 26 |
| Total for 1913 | **$203,676 02** | **$199,582 63** | **$860 46** | 27 |
| **1914** | | | | |
| Revenue Expenditures | $193,683 54 | $190,658 52 | $990 00 | 28 |
| Corporate Stock Expenditures | .......... | .......... | .......... | 29 |
| Total for 1914 | **$193,683 54** | **$190,658 52** | **$990 00** | 30 |

NEW YORK

MADE FROM REVENUE AND FROM CORPORATE STOCK FUNDS FOR THE DEPARTMENTS, ACCORDING TO OBJECTS OF EXPENDITURE:

| LINE No. | Purchase of Equipment | Materials | Contract or Open Order Service | Contingencies | Fixed Charges and Contributions | Unclassified |
|---|---|---|---|---|---|---|
| 1 | .......... | .......... | $7,000 99 | $466 60 | .......... | .......... |
| 2 | .......... | .......... | .......... | .......... | .......... | .......... |
| 3 | .......... | .......... | **$7,000 99** | **$466 60** | .......... | .......... |
| 4 | .......... | .......... | $7,366 30 | $354 08 | .......... | .......... |
| 5 | .......... | .......... | .......... | .......... | .......... | .......... |
| 6 | .......... | .......... | **$7,366 30** | **$354 08** | .......... | .......... |
| 7 | $114 26 | .......... | $2,896 48 | $383 23 | .......... | .......... |
| 8 | .......... | .......... | .......... | .......... | .......... | .......... |
| 9 | **$114 26** | .......... | **$2,896 48** | **$383 23** | .......... | .......... |
| 10 | $980 96 | .......... | $5,120 49 | $400 00 | .......... | .......... |
| 11 | .......... | .......... | .......... | .......... | .......... | .......... |
| 12 | **$980 96** | .......... | **$5,120 49** | **$400 00** | .......... | .......... |
| 13 | $2,211 42 | .......... | $3,327 59 | $400 00 | .......... | .......... |
| 14 | .......... | .......... | .......... | .......... | .......... | .......... |
| 15 | **$2,211 42** | .......... | **$3,327 59** | **$400 00** | .......... | .......... |
| 16 | .......... | .......... | $655 60 | $445 05 | .......... | .......... |
| 17 | .......... | .......... | .......... | .......... | .......... | .......... |
| 18 | .......... | .......... | **$655 60** | **$445 05** | .......... | .......... |
| 10 | .......... | .......... | $506 90 | $457 65 | .......... | .......... |
| 20 | .......... | .......... | .......... | .......... | .......... | .......... |
| 21 | .......... | .......... | **$506 90** | **$457 65** | .......... | .......... |
| 22 | $183 95 | .......... | $356 77 | $481 41 | .......... | .......... |
| 23 | .......... | .......... | .......... | .......... | .......... | .......... |
| 24 | **$183 95** | .......... | **$356 77** | **$481 41** | .......... | .......... |
| 25 | $1,975 81 | .......... | $1,232 37 | $24 75 | .......... | .......... |
| 26 | .......... | .......... | .......... | .......... | .......... | .......... |
| 27 | **$1,975 81** | .......... | **$1,232 37** | **$24 75** | .......... | .......... |
| 28 | $1,493 98 | .......... | $516 04 | $25 00 | .......... | .......... |
| 29 | .......... | .......... | .......... | .......... | .......... | .......... |
| 30 | **$1,493 98** | .......... | **$516 04** | **$25 00** | .......... | .......... |

Comparative Statements Showing Separately the Expenditures
Years 1910 to 1914, Inclusive, Classified by

| | Total | Personal Service | Supplies | Line No. |
|---|---|---|---|---|
| **DISTRICT ATTORNEY, NEW YORK COUNTY** | | | | |
| **1910** | | | | |
| Revenue Expenditures | $371,242 25 | $332,757 63 | $1,549 18 | 1 |
| Corporate Stock Expenditures | .......... | .......... | .......... | 2 |
| Total for 1910 | **$371,242 25** | **$332,757 63** | **$1,549 18** | 3 |
| **1911** | | | | |
| Revenue Expenditures | $409,108 45 | $387,753 89 | $1,550 00 | 4 |
| Corporate Stock Expenditures | .......... | .......... | .......... | 5 |
| Total for 1911 | **$409,108 45** | **$387,753 89** | **$1,550 00** | 6 |
| **1912** | | | | |
| Revenue Expenditures | $450,536 90 | $402,959 42 | $2,041 16 | 7 |
| Corporate Stock Expenditures | .......... | .......... | .......... | 8 |
| Total for 1912 | **$450,536 90** | **$402,959 42** | **$2,041 16** | 9 |
| **1913** | | | | |
| Revenue Expenditures | $469,877 03 | $422,918 62 | $7,808 64 | 10 |
| Corporate Stock Expenditures | .......... | .......... | .......... | 11 |
| Total for 1913 | **$469,877 03** | **$422,918 62** | **$7,808 64** | 12 |
| **1914** | | | | |
| Revenue Expenditures | $522,847 74 | $424,524 92 | $1,777 75 | 13 |
| Corporate Stock Expenditures | .......... | .......... | .......... | 14 |
| Total for 1914 | **$522,847 74** | **$424,524 92** | **$1,777 75** | 15 |
| **COMMISSIONER OF JURORS—NEW YORK COUNTY** | | | | |
| **1910** | | | | |
| Revenue Expenditures | $50,341 57 | $46,122 60 | $1,937 05 | 16 |
| Corporate Stock Expenditures | .......... | .......... | .......... | 17 |
| Total for 1910 | **$50,341 57** | **$46,122 60** | **$1,937 05** | 18 |
| **1911** | | | | |
| Revenue Expenditures | $52,548 46 | $48,185 27 | $2,076 10 | 19 |
| Corporate Stock Expenditures | .......... | .......... | .......... | 20 |
| Total for 1911 | **$52,548 46** | **$48,185 27** | **$2,076 10** | 21 |
| **1912** | | | | |
| Revenue Expenditures | $52,122 28 | $47,642 75 | $2,015 39 | 22 |
| Corporate Stock Expenditures | .......... | .......... | .......... | 23 |
| Total for 1912 | **$52,122 28** | **$47,642 75** | **$2,015 39** | 24 |
| **1913** | | | | |
| Revenue Expenditures | $52,782 22 | $47,927 41 | $4,027 53 | 25 |
| Corporate Stock Expenditures | .......... | .......... | .......... | 26 |
| Total for 1913 | **$52,782 22** | **$47,927 41** | **$4,027 53** | 27 |
| **1914** | | | | |
| Revenue Expenditures | $57,181 14 | $52,417 69 | $3,885 81 | 28 |
| Corporate Stock Expenditures | .......... | .......... | .......... | 29 |
| Total for 1914 | **$57,181 14** | **$52,417 69** | **$3,885 81** | 30 |

NEW YORK

Made from Revenue and from Corporate Stock Funds for the Departments, According to Objects of Expenditure:

| Line No. | Purchase of Equipment | Materials | Contract or Open Order Service | Contingencies | Fixed Charges and Contributions | Unclassified |
|---|---|---|---|---|---|---|
| 1 | .......... | .......... | $2,428 73 | $34,506 71 | .......... | .......... |
| 2 | .......... | .......... | .......... | .......... | .......... | .......... |
| 3 | .......... | .......... | **$2,428 73** | **$34,506 71** | .......... | .......... |
| 4 | $841 96 | .......... | $2,721 44 | $12,321 62 | $576 50 | $3,343 04 |
| 5 | .......... | .......... | .......... | .......... | .......... | .......... |
| 6 | **$841 96** | .......... | **$2,721 44** | **$12,321 62** | **$576 50** | **$3,343 04** |
| 7 | $1,000 00 | .......... | $2,962 41 | $41,573 91 | .......... | .......... |
| 8 | .......... | .......... | .......... | .......... | .......... | .......... |
| 9 | **$1,000 00** | .......... | **$2,962 41** | **$41,573 91** | .......... | .......... |
| 10 | $2,300 00 | .......... | $15,681 65 | $21,168 12 | .......... | .......... |
| 11 | .......... | .......... | .......... | .......... | .......... | .......... |
| 12 | **$2,300 00** | .......... | **$15,681 65** | **$21,168 12** | .......... | .......... |
| 13 | $2,582 00 | .......... | $3,000 00 | $90,963 07 | .......... | .......... |
| 14 | .......... | .......... | .......... | .......... | .......... | .......... |
| 15 | **$2,582 00** | .......... | **$3,000 00** | **$90,963,07** | .......... | .......... |
| 16 | .......... | .......... | $152 65 | $2,129 27 | .......... | .......... |
| 17 | .......... | .......... | .......... | .......... | .......... | .......... |
| 18 | .......... | .......... | **$152 65** | **$2,129 27** | .......... | .......... |
| 19 | .......... | .......... | $167 01 | $2,120 08 | .......... | .......... |
| 20 | .......... | .......... | .......... | .......... | .......... | .......... |
| 21 | .......... | .......... | **$167 01** | **$2,120 08** | .......... | .......... |
| 22 | $154 00 | .......... | $179 99 | $2,130 15 | .......... | .......... |
| 23 | .......... | .......... | .......... | .......... | .......... | .......... |
| 24 | **$154 00** | .......... | **$179 99** | **$2,130 15** | .......... | .......... |
| 25 | $229 08 | .......... | $594 25 | $3 95 | .......... | .......... |
| 26 | .......... | .......... | .......... | .......... | .......... | .......... |
| 27 | **$229 08** | .......... | **$594 25** | **$3 95** | .......... | .......... |
| 28 | $243 00 | .......... | $630 25 | $4 39 | .......... | .......... |
| 29 | .......... | .......... | .......... | .......... | .......... | .......... |
| 30 | **$243 00** | .......... | **$630 25** | **$4 39** | .......... | .......... |

COMPARATIVE STATEMENTS SHOWING SEPARATELY THE EXPENDITURES YEARS 1910 TO 1914, INCLUSIVE, CLASSIFIED BY

| | Total | Personal Service | Supplies | LINE No. |
|---|---|---|---|---|
| **MISCELLANEOUS—NEW YORK COUNTY** | | | | |
| **1910** | | | | |
| Revenue Expenditures | $575,347 82 | $239,235 80 | .......... | 1 |
| Corporate Stock Expenditures | .......... | .......... | .......... | 2 |
| Total for 1910 | **$575,347 82** | **$239,235 80** | .......... | 3 |
| **1911** | | | | |
| Revenue Expenditures | $587,591 28 | $344,500 00 | $998 50 | 4 |
| Corporate Stock Expenditures | .......... | .......... | .......... | 5 |
| Total for 1911 | **$587,591 28** | **$344,500 00** | **$998 50** | 6 |
| **1912** | | | | |
| Revenue Expenditures | $449,071 18 | $426,129 53 | .......... | 7 |
| Corporate Stock Expenditures | .......... | .......... | .......... | 8 |
| Total for 1912 | **$449,071 18** | **$426,129 53** | .......... | 9 |
| **1913** | | | | |
| Revenue Expenditures | $482,962 87 | $409,557 24 | .......... | 10 |
| Corporate Stock Expenditures | .......... | .......... | .......... | 11 |
| Total for 1913 | **$482,962 87** | **$409,557 24** | .......... | 12 |
| **1914** | | | | |
| Revenue Expenditures | $475,295 09 | $411,587 97 | .......... | 13 |
| Corporate Stock Expenditures | .......... | .......... | .......... | 14 |
| Total for 1914 | **$475,295 09** | **$411,587 97** | .......... | 15 |
| **NATIONAL GUARD AND NAVAL MILITIA—NEW YORK COUNTY** | | | | |
| **1910** | | | | |
| Revenue Expenditures | $185,828 75 | $177,828 75 | .......... | 16 |
| Corporate Stock Expenditures | .......... | .......... | .......... | 17 |
| Total for 1910 | **$185,828 75** | **$177,828 75** | .......... | 18 |
| **1911** | | | | |
| Revenue Expenditures | $200,132 25 | $192,132 25 | .......... | 19 |
| Corporate Stock Expenditures | .......... | .......... | .......... | 20 |
| Total for 1911 | **$200,132 25** | **$192,132 25** | .......... | 21 |
| **1912** | | | | |
| Revenue Expenditures | $212,527 50 | $204,527 50 | .......... | 22 |
| Corporate Stock Expenditures | .......... | .......... | .......... | 23 |
| Total for 1912 | **$212,527 50** | **$204,527 50** | .......... | 24 |
| **1913** | | | | |
| Revenue Expenditures | $223,931 00 | $215,931 00 | .......... | 25 |
| Corporate Stock Expenditures | .......... | .......... | .......... | 26 |
| Total for 1913 | **$223,931 00** | **$215,931 00** | .......... | 27 |
| **1914** | | | | |
| Revenue Expenditures | $221,101 00 | $213,101 00 | .......... | 28 |
| Corporate Stock Expenditures | .......... | .......... | .......... | 29 |
| Total for 1914 | **$221,101 00** | **$213,101 00** | .......... | 30 |

NEW YORK

Made from Revenue and from Corporate Stock Funds for the Departments, According to Objects of Expenditure:

| LINE No. | Purchase of Equipment | Materials | Contract or Open Order Service | Contingencies | Fixed Charges and Contributions | Unclassified |
|---|---|---|---|---|---|---|
| 1 | .......... | .......... | $6,574 80 | $12,000 00 | $26,392 46 | $291,144 76 |
| 2 | .......... | .......... | .......... | .......... | .......... | .......... |
| 3 | .......... | .......... | **$6,574 80** | **$12,000 00** | **$26,392 46** | **$291,144 76** |
| 4 | .......... | .......... | .......... | $4,936 90 | $21,807 01 | $215,348 57 |
| 5 | .......... | .......... | .......... | .......... | .......... | .......... |
| 6 | .......... | .......... | .......... | **$4,936 90** | **$21,807 01** | **$215,348 57** |
| 7 | .......... | .......... | .......... | $1,458 00 | $21,483 65 | .......... |
| 8 | .......... | .......... | .......... | .......... | .......... | .......... |
| 9 | .......... | .......... | .......... | **$1,458 00** | **$21,483 65** | .......... |
| 10 | .......... | .......... | $11,118 66 | $1,182 15 | $61,104 82 | .......... |
| 11 | .......... | .......... | .......... | .......... | .......... | .......... |
| 12 | .......... | .......... | **$11,118 66** | **$1.182 15** | **$61,104 82** | .......... |
| 13 | .......... | .......... | .......... | $3,295 72 | $60,411 40 | .......... |
| 14 | .......... | .......... | .......... | .......... | .......... | .......... |
| 15 | .......... | .......... | .......... | **$3,295 72** | **$60,411 40** | .......... |
| 16 | .......... | .......... | $8,000 00 | .......... | .......... | .......... |
| 17 | .......... | .......... | .......... | .......... | .......... | .......... |
| 18 | .......... | .......... | **$8,000 00** | .......... | .......... | .......... |
| 19 | .......... | .......... | $8,000 00 | .......... | .......... | .......... |
| 20 | .......... | .......... | .......... | .......... | .......... | .......... |
| 21 | .......... | .......... | **$8,000 00** | .......... | .......... | .......... |
| 22 | .......... | .......... | $8,000 00 | .......... | .......... | .......... |
| 23 | .......... | .......... | .......... | .......... | .......... | .......... |
| 24 | .......... | .......... | **$8,000 00** | .......... | .......... | .......... |
| 25 | .......... | .......... | $8,000 00 | .......... | .......... | .......... |
| 26 | .......... | .......... | .......... | .......... | .......... | .......... |
| 27 | .......... | .......... | **$8,000 00** | .......... | .......... | .......... |
| 28 | .......... | .......... | $8,000 00 | .......... | .......... | .......... |
| 29 | .......... | .......... | .......... | .......... | .......... | .......... |
| 30 | .......... | .......... | **$8,000 00** | .......... | .......... | .......... |

THE CITY OF

COMPARATIVE STATEMENTS SHOWING SEPARATELY THE EXPENDITURES
YEARS 1910 TO 1914, INCLUSIVE, CLASSIFIED BY

| | Total | Personal Service | Supplies | LINE No. |
|---|---|---|---|---|
| **PUBLIC ADMINISTRATOR—NEW YORK COUNTY** | | | | |
| **1910** | | | | |
| Revenue Expenditures | $26,096 50 | $25,330 00 | $282 06 | 1 |
| Corporate Stock Expenditures | .......... | .......... | .......... | 2 |
| Total for 1910 | **$26,096 50** | **$25,330 00** | **$282 06** | 3 |
| **1911** | | | | |
| Revenue Expenditures | $26,284 87 | $25,530 00 | $191 20 | 4 |
| Corporate Stock Expenditures | .......... | .......... | .......... | 5 |
| Total for 1911 | **$26,284 87** | **$25,530 00** | **$191 20** | 6 |
| **1912** | | | | |
| Revenue Expenditures | $25,377 42 | $24,860 00 | $39 80 | 7 |
| Corporate Stock Expenditures | .......... | .......... | .......... | 8 |
| Total for 1912 | **$25,377 42** | **$24,860 00** | **$39 80** | 9 |
| **1913** | | | | |
| Revenue Expenditures | $26,784 06 | $26,092 83 | $209 11 | 10 |
| Corporate Stock Expenditures | .......... | .......... | .......... | 11 |
| Total for 1913 | **$26,784 06** | **$26,092 83** | **$209 11** | 12 |
| **1914** | | | | |
| Revenue Expenditures | $27,261 86 | $26,650 00 | $210 68 | 13 |
| Corporate Stock Expenditures | .......... | .......... | .......... | 14 |
| Total for 1914 | **$27,261 86** | **$26,650 00** | **$210 68** | 15 |
| **COMMISSIONER OF RECORDS—NEW YORK COUNTY** | | | | |
| **1910** | | | | |
| Revenue Expenditures | $70,243 37 | $67,051 35 | $1,849 08 | 16 |
| Corporate Stock Expenditures | .......... | .......... | .......... | 17 |
| Total for 1910 | **$70,243 37** | **$67,051 35** | **$1,849 08** | 18 |
| **1911** | | | | |
| Revenue Expenditures | $72,461 81 | $69,130 00 | $2,500 00 | 19 |
| Corporate Stock Expenditures | .......... | .......... | .......... | 20 |
| Total for 1911 | **$72,461 81** | **$69,130 00** | **$2,500 00** | 21 |
| **1912** | | | | |
| Revenue Expenditures | $96,523 35 | $92,505 16 | $1,188 44 | 22 |
| Corporate Stock Expenditures | .......... | .......... | .......... | 23 |
| Total for 1912 | **$96,523 35** | **$92,505 16** | **$1,188 44** | 24 |
| **1913** | | | | |
| Revenue Expenditures | $100,300 62 | $93,444 71 | $5,201 83 | 25 |
| Corporate Stock Expenditures | .......... | .......... | .......... | 26 |
| Total for 1913 | **$100,300 62** | **$93,444 71** | **$5,201 83** | 27 |
| **1914** | | | | |
| Revenue Expenditures | $96,680 42 | $92,961 49 | $494 29 | 28 |
| Corporate Stock Expenditures | .......... | .......... | .......... | 29 |
| Total for 1914 | **$96,680 42** | **$92,961 49** | **$494 29** | 30 |

NEW YORK

MADE FROM REVENUE AND FROM CORPORATE STOCK FUNDS FOR THE DEPARTMENTS, ACCORDING TO OBJECTS OF EXPENDITURE:

| LINE No. | Purchase of Equipment | Materials | Contract or Open Order Service | Contingencies | Fixed Charges and Contributions | Unclassified |
|---|---|---|---|---|---|---|
| 1 | .......... | .......... | $196 24 | $288 20 | .......... | .......... |
| 2 | .......... | .......... | .......... | .......... | .......... | .......... |
| 3 | .......... | .......... | **$196 24** | **$288 20** | .......... | .......... |
| 4 | .......... | .......... | $199 36 | $364 31 | .......... | .......... |
| 5 | .......... | .......... | .......... | .......... | .......... | .......... |
| 6 | .......... | .......... | **$199 36** | **$364 31** | .......... | .......... |
| 7 | .......... | .......... | $213 54 | $264 08 | .......... | .......... |
| 8 | .......... | .......... | .......... | .......... | .......... | .......... |
| 9 | .......... | .......... | **$213 54** | **$264 08** | .......... | .......... |
| 10 | $177 45 | .......... | $212 76 | $91 91 | .......... | .......... |
| 11 | .......... | .......... | .......... | .......... | .......... | .......... |
| 12 | **$177 45** | .......... | **$212 76** | **$91 91** | .......... | .......... |
| 13 | $187 45 | .......... | $190 96 | $22 77 | .......... | .......... |
| 14 | .......... | .......... | .......... | .......... | .......... | .......... |
| 15 | **$187 45** | .......... | **$190 96** | **$22 77** | .......... | .......... |
| 16 | $197 50 | $591 89 | $306 40 | $247 15 | .......... | .......... |
| 17 | .......... | .......... | .......... | .......... | .......... | .......... |
| 18 | **$197 50** | **$591 89** | **$306 40** | **$247 15** | .......... | .......... |
| 19 | .......... | $131 60 | $232 00 | $468 21 | .......... | .......... |
| 20 | .......... | .......... | .......... | .......... | .......... | .......... |
| 21 | .......... | **$131 60** | **$232 00** | **$468 21** | .......... | .......... |
| 22 | $2,167 72 | .......... | $368 30 | $293 73 | .......... | .......... |
| 23 | .......... | .......... | .......... | .......... | .......... | .......... |
| 24 | **$2,167 72** | .......... | **$368 30** | **$293 73** | .......... | .......... |
| 25 | $1,116 63 | .......... | $394 70 | $142 75 | .......... | .......... |
| 26 | .......... | .......... | .......... | .......... | .......... | .......... |
| 27 | **$1,116 63** | .......... | **$394 70** | **$142 75** | .......... | .......... |
| 28 | $759 05 | $21 50 | $2,342 45 | $101 64 | .......... | .......... |
| 29 | .......... | .......... | .......... | .......... | .......... | .......... |
| 30 | **$759 05** | **$21 50** | **$2,342 45** | **$101 64** | .......... | .......... |

COMPARATIVE STATEMENTS SHOWING SEPARATELY THE EXPENDITURES
YEARS 1910 TO 1914, INCLUSIVE, CLASSIFIED BY

| | Total | Personal Service | Supplies | LINE No. |
|---|---|---|---|---|
| **COMMISSIONER OF RECORDS, SURROGATES' COURT—NEW YORK COUNTY** | | | | |
| **1910** | | | | |
| Revenue Expenditures | .......... | .......... | .......... | 1 |
| Corporate Stock Expenditures | .......... | .......... | .......... | 2 |
| Total for 1910 | .......... | .......... | .......... | 3 |
| **1911** | | | | |
| Revenue Expenditures | .......... | .......... | .......... | 4 |
| Corporate Stock Expenditures | .......... | .......... | .......... | 5 |
| Total for 1911 | .......... | .......... | .......... | 6 |
| **1912** | | | | |
| Revenue Expenditures | $44,817 93 | $44,243 74 | $530 19 | 7 |
| Corporate Stock Expenditures | .......... | .......... | .......... | 8 |
| Total for 1912 | **$44,817 93** | **$44,243 74** | **$530 19** | 9 |
| **1913** | | | | |
| Revenue Expenditures | $49,961 25 | $48,520 00 | $184 00 | 10 |
| Corporate Stock Expenditures | .......... | .......... | .......... | 11 |
| Total for 1913 | **$49,691 25** | **$48,520 00** | **$184 00** | 12 |
| **1914** | | | | |
| Revenue Expenditures | $47,517 17 | $46,536 13 | $192 35 | 13 |
| Corporate Stock Expenditures | .......... | .......... | .......... | 14 |
| Total for 1914 | **$47,517 17** | **$46,536 13** | **$192 35** | 15 |
| **REGISTER—NEW YORK COUNTY** | | | | |
| **1910** | | | | |
| Revenue Expenditures | $228,750 64 | $223,100 88 | $1,652 58 | 16 |
| Corporate Stock Expenditures | .......... | .......... | .......... | 17 |
| Total for 1910 | **$228,750 64** | **$223,100 88** | **$1,652 58** | 18 |
| **1911** | | | | |
| Revenue Expenditures | $310,302 35 | $306,920 59 | $1,504 54 | 19 |
| Corporate Stock Expenditures | .......... | .......... | .......... | 20 |
| Total for 1911 | **$310,302 35** | **$306,920 59** | **$1,504 54** | 21 |
| **1912** | | | | |
| Revenue Expenditures | $317,650 04 | $311,807 63 | $3,947 24 | 22 |
| Corporate Stock Expenditures | .......... | .......... | .......... | 23 |
| Total for 1912 | **$317,650 04** | **$311,807 63** | **$3 947 24** | 24 |
| **1913** | | | | |
| Revenue Expenditures | $314,615 92 | $311,412 19 | $762 32 | 25 |
| Corporate Stock Expenditures | .......... | .......... | .......... | 26 |
| Total for 1913 | **$314,615 92** | **$311,412 19** | **$762 32** | 27 |
| **1914** | | | | |
| Revenue Expenditures | $279,280 05 | $275,266 88 | $677 42 | 28 |
| Corporate Stock Expenditures | .......... | .......... | .......... | 29 |
| Total for 1914 | **$279,280 05** | **$275,266 88** | **$677 42** | 30 |

NEW YORK

MADE FROM REVENUE AND FROM CORPORATE STOCK FUNDS FOR THE DEPARTMENTS, ACCORDING TO OBJECTS OF EXPENDITURE:

| LINE No. | Purchase of Equipment | Materials | Contract or Open Order Service | Contingencies | Fixed Charges and Contributions | Unclassified |
|---|---|---|---|---|---|---|
| 1 | .......... | .......... | .......... | .......... | .......... | .......... |
| 2 | .......... | .......... | .......... | .......... | .......... | .......... |
| 3 | .......... | .......... | .......... | .......... | .......... | .......... |
| 4 | .......... | .......... | .......... | .......... | .......... | .......... |
| 5 | .......... | .......... | .......... | .......... | .......... | .......... |
| 6 | .......... | .......... | .......... | .......... | .......... | .......... |
| 7 | .......... | .......... | .......... | $44 00 | .......... | .......... |
| 8 | .......... | .......... | .......... | .......... | .......... | .......... |
| 9 | .......... | .......... | .......... | **$44 00** | .......... | .......... |
| 10 | $509 20 | $478 05 | .......... | .......... | .......... | .......... |
| 11 | .......... | .......... | .......... | .......... | .......... | .......... |
| 12 | **$509 20** | **$478 05** | .......... | .......... | .......... | .......... |
| 13 | $366 50 | $422 19 | .......... | .......... | .......... | .......... |
| 14 | .......... | .......... | .......... | .......... | .......... | .......... |
| 15 | **$366 50** | **$422 19** | .......... | .......... | .......... | .......... |
| 16 | .......... | .......... | $3,524 18 | $473 00 | .......... | .......... |
| 17 | .......... | .......... | .......... | .......... | .......... | .......... |
| 18 | .......... | .......... | **$3,524 18** | **$473 00** | .......... | .......... |
| 19 | .......... | .......... | $130 31 | $1,746 91 | .......... | .......... |
| 20 | .......... | .......... | .......... | .......... | .......... | .......... |
| 21 | .......... | .......... | **$130 31** | **$1,746 91** | .......... | .......... |
| 22 | $1,174 29 | .......... | $356 26 | $364 62 | .......... | .......... |
| 23 | .......... | .......... | .......... | .......... | .......... | .......... |
| 24 | **$1,174 29** | .......... | **$356 26** | **$364 62** | .......... | .......... |
| 25 | $989 78 | $576 25 | $863 33 | $12 05 | .......... | .......... |
| 26 | .......... | .......... | .......... | .......... | .......... | .......... |
| 27 | **$989 78** | **$576 25** | **$863 33** | **$12 05** | .......... | .......... |
| 28 | $1,799 97 | $662 25 | $847 03 | $26 50 | .......... | .......... |
| 29 | .......... | .......... | .......... | .......... | .......... | .......... |
| 30 | **$1,799 97** | **$662 25** | **$847 03** | **$26 50** | .......... | .......... |

THE CITY OF

COMPARATIVE STATEMENTS SHOWING SEPARATELY THE EXPENDITURES
YEARS 1910 TO 1914, INCLUSIVE, CLASSIFIED BY

| | Total | Personal Service | Supplies | LINE No. |
|---|---|---|---|---|
| **SHERIFF—NEW YORK COUNTY** | | | | |
| **1910** | | | | |
| Revenue Expenditures | $189,424 01 | $175,081 41 | $4,129 87 | 1 |
| Corporate Stock Expenditures | .......... | .......... | .......... | 2 |
| Total for 1910 | **$189,424 01** | **$175,081 41** | **$4,129 87** | 3 |
| **1911** | | | | |
| Revenue Expenditures | $180,713 59 | $172,383 08 | $4,377 41 | 4 |
| Corporate Stock Expenditures | .......... | .......... | .......... | 5 |
| Total for 1911 | **$180,713 59** | **$172,383 08** | **$4,377 41** | 6 |
| **1912** | | | | |
| Revenue Expenditures | $211,616 74 | $201,638 68 | $4,228 02 | 7 |
| Corporate Stock Expenditures | .......... | .......... | .......... | 8 |
| Total for 1912 | **$211,616 74** | **$201,638 68** | **$4,228 02** | 9 |
| **1913** | | | | |
| Revenue Expenditures | $210,342 18 | $201,259 18 | $4,803 65 | 10 |
| Corporate Stock Expenditures | .......... | .......... | .......... | 11 |
| Total for 1913 | **$210,342 18** | **$201,259 18** | **$4,803 65** | 12 |
| **1914** | | | | |
| Revenue Expenditures | $206,074 60 | $197,424 29 | $4,891 12 | 13 |
| Corporate Stock Expenditures | .......... | .......... | .......... | 14 |
| Total for 1914 | **$206,074 60** | **$197,424 29** | **$4,891 12** | 15 |
| **CHARITABLE INSTITUTIONS—KINGS COUNTY** | | | | |
| **1910** | | | | |
| Revenue Expenditures | $55,735 46 | .......... | .......... | 16 |
| Corporate Stock Expenditures | .......... | .......... | .......... | 17 |
| Total for 1910 | **$55,735 46** | .......... | .......... | 18 |
| **1911** | | | | |
| Revenue Expenditures | $57,911 99 | .......... | .......... | 19 |
| Corporate Stock Expenditures | .......... | .......... | .......... | 20 |
| Total for 1911 | **$57,911 99** | .......... | .......... | 21 |
| **1912** | | | | |
| Revenue Expenditures | $58,343 57 | .......... | .......... | 22 |
| Corporate Stock Expenditures | .......... | .......... | .......... | 23 |
| Total for 1912 | **$58,343 57** | .......... | .......... | 24 |
| **1913** | | | | |
| Revenue Expenditures | $55,192 99 | .......... | .......... | 25 |
| Corporate Stock Expenditures | .......... | .......... | .......... | 26 |
| Total for 1913 | **$55,192 99** | .......... | .......... | 27 |
| **1914** | | | | |
| Revenue Expenditures | $51,042 74 | .......... | .......... | 28 |
| Corporate Stock Expenditures | .......... | .......... | .......... | 29 |
| Total for 1914 | **$51,042 74** | .......... | .......... | 30 |

NEW YORK

MADE FROM REVENUE AND FROM CORPORATE STOCK FUNDS FOR THE DEPARTMENTS, ACCORDING TO OBJECTS OF EXPENDITURE:

| LINE No. | Purchase of Equipment | Materials | Contract or Open Order Service | Contingencies | Fixed Charges and Contributions | Unclassified |
|---|---|---|---|---|---|---|
| 1 | $247 55 | .......... | $6,878 46 | $3,086 72 | .......... | .......... |
| 2 | .......... | .......... | .......... | .......... | .......... | .......... |
| 3 | **$247 55** | .......... | **$6,878 46** | **$3,086 72** | .......... | .......... |
| 4 | $26 75 | .......... | $1,276 47 | $2,649 88 | .......... | .......... |
| 5 | .......... | .......... | .......... | .......... | .......... | .......... |
| 6 | **$26 75** | .......... | **$1,276 47** | **$2,649 88** | .......... | .......... |
| 7 | .......... | .......... | $3,016 09 | $2,733 95 | .......... | .......... |
| 8 | .......... | .......... | .......... | .......... | .......... | .......... |
| 9 | .......... | .......... | **$3,016 09** | **$2,733 95** | .......... | .......... |
| 10 | $256 85 | .......... | $3,760 35 | $262 15 | .......... | .......... |
| 11 | .......... | .......... | .......... | .......... | .......... | .......... |
| 12 | **$256 85** | .......... | **$3,760 35** | **$262 15** | .......... | .......... |
| 13 | $156 83 | .......... | $3,219 03 | $383 33 | .......... | .......... |
| 14 | .......... | .......... | .......... | .......... | .......... | .......... |
| 15 | **$156 83** | .......... | **$3,219 03** | **$383 33** | .......... | .......... |
| 16 | .......... | .......... | .......... | .......... | $55,735 46 | .......... |
| 17 | .......... | .......... | .......... | .......... | .......... | .......... |
| 18 | .......... | .......... | .......... | .......... | **$55,735 46** | .......... |
| 19 | .......... | .......... | .......... | .......... | $57,911 99 | .......... |
| 20 | .......... | .......... | .......... | .......... | .......... | .......... |
| 21 | .......... | .......... | .......... | .......... | **$57,911 99** | .......... |
| 22 | .......... | .......... | .......... | .......... | $58,343 57 | .......... |
| 23 | .......... | .......... | .......... | .......... | .......... | .......... |
| 24 | .......... | .......... | .......... | .......... | **$58,343 57** | .......... |
| 25 | .......... | .......... | .......... | .......... | $55,192 99 | .......... |
| 26 | .......... | .......... | .......... | .......... | .......... | .......... |
| 27 | .......... | .......... | .......... | .......... | **$55,192 99** | .......... |
| 28 | .......... | .......... | .......... | .......... | $51,042 74 | .......... |
| 29 | .......... | .......... | .......... | .......... | .......... | .......... |
| 30 | .......... | .......... | .......... | .......... | **$51,042 74** | .......... |

COMPARATIVE STATEMENTS SHOWING SEPARATELY THE EXPENDITURES
YEARS 1910 TO 1914, INCLUSIVE, CLASSIFIED BY

| | Total | Personal Service | Supplies | LINE No. |
|---|---|---|---|---|
| **CITY RECORD—KINGS COUNTY** | | | | |
| **1910** | | | | |
| Revenue Expenditures | $19,035 52 | .......... | .......... | 1 |
| Corporate Stock Expenditures | .......... | .......... | .......... | 2 |
| Total for 1910 | **$19,035 52** | .......... | .......... | 3 |
| **1911** | | | | |
| Revenue Expenditures | $19,967 45 | .......... | .......... | 4 |
| Corporate Stock Expenditures | .......... | .......... | .......... | 5 |
| Total for 1911 | **$19,967 45** | .......... | .......... | 6 |
| **1912** | | | | |
| Revenue Expenditures | $17,967 15 | .......... | .......... | 7 |
| Corporate Stock Expenditures | .......... | .......... | .......... | 8 |
| Total for 1912 | **$17,967 15** | .......... | .......... | 9 |
| **1913** | | | | |
| Revenue Expenditures | $18,518 32 | .......... | .......... | 10 |
| Corporate Stock Expenditures | .......... | .......... | .......... | 11 |
| Total for 1913 | **$18,518 32** | .......... | .......... | 12 |
| **1914** | | | | |
| Revenue Expenditures | $18,809 71 | .......... | .......... | 13 |
| Corporate Stock Expenditures | .......... | .......... | .......... | 14 |
| Total for 1914 | **$18,809 71** | .......... | .......... | 15 |
| **COUNTY CLERK—KINGS COUNTY** | | | | |
| **1910** | | | | |
| Revenue Expenditures | $88,661 57 | $86,338 62 | .......... | 16 |
| Corporate Stock Expenditures | .......... | .......... | .......... | 17 |
| Total for 1910 | **$88,661 57** | **$86,338 62** | .......... | 18 |
| **1911** | | | | |
| Revenue Expenditures | $89,670 80 | $87,847 18 | .......... | 19 |
| Corporate Stock Expenditures | .......... | .......... | .......... | 20 |
| Total for 1911 | **$89,670 80** | **$87,847 18** | .......... | 21 |
| **1912** | | | | |
| Revenue Expenditures | $98,868 13 | $96,930 86 | $296 82 | 22 |
| Corporate Stock Expenditures | .......... | .......... | .......... | 23 |
| Total for 1912 | **$98,868 13** | **$96,930 86** | **$296 82** | 24 |
| **1913** | | | | |
| Revenue Expenditures | $104,777 13 | $103,051 17 | $621 79 | 25 |
| Corporate Stock Expenditures | .......... | .......... | .......... | 26 |
| Total for 1913 | **$104,777 13** | **$103,051 17** | **$621 79** | 27 |
| **1914** | | | | |
| Revenue Expenditures | $104 290 81 | $103,475 83 | $576 60 | 28 |
| Corporate Stock Expenditures | .......... | .......... | .......... | 29 |
| Total for 1914 | **$104,290 81** | **$103,475 83** | **$576 60** | 30 |

NEW YORK

MADE FROM REVENUE AND FROM CORPORATE STOCK FUNDS FOR THE DEPARTMENTS, ACCORDING TO OBJECTS OF EXPENDITURE:

| LINE No. | Purchase of Equipment | Materials | Contract or Open Order Service | Contingencies | Fixed Charges and Contributions | Unclassified |
|---|---|---|---|---|---|---|
| 1 | .......... | .......... | $19,035 52 | .......... | .......... | .......... |
| 2 | .......... | .......... | .......... | .......... | .......... | .......... |
| 3 | .......... | .......... | **$19,035 52** | .......... | .......... | .......... |
| 4 | .......... | .......... | $19,967 45 | .......... | .......... | .......... |
| 5 | .......... | .......... | .......... | .......... | .......... | .......... |
| 6 | .......... | .......... | **$19,967 45** | .......... | .......... | .......... |
| 7 | .......... | .......... | $17,967 15 | .......... | .......... | .......... |
| 8 | .......... | .......... | .......... | .......... | .......... | .......... |
| 9 | .......... | .......... | **$17,967 15** | .......... | .......... | .......... |
| 10 | .......... | .......... | $18,518 32 | .......... | .......... | .......... |
| 11 | .......... | .......... | .......... | .......... | .......... | .......... |
| 12 | .......... | .......... | **$18,518 32** | .......... | .......... | .......... |
| 13 | .......... | .......... | $18,809 71 | .......... | .......... | .......... |
| 14 | .......... | .......... | .......... | .......... | .......... | .......... |
| 15 | .......... | .......... | **$18,809 71** | .......... | .......... | .......... |
| 16 | .......... | .......... | $899 65 | $1,423 30 | .......... | .......... |
| 17 | .......... | .......... | .......... | .......... | .......... | .......... |
| 18 | .......... | .......... | **$899 65** | **$1,423 30** | .......... | .......... |
| 19 | .......... | .......... | $634 54 | $1,189 08 | .......... | .......... |
| 20 | .......... | .......... | .......... | .......... | .......... | .......... |
| 21 | .......... | .......... | **$634 54** | **$1,189 08** | .......... | .......... |
| 22 | $168 05 | .......... | $1,131 27 | $341 13 | .......... | .......... |
| 23 | .......... | .......... | .......... | .......... | .......... | .......... |
| 24 | **$168 05** | .......... | **$1,131 27** | **$341 13** | .......... | .......... |
| 25 | $170 07 | .......... | $934 10 | .......... | .......... | .......... |
| 26 | .......... | .......... | .......... | .......... | .......... | .......... |
| 27 | **$170 07** | .......... | **$934 10** | .......... | .......... | .......... |
| 28 | $184 56 | .......... | .......... | $53 82 | .......... | .......... |
| 29 | .......... | .......... | .......... | .......... | .......... | .......... |
| 30 | **$184 56** | .......... | .......... | **$53 82** | .......... | .......... |

Comparative Statements Showing Separately the Expenditures
Years 1910 to 1914, Inclusive, Classified by

| | Total | Personal Service | Supplies | Line No. |
|---|---|---|---|---|
| **COUNTY COURT—KINGS COUNTY** | | | | |
| **1910** | | | | |
| Revenue Expenditures | $135,531 10 | $133,972 90 | $669 99 | 1 |
| Corporate Stock Expenditures | .......... | .......... | .......... | 2 |
| Total for 1910 | **$135,531 10** | **$133,972 90** | **$669 99** | 3 |
| **1911** | | | | |
| Revenue Expenditures | $145,356 99 | $141,288 76 | $642 31 | 4 |
| Corporate Stock Expenditures | .......... | .......... | .......... | 5 |
| Total for 1911 | **$145,356 99** | **$141,288 76** | **$642 31** | 6 |
| **1912** | | | | |
| Revenue Expenditures | $161,701 06 | $159,913 30 | $1,052 01 | 7 |
| Corporate Stock Expenditures | .......... | .......... | .......... | 8 |
| Total for 1912 | **$161,701 06** | **$159,913 30** | **$1,052 01** | 9 |
| **1913** | | | | |
| Revenue Expenditures | $172,217 84 | $168,967 93 | $724 37 | 10 |
| Corporate Stock Expenditures | .......... | .......... | .......... | 11 |
| Total for 1913 | **$172,217 84** | **$168,967 93** | **$724 37** | 12 |
| **1914** | | | | |
| Revenue Expenditures | $194,819 52 | $190,269 62 | $646 07 | 13 |
| Corporate Stock Expenditures | .......... | .......... | .......... | 14 |
| Total for 1914 | **$194,819 52** | **$190,269 62** | **$646 07** | 15 |
| **SUPREME COURT, SECOND DEPARTMENT (KINGS COUNTY)** | | | | |
| **1910** | | | | |
| Revenue Expenditures | $371,824 57 | $366,946 55 | $1,736 54 | 16 |
| Corporate Stock Expenditures | .......... | .......... | .......... | 17 |
| Total for 1910 | **$371,824 57** | **$366,946 55** | **$1,736 54** | 18 |
| **1911** | | | | |
| Revenue Expenditures | $375,855 58 | $370,869 21 | $1,875 48 | 19 |
| Corporate Stock Expenditures | .......... | .......... | .......... | 20 |
| Total for 1911 | **$375,855 58** | **$370,869 21** | **$1,875 48** | 21 |
| **1912** | | | | |
| Revenue Expenditures | $407,005 14 | $405,727 26 | .......... | 22 |
| Corporate Stock Expenditures | .......... | .......... | .......... | 23 |
| Total for 1912 | **$407,005 14** | **$405,727 26** | .......... | 24 |
| **1913** | | | | |
| Revenue Expenditures | $427,993 31 | $427,006 30 | $44 00 | 25 |
| Corporate Stock Expenditures | .......... | .......... | .......... | 26 |
| Total for 1913 | **$427,993 31** | **$427,006 30** | **$44 00** | 27 |
| **1914** | | | | |
| Revenue Expenditures | $466,314 53 | $463,303 96 | .......... | 28 |
| Corporate Stock Expenditures | .......... | .......... | .......... | 29 |
| Total for 1914 | **$466,314 53** | **$463,303 96** | .......... | 30 |

NEW YORK

MADE FROM REVENUE AND FROM CORPORATE STOCK FUNDS FOR THE DEPARTMENTS, ACCORDING TO OBJECTS OF EXPENDITURE:

| LINE No. | Purchase of Equipment | Materials | Contract or Open Order Service | Contingencies | Fixed Charges and Contributions | Unclassified |
|---|---|---|---|---|---|---|
| 1 | .......... | .......... | $888 21 | .......... | .......... | .......... |
| 2 | .......... | .......... | .......... | .......... | .......... | .......... |
| 3 | .......... | .......... | **$888 21** | .......... | .......... | .......... |
| 4 | $2,591 88 | .......... | $363 14 | $470 90 | .......... | .......... |
| 5 | .......... | .......... | .......... | .......... | .......... | .......... |
| 6 | **$2,591 88** | .......... | **$363 14** | **$470 90** | .......... | .......... |
| 7 | .......... | .......... | $68 21 | $667 54 | .......... | .......... |
| 8 | .......... | .......... | .......... | .......... | .......... | .......... |
| 9 | .......... | .......... | **$68 21** | **$667 54** | .......... | .......... |
| 10 | $181 30 | .......... | $2,170 77 | $173 47 | .......... | .......... |
| 11 | .......... | .......... | .......... | .......... | .......... | .......... |
| 12 | **$181 30** | .......... | **$2,170 77** | **$173 47** | .......... | .......... |
| 13 | $345 65 | .......... | $1,351 03 | $100 00 | $2,107 15 | .......... |
| 14 | .......... | .......... | .......... | .......... | .......... | .......... |
| 15 | **$345 65** | | **$1,351 03** | **$100 00** | **$2,107 15** | .......... |
| 16 | $986 50 | .......... | $569 01 | $1,585 97 | .......... | .......... |
| 17 | .......... | .......... | .......... | .......... | .......... | .......... |
| 18 | **$986 50** | .......... | **$569 01** | **$1,585 97** | .......... | .......... |
| 19 | $998 38 | .......... | $840 06 | $1,272 45 | .......... | .......... |
| 20 | .......... | .......... | .......... | .......... | .......... | .......... |
| 21 | **$998 38** | .......... | **$840 06** | **$1,272 45** | .......... | .......... |
| 22 | .......... | .......... | .......... | $1,277 88 | .......... | .......... |
| 23 | .......... | .......... | .......... | .......... | .......... | .......... |
| 24 | .......... | .......... | .......... | **$1,277 88** | .......... | .......... |
| 25 | .......... | .......... | $465 19 | $477 82 | .......... | .......... |
| 26 | .......... | .......... | .......... | .......... | .......... | .......... |
| 27 | .......... | .......... | **$465 19** | **$477 82** | .......... | .......... |
| 28 | .......... | .......... | $431 51 | $2,579 06 | .......... | .......... |
| 29 | .......... | .......... | .......... | .......... | .......... | .......... |
| 30 | .......... | .......... | **$431 51** | **$2,579 06** | .......... | .......... |

COMPARATIVE STATEMENTS SHOWING SEPARATELY THE EXPENDITURES
YEARS 1910 TO 1914, INCLUSIVE, CLASSIFIED BY

| | Total | Personal Service | Supplies | LINE No. |
|---|---|---|---|---|
| **SUPREME COURT LIBRARY IN THE BOROUGH OF BROOKLYN** | | | | |
| **1910** | | | | |
| Revenue Expenditures | $9,191 67 | $8,591 67 | .......... | 1 |
| Corporate Stock Expenditures | .......... | .......... | .......... | 2 |
| Total for 1910 | **$9,191 67** | **$8,591 67** | .......... | 3 |
| **1911** | | | | |
| Revenue Expenditures | $9,400 00 | $8,800 00 | .......... | 4 |
| Corporate Stock Expenditures | .......... | .......... | .......... | 5 |
| Total for 1911 | **$9,400 00** | **$8,800 00** | .......... | 6 |
| **1912** | | | | |
| Revenue Expenditures | $9,400 00 | $8,800 00 | .......... | 7 |
| Corporate Stock Expenditures | .......... | .......... | .......... | 8 |
| Total for 1912 | **$9,400 00** | **$8,800 00** | .......... | 9 |
| **1913** | | | | |
| Revenue Expenditures | $9,208 77 | $8,233 87 | .......... | 10 |
| Corporate Stock Expenditures | .......... | .......... | .......... | 11 |
| Total for 1913 | **$9,208 77** | **$8,233 87** | .......... | 12 |
| **1914** | | | | |
| Revenue Expenditures | $9,199 69 | $8,200 00 | .......... | 13 |
| Corporate Stock Expenditures | .......... | .......... | .......... | 14 |
| Total for 1914 | **$9,199 69** | **$8,200 00** | .......... | 15 |
| **SURROGATE'S COURT—KINGS COUNTY** | | | | |
| **1910** | | | | |
| Revenue Expenditures | $92,661 24 | $90,903 36 | $1,177 94 | 16 |
| Corporate Stock Expenditures | .......... | .......... | .......... | 17 |
| Total for 1910 | **$92,661 24** | **$90,903 36** | **$1,177 94** | 18 |
| **1911** | | | | |
| Revenue Expenditures | $91,423 92 | $89,904 89 | $994 51 | 19 |
| Corporate Stock Expenditures | .......... | .......... | .......... | 20 |
| Total for 1911 | **$91,423 92** | **$89,904 89** | **$994 51** | 21 |
| **1912** | | | | |
| Revenue Expenditures | $102,396 12 | $100,700 41 | $961 65 | 22 |
| Corporate Stock Expenditures | .......... | .......... | .......... | 23 |
| Total for 1912 | **$102,396 12** | **$100.700 41** | **$961 65** | 24 |
| **1913** | | | | |
| Revenue Expenditures | $104,787 35 | $103,106 00 | $684 29 | 25 |
| Corporate Stock Expenditures | .......... | .......... | .......... | 26 |
| Total for 1913 | **$104,787 35** | **$103,106 00** | **$684 29** | 27 |
| **1914** | | | | |
| Revenue Expenditures | $109,309 33 | $107,444 75 | $449 37 | 28 |
| Corporate Stock Expenditures | .......... | .......... | .......... | 29 |
| Total for 1914 | **$109,309 33** | **$107,444 75** | **$449 37** | 30 |

NEW YORK

MADE FROM REVENUE AND FROM CORPORATE STOCK FUNDS FOR THE DEPARTMENTS, ACCORDING TO OBJECTS OF EXPENDITURE:

| LINE No. | Purchase of Equipment | Materials | Contract or Open Order Service | Contingencies | Fixed Charges and Contributions | Unclassified |
|---|---|---|---|---|---|---|
| 1 | .......... | .......... | .......... | $600 00 | .......... | .......... |
| 2 | .......... | .......... | .......... | .......... | .......... | .......... |
| 3 | .......... | .......... | .......... | **$600 00** | .......... | .......... |
| 4 | .......... | .......... | .......... | $600 00 | .......... | .......... |
| 5 | .......... | .......... | .......... | .......... | .......... | .......... |
| 6 | .......... | .......... | .......... | **$600 00** | .......... | .......... |
| 7 | .......... | .......... | .......... | $600 00 | .......... | .......... |
| 8 | .......... | .......... | .......... | .......... | .......... | .......... |
| 9 | .......... | .......... | .......... | **$600 00** | .......... | .......... |
| 10 | .......... | .......... | .......... | $974 90 | .......... | .......... |
| 11 | .......... | .......... | .......... | .......... | .......... | .......... |
| 12 | .......... | .......... | .......... | **$974 90** | .......... | .......... |
| 13 | .......... | .......... | .......... | $999 69 | .......... | .......... |
| 14 | .......... | .......... | .......... | .......... | .......... | .......... |
| 15 | .......... | .......... | .......... | **$999 69** | .......... | .......... |
| 16 | .......... | .......... | $152 94 | $427 00 | .......... | .......... |
| 17 | .......... | .......... | .......... | .......... | .......... | .......... |
| 18 | .......... | .......... | **$152 94** | **$427 00** | .......... | .......... |
| 19 | .......... | .......... | $225 42 | $299 10 | .......... | .......... |
| 20 | .......... | .......... | .......... | .......... | .......... | .......... |
| 21 | .......... | .......... | **$225 42** | **$299 10** | .......... | .......... |
| 22 | .......... | .......... | $455 82 | $278 24 | .......... | .......... |
| 23 | .......... | .......... | .......... | .......... | .......... | .......... |
| 24 | .......... | .......... | **$455 82** | **$278 24** | .......... | .......... |
| 25 | $552 50 | .......... | $443 06 | $1 50 | .......... | .......... |
| 26 | .......... | .......... | .......... | .......... | .......... | .......... |
| 27 | **$552 50** | .......... | **$443 06** | **$1 50** | .......... | .......... |
| 28 | $1,047 85 | .......... | $367 36 | .......... | .......... | .......... |
| 29 | .......... | .......... | .......... | .......... | .......... | .......... |
| 30 | **$1,047 85** | .......... | **$367 36** | .......... | .......... | .......... |

Comparative Statements Showing Separately the Expenditures
Years 1910 to 1914, Inclusive, Classified by

| | Total | Personal Service | Supplies | Line No. |
|---|---|---|---|---|
| **DISTRICT ATTORNEY—KINGS COUNTY** | | | | |
| **1910** | | | | |
| Revenue Expenditures | $118,229 69 | $105,873 25 | $1,392 00 | 1 |
| Corporate Stock Expenditures | .......... | .......... | .......... | 2 |
| Total for 1910 | **$118,229 69** | **$105,873 25** | **$1,392 00** | 3 |
| **1911** | | | | |
| Revenue Expenditures | $131,673 08 | $120,662 26 | $279 55 | 4 |
| Corporate Stock Expenditures | .......... | .......... | .......... | 5 |
| Total for 1911 | **$131,673 08** | **$120,662 26** | **$279 55** | 6 |
| **1912** | | | | |
| Revenue Expenditures | $113,944 87 | $101,613 37 | $907 59 | 7 |
| Corporate Stock Expenditures | .......... | .......... | .......... | 8 |
| Total for 1912 | **$113,944 87** | **$101,613 37** | **$907 59** | 9 |
| **1913** | | | | |
| Revenue Expenditures | $129,896 16 | $119,747 14 | $2,015 00 | 10 |
| Corporate Stock Expenditures | .......... | .......... | .......... | 11 |
| Total for 1913 | **$129,896 16** | **$119,747 14** | **$2,015 00** | 12 |
| **1914** | | | | |
| Revenue Expenditures | $140,028 28 | $127,511 21 | $2,498 61 | 13 |
| Corporate Stcok Expenditures | .......... | .......... | .......... | 14 |
| Total for 1914 | **$140,028 28** | **$127,511 21** | **$2,498 61** | 15 |
| **COMMISSIONER OF JURORS—KINGS COUNTY** | | | | |
| **1910** | | | | |
| Revenue Expenditures | $37,335 10 | $35,725 48 | $135 35 | 16 |
| Corporate Stock Expenditures | .......... | .......... | .......... | 17 |
| Total for 1910 | **$37,335 10** | **$35,725 48** | **$135 35** | 18 |
| **1911** | | | | |
| Revenue Expenditures | $37,615 12 | $35,617 96 | $151 01 | 19 |
| Corporate Stock Expenditures | .......... | .......... | .......... | 20 |
| Total for 1911 | **$37,615 12** | **$35,617 96** | **$151 01** | 21 |
| **1912** | | | | |
| Revenue Expenditures | $41,846 42 | $38,163 44 | $454 52 | 22 |
| Corporate Stock Expenditures | .......... | .......... | .......... | 23 |
| Total for 1912 | **$41,846 42** | **$38,163 44** | **$454 52** | 24 |
| **1913** | | | | |
| Revenue Expenditures | $40,261 44 | $38,190 00 | $1,318 16 | 25 |
| Corporate Stock Expenditures | .......... | .......... | .......... | 26 |
| Total for 1913 | **$40,261 44** | **$38,190 00** | **$1,318 16** | 27 |
| **1914** | | | | |
| Revenue Expenditures | $40,973 03 | $38,794 84 | $1,682 72 | 28 |
| Corporate Stock Expenditures | .......... | .......... | .......... | 29 |
| Total for 1914 | **$40,973 03** | **$38,794 84** | **$1,682 72** | 30 |

NEW YORK

MADE FROM REVENUE AND FROM CORPORATE STOCK FUNDS FOR THE DEPARTMENTS, ACCORDING TO OBJECTS OF EXPENDITURE:

| LINE No. | Purchase of Equipment | Materials | Contract or Open Order Service | Contingencies | Fixed Charges and Contributions | Unclassified |
|---|---|---|---|---|---|---|
| 1 | .......... | .......... | $1,966 34 | $8,998 10 | .......... | .......... |
| 2 | .......... | .......... | .......... | .......... | .......... | .......... |
| 3 | .......... | .......... | **$1,966 34** | **$8,998 10** | .......... | .......... |
| 4 | $114 50 | .......... | $1,131 95 | $9,484 82 | .......... | .......... |
| 5 | .......... | .......... | .......... | .......... | .......... | .......... |
| 6 | **$114 50** | .......... | **$1,131 95** | **$9,484 82** | .......... | .......... |
| 7 | $899 81 | .......... | $969 96 | $9,554 14 | .......... | .......... |
| 8 | .......... | .......... | .......... | .......... | .......... | .......... |
| 9 | **$899 81** | .......... | **$969 96** | **$9,554 14** | .......... | .......... |
| 10 | $975 00 | .......... | $2,019 75 | $5,139 27 | .......... | .......... |
| 11 | .......... | .......... | .......... | .......... | .......... | .......... |
| 12 | **$975 00** | .......... | **$2,019 75** | **$5,139 27** | .......... | .......... |
| 13 | $824 01 | .......... | $3,234 54 | $5,959 91 | .......... | .......... |
| 14 | .......... | .......... | .......... | .......... | .......... | .......... |
| 15 | **$824 01** | .......... | **$3,234 54** | **$5 959 91** | .......... | .......... |
| 16 | .......... | .......... | $155 18 | $1,319 09 | .......... | .......... |
| 17 | .......... | .......... | .......... | .......... | .......... | .......... |
| 18 | .......... | .......... | **$155 18** | **$1,319 09** | .......... | .......... |
| 19 | .......... | .......... | $142 74 | $1,703 41 | .......... | .......... |
| 20 | .......... | .......... | .......... | .......... | .......... | .......... |
| 21 | .......... | .......... | **$142 74** | **$1,703 41** | .......... | .......... |
| 22 | $1,733 19 | .......... | $150 87 | $1,344 40 | .......... | .......... |
| 23 | .......... | .......... | .......... | .......... | .......... | .......... |
| 24 | **$1,733 19** | .......... | **$150 87** | **$1,344 40** | .......... | .......... |
| 25 | $555 31 | .......... | $197 97 | .......... | .......... | .......... |
| 26 | .......... | .......... | .......... | .......... | .......... | .......... |
| 27 | **$555 31** | .......... | **$197 97** | .......... | .......... | .......... |
| 28 | $256 73 | .......... | $233 74 | $5 00 | .......... | .......... |
| 29 | .......... | .......... | .......... | .......... | .......... | .......... |
| 30 | **$256 73** | .......... | **$233 74** | **$5 00** | .......... | .......... |

Comparative Statements Showing Separately the Expenditures Years 1910 to 1914, Inclusive, Classified by

| | Total | Personal Service | Supplies | Line No. |
|---|---|---|---|---|
| **MISCELLANEOUS—KINGS COUNTY** | | | | |
| **1910** | | | | |
| Revenue Expenditures | $126,103 74 | $104,925 04 | .......... | 1 |
| Corporate Stock Expenditures | .......... | .......... | .......... | 2 |
| Total for 1910 | **$126,103 74** | **$104,925 04** | .......... | 3 |
| **1911** | | | | |
| Revenue Expenditures | $174,540 02 | $108,884 95 | .......... | 4 |
| Corporate Stock Expenditures | .......... | .......... | .......... | 5 |
| Total for 1911 | **$174,540 02** | **$108,884 95** | .......... | 6 |
| **1912** | | | | |
| Revenue Expenditures | $127,689 95 | $109,149 65 | .......... | 7 |
| Corporate Stock Expenditures | .......... | .......... | .......... | 8 |
| Total for 1912 | **$127,689 95** | **$109,149 65** | .......... | 9 |
| **1913** | | | | |
| Revenue Expenditures | $141,000 60 | $114,423 76 | .......... | 10 |
| Corporate Stock Expenditures | .......... | .......... | .......... | 11 |
| Total for 1913 | **$141,000 60** | **$114,423 76** | .......... | 12 |
| **1914** | | | | |
| Revenue Expenditures | $146,846 34 | $120,193 34 | .......... | 13 |
| Corporate Stock Expenditures | .......... | .......... | .......... | 14 |
| Total for 1914 | **$146,846 34** | **$120,193 34** | .......... | 15 |
| **NATIONAL GUARD AND NAVAL MILITIA—KINGS COUNTY** | | | | |
| **1910** | | | | |
| Revenue Expenditures | $135,867 50 | $135,867 50 | .......... | 16 |
| Corporate Stock Expenditures | .......... | .......... | .......... | 17 |
| Total for 1910 | **$135,867 50** | **$135,867 50** | .......... | 18 |
| **1911** | | | | |
| Revenue Expenditures | $141,277 50 | $141,277 50 | .......... | 19 |
| Corporate Stock Expenditures | .......... | .......... | .......... | 20 |
| Total for 1911 | **$141,277 50** | **$141,277 50** | .......... | 21 |
| **1912** | | | | |
| Revenue Expenditures | $144,797 25 | $144,797 25 | .......... | 22 |
| Corporate Stock Expenditures | .......... | .......... | .......... | 23 |
| Total for 1912 | **$144,797 25** | **$144,797 25** | .......... | 24 |
| **1913** | | | | |
| Revenue Expenditures | $144,108 25 | $144,108 25 | .......... | 25 |
| Corporate Stock Expenditures | .......... | .......... | .......... | 26 |
| Total for 1913 | **$144,108 25** | **$144,108 25** | .......... | 27 |
| **1914** | | | | |
| Revenue Expenditures | $154,855 75 | $154,855 75 | .......... | 28 |
| Corporate Stock Expenditures | .......... | .......... | .......... | 29 |
| Total for 1914 | **$154,855 75** | **$154,855 75** | .......... | 30 |

NEW YORK

MADE FROM REVENUE AND FROM CORPORATE STOCK FUNDS FOR THE DEPARTMENTS, ACCORDING TO OBJECTS OF EXPENDITURE:

| LINE No. | Purchase of Equipment | Materials | Contract or Open Order Service | Contingencies | Fixed Charges and Contributions | Unclassified |
|---|---|---|---|---|---|---|
| 1 | .......... | .......... | $6,000 00 | $5,000 00 | $1,000 00 | $9,178 70 |
| 2 | .......... | .......... | .......... | .......... | .......... | .......... |
| 3 | .......... | .......... | **$6,000 00** | **$5,000 00** | **$1,000 00** | **$9,178 70** |
| 4 | .......... | .......... | $1,706 00 | $2,924 00 | $2,200 00 | $58,825 07 |
| 5 | .......... | .......... | .......... | .......... | .......... | .......... |
| 6 | .......... | .......... | **$1,706 00** | **$2,924 00** | **$2,200 00** | **$58,825 07** |
| 7 | .......... | .......... | .......... | $3,944 30 | $14,596 00 | .......... |
| 8 | .......... | .......... | .......... | .......... | .......... | .......... |
| 9 | .......... | .......... | .......... | **$3,944 30** | **$14,596 00** | .......... |
| 10 | .......... | .......... | .......... | $3,172 85 | $23,403 99 | .......... |
| 11 | .......... | .......... | .......... | .......... | .......... | .......... |
| 12 | .......... | .......... | .......... | **$3,172 85** | **$23,403 99** | .......... |
| 13 | .......... | .......... | .......... | $3,249 00 | $23,404 00 | .......... |
| 14 | .......... | .......... | .......... | .......... | .......... | .......... |
| 15 | .......... | .......... | .......... | **$3,249 00** | **$23,404 00** | .......... |
| 16 | .......... | .......... | .......... | .......... | .......... | .......... |
| 17 | .......... | .......... | .......... | .......... | .......... | .......... |
| 18 | .......... | .......... | .......... | .......... | .......... | .......... |
| 19 | .......... | .......... | .......... | .......... | .......... | .......... |
| 20 | .......... | .......... | .......... | .......... | .......... | .......... |
| 21 | .......... | .......... | .......... | .......... | .......... | .......... |
| 22 | .......... | .......... | .......... | .......... | .......... | .......... |
| 23 | .......... | .......... | .......... | .......... | .......... | .......... |
| 24 | .......... | .......... | .......... | .......... | .......... | .......... |
| 25 | .......... | .......... | .......... | .......... | .......... | .......... |
| 26 | .......... | .......... | .......... | .......... | .......... | .......... |
| 27 | .......... | .......... | .......... | .......... | .......... | .......... |
| 28 | .......... | .......... | .......... | .......... | .......... | .......... |
| 29 | .......... | .......... | .......... | .......... | .......... | .......... |
| 30 | .......... | .......... | .......... | .......... | .......... | .......... |

COMPARATIVE STATEMENTS SHOWING SEPARATELY THE EXPENDITURES
YEARS 1910 TO 1914, INCLUSIVE, CLASSIFIED BY

| | Total | Personal Service | Supplies | LINE No. |
|---|---|---|---|---|
| **PUBLIC ADMINISTRATOR—KINGS COUNTY** | | | | |
| **1910** | | | | |
| Revenue Expenditures | .......... | .......... | .......... | 1 |
| Corporate Stock Expenditures | .......... | .......... | .......... | 2 |
| Total for 1910 | .......... | .......... | .......... | 3 |
| **1911** | | | | |
| Revenue Expenditures | .......... | .......... | .......... | 4 |
| Corporate Stock Expenditures | .......... | .......... | .......... | 5 |
| Total for 1911 | .......... | .......... | .......... | 6 |
| **1912** | | | | |
| Revenue Expenditures | $12,613 83 | $11,247 03 | $347 09 | 7 |
| Corporate Stock Expenditures | .......... | .......... | .......... | 8 |
| Total for 1912 | **$12,613 83** | **$11,247 03** | **$347 09** | 9 |
| **1913** | | | | |
| Revenue Expenditures | $12,128 06 | $11,019 84 | $189 00 | 10 |
| Corporate Stock Expenditures | .......... | .......... | .......... | 11 |
| Total for 1913 | **$12,128 06** | **$11,019 84** | **$189 00** | 12 |
| **1914** | | | | |
| Revenue Expenditures | $12,057 13 | $11,320 00 | $303 21 | 13 |
| Corporate Stock Expenditures | .......... | .......... | .......... | 14 |
| Total for 1914 | **$12,057 13** | **$11,320 00** | **$303 21** | 15 |
| **COMMISSIONER OF RECORDS—KINGS COUNTY** | | | | |
| **1910** | | | | |
| Revenue Expenditures | $98,844 68 | $97,382 88 | $979 74 | 16 |
| Corporate Stock Expenditures | .......... | .......... | .......... | 17 |
| Total for 1910 | **$98,844 68** | **$97,382 88** | **$979 74** | 18 |
| **1911** | | | | |
| Revenue Expenditures | $98,706 32 | $96,753 79 | $1,550 33 | 19 |
| Corporate Stock Expenditures | .......... | .......... | .......... | 20 |
| Total for 1911 | **$98,706 32** | **$96,753 79** | **$1,550 33** | 21 |
| **1912** | | | | |
| Revenue Expenditures | $97,878 01 | $96,769 50 | $641 76 | 22 |
| Corporate Stock Expenditures | .......... | .......... | .......... | 23 |
| Total for 1912 | **$97,878 01** | **$96,769 50** | **$641 76** | 24 |
| **1913** | | | | |
| Revenue Expenditures | $99,384 24 | $97,412 89 | $406 24 | 25 |
| Corporate Stock Expenditures | .......... | .......... | .......... | 26 |
| Total for 1913 | **$99,384 24** | **$97,412 89** | **$406 24** | 27 |
| **1914** | | | | |
| Revenue Expenditures | $98,730 49 | $96,931 51 | $270 77 | 28 |
| Corporate Stock Expenditures | .......... | .......... | .......... | 29 |
| Total for 1914 | **$98,730 49** | **$96,931 51** | **$270 77** | 30 |

NEW YORK

MADE FROM REVENUE AND FROM CORPORATE STOCK FUNDS FOR THE DEPARTMENTS, ACCORDING TO OBJECTS OF EXPENDITURE:

| LINE No. | Purchase of Equipment | Materials | Contract or Open Order Service | Contingencies | Fixed Charges and Contributions | Unclassified |
|---|---|---|---|---|---|---|
| 1 | .......... | .......... | .......... | .......... | .......... | .......... |
| 2 | .......... | .......... | .......... | .......... | .......... | .......... |
| 3 | .......... | .......... | .......... | .......... | .......... | .......... |
| 4 | .......... | .......... | .......... | .......... | .......... | .......... |
| 5 | .......... | .......... | .......... | .......... | .......... | .......... |
| 6 | .......... | .......... | .......... | .......... | .......... | .......... |
| 7 | $824 03 | .......... | $191 68 | $4 00 | .......... | .......... |
| 8 | .......... | .......... | .......... | .......... | .......... | .......... |
| 9 | **$824 03** | .......... | **$191 68** | **$4 00** | .......... | .......... |
| 10 | $377 10 | .......... | $542 12 | .......... | .......... | .......... |
| 11 | .......... | .......... | .......... | .......... | .......... | .......... |
| 12 | **$377 10** | .......... | **$542 12** | .......... | .......... | .......... |
| 13 | $23 40 | .......... | $401 87 | $8 65 | .......... | .......... |
| 14 | .......... | .......... | .......... | .......... | .......... | .......... |
| 15 | **$23 40** | .......... | **$401 87** | **$8 65** | .......... | .......... |
| 16 | .......... | .......... | $374 39 | $107 67 | .......... | .......... |
| 17 | .......... | .......... | .......... | .......... | .......... | .......... |
| 18 | .......... | .......... | **$374 39** | **$107 67** | .......... | .......... |
| 19 | .......... | .......... | $294 34 | $107 86 | .......... | .......... |
| 20 | .......... | .......... | .......... | .......... | .......... | .......... |
| 21 | .......... | .......... | **$294 34** | **$107 86** | .......... | .......... |
| 22 | $89 88 | .......... | $234 07 | $142 80 | .......... | .......... |
| 23 | .......... | .......... | .......... | .......... | .......... | .......... |
| 24 | **$89 88** | .......... | **$234 07** | **$142 80** | .......... | .......... |
| 25 | $584 14 | $499 65 | $439 82 | $41 50 | .......... | .......... |
| 26 | .......... | .......... | .......... | .......... | .......... | .......... |
| 27 | **$584 14** | **$499 65** | **$439 82** | **$41 50** | .......... | .......... |
| 28 | $404 05 | $779 47 | $317 93 | $26 76 | .......... | .......... |
| 29 | .......... | .......... | .......... | .......... | .......... | .......... |
| 30 | **$404 05** | **$779 47** | **$317 93** | **$26 76** | .......... | .......... |

COMPARATIVE STATEMENTS SHOWING SEPARATELY THE EXPENDITURES
YEARS 1910 TO 1914, INCLUSIVE, CLASSIFIED BY

| | Total | Personal Service | Supplies | LINE No. |
|---|---|---|---|---|
| **REGISTER—KINGS COUNTY** | | | | |
| **1910** | | | | |
| Revenue Expenditures | $220,241 08 | $207,738 37 | $1,102 08 | 1 |
| Corporate Stock Expenditures | .......... | .......... | .......... | 2 |
| Total for 1910 | **$220,241 08** | **$207,738 37** | **$1,102 08** | 3 |
| **1911** | | | | |
| Revenue Expenditures | $216,472 89 | $203,589 58 | $1,483 86 | 4 |
| Corporate Stock Expenditures | .......... | .......... | .......... | 5 |
| Total for 1911 | **$216,472 89** | **$203,589 58** | **$1,483 86** | 6 |
| **1912** | | | | |
| Revenue Expenditures | $218,223 69 | $215,081 20 | $983 88 | 7 |
| Corporate Stock Expenditures | .......... | .......... | .......... | 8 |
| Total for 1912 | **$218,223 69** | **$215,081 20** | **$983 88** | 9 |
| **1913** | | | | |
| Revenue Expenditures | $216,268 06 | $214,161 76 | $437 70 | 10 |
| Corporate Stock Expenditures | .......... | .......... | .......... | 11 |
| Total for 1913 | **$216,268 06** | **$214,161 76** | **$437 70** | 12 |
| **1914** | | | | |
| Revenue Expenditures | $197,880 05 | $196,775 11 | $273 03 | 13 |
| Corporate Stock Expenditures | .......... | .......... | .......... | 14 |
| Total for 1914 | **$197,880 05** | **$196,775 11** | **$273 03** | 15 |
| **SHERIFF—KINGS COUNTY** | | | | |
| **1910** | | | | |
| Revenue Expenditures | $85,601 44 | $79,164 75 | $3,572 19 | 16 |
| Corporate Stock Expenditures | .......... | .......... | .......... | 17 |
| Total for 1910 | **$85,601 44** | **$79,164 75** | **$3,572 19** | 18 |
| **1911** | | | | |
| Revenue Expenditures | $87,123 44 | $80,569 79 | $4,142 35 | 19 |
| Corporate Stock Expenditures | .......... | .......... | .......... | 20 |
| Total for 1911 | **$87,123 44** | **$80,569 79** | **$4,142 35** | 21 |
| **1912** | | | | |
| Revenue Expenditures | $88,365 26 | $81,294 35 | $4,192 00 | 22 |
| Corporate Stock Expenditures | .......... | .......... | .......... | 23 |
| Total for 1912 | **$88,365 26** | **$81,294 35** | **$4,192 00** | 24 |
| **1913** | | | | |
| Revenue Expenditures | $91,637 78 | $83,544 45 | $4,101 88 | 25 |
| Corporate Stock Expenditures | .......... | .......... | .......... | 26 |
| Total for 1913 | **$91,637 78** | **$83,544 45** | **$4,101 88** | 27 |
| **1914** | | | | |
| Revenue Expenditures | $95,963 53 | $85,258 71 | $3,533 28 | 28 |
| Corporate Stock Expenditures | .......... | .......... | .......... | 29 |
| Total for 1914 | **$95,963 53** | **$85,258 71** | **$3,533 28** | 30 |

# NEW YORK

MADE FROM REVENUE AND FROM CORPORATE STOCK FUNDS FOR THE DEPARTMENTS, ACCORDING TO OBJECTS OF EXPENDITURE:

| LINE No. | Purchase of Equipment | Materials | Contract or Open Order Service | Contingencies | Fixed Charges and Contributions | Unclassified |
|---|---|---|---|---|---|---|
| 1 | .......... | .......... | $9,509 60 | $1,891 03 | .......... | .......... |
| 2 | .......... | .......... | .......... | .......... | .......... | .......... |
| 3 | .......... | .......... | **$9,509 60** | **$1,891 03** | .......... | .......... |
| 4 | .......... | .......... | $9,749 86 | $1,649 59 | .......... | .......... |
| 5 | .......... | .......... | .......... | .......... | .......... | .......... |
| 6 | .......... | .......... | **$9,749 86** | **$1,649 59** | .......... | .......... |
| 7 | $596 53 | .......... | $562 65 | $999 43 | .......... | .......... |
| 8 | .......... | .......... | .......... | .......... | .......... | .......... |
| 9 | **$596 53** | .......... | **$562 65** | **$999 43** | .......... | .......... |
| 0 | $1,097 03 | .......... | $474 29 | $97 28 | .......... | .......... |
| 1 | .......... | .......... | .......... | .......... | .......... | .......... |
| 2 | **$1,097 03** | .......... | **$474 29** | **$97 28** | .......... | .......... |
| 3 | $335 80 | .......... | $450 35 | $45 76 | .......... | .......... |
| 4 | .......... | .......... | .......... | .......... | .......... | .......... |
| 5 | **$335 80** | .......... | **$450 35** | **$45 76** | .......... | .......... |
| 6 | .......... | .......... | $694 29 | $2,170 21 | .......... | .......... |
| 7 | .......... | .......... | .......... | .......... | .......... | .......... |
| 8 | .......... | .......... | **$694 29** | **$2,170 21** | .......... | .......... |
| 9 | .......... | .......... | $700 52 | $1,710 78 | .......... | .......... |
| 0 | .......... | .......... | .......... | .......... | .......... | .......... |
| 1 | .......... | .......... | **$700 52** | **$1,710 78** | .......... | .......... |
| 2 | .......... | .......... | $641 83 | $2,237 08 | .......... | .......... |
| 3 | .......... | .......... | .......... | .......... | .......... | .......... |
| 4 | .......... | .......... | **$641 83** | **$2,237 08** | .......... | .......... |
| 5 | $106 90 | .......... | $1,730 08 | $2,154 47 | .......... | .......... |
| 6 | .......... | .......... | .......... | .......... | .......... | .......... |
| 7 | **$106 90** | .......... | **$1,730 08** | **$2,154 47** | .......... | .......... |
| 8 | $3,891 13 | .......... | $2,859 64 | $318 27 | $102 50 | .......... |
| 9 | .......... | .......... | .......... | .......... | .......... | .......... |
| 0 | **$3,891 13** | .......... | **$2,859 64** | **$318 27** | **$102 50** | .......... |

Comparative Statements Showing Separately the Expenditures
Years 1910 to 1914, Inclusive, Classified by

| | Total | Personal Service | Supplies | LINE No. |
|---|---|---|---|---|
| **CHARITABLE INSTITUTIONS—QUEENS COUNTY** | | | | |
| **1910** | | | | |
| Revenue Expenditures | $5,244 05 | .......... | .......... | 1 |
| Corporate Stock Expenditures | .......... | .......... | .......... | 2 |
| Total for 1910 | **$5,244 05** | .......... | .......... | 3 |
| **1911** | | | | |
| Revenue Expenditures | $6,415 41 | .......... | .......... | 4 |
| Corporate Stock Expenditures | .......... | .......... | .......... | 5 |
| Total for 1911 | **$6,415 41** | .......... | .......... | 6 |
| **1912** | | | | |
| Revenue Expenditures | $5,920 50 | .......... | .......... | 7 |
| Corporate Stock Expenditures | .......... | .......... | .......... | 8 |
| Total for 1912 | **$5,920 50** | .......... | .......... | 9 |
| **1913** | | | | |
| Revenue Expenditures | $6,374 61 | .......... | .......... | 10 |
| Corporate Stock Expenditures | .......... | .......... | .......... | 11 |
| Total for 1913 | **$6,374 61** | .......... | .......... | 12 |
| **1914** | | | | |
| Revenue Expenditures | $5,668 71 | .......... | .......... | 13 |
| Corporate Stock Expenditures | .......... | .......... | .......... | 14 |
| Total for 1914 | **$5,668 71** | .......... | .......... | 15 |
| **CITY RECORD—QUEENS COUNTY** | | | | |
| **1910** | | | | |
| Revenue Expenditures | $3,648 58 | .......... | .......... | 16 |
| Corporate Stock Expenditures | .......... | .......... | .......... | 17 |
| Total for 1910 | **$3,648 58** | .......... | .......... | 18 |
| **1911** | | | | |
| Revenue Expenditures | $3,062 83 | .......... | .......... | 19 |
| Corporate Stock Expenditures | .......... | .......... | .......... | 20 |
| Total for 1911 | **$3,062 83** | .......... | .......... | 21 |
| **1912** | | | | |
| Revenue Expenditures | $2,157 27 | .......... | .......... | 22 |
| Corporate Stock Expenditures | .......... | .......... | .......... | 23 |
| Total for 1912 | **$2,157 27** | .......... | .......... | 24 |
| **1913** | | | | |
| Revenue Expenditures | $3,780 61 | .......... | .......... | 25 |
| Corporate Stock Expenditures | .......... | .......... | .......... | 26 |
| Total for 1913 | **$3,780 61** | .......... | .......... | 27 |
| **1914** | | | | |
| Revenue Expenditures | $3,989 95 | .......... | .......... | 28 |
| Corporate Stock Expenditures | .......... | .......... | .......... | 29 |
| Total for 1914 | **$3,989 95** | .......... | .......... | 30 |

NEW YORK

Made from Revenue and from Corporate Stock Funds for the Departments, According to Objects of Expenditure:

| LINE No. | Purchase of Equipment | Materials | Contract or Open Order Service | Contingencies | Fixed Charges and Contributions | Unclassified |
|---|---|---|---|---|---|---|
| 1 | .......... | .......... | .......... | .......... | $5,244 05 | .......... |
| 2 | .......... | .......... | .......... | .......... | .......... | .......... |
| 3 | .......... | .......... | .......... | .......... | **$5,244 05** | .......... |
| 4 | .......... | .......... | .......... | .......... | $6,415 41 | .......... |
| 5 | .......... | .......... | .......... | .......... | .......... | .......... |
| 6 | .......... | .......... | .......... | .......... | **$6,415 41** | .......... |
| 7 | .......... | .......... | .......... | .......... | $5,920 50 | .......... |
| 8 | .......... | .......... | .......... | .......... | .......... | .......... |
| 9 | .......... | .......... | .......... | .......... | **$5,920 50** | .......... |
| 10 | .......... | .......... | .......... | .......... | $6,374 61 | .......... |
| 11 | .......... | .......... | .......... | .......... | .......... | .......... |
| 12 | .......... | .......... | .......... | .......... | **$6,374 61** | .......... |
| 13 | .......... | .......... | .......... | .......... | $5,668 71 | .......... |
| 14 | .......... | .......... | .......... | .......... | .......... | .......... |
| 15 | .......... | .......... | .......... | .......... | **$5,668 71** | .......... |
| 16 | .......... | .......... | $3,648 58 | .......... | .......... | .......... |
| 17 | .......... | .......... | .......... | .......... | .......... | .......... |
| 18 | .......... | .......... | **$3,648 58** | .......... | .......... | .......... |
| 19 | .......... | .......... | $3,062 83 | .......... | .......... | .......... |
| 20 | .......... | .......... | .......... | .......... | .......... | .......... |
| 21 | .......... | .......... | **$3,062 83** | .......... | .......... | .......... |
| 22 | .......... | .......... | $2,157 27 | .......... | .......... | .......... |
| 23 | .......... | .......... | .......... | .......... | .......... | .......... |
| 24 | .......... | .......... | **$2,157 27** | .......... | .......... | .......... |
| 25 | .......... | .......... | $3,780 61 | .......... | .......... | .......... |
| 26 | .......... | .......... | .......... | .......... | .......... | .......... |
| 27 | .......... | .......... | **$3,780 61** | .......... | .......... | .......... |
| 28 | .......... | .......... | $3,989 95 | .......... | .......... | .......... |
| 29 | .......... | .......... | .......... | .......... | .......... | .......... |
| 30 | .......... | .......... | **$3,989 95** | .......... | .......... | .......... |

Comparative Statements Showing Separately the Expenditures
Years 1910 to 1914, Inclusive, Classified by

| | Total | Personal Service | Supplies | Line No. |
|---|---|---|---|---|
| **COUNTY CLERK—QUEENS COUNTY** | | | | |
| **1910** | | | | |
| Revenue Expenditures | $27,212 54 | $21,780 07 | $1,774 00 | 1 |
| Corporate Stock Expenditures | .......... | .......... | .......... | 2 |
| Total for 1910 | **$27,212 54** | **$21,780 07** | **$1,774 00** | 3 |
| **1911** | | | | |
| Revenue Expenditures | $37,086 02 | $34,054 74 | .......... | 4 |
| Corporate Stock Expenditures | .......... | .......... | .......... | 5 |
| Total for 1911 | **$37,086 02** | **$34,054 74** | .......... | 6 |
| **1912** | | | | |
| Revenue Expenditures | $77,643 53 | $33,492 90 | $594 00 | 7 |
| Corporate Stock Expenditures | .......... | .......... | .......... | 8 |
| Total for 1912 | **$77,643 53** | **$33,492 90** | **$594 00** | 9 |
| **1913** | | | | |
| Revenue Expenditures | $107,228 67 | $97,638 31 | $1,148 90 | 10 |
| Corporate Stock Expenditures | .......... | .......... | .......... | 11 |
| Total for 1913 | **$107,228 67** | **$97,638 31** | **$1,148 90** | 12 |
| **1914** | | | | |
| Revenue Expenditures | $127,866 34 | $120,093 15 | $2,199 13 | 13 |
| Corporate Stock Expenditures | .......... | .......... | .......... | 14 |
| Total for 1914 | **$127,866 34** | **$120,093 15** | **$2,199 13** | 15 |
| **COUNTY COURT—QUEENS COUNTY** | | | | |
| **1910** | | | | |
| Revenue Expenditures | .......... | .......... | .......... | 16 |
| Corporate Stock Expenditures | .......... | .......... | .......... | 17 |
| Total for 1910 | .......... | .......... | .......... | 18 |
| **1911** | | | | |
| Revenue Expenditures | $33,139 66 | $31,822 00 | $999 81 | 19 |
| Corporate Stock Expenditures | .......... | .......... | .......... | 20 |
| Total for 1911 | **$33,139 66** | **$31,822 00** | **$999 81** | 21 |
| **1912** | | | | |
| Revenue Expenditures | $39,904 23 | $38,501 00 | $790 98 | 22 |
| Corporate Stock Expenditures | .......... | .......... | .......... | 23 |
| Total for 1912 | **$39,904 23** | **$38,501 00** | **$790 98** | 24 |
| **1913** | | | | |
| Revenue Expenditures | $43,022 73 | $41,672 73 | $435 21 | 25 |
| Corporate Stock Expenditures | .......... | .......... | .......... | 26 |
| Total for 1913 | **$43,022 73** | **$41,672 73** | **$435 21** | 27 |
| **1914** | | | | |
| Revenue Expenditures | $42,428 26 | $41,800 00 | $141 64 | 28 |
| Corporate Stock Expenditures | .......... | .......... | .......... | 29 |
| Total for 1914 | **$42,428 26** | **$41,800 00** | **$141 64** | 30 |

NEW YORK

MADE FROM REVENUE AND FROM CORPORATE STOCK FUNDS FOR THE DEPARTMENTS, ACCORDING TO OBJECTS OF EXPENDITURE:

| LINE No. | Purchase of Equipment | Materials | Contract or Open Order Service | Contingencies | Fixed Charges and Contributions | Unclassified |
|---|---|---|---|---|---|---|
| 1 | $1,688 50 | .......... | $1,969 97 | .......... | .......... | .......... |
| 2 | .......... | .......... | .......... | .......... | .......... | .......... |
| 3 | **$1,688 50** | .......... | **$1,969 97** | .......... | .......... | .......... |
| 4 | $173 32 | .......... | $2,857 96 | .......... | .......... | .......... |
| 5 | .......... | .......... | .......... | .......... | .......... | .......... |
| 6 | **$173 32** | .......... | **$2,857 96** | .......... | .......... | .......... |
| 7 | $5,698 00 | .......... | $37,858 63 | .......... | .......... | .......... |
| 8 | .......... | .......... | .......... | .......... | .......... | .......... |
| 9 | **$5,698 00** | .......... | **$37,858 63** | .......... | .......... | .......... |
| 10 | $7,640 71 | .......... | $783 75 | $17 00 | .......... | .......... |
| 11 | .......... | .......... | .......... | .......... | .......... | .......... |
| 12 | **$7,640 71** | .......... | **$783 75** | **$17 00** | .......... | .......... |
| 13 | $3,480 25 | .......... | $2,093 81 | .......... | .......... | .......... |
| 14 | .......... | .......... | .......... | .......... | .......... | .......... |
| 15 | **$3,480 25** | .......... | **$2,093 81** | .......... | .......... | .......... |
| 16 | .......... | .......... | .......... | .......... | .......... | .......... |
| 17 | .......... | .......... | .......... | .......... | .......... | .......... |
| 18 | .......... | .......... | .......... | .......... | .......... | .......... |
| 19 | .......... | .......... | $167 85 | $150 00 | .......... | .......... |
| 20 | .......... | .......... | .......... | .......... | .......... | .......... |
| 21 | .......... | .......... | **$167 85** | **$150 00** | .......... | .......... |
| 22 | $161 80 | .......... | $178 57 | $271 88 | .......... | .......... |
| 23 | .......... | .......... | .......... | .......... | .......... | .......... |
| 24 | **$161 80** | .......... | **$178 57** | **$271 88** | .......... | .......... |
| 25 | $229 80 | .......... | $684 99 | .......... | .......... | .......... |
| 26 | .......... | .......... | .......... | .......... | .......... | .......... |
| 27 | **$229 80** | .......... | **$684 99** | .......... | .......... | .......... |
| 28 | $284 65 | .......... | $179 07 | $22 90 | .......... | .......... |
| 29 | .......... | .......... | .......... | .......... | .......... | .......... |
| 30 | **$284 65** | .......... | **$179 07** | **$22 90** | .......... | .......... |

COMPARATIVE STATEMENTS SHOWING SEPARATELY THE EXPENDITURES
YEARS 1910 TO 1914, INCLUSIVE, CLASSIFIED BY

| | Total | Personal Service | Supplies | LINE No. |
|---|---|---|---|---|
| **SUPREME COURT, QUEENS COUNTY** | | | | |
| **1910** | | | | |
| Revenue Expenditures | $146,779 64 | $141,733 65 | $369 90 | 1 |
| Corporate Stock Expenditures | .......... | .......... | .......... | 2 |
| Total for 1910 | **$146,779 64** | **$141,733 65** | **$369 90** | 3 |
| **1911** | | | | |
| Revenue Expenditures | $69,953 19 | $68,177 16 | $1,287 14 | 4 |
| Corporate Stock Expenditures | .......... | .......... | .......... | 5 |
| Total for 1911 | **$69,953 19** | **$68,177 16** | **$1,287 14** | 6 |
| **1912** | | | | |
| Revenue Expenditures | $73,714 73 | $73,271 75 | .......... | 7 |
| Corporate Stock Expenditures | .......... | .......... | .......... | 8 |
| Total for 1912 | **$73,714 73** | **$73,271 75** | .......... | 9 |
| **1913** | | | | |
| Revenue Expenditures | $94,715 94 | $94,615 94 | $100 00 | 10 |
| Corporate Stock Expenditures | .......... | .......... | .......... | 11 |
| Total for 1913 | **$94,715 94** | **$94,615 94** | **$100 00** | 12 |
| **1914** | | | | |
| Revenue Expenditures | $95,586 38 | $95,486 38 | .......... | 13 |
| Corporate Stock Expenditures | .......... | .......... | .......... | 14 |
| Total for 1914 | **$95,586 38** | **$95,486 38** | .......... | 15 |
| **SUPREME COURT LIBRARY—QUEENS COUNTY** | | | | |
| **1910** | | | | |
| Revenue Expenditures | .......... | .......... | .......... | 16 |
| Corporate Stock Expenditures | .......... | .......... | .......... | 17 |
| Total for 1910 | .......... | .......... | .......... | 18 |
| **1911** | | | | |
| Revenue Expenditures | .......... | .......... | .......... | 19 |
| Corporate Stock Expenditures | .......... | .......... | .......... | 20 |
| Total for 1911 | .......... | .......... | .......... | 21 |
| **1912** | | | | |
| Revenue Expenditures | $2,272 65 | $1,741 67 | $93 70 | 22 |
| Corporate Stock Expenditures | .......... | .......... | .......... | 23 |
| Total for 1912 | **$2,272 65** | **$1,741 67** | **$93 70** | 24 |
| **1913** | | | | |
| Revenue Expenditures | $2,566 43 | $1,800 00 | $10 00 | 25 |
| Corporate Stock Expenditures | .......... | .......... | .......... | 26 |
| Total for 1913 | **$2,566 43** | **$1,800 00** | **$10 00** | 27 |
| **1914** | | | | |
| Revenue Expenditures | $2,308 06 | $1,992 50 | .......... | 28 |
| Corporate Stock Expenditures | .......... | .......... | .......... | 29 |
| Total for 1914 | **$2,308 06** | **$1,992 50** | .......... | 30 |

NEW YORK

MADE FROM REVENUE AND FROM CORPORATE STOCK FUNDS FOR THE DEPARTMENTS, ACCORDING TO OBJECTS OF EXPENDITURE:

| LINE No. | Purchase of Equipment | Materials | Contract or Open Order Service | Contingencies | Fixed Charges and Contributions | Unclassified |
|---|---|---|---|---|---|---|
| 1 | $172 13 | .......... | $2,472 32 | $2,031 64 | .......... | .......... |
| 2 | .......... | .......... | .......... | .......... | .......... | .......... |
| 3 | **$172 13** | .......... | **$2,472 32** | **$2,031 64** | .......... | .......... |
| 4 | .......... | .......... | $288 99 | $199 90 | .......... | .......... |
| 5 | .......... | .......... | .......... | .......... | .......... | .......... |
| 6 | .......... | .......... | **$288 99** | **$199 90** | .......... | .......... |
| 7 | .......... | .......... | $292 98 | $150 00 | .......... | .......... |
| 8 | .......... | .......... | .......... | .......... | .......... | .......... |
| 9 | .......... | .......... | **$292 98** | **$150 00** | .......... | .......... |
| 10 | .......... | .......... | .......... | .......... | .......... | .......... |
| 11 | .......... | .......... | .......... | .......... | .......... | .......... |
| 12 | .......... | .......... | .......... | .......... | .......... | .......... |
| 13 | .......... | .......... | .......... | $100 00 | .......... | .......... |
| 14 | .......... | .......... | .......... | .......... | .......... | .......... |
| 15 | .......... | .......... | .......... | **$100 00** | .......... | .......... |
| 16 | .......... | .......... | .......... | .......... | .......... | .......... |
| 17 | .......... | .......... | .......... | .......... | .......... | .......... |
| 18 | .......... | .......... | .......... | .......... | .......... | .......... |
| 19 | .......... | .......... | .......... | .......... | .......... | .......... |
| 20 | .......... | .......... | .......... | .......... | .......... | .......... |
| 21 | .......... | .......... | .......... | .......... | .......... | .......... |
| 22 | $398 90 | .......... | $21 13 | $17 25 | .......... | .......... |
| 23 | .......... | .......... | .......... | .......... | .......... | .......... |
| 24 | **$398 90** | .......... | **$21 13** | **$17 25** | .......... | .......... |
| 25 | $505 13 | .......... | $157 70 | .......... | $93 60 | .......... |
| 26 | .......... | .......... | .......... | .......... | .......... | .......... |
| 27 | **$505 13** | .......... | **$157 70** | .......... | **$93 60** | .......... |
| 28 | .......... | .......... | .......... | $221 96 | $93 60 | .......... |
| 29 | .......... | .......... | .......... | .......... | .......... | .......... |
| 30 | .......... | .......... | .......... | **$221 96** | **$93 60** | .......... |

COMPARATIVE STATEMENTS SHOWING SEPARATELY THE EXPENDITURES
YEARS 1910 TO 1914, INCLUSIVE, CLASSIFIED BY

| | Total | Personal Service | Supplies | LINE No. |
|---|---|---|---|---|
| **SURROGATE'S COURT—QUEENS COUNTY** | | | | |
| **1910** | | | | |
| Revenue Expenditures | $17,822 67 | $16,786 04 | $559 72 | 1 |
| Corporate Stock Expenditures | .......... | .......... | .......... | 2 |
| Total for 1910 | **$17,822 67** | **$16,786 04** | **$559 72** | 3 |
| **1911** | | | | |
| Revenue Expenditures | $23,348 18 | $22,576 99 | $257 10 | 4 |
| Corporate Stock Expenditures | .......... | .......... | .......... | 5 |
| Total for 1911 | **$23,348 18** | **$22,576 99** | **$257 10** | 6 |
| **1912** | | | | |
| Revenue Expenditures | $23,793 60 | $22,941 43 | $145 00 | 7 |
| Corporate Stock Expenditures | .......... | .......... | .......... | 8 |
| Total for 1912 | **$23,793 60** | **$22,941 43** | **$145 00** | 9 |
| **1913** | | | | |
| Revenue Expenditures | $23,946 59 | $23,125 10 | $545 54 | 10 |
| Corporate Stock Expenditures | .......... | .......... | .......... | 11 |
| Total for 1913 | **$23,946 59** | **$23,125 10** | **$545 54** | 12 |
| **1914** | | | | |
| Revenue Expenditures | $26,898 03 | $24,065 32 | $220 46 | 13 |
| Corporate Stock Expenditures | .......... | .......... | .......... | 14 |
| Total for 1914 | **$26,898 03** | **$24,065 32** | **$220 46** | 15 |
| **DISTRICT ATTORNEY—QUEENS COUNTY** | | | | |
| **1910** | | | | |
| Revenue Expenditures | $30,740 49 | $26,268 98 | $196 23 | 16 |
| Corporate Stock Expenditures | .......... | .......... | .......... | 17 |
| Total for 1910 | **$30,740 49** | **$26,268 98** | **$196 23** | 18 |
| **1911** | | | | |
| Revenue Expenditures | $38,319 94 | $35,599 99 | $658 56 | 19 |
| Corporate Stock Expenditures | .......... | .......... | .......... | 20 |
| Total for 1911 | **$38,319 94** | **$35,599 99** | **$658 56** | 21 |
| **1912** | | | | |
| Revenue Expenditures | $32,176 02 | $29,940 22 | $199 13 | 22 |
| Corporate Stock Expenditures | .......... | .......... | .......... | 23 |
| Total for 1912 | **$32,176 02** | **$29,940 22** | **$199 13** | 24 |
| **1913** | | | | |
| Revenue Expenditures | $35,872 22 | $33,786 78 | $266 77 | 25 |
| Corporate Stock Expenditures | .......... | .......... | .......... | 26 |
| Total for 1913 | **$35,872 22** | **$33,786 78** | **$266 77** | 27 |
| **1914** | | | | |
| Revenue Expenditures | $40,747 17 | $36,160 96 | $202 74 | 28 |
| Corporate Stock Expenditures | .......... | .......... | .......... | 29 |
| Total for 1914 | **$40,747 17** | **$36,160 96** | **$202 74** | 30 |

NEW YORK

MADE FROM REVENUE AND FROM CORPORATE STOCK FUNDS FOR THE DEPARTMENTS, ACCORDING TO OBJECTS OF EXPENDITURE:

| LINE No. | Purchase of Equipment | Materials | Contract or Open Order Service | Contingencies | Fixed Charges and Contributions | Unclassified |
|---|---|---|---|---|---|---|
| 1 | .......... | .......... | $230 78 | $246 13 | .......... | .......... |
| 2 | .......... | .......... | .......... | .......... | .......... | .......... |
| 3 | .......... | .......... | **$230 78** | **$246 13** | .......... | .......... |
| 4 | .......... | .......... | $239 79 | $274 30 | .......... | .......... |
| 5 | .......... | .......... | .......... | .......... | .......... | .......... |
| 6 | .......... | .......... | **$239 79** | **$274 30** | .......... | .......... |
| 7 | $98 40 | .......... | $262 02 | $346 75 | .......... | .......... |
| 8 | .......... | .......... | .......... | .......... | .......... | .......... |
| 9 | **$98 40** | .......... | **$262 02** | **$346 75** | .......... | .......... |
| 10 | $42 90 | .......... | $233 05 | .......... | .......... | .......... |
| 11 | .......... | .......... | .......... | .......... | .......... | .......... |
| 12 | **$42 90** | .......... | **$233 05** | .......... | .......... | .......... |
| 13 | $167 00 | .......... | $2,433 25 | $12 00 | .......... | .......... |
| 14 | .......... | .......... | .......... | .......... | .......... | .......... |
| 15 | **$167 00** | .......... | **$2,433 25** | **$12 00** | .......... | .......... |
| 16 | .......... | .......... | $374 56 | $3,900 72 | .......... | .......... |
| 17 | .......... | .......... | .......... | .......... | .......... | .......... |
| 18 | .......... | .......... | **$374 56** | **$3,900 72** | .......... | .......... |
| 19 | $3 41 | .......... | $634 12 | $1,423 86 | .......... | .......... |
| 20 | .......... | .......... | .......... | .......... | .......... | .......... |
| 21 | **$3 41** | .......... | **$634 12** | **$1,423 86** | .......... | .......... |
| 22 | .......... | .......... | $463 67 | $1,573 00 | .......... | .......... |
| 23 | .......... | .......... | .......... | .......... | .......... | .......... |
| 24 | .......... | .......... | **$463 67** | **$1,573 00** | .......... | .......... |
| 25 | $52 00 | .......... | $488 99 | $1,277 68 | .......... | .......... |
| 26 | .......... | .......... | .......... | .......... | .......... | .......... |
| 27 | **$52 00** | .......... | **$488 99** | **$1,277 68** | .......... | .......... |
| 28 | $314 88 | .......... | $2,142 28 | $1,926 31 | .......... | .......... |
| 29 | .......... | .......... | .......... | .......... | .......... | .......... |
| 30 | **$314 88** | .......... | **$2,142 28** | **$1,926 31** | .......... | .......... |

COMPARATIVE STATEMENTS SHOWING SEPARATELY THE EXPENDITURES
YEARS 1910 TO 1914, INCLUSIVE, CLASSIFIED BY

| | Total | Personal Service | Supplies | LINE No. |
|---|---|---|---|---|
| **COMMISSIONER OF JURORS—QUEENS COUNTY** | | | | |
| **1910** | | | | |
| Revenue Expenditures | $11,708 16 | $11,119 70 | $481 15 | 1 |
| Corporate Stock Expenditures | .......... | .......... | .......... | 2 |
| Total for 1910 | **$11,708 16** | **$11,119 70** | **$481 15** | 3 |
| **1911** | | | | |
| Revenue Expenditures | $11,779 12 | $11,121 18 | $495 50 | 4 |
| Corporate Stock Expenditures | .......... | .......... | .......... | 5 |
| Total for 1911 | **$11,779 12** | **$11,121 18** | **$495 50** | 6 |
| **1912** | | | | |
| Revenue Expenditures | $10,732 04 | $9,937 12 | $18 55 | 7 |
| Corporate Stock Expenditures | .......... | .......... | .......... | 8 |
| Total for 1912 | **$10,732 04** | **$9,937 12** | **$18 55** | 9 |
| **1913** | | | | |
| Revenue Expenditures | $12,626 86 | $11,771 33 | $741 85 | 10 |
| Corporate Stock Expenditures | .......... | .......... | .......... | 11 |
| Total for 1913 | **$12,626 86** | **$11,771 33** | **$741 85** | 12 |
| **1914** | | | | |
| Revenue Expenditures | $12,253 88 | $11,499 50 | $616 00 | 13 |
| Corporate Stock Expenditures | .......... | .......... | .......... | 14 |
| Total for 1914 | **$12,253 88** | **$11,499 50** | **$616 00** | 15 |
| **MISCELLANEOUS—QUEENS COUNTY** | | | | |
| **1910** | | | | |
| Revenue Expenditures | $14,296 30 | $700 00 | .......... | 16 |
| Corporate Stock Expenditures | .......... | .......... | .......... | 17 |
| Total for 1910 | **$14,296 30** | **$700 00** | .......... | 18 |
| **1911** | | | | |
| Revenue Expenditures | $51,899 64 | $36,919 73 | .......... | 19 |
| Corporate Stock Expenditures | .......... | .......... | .......... | 20 |
| Total for 1911 | **$51,899 64** | **$36,919 73** | .......... | 21 |
| **1912** | | | | |
| Revenue Expenditures | $33,517 90 | $32,662 00 | .......... | 22 |
| Corporate Stock Expenditures | .......... | .......... | .......... | 23 |
| Total for 1912 | **$33,517 90** | **$32,662 00** | .......... | 24 |
| **1913** | | | | |
| Revenue Expenditures | $38,242 52 | $36,700 00 | .......... | 25 |
| Corporate Stock Expenditures | .......... | .......... | .......... | 26 |
| Total for 1913 | **$38,242 52** | **$36,700 00** | .......... | 27 |
| **1914** | | | | |
| Revenue Expenditures | $38,801 57 | $36,862 92 | .......... | 28 |
| Corporate Stock Expenditures | .......... | .......... | .......... | 29 |
| Total for 1914 | **$38,801 57** | **$36,862 92** | .......... | 30 |

NEW YORK

MADE FROM REVENUE AND FROM CORPORATE STOCK FUNDS FOR THE DEPARTMENTS, ACCORDING TO OBJECTS OF EXPENDITURE:

| LINE No. | Purchase of Equipment | Materials | Contract or Open Order Service | Contingencies | Fixed Charges and Contributions | Unclassified |
|---|---|---|---|---|---|---|
| 1 | .......... | .......... | $61 31 | $46 00 | .......... | .......... |
| 2 | .......... | .......... | .......... | .......... | .......... | .......... |
| 3 | .......... | .......... | **$61 31** | **$46 00** | .......... | .......... |
| 4 | .......... | .......... | $52 86 | $109 58 | .......... | .......... |
| 5 | .......... | .......... | .......... | .......... | .......... | .......... |
| 6 | .......... | .......... | **$52 86** | **$109 58** | .......... | .......... |
| 7 | .......... | .......... | $53 91 | $722 46 | .......... | .......... |
| 8 | .......... | .......... | .......... | .......... | .......... | .......... |
| 9 | .......... | .......... | **$53 91** | **$722 46** | .......... | .......... |
| 10 | $7 20 | .......... | $106 48 | .......... | .......... | .......... |
| 11 | .......... | .......... | .......... | .......... | .......... | .......... |
| 12 | **$7 20** | .......... | **$106 48** | .......... | .......... | .......... |
| 13 | .......... | .......... | $119 38 | $19 00 | .......... | .......... |
| 14 | .......... | .......... | .......... | .......... | .......... | .......... |
| 15 | .......... | .......... | **$119 38** | **$19 00** | .......... | .......... |
| 16 | .......... | .......... | $2,000 00 | $3,752 70 | .......... | $7,843 60 |
| 17 | .......... | .......... | ....... | .......... | .......... | .......... |
| 18 | .......... | .......... | **$2,000 00** | **$3,752 70** | .......... | **$7,843 60** |
| 19 | .......... | .......... | $640 00 | $280 80 | .......... | $14,059 11 |
| 20 | .......... | .......... | .......... | .......... | .......... | .......... |
| 21 | .......... | .......... | **$640 00** | **$280 80** | .......... | **$14,059 11** |
| 22 | .......... | .......... | .......... | $855 90 | .......... | .......... |
| 23 | .......... | .......... | .......... | .......... | .......... | .......... |
| 24 | .......... | .......... | .......... | **$855 90** | .......... | .......... |
| 25 | .......... | .......... | .......... | $1,542 52 | .......... | .......... |
| 26 | .......... | .......... | .......... | .......... | .......... | .......... |
| 27 | .......... | .......... | .......... | **$1,542 52** | .......... | .......... |
| 28 | .......... | .......... | .......... | $1,938 65 | .......... | .......... |
| 29 | .......... | .......... | .......... | .......... | .......... | .......... |
| 30 | .......... | .......... | .......... | **$1,938 65** | .......... | .......... |

Comparative Statements Showing Separately the Expenditures
Years 1910 to 1914, Inclusive, Classified by

| | Total | Personal Service | Supplies | Line No. |
|---|---|---|---|---|
| **NATIONAL GUARD AND NAVAL MILITIA—QUEENS COUNTY** | | | | |
| **1910** | | | | |
| Revenue Expenditures | $5,020 00 | $5,020 00 | .......... | 1 |
| Corporate Stock Expenditures | .......... | .......... | .......... | 2 |
| Total for 1910 | **$5,020 00** | **$5,020 00** | .......... | 3 |
| **1911** | | | | |
| Revenue Expenditures | $5,110 00 | $5,110 00 | .......... | 4 |
| Corporate Stock Expenditures | .......... | .......... | .......... | 5 |
| Total for 1911 | **$5,110 00** | **$5,110 00** | .......... | 6 |
| **1912** | | | | |
| Revenue Expenditures | $5,124 00 | $5,124 00 | .......... | 7 |
| Corporate Stock Expenditures | .......... | .......... | .......... | 8 |
| Total for 1912 | **$5,124 00** | **$5,124 00** | .......... | 9 |
| **1913** | | | | |
| Revenue Expenditures | $5,110 00 | $5,110 00 | .......... | 10 |
| Corporate Stock Expenditures | .......... | .......... | .......... | 11 |
| Total for 1913 | **$5,110 00** | **$5,110 00** | .......... | 12 |
| **1914** | | | | |
| Revenue Expenditures | $5,110 00 | $5,110 00 | .......... | 13 |
| Corporate Stock Expenditures | .......... | .......... | .......... | 14 |
| Total for 1914 | **$5,110 00** | **$5,110 00** | .......... | 15 |
| **PUBLIC ADMINISTRATOR—QUEENS COUNTY** | | | | |
| **1910** | | | | |
| Revenue Expenditures | $1,200 00 | $1,200 00 | .......... | 16 |
| Corporate Stock Expenditures | .......... | .......... | .......... | 17 |
| Total for 1910 | **$1,200 00** | **$1,200 00** | .......... | 18 |
| **1911** | | | | |
| Revenue Expenditures | $1,200 00 | $1,200 00 | .......... | 19 |
| Corporate Stock Expenditures | .......... | .......... | .......... | 20 |
| Total for 1911 | **$1,200 00** | **$1,200 00** | .......... | 21 |
| **1912** | | | | |
| Revenue Expenditures | $1,200 00 | $1,200 00 | .......... | 22 |
| Corporate Stock Expenditures | .......... | .......... | .......... | 23 |
| Total for 1912 | **$1,200 00** | **$1,200 00** | .......... | 24 |
| **1913** | | | | |
| Revenue Expenditures | $1,200 00 | $1,200 00 | .......... | 25 |
| Corporate Stock Expenditures | .......... | .......... | .......... | 26 |
| Total for 1913 | **$1,200 00** | **$1,200 00** | .......... | 27 |
| **1914** | | | | |
| Revenue Expenditures | $1,306 00 | $1,200 00 | .......... | 28 |
| Corporate Stock Expenditures | .......... | .......... | .......... | 29 |
| Total for 1914 | **$1,306 00** | **$1,200 00** | .......... | 30 |

NEW YORK

MADE FROM REVENUE AND FROM CORPORATE STOCK FUNDS FOR THE DEPARTMENTS, ACCORDING TO OBJECTS OF EXPENDITURE:

| LINE No. | Purchase of Equipment | Materials | Contract or Open Order Service | Contingencies | Fixed Charges and Contributions | Unclassified |
|---|---|---|---|---|---|---|
| 1 | .......... | .......... | .......... | .......... | .......... | .......... |
| 2 | .......... | .......... | .......... | .......... | .......... | .......... |
| 3 | .......... | .......... | .......... | .......... | .......... | .......... |
| 4 | .......... | .......... | .......... | .......... | .......... | .......... |
| 5 | .......... | .......... | .......... | .......... | .......... | .......... |
| 6 | .......... | .......... | .......... | .......... | .......... | .......... |
| 7 | .......... | .......... | .......... | .......... | .......... | .......... |
| 8 | .......... | .......... | .......... | .......... | .......... | .......... |
| 9 | .......... | .......... | .......... | .......... | .......... | .......... |
| 10 | .......... | .......... | .......... | .......... | .......... | .......... |
| 11 | .......... | .......... | .......... | .......... | .......... | .......... |
| 12 | .......... | .......... | .......... | .......... | .......... | .......... |
| 13 | .......... | .......... | .......... | .......... | .......... | .......... |
| 14 | .......... | .......... | .......... | .......... | .......... | .......... |
| 15 | .......... | .......... | .......... | .......... | .......... | .......... |
| 16 | .......... | .......... | .......... | .......... | .......... | .......... |
| 17 | .......... | .......... | .......... | .......... | .......... | .......... |
| 18 | .......... | .......... | .......... | .......... | .......... | .......... |
| 19 | .......... | .......... | .......... | .......... | .......... | .......... |
| 20 | .......... | .......... | .......... | .......... | .......... | .......... |
| 21 | .......... | .......... | .......... | .......... | .......... | .......... |
| 22 | .......... | .......... | .......... | .......... | .......... | .......... |
| 23 | .......... | .......... | .......... | .......... | .......... | .......... |
| 24 | .......... | .......... | .......... | .......... | .......... | .......... |
| 25 | .......... | .......... | .......... | .......... | .......... | .......... |
| 26 | .......... | .......... | .......... | .......... | .......... | .......... |
| 27 | .......... | .......... | .......... | .......... | .......... | .......... |
| 28 | .......... | .......... | .......... | $106 00 | .......... | .......... |
| 29 | .......... | .......... | .......... | .......... | .......... | .......... |
| 30 | .......... | .......... | .......... | **$106 00** | .......... | .......... |

COMPARATIVE STATEMENTS SHOWING SEPARATELY THE EXPENDITURES
YEARS 1910 TO 1914, INCLUSIVE, CLASSIFIED BY

| | Total | Personal Service | Supplies | LINE No. |
|---|---|---|---|---|
| **SHERIFF—QUEENS COUNTY** | | | | |
| **1910** | | | | |
| Revenue Expenditures | $77,790 27 | $55,891 25 | $19,654 65 | 1 |
| Corporate Stock Expenditures | .......... | .......... | .......... | 2 |
| Total for 1910 | **$77,790 27** | **$55,891 25** | **$19,654 65** | 3 |
| **1911** | | | | |
| Revenue Expenditures | $75,381 68 | $57,632 62 | $15,874 92 | 4 |
| Corporate Stock Expenditures | .......... | .......... | .......... | 5 |
| Total for 1911 | **$75,381 68** | **$57,632 62** | **$15,874 92** | 6 |
| **1912** | | | | |
| Revenue Expenditures | $71,355 14 | $49,703 26 | $10,729 22 | 7 |
| Corporate Stock Expenditures | .......... | .......... | .......... | 8 |
| Total for 1912 | **$71,355 14** | **$49,703 26** | **$10,729 22** | 9 |
| **1913** | | | | |
| Revenue Expenditures | $52,046 22 | $45,152 15 | $1,104 29 | 10 |
| Corporate Stock Expenditures | .......... | .......... | .......... | 11 |
| Total for 1913 | **$52,046 22** | **$45,152 15** | **$1,104 29** | 12 |
| **1914** | | | | |
| Revenue Expenditures | $44,692 01 | $41,873 69 | $661 52 | 13 |
| Corporate Stock Expenditures | .......... | .......... | .......... | 14 |
| Total for 1914 | **$44,692 01** | **$41,873 69** | **$661 52** | 15 |
| **CHARITABLE INSTITUTIONS—RICHMOND COUNTY** | | | | |
| **1910** | | | | |
| Revenue Expenditures | $1,179 45 | .......... | .......... | 16 |
| Corporate Stock Expenditures | .......... | .......... | .......... | 17 |
| Total for 1910 | **$1,179 45** | .......... | .......... | 18 |
| **1911** | | | | |
| Revenue Expenditures | $1,518 83 | .......... | .......... | 19 |
| Corporate Stock Expenditures | .......... | .......... | .......... | 20 |
| Total for 1911 | **$1,518 83** | .......... | .......... | 21 |
| **1912** | | | | |
| Revenue Expenditures | $1,566 41 | .......... | .......... | 22 |
| Corporate Stock Expenditures | .......... | .......... | .......... | 23 |
| Total for 1912 | **$1,566 41** | .......... | .......... | 24 |
| **1913** | | | | |
| Revenue Expenditures | $1,289 18 | .......... | .......... | 25 |
| Corporate Stock Expenditures | .......... | .......... | .......... | 26 |
| Total for 1913 | **$1,289 18** | .......... | .......... | 27 |
| **1914** | | | | |
| Revenue Expenditures | $1,068 39 | .......... | .......... | 28 |
| Corporate Stock Expenditures | .......... | .......... | .......... | 29 |
| Total for 1914 | **$1,068 39** | .......... | .......... | 30 |

NEW YORK

MADE FROM REVENUE AND FROM CORPORATE STOCK FUNDS FOR THE DEPARTMENTS, ACCORDING TO OBJECTS OF EXPENDITURE:

| LINE No. | Purchase of Equipment | Materials | Contract or Open Order Service | Contingencies | Fixed Charges and Contributions | Unclassified |
|---|---|---|---|---|---|---|
| 1 | .......... | .......... | $541 81 | $1,702 56 | .......... | .......... |
| 2 | .......... | .......... | .......... | .......... | .......... | .......... |
| 3 | .......... | .......... | **$541 81** | **$1,702 56** | .......... | .......... |
| 4 | .......... | .......... | $530 20 | $1,343 94 | .......... | .......... |
| 5 | .......... | .......... | .......... | .......... | .......... | .......... |
| 6 | .......... | .......... | **$530 20** | **$1,343 94** | .......... | .......... |
| 7 | .......... | .......... | $7,958 73 | $2,963 93 | .......... | .......... |
| 8 | .......... | .......... | .......... | .......... | .......... | .......... |
| 9 | .......... | .......... | **$7,958 73** | **$2,963 93** | .......... | .......... |
| 10 | $184 97 | .......... | $5,072 81 | $532 00 | .......... | .......... |
| 11 | .......... | .......... | .......... | .......... | .......... | .......... |
| 12 | **$184 97** | .......... | **$5,072 81** | **$532 00** | .......... | .......... |
| 13 | .......... | .......... | $2,098 80 | $58 00 | .......... | .......... |
| 14 | .......... | .......... | .......... | .......... | .......... | .......... |
| 15 | .......... | .......... | **$2,098 80** | **$58 00** | .......... | .......... |
| 16 | .......... | .......... | .......... | .......... | $1,179 45 | .......... |
| 17 | .......... | .......... | .......... | .......... | .......... | .......... |
| 18 | .......... | .......... | .......... | .......... | **$1,179 45** | .......... |
| 19 | .......... | .......... | .......... | .......... | $1,518 83 | .......... |
| 20 | .......... | .......... | .......... | .......... | .......... | .......... |
| 21 | .......... | .......... | .......... | .......... | **$1,518 83** | .......... |
| 22 | .......... | .......... | .......... | .......... | $1,566 41 | .......... |
| 23 | .......... | .......... | .......... | .......... | .......... | .......... |
| 24 | .......... | .......... | .......... | .......... | **$1,566 41** | .......... |
| 25 | .......... | .......... | .......... | .......... | $1,289 18 | .......... |
| 26 | .......... | .......... | .......... | .......... | .......... | .......... |
| 27 | .......... | .......... | .......... | .......... | **$1,289 18** | .......... |
| 28 | .......... | .......... | .......... | .......... | $1,068 39 | .......... |
| 29 | .......... | .......... | .......... | .......... | .......... | .......... |
| 30 | .......... | .......... | .......... | .......... | **$1,068 39** | .......... |

Comparative Statements Showing Separately the Expenditures
Years 1910 to 1914, Inclusive, Classified by

| | Total | Personal Service | Supplies | Line No. |
|---|---|---|---|---|
| **CITY RECORD—RICHMOND COUNTY** | | | | |
| **1910** | | | | |
| Revenue Expenditures | $2,712 72 | .......... | .......... | 1 |
| Corporate Stock Expenditures | .......... | .......... | .......... | 2 |
| Total for 1910 | **$2,712 72** | .......... | .......... | 3 |
| **1911** | | | | |
| Revenue Expenditures | $1,490 24 | .......... | .......... | 4 |
| Corporate Stock Expenditures | .......... | .......... | .......... | 5 |
| Total for 1911 | **$1,490 24** | .......... | .......... | 6 |
| **1912** | | | | |
| Revenue Expenditures | $2,529 45 | .......... | .......... | 7 |
| Corporate Stock Expenditures | .......... | .......... | .......... | 8 |
| Total for 1912 | **$2,529 45** | .......... | .......... | 9 |
| **1913** | | | | |
| Revenue Expenditures | $2,434 39 | .......... | .......... | 10 |
| Corporate Stock Expenditures | .......... | .......... | .......... | 11 |
| Total for 1913 | **$2,434 39** | .......... | .......... | 12 |
| **1914** | | | | |
| Revenue Expenditures | $1,720 69 | .......... | .......... | 13 |
| Corporate Stock Expenditures | .......... | .......... | .......... | 13 |
| Total for 1914 | **$1,720 69** | .......... | .......... | 15 |
| **COUNTY CLERK—RICHMOND COUNTY** | | | | |
| **1910** | | | | |
| Revenue Expenditures | $20,297 94 | $19,853 99 | $91 52 | 16 |
| Corporate Stock Expenditures | .......... | .......... | .......... | 17 |
| Total for 1910 | **$20,297 94** | **$19,853 99** | **$91 52** | 18 |
| **1911** | | | | |
| Revenue Expenditures | $18,786 07 | $18,461 95 | $96 55 | 19 |
| Corporate Stock Expenditures | .......... | .......... | .......... | 20 |
| Total for 1911 | **$18,786 07** | **$18,461 95** | **$96 55** | 21 |
| **1912** | | | | |
| Revenue Expenditures | $18,743 30 | $18,459 90 | .......... | 22 |
| Corporate Stock Expenditures | .......... | .......... | .......... | 23 |
| Total for 1912 | **$18,743 30** | **$18,459 90** | .......... | 24 |
| **1913** | | | | |
| Revenue Expenditures | $22,715 45 | $22,015 06 | $119 73 | 25 |
| Corporate Stock Expenditures | .......... | .......... | .......... | 26 |
| Total for 1913 | **$22,715 45** | **$22,015 06** | **$119 73** | 27 |
| **1914** | | | | |
| Revenue Expenditures | $21,231 32 | $20,650 08 | $99 80 | 28 |
| Corporate Stock Expenditures | .......... | .......... | .......... | 29 |
| Total for 1914 | **$21,231 32** | **$20,650 08** | **$99 80** | 30 |

NEW YORK

MADE FROM REVENUE AND FROM CORPORATE STOCK FUNDS FOR THE DEPARTMENTS, ACCORDING TO OBJECTS OF EXPENDITURE:

| LINE No. | Purchase of Equipment | Materials | Contract or Open Order Service | Contingencies | Fixed Charges and Contributions | Unclassified |
|---|---|---|---|---|---|---|
| 1 | .......... | .......... | $2,712 72 | .......... | .......... | .......... |
| 2 | .......... | .......... | .......... | .......... | .......... | .......... |
| 3 | .......... | .......... | **$2,712 72** | .......... | .......... | .......... |
| 4 | .......... | .......... | $1,490 24 | .......... | .......... | .......... |
| 5 | .......... | .......... | .......... | .......... | .......... | .......... |
| 6 | .......... | .......... | **$1,490 24** | .......... | .......... | .......... |
| 7 | .......... | .......... | $2,529 45 | .......... | .......... | .......... |
| 8 | .......... | .......... | .......... | .......... | .......... | .......... |
| 9 | .......... | .......... | **$2,529 45** | .......... | .......... | .......... |
| 10 | .......... | .......... | $2,434 39 | .......... | .......... | .......... |
| 11 | .......... | .......... | .......... | .......... | .......... | .......... |
| 12 | .......... | .......... | **$2,434 39** | .......... | .......... | .......... |
| 13 | .......... | .......... | $1,720 69 | .......... | .......... | .......... |
| 14 | .......... | .......... | .......... | .......... | .......... | .......... |
| 15 | .......... | .......... | **$1,720 69** | .......... | .......... | .......... |
| 16 | .......... | .......... | $305 85 | $46 58 | .......... | .......... |
| 17 | .......... | .......... | .......... | .......... | .......... | .......... |
| 18 | .......... | .......... | **$305 85** | **$46 58** | .......... | .......... |
| 19 | .......... | .......... | $180 09 | $47 48 | .......... | .......... |
| 20 | .......... | .......... | .......... | .......... | .......... | .......... |
| 21 | .......... | .......... | **$180 09** | **$47 48** | .......... | .......... |
| 22 | .......... | .......... | $106 40 | $177 00 | .......... | .......... |
| 23 | .......... | .......... | .......... | .......... | .......... | .......... |
| 24 | .......... | .......... | **$106 40** | **$177 00** | .......... | .......... |
| 25 | $441 00 | .......... | $139 66 | .......... | .......... | .......... |
| 26 | .......... | .......... | .......... | .......... | .......... | .......... |
| 27 | **$441 00** | .......... | **$139 66** | .......... | .......... | |
| 28 | $371 06 | .......... | $100 38 | $10 00 | .......... | .......... |
| 29 | .......... | .......... | .......... | .......... | .......... | .......... |
| 30 | **$371 06** | .......... | **$100 38** | **$10 00** | .......... | .......... |

COMPARATIVE STATEMENTS SHOWING SEPARATELY THE EXPENDITURES
YEARS 1910 TO 1914, INCLUSIVE, CLASSIFIED BY

| | Total | Personal Service | Supplies | LINE No. |
|---|---|---|---|---|
| **COUNTY COURT AND SURROGATE'S COURT —RICHMOND COUNTY** | | | | |
| **1910** | | | | |
| Revenue Expenditures | $18,618 56 | $18,150 00 | .......... | 1 |
| Corporate Stock Expenditures | .......... | .......... | .......... | 2 |
| Total for 1910 | **$18,618 56** | **$18,150 00** | .......... | 3 |
| **1911** | | | | |
| Revenue Expenditures | $18,399 15 | $17,928 75 | .......... | 4 |
| Corporate Stock Expenditures | .......... | .......... | .......... | 5 |
| Total for 1911 | **$18,399 15** | **$17,928 75** | .......... | 6 |
| **1912** | | | | |
| Revenue Expenditures | $23,166 68 | $22,766 68 | $191 43 | 7 |
| Corporate Stock Expenditures | .......... | .......... | .......... | 8 |
| Total for 1912 | **$23,166 68** | **$22,766 68** | **$191 43** | 9 |
| **1913** | | | | |
| Revenue Expenditures | $21,509 51 | $21,100 00 | $127 08 | 10 |
| Corporate Stock Expenditures | .......... | .......... | .......... | 11 |
| Total for 1913 | **$21,509 51** | **$21,100 00** | **$127 08** | 12 |
| **1914** | | | | |
| Revenue Expenditures | $21,562 55 | $21,100 00 | $170 29 | 13 |
| Corporate Stock Expenditures | .......... | .......... | .......... | 14 |
| Total for 1914 | **$21,562 55** | **$21,100 00** | **$170 29** | 15 |
| **SUPREME COURT—RICHMOND COUNTY** | | | | |
| **1910** | | | | |
| Revenue Expenditures | $10,962 51 | $10,962 51 | .......... | 16 |
| Corporate Stock Expenditures | .......... | .......... | .......... | 17 |
| Total for 1910 | **$10,962 51** | **$10,962 51** | .......... | 18 |
| **1911** | | | | |
| Revenue Expenditures | $12,726 45 | $12,605 47 | .......... | 19 |
| Corporate Stock Expenditures | .......... | .......... | .......... | 20 |
| Total for 1911 | **$12,726 45** | **$12,605 47** | .......... | 21 |
| **1912** | | | | |
| Revenue Expenditures | $12,962 68 | $12,929 08 | $33 60 | 22 |
| Corporate Stock Expenditures | .......... | .......... | .......... | 23 |
| Total for 1912 | **$12,962 68** | **$12,929 08** | **$33 60** | 24 |
| **1913** | | | | |
| Revenue Expenditures | $18,328 55 | $18,263 35 | .......... | 25 |
| Corporate Stock Expenditures | .......... | .......... | .......... | 26 |
| Total for 1913 | **$18,328 55** | **$18,263 35** | .......... | 27 |
| **1914** | | | | |
| Revenue Expenditures | $19,219 73 | $19,165 33 | .......... | 28 |
| Corporate Stock Expenditures | .......... | .......... | .......... | 29 |
| Total for 1914 | **$19,219 73** | **$19,165 33** | .......... | 30 |

## NEW YORK

MADE FROM REVENUE AND FROM CORPORATE STOCK FUNDS FOR THE DEPARTMENTS, ACCORDING TO OBJECTS OF EXPENDITURE:

| LINE No. | Purchase of Equipment | Materials | Contract or Open Order Service | Contingencies | Fixed Charges and Contributions | Unclassified |
|---|---|---|---|---|---|---|
| 1 | .......... | .......... | $69 81 | $398 75 | .......... | .......... |
| 2 | .......... | .......... | .......... | .......... | .......... | .......... |
| 3 | .......... | .......... | **$69 81** | **$398 75** | .......... | .......... |
| 4 | .......... | .......... | $78 76 | $391 64 | .......... | .......... |
| 5 | .......... | .......... | .......... | .......... | .......... | .......... |
| 6 | .......... | .......... | **$78 76** | **$391 64** | .......... | .......... |
| 7 | .......... | .......... | $108 57 | $100 00 | .......... | .......... |
| 8 | .......... | .......... | .......... | .......... | .......... | .......... |
| 9 | .......... | .......... | **$108 57** | **$100 00** | .......... | .......... |
| 10 | $98 65 | .......... | $164 58 | $19 20 | .......... | .......... |
| 11 | .......... | .......... | .......... | .......... | .......... | .......... |
| 12 | **$98 65** | .......... | **$164 58** | **$19 20** | .......... | .......... |
| 13 | $126 90 | .......... | $141 26 | $24 10 | .......... | .......... |
| 14 | .......... | .......... | .......... | .......... | .......... | .......... |
| 15 | **$126 90** | .......... | **$141 26** | **$24 10** | .......... | .......... |
| 16 | .......... | .......... | .......... | .......... | .......... | .......... |
| 17 | .......... | .......... | .......... | .......... | .......... | .......... |
| 18 | .......... | .......... | .......... | .......... | .......... | .......... |
| 19 | .......... | .......... | .......... | $120 98 | .......... | .......... |
| 20 | .......... | .......... | .......... | .......... | .......... | .......... |
| 21 | .......... | .......... | .......... | **$120 98** | .......... | .......... |
| 22 | .......... | .......... | .......... | .......... | .......... | .......... |
| 23 | .......... | .......... | .......... | .......... | .......... | .......... |
| 24 | .......... | .......... | .......... | .......... | .......... | .......... |
| 25 | .......... | .......... | .......... | $65 20 | .......... | .......... |
| 26 | .......... | .......... | .......... | .......... | .......... | .......... |
| 27 | .......... | .......... | .......... | **$65 20** | .......... | .......... |
| 28 | .......... | .......... | .......... | $54 40 | .......... | .......... |
| 29 | .......... | .......... | .......... | .......... | .......... | .......... |
| 30 | .......... | .......... | .......... | **$54 40** | .......... | .......... |

Comparative Statements Showing Separately the Expenditures
Years 1910 to 1914, Inclusive, Classified by

| | Total | Personal Service | Supplies | Line No. |
|---|---|---|---|---|
| **DISTRICT ATTORNEY—RICHMOND COUNTY** | | | | |
| **1910** | | | | |
| Revenue Expenditures | $12,220 43 | $10,074 60 | .......... | 1 |
| Corporate Stock Expenditures | .......... | .......... | .......... | 2 |
| Total for 1910 | **$12,220 43** | **$10,074 60** | .......... | 3 |
| **1911** | | | | |
| Revenue Expenditures | $12,657 86 | $11,681 08 | .......... | 4 |
| Corporate Stock Expenditures | .......... | .......... | .......... | 5 |
| Total for 1911 | **$12,657 86** | **$11,681 08** | .......... | 6 |
| **1912** | | | | |
| Revenue Expenditures | $13,533 17 | $10,950 00 | $178 60 | 7 |
| Corporate Stock Expenditures | .......... | .......... | .......... | 8 |
| Total for 1912 | **$13,533 17** | **$10,950 00** | **$178 60** | 9 |
| **1913** | | | | |
| Revenue Expenditures | $15,242 51 | $13,899 40 | $98 70 | 10 |
| Corporate Stock Expenditures | .......... | .......... | .......... | 11 |
| Total for 1913 | **$15,242 51** | **$13,899 40** | **$98 70** | 12 |
| **1914** | | | | |
| Revenue Expenditures | $24,773 75 | $18,332 89 | $77 80 | 13 |
| Corporate Stock Expenditures | .......... | .......... | .......... | 14 |
| Total for 1914 | **$24,773 75** | **$18,332 89** | **$77 80** | 15 |
| **COMMISSIONER OF JURORS—RICHMOND COUNTY** | | | | |
| **1910** | | | | |
| Revenue Expenditures | $4,137 18 | $3,974 60 | $107 60 | 16 |
| Corporate Stock Expenditures | .......... | .......... | .......... | 17 |
| Total for 1910 | **$4,137 18** | **$3,974 60** | **$107 60** | 18 |
| **1911** | | | | |
| Revenue Expenditures | $4,172 57 | $3,987 00 | $114 00 | 19 |
| Corporate Stock Expenditures | .......... | .......... | .......... | 20 |
| Total for 1911 | **$4,172 57** | **$3,987 00** | **$114 00** | 21 |
| **1912** | | | | |
| Revenue Expenditures | $4,250 14 | $4,050 00 | $110 00 | 22 |
| Corporate Stock Expenditures | .......... | .......... | .......... | 23 |
| Total for 1912 | **$4,250 14** | **$4,050 00** | **$110 00** | 24 |
| **1913** | | | | |
| Revenue Expenditures | $4,273 57 | $4,050 00 | $133 00 | 25 |
| Corporate Stock Expenditures | .......... | .......... | .......... | 26 |
| Total for 1913 | **$4,273 57** | **$4,050 00** | **$133 00** | 27 |
| **1914** | | | | |
| Revenue Expenditures | $4,208 78 | $3,968 68 | .......... | 28 |
| Corporate Stock Expenditures | .......... | .......... | .......... | 29 |
| Total for 1914 | **$4,208 78** | **$3,968 68** | .......... | 30 |

NEW YORK

MADE FROM REVENUE AND FROM CORPORATE STOCK FUNDS FOR THE DEPARTMENTS, ACCORDING TO OBJECTS OF EXPENDITURE:

| LINE No. | Purchase of Equipment | Materials | Contract or Open Order Service | Contingencies | Fixed Charges and Contributions | Unclassified |
|---|---|---|---|---|---|---|
| 1 | .......... | .......... | .......... | $2,145 83 | .......... | .......... |
| 2 | .......... | .......... | .......... | .......... | .......... | .......... |
| 3 | .......... | .......... | .......... | **$2,145 83** | .......... | .......... |
| 4 | .......... | .......... | .......... | $976 78 | .......... | .......... |
| 5 | .......... | .......... | .......... | .......... | .......... | .......... |
| 6 | .......... | .......... | .......... | **$976 78** | .......... | .......... |
| 7 | .......... | .......... | $1,557 65 | $846 92 | .......... | .......... |
| 8 | .......... | .......... | .......... | .......... | .......... | .......... |
| 9 | .......... | .......... | **$1,557 65** | **$846 92** | .......... | .......... |
| 10 | $74 95 | .......... | $618 04 | $551 42 | .......... | .......... |
| 11 | .......... | .......... | .......... | .......... | .......... | .......... |
| 12 | **$74 95** | .......... | **$618 04** | **$551 42** | .......... | .......... |
| 13 | $508 58 | .......... | $499 43 | $5,355 05 | .......... | .......... |
| 14 | .......... | .......... | .......... | .......... | .......... | .......... |
| 15 | **$508 58** | .......... | **$499 43** | **$5,355 05** | .......... | .......... |
| 16 | .......... | .......... | .......... | $54 98 | .......... | .......... |
| 17 | .......... | .......... | .......... | .......... | .......... | .......... |
| 18 | .......... | .......... | .......... | **$54 98** | .......... | .......... |
| 19 | .......... | .......... | $57 02 | $14 55 | .......... | .......... |
| 20 | .......... | .......... | .......... | .......... | .......... | .......... |
| 21 | .......... | .......... | **$57 02** | **$14 55** | .......... | .......... |
| 22 | .......... | .......... | $70 54 | $19 60 | .......... | .......... |
| 23 | .......... | .......... | .......... | .......... | .......... | .......... |
| 24 | .......... | .......... | **$70 54** | **$19 60** | .......... | .......... |
| 25 | .......... | .......... | $90 57 | .......... | .......... | .......... |
| 26 | .......... | .......... | .......... | .......... | .......... | .......... |
| 27 | .......... | .......... | **$90 57** | .......... | .......... | .......... |
| 28 | .......... | .......... | .......... | $240 10 | .......... | .......... |
| 29 | .......... | .......... | .......... | .......... | .......... | .......... |
| 30 | .......... | .......... | .......... | **$240 10** | .......... | .......... |

COMPARATIVE STATEMENTS SHOWING SEPARATELY THE EXPENDITURES
YEARS 1910 TO 1914, INCLUSIVE, CLASSIFIED BY

| | Total | Personal Service | Supplies | LINE No. |
|---|---|---|---|---|
| **MISCELLANEOUS—RICHMOND COUNTY** | | | | |
| **1910** | | | | |
| Revenue Expenditures | $17,891 13 | $7,784 50 | .......... | 1 |
| Corporate Stock Expenditures | .......... | .......... | .......... | 2 |
| Total for 1910 | **$17,891 13** | **$7,784 50** | .......... | 3 |
| **1911** | | | | |
| Revenue Expenditures | $11,648 12 | $7,456 00 | .......... | 4 |
| Corporate Stock Expenditures | .......... | .......... | .......... | 5 |
| Total for 1911 | **$11,648 12** | **$7,456 00** | .......... | 6 |
| **1912** | | | | |
| Revenue Expenditures | $12,505 00 | $11,705 83 | .......... | 7 |
| Corporate Stock Expenditures | .......... | .......... | .......... | 8 |
| Total for 1912 | **$12,505 00** | **$11,705 83** | .......... | 9 |
| **1913** | | | | |
| Revenue Expenditures | $12,505 00 | $11,511 66 | .......... | 10 |
| Corporate Stock Expenditures | .......... | .......... | .......... | 11 |
| Total for 1913 | **$12,505 00** | **$11,511 66** | .......... | 12 |
| **1914** | | | | |
| Revenue Expenditures | $9,858 00 | $8,008 50 | .......... | 13 |
| Corporate Stock Expenditures | .......... | .......... | .......... | 14 |
| Total for 1914 | **$9,858 00** | **$8,008 50** | .......... | 15 |
| **NATIONAL GUARD AND NAVAL MILITIA—RICHMOND COUNTY** | | | | |
| **1910** | | | | |
| Revenue Expenditures | .......... | .......... | .......... | 16 |
| Corporate Stock Expenditures | .......... | .......... | .......... | 17 |
| Total for 1910 | .......... | .......... | .......... | 18 |
| **1911** | | | | |
| Revenue Expenditures | .......... | .......... | .......... | 19 |
| Corporate Stock Expenditures | .......... | .......... | .......... | 20 |
| Total for 1911 | .......... | .......... | .......... | 21 |
| **1912** | | | | |
| Revenue Expenditures | .......... | .......... | .......... | 22 |
| Corporate Stock Expenditures | .......... | .......... | .......... | 23 |
| Total for 1912 | .......... | .......... | .......... | 24 |
| **1913** | | | | |
| Revenue Expenditures | $1,460 00 | $1,460 00 | .......... | 25 |
| Corporate Stock Expenditures | .......... | .......... | .......... | 26 |
| Total for 1913 | **$1,460 00** | **$1,460 00** | .......... | 27 |
| **1914** | | | | |
| Revenue Expenditures | $5,969 00 | $5,969 00 | .......... | 28 |
| Corporate Stock Expenditures | .......... | .......... | .......... | 29 |
| Total for 1914 | **$5,969 00** | **$5,969 00** | .......... | 30 |

NEW YORK

MADE FROM REVENUE AND FROM CORPORATE STOCK FUNDS FOR THE DEPARTMENTS, ACCORDING TO OBJECTS OF EXPENDITURE:

| LINE No. | Purchase of Equipment | Materials | Contract or Open Order Service | Contingencies | Fixed Charges and Contributions | Unclassified |
|---|---|---|---|---|---|---|
| 1 | .......... | .......... | $1,950 00 | $721 23 | $25 00 | $7,410 40 |
| 2 | .......... | .......... | .......... | .......... | .......... | .......... |
| 3 | .......... | .......... | **$1,950 00** | **$721 23** | **$25 00** | **$7,410 40** |
| 4 | .......... | .......... | $219 20 | $651 97 | $25 00 | $3,295 95 |
| 5 | .......... | .......... | .......... | .......... | .......... | .......... |
| 6 | .......... | .......... | **$219 20** | **$651 97** | **$25 00** | **$3,295 95** |
| 7 | .......... | .......... | .......... | $774 17 | $25 00 | .......... |
| 8 | .......... | .......... | .......... | .......... | .......... | .......... |
| 9 | .......... | .......... | .......... | **$774 17** | **$25 00** | .......... |
| 10 | .......... | .......... | .......... | $968 34 | $25 00 | .......... |
| 11 | .......... | .......... | .......... | .......... | .......... | .......... |
| 12 | .......... | .......... | .......... | **$968 34** | **$25 00** | .......... |
| 13 | .......... | .......... | .......... | $924 50 | $925 00 | .......... |
| 14 | .......... | .......... | .......... | .......... | .......... | .......... |
| 15 | .......... | .......... | .......... | **$924 50** | **$925 00** | .......... |
| 16 | .......... | .......... | .......... | .......... | .......... | .......... |
| 17 | .......... | .......... | .......... | .......... | .......... | .......... |
| 18 | .......... | .......... | .......... | .......... | .......... | .......... |
| 19 | .......... | .......... | .......... | .......... | .......... | .......... |
| 20 | .......... | .......... | .......... | .......... | .......... | .......... |
| 21 | .......... | .......... | .......... | .......... | .......... | .......... |
| 22 | .......... | .......... | .......... | .......... | .......... | .......... |
| 23 | .......... | .......... | .......... | .......... | .......... | .......... |
| 24 | .......... | .......... | .......... | .......... | .......... | .......... |
| 25 | .......... | .......... | .......... | .......... | .......... | .......... |
| 26 | .......... | .......... | .......... | .......... | .......... | .......... |
| 27 | .......... | .......... | .......... | .......... | .......... | .......... |
| 28 | .......... | .......... | .......... | .......... | .......... | .......... |
| 29 | .......... | .......... | .......... | .......... | .......... | .......... |
| 30 | .......... | .......... | .......... | .......... | .......... | .......... |

COMPARATIVE STATEMENTS SHOWING SEPARATELY THE EXPENDITURES
YEARS 1910 TO 1914, INCLUSIVE, CLASSIFIED BY

| | Total | Personal Service | Supplies | LINE No. |
|---|---|---|---|---|
| **SHERIFF—RICHMOND COUNTY** | | | | |
| **1910** | | | | |
| Revenue Expenditures | $23,450 80 | $14,272 80 | $8,310 69 | 1 |
| Corporate Stock Expenditures | .......... | .......... | .......... | 2 |
| Total for 1910 | **$23,450 80** | **$14,272 80** | **$8,310 69** | 3 |
| **1911** | | | | |
| Revenue Expenditures | $27,785 93 | $15,986 27 | $11,218 30 | 4 |
| Corporate Stock Expenditures | .......... | .......... | .......... | 5 |
| Total for 1911 | **$27,785 93** | **$15,986 27** | **$11,218 30** | 6 |
| **1912** | | | | |
| Revenue Expenditures | $30,241 93 | $20,721 00 | $8,459 98 | 7 |
| Corporate Stock Expenditures | .......... | .......... | .......... | 8 |
| Total for 1912 | **$30,241 93** | **$20,721 00** | **$8,459 98** | 9 |
| **1913** | | | | |
| Revenue Expenditures | $33,073 32 | $19,774 00 | $11,681 94 | 10 |
| Corporate Stock Expenditures | .......... | .......... | .......... | 11 |
| Total for 1913 | **$33,073 32** | **$19,774 00** | **$11,681 94** | 12 |
| **1914** | | | | |
| Revenue Expenditures | $32,259 90 | $21,995 50 | $8,365 88 | 13 |
| Corporate Stock Expenditures | .......... | .......... | .......... | 14 |
| Total for 1914 | **$32,259 90** | **$21,995 50** | **$8,365 88** | 15 |
| **CHARITABLE INSTITUTIONS—BRONX COUNTY** | | | | |
| **1910** | | | | |
| Revenue Expenditures | .......... | .......... | .......... | 16 |
| Corporate Stock Expenditures | .......... | .......... | .......... | 17 |
| Total for 1910 | .......... | .......... | .......... | 18 |
| **1911** | | | | |
| Revenue Expenditures | .......... | .......... | .......... | 19 |
| Corporate Stock Expenditures | .......... | .......... | .......... | 20 |
| Total for 1911 | .......... | .......... | .......... | 21 |
| **1912** | | | | |
| Revenue Expenditures | .......... | .......... | .......... | 22 |
| Corporate Stock Expenditures | .......... | .......... | .......... | 23 |
| Total for 1912 | .......... | .......... | .......... | 24 |
| **1913** | | | | |
| Revenue Expenditures | .......... | .......... | .......... | 25 |
| Corporate Stock Expenditures | .......... | .......... | .......... | 26 |
| Total for 1913 | .......... | .......... | .......... | 27 |
| **1914** | | | | |
| Revenue Expenditures | $24,621 52 | .......... | .......... | 28 |
| Corporate Stock Expenditures | .......... | .......... | .......... | 29 |
| Total for 1914 | **$24,621 52** | .......... | .......... | 30 |

NEW YORK

Made from Revenue and from Corporate Stock Funds for the Departments, According to Objects of Expenditure:

| LINE No. | Purchase of Equipment | Materials | Contract or Open Order Service | Contingencies | Fixed Charges and Contributions | Unclassified |
|---|---|---|---|---|---|---|
| 1 | .......... | .......... | $179 76 | $687 55 | .......... | .......... |
| 2 | .......... | .......... | .......... | .......... | .......... | .......... |
| 3 | .......... | .......... | **$179 76** | **$687 55** | .......... | .......... |
| 4 | .......... | .......... | $266 73 | $314 63 | .......... | .......... |
| 5 | .......... | .......... | .......... | .......... | .......... | .......... |
| 6 | .......... | .......... | **$266 73** | **$314 63** | .......... | .......... |
| 7 | .......... | .......... | $760 86 | $300 09 | .......... | .......... |
| 8 | .......... | .......... | .......... | .......... | .......... | .......... |
| 9 | .......... | .......... | **$760 86** | **$300 09** | .......... | .......... |
| 10 | $874 65 | .......... | $540 99 | $201 74 | .......... | .......... |
| 11 | .......... | .......... | .......... | .......... | .......... | .......... |
| 12 | **$874 65** | .......... | **$540 99** | **$201 74** | .......... | .......... |
| 13 | $901 32 | .......... | $694 84 | $302 36 | .......... | .......... |
| 14 | .......... | .......... | .......... | .......... | .......... | .......... |
| 15 | **$901 32** | .......... | **$694 84** | **$302 36** | .......... | .......... |
| 16 | .......... | .......... | .......... | .......... | .......... | .......... |
| 17 | .......... | .......... | .......... | .......... | .......... | .......... |
| 18 | .......... | .......... | .......... | .......... | .......... | .......... |
| 19 | .......... | .......... | .......... | .......... | .......... | .......... |
| 20 | .......... | .......... | .......... | .......... | .......... | .......... |
| 21 | .......... | .......... | .......... | .......... | .......... | .......... |
| 22 | .......... | .......... | .......... | .......... | .......... | .......... |
| 23 | .......... | .......... | .......... | .......... | .......... | .......... |
| 24 | .......... | .......... | .......... | .......... | .......... | .......... |
| 25 | .......... | .......... | .......... | .......... | .......... | .......... |
| 26 | .......... | .......... | .......... | .......... | .......... | .......... |
| 27 | .......... | .......... | .......... | .......... | .......... | .......... |
| 28 | .......... | .......... | .......... | .......... | $24,621 52 | .......... |
| 29 | .......... | .......... | .......... | .......... | .......... | .......... |
| 30 | .......... | .......... | .......... | .......... | **$24,621 52** | .......... |

COMPARATIVE STATEMENTS SHOWING SEPARATELY THE EXPENDITURES
YEARS 1910 TO 1914, INCLUSIVE, CLASSIFIED BY

| | Total | Personal Service | Supplies | LINE No. |
|---|---|---|---|---|
| **BOARD OF CITY RECORD—BRONX COUNTY** | | | | |
| **1910** | | | | |
| Revenue Expenditures | .......... | .......... | .......... | 1 |
| Corporate Stock Expenditures | .......... | .......... | .......... | 2 |
| Total for 1910 | .......... | .......... | .......... | 3 |
| **1911** | | | | |
| Revenue Expenditures | .......... | .......... | .......... | 4 |
| Corporate Stock Expenditures | .......... | .......... | .......... | 5 |
| Total for 1911 | .......... | .......... | .......... | 6 |
| **1912** | | | | |
| Revenue Expenditures | .......... | .......... | .......... | 7 |
| Corporate Stock Expenditures | .......... | .......... | .......... | 8 |
| Total for 1912 | .......... | .......... | .......... | 9 |
| **1913** | | | | |
| Revenue Expenditures | .......... | .......... | .......... | 10 |
| Corporate Stock Expenditures | .......... | .......... | .......... | 11 |
| Total for 1913 | .......... | .......... | .......... | 12 |
| **1914** | | | | |
| Revenue Expenditures | $11,799 30 | .......... | .......... | 13 |
| Corporate Stock Expenditures | .......... | .......... | .......... | 14 |
| Total for 1914 | **$11,799 30** | .......... | .......... | 15 |
| **COUNTY CLERK—BRONX COUNTY** | | | | |
| **1910** | | | | |
| Revenue Expenditures | .......... | .......... | .......... | 16 |
| Corporate Stock Expenditures | .......... | .......... | .......... | 17 |
| Total for 1910 | .......... | .......... | .......... | 18 |
| **1911** | | | | |
| Revenue Expenditures | .......... | .......... | .......... | 19 |
| Corporate Stock Expenditures | .......... | .......... | .......... | 20 |
| Total for 1911 | .......... | .......... | .......... | 21 |
| **1912** | | | | |
| Revenue Expenditures | .......... | .......... | .......... | 22 |
| Corporate Stock Expenditures | .......... | .......... | .......... | 23 |
| Total for 1912 | .......... | .......... | .......... | 24 |
| **1913** | | | | |
| Revenue Expenditures | .......... | .......... | .......... | 25 |
| Corporate Stock Expenditures | .......... | .......... | .......... | 26 |
| Total for 1913 | .......... | .......... | .......... | 27 |
| **1914** | | | | |
| Revenue Expenditures | $64,743 72 | $61,093 84 | $454 72 | 28 |
| Corporate Stock Expenditures | .......... | .......... | .......... | 29 |
| Total for 1914 | **$64,743 72** | **$61,093 84** | **$454 72** | 30 |

NEW YORK

MADE FROM REVENUE AND FROM CORPORATE STOCK FUNDS FOR THE DEPARTMENTS, ACCORDING TO OBJECTS OF EXPENDITURE:

| LINE No. | Purchase of Equipment | Materials | Contract or Open Order Service | Contingencies | Fixed Charges and Contributions | Unclassified |
|---|---|---|---|---|---|---|
| 1 | .......... | .......... | .......... | .......... | .......... | .......... |
| 2 | .......... | .......... | .......... | .......... | .......... | .......... |
| 3 | .......... | .......... | .......... | .......... | .......... | .......... |
| 4 | .......... | .......... | .......... | .......... | .......... | .......... |
| 5 | .......... | .......... | .......... | .......... | .......... | .......... |
| 6 | .......... | .......... | .......... | .......... | .......... | .......... |
| 7 | .......... | .......... | .......... | .......... | .......... | .......... |
| 8 | .......... | .......... | .......... | .......... | .......... | .......... |
| 9 | .......... | .......... | .......... | .......... | .......... | .......... |
| 10 | .......... | .......... | .......... | .......... | .......... | .......... |
| 11 | .......... | .......... | .......... | .......... | .......... | .......... |
| 12 | .......... | .......... | .......... | .......... | .......... | .......... |
| 13 | .......... | .......... | $11,799 30 | .......... | .......... | .......... |
| 14 | .......... | .......... | .......... | .......... | .......... | .......... |
| 15 | .......... | .......... | **$11,799 30** | .......... | .......... | .......... |
| 16 | .......... | .......... | .......... | .......... | .......... | .......... |
| 17 | .......... | .......... | .......... | .......... | .......... | .......... |
| 18 | .......... | .......... | .......... | .......... | .......... | .......... |
| 19 | .......... | .......... | .......... | .......... | .......... | .......... |
| 20 | .......... | .......... | .......... | .......... | .......... | .......... |
| 21 | .......... | .......... | .......... | .......... | .......... | .......... |
| 22 | .......... | .......... | .......... | .......... | .......... | .......... |
| 23 | .......... | .......... | .......... | .......... | .......... | .......... |
| 24 | .......... | .......... | .......... | .......... | .......... | .......... |
| 25 | .......... | .......... | .......... | .......... | .......... | .......... |
| 26 | .......... | .......... | .......... | .......... | .......... | .......... |
| 27 | .......... | .......... | .......... | .......... | .......... | .......... |
| 28 | $1,925 00 | .......... | $1,058 62 | $211 54 | .......... | .......... |
| 29 | .......... | .......... | .......... | .......... | .......... | .......... |
| 30 | **$1,925 00** | .......... | **$1,058 62** | **$211 54** | .......... | .......... |

COMPARATIVE STATEMENTS SHOWING SEPARATELY THE EXPENDITURES
YEARS 1910 TO 1914, INCLUSIVE, CLASSIFIED BY

| | Total | Personal Service | Supplies | LINE No. |
|---|---|---|---|---|
| **COUNTY COURT—BRONX COUNTY** | | | | |
| **1910** | | | | |
| Revenue Expenditures | .......... | .......... | .......... | 1 |
| Corporate Stock Expenditures | .......... | .......... | .......... | 2 |
| Total for 1910 | .......... | .......... | .......... | 3 |
| **1911** | | | | |
| Revenue Expenditures | .......... | .......... | .......... | 4 |
| Corporate Stock Expenditures | .......... | .......... | .......... | 5 |
| Total for 1911 | .......... | .......... | .......... | 6 |
| **1912** | | | | |
| Revenue Expenditures | .......... | .......... | .......... | 7 |
| Corporate Stock Expenditures | .......... | .......... | .......... | 8 |
| Total for 1912 | .......... | .......... | .......... | 9 |
| **1913** | | | | |
| Revenue Expenditures | .......... | .......... | .......... | 10 |
| Corporate Stock Expenditures | .......... | .......... | .......... | 11 |
| Total for 1913 | .......... | .......... | .......... | 12 |
| **1914** | | | | |
| Revenue Expenditures | $37,260 01 | $33,446 35 | $693 30 | 13 |
| Corporate Stock Expenditures | .......... | .......... | .......... | 14 |
| Total for 1914 | **$37,260 01** | **$33,446 35** | **$693 30** | 15 |
| **SURROGATE'S COURT—BRONX COUNTY** | | | | |
| **1910** | | | | |
| Revenue Expenditures | .......... | .......... | .......... | 16 |
| Corporate Stock Expenditures | .......... | .......... | .......... | 17 |
| Total for 1910 | .......... | .......... | .......... | 18 |
| **1911** | | | | |
| Revenue Expenditures | .......... | .......... | .......... | 19 |
| Corporate Stock Expenditures | .......... | .......... | .......... | 20 |
| Total for 1911 | .......... | .......... | .......... | 21 |
| **1912** | | | | |
| Revenue Expenditures | .......... | .......... | .......... | 22 |
| Corporate Stock Expenditures | .......... | .......... | .......... | 23 |
| Total for 1912 | .......... | .......... | .......... | 24 |
| **1913** | | | | |
| Revenue Expenditures | .......... | .......... | .......... | 25 |
| Corporate Stock Expenditures | .......... | .......... | .......... | 26 |
| Total for 1913 | .......... | .......... | .......... | 27 |
| **1914** | | | | |
| Revenue Expenditures | $35,039 17 | $33,201 61 | $636 00 | 28 |
| Corporate Stock Expenditures | .......... | .......... | .......... | 29 |
| Total for 1914 | **$35,039 17** | **$33,201 61** | **$636 00** | 30 |

NEW YORK

MADE FROM REVENUE AND FROM CORPORATE STOCK FUNDS FOR THE DEPARTMENTS, ACCORDING TO OBJECTS OF EXPENDITURE:

| LINE No. | Purchase of Equipment | Materials | Contract or Open Order Service | Contingencies | Fixed Charges and Contributions | Unclassified |
|---|---|---|---|---|---|---|
| 1 | .......... | .......... | .......... | .......... | .......... | .......... |
| 2 | .......... | .......... | .......... | .......... | .......... | .......... |
| 3 | .......... | .......... | .......... | .......... | .......... | .......... |
| 4 | .......... | .......... | .......... | .......... | .......... | .......... |
| 5 | .......... | .......... | .......... | .......... | .......... | .......... |
| 6 | .......... | .......... | .......... | .......... | .......... | .......... |
| 7 | .......... | .......... | .......... | .......... | .......... | .......... |
| 8 | .......... | .......... | .......... | .......... | .......... | .......... |
| 9 | .......... | .......... | .......... | .......... | .......... | .......... |
| 10 | .......... | .......... | .......... | .......... | .......... | .......... |
| 11 | .......... | .......... | .......... | .......... | .......... | .......... |
| 12 | .......... | .......... | .......... | .......... | .......... | .......... |
| 13 | $2,652 82 | .......... | $304 97 | $162 57 | .......... | .......... |
| 14 | .......... | .......... | .......... | .......... | .......... | .......... |
| 15 | **$2,652 82** | .......... | **$304 97** | **$162 57** | .......... | .......... |
| 16 | .......... | .......... | .......... | .......... | .......... | .......... |
| 17 | .......... | .......... | .......... | .......... | .......... | .......... |
| 18 | .......... | .......... | .......... | .......... | .......... | .......... |
| 19 | .......... | .......... | .......... | .......... | .......... | .......... |
| 20 | .......... | .......... | .......... | .......... | .......... | .......... |
| 21 | .......... | .......... | .......... | .......... | .......... | .......... |
| 22 | .......... | .......... | .......... | .......... | .......... | .......... |
| 23 | .......... | .......... | .......... | .......... | .......... | .......... |
| 24 | .......... | .......... | .......... | .......... | .......... | .......... |
| 25 | .......... | .......... | .......... | .......... | .......... | .......... |
| 26 | .......... | .......... | .......... | .......... | .......... | .......... |
| 27 | .......... | .......... | .......... | .......... | .......... | .......... |
| 28 | $1,145 56 | .......... | .......... | $56 00 | .......... | .......... |
| 29 | .......... | .......... | .......... | .......... | .......... | .......... |
| 30 | **$1,145 56** | .......... | .......... | **$56 00** | .......... | .......... |

Comparative Statements Showing Separately the Expenditures
Years 1910 to 1914, Inclusive, Classified by

| | Total | Personal Service | Supplies | Line No. |
|---|---|---|---|---|
| **DISTRICT ATTORNEY—BRONX COUNTY** | | | | |
| **1910** | | | | |
| Revenue Expenditures.......................... | .......... | .......... | .......... | 1 |
| Corporate Stock Expenditures.................. | .......... | .......... | .......... | 2 |
| Total for 1910............................ | .......... | .......... | .......... | 3 |
| **1911** | | | | |
| Revenue Expenditures.......................... | .......... | .......... | .......... | 4 |
| Corporate Stock Expenditures.................. | .......... | .......... | .......... | 5 |
| Total for 1911............................ | .......... | .......... | .......... | 6 |
| **1912** | | | | |
| Revenue Expenditures.......................... | .......... | .......... | .......... | 7 |
| Corporate Stock Expenditures.................. | .......... | .......... | .......... | 8 |
| Total for 1912............................ | .......... | .......... | .......... | 9 |
| **1913** | | | | |
| Revenue Expenditures.......................... | .......... | .......... | .......... | 10 |
| Corporate Stock Expenditures.................. | .......... | .......... | .......... | 11 |
| Total for 1913............................ | .......... | .......... | .......... | 12 |
| **1914** | | | | |
| Revenue Expenditures.......................... | $90,188 79 | $77,724 18 | $1,103 53 | 13 |
| Corporate Stock Expenditures.................. | .......... | .......... | .......... | 14 |
| Total for 1914............................ | **$90,188 79** | **$77,724 18** | **$1,103 53** | 15 |
| **BRONX COUNTY LAW LIBRARY** | | | | |
| **1910** | | | | |
| Revenue Expenditures.......................... | .......... | .......... | .......... | 16 |
| Corporate Stock Expenditures.................. | .......... | .......... | .......... | 17 |
| Total for 1910............................ | .......... | .......... | .......... | 18 |
| **1911** | | | | |
| Revenue Expenditures.......................... | .......... | .......... | .......... | 19 |
| Corporate Stock Expenditures.................. | .......... | .......... | .......... | 20 |
| Total for 1911............................ | .......... | .......... | .......... | 21 |
| **1912** | | | | |
| Revenue Expenditures.......................... | .......... | .......... | .......... | 22 |
| Corporate Stock Expenditures.................. | .......... | .......... | .......... | 23 |
| Total for 1912............................ | .......... | .......... | .......... | 24 |
| **1913** | | | | |
| Revenue Expenditures.......................... | .......... | .......... | .......... | 25 |
| Corporate Stock Expenditures.................. | .......... | .......... | .......... | 26 |
| Total for 1913............................ | .......... | .......... | .......... | 27 |
| **1914** | | | | |
| Revenue Expenditures.......................... | $5,328 38 | $449 16 | .......... | 28 |
| Corporate Stock Expenditures.................. | .......... | .......... | .......... | 29 |
| Total for 1914............................ | **$5,328 38** | **$449 16** | .......... | 30 |

## NEW YORK

Made from Revenue and from Corporate Stock Funds for the Departments, According to Objects of Expenditure:

| Line No. | Purchase of Equipment | Materials | Contract or Open Order Service | Contingencies | Fixed Charges and Contributions | Unclassified |
|---|---|---|---|---|---|---|
| 1 | .......... | .......... | .......... | .......... | .......... | .......... |
| 2 | .......... | .......... | .......... | .......... | .......... | .......... |
| 3 | .......... | .......... | .......... | .......... | .......... | .......... |
| 4 | .......... | .......... | .......... | .......... | .......... | .......... |
| 5 | .......... | .......... | .......... | .......... | .......... | .......... |
| 6 | .......... | .......... | .......... | .......... | .......... | .......... |
| 7 | .......... | .......... | .......... | .......... | .......... | .......... |
| 8 | .......... | .......... | .......... | .......... | .......... | .......... |
| 9 | .......... | .......... | .......... | .......... | .......... | .......... |
| 10 | .......... | .......... | .......... | .......... | .......... | .......... |
| 11 | .......... | .......... | .......... | .......... | .......... | .......... |
| 12 | .......... | .......... | .......... | .......... | .......... | .......... |
| 13 | $2,568 55 | .......... | $1,644 45 | $7,148 08 | .......... | .......... |
| 14 | .......... | .......... | .......... | .......... | .......... | .......... |
| 15 | **$2,568 55** | .......... | **$1,644 45** | **$7,148 08** | .......... | .......... |
| 16 | .......... | .......... | .......... | .......... | .......... | .......... |
| 17 | .......... | .......... | .......... | .......... | .......... | .......... |
| 18 | .......... | .......... | .......... | .......... | .......... | .......... |
| 19 | .......... | .......... | .......... | .......... | .......... | .......... |
| 20 | .......... | .......... | .......... | .......... | .......... | .......... |
| 21 | .......... | .......... | .......... | .......... | .......... | .......... |
| 22 | .......... | .......... | .......... | .......... | .......... | .......... |
| 23 | .......... | .......... | .......... | .......... | .......... | .......... |
| 24 | .......... | .......... | .......... | .......... | .......... | .......... |
| 25 | .......... | .......... | .......... | .......... | .......... | .......... |
| 26 | .......... | .......... | .......... | .......... | .......... | .......... |
| 27 | .......... | .......... | .......... | .......... | .......... | .......... |
| 28 | $4,879 22 | .......... | .......... | .......... | .......... | .......... |
| 29 | .......... | .......... | .......... | .......... | .......... | .......... |
| 30 | **$4,879 22** | .......... | .......... | .......... | .......... | .......... |

COMPARATIVE STATEMENTS SHOWING SEPARATELY THE EXPENDITURES YEARS 1910 TO 1914, INCLUSIVE, CLASSIFIED BY

| | Total | Personal Service | Supplies | LINE No. |
|---|---|---|---|---|
| **COMMISSIONER OF JURORS—BRONX COUNTY** | | | | |
| **1910** | | | | |
| Revenue Expenditures | .......... | .......... | .......... | 1 |
| Corporate Stock Expenditures | .......... | .......... | .......... | 2 |
| Total for 1910 | .......... | .......... | .......... | 3 |
| **1911** | | | | |
| Revenue Expenditures | .......... | .......... | .......... | 4 |
| Corporate Stock Expenditures | .......... | .......... | .......... | 5 |
| Total for 1911 | .......... | .......... | .......... | 6 |
| **1912** | | | | |
| Revenue Expenditures | .......... | .......... | .......... | 7 |
| Corporate Stock Expenditures | .......... | .......... | .......... | 8 |
| Total for 1912 | .......... | .......... | .......... | 9 |
| **1913** | | | | |
| Revenue Expenditures | $14,501 45 | $9,402 28 | $85 85 | 10 |
| Corporate Stock Expenditures | .......... | .......... | .......... | 11 |
| Total for 1913 | **$14,501 45** | **$9,402 28** | **$85 85** | 12 |
| **1914** | | | | |
| Revenue Expenditures | $23,864 09 | $21,232 90 | $1,659 57 | 13 |
| Corporate Stock Expenditures | .......... | .......... | .......... | 14 |
| Total for 1914 | **$23,864 09** | **$21,232 90** | **$1,659 57** | 15 |
| **MISCELLANEOUS—BRONX COUNTY** | | | | |
| **1910** | | | | |
| Revenue Expenditures | .......... | .......... | .......... | 16 |
| Corporate Stock Expenditures | .......... | .......... | .......... | 17 |
| Total for 1910 | .......... | .......... | .......... | 18 |
| **1911** | | | | |
| Revenue Expenditures | .......... | .......... | .......... | 19 |
| Corporate Stock Expenditures | .......... | .......... | .......... | 20 |
| Total for 1911 | .......... | .......... | .......... | 21 |
| **1912** | | | | |
| Revenue Expenditures | .......... | .......... | .......... | 22 |
| Corporate Stock Expenditures | .......... | .......... | .......... | 23 |
| Total for 1912 | .......... | .......... | .......... | 24 |
| **1913** | | | | |
| Revenue Expenditures | .......... | .......... | .......... | 25 |
| Corporate Stock Expenditures | .......... | .......... | .......... | 26 |
| Total for 1913 | .......... | .......... | .......... | 27 |
| **1914** | | | | |
| Revenue Expenditures | $14,146 38 | $12,223 98 | .......... | 28 |
| Corporate Stock Expenditures | .......... | .......... | .......... | 29 |
| Total for 1914 | **$14,146 38** | **$12,223 98** | .......... | 30 |

NEW YORK

Made from Revenue and from Corporate Stock Funds for the Departments, According to Objects of Expenditure:

| LINE No. | Purchase of Equipment | Materials | Contract or Open Order Service | Contingencies | Fixed Charges and Contributions | Unclassified |
|---|---|---|---|---|---|---|
| 1 | .......... | .......... | .......... | .......... | .......... | .......... |
| 2 | .......... | .......... | .......... | .......... | .......... | .......... |
| 3 | .......... | .......... | .......... | .......... | .......... | .......... |
| 4 | .......... | .......... | .......... | .......... | .......... | .......... |
| 5 | .......... | .......... | .......... | .......... | .......... | .......... |
| 6 | .......... | .......... | .......... | .......... | .......... | .......... |
| 7 | .......... | .......... | .......... | .......... | .......... | .......... |
| 8 | .......... | .......... | .......... | .......... | .......... | .......... |
| 9 | .......... | .......... | .......... | .......... | .......... | .......... |
| 10 | $3,191 67 | .......... | $1,338 91 | $3 30 | $479 44 | .......... |
| 11 | .......... | .......... | .......... | .......... | .......... | .......... |
| 12 | **$3,191 67** | .......... | **$1,338 91** | **$3 30** | **$479 44** | .......... |
| 13 | $316 17 | .......... | $193 04 | $97 79 | $319 62 | .......... |
| 14 | .......... | .......... | .......... | .......... | .......... | .......... |
| 15 | **$361 17** | .......... | **$193 04** | **$79 97** | **$319 62** | .......... |
| 16 | .......... | .......... | .......... | .......... | .......... | .......... |
| 17 | .......... | .......... | .......... | .......... | .......... | .......... |
| 18 | .......... | .......... | .......... | .......... | .......... | .......... |
| 19 | .......... | .......... | .......... | .......... | .......... | .......... |
| 20 | .......... | .......... | .......... | .......... | .......... | .......... |
| 21 | .......... | .......... | .......... | .......... | .......... | .......... |
| 22 | .......... | .......... | .......... | .......... | .......... | .......... |
| 23 | .......... | .......... | .......... | .......... | .......... | .......... |
| 24 | .......... | .......... | .......... | .......... | .......... | .......... |
| 25 | .......... | .......... | .......... | .......... | .......... | .......... |
| 26 | .......... | .......... | .......... | .......... | .......... | .......... |
| 27 | .......... | .......... | .......... | .......... | .......... | .......... |
| 28 | .......... | .......... | .......... | $4 65 | $1,917 75 | .......... |
| 29 | .......... | .......... | .......... | .......... | .......... | .......... |
| 30 | .......... | .......... | .......... | **$4 65** | **$1,917 75** | .......... |

COMPARATIVE STATEMENTS SHOWING SEPARATELY THE EXPENDITURES
YEARS 1910 TO 1914, INCLUSIVE, CLASSIFIED BY

| | Total | Personal Service | Supplies | LINE No. |
|---|---|---|---|---|
| **NATIONAL GUARD AND NAVAL MILITIA—BRONX COUNTY** | | | | |
| **1910** | | | | |
| Revenue Expenditures | .......... | .......... | .......... | 1 |
| Corporate Stock Expenditures | .......... | .......... | .......... | 2 |
| Total for 1910 | .......... | .......... | .......... | 3 |
| **1911** | | | | |
| Revenue Expenditures | .......... | .......... | .......... | 4 |
| Corporate Stock Expenditures | .......... | .......... | .......... | 5 |
| Total for 1911 | .......... | .......... | .......... | 6 |
| **1912** | | | | |
| Revenue Expenditures | .......... | .......... | .......... | 7 |
| Corporate Stock Expenditures | .......... | .......... | .......... | 8 |
| Total for 1912 | .......... | .......... | .......... | 9 |
| **1913** | | | | |
| Revenue Expenditures | .......... | .......... | .......... | 10 |
| Corporate Stock Expenditures | .......... | .......... | .......... | 11 |
| Total for 1913 | .......... | .......... | .......... | 12 |
| **1914** | | | | |
| Revenue Expenditures | $29,052 00 | $29,052 00 | .......... | 13 |
| Corporate Stock Expenditures | .......... | .......... | .......... | 14 |
| Total for 1914 | **$29,052 00** | **$29,052 00** | .......... | 15 |
| **PUBLIC ADMINISTRATOR—BRONX COUNTY** | | | | |
| **1910** | | | | |
| Revenue Expenditures | .......... | .......... | .......... | 16 |
| Corporate Stock Expenditures | .......... | .......... | .......... | 17 |
| Total for 1910 | .......... | .......... | .......... | 18 |
| **1911** | | | | |
| Revenue Expenditures | .......... | .......... | .......... | 19 |
| Corporate Stock Expenditures | .......... | .......... | .......... | 20 |
| Total for 1911 | .......... | .......... | .......... | 21 |
| **1912** | | | | |
| Revenue Expenditures | .......... | .......... | .......... | 22 |
| Corporate Stock Expenditures | .......... | .......... | .......... | 23 |
| Total for 1912 | .......... | .......... | .......... | 24 |
| **1913** | | | | |
| Revenue Expenditures | .......... | .......... | .......... | 25 |
| Corporate Stock Expenditures | .......... | .......... | .......... | 26 |
| Total for 1913 | .......... | .......... | .......... | 27 |
| **1914** | | | | |
| Revenue Expenditures | $5,708 52 | $4,699 20 | $174 75 | 28 |
| Corporate Stock Expenditures | .......... | .......... | .......... | 29 |
| Total for 1914 | **$5,708 52** | **$4,699 20** | **$174 75** | 30 |

## NEW YORK

MADE FROM REVENUE AND FROM CORPORATE STOCK FUNDS FOR THE DEPARTMENTS, ACCORDING TO OBJECTS OF EXPENDITURE:

| LINE No. | Purchase of Equipment | Materials | Contract or Open Order Service | Contingencies | Fixed Charges and Contributions | Unclassified |
|---|---|---|---|---|---|---|
| 1 | .......... | .......... | .......... | .......... | .......... | .......... |
| 2 | .......... | .......... | .......... | .......... | .......... | .......... |
| 3 | .......... | .......... | .......... | .......... | .......... | .......... |
| 4 | .......... | .......... | .......... | .......... | .......... | .......... |
| 5 | .......... | .......... | .......... | .......... | .......... | .......... |
| 6 | .......... | .......... | .......... | .......... | .......... | .......... |
| 7 | .......... | .......... | .......... | .......... | .......... | .......... |
| 8 | .......... | .......... | .......... | .......... | .......... | .......... |
| 9 | .......... | .......... | .......... | .......... | .......... | ........ |
| 10 | .......... | .......... | .......... | .......... | .......... | .......... |
| 11 | .......... | .......... | .......... | .......... | .......... | .......... |
| 12 | .......... | .......... | .......... | .......... | .......... | .......... |
| 13 | .......... | .......... | .......... | .......... | .......... | .......... |
| 14 | .......... | .......... | .......... | .......... | .......... | .......... |
| 15 | .......... | .......... | .......... | .......... | .......... | .......... |
| 16 | .......... | .......... | .......... | .......... | .......... | .......... |
| 17 | .......... | .......... | .......... | .......... | .......... | .......... |
| 18 | .......... | .......... | .......... | .......... | .......... | .......... |
| 19 | .......... | .......... | .......... | .......... | .......... | .......... |
| 20 | .......... | .......... | .......... | .......... | .......... | .......... |
| 21 | .......... | .......... | .......... | .......... | .......... | .......... |
| 22 | .......... | .......... | .......... | .......... | .......... | .......... |
| 23 | .......... | .......... | .......... | .......... | .......... | .......... |
| 24 | .......... | .......... | .......... | .......... | .......... | .......... |
| 25 | .......... | .......... | .......... | .......... | .......... | .......... |
| 26 | .......... | .......... | .......... | .......... | .......... | .......... |
| 27 | .......... | .......... | .......... | .......... | .......... | .......... |
| 28 | $796 88 | .......... | $23 95 | $13 74 | .......... | .......... |
| 29 | .......... | .......... | .......... | .......... | .......... | .......... |
| 30 | **$796 88** | .......... | **$23 95** | **$13 74** | .......... | .......... |

COMPARATIVE STATEMENTS SHOWING SEPARATELY THE EXPENDITURES
YEARS 1910 TO 1914, INCLUSIVE, CLASSIFIED BY

| | Total | Personal Service | Supplies | LINE No. |
|---|---|---|---|---|
| **REGISTER—BRONX COUNTY** | | | | |
| **1910** | | | | |
| Revenue Expenditures | .......... | .......... | .......... | 1 |
| Corporate Stock Expenditures | .......... | .......... | .......... | 2 |
| Total for 1910 | .......... | .......... | .......... | 3 |
| **1911** | | | | |
| Revenue Expenditures | .......... | .......... | .......... | 4 |
| Corporate Stock Expenditures | .......... | .......... | .......... | 5 |
| Total for 1911 | .......... | .......... | .......... | 6 |
| **1912** | | | | |
| Revenue Expenditures | .......... | .......... | .......... | 7 |
| Corporate Stock Expenditures | .......... | .......... | .......... | 8 |
| Total for 1912 | .......... | .......... | .......... | 9 |
| **1913** | | | | |
| Revenue Expenditures | .......... | .......... | .......... | 10 |
| Corporate Stock Expenditures | .......... | .......... | .......... | 11 |
| Total for 1913 | .......... | .......... | .......... | 12 |
| **1914** | | | | |
| Revenue Expenditures | $97,318 11 | $85,803 66 | $4,009 03 | 13 |
| Corporate Stock Expenditures | .......... | .......... | .......... | 14 |
| Total for 1914 | **$97,318 11** | **$85,803 66** | **$4,009 03** | 15 |
| **SHERIFF—BRONX COUNTY** | | | | |
| **1910** | | | | |
| Revenue Expenditures | .......... | .......... | .......... | 16 |
| Corporate Stock Expenditures | .......... | .......... | .......... | 17 |
| Total for 1910 | .......... | .......... | .......... | 18 |
| **1911** | | | | |
| Revenue Expenditures | .......... | .......... | .......... | 19 |
| Corporate Stock Expenditures | .......... | .......... | .......... | 20 |
| Total for 1911 | .......... | .......... | .......... | 21 |
| **1912** | | | | |
| Revenue Expenditures | .......... | .......... | .......... | 22 |
| Corporate Stock Expenditures | .......... | .......... | .......... | 23 |
| Total for 1912 | .......... | .......... | .......... | 24 |
| **1913** | | | | |
| Revenue Expenditures | .......... | .......... | .......... | 25 |
| Corporate Stock Expenditures | .......... | .......... | .......... | 26 |
| Total for 1913 | .......... | .......... | .......... | 27 |
| **1914** | | | | |
| Revenue Expenditures | $98,289 94 | $85,989 44 | $6,046 83 | 28 |
| Corporate Stock Expenditures | .......... | .......... | .......... | 29 |
| Total for 1914 | **$98,289 94** | **$85,989 44** | **$6,046 83** | 30 |

NEW YORK

Made from Revenue and from Corporate Stock Funds for the Departments, According to Objects of Expenditure:

| LINE No. | Purchase of Equipment | Materials | Contract or Open Order Service | Contingencies | Fixed Charges and Contributions | Unclassified |
|---|---|---|---|---|---|---|
| 1 | .......... | .......... | .......... | .......... | .......... | .......... |
| 2 | .......... | .......... | .......... | .......... | .......... | .......... |
| 3 | .......... | .......... | .......... | .......... | .......... | .......... |
| 4 | .......... | .......... | .......... | .......... | .......... | .......... |
| 5 | .......... | .......... | .......... | .......... | .......... | .......... |
| 6 | .......... | .......... | .......... | .......... | .......... | .......... |
| 7 | .......... | .......... | .......... | .......... | .......... | .......... |
| 8 | .......... | .......... | .......... | .......... | .......... | .......... |
| 9 | .......... | .......... | .......... | .......... | .......... | .......... |
| 10 | .......... | .......... | .......... | .......... | .......... | .......... |
| 11 | .......... | .......... | .......... | .......... | .......... | .......... |
| 12 | .......... | .......... | .......... | .......... | .......... | .......... |
| 13 | $6,701 00 | .......... | $543 57 | $260 85 | .......... | .......... |
| 14 | .......... | .......... | .......... | .......... | .......... | .......... |
| 15 | **$6,701 00** | .......... | **$543 57** | **$260 85** | .......... | .......... |
| 16 | .......... | .......... | .......... | .......... | .......... | .......... |
| 17 | .......... | .......... | .......... | .......... | .......... | .......... |
| 18 | .......... | .......... | .......... | .......... | .......... | .......... |
| 19 | .......... | .......... | .......... | .......... | .......... | .......... |
| 20 | .......... | .......... | .......... | .......... | .......... | .......... |
| 21 | .......... | .......... | .......... | .......... | .......... | .......... |
| 22 | .......... | .......... | .......... | .......... | .......... | .......... |
| 23 | .......... | .......... | .......... | .......... | .......... | .......... |
| 24 | .......... | .......... | .......... | .......... | .......... | .......... |
| 25 | .......... | .......... | .......... | .......... | .......... | .......... |
| 26 | .......... | .......... | .......... | .......... | .......... | .......... |
| 27 | .......... | .......... | .......... | .......... | .......... | .......... |
| 28 | $2,461 28 | .......... | $3,057 39 | $735 00 | .......... | .......... |
| 29 | .......... | .......... | .......... | .......... | .......... | .......... |
| 30 | **$2,461 28** | .......... | **$3,057 39** | **$735 00** | .......... | .......... |

# SECTION II

## DETAILED STATEMENTS OF UNIT COSTS AND FUNCTIONAL EXPENSES OF THE PRINCIPAL LARGER DEPARTMENTS

DEPARTMENT

COMPARATIVE SUMMARY OF EXPENSES

| | 1913 | | LINE No. |
|---|---|---|---|
| | Total | Administration and Unclassified | |
| GENERAL ADMINISTRATION | **$94,512 80** | **$94,512 80** | 1 |
| EAST RIVER BRIDGES: | | | |
| Division Administration | $7,621 49 | $7,621 49 | 2 |
| New York and Brooklyn (Suspension) | 334,727 94 | *76,352 96 | 3 |
| Williamsburg (Suspension) | 238,685 08 | *41,515 65 | 4 |
| Manhattan (Suspension) | 62,632 74 | *8,624 47 | 5 |
| Queensboro (Cantilever) | 89,433 98 | *16,082 21 | 6 |
| Total East River Bridges | **$733,101 23** | **$150,196 78** | 7 |
| HARLEM RIVER, MANHATTAN AND BRONX BRIDGES: | | | |
| Division Administration | $16,103 52 | $16,103 52 | 8 |
| Undistributed Shop Expense | 5,152 36 | 5,152 36 | 9 |
| Undistributed Storehouse Expense | 6,776 82 | 6,776 82 | 10 |
| Undistributed Stable Expense | 4,229 68 | 4,229 68 | 11 |
| 135th Street Bridge (Bascule) | 3,182 73 | .......... | 12 |
| Westchester Avenue Bridge (Retractile) | 4,981 09 | .......... | 13 |
| Unionport Bridge (Swing) | 5,468 21 | .......... | 14 |
| Pelham Bridge (Bascule) | 7,964 65 | .......... | 15 |
| City Island Bridge (Swing) | 17,081 03 | .......... | 16 |
| Eastchester Bridge (Swing) | 7,100 25 | .......... | 17 |
| Willis Avenue Bridge (Swing) | 47,448 22 | .......... | 18 |
| 3rd Avenue Bridge (Swing) | 44,137 30 | .......... | 19 |
| Madison Avenue Bridge (Swing) | 19,820 64 | .......... | 20 |
| 145th Street Bridge (Swing) | 27,057 89 | .......... | 21 |
| Macomb's Dam Bridge (Swing) | 23,524 10 | .......... | 22 |
| New York and Putnam Bridge (Swing) | 3,623 60 | .......... | 23 |
| Washington Bridge (Steel Arches) | 5,507 36 | .......... | 24 |
| University Heights Bridge (Swing) | 15,000 13 | .......... | 25 |
| Ship Canal Bridge (Swing) | 18,868 98 | .......... | 26 |
| Broadway Bridge (Fixed) | .......... | .......... | 27 |
| Kings Bridge (Fixed) | 66 49 | .......... | 28 |
| Operation and Maintenance Costs Undistributed | 21,118 73 | .......... | 29 |
| Total Harlem River, Manhattan and Bronx Bridges | **$304,213 78** | **$32,262 38** | 30 |
| BROOKLYN BOROUGH BRIDGES: | | | |
| Divisional Administration | $9,814 08 | $9,814 08 | 31 |
| Undistributed Stable Expense | 513 48 | 513 48 | 32 |
| Hamilton Avenue Bridge (Bascule) | 9,959 37 | .......... | 33 |
| Ninth Street Bridge (Bascule) | 8,068 40 | .......... | 34 |
| Third Street Bridge (Bascule) | 10,824 80 | .......... | 35 |
| Carroll Street Bridge (Retractile) | 6,550 51 | .......... | 36 |
| Union Street Bridge (Bascule) | 5,596 62 | .......... | 37 |
| Washington Avenue Bridge (Retractile) | 8,720 77 | .......... | 38 |
| Harway Avenue Bridge (Bascule) | 4,730 23 | .......... | 39 |
| Third Avenue Bridge (Fixed) | .......... | .......... | 40 |
| Ocean Avenue Bridge (Fixed) | 2,182 05 | .......... | 41 |
| Shell Road Bridge (Fixed) | 15 62 | .......... | 42 |
| Vernon Avenue Bridge (Bascule) | 38,327 47 | .......... | 43 |
| Greenpoint Avenue Bridge (Swing) | 10,243 62 | .......... | 44 |
| Meeker Avenue Bridge (Swing) | 13,231 63 | .......... | 45 |
| Grand Street Bridge (Swing) | 9,047 45 | .......... | 46 |
| Metropolitan Avenue Bridge (Swing) | 9,506 38 | .......... | 47 |
| Metropolitan Avenue Bridge (Fixed) | 117 07 | .......... | 48 |
| Total Brooklyn Borough Bridges | **$147,449 55** | **$10,327 56** | 49 |

NEW YORK

OF BRIDGES

FOR THE YEARS 1913, AND 1914.

| LINE No. | 1913 | | 1914 | | | |
|---|---|---|---|---|---|---|
| | Operation | Maintenance | Total | Administration and Unclassified | Operation | Maintenance |
| 1 | .......... | .......... | **$90,845 63** | **$90,845 63** | .......... | .......... |
| 2 | .......... | .......... | $6,516 37 | $6,516 37 | .......... | .......... |
| 3 | $80,689 02 | $177,685 96 | 352,688 43 | *75,740 25 | $88,573 35 | $188,374 83 |
| 4 | 63,397 68 | 133,771 75 | 198,997 37 | *38,431 85 | 67,992 87 | 92,572 65 |
| 5 | 31,234 97 | 22,773 30 | 60,112 14 | *8,478 34 | 31,566 97 | 20,066 83 |
| 6 | 38,841 35 | 34,510 42 | 86,941 08 | *15,296 69 | 37,741 18 | 33,903 21 |
| 7 | **$214,163 02** | **$368,741 43** | **$705,255 39** | **$144,463 50** | **$225,874 37** | **$334,917 52** |
| 8 | .......... | .......... | $18,317 11 | $18,317 11 | .......... | .......... |
| 9 | .......... | .......... | 8,656 67 | 8,656 67 | .......... | .......... |
| 10 | .......... | .......... | 3,798 82 | 3,798 82 | .......... | .......... |
| 11 | .......... | .......... | 3,085 69 | 3,085 69 | .......... | .......... |
| 12 | $2,471 03 | $711 70 | 2,997 06 | .......... | $2,263 28 | $733 78 |
| 13 | 4,556 48 | 424 61 | 5,799 55 | .......... | 4,936 30 | 863 25 |
| 14 | 3,831 62 | 1,636 59 | 5,455 75 | .......... | 3,905 42 | 1,550 33 |
| 15 | 7,496 13 | 468 52 | 7,006 36 | .......... | 6,678 96 | 327 40 |
| 16 | 3,815 26 | 13,265 77 | 4,183 71 | .......... | 3,218 09 | 965 62 |
| 17 | 3,843 44 | 3,256 81 | 4,915 65 | .......... | 3,763 80 | 1,151 85 |
| 18 | 30,047 35 | 17,400 87 | 33,099 15 | .......... | 28,103 17 | 4,995 98 |
| 19 | 27,174 76 | 16,962 54 | 41,476 25 | .......... | 28,081 10 | 13,395 15 |
| 20 | 19,618 47 | 202 17 | 20,470 35 | .......... | 20,101 59 | 368 76 |
| 21 | 21,256 60 | 5,801 29 | 23,597 70 | .......... | 22,897 09 | 700 61 |
| 22 | 21,285 92 | 2,238 18 | 26,786 24 | .......... | 21,233 43 | 5,552 81 |
| 23 | 3,573 97 | 49 63 | 3,786 04 | .......... | 3,629 94 | 156 10 |
| 24 | 4,060 14 | 1,447 22 | 20,766 87 | .......... | 4,219 54 | 16,547 33 |
| 25 | 14,021 91 | 978 22 | 18,604 24 | .......... | 13,683 16 | 4,921 08 |
| 26 | 16,784 65 | 2,084 33 | 17,671 08 | .......... | 16,500 62 | 1,170 46 |
| 27 | .......... | .......... | 35 26 | .......... | .......... | 35 26 |
| 28 | .......... | 66 49 | .......... | .......... | .......... | .......... |
| 29 | 7,046 04 | 14,072 69 | 17,146 49 | .......... | 6,945 35 | 10,201 14 |
| 30 | **$190,883 77** | **$81,067 63** | **$287,656 04** | **$33,858 29** | **$190,160 84** | **$63,636 91** |
| 31 | .......... | .......... | $10,317 30 | $10,317 30 | .......... | .......... |
| 32 | .......... | .......... | 427 15 | 427 15 | .......... | .......... |
| 33 | $7,346 89 | $2,612 48 | 7,951 64 | .......... | $7,052 99 | $898 65 |
| 34 | 7,358 24 | 710 16 | 9,939 94 | .......... | 7,258 37 | 2,681 57 |
| 35 | 6,724 50 | 4,100 30 | 9,850 02 | .......... | 6,812 10 | 3,037 92 |
| 36 | 5,319 47 | 1,231 04 | 6,673 64 | .......... | 5,098 15 | 1,575 49 |
| 37 | 4,820 41 | 776 21 | 6,560 14 | .......... | 5,018 54 | 1,541 60 |
| 38 | 7,636 92 | 1,083 85 | 8,306 36 | .......... | 7,399 76 | 906 60 |
| 39 | 4,502 81 | 227 42 | 5,068 00 | .......... | 3,903 21 | 1,164 79 |
| 40 | .......... | .......... | .......... | .......... | .......... | .......... |
| 41 | .......... | 2,182 05 | 138 69 | .......... | 10 75 | 127 94 |
| 42 | .......... | 15 62 | 178 54 | .......... | .......... | 178 54 |
| 43 | 25,026 09 | 13,301 38 | 32,814 07 | .......... | 26,877 69 | 5,936 38 |
| 44 | 8,807 04 | 1,436 58 | 10,989 33 | .......... | 9,683 04 | 1,306 29 |
| 45 | 9,836 54 | 3,395 09 | 10,089 10 | .......... | 9,463 20 | 625 90 |
| 46 | 7,258 60 | 1,788 85 | 10,250 03 | .......... | 8,773 96 | 1,476 07 |
| 47 | 7,812 06 | 1,694 32 | 8,183 55 | .......... | 7,155 34 | 1,028 21 |
| 48 | .......... | 117 07 | .......... | .......... | .......... | .......... |
| 49 | **$102,449 57** | **$34,672 42** | **$137,737 50** | **$10,744 45** | **$104,507 10** | **$22,485 95** |

DEPARTMENT

COMPARATIVE SUMMARY OF EXPENSES

| | 1913 | | LINE No. |
|---|---|---|---|
| | Total | Administration and Unclassified | |
| QUEENS BOROUGH BRIDGES: | | | |
| Baden Avenue Bridge (Retractile) | $5,373 51 | .......... | 1 |
| Flushing Creek Bridge (Bascule) | 8,186 79 | .......... | 2 |
| Strongs Causeway Bridge (Swing) | 921 71 | .......... | 3 |
| Little Neck Bridge (Swing) | 540 68 | .......... | 4 |
| Hunters Point Avenue Bridge (Bascule) | 2,675 42 | .......... | 5 |
| Total Queens Borough Bridges | **$17,698 11** | .......... | 6 |
| RICHMOND BOROUGH BRIDGES: | | | |
| Lemon Creek Bridge (Draw) | $2,109 48 | .......... | 7 |
| Fresh Kills Bridge (Swing) | 5,039 83 | .......... | 8 |
| Total Richmond Borough Bridges | **$7,149 31** | .......... | 9 |
| UNDISTRIBUTED EXPENSES: | | | |
| Automobile Service | $7,896 39 | $7,896 39 | 10 |
| Municipal Building | 3,742 99 | .......... | 11 |
| Miscellaneous Expenses | 14,329 56 | .......... | 12 |
| Total Undistributed Expenses | **$25,968 94** | **$7,896 39** | 13 |
| Departmental Totals | **$1,330,093 72** | **$295,195 91** | 14 |

* These items are made up as follows:

| | 1913 | | LINE No. |
|---|---|---|---|
| | New York and Brooklyn | Williamsburg | |
| Administration | $21,948 66 | $20,335 71 | 1 |
| Comfort Stations | 12,590 25 | 8,076 47 | 2 |
| Shops (Undistributed Expense) | 31,902 75 | 6,446 59 | 3 |
| Storehouse (Undistributed Expense) | 2,994 44 | 6,656 88 | 4 |
| Stable (Undistributed Expense) | 6,916 86 | .......... | 5 |
| Total | **$76,352 96** | **$41,515 65** | 6 |

NEW YORK

OF BRIDGES

FOR THE YEARS 1913, AND 1914.

| LINE No. | 1913 | | 1914 | | | |
|---|---|---|---|---|---|---|
| | Operation | Maintenance | Total | Administration and Unclassified | Operation | Maintenance |
| 1 | $4,391 94 | $981 57 | $6,107 21 | .......... | $5,549 76 | $557 45 |
| 2 | 7,052 00 | 1,134 79 | 7,849 92 | .......... | 7,067 72 | 782 20 |
| 3 | 850 24 | 71 47 | 1,375 14 | .......... | 799 50 | 575 64 |
| 4 | 509 43 | 31 25 | 789 69 | .......... | 655 25 | 134 44 |
| 5 | 2,574 82 | 100 60 | 3,474 96 | .......... | 3,035 43 | 439 53 |
| 6 | **$15,378 43** | **$2,319 68** | **$19,596 92** | .......... | **$17,107 66** | **$2,489 26** |
| 7 | $868 90 | $1,240 58 | $990 12 | .......... | $905 48 | $84 64 |
| 8 | 1,149 58 | 3,890 25 | 1,722 44 | .......... | 956 37 | 766 07 |
| 9 | **$2,018 48** | **$5,130 83** | **$2,712 56** | .......... | **$1,861 85** | **$850 71** |
| 10 | .......... | .......... | $8,719 54 | $8,719 54 | .......... | .......... |
| 11 | $2,857 99 | $885 00 | 2,744 33 | .......... | .......... | $2,744 33 |
| 12 | 3,913 94 | 10,415 62 | 24,865 15 | .......... | $3,940 37 | 20,924 78 |
| 13 | **$6,771 93** | **$11,300 62** | **$36,329 02** | **$8,719 54** | **$3,940 37** | **$23,669 11** |
| 14 | **$531,665 20** | **$503,232 61** | **$1,280,133 06** | **$288,631 41** | **$543,452 19** | **$448,049 46** |

| LINE No. | 1913 | | 1914 | | | |
|---|---|---|---|---|---|---|
| | Manhattan | Queensboro | New York and Brooklyn | Williamsburg | Manhattan | Queensboro |
| 1 | $6,199 11 | $11,999 87 | $20,539 20 | $19,462 73 | $6,051 29 | $12,182 46 |
| 2 | 2,425 36 | .......... | 11,816 12 | 7,468 66 | 2,427 05 | .......... |
| 3 | .......... | 958 49 | 30,243 89 | 5,775 15 | .......... | 499 35 |
| 4 | .......... | 3,123 85 | 5,740 21 | 5,725 31 | .......... | 2,614 88 |
| 5 | .......... | .......... | 7,400 83 | .......... | .......... | .......... |
| 6 | **$8,624 47** | **$16,082 21** | **$75,740 25** | **$38,431 85** | **$8,478 34** | **$15,296 69** |

# THE CITY OF

## DEPARTMENT OF WATER SUPPLY

### Comparative Summary for the Years 1913 and 1914, of Revenue

| | Line No. |
|---|---|
| **Revenues:** | |
| Sale of Water: | |
| Meter Rates (including accounts) | 1 |
| Frontage Rates | 2 |
| Building Purposes | 3 |
| Shipping | 4 |
| Street Sprinkling | 5 |
| Hose Permits | 6 |
| Total | 7 |
| Penalties: | |
| Meter Rates | 8 |
| Frontage Rates | 9 |
| Total | 10 |
| Miscellaneous: | |
| Sale of Ashes | 11 |
| Sale of Old Material | 12 |
| Pole License Fees | 13 |
| Unenumerated | 14 |
| Total | 15 |
| Total Revenues | 16 |
| **Expenditures:** | |
| General Administration—including Offices of Commissioner, Deputy Commissioners, Bureau of Audit and Accounts, Bureau of Supplies, and Motor Vehicles | 17 |
| Water Supply: | |
| Administration | 18 |
| Collection and Storage System—including Watersheds, Wells, Aqueducts, Reservoirs, Dams, Filtration and Purification Plants, Basins, etc | 19 |
| Purchased Water | 20 |
| Pumping—Low Pressure | 21 |
| Pumping—High Pressure | 22 |
| Distribution System (excluding recoverable expenditures) | 23 |
| Analyzing and Testing (Laboratories) | 24 |
| Undistributed Expenses: | |
| Machine Shops | 25 |
| Stables | 26 |
| Total | 27 |
| Water Revenue Collection: | |
| Administration and Office Expenses | 28 |
| Inspection: | |
| General | 29 |
| Meter Testing Station | 30 |
| Patrol Boat | 31 |
| Total | 32 |
| Total Expenses of Administration—Operation and Maintenance | 33 |
| Taxes (Accrued, Based on 1914 Budget Allowance) (Note No. 2) | 34 |
| Total | 35 |
| Balance—Excess of Revenues over Expenses before charging Interest, Amortization and Depreciation | 36 |
| Total | 37 |

Note No. 1—There are outstanding bills amounting to $34,572.76 for purchased water for 1914, not

Note No. 2—Taxes on watershed and aqueduct lands outside City of New York.

NEW YORK

GAS AND ELECTRICITY.

AND EXPENSES RELATING TO THE SUPPLY AND SALE OF WATER:

| LINE No. | 1913 | | 1914 | |
|---|---|---|---|---|
| | Items | Total | Items | Total |
| 1 | $6,279,482 47 | | $6,517,067 21 | |
| 2 | 5,985,849 56 | | 6,139,327 97 | |
| 3 | 181,779 10 | | 180,818 32 | |
| 4 | 43,982 66 | | 46,220 66 | |
| 5 | 5,372 32 | | 4,867 31 | |
| 6 | 9,835 00 | | 19,325 62 | |
| 7 | | **$12,506,301 11** | | **$12,907,627 09** |
| 8 | $95,478 28 | | $94,087 95 | |
| 9 | 139,893 26 | | 158,559 22 | |
| 10 | | **$235,371 54** | | **$252,647 17** |
| 11 | $892 75 | | $1,624 00 | |
| 12 | 8,454 62 | | 16,137 56 | |
| 13 | 2,030 50 | | 1,764 33 | |
| 14 | .......... | | 1,041 03 | |
| 15 | | **$11,377 87** | | **$20,566 92** |
| 16 | | **$12,753,050 52** | | **$13,180,841 18** |
| 17 | .......... | **$269,443 43** | .......... | **$273,222 89** |
| 18 | $90,771 50 | | $93,289 46 | |
| 19 | 442,002 64 | | 419,535 04 | |
| 20 | 150,619 51 | | (See Note No. 1) | |
| 21 | 1,489,252 85 | | 1,411,213 14 | |
| 22 | 247,268 43 | | 233,698 73 | |
| 23 | 919,524 42 | | 830,009 17 | |
| 24 | 40,151 77 | | 31,291 73 | |
| 25 | 16,015 71 | | 16,331 63 | |
| 26 | 22,890 32 | | 18,292 78 | |
| 27 | | **$3,418,497 15** | | **$3,053,661 68** |
| 28 | $297,168 58 | | $284,633 69 | |
| 29 | 340,316 08 | | 327,319 36 | |
| 30 | 45,993 50 | | 43,147 64 | |
| 31 | 5,111 89 | | 5,468 55 | |
| 32 | | **$688,590 05** | | **$660,569 24** |
| 33 | .......... | **$4,376,530 63** | .......... | **$3,987,453 81** |
| 34 | .......... | **195,850 00** | .......... | **200,000 00** |
| 35 | .......... | **$4,572,380 63** | .......... | **$4,187,453 81** |
| 36 | .......... | **8,180,669 89** | .......... | **8,993,387 37** |
| 37 | .......... | **$12,753,050 52** | .......... | **$13,180,841 18** |

entered on books and held for lack of appropriation.

## THE CITY OF

### DEPARTMENT OF WATER SUPPLY,

COMPARATIVE SUMMARY FOR THE YEARS 1913 AND 1914 OF EXPENSES INCURRED BY THE BUREAU OF PUBLIC BUILDINGS, ETC., AND (2) IN INSPECTING

| | | LINE No. |
|---|---|---|
| I. | Administration of Bureau of Gas and Electricity | 1 |
| II. | Supplying Heat, Light and Power for Public Purposes: | |
| | Street and Park Lighting | 2 |
| | Lighting Markets | 3 |
| | Lighting Public Buildings | 4 |
| | Lighting Pumping Stations | 5 |
| | *Electric Current for High-Pressure Fire Service | 6 |
| | Heat and Power for City Departments | 7 |
| | Rental of Gas Regulators | 8 |
| | Maintenance of Lamp Posts (Recoverable Expenditure) | 9 |
| | Gas Examination, Operation and Maintenance of Photometric Stations | 10 |
| | Inspection of Lamps and Lighting | 11 |
| III. | Inspection of Electrical Construction and Equipment | 12 |
| | Total Expenses of Bureau of Gas and Electricity | 13 |

* This item is also included under caption "Power" in Annual Statement of High Pressure Pumping

## THE CITY OF

### DEPARTMENT OF WATER SUPPLY,

SUMMARY FOR THE YEAR 1914 OF CAPITAL OUTLAYS FOR CONSTRUCTION, ACQUISITION OF REAL

| | | | |
|---|---|---|---|
| COLLECTION AND STORAGE: | | | |
| Land, Reservations and Water Rights | | $36,981 13 | |
| Reservoirs, Dams, etc | | 278 61 | |
| Wells | | 4,758 87 | |
| Infiltration Galleries, etc | | 1,352 59 | |
| Bridges and Similar Structures | | 158,325 59 | |
| Roads, Crossings, etc | | 1,009 60 | |
| Buildings and Dwellings | | 17,785 88 | |
| Aqueducts and Conduits | | 6,364 04 | |
| Reservoirs (distribution) | | 334 25 | |
| Sewage Disposal Plant | | 811 20 | |
| Total, Collection and Storage | | | **$228,001 76** |
| PURIFICATION: | | | |
| Filter Plants, Basins, etc | | $2,266 01 | |
| Total, Purification | | | **$2,266 01** |
| PUMPING: | | | |
| Buildings and Grounds | | $27,594 52 | |
| Plant, Machinery and Equipment | | 71,475 39 | |
| Total, Pumping | | | **$99,069 91** |
| DISTRIBUTION: | | | |
| Mains and Appurtenances: | | | |
| Manhattan and The Bronx | $1,034,142 23 | | |
| Brooklyn | 471,787 76 | | |
| Queens | 178,642 61 | | |
| Richmond | 156,845 13 | | |
| Total, all Boroughs | | $1,841 417 73 | |

# NEW YORK

## GAS AND ELECTRICITY

GAS AND ELECTRICITY: (1) IN SUPPLYING HEAT, LIGHT AND POWER FOR CITY STREETS AND PARKS, ELECTRICAL CONSTRUCTION AND EQUIPMENT.

| LINE No. | 1913 | | 1914 | |
|---|---|---|---|---|
| | Items | Totals | Items | Totals |
| 1 | .......... | **$79,134 05** | .......... | **$84,339 49** |
| 2 | $3,301,171 93 | | $2,539,691 75 | |
| 3 | 374 17 | | 210 00 | |
| 4 | 889,673 31 | | 1,163,421 56 | |
| 5 | 1,091 10 | | 2,072 95 | |
| 6 | 129,958 26 | | 21,957 00 | |
| 7 | 85,682 15 | | 95,492 36 | |
| 8 | 6,384 57 | | 3,746 20 | |
| 9 | 36,859 47 | | 15,378 44 | |
| 10 | 14,744 63 | | 15,234 48 | |
| 11 | 138,139 87 | | 142,550 20 | |
| | | **$4,604,079 46** | | **$3,999,754 94** |
| 12 | .......... | **$114,361 02** | .......... | **$110,874 05** |
| 13 | .......... | **$4,797,574 53** | .......... | **$4,194,968 48** |

Stations.

# NEW YORK

## GAS AND ELECTRICITY

ESTATE AND IMPROVEMENTS OF PROPERTY RELATING TO THE CROTON WATER SUPPLY.

| | | | |
|---|---|---|---|
| Fire Hydrants and Connections: | | | |
| Manhattan and The Bronx | $207,773 70 | | |
| Brooklyn | 30,174 28 | | |
| Queens | 4,536 51 | | |
| Richmond | 4,806 00 | | |
| Total, all Boroughs | | $247,290 49 | |
| Fountains, Troughs and Miscellaneous | | $2,358 05 | |
| Total, Distribution | | | **$2,091,066 27** |
| ANALYZING AND TESTING: | | | |
| Laboratories | | $8,807 48 | |
| Total, Analyzing and Testing | | | **$8,807 48** |
| WATER REVENUE COLLECTION: | | | |
| Meters | | $1,041 96 | |
| Total, Water Revenue Collection | | | **$1,041 96** |
| GENERAL: | | | |
| Buildings, Shops, etc. | | $72,453 20 | |
| Miscellaneous (undistributed) | | 31,537 87 | |
| Total, General | | | **$103,991 07** |
| Grand Total | | | **$2,534,244 46** |

THE CITY OF

DEPARTMENT OF

Comparative Summary for the Years 1913 and 1914, of Expenses Incurred in the Operation

| | LINE No. |
|---|---|
| GENERAL ADMINISTRATION: | |
| Office of Commissioner, Deputies, Secretaries, and Chief Clerk | 1 |
| Operation and Maintenance of Commissioner's Automobile | 2 |
| Office of Auditor | 3 |
| Operation and Maintenance of Office Building and Plant | 4 |
| Total | 5 |
| RECEIVING, STORING, AND ISSUING OF SUPPLIES: | |
| Offices and Plant at West 57th St., West 80th St., West 75th St., Timber Basin, and Shermans Creek | 6 |
| St. George, S. I., Storehouse | 7 |
| Auto Truck | 8 |
| Concrete and Granite Plant | 9 |
| Total | 10 |
| SUPERINTENDENCE OF WATERFRONT: | |
| Office of Superintendent of Docks | 11 |
| Automobile of Superintendent | 12 |
| Launch "Jamaica" | 13 |
| Supervision of Watchmen, and Care of Time Clocks and Dials | 14 |
| Total | 15 |
| ENGINEERING SUPERVISION: | |
| Offices of Chief Engineer and Deputy | 16 |
| Automobile of Chief Engineer | 17 |
| Division Offices and Plant | 18 |
| Supervision of Watchmen, and Care of Time Clocks and Dials | 19 |
| Total | 20 |
| OPERATION AND MAINTENANCE OF FLOATING PLANT: | |
| Tugs | 21 |
| Launches | 22 |
| Pile Drivers, Derricks, and Miscellaneous Floating Plant | 23 |
| Total | 24 |
| MECHANICAL ENGINEERING: | |
| Offices and Plant—Undistributed Expenses | 25 |
| PATROL OF WATERFRONT AND COLLECTION OF WHARFAGE REVENUES: | |
| Operation and Maintenance | 26 |
| CARE AND MAINTENANCE OF WATERFRONT PROPERTIES: | |
| Cleaning and Sweeping Piers and Marginal Streets | 27 |
| Removal of Encumbrances | 28 |
| Repairs and Maintenance of Piers, Bulkheads, and Marginal Streets | 29 |
| Miscellaneous Items | 30 |
| Supervision of Permits | 31 |
| Operation and Maintenance of Recreation Structures | 32 |
| Total | 33 |
| OPERATION AND MAINTENANCE OF MUNICIPAL FERRIES: | |
| Superintendence | 34 |
| Ferry Boats | 35 |
| Terminals | 36 |
| Total | 37 |
| SUBSIDY TO ROOSEVELT STREET FERRY | 38 |
| MISCELLANEOUS WAGE ALLOWANCES (INJURIES, VETERANS, ETC.) | 39 |
| Departmental Total | 40 |

Note: (a) Distributed over the various functions for the year 1914.

NEW YORK

DOCKS AND FERRIES

and Maintenance of Docks and Ferries, and the Collection of Wharfage Revenues:

| LINE No. | Year Ended Dec. 31, 1913 | | | Year Ended Dec. 31, 1914 | | |
|---|---|---|---|---|---|---|
| | Tax Levy | Corporate Stock | Total | Tax Levy | Corporate Stock | Total |
| 1 | $75,992 74 | $123 17 | $76,115 91 | $69,443 39 | $847 02 | $70,290 41 |
| 2 | 7,763 63 | 46 84 | 7,810 47 | 6,880 72 | 53 26 | 6,933 98 |
| 3 | 41,373 80 | .......... | 41,373 80 | 41,267 28 | .......... | 41,267 28 |
| 4 | 39,349 62 | 5,289 07 | 44,638 69 | 36,547 29 | 1,722 75 | 38,270 04 |
| 5 | **$164,479 79** | **$5,459 08** | **$169,938 87** | **$154,138 68** | **$2,623 03** | **$156,761 71** |
| 6 | $36,548 20 | $95,324 95 | $131,873 15 | $30,961 96 | $78,056 94 | $109,018 90 |
| 7 | 4,769 16 | 11,878 35 | 16,647 51 | 5,474 91 | 12,264 78 | 17,739 69 |
| 8 | .......... | .......... | .......... | 3,372 78 | 1,180 80 | 4,553 58 |
| 9 | .......... | .......... | .......... | 437 76 | 8,954 05 | 9,391 81 |
| 10 | **$41,317 36** | **$107,203 30** | **$148,520 66** | **$40,247 41** | **$100,456 57** | **$140,703 98** |
| 11 | $19,471 86 | $163 98 | $19,635 84 | $17,526 41 | $54 40 | $17,580 81 |
| 12 | 3,698 96 | 14 87 | 3,713 83 | 4,323 90 | 4 01 | 4,327 91 |
| 13 | 2,114 77 | 461 53 | 2,576 30 | 2,866 50 | 383 18 | 3,249 68 |
| 14 | 5,862 21 | .......... | 5,862 21 | 5,240 24 | .......... | 5,240 24 |
| 15 | **$31,147 80** | **$640 38** | **$31,788 18** | **$29,957 05** | **$441 59** | **$30,398 64** |
| 16 | $9,627 87 | $32,885 60 | $42,513 47 | $8,589 13 | $30,617 52 | $39,206 65 |
| 17 | 1,464 95 | 1,435 12 | 2,900 07 | 1,778 83 | 1,304 13 | 3,082 96 |
| 18 | 41,834 14 | 103,768 60 | 145,602 74 | 50,986 65 | 106,425 80 | 157,412 45 |
| 19 | 3,046 66 | 11,853 61 | 14,900 27 | 3,097 42 | 11,309 11 | 14,406 53 |
| 20 | **$55,973 62** | **$149,942 93** | **$205,916 55** | **$64,452 03** | **$149,656 56** | **$214,108 59** |
| 21 | $17,927 17 | $65,328 40 | $83,255 57 | $16,537 52 | $47,623 22 | $64,160 74 |
| 22 | 15,734 43 | 42,428 73 | 58,163 16 | 12,665 31 | 31,074 29 | 43,739 60 |
| 23 | 51,104 75 | 109,397 30 | 160,502 05 | 46,043 93 | 87,526 51 | 133,570 44 |
| 24 | **$84,766 35** | **$217,154 43** | **$301,920 78** | **$75,246 76** | **$166,224 02** | **$241,470 78** |
| 25 | **$61,319 13** | **$72,096 04** | **$133,415 17** | **$56,281 76** | **$80,332 08** | **$136,613 84** |
| 26 | **$88,443 97** | **$264 33** | **$88,708 30** | **$83,808 36** | **$214 25** | **$84,022 61** |
| 27 | $225,460 70 | $818 22 | $226,278 92 | $209,792 69 | $77 30 | $209,869 99 |
| 28 | 5,263 24 | .......... | 5,263 24 | 2,526 33 | 1,178 56 | 3,704 89 |
| 29 | 252,791 09 | 42,440 55 | 295,231 64 | 328,296 37 | 23,434 15 | 351,730 52 |
| 30 | 10,724 62 | 16,655 89 | 27,380 51 | 7,885 71 | 17,229 74 | 25,115 45 |
| 31 | 24,444 50 | 15,090 70 | 39,535 20 | 19,575 10 | 9,003 50 | 28,578 60 |
| 32 | 117,956 49 | 789 30 | 118,745 79 | 80,760 74 | 1,275 19 | 82,035 93 |
| 33 | **$636,640 64** | **$75,794 66** | **$712,435 30** | **$648,836 94** | **$52,198 44** | **$701,035 38** |
| 34 | $42,760 40 | $673 39 | $43,433 79 | $38,902 05 | $21 76 | $38,923 81 |
| 35 | 1,078,858 03 | 6,714 25 | 1,085,572 28 | 943,816 53 | 1,121 55 | 944,938 08 |
| 36 | 252,344 97 | 3,401 30 | 255,746 27 | 237,381 89 | 2,293 79 | 239,675 68 |
| 37 | **$1,373,963 40** | **$10,788 94** | **$1,384,752 34** | **$1,220,100 47** | **$3,437 10** | **$1,223,537 57** |
| 38 | **$132,000 00** | .......... | **$132,000 00** | **$132,000 00** | .......... | **$132,000 00** |
| 39 | **$9,101 36** | **$26,838 20** | **$35,939 56** | (a) | (a) | (a) |
| 40 | **$2,679,153 42** | **$666,182 29** | **$3,345,335 71** | **$2,505,069 46** | **$555,583 64** | **$3,060,653 10** |

# THE CITY OF NEW YORK

## DEPARTMENT OF DOCKS AND FERRIES

### Comparative Statement of Revenues Earned for Years 1913 and 1914.

| | 1913 | 1914 |
|---|---|---|
| Dock and Slip Rents accrued from leased City Wharf Property, and Revenue from Permits | $4,344,590 27 | $4,534,038 69 |
| Wharfage accrued from unleased City Wharf Property | 252,825 52 | 244,144 20 |
| Total | **$4,597,415 79** | **$4,778,182 89** |
| Ferry Rents accrued from leases of Ferry Franchises of City Wharf Property used for ferry purposes | **$317,319 09** | **$307,560 59** |
| Receipts from Operation of Municipal Ferries: | | |
| Staten Island Traffic and Privileges | $865,526 26 | $857,793 98 |
| 39th Street, South Brooklyn, Traffic and Privileges | 230,889 38 | 222,345 54 |
| Total | **$1,096,415 64** | **$1,080,139 52** |
| Miscellaneous Revenue Received: | | |
| Sale of Old Materials | $195 30 | .......... |
| Filling-in Privileges | .......... | $217 50 |
| Miscellaneous | 47 95 | 12 95 |
| Total | **$243 25** | **$230 45** |
| Total Revenue | **$6,011,393 77** | **$6,166,113 45** |

# THE CITY OF NEW YORK

## BELLEVUE AND ALLIED HOSPITALS

COMPARATIVE SUMMARY FOR THE YEARS 1913 AND 1914 OF UNIT COSTS OF WORK PERFORMED AND SERVICE RENDERED:

| Functions | Description | Units of Service Number | | Cost per Unit | |
|---|---|---|---|---|---|
| | | 1913 | 1914 | 1913 | 1914 |
| BELLEVUE HOSPITAL: | | | | | |
| Hospital Service | Day's Treatment | 454,770 | 495,108 | $1.89 | $1.75 |
| Dispensary Service | Cases Treated | 40,340 | 43,960 | .4502 | .3539 |
| Dispensary Service | Visits | 141,180 | 153,406 | .1286 | .1014 |
| Day Camp Service | Day's Treatment | 32,257 | 31,617 | .37 | .3294 |
| GOUVERNEUR HOSPITAL: | | | | | |
| Hospital Service | Day's Treatment | 65,367 | 75,926 | $2.14 | $1.92 |
| Dispensary Service | Cases Treated | 60,904 | 64,888 | .3124 | .2756 |
| Dispensary Service | Visits | 133,199 | 140,662 | .1428 | .1271 |
| Day Camp Service | Day's Treatment | 27,430 | 28,119 | .55 | .5607 |
| HARLEM HOSPITAL: | | | | | |
| Hospital Service | Day's Treatment | 71,743 | 77,576 | $1.96 | $1.94 |
| Dispensary Service | Cases Treated | 36,800 | 33,706 | .2796 | .2755 |
| Dispensary Service | Visits | 98,113 | 93,043 | .1049 | .0998 |
| FORDHAM HOSPITAL: | | | | | |
| Hospital Service | Day's Treatment | 65,069 | 69,194 | $2.05 | $2.07 |
| Dispensary Service | Cases Treated | 15,875 | 16,197 | .2237 | .2171 |
| Dispensary Service | Visits | 45,096 | 43,002 | .0787 | .0817 |

THE CITY OF

BELLEVUE AND

COMPARATIVE SUMMARY FOR THE YEARS 1913 AND 1914 OF EXPENSES

| | LINE No. |
|---|---|
| GENERAL ADMINISTRATION: | |
| Executive | 1 |
| Audit and Accounts | 2 |
| Purchase and Storage of Supplies | 3 |
| Engineering Supervision | 4 |
| Total, General Administration | 5 |
| BELLEVUE HOSPITAL: | |
| Hospital Service: | |
| Administration | 6 |
| Professional Care of Patients | 7 |
| Kitchen, Dining Rooms and Pantries | 8 |
| Housekeeping | 9 |
| Plant Service | 10 |
| Ambulance Service | 11 |
| Total, Hospital Service | 12 |
| Dispensary Service | 13 |
| Day Camp—Boat Southfield | 14 |
| Total, Bellevue Hospital | 15 |
| GOUVERNEUR HOSPITAL: | |
| Hospital Service: | |
| Administration | 16 |
| Professional Care of Patients | 17 |
| Kitchen, Dining Rooms and Pantries | 18 |
| Housekeeping | 19 |
| Plant Service | 20 |
| Ambulance Service | 21 |
| Total, Hospital Service | 22 |
| Dispensary Service | 23 |
| Day Camp—Boat Westfield | 24 |
| Total, Gouverneur Hospital | 25 |
| HARLEM HOSPITAL. | |
| Hospital Service: | |
| Administration | 26 |
| Professional Care of Patients | 27 |
| Kitchen, Dining Rooms and Pantries | 28 |
| Housekeeping | 29 |
| Plant Service | 30 |
| Ambulance Service | 31 |
| Total, Hospital Service | 32 |
| Dispensary Service | 33 |
| Total, Harlem Hospital | 34 |
| FORDHAM HOSPITAL. | |
| Hospital Service: | |
| Administration | 35 |
| Professional Care of Patients | 36 |
| Kitchen, Dining Rooms and Pantries | 37 |
| Housekeeping | 38 |
| Plant Service | 39 |
| Ambulance Service | 40 |
| Total, Hospital Service | 41 |
| Dispensary Service | 42 |
| Total, Harlem Hospital | 43 |
| Departmental Totals | 44 |

# NEW YORK

## ALLIED HOSPITALS.

Classified According to Functions Performed or Character of Work Done.

| Line No. | 1913 | | 1914 | |
|---|---|---|---|---|
| | Items | Totals | Items | Totals |
| 1 | .......... | $19,442 06 | .......... | $21,763 49 |
| 2 | .......... | 11,872 72 | .......... | 14,601 37 |
| 3 | .......... | 8,215 89 | .......... | 9,018 02 |
| 4 | .......... | 4,644 59 | .......... | 4,599 09 |
| 5 | | **$44,175 26** | | **$49,981 97** |
| 6 | $43,515 50 | | $41,153 27 | |
| 7 | 470,526 71 | | 507,659 16 | |
| 8 | 141,674 74 | | 129,434 67 | |
| 9 | 44,452 92 | | 39,455 53 | |
| 10 | 131,582 49 | | 122,508 01 | |
| 11 | 30,301 58 | | 28,973 89 | |
| 12 | | **$862,053 94** | | **$869,184 53** |
| 13 | .......... | **18,164 62** | .......... | **15,561 70** |
| 14 | .......... | **12,027 60** | .......... | **10,416 56** |
| 15 | .......... | **$892,246 16** | .......... | **$895,162 79** |
| 16 | $7,411 43 | | $7,434 20 | |
| 17 | 41,799 87 | | 52,879 01 | |
| 18 | 41,871 66 | | 35,551 23 | |
| 19 | 11,959 51 | | 13,057 08 | |
| 20 | 32,727 49 | | 31,244 14 | |
| 21 | 4,510 34 | | 5,616 83 | |
| 22 | | **$140,280 30** | | **$145,782 49** |
| 23 | .......... | **19,030 75** | .......... | **17,881 22** |
| 24 | .......... | **14,918 88** | .......... | **15,769 13** |
| 25 | | **$174,229 93** | | **$179,432 84** |
| 26 | $10,871 13 | | $10,235 22 | |
| 27 | 39,859 90 | | 56,812 80 | |
| 28 | 38,603 15 | | 32,356 72 | |
| 29 | 10,119 24 | | 8,527 97 | |
| 30 | 35,630 11 | | 36,389 04 | |
| 31 | 5,894 76 | | 6,301 62 | |
| 32 | | **$140,978 29** | | **$150,623 37** |
| 33 | .......... | **10,292 67** | .......... | **9,286 09** |
| 34 | | **$151,270 96** | | **$159,909 46** |
| 35 | $7,556 41 | | $7,237 74 | |
| 36 | 42,122 13 | | 57,352 21 | |
| 37 | 31,713 30 | | 26,767 35 | |
| 38 | 7,440 37 | | 7,311 87 | |
| 39 | 33,442 22 | | 35,400 62 | |
| 40 | 11,393 09 | | 9,369 56 | |
| 41 | | **$133,667 52** | | **$143,439 35** |
| 42 | .......... | **3,552 41** | .......... | **3,517 25** |
| 43 | | **$137,219 93** | | **$146,956 60** |
| 44 | | **$1,399,142 24** | | **$1,431,443 66** |

## THE CITY OF

### DEPARTMENT OF HEALTH

COMPARATIVE SUMMARY OF EXPENSES FOR THE YEARS 1913 AND 1914 CLASSIFIED

| | LINE No. |
|---|---|
| GENERAL ADMINISTRATION AND UNDISTRIBUTED EXPENSES: | |
| Executive | 1 |
| Audit and Accounts | 2 |
| Purchase and Storage of Supplies | 3 |
| Medical Supervision | 4 |
| Care of Offices | 5 |
| Automobile Service | 6 |
| Sale of Laboratory Products | 7 |
| Total | 8 |
| KEEPING OF RECORDS: | |
| Administration | 9 |
| Tabulation of Vital Statistics | 10 |
| Searching and Transcribing Records | 11 |
| Book Bindery | 12 |
| Total | 13 |
| PROMOTION OF CHILD HYGIENE: | |
| Administration | 14 |
| Supervision of Midwives | 15 |
| Issuance of Employment Certificates | 16 |
| Inspection of Institutions for Dependent Children | 17 |
| Inspection of School Children | 18 |
| Clinics for School Children | 19 |
| Infants' Milk Stations | 20 |
| Vaccinations | 21 |
| Total | 22 |
| PREVENTION AND SUPPRESSION OF INFECTIOUS DISEASES: | |
| Administration | 23 |
| Stables and Wagon Repair Shops | 24 |
| Laboratories | 25 |
| Medical Inspection, General | 26 |
| Medical Inspection of Typhoid | 27 |
| Animal Inspection | 28 |
| Inspection of Institutions | 29 |
| Disinfection | 30 |
| Hospital Admission Bureau | 31 |
| Tuberculosis Clinics | 32 |
| Tuberculosis Day Camp | 33 |
| Clinics, Venereal Diseases | 34 |
| Rabies Clinics | 35 |
| Total | 36 |
| GENERAL SANITARY AND FOOD INSPECTION SERVICE: | |
| Administration | 37 |
| General Sanitary Inspection | 38 |
| Food Inspection | 39 |
| Milk Inspection, City | 40 |
| Milk Inspection, Country | 41 |
| Total | 42 |
| LABORATORY SERVICE: | |
| Administration and Research and Vaccine Laboratory | 43 |
| Chemical Laboratory | 44 |
| Drug Laboratory | 45 |
| Total | 46 |
| Total, Other than Hospital Service | 47 |

NEW YORK

(Exclusive of Hospitals),

According to Functions Performed or Character of Work Done.

| Line No. | 1913 | | 1914 | |
|---|---|---|---|---|
| | Items | Total | Items | Total |
| 1 | $147,654 25 | | $139,817 69 | |
| 2 | 23,309 25 | | 22,242 62 | |
| 3 | 18,459 98 | | 19,600 27 | |
| 4 | 9,010 44 | | 156 15 | |
| 5 | (c) 134,602 39 | | 61,355 53 | |
| 6 | 18,211 90 | | 17,760 12 | |
| 7 | .......... | | (a) 6,423 86 | |
| 8 | | $351,248 21 | | $267,356 24 |
| 9 | $7,333 29 | | $6,098 86 | |
| 10 | 7,237 44 | | 7,896 93 | |
| 11 | 47,080 09 | | 48,167 78 | |
| 12 | 3,304 65 | | 3,254 10 | |
| 13 | | 64,955 47 | | 65,417 67 |
| 14 | (b) $58,075 20 | | $35,376 62 | |
| 15 | 14,270 35 | | 16,666 29 | |
| 16 | 16,737 57 | | 16,912 62 | |
| 17 | 3,275 00 | | 11,150 00 | |
| 18 | 326,610 30 | | 329,760 06 | |
| 19 | 77,425 81 | | 85,043 95 | |
| 20 | 140,787 26 | | 152,628 37 | |
| 21 | .......... | | 10,427 67 | |
| 22 | | 637,181 49 | | 657,965 58 |
| 23 | (b) $82,696 67 | | $56,478 98 | |
| 24 | 84,705 71 | | 60,955 57 | |
| 25 | 65,383 94 | | 44,332 60 | |
| 26 | 209,552 54 | | 245,708 21 | |
| 27 | .......... | | 11,794 13 | |
| 28 | 10,658 36 | | 11,278 10 | |
| 29 | .......... | | 13,523 33 | |
| 30 | 47,546 12 | | 37,242 46 | |
| 31 | 18,886 20 | | 17,468 30 | |
| 32 | 80,384 77 | | 74,155 23 | |
| 33 | 28,771 41 | | 26,936 24 | |
| 34 | .......... | | 14,187 43 | |
| 35 | .......... | | 1,668 79 | |
| 36 | | 628,585 72 | | 615,729 37 |
| 37 | $84,786 64 | | $87,739 77 | |
| 38 | 207,625 08 | | 189,536 62 | |
| 39 | 83,003 91 | | 112,434 57 | |
| 40 | 56,285 14 | | 32,672 00 | |
| 41 | 56,021 04 | | 49,968 07 | |
| 42 | | 487,721 81 | | 472,351 03 |
| 43 | $161,497 89 | | $157,398 07 | |
| 44 | 16,760 19 | | 19,635 52 | |
| 45 | 8,490 87 | | 9,236 92 | |
| 46 | | 186,748 95 | | 186,270 51 |
| 47 | | $2,356,441 65 | | $2,265,090 40 |

(a) Included under "General Administration, Executive," during 1913.
(b) Includes direct supervision of the various activities during 1913.
(c) Does not include rentals.

# THE CITY OF NEW YORK

## DEPARTMENT OF HEALTH—Hospitals

### Comparative Summary for the Years 1913 and 1914, of Functional Costs of Work Performed and Service Rendered

| Function | 1913 | 1914 |
|---|---|---|
| General Administration | **$3,978 81** | **$4,236 90** |
| Willard Parker Hospital: | | |
| Administration | $13,345 85 | $14,973 88 |
| Professional Care of Patients | 86,207 67 | 104,919 10 |
| Kitchen and Dining Rooms | 65,058 11 | 67,327 56 |
| Housekeeping | 9,787 19 | 11,570 83 |
| Plant Service | 46,235 84 | 54,676 70 |
| Total Hospital Service | **$220,634 66** | **$253,468 07** |
| Riverside Hospital: | | |
| Administration | $9,668 57 | $10,347 06 |
| Professional Care of Patients | 66,441 28 | 65,775 34 |
| Kitchen and Dining Rooms | 94,630 00 | 88,718 48 |
| Housekeeping | 19,768 09 | 28,048 36 |
| Plant Service | 57,465 19 | 51,851 35 |
| Steamboats, Launches and Docks | 39,766 24 | 40,974 32 |
| Stables | 2,465 24 | 2,398 58 |
| Total Hospital Service | **$290,204 61** | **$288,113 49** |
| Kingston Avenue Hospital: | | |
| Administration | $12,554 88 | $13,793 29 |
| Professional Care of Patients | 53,942 57 | 56,838 04 |
| Kitchen and Dining Rooms | 42,668 89 | 40,281 60 |
| Housekeeping | 16,841 69 | 18,770 55 |
| Plant Service | 65,092 78 | 57,156 92 |
| Total Hospital Service | **$191,100 81** | **$186,840 40** |
| Tuberculosis Sanatorium: Otisville: | | |
| Administration | $26,613 04 | $25,137 25 |
| Professional Care of Patients | 56,816 76 | 60,467 75 |
| Kitchen and Dining Rooms | 106,385 47 | 96,506 50 |
| Laundry and Power Plant | 11,196 56 | 10,551 10 |
| Stables | 12,956 91 | 10,553 41 |
| Operation and Maintenance of Plant | 4,983 20 | 2,801 30 |
| Undistributed Shop Expenses | 43,728 06 | 14,969 22 |
| Net Loss on Productive Departments | 4,200 32 | 5,084 90 |
| Total Hospital Service | **$266,880 32** | **$226,071 43** |
| Total Department of Health—Hospitals | **$972,799 21** | **$958,730 29** |
| Total Department of Health Other Than Hospitals | **2,356,441 65** | **2,265,090 40** |
| Total Department of Health | **$3,329,240 86** | **$3,223,820 69** |

# THE CITY OF NEW YORK

## DEPARTMENT OF HEALTH

### Comparative Summary for the Years 1913 and 1914 of Unit Costs of Work Performed and Service Rendered

| Functions | Description | Number 1913 | Number 1914 | Cost per Unit 1913 | Cost per Unit 1914 |
|---|---|---|---|---|---|
| | Units of Service | | | | |
| **Keeping of Records:** | | | | | |
| Tabulation of Vital Statistics..... | Certificates Tabulated ... | 256,871 | 274,517 | $0.028 | $0.028 |
| Searching and Transcribing Records.................. | Searches Made.......... | 190,490 | 170,695 | .247 | .28 |
| **Promoting Child Hygiene:** | | | | | |
| Supervision of Midwives......... | Inspections............. | 49,494 | 54,029 | .288 | .308 |
| Issuance of Employment Certificates................ | Certificates Issued....... | 42,167 | 33,555 | .3969 | .50 |
| Inspection of Institutions for Dependent Children......... | Inspections............. | 26,825 | 25,515 | .122 | .437 |
| Inspection of School Children..... | Net Enrollment of Pupils. | 804,237 | 832,195 | .41 | .396 |
| Clinics for School Children....... | Operations and Treatments .............. | 196,674 | 198,973 | .3935 | .42 |
| Infants Milk Stations............ | Examinations and Treatments .............. | 1,024,910 | 1,109,428 | .1375 | .13 |
| Vaccinations.................... | Vaccinations Made...... | ....... | 140,884 | ..... | .07 |
| **Prevention and Suppression of Infectious Diseases:** | | | | | |
| Medical Inspections, | Visits by Inspectors...... | 430,880 | 419,899 | .486 | .585 |
| Animal Inspections, | Examinations Made...... | 41,394 | 65,484 | .257 | .172 |
| Disinfections.................. | Rooms Disinfected....... | 46,638 | 46,905 | 1.019 | .79 |
| Stables......................... | Miles.................. | 186,692 | 128,783 | .447 | .46 |
| Tuberculosis Clinics............. | Patients Treated........ | 110,729 | 158,193 | .725 | .46 |
| Tuberculosis Day Camp......... | Patient Days........... | 50,306 | 83,690 | .571 | .32 |
| **General Sanitary and Food Inspection:** | | | | | |
| General Sanitary Inspection...... | Inspections............. | 300,069 | 441,291 | .69 | .42 |
| Food Inspection................ | Inspections............. | 376,808 | 379,302 | .22 | .296 |
| Milk Inspection, City........... | Inspections............. | 137,386 | 144,706 | .409 | .22 |
| Milk Inspection, Country........ | Inspections............. | 29,211 | 22,619 | 1.91 | 2.20 |
| **Laboratory Service:** | | | | | |
| Chemical Laboratory............ | Analyses ............... | 15,142 | 14,190 | 1.106 | 1.38 |
| **Hospital Service:** | | | | | |
| Willard Parker Hospital......... | Patient Days........... | 90,560 | 112,660 | 2.43 | 2.25 |
| Riverside...................... | Patient Days........... | 127,774 | 122,899 | 2.27 | 2.34 |
| Kingston Avenue Hospital....... | Patient Days........... | 74,105 | 77,927 | 2.57 | 2.39 |
| Tuberculosis Sanatorium, Otisville, N. Y...................... | Patient Days........... | 185,745 | 203,135 | 1.43 | 1.11 |

## DEPARTMENT OF STREET CLEANING—BOROUGHS

Summary of Expenses for the Year 1914, Classified According

| | General | Line No. |
|---|---|---|
| **Administration and Undistributed Expenses:** | | |
| Executive | $71,831 59 | 1 |
| Offices of Deputy Commissioners | .......... | 2 |
| District and Section Supervision | .......... | 3 |
| Audit and Accounts | 64,659 81 | 4 |
| Purchase and Storage of Supplies | 14,184 68 | 5 |
| Automobile Service | 6,824 99 | 6 |
| Medical and Surgical Service | 21,679 84 | 7 |
| Operation and Maintenance of Stables | .......... | 8 |
| Maintenance of Horse Drawn Equipment | .......... | 9 |
| Repair Shops, Overhead | .......... | 10 |
| Miscellaneous | 17,661 41 | 11 |
| Total, Administration and Undistributed Expenses | **$196,842 32** | 12 |
| Sweeping and Cleaning | .......... | 13 |
| Collection of Refuse | .......... | 14 |
| **Final Disposition of Refuse:** | | |
| Water Front Dumps | .......... | 15 |
| Scows and Launches | .......... | 16 |
| Land Fills | .......... | 17 |
| Other | .......... | 18 |
| Total, Final Disposition of Refuse | .......... | 19 |
| Snow Removal | .......... | 20 |
| Storage of Street Incumbrances | .......... | 21 |
| Departmental Total | **$196,842 32** | 22 |

Statistics and

| Function | |
|---|---|
| Collection of Refuse | 23 |
| Final Disposition of Refuse | 24 |
| Snow Removal | 25 |
| Operation and Maintenance of Stables | 26 |

NEW YORK

OF MANHATTAN, THE BRONX AND BROOKLYN

TO FUNCTIONS PERFOMRED OR CHARACTER OF WORK DONE:

| LINE No. | Borough of Manhattan | Borough of The Bronx | Borough of Brooklyn | Total |
|---|---|---|---|---|
| 1 | .......... | .......... | .......... | $71,831 59 |
| 2 | $7,774 11 | $10,349 95 | $14,656 05 | 32,780 11 |
| 3 | 259,756 99 | 34,149 45 | 157,954 15 | 451,860 59 |
| 4 | .......... | .......... | .......... | 64,659 81 |
| 5 | 4,682 22 | 824 04 | 5,047 60 | 24,738 54 |
| 6 | 3,800 07 | 5,530 46 | 5,347 30 | 21,502 82 |
| 7 | .......... | .......... | .......... | 21,679 84 |
| 8 | 636,315 65 | 147,957 14 | 465,128 18 | 1,249,400 97 |
| 9 | 94,721 30 | 21,010 94 | 58,769 29 | 174,501 53 |
| 10 | 15,732 20 | 768 45 | 7,915 89 | 24,416 54 |
| 11 | 24,034 14 | 7,035 31 | 20,442 74 | 69,173 60 |
| 12 | **$1,046,816 68** | **$227,625 74** | **$735,261 20** | **$2,206,545 94** |
| 13 | **$1,422,633 60** | **$245,968 20** | **$762,065 66** | **$2,430,667 46** |
| 14 | **$720,484 92** | **$182,781 86** | **$563,187 90** | **$1,466,454 68** |
| 15 | $144,292 62 | $10,868 92 | $15,935 76 | $171,097 30 |
| 16 | 7,410 87 | .......... | .......... | 7,410 87 |
| 17 | 2,545 29 | 9,487 60 | 38,081 55 | 50,114 44 |
| 18 | 644,920 26 | 72,686 53 | 663,485 37 | 1,381,092 16 |
| 19 | **$799,169 04** | **$93,043 05** | **$717,502 68** | **$1,609,714 77** |
| 20 | **$1,661,693 85** | **$131,393 35** | **$653,649 05** | **$2,446,736 25** |
| 21 | **$15,481 03** | .......... | **$2,036 02** | **$17,517 05** |
| 22 | **$5,666,279 12** | **$880,812 20** | **$3,433,702 51** | **$10,177,636 15** |

UNIT COSTS:

| | Unit of Service | | Total Cost | Cost per Unit |
|---|---|---|---|---|
| | Description | Number | | |
| 23 | Loads Collected | 3,683,406 | $1,466,454 68 | $ .3981 |
| 24 | Loads Disposed | 3,270,743 | 1,609,714 77 | .4921 |
| 25 | Cubic Yards Removed | 5,180,826.89 | 2,446,736 25 | .4722 |
| 26 | Horse Working Days | 688,375 | 1,249,400 97 | 1.8118 |

THE CITY OF

PRESIDENT OF THE

COMPARATIVE SUMMARY STATEMENT OF EXPENSES

| | LINE No. |
|---|---|
| **ADMINISTRATIVE OFFICES:** | |
| Office of the Borough President | 1 |
| Office of the Commissioner of Public Works | 2 |
| Office of the Assistant Commissioner of Public Works | 3 |
| Office of the Consulting Engineer | 4 |
| Total, Administrative Offices | 5 |
| **BUREAU OF HIGHWAYS:** | |
| Administration and Undistributed Expenses: | |
| Executive | 6 |
| Engineering | 7 |
| Chemical Laboratory | 8 |
| Permit Division | 9 |
| Maintenance of Pavements (other than stone): | |
| Administration and Equipment | 10 |
| Sheet Asphalt | 11 |
| Wood Block | 12 |
| Asphalt Blocks | 13 |
| Asphalt Plant | 14 |
| Maintenance of Roadways, Viaducts and Stone Pavements: | |
| Administration, Equipment, Stores and Live Stock | 15 |
| Stone Block Repairs | 16 |
| Macadam and Dirt Repairs | 17 |
| Fences Repaired | 18 |
| Viaducts | 19 |
| Maintenance of Side Walks, Street Signs and Control of Encumbrances: | |
| Administration, Equipment and Stores | 20 |
| Sidewalk Repairs | 21 |
| Street Signs | 22 |
| Encumbrances | 23 |
| Total Bureau of Highways | 24 |
| **BUREAU OF SEWERS:** | |
| Executive | 25 |
| Supervision, Stores and Equipment Service | 26 |
| Cleaning Sewers | 27 |
| Cleaning Basins | 28 |
| Repairs to Sewer System | 29 |
| Total, Bureau of Sewers | 30 |
| **BUREAU OF DESIGN AND SURVEY:** | |
| Executive | 31 |
| Designing and Surveying | 32 |
| Total, Bureau of Design and Survey | 33 |
| **BUREAU OF PUBLIC BUILDINGS AND OFFICES:** | |
| Administration | 34 |
| Operation and Maintenance of Offices and Office Buildings: | |
| Supervision | 35 |
| Municipal Building | 36 |

NEW YORK

BOROUGH OF MANHATTAN

FOR THE YEARS 1913 AND 1914.

| LINE No. | 1913 | | 1914 | |
|---|---|---|---|---|
| | Items | Total | Items | Total |
| 1 | .......... | $28,865 76 | .......... | $30,784 67 |
| 2 | .......... | 38,843 41 | .......... | 35,353 26 |
| 3 | .......... | 75,314 28 | .......... | 76,580 49 |
| 4 | .......... | 27,943 04 | .......... | 30,460 51 |
| 5 | .......... | **$170,966 49** | .......... | **$173,178 93** |
| 6 | $31,192 49 | | $24,825 60 | |
| 7 | 15,207 80 | | 11,299 69 | |
| 8 | 3,788 46 | | 4,795 07 | |
| 9 | 5,999 78 | | 7,190 82 | |
| | | **$56,188 53** | | **$48,111 18** |
| 10 | $51,799 40 | | $32,424 10 | |
| 11 | 528,130 29 | | 278,020 11 | |
| 12 | 17,785 80 | | 12,520 73 | |
| 13 | 71,085 19 | | 47,028 90 | |
| 14 | .......... | | 24,172 99 | |
| | | **$668,800 68** | | **$394,166 83** |
| 15 | $50,215 02 | | $51,937 29 | |
| 16 | 303,621 62 | | 248,905 08 | |
| 17 | 32,151 16 | | 30,804 12 | |
| 18 | 413 06 | | 16 01 | |
| 19 | 2,125 37 | | 9,879 67 | |
| | | **$388,526 23** | | **$341,542 17** |
| 20 | $29,071 57 | | $25,759 26 | |
| 21 | 21,637 62 | | 8,063 37 | |
| 22 | 22,039 91 | | 7,113 07 | |
| 23 | 9,427 35 | | 5,277 99 | |
| | | **$82,176 45** | | **$46,213 69** |
| 24 | | **$1,195,691 89** | | **$830,033 87** |
| 25 | .......... | $35,617 93 | .......... | $36,633 18 |
| 26 | .......... | 27,954 42 | .......... | 36,802 83 |
| 27 | .......... | 69,016 86 | .......... | 61,559 34 |
| 28 | .......... | 23,492 96 | .......... | 32,416 11 |
| 29 | .......... | 80,039 58 | .......... | 60,880 78 |
| 30 | .......... | **$236,121 75** | .......... | **$228,292 24** |
| 31 | .......... | $13,791 12 | .......... | $9,130 60 |
| 32 | .......... | 34,629 89 | .......... | 36,324 87 |
| 33 | .......... | **$48,421 01** | .......... | **$45,455 47** |
| 34 | .......... | **$45,394 53** | .......... | **$40,587 52** |
| 35 | $2,639 05 | | $2,039 09 | |
| 36 | 21,042 98 | | 186,433 53 | |

PRESIDENT OF THE

COMPARATIVE SUMMARY STATEMENT OF EXPENSES

| | LINE No. |
|---|---|
| BUREAU OF PUBLIC BUILDINGS AND OFFICES—*Continued* | |
| City Hall | 1 |
| County Court House | 2 |
| City Court House | 3 |
| Hall of Records | 4 |
| Criminal Court Building | 5 |
| Jefferson Market Court Building | 6 |
| 300 Mulberry Street | 7 |
| New Children's Court Building | 8 |
| Children's Court Building | 9 |
| West 54th Street Court Building | 10 |
| East 57th Street Court Building | 11 |
| Harlem Court Building | 12 |
| Municipal Courts | 13 |
| Bureau of Licenses—57 Chambers Street | 14 |
| City Paymaster | 15 |
| Undistributed Expenses: | |
| Mechanics' Squads | 16 |
| Snow Removal | 17 |
| Miscellaneous | 18 |
| Operation and Maintenance of Baths and Comfort Stations: | |
| Supervision | 19 |
| Baths—Permanent: | |
| Oliver Street | 20 |
| Rutgers Place | 21 |
| Allen Street | 22 |
| Rivington Street | 23 |
| Carmine Street | 24 |
| East 11th Street | 25 |
| East 23d Street | 26 |
| West 28th Street | 27 |
| West 41st Street | 28 |
| East 54th Street | 29 |
| West 60th Street | 30 |
| East 76th Street | 31 |
| East 109th Street | 32 |
| Baths—Floating | 33 |
| Comfort Stations: | |
| Battery Park | 34 |
| Hanover Square | 35 |
| Washington Market | 36 |
| Mail Street | 37 |
| Chatham Square | 38 |
| Delancey Street | 39 |
| Abingdon Square | 40 |
| Greeley Square | 41 |
| Queensboro Bridge | 42 |
| Long Acre Square | 43 |
| Park Avenue | 44 |
| 129th Street | 45 |
| Willis Avenue Bridge | 46 |
| Care of Market Buildings and Places | 47 |
| Supreme Court | 48 |
| Total Bureau of Public Buildings and Offices | 49 |
| BUREAU OF BUILDINGS: | |
| Executive | 50 |
| Violations | 51 |
| New Building Construction and Alteration | 52 |
| Total Bureau of Buildings | 53 |
| Grand Total | 54 |

NEW YORK

BOROUGH OF MANHATTAN

FOR THE YEARS 1913 AND 1914—*Continued.*

| LINE No. | 1913 | | 1914 | |
|---|---|---|---|---|
| | Items | Total | Items | Total |
| 1 | $37,490 39 | | $61,127 86 | |
| 2 | 32,794 55 | | 31,302 70 | |
| 3 | 14,954 92 | | 15,623 13 | |
| 4 | 76,103 19 | | 80,656 16 | |
| 5 | 66,395 94 | | 62,627 34 | |
| 6 | 8,107 41 | | 8,893 43 | |
| 7 | 3,026 04 | | 1,987 39 | |
| 8 | .......... | | 1,035 25 | |
| 9 | 5,864 83 | | 5,757 11 | |
| 10 | 17,999 47 | | 19,390 99 | |
| 11 | 21,975 74 | | 11,877 23 | |
| 12 | 16,920 02 | | 15,308 13 | |
| 13 | 27,544 31 | | 23,929 99 | |
| 14 | 2,250 42 | | 3,910 89 | |
| 15 | 2,949 33 | | 1,143 12 | |
| 16 | 3,712 91 | | 4,118 65 | |
| 17 | .......... | | 20,745 62 | |
| 18 | 8,372 98 | | 11,340 87 | |
| | | **$370,144 48** | | **$569,248 48** |
| 19 | $2,179 71 | | $2,320 80 | |
| 20 | 18,108 58 | | 16,832 43 | |
| 21 | 33,049 86 | | 30,560 89 | |
| 22 | 20,651 15 | | 18,408 46 | |
| 23 | 22,406 76 | | 20,695 15 | |
| 24 | 16,950 42 | | 16,708 45 | |
| 25 | 18,795 62 | | 17,131 09 | |
| 26 | 24,406 56 | | 24,377 48 | |
| 27 | .......... | | 470 07 | |
| 28 | 18,556 11 | | 16,638 42 | |
| 29 | 19,210 36 | | 21,193 51 | |
| 30 | 24,416 73 | | 19,276 30 | |
| 31 | 17,906 11 | | 15,510 55 | |
| 32 | 19,088 13 | | 17,206 55 | |
| 33 | 24,294 24 | | 31,753 81 | |
| 34 | 5,631 48 | | 5,603 14 | |
| 35 | 5,682 57 | | 4,062 36 | |
| 36 | 1,924 53 | | 2,184 77 | |
| 37 | 7,080 72 | | 5,565 13 | |
| 38 | 6,336 78 | | 5,971 45 | |
| 39 | 7,007 80 | | 6,266 07 | |
| 40 | .......... | | 3,542 52 | |
| 41 | 6,203 83 | | 5,558 70 | |
| 42 | .......... | | 806 67 | |
| 43 | 6,694 05 | | 6,218 01 | |
| 44 | 6,406 03 | | 5,566 90 | |
| 45 | 42 47 | | 4,994 99 | |
| 46 | 5,345 84 | **$338,382 44** | 6,129 79 | **$331,554 46** |
| 47 | .......... | **34,894 27** | .......... | **73,828 11** |
| 48 | .......... | **24,878 01** | .......... | **17,016 90** |
| 49 | .......... | **$813,693 73** | .......... | **$1,032,235 47** |
| 50 | .......... | $63,778 08 | .......... | $48,100 38 |
| 51 | .......... | 39,722 90 | .......... | 43,648 46 |
| 52 | .......... | 251,400 83 | .......... | 241,820 46 |
| 53 | .......... | **$354,901 81** | .......... | **$333,569 30** |
| 54 | .......... | **$2,819,796 68** | .......... | **$2,642,765 28** |

# THE CITY OF

## OFFICE OF THE PRESIDENT OF THE

Comparative Summary for the Years 1913 and 1914 of Expenses Incurred in the Care of Highways,

| | Line No. |
|---|---|
| **Bureau of Administration:** | |
| Office of the President of the Borough | 1 |
| Office of the Commissioner and Assistant Commissioner of Public Works | 2 |
| Office of the Consulting Engineer | 3 |
| Secretarial Work for Local Improvement Boards | 4 |
| Auditing and Accounting | 5 |
| Pay Roll Division | 6 |
| Contracts and Specifications | 7 |
| Municipal Library | 8 |
| Total, Bureau of Administration | 9 |
| **General Engineering:** | |
| Chief Engineer of Sewers and Highways | 10 |
| Topographical Bureau | 11 |
| Bureau of Design | 12 |
| Total, General Engineering | 13 |
| **Bureau of Highways:** | |
| Administration and Undistributed Expenses: | |
| Executive | 14 |
| Engineering Supervision and Inspection | 15 |
| Stores and Shops | 16 |
| Stable and Garage | 17 |
| General, Equipment and Motor Vehicle Service | 18 |
| Maintenance of Permanent Pavements: | |
| Asphalt Sheet Pavement | 19 |
| Asphalt Block Pavement | 20 |
| Bituminous Pavement | 21 |
| Granite Block Pavement—on Sand | 22 |
| Granite Block Pavement—Tar and Gravel | 23 |
| Granite Block Pavement—Grout Joints | 24 |
| Wood Block Pavement | 25 |
| Brick Pavement | 26 |
| Maintenance of Macadam and Dirt Roads: | |
| Macadam Pavements | 27 |
| Macadam Pavements—Special Bituminous | 28 |
| Earth Roads | 29 |
| Iron Slag Pavement | 30 |
| Water Sprinkling | 31 |
| Maintenance of Walks, Steps, Curbs and Gutters: | |
| Crosswalks | 32 |
| Sidewalks | 33 |
| Steps | 34 |
| Curbing | 35 |
| Gutters | 36 |
| Maintenance of Bridges, Viaducts and Transverse Roads | 37 |
| Maintenance of Ditches and Deep Gutters | 38 |
| Maintenance of Street Signs | 39 |
| Control of Street and Sidewalk Encumbrances | 40 |
| Control of Sub-surface Construction under City Streets | 41 |
| Maintenance of Guard Rails | 42 |
| Cutting Grass | 43 |
| Temporary Repairs | 44 |
| Snow Removal | 45 |
| Miscellaneous | 46 |
| Total, Bureau of Highways | 47 |

# NEW YORK

## BOROUGH OF THE BRONX.

### SEWERS, PUBLIC BUILDINGS AND OFFICES, IN THE ENFORCEMENT OF BUILDING REGULATIONS, ETC.

| LINE No. | 1913 | | 1914 | |
|---|---|---|---|---|
| | Items | Total | Items | Total |
| 1 | .......... | $24,070 25 | .......... | $29,006 34 |
| 2 | .......... | 17,625 81 | .......... | 18,016 23 |
| 3 | .......... | 13,029 30 | .......... | 13,374 86 |
| 4 | .......... | 1,987 99 | .......... | 2,219 03 |
| 5 | .......... | 14,914 44 | .......... | 14,019 16 |
| 6 | .......... | 7,739 00 | .......... | 4,992 04 |
| 7 | .......... | 4,076 32 | .......... | 3,601 43 |
| 8 | .......... | 2,437 11 | .......... | 2,273 20 |
| 9 | .......... | **$85,880 22** | .......... | **$87,502 29** |
| 10 | .......... | $3,726 44 | .......... | $6,116 86 |
| 11 | .......... | 31,091 89 | .......... | 65,045 45 |
| 12 | .......... | 41,775 04 | .......... | 25,447 32 |
| 13 | .......... | **$76,593 37** | .......... | **$96,609 63** |
| 14 | $23,685 88 | | $26,800 77 | |
| 15 | 24,760 21 | | 30,760 40 | |
| 16 | 14,728 55 | | 18,729 68 | |
| 17 | 24,030 44 | | 26,668 38 | |
| 18 | 49,901 12 | **$137,106 20** | 68,673 10 | **$171,632 33** |
| 19 | $21,674 16 | | $20,255 76 | |
| 20 | 47,028 47 | | 14,258 59 | |
| 21 | 48 18 | | 193 20 | |
| 22 | 31,182 08 | | 27,572 09 | |
| 23 | 4,000 64 | | 9,664 45 | |
| 24 | 443 54 | | 1,922 38 | |
| 25 | 1,767 43 | | 1,150 05 | |
| 26 | .......... | **106,144 50** | 17.98 | **75,034 50** |
| 27 | $232,945 52 | | $153,933 42 | |
| 28 | 5,599 41 | | 2,559 33 | |
| 29 | 89,700 09 | | 97,905 52 | |
| 30 | 37 50 | | 98 27 | |
| 31 | 10,665 03 | **338,947 55** | 7,978 08 | **262,474 62** |
| 32 | $13,678 89 | | $13,885 75 | |
| 33 | 6,193 57 | | 5,261 08 | |
| 34 | 6,437 85 | | 7,369 78 | |
| 35 | 1,747 54 | | 3,550 94 | |
| 36 | 3,740 87 | **31,798 72** | 4,147 73 | **34,215 28** |
| 37 | .......... | **26,118 42** | .......... | **22,051 13** |
| 38 | .......... | **615 91** | .......... | **37 57** |
| 39 | .......... | **6,371 90** | .......... | **5,222 87** |
| 40 | .......... | **6,079 95** | .......... | **2,451 98** |
| 41 | .......... | **7,953 45** | .......... | **18,263 98** |
| 42 | .......... | **883 01** | .......... | **1,034 16** |
| 43 | .......... | **1,821 58** | .......... | **3,043 61** |
| 44 | .......... | **2,321 04** | .......... | **6,617 49** |
| 45 | .......... | .......... | .......... | **11,785 13** |
| 46 | .......... | **3,940 09** | .......... | **1,561 59** |
| 47 | .......... | **$670,102 32** | .......... | **$615,426 24** |

OFFICE OF THE PRESIDENT O

COMPARATIVE SUMMARY FOR THE YEARS 1913 AND 1914 OF EXPENSES INCURRED IN THE CARE OF HIGHWAY

| | LINE No |
|---|---|
| **BUREAU OF SEWERS:** | |
| Administration and Undistributed Expenses: | |
| Executive | |
| Engineering Supervision | |
| Stables, Stores, Shops, Motor Vehicle Service, etc. | |
| Operation and Maintenance of Cement Laboratory | |
| Operation and Maintenance of Sewer System: | |
| Pipe Sewers | |
| Brick and Concrete Sewers | |
| Pipe Drains or Culverts | |
| Stone Drains or Culverts | |
| Box Drains or Culverts | |
| Open Drains or Ditches | 1 |
| Receiving or Catch Basins | 1 |
| Manholes | 1 |
| Flush Tanks | 1 |
| Total, Bureau of Sewers | 1 |
| **BUREAU OF PUBLIC BUILDINGS AND OFFICES:** | |
| Administration | 1 |
| Operation and Maintenance of Buildings and Offices: | |
| Municipal Building | 1 |
| City Clerk and Marriage License Bureau | 1 |
| Engineer's Office (242nd Street and Broadway) | 1 |
| Engineer's Office (507 Tremont Avenue) | 1 |
| Engineer's Office (1517 Williamsbridge Road) | 2 |
| Engineer's Office (1519 Williamsbridge Road) | 2 |
| Court House (161st Street and 3rd Avenue) | 2 |
| Court House (162nd Street and Brook Avenue) | 2 |
| Municipal Court House—Westchester | 2 |
| Magistrate's Court | 2 |
| Children's Court | 2 |
| Supreme Court | 2 |
| County Judge | 2 |
| Surrogate | 2 |
| District Attorney's Office | 3 |
| District Attorney's Library | 3 |
| County Clerk | 3 |
| Jail | 3 |
| Register | 3 |
| Miscellaneous | 3 |
| Operation and Maintenance of Baths: | |
| Elton Avenue Bath | 3 |
| Floating Baths | 3 |
| Total, Bureau of Public Buildings and Offices | 3 |
| **BUREAU OF BUILDINGS:** | |
| Administration and Clerical Work | 3 |
| Inspections | 4 |
| Total, Bureau of Buildings | 4 |
| Grand Total | 4 |

NEW YORK

THE BOROUGH OF THE BRONX—*Continued*

SEWERS, PUBLIC BUILDINGS AND OFFICES, IN THE ENFORCEMENT OF BUILDING REGULATIONS, ETC.

| LINE No. | 1913 | | 1914 | |
|---|---|---|---|---|
| | Items | Total | Items | Total |
| 1 | $8,672 80 | | $8,246 79 | |
| 2 | 37,427 79 | | 44,680 72 | |
| 3 | 33,813 81 | | 29,822 39 | |
| 4 | 1,123 55 | | 456 12 | |
| | | **$81,037 95** | | **$83,206 02** |
| 5 | $16,131 72 | | $12,915 80 | |
| 6 | 9,422 70 | | 9,577 34 | |
| 7 | 1,812 42 | | 665 19 | |
| 8 | 12,208 41 | | 7,119 98 | |
| 9 | 1,998 36 | | 2,537 31 | |
| 10 | 2,968 26 | | 2,768 10 | |
| 11 | 27,612 72 | | 27,037 51 | |
| 12 | 2,545 63 | | 1,123 32 | |
| 13 | 26.51 | | 26 00 | |
| | | **74,726 73** | | **63,770 55** |
| 14 | | **$155,764 68** | | **$146,976 57** |
| 15 | .......... | **$12,676 77** | .......... | **$11,498 14** |
| 16 | $26,948 21 | | $25,993 62 | |
| 17 | 287 93 | | 202 99 | |
| 18 | 1,043 06 | | 1,023 15 | |
| 19 | 897 55 | | 879 74 | |
| 20 | 1,352 96 | | 905 51 | |
| 21 | 4,040 44 | | 3,789 26 | |
| 22 | 11.75 | | 14,427 71 | |
| 23 | 8,055 18 | | 8,643 44 | |
| 24 | 1,418 98 | | 2,684 85 | |
| 25 | 1,460 82 | | 1,590 75 | |
| 26 | .......... | | 2,111 72 | |
| 27 | .......... | | 5,551 30 | |
| 28 | .......... | | 2,383 02 | |
| 29 | .......... | | 2,993 20 | |
| 30 | .......... | | 3,583 03 | |
| 31 | .......... | | 203 04 | |
| 32 | .......... | | 2,837 44 | |
| 33 | .......... | | 57 60 | |
| 34 | .......... | | 3,991 82 | |
| 35 | 857 28 | | 115 37 | |
| | | **46,374 16** | | **83,969 16** |
| 36 | $18,562 13 | | $20,154 93 | |
| 37 | 5,172 35 | | 731 00 | |
| | | **23,734 48** | | **20,885 93** |
| 38 | | **$82,785 41** | | **$116,353 23** |
| 39 | .......... | **$35,976 36** | .......... | **$36,638 33** |
| 40 | .......... | **81,095 84** | .......... | **80,020 22** |
| 41 | | **$117,072 20** | | **$116,658 55** |
| 42 | | **$1,188,198 20** | | **$1,179,526 51** |

OFFICE OF THE PRESIDENT O

COMPARATIVE SUMMARY, FOR THE YEARS 1913 AND 1914, OF EXPENSES INCURRED IN THE CA
REGULATION

| |
|---|
| **ADMINISTRATION OFFICES:** |
| Office of the Borough President |
| Office of the Commissioner of Public Works |
| Office of the Assistant Commissioner of Public Works |
| Office of the Consulting Engineer |
| Total, Administration Offices |
| **BUREAU OF HIGHWAYS:** |
| Administration and Undistributed Expenses: |
| Executive |
| Supervision, Stores and Equipment Service |
| Making of Surveys, Plans and Specifications |
| Operation and Maintenance of Testing Laboratory |
| Miscellaneous, including Vacations |
| Maintenance of Pavements: |
| Asphalt Plant |
| Asphalt Pavements |
| Granite Pavement, Sand Foundation |
| Tar, Gravel and Granite Pavement |
| Wood Block Pavement |
| Belgian Block Pavement |
| Pavement Foundations |
| Unclassified Emergency Work |
| Maintenance of Macadam and Dirt Roads: |
| Macadam Pavements |
| Dirt Roads—Repaired by Hand |
| Dirt Roads—Repaired by Machine |
| Oil Sprinkling |
| Water Sprinkling |
| Maintenance of Walks, Curbs and Gutters: |
| Bluestone Sidewalks |
| Ash Sidewalks |
| Cement Sidewalks |
| Gutters |
| Maintenance of Bridges |
| Cleaning and Construction of Cesspools |
| Control of Street and Sidewalk Encumbrances |
| Total, Bureau of Highways |
| **BUREAU OF SEWERS:** |
| Administration and Undistributed Expenses: |
| Executive |
| Supervision, Stores and Equipment Service |
| Vacations |
| Miscellaneous |

NEW YORK

THE BOROUGH OF BROOKLYN

OF HIGHWAYS, SEWERS, PUBLIC BUILDINGS AND OFFICES, IN THE ENFORCEMENT OF BUILDING ETC.

| LINE No. | 1913 | | 1914 | |
|---|---|---|---|---|
| | Items | Totals | Items | Totals |
| 1 | .......... | $56,193 64 | .......... | $54,959 47 |
| 2 | .......... | 18,949 96 | .......... | 17,345 49 |
| 3 | .......... | 10,337 25 | .......... | 10,611 64 |
| 4 | .......... | 6,816 70 | .......... | 8,175 53 |
| 5 | .......... | **$92,297 55** | .......... | **$91,092 13** |
| 6 | $44,618 44 | | $36,757 31 | |
| 7 | 137,404 64 | | 154,937 83 | |
| 8 | 24,603 87 | | 24,715 14 | |
| 9 | 6,243 04 | | 7,889 29 | |
| 10 | 67,908 37 | | 66,727 61 | |
| | | **$280,778 36** | | **$291,027 18** |
| 11 | $80,017 98 | | $60,308 95 | |
| 12 | 101,803 60 | | 87,001 40 | |
| 13 | 103,478 77 | | 36,507 60 | |
| 14 | 32,507 50 | | 22,958 87 | |
| 15 | 1,443 99 | | 30,102 84 | |
| 16 | 18,985 22 | | 3,870 37 | |
| 17 | 9,333 10 | | 10,346 78 | |
| 18 | 20,519 48 | | 21,925 89 | |
| | | **368,089 64** | | **273,022 70** |
| 19 | $59,503 80 | | $69,086 75 | |
| 20 | 21,842 52 | | 29,194 33 | |
| 21 | 15,304 23 | | 17,135 10 | |
| 22 | 35,817 86 | | 34,305 26 | |
| 23 | 10,559 96 | | 14,845 13 | |
| | | **143,028 37** | | **164,566 57** |
| 24 | $46,252 99 | | $15,385 84 | |
| 25 | 8,762 03 | | 7,710 69 | |
| 26 | 8,614 38 | | 4,019 32 | |
| 27 | 5,584 73 | | 3,773 99 | |
| | | **69,214 13** | | **30,889 84** |
| 28 | .......... | **5,797 34** | .......... | **4,506 14** |
| 29 | .......... | **7,816 75** | .......... | **4,677 07** |
| 30 | .......... | **23,781 26** | .......... | **23,949 61** |
| 31 | .......... | **$898,505 85** | .......... | **$792,639 11** |
| 32 | $27,544 49 | | $24,915 01 | |
| 33 | 139,725 63 | | 130,121 04 | |
| 34 | .......... | | 14,553 04 | |
| 35 | 1,404 18 | | 1,565 65 | |
| | | **$168,674 30** | | **$171,154 74** |

THE CITY OF

OFFICE OF THE PRESIDENT OF

COMPARATIVE SUMMARY, FOR THE YEARS 1913 AND 1914, OF EXPENSES INCURRED IN THE CARE
REGULATIONS,

| | LINE No. |
|---|---|
| Operation and Maintenance of Sewers: | |
| Repairs and Cleaning of Pipe Sewers | 1 |
| Repairs and Cleaning of Brick and Cement Sewers | 2 |
| Repairs to Sewers Unclassified (Contract Service) | 3 |
| Repairs to Manholes | 4 |
| Repairs and Cleaning of Catch Basins | 5 |
| Dredging Sewer Outlets | 6 |
| Operation and Maintenance of Gowanus Flushing Tunnel | 7 |
| Operation and Maintenance of Sewage Disposal Works: | |
| Caisson No. 2 | 8 |
| Caisson No. 3 | 9 |
| Caisson No. 4 | 10 |
| 26th Ward Disposal Works | 11 |
| Experimental Plant, 26th Ward Disposal Works | 12 |
| Total, Bureau of Sewers | 13 |
| TOPOGRAPHICAL BUREAU: | |
| Administration | 14 |
| Preparing Plans and Specifications | 15 |
| Total, Topographical Bureau | 16 |
| BUREAU OF PUBLIC BUILDINGS AND OFFICES: | |
| Administration and Undistributed Expenses | 17 |
| Operation and Maintenance of Offices and Office Buildings: | |
| Supervision | 18 |
| Borough President's Offices | 19 |
| Borough Hall | 20 |
| Municipal Building | 21 |
| Court House | 22 |
| Hall of Records | 23 |
| Raymond Street Jail | 24 |
| Brooklyn Disciplinary Training School | 25 |
| Courts of Special Sessions, Supreme Court and Appellate Division | 26 |
| Magistrates' Courts | 27 |
| Municipal Courts | 28 |
| Children's Court and Court of Domestic Relations | 29 |
| Undistributed Expenses | 30 |
| Operation and Maintenance of Baths and Comfort Stations: | |
| Supervision | 31 |
| Baths—Permanent: | |
| Coney Island | 32 |
| Hicks Street | 33 |
| Pitkin Avenue | 34 |
| Montrose Avenue | 35 |
| Huron Street | 36 |
| Duffield Street | 37 |
| Hamburg Avenue | 38 |
| Fourth Avenue | 39 |
| Baths—Floating | 40 |

NEW YORK

THE BOROUGH OF BROOKLYN

OF HIGHWAYS, SEWERS, PUBLIC BUILDINGS AND OFFICES, IN THE ENFORCEMENT OF BUILDING ETC.—*Continued*

| LINE No. | 1913 Items | 1913 Totals | 1914 Items | 1914 Totals |
|---|---|---|---|---|
| 1 | $45,024 40 | | $38,300 82 | |
| 2 | 15,809 44 | | 5,024 63 | |
| 3 | 6,398 59 | | 13,632 98 | |
| 4 | 4,094 88 | | 4,855 73 | |
| 5 | 53,928 43 | | 54,164 78 | |
| 6 | 13,107 66 | | 8,750 26 | |
| 7 | 10,678 54 | | 12,765 89 | |
| | | **$149,041 94** | | **$137,495 09** |
| 8 | $19,137 10 | | $16,569 10 | |
| 9 | 12,202 74 | | 12,300 88 | |
| 10 | 12,474 55 | | 12,495 28 | |
| 11 | 29,777 72 | | 27,994 73 | |
| 12 | 23,964 32 | | 10,263 60 | |
| | | **$97,556 43** | | **$79,623 59** |
| 13 | .......... | **$415,272 67** | .......... | **$388,273 42** |
| 14 | .......... | **$328 60** | .......... | **$25,114 04** |
| 15 | .......... | .......... | .......... | **36,845 41** |
| 16 | .......... | **$328 60** | .......... | **$61,959 45** |
| 17 | .......... | **$50,278 62** | .......... | **$50,003 10** |
| 18 | $145 19 | | $1,158 50 | |
| 19 | $9,068 04 | | $10,722 13 | |
| 20 | 33,801 72 | | 35,065 68 | |
| 21 | 34,608 07 | | 22,578 03 | |
| 22 | 38,232 02 | | 37,545 38 | |
| 23 | 44,915 66 | | 45,059 65 | |
| 24 | 4,888 50 | | 4,739 60 | |
| 25 | 5,098 19 | | 3,622 25 | |
| 26 | 19,406 64 | | 16,138 39 | |
| 27 | 10,556 84 | | 12,441 27 | |
| 28 | 7,876 53 | | 7,345 07 | |
| 29 | 3,892 54 | | 3,743 36 | |
| 30 | 8,555 13 | | 3,715 65 | |
| | | **$221,045 07** | | **$203,874 96** |
| 31 | $5,039 80 | | $5,704 28 | |
| 32 | 27,473 83 | | 28,028 82 | |
| 33 | 17,310 75 | | 18,941 40 | |
| 34 | 26,659 05 | | 26,836 45 | |
| 35 | 26,045 92 | | 25,291 32 | |
| 36 | 23,118 23 | | 23,487 76 | |
| 37 | 17,906 16 | | 18,962 16 | |
| 38 | 20,800 16 | | 21,614 62 | |
| 39 | 26,111 13 | | 25,728 97 | |
| 40 | 14,661 24 | | 6,206 05 | |

THE CITY OF

OFFICE OF THE PRESIDENT OF

COMPARATIVE SUMMARY, FOR THE YEARS 1913 AND 1914, OF EXPENSES INCURRED IN THE CARE
REGULATIONS,

| | LINE No. |
|---|---|
| Comfort Stations: | |
| Borough Hall | 1 |
| Reid Avenue | 2 |
| Lorimer Street | 3 |
| Hamilton Avenue | 4 |
| Greenpoint Avenue | 5 |
| Liberty Avenue | 6 |
| Plaza | 7 |
| Operation and Maintenance of Market Buildings and Places | 8 |
| Maintenance of Street Signs | 9 |
| Total, Bureau of Public Buildings and Offices | 10 |
| BUREAU OF BUILDINGS: | |
| Administration and Undistributed Expenses | 11 |
| Inspection of Structural Conditions in Existing Buildings | 12 |
| Recording and Reporting Violations of Legal Regulations | 13 |
| Control of Building Construction and Alterations: | |
| Administration | 14 |
| Examination of Plans | 15 |
| Inspection—Plumbing | 16 |
| Inspection—Iron and Steel Work | 17 |
| Inspection—Masonry and Carpentry | 18 |
| Inspection—Plastering | 19 |
| Inspection—Elevators | 20 |
| Total, Bureau of Buildings | 21 |
| BUREAU OF SUBSTRUCTURES: | |
| Control of Subsurface Work beneath City Streets | 22 |
| Department Total | 23 |

NEW YORK

THE BOROUGH OF BROOKLYN

OF HIGHWAYS, SEWERS, PUBLIC BUILDINGS AND OFFICES, IN THE ENFORCEMENT OF BUILDIN
ETC.—*Continued.*

| LINE No. | 1913 | | 1914 | |
|---|---|---|---|---|
| | Items | Totals | Items | Totals |
| 1 | $5,070 23 | | $4,993 33 | |
| 2 | 5,343 10 | | 5,192 38 | |
| 3 | 5,239 22 | | 5,320 89 | |
| 4 | 5,366 19 | | 5,354 77 | |
| 5 | 5,499 62 | | 5,578 82 | |
| 6 | 5,373 91 | | 5,497 71 | |
| 7 | 243 04 | | 4,779 61 | |
| | | **$237,261 58** | | **$237,519 34** |
| 8 | .......... | **$17,938 92** | .......... | **$17,666 40** |
| 9 | .......... | **5,682 57** | .......... | **5,442 47** |
| 10 | .......... | **$532,206 76** | .......... | **$514,506 27** |
| 11 | .......... | **$28,939 20** | .......... | **$29,885 13** |
| 12 | .......... | **17,998 92** | .......... | **13,865 29** |
| 13 | .......... | **8,537 83** | .......... | **8,755 00** |
| 14 | $5,301 02 | | $4,424 50 | |
| 15 | 26,901 14 | | 28,220 75 | |
| 16 | 27,420 63 | | 28,229 71 | |
| 17 | 2,808 03 | | 2,841 32 | |
| 18 | 68,513 76 | | 67,216 57 | |
| 19 | 2,400 00 | | 2,399 33 | |
| 20 | 2,689 81 | | 2,700 00 | |
| | | **136,034 39** | | **136,032 18** |
| 21 | .......... | **$191,510 34** | .......... | **$188,537 60** |
| 22 | .......... | **$24,835 53** | .......... | **$24,459 01** |
| 23 | .......... | **$2,154,957 30** | .......... | **$2,061,466 99** |

THE CITY OF

OFFICE OF THE PRESIDENT OF

COMPARATIVE SUMMARY, FOR THE YEARS 1913 AND 1914, OF EXPENSES INCURRED
ENFORCEMENT OF

| | LINE No. |
|---|---|
| **ADMINISTRATIVE OFFICES:** | |
| Offices of the President of the Borough | 1 |
| Offices of the Commissioner and Assistant Commissioner of Public Works | 2 |
| Bureau of Audit and Accounts and Payroll Division | 3 |
| Office of the Consulting Engineer | 4 |
| Secretarial Work for Local Improvement Board | 5 |
| Total, Administrative Offices | 6 |
| **BUREAU OF HIGHWAYS:** | |
| Administration and Undistributed Expenses: | |
| Executive | 7 |
| Supervision, Stores and Equipment Service | 8 |
| Making of Surveys, Plans and Specifications | 9 |
| Operation and Maintenance of Testing Laboratory | 10 |
| Investigation of Complaints and General Inspection | 11 |
| Miscellaneous | 12 |
| Total | 13 |
| Maintenance of Pavements: | |
| Asphalt Plant | 14 |
| Asphalt and Block Pavement | 15 |
| Asphalt Sheet Pavement | 16 |
| Granite Pavement | 17 |
| Brick Pavement | 18 |
| Wood Block Pavement | 19 |
| Asphaltic Concrete Pavement | 20 |
| Belgian Block Pavement | 21 |
| Headers | 22 |
| Miscellaneous | 23 |
| Total | 24 |
| Maintenance of Macadam and Dirt Roads: | |
| Dirt Roads | 25 |
| Dirt Wings | 26 |
| Macadam Pavement | 27 |
| Total | 28 |
| Maintenance of Walks, Curbs and Gutters: | |
| Crosswalks | 29 |
| Sidewalks | 30 |
| Curbs | 31 |
| Gutters | 32 |
| Total | 33 |
| Maintenance of Bridges, Viaducts and Retaining Walls: | |
| Bridges and Viaducts | 34 |
| Retaining Walls | 35 |
| Total | 36 |
| Maintenance of Catch Basins, Cesspools, Culverts and Drains: | |
| Catch Basins and Cesspools | 37 |
| Culverts and Drains | 38 |
| Total | 39 |

NEW YORK

THE BOROUGH OF QUEENS.

IN THE CARE OF HIGHWAYS, SEWERS, PUBLIC BUILDINGS AND OFFICES, IN THE BUILDING REGULATIONS, ETC.:

| LINE No. | 1913 | | 1914 | |
|---|---|---|---|---|
| | Items | Totals | Items | Totals |
| 1 | .......... | $28,330 62 | .......... | $42,867 28 |
| 2 | .......... | 11,411 68 | .......... | 11,754 24 |
| 3 | .......... | 25,966 65 | .......... | 26,035 44 |
| 4 | .......... | 9,154 70 | .......... | 9,016 40 |
| 5 | .......... | 3,543 02 | .......... | 3,365 09 |
| 6 | .......... | **$78,406 67** | .......... | **$93,038 45** |
| 7 | .......... | | $21,458 32 | |
| 8 | .......... | | 212,932 43 | |
| 9 | .......... | | 12,254 27 | |
| 10 | .......... | | 2,410 42 | |
| 11 | .......... | | 10,785 97 | |
| 12 | .......... | | 32,767 63 | |
| 13 | .......... | | .......... | **$292,609 04** |
| 14 | .......... | | $22,359 97 | |
| 15 | .......... | | 10,913 35 | |
| 16 | .......... | | 24,717 52 | |
| 17 | .......... | | 23,008 82 | |
| 18 | .......... | | 25,557 79 | |
| 19 | .......... | | 11,788 82 | |
| 20 | .......... | | 16,050 97 | |
| 21 | .......... | | 10,122 88 | |
| 22 | .......... | | 1,615 19 | |
| 23 | .......... | | 2,790 70 | |
| 24 | .......... | | .......... | **$148,926 01** |
| 25 | .......... | | $94,853 09 | |
| 26 | .......... | | 14,725 76 | |
| 27 | .......... | | 199,724 30 | |
| 28 | .......... | | .......... | **$309,303 15** |
| 29 | .......... | | $4,228 66 | |
| 30 | .......... | | 5,044 99 | |
| 31 | .......... | | 2,957 81 | |
| 32 | .......... | | 58,127 69 | |
| 33 | .......... | | .......... | **$70,359 15** |
| 34 | .......... | | $5,095 70 | |
| 35 | .......... | | 6,024 79 | |
| 36 | .......... | | .......... | **$11,120 49** |
| 37 | .......... | | $2,894 75 | |
| 38 | .......... | | 11,381 64 | |
| 39 | .......... | | .......... | **$14,276 39** |

THE CITY OF

OFFICE OF THE PRESIDENT OF

COMPARATIVE SUMMARY, FOR THE YEARS 1913 AND 1914, OF EXPENSES INCURRED
ENFORCEMENT OF

| | LINE No. |
|---|---|
| Bureau of Highways—*Continued* | |
| Maintenance of Street Signs | 1 |
| Control of Street and Sidewalk Incumbrances | 2 |
| Total, Bureau of Highways | 3 |
| BUREAU OF SEWERS. | |
| Administration and Undistributed Expenses: | |
| Executive | 4 |
| Supervision, Stores and Equipment Service | 5 |
| Making of Surveys, Plans and Specifications | 6 |
| Investigation of Complaints and General Inspection | 7 |
| Total | 8 |
| Operation and Maintenance of Sewer System: | |
| Sewers | 9 |
| Manholes | 10 |
| Catch Basins | 11 |
| Culverts | 12 |
| Drains | 13 |
| Miscellaneous | 14 |
| Total | 15 |
| Operation and Maintenance of Disposal Works: | |
| Flushing Screen House | 16 |
| Far Rockaway Disposal Plant | 17 |
| Jamaica Disposal Plant | 18 |
| Newtown Disposal Plant | 19 |
| Total | 20 |
| Total, Bureau of Sewers | 21 |
| TOPOGRAPHICAL BUREAU: | |
| Preparing City Map or Plan | 22 |
| BUREAU OF STREET CLEANING: | |
| Administration | 23 |
| Street Sweeping | 24 |
| Carting | 25 |
| Final Disposition: | |
| Incineration | 26 |
| Dumps | 27 |
| Scow Service—Fifth Ward (Contract) | 28 |
| Snow Removal | 29 |
| Total, Bureau of Street Cleaning | 30 |
| BUREAU OF PUBLIC BUILDINGS AND OFFICES: | |
| Administration | 31 |
| Operation and Maintenance of Offices and Office Buildings: | |
| Supervision and Undistributed Expenses | 32 |
| Town Hall, Flushing | 33 |
| Town Hall, Jamaica | 34 |
| Town Hall, Newtown | 35 |
| Queens County Court House | 36 |
| County Building, Jamaica | 37 |
| Village Hall, Far Rockaway | 38 |
| Borough Hall, L. I. City | 39 |
| Municipal Building, L. I. City | 40 |
| St. Mary's Lyceum, L. I. City (Court Rooms) | 41 |
| Total | 42 |

NEW YORK

THE BOROUGH OF QUEENS—*Continued.*

IN THE CARE OF HIGHWAYS, SEWERS, PUBLIC BUILDINGS AND OFFICES, IN THE BUILDING REGULATIONS, ETC.:—*Continued.*

| LINE No. | 1913 | | 1914 | |
|---|---|---|---|---|
| | Items | Totals | Items | Totals |
| 1 | .......... | | .......... | **$7,450 53** |
| 2 | .......... | | .......... | **1,366 12** |
| 3 | | **$819,880 75** | | ***$855,410 88** |
| 4 | $17,455 46 | | $8,568 96 | |
| 5 | 20,948 94 | | 31,178 05 | |
| 6 | 9,598 44 | | 21,687 62 | |
| 7 | 12,469 86 | | 10,006 10 | |
| 8 | | **$60,472 70** | | **$71,440 73** |
| 9 | $39,566 38 | | $32,835 83 | |
| 0 | 3,325 65 | | 3,311 03 | |
| 1 | 28,156 79 | | 30,043 59 | |
| 2 | 453 40 | | 288 49 | |
| 3 | 13,242 91 | | 16,902 85 | |
| 4 | 837 50 | | 334 00 | |
| 5 | .......... | **$85,582 63** | .......... | **$83,715 79** |
| 6 | .......... | | $3,651 30 | |
| 7 | $27,751 06 | | 27,843 77 | |
| 8 | 14,885 38 | | 16,945 62 | |
| 9 | 15,496 16 | | 20,918 20 | |
| 0 | | **$58,132 60** | | **$69,358 89** |
| 1 | | **$204,187 93** | | **$224,515 41** |
| 2 | | .......... | | **$209,195 47** |
| 3 | .......... | **$12,783 22** | .......... | **$11,976 24** |
| 4 | .......... | **138,328 75** | .......... | **123,501 57** |
| 5 | .......... | **317,006 68** | .......... | **328,277 23** |
| 6 | $8,575 82 | .......... | $8,252 73 | .......... |
| 7 | 18,973 34 | .......... | 22,679 07 | .......... |
| 8 | 8,500 00 | **36,049 16** | 5,052 50 | **35,984 30** |
| 9 | .......... | **1,895 78** | .......... | **56,524 05** |
| 0 | | **$506,063 59** | | **$556,263 39** |
| 1 | .......... | **$8,353 11** | .......... | **$6,181 43** |
| 2 | $4,612 40 | | $7,758 96 | |
| 3 | 5,687 83 | | 5,268 02 | |
| 4 | 5,487 35 | | 7,313 74 | |
| 5 | 2,556 45 | | 2,732 58 | |
| 6 | 31,269 74 | | 28,805 14 | |
| 7 | 5,130 32 | | 5,050 06 | |
| 8 | 1,542 36 | | 1,089 05 | |
| 9 | 15,465 99 | | 14,652 55 | |
| 0 | 1,047 95 | | 304 18 | |
| 1 | 1,996 67 | | 3,465 07 | |
| 2 | .......... | **$74,797 06** | .......... | **$76,439 35** |

OFFICE OF THE PRESIDENT OF

Comparative Summary for the Years 1913 and 1914, of Expenses Incurred
Enforcement of

| | Line No. |
|---|---|
| Bureau of Public Buildings and Offices—*Continued* | |
| Operation and Maintenance of Baths and Comfort Stations: | |
| Interior Bath, L. I. City | 1 |
| Floating Bath, L. I. City | 2 |
| Comfort Station, Jamaica | 3 |
| Total | 4 |
| Telephone Service, Borough President's Department | 5 |
| Work for Other Bureaus, Borough President's Department | 6 |
| Total, Bureau of Public Buildings and Offices | 7 |
| Bureau of Buildings: | |
| Administration | 8 |
| Recording and Reporting Violations of Building Regulations | 9 |
| Inspection of Structural Conditions in Existing Buildings | 10 |
| Regulation of New Building Construction and Alterations: | |
| Supervision | 11 |
| Examination of Plans and Specifications | 12 |
| Inspection | 13 |
| Total | 14 |
| Total, Bureau of Buildings | 15 |
| Departmental Total | 16 |

* Includes $32,000 charged to expense account (at regular rates) for materials which cost the depart-

NEW YORK

THE BOROUGH OF QUEENS—*Continued*

IN THE CARE OF HIGHWAYS, SEWERS, PUBLIC BUILDINGS AND OFFICES, IN THE BUILDING REGULATIONS, ETC.:—*Continued*

| LINE No. | 1913 Items | 1913 Totals | 1914 Items | 1914 Totals |
|---|---|---|---|---|
| 1 | $6,466 30 | | $5,885 15 | |
| 2 | 2,751 59 | | 181 00 | |
| 3 | 1,170 22 | | 2,321 16 | |
| 4 | .......... | **$10,388 11** | .......... | **$8,387 31** |
| 5 | .......... | **$3,864 31** | .......... | **$2,284 69** |
| 6 | .......... | **687 91** | .......... | **1,599 71** |
| 7 | .......... | **$98,090 50** | .......... | **$94,892 49** |
| 8 | .......... | **$21,053 65** | .......... | **$21,576 37** |
| 9 | .......... | **1,194 76** | .......... | **1,520 37** |
| 10 | .......... | **813 32** | .......... | **1,224 05** |
| 11 | $2,056 78 | | $3,514 97 | |
| 12 | 7,163 14 | | 8,548 45 | |
| 13 | 46,519 06 | | 43,946 84 | |
| 14 | .......... | **$55,738 98** | .......... | **$56,010 26** |
| 15 | .......... | **$78,800 71** | .......... | **$80,331 05** |
| 16 | .......... | **$1,785,430 15** | .......... | ***$2,113,647 14** |

ment nothing.

## THE CITY OF

### DEPARTMENT OF PARKS—

SUMMARY FOR THE YEAR 1914 OF EXPENSES CLASSIFIED ACCORDING

| | Supervision and Unclassified Expenses | LINE No. |
|---|---|---|
| PARK BOARD | **$30,039 77** | 1 |
| BOROUGHS OF MANHATTAN AND RICHMOND: | | |
| General Administration | $77,361 41 | 2 |
| Operation and Maintenance of Parks and Playgrounds—Manhattan | 77,414 74 | 3 |
| Operation and Maintenance of Parks and Playgrounds—Richmond | 994 48 | 4 |
| Operation and Maintenance of Parkways—Manhattan | 2,435 91 | 5 |
| Operation and Maintenance of Recreation Piers | .......... | 6 |
| City Streets—Care of Trees and Snow Removal | 4,135 91 | 7 |
| Music and Celebrations | 56,654 40 | 8 |
| Menagerie | 40,213 49 | 9 |
| Undistributed Expenses | 146,809 71 | 10 |
| Work Done for Other Departments | 165 85 | 11 |
| Total, Boroughs of Manhattan and Richmond | **$406,185 90** | 12 |
| BOROUGH OF BROOKLYN: | | |
| General Administration | $47,840 63 | 13 |
| Operation and Maintenance of Parks and Playgrounds | 67,287 65 | 14 |
| Operation and Maintenance of Parkways | 13,494 34 | 15 |
| City Streets—Care of Trees | .......... | 16 |
| Music and Celebrations | 20,205 73 | 17 |
| Menagerie | 22,422 99 | 18 |
| Undistributed Expenses | 96,431 67 | 19 |
| Total, Borough of Brooklyn | **$267,683 01** | 20 |
| BOROUGH OF THE BRONX: | | |
| General Administration | $34,172 51 | 21 |
| Operation and Maintenance of Parks and Playgrounds | 29,734 07 | 22 |
| Operation and Maintenance of Parkways | 4,190 60 | 23 |
| City Streets—Care of Trees | .......... | 24 |
| Music and Celebrations | 6,099 11 | 25 |
| Omnibus Line Operation | 11,160 61 | 26 |
| Undistributed Expenses | 49,013 20 | 27 |
| Total, Borough of The Bronx | **$134,370 10** | 28 |
| BOROUGH OF QUEENS: | | |
| General Administration | $27,894 07 | 29 |
| Operation and Maintenance of Improved Parks | 4,526 99 | 30 |
| Care of Undeveloped Park Areas | 1,113 10 | 31 |
| City Streets—Care of Trees | 6,063 76 | 32 |
| Music and Celebrations | 4,221 26 | 33 |
| Menagerie—Forest Park | 750 18 | 34 |
| Undistributed Expenses | 51,544 33 | 35 |
| Total, Borough of Queens | **$96,113 69** | 36 |
| Total, All Boroughs | **$934,392 47** | 37 |

NEW YORK

ALL BOROUGHS

TO FUNCTIONS PERFORMED OR CHARACTER OF WORK DONE

| LINE No. | Care of Roads, Paths and Driveways | Care of Grounds Including Trees and Plants | Playgrounds, Athletic Fields and School Farms | Care of Bath Houses and Comfort Stations | Operation and Maintenance of Other Park Buildings, Improvements and Properties | Total |
|---|---|---|---|---|---|---|
| 1 | .......... | .......... | .......... | .......... | .......... | **$30,039 77** |
| 2 | .......... | .......... | .......... | .......... | .......... | $77,361 41 |
| 3 | $156,264 98 | $113,792 84 | $124,360 63 | $120,391 35 | $65,627 40 | 657,851 94 |
| 4 | 2,077 52 | 710 75 | 728 86 | .......... | 503 63 | 5,015 24 |
| 5 | 7,132 35 | 9,962 38 | .......... | 570 15 | 5,787 60 | 25,888 39 |
| 6 | .......... | .......... | 919 61 | .......... | .......... | 919 61 |
| 7 | .......... | 11,198 13 | .......... | .......... | .......... | 15,334 04 |
| 8 | .......... | .......... | .......... | .......... | .......... | 56,654 40 |
| 9 | .......... | .......... | .......... | .......... | .......... | 40,213 49 |
| 10 | .......... | 33,879 45 | .......... | .......... | 2,103 21 | 182,792 37 |
| 11 | .......... | .......... | .......... | .......... | .......... | 165 85 |
| 12 | **$165,474 85** | **$169,543 55** | **$126,009 10** | **$120,961 50** | **$74,021 84** | **$1,062,196 74** |
| 13 | .......... | .......... | .......... | .......... | .......... | $47,840 63 |
| 14 | $75,655 43 | $123,709 28 | $41,979 77 | $61,568 85 | $59,293 33 | 429,494 31 |
| 15 | 101,415 69 | 17,550 32 | .......... | .......... | 5,956 95 | 138,417 30 |
| 16 | .......... | 49,000 33 | .......... | .......... | .......... | 49,000 33 |
| 17 | .......... | .......... | .......... | .......... | .......... | 20,205 73 |
| 18 | .......... | .......... | .......... | .......... | .......... | 22,422 99 |
| 19 | .......... | 33,878 67 | .......... | .......... | 13,219 81 | 143,530 15 |
| 20 | **$177,071 12** | **$224,138 60** | **$41,979 77** | **$61,568 85** | **$78,470 09** | **$850,911 44** |
| 21 | .......... | .......... | .......... | .......... | .......... | $34,172 51 |
| 22 | $74,320 70 | $50,185 11 | $45,177 59 | $23,808 84 | $26,352 12 | 249,578 43 |
| 23 | 46,933 40 | 4,592 71 | 97 37 | .......... | 595 33 | 56,409 41 |
| 24 | .......... | 17,177 15 | .......... | .......... | .......... | 17,177 15 |
| 25 | .......... | .......... | .......... | .......... | .......... | 6,099 11 |
| 26 | .......... | .......... | .......... | .......... | .......... | 11,160 61 |
| 27 | 4,166 88 | 39,343 11 | .......... | .......... | 7,436 08 | 99,959 27 |
| 28 | **$125,420 98** | **$111,298 08** | **$45,274 96** | **$23,808 84** | **$34,383 53** | **$474,556 49** |
| 29 | .......... | .......... | .......... | .......... | .......... | $27,894 07 |
| 30 | $16,975 31 | $22,870 66 | $7,968 17 | $4,245 10 | $17,165 08 | 73,751 31 |
| 31 | 851 93 | 1,207 07 | .......... | .......... | 196 37 | 3,368 47 |
| 32 | .......... | 13,874 36 | .......... | .......... | .......... | 19,938 12 |
| 33 | .......... | .......... | .......... | .......... | .......... | 4,221 26 |
| 34 | .......... | .......... | .......... | .......... | .......... | 750 18 |
| 35 | .......... | .......... | .......... | .......... | .......... | 51,544 33 |
| 36 | **$17,827 24** | **$37,952 09** | **$7,968 17** | **$4,245 10** | **$17,361 45** | **$181,467 74** |
| 37 | **$485,794 19** | **$542,932 32** | **$221,232 00** | **$210,584 29** | **$204,236 91** | **$2,599,172 18** |

DEPARTMENT OF PARKS—BOROUGHS OF

SUMMARY FOR THE YEAR 1914 OF EXPENSES FOR EACH PARK, CLASSIFIED

| | Supervision and Unclassified Expenses | LINE No. |
|---|---|---|
| GENERAL ADMINISTRATION | **$77,361 41** | 1 |
| OPERATION AND MAINTENANCE OF PARKS AND PLAYGROUNDS—MANHATTAN: | | |
| Abingdon Square | | 2 |
| Battery Park | $1,727 72 | 3 |
| Bennet Field | .......... | 4 |
| Bryant Park | 1,343 73 | 5 |
| Carmensville Playground—152d Street and Amsterdam Avenue | 2 26 | 6 |
| Central Park | 24,066 15 | 7 |
| Chelsea Park | 1,349 70 | 8 |
| Cherry and Market Streets Playground | .......... | 9 |
| City Hall Park | 1,097 14 | 10 |
| Clark Playground | .......... | 11 |
| Colonial Park | 1,320 92 | 12 |
| Columbus Park | 1,034 97 | 13 |
| Corlear's Hook Park | 436 58 | 14 |
| De Witt Clinton Park | 681 35 | 15 |
| Hamilton Fish Park | 443 41 | 16 |
| Five Points Playground | .......... | 17 |
| 5th Avenue and 138th Street Playground | .......... | 18 |
| Fort Washington Park | 202 66 | 19 |
| Grace Playground | .......... | 20 |
| Highbridge Park | 215 95 | 21 |
| Hudson Park | 917 55 | 22 |
| Isham Park | 506 72 | 23 |
| Jasper Oval | .......... | 24 |
| Jeanette Park | .......... | 25 |
| Jackson Square | .......... | 26 |
| John Jay Park | 264 44 | 27 |
| Thomas Jefferson Park | 2,486 60 | 28 |
| Madison Square Park | 486 01 | 29 |
| Manhattan Square Park | 743 65 | 30 |
| Morningside Park | 2,472 55 | 31 |
| Roger Morris Park | 309 14 | 32 |
| Mount Morris Park | 1,749 61 | 33 |
| Queensboro Playground | .......... | 34 |
| Riverside Park | 11,520 10 | 35 |
| Ryan Park | .......... | 36 |
| St. Gabriel's Park | 1,227 49 | 37 |
| St. Nicholas Park | 1,305 96 | 38 |
| Carl Schurz Park | 2,123 51 | 39 |
| Wm. H. Seward Park | 2,190 54 | 40 |
| Stuyvesant Park | 1,145 32 | 41 |
| 17th and 18th Streets, Avenue C and East River Park | 113 46 | 42 |
| 67th Street and West End Avenue Playground | .......... | 43 |
| Tompkins Square | 1,891 36 | 44 |
| Union Square | 745 74 | 45 |
| Washington Square | 699 54 | 46 |
| Water Gate Playground | .......... | 47 |
| West 59th Street Playground | .......... | 48 |
| West 122nd Street | .......... | 49 |
| Yorkville Playground | .......... | 50 |
| Small Parks, Squares and Triangles | 3,444 57 | 51 |
| Small Playgrounds | .......... | 52 |
| Undistributed Expenses | 7,148 34 | 53 |
| Total, Operation and Maintenance of Parks and Playgrounds—Manhattan | **$77,414 74** | 54 |
| OPERATION AND MAINTENANCE OF PARKS AND PLAYGROUNDS—RICHMOND: | | |
| Silver Lake | $408 36 | 55 |
| Washington Park | 262 70 | 56 |

# NEW YORK

## MANHATTAN AND RICHMOND

According to Functions Performed or Character of Work Done:

| LINE No. | Care of Roads, Paths and Driveways | Care of Grounds Including Trees and Plants | Playgrounds Athletic Fields and School Farms | Care of Bath Houses and Comfort Stations | Operation and Maintenance of Other Park Buildings Improvements and Properties | Total |
|---|---|---|---|---|---|---|
| 1 | .......... | .......... | .......... | .......... | .......... | **$77,361 41** |
| 2 | .......... | .......... | $287 28 | .......... | .......... | $287 28 |
| 3 | $4,740 98 | $2,230 79 | 912 26 | $1,836 95 | $1,194 69 | 12,643 39 |
| 4 | .......... | .......... | 347 70 | .......... | .......... | 347 70 |
| 5 | 3,255 92 | 2,558 38 | .......... | 4,465 26 | 295 05 | 11,918 34 |
| 6 | .......... | 83 07 | 3,454 91 | .......... | 3,530 57 | 7,070 81 |
| 7 | 65,163 59 | 60,034 65 | 7,189 84 | 22,074 21 | 19,433 01 | 197,961 45 |
| 8 | 1,113 04 | 311 15 | 3,960 46 | 3,373 12 | 224 20 | 10,331 67 |
| 9 | .......... | .......... | 2,264 52 | .......... | .......... | 2,264 52 |
| 10 | 5,232 29 | 2,444 65 | .......... | .......... | 488 50 | 9,262 58 |
| 11 | .......... | .......... | 526 14 | .......... | .......... | 526 14 |
| 12 | 2,555 78 | 788 68 | 1,146 38 | .......... | 279 27 | 6,091 03 |
| 13 | 1,302 87 | 70 92 | 1,217 99 | 3,474 59 | 129 00 | 7,230 34 |
| 14 | 1,698 32 | 553 42 | 5,037 56 | 2,754 74 | 411 18 | 10,891 80 |
| 15 | 2,084 82 | 334 01 | 7,811 94 | 8,267 87 | 826 38 | 20,006 37 |
| 16 | 1,908 78 | 458 55 | 5,584 68 | 4,710 52 | 357 47 | 13,463 41 |
| 17 | .......... | .......... | 1,483 66 | .......... | 577 23 | 2,060 89 |
| 18 | .......... | .......... | 693 20 | .......... | .......... | 693 20 |
| 19 | 1,064 46 | 233 88 | .......... | 17 17 | 284 13 | 1,802 30 |
| 20 | .......... | .......... | 178 15 | .......... | 16 46 | 194 61 |
| 21 | 335 92 | 1,177 01 | 1,069 64 | .......... | 694 76 | 3,493 28 |
| 22 | 1,185 00 | 469 99 | 2,594 48 | 2,750 82 | 672 75 | 8,590 59 |
| 23 | 717 39 | 953 53 | 1,321 68 | .......... | 432 55 | 3,931 87 |
| 24 | .......... | .......... | 2,211 58 | .......... | 12 77 | 2,224 35 |
| 25 | .......... | .......... | 121 57 | .......... | .......... | 121 57 |
| 26 | .......... | .......... | 258 58 | .......... | .......... | 258 58 |
| 27 | 5 12 | 101 17 | 4,065 47 | .......... | 2,926 50 | 7,362 70 |
| 28 | 2,155 88 | 258 96 | 9,327 29 | 8,561 45 | 1,684 23 | 24,474 41 |
| 29 | 2,710 44 | 2,817 14 | .......... | 2,983 77 | 240 93 | 9,238 29 |
| 30 | 748 27 | 175 75 | .......... | .......... | 9 89 | 1,677 56 |
| 31 | 4,829 23 | 826 91 | 8 24 | 1,920 28 | 614 51 | 10,671 72 |
| 32 | 646 20 | 468 55 | .......... | .......... | 44 30 | 1,468 19 |
| 33 | 2,844 48 | 1,578 66 | 263 28 | 3,161 24 | 318 75 | 9,916 02 |
| 34 | .......... | 12 56 | 3,214 99 | .......... | 1,021 79 | 4,249 34 |
| 35 | 24,244 77 | 12,690 54 | 1,056 37 | 16,039 29 | 3,758 54 | 69,309 61 |
| 36 | .......... | .......... | 1,463 73 | .......... | 81 00 | 1,544 73 |
| 37 | 1,409 77 | 752 48 | 4,140 54 | .......... | 439 33 | 7,969 01 |
| 38 | 2,587 76 | 752 34 | 148 41 | .......... | 503 17 | 5,297 64 |
| 39 | 2,111 23 | 352 87 | 2,417 78 | 3,640 09 | 462 20 | 11,107 68 |
| 40 | 2,029 28 | 799 36 | 4,739 85 | 10,820 54 | 833 08 | 21,412 65 |
| 41 | 1,756 72 | 1,481 17 | .......... | 1,487 08 | 198 57 | 6,068 86 |
| 42 | 641 86 | 79 54 | 1,836 61 | 1,465 34 | 178 72 | 4,315 53 |
| 43 | .......... | .......... | 290 90 | .......... | .......... | 290 90 |
| 44 | 2,899 54 | 2,293 54 | 4,788 99 | 3,390 99 | 560 18 | 15,824 60 |
| 45 | 1,427 27 | 536 48 | .......... | 3,607 26 | 167 48 | 6,484 23 |
| 46 | 3,445 38 | 2,424 63 | .......... | 1,662 48 | 791 95 | 9,023 98 |
| 47 | .......... | .......... | 1,004 72 | .......... | .......... | 1,004 72 |
| 48 | .......... | .......... | 3,098 01 | .......... | 2,316 88 | 5,414 89 |
| 49 | 43 16 | .......... | .......... | .......... | .......... | 43 16 |
| 50 | .......... | .......... | 5,810 44 | .......... | 3,700 35 | 9,510 79 |
| 51 | 5,937 41 | 2,042 22 | 2 74 | 5,268 64 | 1,489 77 | 18,185 35 |
| 52 | .......... | .......... | 253 42 | .......... | .......... | 253 42 |
| 53 | 1,432 05 | 10,645 29 | 26,754 65 | 2,657 65 | 13,425 31 | 62,063 29 |
| 54 | **$156,264 98** | **$113,792 84** | **$124,360 63** | **$120,391 35** | **$65,627 40** | **$657,851 94** |
| 55 | $314 38 | $144 50 | .......... | .......... | .......... | $867 24 |
| 56 | 969 82 | 276 25 | .......... | .......... | $380 76 | 1,889 53 |

DEPARTMENT OF PARKS—BOROUGH OF

SUMMARY FOR THE YEAR 1914 OF EXPENSES FOR EACH PARK, CLASSIFIED

| | Supervision and Unclassified Expenses | LINE No. |
|---|---|---|
| OPERATION AND MAINTENANCE—*Continued* | | |
| Broadway, Bennett Street, Heberton Avenue, Vreeland Street, Port Richmond.. | $234 98 | 1 |
| Maine and Willard Avenues, Westerleigh | 88 44 | 2 |
| Alaska Field | .......... | 3 |
| Curtis Field | .......... | 4 |
| St. Peter's Field | .......... | 5 |
| Total, Operation and Maintenance of Parks and Playgrounds—Richmond | **$994 48** | 6 |
| OPERATION AND MAINTENANCE OF PARKWAYS—MANHATTAN: | | |
| Broadway | $249 30 | 7 |
| Delancey Street | 118 46 | 8 |
| Harlem River Driveway | 1,476 37 | 9 |
| Park Avenue | 290 12 | 10 |
| Seventh Avenue | 134 20 | 11 |
| Washington Bridge | 167 46 | 12 |
| Total, Operation and Maintenance of Parkways—Manhattan | **$2,435 91** | 13 |
| OPERATION AND MAINTENANCE OF RECREATION PIERS: | | |
| East 3d Street Pier | .......... | 14 |
| Market Street Pier | .......... | 15 |
| East 24th Street Pier | .......... | 16 |
| East 112th Street Pier | .......... | 17 |
| West 50th Street Pier | .......... | 18 |
| Barrow Street Pier | .......... | 19 |
| West 129th Street Pier | .......... | 20 |
| Albany Street Pier | .......... | 21 |
| Total, Operation and Maintenance of Recreation Piers | .......... | 22 |
| CITY STREETS: | | |
| Care of Trees—Manhattan | .......... | 23 |
| Care of Trees—Richmond | .......... | 24 |
| Snow Removal | $4,135 91 | 25 |
| Total, City Streets | **$4,135 91** | 26 |
| MUSIC AND CELEBRATIONS | **$56,654 40** | 27 |
| MENAGERIE | **$40,213 49** | 28 |
| UNDISTRIBUTED EXPENSES: | | |
| Automobile Service | $8,330 18 | 29 |
| General Park Equipment | 17,546 81 | 30 |
| Greenhouses and Nursery | .......... | 31 |
| Stables | 66,749 95 | 32 |
| Manure Pit | 7,395 19 | 33 |
| Shops-Overhead | 32,868 62 | 34 |
| 79th Street Storage Yard | 5,302 93 | 35 |
| 97th Street Storage Yard | 5,967 60 | 36 |
| Miscellaneous Expenses | 2,648 43 | 37 |
| Small Buildings, all Parks except Central Park | .......... | 38 |
| Total, Undistributed Expenses | **$146,809 71** | 39 |
| Work Done for Other Departments | **$165 85** | 40 |
| Departmental Totals | **$406,185 90** | 41 |

NEW YORK

MANHATTAN AND RICHMOND—*Continued*

According to Functions Performed or Character of Work Done—*Continued*

| Line No. | Care of Roads, Paths and Driveways | Care of Grounds Including Trees and Plants | Playgrounds Athletic Fields and School Farms | Care of Bath Houses and Comfort Stations | Operation and Maintenance of Other Park Buildings, Improvements and Properties | Total |
|---|---|---|---|---|---|---|
| 1 | $732 07 | $202 50 | .......... | .......... | $122 87 | $1,292 42 |
| 2 | 61 25 | 87 50 | $275 83 | .......... | .......... | 513 02 |
| 3 | .......... | .......... | 1 21 | .......... | .......... | 1 21 |
| 4 | .......... | .......... | 4 05 | .......... | .......... | 4 05 |
| 5 | .......... | .......... | 447 77 | .......... | .......... | 447 77 |
| 6 | **$2,077 52** | **$710 75** | **$728 86** | .......... | **$503 63** | **$5,015 24** |
| 7 | $748 31 | $5,018 11 | .......... | .......... | $650 79 | $6,666 51 |
| 8 | 739 73 | 613 95 | .......... | .......... | 163 12 | 1,635 26 |
| 9 | 4,610 17 | 322 16 | .......... | $570 15 | 1,597 43 | 8,576 28 |
| 10 | 283 97 | 3,049 07 | .......... | .......... | 3,082 16 | 6,705 32 |
| 11 | 82 03 | 758 59 | .......... | .......... | 266 66 | 1,241 48 |
| 12 | 668 14 | 200 50 | .......... | .......... | 27 44 | 1,063 54 |
| 13 | **$7,132 35** | **$9,962 38** | .......... | **$570 15** | **$5,787 60** | **$25,888 39** |
| 14 | .......... | .......... | $158 61 | .......... | .......... | $158 61 |
| 15 | .......... | .......... | 72 29 | .......... | .......... | 72 29 |
| 16 | .......... | .......... | 163 22 | .......... | .......... | 163 22 |
| 17 | .......... | .......... | 119 26 | .......... | .......... | 119 26 |
| 18 | .......... | .......... | 160 02 | .......... | .......... | 160 02 |
| 19 | .......... | .......... | 110 01 | .......... | .......... | 110 01 |
| 20 | .......... | .......... | 120 20 | .......... | .......... | 120 20 |
| 21 | .......... | .......... | 16 00 | .......... | .......... | 16 00 |
| 22 | .......... | .......... | **$919 61** | .......... | .......... | **$919 61** |
| 23 | .......... | $7,621 59 | .......... | .......... | .......... | $7,621 59 |
| 24 | .......... | 3,576 54 | .......... | .......... | .......... | 3,576 54 |
| 25 | .......... | .......... | .......... | .......... | .......... | 4,135 91 |
| 26 | .......... | **$11,198 13** | .......... | .......... | .......... | **$15,334 04** |
| 27 | .......... | .......... | .......... | .......... | .......... | **$56,654 40** |
| 28 | .......... | .......... | .......... | .......... | .......... | **$40,213 49** |
| 29 | .......... | .......... | .......... | .......... | .......... | $8,330 18 |
| 30 | .......... | .......... | .......... | .......... | .......... | 17,546 81 |
| 31 | .......... | $33,879 45 | .......... | .......... | .......... | 33,879 45 |
| 32 | .......... | .......... | .......... | .......... | .......... | 66,749 95 |
| 33 | .......... | .......... | .......... | .......... | .......... | 7,395 19 |
| 34 | .......... | .......... | .......... | .......... | .......... | 32,868 62 |
| 35 | .......... | .......... | .......... | .......... | .......... | 5,302 93 |
| 36 | .......... | .......... | .......... | .......... | .......... | 5,967 60 |
| 37 | .......... | .......... | .......... | .......... | .......... | 2,648 43 |
| 38 | .......... | .......... | .......... | .......... | $2,103 21 | 2,103 21 |
| 39 | .......... | **$33,879 45** | .......... | .......... | **$2,103 21** | **$182,792 37** |
| 40 | .......... | .......... | .......... | .......... | .......... | **$165 85** |
| 41 | **$165,474 85** | **$169,543 55** | **$126,009 10** | **$120,961 50** | **$74,021 84** | **$1,062,196 74** |

## DEPARTMENT OF PARKS—

### Comparative Summary of Expenses for the Years 1913 and 1914

| | Supervision and Unclassified Expenses | Care of Roads, Paths and Driveways | Line No. |
|---|---|---|---|
| General Administration | *$39,295 50* | .......... | 1 |
| | 34,172 51 | .......... | 2 |
| Operation and Maintenance of Parks and Playgrounds: | | | |
| Bronx Park | *$3,352 08* | *$4,578 90* | 3 |
| | 1,796 50 | 3,864 45 | 4 |
| Claremont Park | *1,906 75* | *3,156 05* | 5 |
| | 2,354 34 | 3,773 34 | 6 |
| Crotona Park | *4,737 49* | *12,119 15* | 7 |
| | 4,824 34 | 18,598 53 | 8 |
| De Voe Park | *184 83* | *1,224 75* | 9 |
| | 325 05 | 780 12 | 10 |
| Echo Park | *976 33* | *737 50* | 11 |
| | 1,075 13 | 902 66 | 12 |
| McCombs Dam Park | *3,497 22* | *3,791 47* | 13 |
| | 2,412 00 | 5,585 18 | 14 |
| Melrose Park | .......... | *184 00* | 15 |
| | .......... | 93 13 | 16 |
| Pelham Bay Park | *7,553 96* | *16,293 91* | 17 |
| | 5,714 02 | 17,019 14 | 18 |
| Poe Park | *103 94* | *555 88* | 19 |
| | 160 60 | 370 38 | 20 |
| St. James Park | *1,334 23* | *1,883 91* | 21 |
| | 904 71 | 1,196 25 | 22 |
| St. Mary's Park | *2,945 03* | *10,568 59* | 23 |
| | 2,265 75 | 3,691 30 | 24 |
| Franz Sigel Park | *2,088 19* | *3,211 35* | 25 |
| | 1,287 75 | 2,279 19 | 26 |
| University Park | *96 46* | *323 31* | 27 |
| | 160 60 | 245 19 | 28 |
| Van Cortlandt Park | *6,941 19* | *13,344 74* | 29 |
| | 6,225 54 | 13,743 98 | 30 |
| Washington Bridge Park | *65 47* | *542 64* | 31 |
| | 27 50 | 447 50 | 32 |
| Small Parks, Squares and Triangles | *102 34* | *1,068 81* | 33 |
| | 200 24 | 1,730 36 | 34 |
| Total Parks and Playgrounds | *$35,885 51* | *$73,584 96* | 35 |
| | 29,734 07 | 74,320 70 | 36 |
| Operation and Maintenance of Parkways: | | | |
| Bronx and Pelham Parkway | *$2,462 25* | *$15,082 22* | 37 |
| | 1,621 67 | 14,430 91 | 38 |
| Crotona Parkway | *15 02* | *1,041 87* | 39 |
| | .......... | 485 57 | 40 |
| Mosholu Parkway | *1,486 32* | *5,601 35* | 41 |
| | 1,211 18 | 11,152 77 | 42 |
| Roads in N. Y. Botanical Garden | *354 00* | *1,666 32* | 43 |
| | .......... | 2,356 32 | 44 |
| Spuyten Duyvil Parkway | *1,306 27* | *4,147 09* | 45 |
| | 1,357 75 | 18,507 83 | 46 |
| Total Parkways | *$5,623 86* | *$27,538 85* | 47 |
| | 4,190 60 | 46,933 40 | 48 |

Note—1913 Expenses in Italics. 1914 Expenses in Roman.

NEW YORK

BOROUGH OF THE BRONX

(SEE NOTE), ON BASIS OF COST BY FUNCTIONS FOR EACH PARK

| LINE No. | Care of Grounds Including Trees and Plants | Playgrounds and Athletic Fields | Care of Bath Houses and Comfort Stations | Operation and Maintenance of Other Park Buildings Improvements and Properties | Total |
|---|---|---|---|---|---|
| 1 | .......... | .......... | .......... | .......... | *$39,295 50* |
| 2 | .......... | .......... | .......... | .......... | 34,172 51 |
| 3 | *$5,490 87* | *$174 85* | *$374 40* | *$2,732 41* | *$16,703 51* |
| 4 | 3,556 41 | 536 32 | 429 17 | 1,638 33 | 11,821 18 |
| 5 | *6,413 42* | *780 91* | *951 61* | *4,047 07* | *17,255 81* |
| 6 | 4,762 91 | 1,877 11 | 1,077 35 | 3,841 20 | 17,686 25 |
| 7 | *8,245 59* | *2,349 15* | *2,712 03* | *757 35* | *30,920 76* |
| 8 | 6,157 16 | 5,890 50 | 2,973 34 | 1,915 09 | 40,358 96 |
| 9 | *878 79* | *481 17* | .......... | *302 77* | *3,072 31* |
| 10 | 2,120 80 | 175 50 | .......... | 28 05 | 3,429 52 |
| 11 | *1,524 33* | .......... | .......... | *346 94* | *3,585 10* |
| 12 | 1,436 07 | 96 44 | .......... | 511 40 | 4,021 70 |
| 13 | *2,098 01* | *2,891 21* | *195 29* | *2,803 02* | *15,276 22* |
| 14 | 2,874 51 | 6,472 18 | 1,506 19 | 1,543 74 | 20,393 80 |
| 15 | *3 75* | .......... | .......... | .......... | *187 75* |
| 16 | 439 75 | .......... | .......... | 147 98 | 680 86 |
| 17 | *18,284 74* | *9,273 75* | *8,623 47* | *5,367 85* | *65,397 68* |
| 18 | 8,082 87 | 9,229 31 | 8,094 03 | 2,804 08 | 50,943 45 |
| 19 | *318 18* | *26 25* | .......... | *1,245 27* | *2,249 52* |
| 20 | 498 18 | .......... | .......... | 357 77 | 1,386 93 |
| 21 | *1,649 62* | *280 24* | *1,401 30* | *41 75* | *6,591 05* |
| 22 | 1,747 29 | 1,121 71 | 1,200 92 | 225 95 | 6,396 83 |
| 23 | *2,383 20* | *339 59* | *1,903 40* | *453 34* | *18,593 15* |
| 24 | 3,632 88 | 1,753 45 | 4,779 68 | 1,432 32 | 17,555 38 |
| 25 | *1,360 13* | *48 75* | *1,329 29* | *95 27* | *8,132 98* |
| 26 | 1,479 60 | 122 56 | 1,212 70 | 165 25 | 6,547 05 |
| 27 | *599 33* | .......... | .......... | .......... | *1,019 10* |
| 28 | 583 13 | .......... | .......... | 24 00 | 1,012 92 |
| 29 | *13,496 74* | *8,179 77* | *2,447 76* | *10,049 57* | *54,459 77* |
| 30 | 10,167 20 | 17,820 71 | 2,474 56 | 10,715 30 | 61,147 29 |
| 31 | *843 11* | *17 50* | *162 48* | *93 73* | *1,724 93* |
| 32 | 810 50 | .......... | 60 90 | 70 38 | 1,416 78 |
| 33 | *1,055 63* | .......... | .......... | *1,153 12* | *3,379 90* |
| 34 | 1,835 85 | 81 80 | .......... | 931 28 | 4,779 53 |
| 35 | *$64,645 44* | *$24,843 14* | *$20,101 03* | *$29,489 46* | *$248,549 54* |
| 36 | 50,185 11 | 45,177 59 | 23,808 84 | 26,352 12 | 249,578 43 |
| 37 | *$4,352 02* | .......... | .......... | *$132 58* | *$22,029 07* |
| 38 | 2,041 31 | .......... | .......... | 375 27 | 18,469 16 |
| 39 | *104 69* | .......... | .......... | *1 25* | *1,162 83* |
| 40 | 177 87 | .......... | .......... | 6 25 | 669 69 |
| 41 | *2,825 80* | .......... | .......... | *156 70* | *10,070 17* |
| 42 | 1,962 09 | $97 37 | .......... | 146 06 | 14,569 47 |
| 43 | .......... | .......... | .......... | .......... | *2,020 32* |
| 44 | .......... | .......... | .......... | .......... | 2,356 32 |
| 45 | *789 10* | .......... | .......... | *8 75* | *6,251 21* |
| 46 | 411 44 | .......... | .......... | 67 75 | 20,344 77 |
| 47 | *$8,071 61* | .......... | .......... | *$299 28* | *$41,533 60* |
| 48 | 4,592 71 | $97 37 | .......... | 595 33 | 56,409 41 |

DEPARTMENT OF PARKS—

COMPARATIVE SUMMARY OF EXPENSES FOR THE YEARS 1913 AND 1914

| | Supervision and Unclassified Expenses | Care of Roads, Paths and Driveways | LINE No. |
|---|---|---|---|
| CITY STREETS—CARE OF TREES | .......... | .......... | 1 |
| | .......... | .......... | 2 |
| OMNIBUS LINE OPERATION | $11,160 61 | .......... | 3 |
| MUSIC AND CELEBRATIONS | *$6,763 65* | .......... | 4 |
| | 6,099 11 | .......... | 5 |
| UNDISTRIBUTED EXPENSES: | | | |
| Automobile Service | *$4,953 50* | .......... | 6 |
| | 6,637 20 | .......... | 7 |
| Supervision and General Expense Undistributed | .......... | .......... | 8 |
| | 3,850 19 | .......... | 9 |
| General Park Equipment | *9,825 51* | .......... | 10 |
| | 7,452 92 | .......... | 11 |
| Greenhouses and Nursery | .......... | .......... | 12 |
| | .......... | .......... | 13 |
| Stables | *21,980 59* | .......... | 14 |
| | 22,371 66 | .......... | 15 |
| Shops | *9,689 62* | .......... | 16 |
| | 8,701 23 | .......... | 17 |
| Stone Crushing | .......... | $4,166 88 | 18 |
| Total Undistributed Expenses | *$46,449 22* | .......... | 19 |
| | 49,013 20 | $4,166 88 | 20 |
| Departmental Total | *$134,017 74* | *$101,123 81* | 21 |
| | 134,370 10 | 125,420 98 | 22 |

NOTE—1913 Expenses in Italics 1914 Expenses in Roman.

NEW YORK

BOROUGH OF THE BRONX—*Continued*

(SEE NOTE), ON BASIS OF COST BY FUNCTIONS FOR EACH PARK—*Continued*

| LINE No. | Care of Grounds Including Trees and Plants | Playgrounds and Athletic Fields | Care of Bath Houses and Comfort Stations | Operation and Maintenance of Other Park Buildings Improvements and Properties | Total |
|---|---|---|---|---|---|
| 1 | *$21,220 10* | .......... | .......... | .......... | *$21,220 10* |
| 2 | 17,177 15 | .......... | .......... | .......... | 17,177 15 |
| 3 | .......... | .......... | .......... | .......... | $11,160 61 |
| 4 | .......... | .......... | .......... | .......... | *$6,763 65* |
| 5 | .......... | .......... | .......... | .......... | 6,099 11 |
| 6 | .......... | .......... | .......... | .......... | *$4,953 50* |
| 7 | .......... | .......... | .......... | .......... | 6,637 20 |
| 8 | .......... | .......... | .......... | *$7,342 35* | *7,342 35* |
| 9 | $2,226 50 | .......... | .......... | 7,436 08 | 13,512 77 |
| 10 | .......... | .......... | .......... | .......... | *9,825 51* |
| 11 | .......... | .......... | .......... | .......... | 7,452 92 |
| 12 | *37,763 00* | .......... | .......... | .......... | *37,763 00* |
| 13 | 37,116 61 | .......... | .......... | .......... | 37,116 61 |
| 14 | .......... | .......... | .......... | .......... | *21,980 59* |
| 15 | .......... | .......... | .......... | .......... | 22,371 66 |
| 16 | .......... | .......... | .......... | .......... | *9,689 62* |
| 17 | .......... | .......... | .......... | .......... | 8,701 23 |
| 18 | .......... | .......... | .......... | .......... | 4,166 88 |
| 19 | *$37,763 00* | .......... | .......... | *$7,342 35* | *$91,554 57* |
| 20 | 39,343 11 | .......... | .......... | 7,436 08 | 99,959 27 |
| 21 | *$131,700 15* | *$24,843 14* | *$20,101 03* | *$37,131 09* | *$448,916 96* |
| 22 | 111,298 08 | 45,274 96 | 23,808 84 | 34,383 53 | 474,556 49 |

DEPARTMENT OF PARKS,

Summary for the Year 1914 of Expenses for Each Park, Classified

| | Supervision and Unclassified Expenses | Care of Roads, Paths and Driveways | Line No. |
|---|---|---|---|
| General Administration | **$47,840 63** | .......... | 1 |
| Operation and Maintenance of Parks and Playgrounds: | | | |
| Ammerfort Park | $773 88 | $502 63 | 2 |
| Bedford Park | 1,288 09 | 1,187 38 | 3 |
| Bensonhurst Park | 682 05 | 1,311 16 | 4 |
| Borough Hall Park | 235 61 | 1,734 14 | 5 |
| Bushwick Park | 1,279 27 | 1,744 95 | 6 |
| Bushwick Playground | 1,072 21 | 30 76 | 7 |
| Canarsie Park | 791 05 | 450 37 | 8 |
| Carroll Park | 1,059 58 | 997 05 | 9 |
| City Park | 1,122 70 | 1,111 52 | 10 |
| Cooper Park | 1,430 70 | 816 81 | 11 |
| Dreamland Park | 1,187 80 | 107 96 | 12 |
| Dyker Beach Park | 785 86 | 2,815 88 | 13 |
| Fort Greene Park | 1,596 30 | 4,186 01 | 14 |
| Fort Hamilton Park | 1,011 07 | 502 37 | 15 |
| Fulton Park | 1,041 25 | 649 43 | 16 |
| Highland Park | 798 82 | 2,650 80 | 17 |
| Irving Square Park | 1,040 14 | 734 90 | 18 |
| Lincoln Terrace Park | 1,204 37 | 1,400 82 | 19 |
| Linton Park | 710 09 | 730 47 | 20 |
| McCarren Park | 2,630 81 | 1,026 33 | 21 |
| McKibben Playground | 1,034 07 | 125 64 | 22 |
| McKinley Park | 1,310 81 | 534 13 | 23 |
| McLaughlin Park | 1,456 22 | 591 50 | 24 |
| New Lots Playground | 1,362 86 | 136 29 | 25 |
| Parade Ground | 1,604 06 | 316 04 | 26 |
| Prospect Park | 26,546 03 | 36,910 98 | 27 |
| Red Hook Park | 887 11 | 1,382 18 | 28 |
| Red Hook Playground | 459 51 | 227 23 | 29 |
| Saratoga Square | 1,062 25 | 747 85 | 30 |
| Seaside Park | 3,715 07 | 2,771 68 | 31 |
| Sunset Park | 1,708 91 | 2,581 78 | 32 |
| Tompkins Park | 1,142 92 | 1,523 52 | 33 |
| Williamsburg Bridge Park | 1,134 00 | 180 64 | 34 |
| Winthrop Park | 1,496 94 | 1,989 71 | 35 |
| Small Parks, Squares and Triangles | 625 24 | 944 52 | 36 |
| Temporary Summer Playgrounds | .......... | .......... | 37 |
| Total Operation and Maintenance of Parks and Playgrounds | **$67,287 65** | **$75,655 43** | 38 |
| Operation and Maintenance of Parkways: | | | |
| Bay Parkway | $901 25 | $9,348 94 | 39 |
| Bay Ridge Parkway and Shore Road | 1,727 84 | 7,645 62 | 40 |
| Eastern Parkway | 2,649 18 | 14,539 64 | 41 |
| Fort Hamilton Avenue | 1,791 58 | 11,285 02 | 42 |
| Ocean Parkway | 3,542 55 | 26,463 00 | 43 |
| Eastern Parkway Extension | 1,059 81 | 9,350 69 | 44 |
| Streets Contiguous to Prospect Park | 55 11 | 7,822 88 | 45 |
| Twenty-Sixth Ward Streets | 1,767 02 | 14,959 90 | 46 |
| Total Operation and Maintenance of Parkways | **$13,494 34** | **$101,415 69** | 47 |
| City Streets—Care of Trees | .......... | .......... | 48 |

NEW YORK

BOROUGH OF BROOKLYN

ACCORDING TO FUNCTIONS PERFORMED OR CHARACTER OF WORK DONE:

| LINE No. | Care of Grounds Including Trees and Plants | Playgrounds Athletic Fields and School Farms | Care of Bath Houses and Comfort Stations | Operation and Maintenance of Other Park Buildings Improvements and Properties | Total |
|---|---|---|---|---|---|
| 1 | .......... | .......... | .......... | .......... | **$47,840 63** |
| 2 | $728 95 | .......... | .......... | $19 49 | $2,024 95 |
| 3 | 1,268 83 | .......... | $1,306 14 | 36 12 | 5,086 56 |
| 4 | 453 85 | .......... | .......... | 117 22 | 2,564 28 |
| 5 | 954 57 | .......... | .......... | 75 71 | 3,000 03 |
| 6 | 892 33 | .......... | 1,567 93 | 591 59 | 6,076 07 |
| 7 | 84 45 | $2,925 24 | 1,263 23 | 8 53 | 5,384 42 |
| 8 | 505 15 | .......... | 237 61 | 39 56 | 2,023 74 |
| 9 | 614 07 | .......... | 1,638 25 | 140 41 | 4,449 36 |
| 10 | 1,910 33 | 986 21 | 1,868 00 | 336 65 | 7,335 41 |
| 11 | 1,427 48 | .......... | 1,301 59 | 133 69 | 5,110 27 |
| 12 | 1,797 98 | .......... | 4,914 62 | 3,381 24 | 11,389 60 |
| 13 | 63 84 | .......... | .......... | 3,075 17 | 6,740 75 |
| 14 | 3,183 49 | .......... | 2,518 05 | 5,121 43 | 16,605 28 |
| 15 | 695 66 | .......... | .......... | 30 09 | 2,239 19 |
| 16 | 457 09 | .......... | 1,025 23 | 51 36 | 3,224 36 |
| 17 | 1,993 20 | 1,438 05 | .......... | 378 73 | 7,259 60 |
| 18 | 1,071 98 | .......... | 1,164 93 | 367 45 | 4,379 40 |
| 19 | 1,294 68 | .......... | 2,222 79 | 368 46 | 6,491 12 |
| 20 | 1,016 15 | .......... | .......... | 745 45 | 3,202 16 |
| 21 | 8,250 56 | 12,758 97 | 2,931 47 | 151 65 | 27,749 79 |
| 22 | 2 19 | 4,089 03 | 1,019 92 | 402 13 | 6,672 98 |
| 23 | 1,427 79 | .......... | 857 94 | 23 58 | 4,154 25 |
| 24 | 498 56 | 3,646 41 | 1,428 99 | 559 74 | 8,181 42 |
| 25 | 74 90 | 2,688 22 | 1,126 42 | 48 28 | 5,436 97 |
| 26 | 1,607 44 | 1,374 13 | .......... | 4,606 20 | 9,507 87 |
| 27 | 70,831 65 | 3,128 51 | 20,746 77 | 35,006 50 | 193,170 44 |
| 28 | 901 02 | .......... | 929 48 | 330 77 | 4,430 56 |
| 29 | 198 30 | 3,160 47 | 643 80 | 92 82 | 4,782 13 |
| 30 | 1,616 83 | .......... | 1,160 70 | 56 55 | 4,644 18 |
| 31 | 7,581 34 | .......... | 3,699 95 | 766 19 | 18,534 23 |
| 32 | 5,281 85 | .......... | 2,913 59 | 780 03 | 13,266 16 |
| 33 | 1,399 52 | .......... | 1,449 08 | 84 13 | 5,599 17 |
| 34 | 46 70 | 3,520 35 | 81 04 | 103 23 | 5,065 96 |
| 35 | 2,470 73 | .......... | 1,551 33 | 854 24 | 8,362 95 |
| 36 | 1,105 82 | .......... | .......... | 408 94 | 3,084 52 |
| 37 | .......... | 2,264 18 | .......... | .......... | 2,264 18 |
| 38 | **$123,709 28** | **$41,979 77** | **$61,568 85** | **$59,293 33** | **$429,494 31** |
| 39 | $45 19 | .......... | .......... | $23 13 | $10,318 51 |
| 40 | 1,480 48 | .......... | .......... | 2,259 00 | 13,112 94 |
| 41 | 3,363 94 | .......... | .......... | 55 92 | 20,608 68 |
| 42 | 50 00 | .......... | .......... | 67 95 | 13,194 55 |
| 43 | 12,515 14 | .......... | .......... | 3,488 37 | 46,009 06 |
| 44 | 17 50 | .......... | .......... | 17 85 | 10,445 85 |
| 45 | 78 07 | .......... | .......... | 44 73 | 8,000 79 |
| 46 | .......... | .......... | .......... | .......... | 16,726 92 |
| 47 | **$17,550 32** | .......... | .......... | **$5,956 95** | **$138,417 30** |
| 48 | **$49,000 33** | .......... | .......... | .......... | **$49,000 33** |

THE CITY OF

DEPARTMENT OF PARKS,

SUMMARY FOR THE YEAR 1914 OF EXPENSES FOR EACH PARK, CLASSIFIED

| | Supervision and Unclassified Expenses | Care of Roads, Paths and Driveways | LINE No. |
|---|---|---|---|
| MUSIC AND CELEBRATIONS | **$20,205 73** | .......... | 1 |
| MENAGERIE | **$22,422 99** | .......... | 2 |
| UNDISTRIBUTED EXPENSES: | | | |
| Undistributed Supervision and General Expenses | $21,469 79 | .......... | 3 |
| Automobile Service | 7,300 23 | .......... | 4 |
| General Park Equipment | 18,036 13 | .......... | 5 |
| Pumping Station | 1,039 46 | .......... | 6 |
| Greenhouses and Nursery | .......... | .......... | 7 |
| Stables | 28,388 80 | .......... | 8 |
| Shops (overhead) | 10,799 13 | .......... | 9 |
| Extraordinary Expenses | 9,398 13 | .......... | 10 |
| Total Undistributed Expenses | **$96,431 67** | .......... | 11 |
| Departmental Total | **$267,683 01** | **$177,071 12** | 12 |

NEW YORK

BOROUGH OF BROOKLYN—*Continued.*

ACCORDING TO FUNCTIONS PERFORMED OR CHARACTER OF WORK DONE—*Continued*

| LINE No. | Care of Grounds Including Trees and Plants | Playgrounds Athletic Fields and School Farms | Care of Bath Houses and Comfort Stations | Operation and Maintenance of Other Park Buildings Improvements and Properties | Total |
|---|---|---|---|---|---|
| 1 | .......... | .......... | .......... | .......... | **$20,205 73** |
| 2 | .......... | .......... | .......... | .......... | **$22,422 99** |
| 3 | $1,852 56 | .......... | .......... | .......... | $23,322 35 |
| 4 | .......... | .......... | .......... | .......... | 7,300 23 |
| 5 | .......... | .......... | .......... | $7,803 82 | 25,839 95 |
| 6 | .......... | .......... | .......... | .......... | 1,039 46 |
| 7 | 32,026 11 | .......... | .......... | .......... | 32,026 11 |
| 8 | .......... | .......... | .......... | .......... | 28,388 80 |
| 9 | .......... | .......... | .......... | 5,415 99 | 16,215 12 |
| 10 | .......... | .......... | .......... | .......... | 9,398 13 |
| 11 | **$33,878 67** | .......... | .......... | **$13,219 81** | **$143,530 15** |
| 12 | **$224,138 60** | **$41,979 77** | **$61,568 85** | **$78,470 09** | **$850,911 44** |

DEPARTMENT OF PARKS—

COMPARATIVE SUMMARY OF EXPENSES FOR THE YEARS 1913 AND 1914

| | Supervision and Unclassified Expenses | Care of Roads, Paths and Driveways | LINE No. |
|---|---|---|---|
| GENERAL ADMINISTRATION | *$29,618 54* | .......... | 1 |
| | 27,894 07 | .......... | 2 |
| OPERATION AND MAINTENANCE OF IMPROVED PARKS: | | | |
| College Point | *$75 96* | *$330 98* | 3 |
| | 19 40 | 336 10 | 4 |
| Flushing | *75 47* | *289 17* | 5 |
| | 42 70 | 422 14 | 6 |
| Forest | *2,024 93* | *11,955 97* | 7 |
| | 1,507 27 | 7,791 37 | 8 |
| Highland | *1,074 00* | *3,293 82* | 9 |
| | 241 22 | 1,384 38 | 10 |
| Kissena Lake | *184 37* | *854 67* | 11 |
| | 973 88 | 4,639 11 | 12 |
| Kings | *420 51* | *1,429 50* | 13 |
| | 940 83 | 1,315 80 | 14 |
| Linden | *217 11* | *255 62* | 15 |
| | 89 39 | 422 10 | 16 |
| Rockaway | *71 83* | .......... | 17 |
| | 114 30 | .......... | 18 |
| Upland | *53 45* | *314 82* | 19 |
| | 16 94 | 419 68 | 20 |
| Ashmead | .......... | .......... | 21 |
| Small Parks and Gores | *473 70* | *187 69* | 22 |
| | 581 06 | 244 63 | 23 |
| Total, Improved Parks | *$4,671 33* | *$18,912 24* | 24 |
| | 4,526 99 | 16,975 31 | 25 |
| CARE OF UNDEVELOPED PARK AREAS: | | | |
| Leavitt Park | *$3,189 35* | .......... | 26 |
| | 238 71 | .......... | 27 |
| Rainey Park | *545 78* | .......... | 28 |
| | 775 41 | $2 50 | 29 |
| Wayanda Park | *1,567 25* | .......... | 30 |
| | 63 60 | 849 43 | 31 |
| Astoria Park | 3 00 | .......... | 32 |
| Baisley's Pond | 32 38 | .......... | 33 |
| Total, Undeveloped Park Areas | *$5,302 38* | .......... | 34 |
| | 1,113 10 | $851 93 | 35 |
| CITY STREETS: | | | |
| Care of Trees | *$3,219 37* | .......... | 36 |
| | 6,063 76 | .......... | 37 |
| MENAGERIE, FOREST PARK | $750 18 | .......... | 38 |
| MUSIC AND CELEBRATIONS | *$3,399 61* | .......... | 39 |
| | 4,221 26 | .......... | 40 |
| UNDISTRIBUTED EXPENSES: | | | |
| Automobile Service | *$4,633 93* | .......... | 41 |
| | 8,784 25 | .......... | 42 |
| Wood Service | 1,485 81 | .......... | 43 |
| General Park Equipment | *8,587 81* | .......... | 44 |
| | 7,311 21 | .......... | 45 |

NOTE—1913 Expenses in Italics. 1914 Expenses in Roman

NEW YORK

BOROUGH OF QUEENS

(SEE NOTE), ON BASIS OF COST BY FUNCTIONS FOR EACH PARK:

| LINE No. | Care of Grounds Including Trees and Plants | Playgrounds and Athletic Fields | Pumping and Comfort Stations and Bath Houses | Operation and Maintenance of Other Park Buildings, Improvements and Properties | Total |
|---|---|---|---|---|---|
| 1 | | | | | *$29,618 54* |
| 2 | | | | | 27,894 07 |
| 3 | *$702 30* | | | *$94 77* | *$1,204 01* |
| 4 | 718 52 | | | 70 91 | 1,144 93 |
| 5 | *742 25* | *$574 00* | | *525 40* | *2,206 29* |
| 6 | 645 69 | | | 220 47 | 1,331 00 |
| 7 | *8,200 06* | *5,552 24* | *$3,446 31* | *10,463 06* | *41,642 57* |
| 8 | 8,059 66 | 6,939 75 | 2,532 36 | 14,670 48 | 41,500 89 |
| 9 | *3,008 56* | | *1,491 65* | *1,431 16* | *10,299 19* |
| 10 | 2,886 76 | | 1,712 74 | 332 20 | 6,557 30 |
| 11 | *2,574 29* | *212 77* | | *71 87* | *3,897 97* |
| 12 | 3,899 55 | 202 75 | | 552 72 | 10,268 01 |
| 13 | *3,272 36* | *81 91* | | *1,854 65* | *7,058 93* |
| 14 | 1,948 14 | 66 65 | | 608 95 | 4,880 37 |
| 15 | *2,311 94* | | | *128 65* | *2,913 32* |
| 16 | 1,098 20 | | | 441 12 | 2,050 81 |
| 17 | *1,736 23* | | | *8,184 13* | *9,992 19* |
| 18 | 2,383 30 | | | 202 26 | 2,699 86 |
| 19 | *946 19* | | | *107 41* | *1,421 87* |
| 20 | 885 35 | | | 53 73 | 1,375 70 |
| 21 | | 759 02 | | 12 24 | 771 26 |
| 22 | *503 14* | | | *8 52* | *1,173 05* |
| 23 | 345 49 | | | | 1,171 18 |
| 24 | *$23,997 32* | *$6,420 92* | *$4,937 96* | *$22,869 62* | *$81,809 39* |
| 25 | 22,870 66 | 7,968 17 | 4,245 10 | 17,165 08 | 73,751 31 |
| 26 | | | | | *$3,189 35* |
| 27 | | | | | 238 71 |
| 28 | | | | *$97 38* | *643 16* |
| 29 | $820 32 | | | 196 37 | 1,794 60 |
| 30 | | | | | *1,567 25* |
| 31 | 159 00 | | | | 1,072 03 |
| 32 | | | | | 3 00 |
| 33 | 227 75 | | | | 260 13 |
| 34 | | | | *$97 38* | *$5,399 76* |
| 35 | $1,207 07 | | | 196 37 | 3,368 47 |
| 36 | *$12,259 05* | | | | *$15,478 42* |
| 37 | 13,874 36 | | | | 19,938 12 |
| 38 | | | | | $750 18 |
| 39 | | | | | *$3,399 61* |
| 40 | | | | | 4,221 26 |
| 41 | | | | | *$4,633 93* |
| 42 | | | | | 8,784 25 |
| 43 | | | | | 1,485 81 |
| 44 | | | | | *8,587 81* |
| 45 | | | | | 7,311 21 |

COMPARATIVE SUMMARY OF EXPENSES FOR THE YEARS 1913 AND 1914

| | Supervision and Unclassified Expenses | Care of Roads, Paths and Driveways | LINE No. |
|---|---|---|---|
| UNDISTRIBUTED EXPENSES—*Continued* | | | |
| Stables | *$10,658 31* | .......... | 1 |
| | 9,321 01 | .......... | 2 |
| Greenhouses and Nurseries | *16,509 85* | .......... | 3 |
| | 19,215 41 | .......... | 4 |
| Storehouse | *1,123 58* | .......... | 5 |
| | 1,741 29 | .......... | 6 |
| Shops (Overhead) | *5,148 19* | .......... | 7 |
| | 3,685 35 | .......... | 8 |
| Total, Undistributed Expenses | *$46,661 67* | .......... | 9 |
| | 51,544 33 | .......... | 10 |
| Departmental Total | *$92,872 90* | *$18,912 24* | 11 |
| | 96,113 69 | 17,827 24 | 12 |

NOTE—1913 Expenses in Italics 1914 Expenses in Roman

NEW YORK

BOROUGH OF QUEENS—*Continued*

(SEE NOTE), ON BASIS OF COST BY FUNCTIONS FOR EACH PARK:—*Continued*

| LINE No. | Care of Grounds Including Trees and Plants | Playgrounds and Athletic Fields | Pumping and Comfort Stations and Bath Houses | Operation and Maintenance of Other Park Buildings, Improvements and Properties | Total |
|---|---|---|---|---|---|
| 1 | .......... | .......... | .......... | .......... | *$10,658 31* |
| 2 | .......... | .......... | .......... | .......... | 9,321 01 |
| 3 | .......... | .......... | .......... | .......... | *16,509 85* |
| 4 | .......... | .......... | .......... | .......... | 19,215 41 |
| 5 | .......... | .......... | .......... | .......... | *1,123 58* |
| 6 | .......... | .......... | .......... | .......... | 1,741 29 |
| 7 | .......... | .......... | .......... | .......... | *5,148 19* |
| 8 | .......... | .......... | .......... | .......... | 3,685 35 |
| 9 | .......... | .......... | .......... | .......... | *$46,661 67* |
| 10 | .......... | .......... | .......... | .......... | 51,544 33 |
| 11 | *$36,256 37* | *$6,420 92* | *$4,937 96* | *$22,967 00* | *$182,367 39* |
| 12 | 37,952 09 | 7,968 17 | 4,245 10 | 17,361 45 | 181,467 74 |

FIRE

COMPARATIVE SUMMARY OF EXPENSES FOR THE

| | LINE No. |
|---|---|
| **ADMINISTRATION:** | |
| Office of Commissioner and Deputy: | |
| Manhattan, Bronx and Richmond | 1 |
| Office of Deputy Commissioner: | |
| Brooklyn and Queens | 2 |
| Division of Pensions | 3 |
| Division of Audit and Accounts | 4 |
| Total Administration | 5 |
| **FIRE FIGHTING—DEPARTMENTAL:** | |
| Office, Chief of Department, Deputies, etc | 6 |
| Operation and Maintenance of Engine Companies: | |
| Manhattan, Bronx and Richmond | 7 |
| Brooklyn and Queens | 8 |
| Operation and Maintenance of Hook and Ladder Companies: | |
| Manhattan, Bronx and Richmond | 9 |
| Brooklyn and Queens | 10 |
| Operation and Maintenance of Hose Companies: | |
| Manhattan, Bronx and Richmond | 11 |
| Brooklyn and Queens | 12 |
| Operation and Maintenance of Boats | 13 |
| Medical and Surgical Office | 14 |
| Repair Shops: | |
| Manhattan, Bronx and Richmond | 15 |
| Brooklyn and Queens | 16 |
| Marine Division | 17 |
| Hospital and Training Stables: | |
| Manhattan, Bronx and Richmond | 18 |
| Brooklyn and Queens | 19 |
| Fire Alarm Telegraph: | |
| Manhattan | 20 |
| Bronx | 21 |
| Richmond | 22 |
| Brooklyn and Queens | 23 |
| Fuel Depots | 24 |
| Spare Apparatus | 25 |
| Total Fire Fighting—Departmental | 26 |
| **FIRE FIGHTING—VOLUNTEER COMPANIES:** | |
| Queens and Richmond | 27 |
| **FIRE PREVENTION:** | |
| Administration: | |
| Manhattan, Bronx and Richmond | 28 |
| Brooklyn and Queens | 29 |
| Inspection: | |
| Manhattan, Bronx and Richmond | 30 |
| Brooklyn and Queens | 31 |

NEW YORK

DEPARTMENT

YEARS ENDED DECEMBER 31, 1913 AND 1914

| LINE No. | 1913 Items | 1913 Total | 1914 Items | 1914 Total |
|---|---|---|---|---|
| 1 | .......... | $44,984 00 | .......... | $44,503 70 |
| 2 | .......... | 11,745 74 | .......... | 12,981 80 |
| 3 | .......... | 4,971 48 | .......... | 5,497 47 |
| 4 | .......... | 11,008 55 | .......... | 10,848 04 |
| 5 | .......... | **$72,709 77** | .......... | **$73,831 01** |
| 6 | .......... | **$262,214 06** | .......... | **$279,451 77** |
| 7 | $2,751,259 37 | | $2,848,914 91 | |
| 8 | 2,179,249 47 | | 2,218,911 50 | |
| | | **4,930,508 84** | | **5,067,826 41** |
| 9 | $1,346,379 25 | | $1,514,131 70 | |
| 10 | 729,976 92 | | 816,887 62 | |
| | | **2,076,356 17** | | **2,331,019 32** |
| 11 | $12,046 07 | | $12,171 21 | |
| 12 | 102,761 40 | | 106,684 44 | |
| | | **114,807 47** | | **118,855 65** |
| 13 | .......... | **464,889 40** | .......... | **477,544 67** |
| 14 | .......... | **50,592 16** | .......... | **43,642 95** |
| 15 | $59,063 72 | | $55,424 92 | |
| 16 | 33,703 85 | | 35,262 86 | |
| 17 | 976 15 | | 722 09 | |
| | | **93,743 72** | | **91,409 87** |
| 18 | $51,405 41 | | $46,811 90 | |
| 19 | 37,681 30 | | 40,189 51 | |
| | | **89,086 71** | | **87,001 41** |
| 20 | $101,468 12 | | $99,577 96 | |
| 21 | 19,097 29 | | 17,849 47 | |
| 22 | 19,839 37 | | 18,034 07 | |
| 23 | 76,277 77 | | 72,650 69 | |
| | | **216,682 55** | | **208,112 19** |
| 24 | .......... | **1,127 29** | .......... | **2,023 28** |
| 25 | .......... | **5,014 10** | .......... | .......... |
| 26 | .......... | **$8,305,022 47** | .......... | **$8,706,887 52** |
| 27 | .......... | **$62,524 86** | .......... | **$44,706 14** |
| 28 | $20,352 49 | | $19,146 26 | |
| 29 | 6,047 28 | | 8,516 48 | |
| | | **$26,399 77** | | **$27,662 74** |
| 30 | $94,747 71 | | $120,216 76 | |
| 31 | 36,827 33 | | 46,679 73 | |
| | | **$131,575 04** | | **$166,896 49** |

Comparative Summary of Expenses for the

| | LINE No. |
|---|---|
| Fire Prevention—*Continued* | |
| Investigation: | |
| Manhattan, Bronx and Richmond | 1 |
| Brooklyn and Queens | 2 |
| Regulation: | |
| Manhattan, Bronx and Richmond | 3 |
| Brooklyn and Queens | 4 |
| Total Fire Prevention | 5 |
| Undistributed Expense: | |
| Repairs and Supplies—Purchasing Division | 6 |
| Storage of Supplies | 7 |
| Printing Office | 8 |
| Operation and Maintenance of Automobiles | 9 |
| Care of Buildings and Grounds: | |
| Office, Division of Buildings | 10 |
| Third Street Shop and Storehouse | 11 |
| Headquarters Building—67th and 68th Streets | 12 |
| Headquarters Building—365 Jay Street, Brooklyn | 13 |
| Headquarters Building—Municipal Building | 14 |
| Other Buildings | 15 |
| Total Undistributed Expense | 16 |
| Work Done for Other Departments | 17 |
| Departmental Total | 18 |

NEW YORK

DEPARTMENT

YEARS ENDED DECEMBER 31, 1913 AND 1914—*Continued*

| LINE No. | 1913 Items | 1913 Total | 1914 Items | 1914 Total |
|---|---|---|---|---|
| 1 | $38,098 37 | | $38,228 99 | |
| 2 | 18,437 60 | | 19,786 55 | |
| | | **$56,535 97** | | **$58,015 54** |
| 3 | $34,664 54 | | 35,503 01 | |
| 4 | 20,287 32 | | 21,259 86 | |
| | | **54,951 86** | | **56,762 87** |
| 5 | .......... | **$269,462 64** | .......... | **$309,337 64** |
| 6 | .......... | **$24,836 49** | .......... | **$21,718 53** |
| 7 | .......... | **8,620 77** | .......... | **7,276 56** |
| 8 | .......... | **3,992 78** | .......... | **3,917 84** |
| 9 | .......... | **45,787 37** | .......... | **47,029 36** |
| 10 | $20,061 65 | | $15,605 64 | |
| 11 | 6,732 69 | | 25,692 96 | |
| 12 | 24,547 45 | | 19,896 92 | |
| 13 | 8,980 88 | | 11,071 33 | |
| 14 | .......... | | 2,188 99 | |
| 15 | 5,513 60 | | 1,098 66 | |
| | | **65,836 27** | | **75,554 50** |
| 16 | | **$149,073 68** | | **$155,496 79** |
| 17 | .......... | | .......... | **$2,001 43** |
| 18 | .......... | **$8,858,793 42** | .......... | **$9,292,260 53** |

## NATIONAL GUARD

Comparative Summary for the Years 1913 and 1914

| | Line No. |
|---|---|
| Headquarters Division, N. G., N. Y. | 1 |
| Armory Board | 2 |
| Borough of Manhattan: | |
| Seventh Regiment | 3 |
| Eighth Regiment | 4 |
| Ninth Regiment | 5 |
| Twelfth Regiment | 6 |
| Twenty-Second Regiment | 7 |
| Sixty-Ninth Regiment | 8 |
| Seventy-First Regiment | 9 |
| First Squadron Cavalry | 10 |
| First Regiment Field Artillery | 11 |
| Third Ambulance and First Field Hospital | 12 |
| First Battalion Naval Militia | 13 |
| Total | 14 |
| Borough of The Bronx: | |
| Second Battalion, Second Regiment, Field Artillery | 15 |
| Borough of Brooklyn: | |
| Thirteenth Coast Artillery | 16 |
| Fourteenth Regiment | 17 |
| Twenty-Third Regiment | 18 |
| Forty-Seventh Regiment | 19 |
| Second Regiment Cavalry | 20 |
| Second Regiment Field Artillery | 21 |
| Second Company Signal Corps | 22 |
| Second Battalion Naval Militia | 23 |
| Total | 24 |
| Borough of Queens: | |
| Company "I," Tenth Regiment | 25 |
| Borough of Richmond: | |
| Troop "F," Second Regiment Cavalry | 26 |
| Department Total | 27 |

NEW YORK

AND NAVAL MILITIA

OF EXPENSES FOR EACH INDEPENDENT MILITIA UNIT:

| LINE No. | 1913 Items | 1913 Total | 1914 Items | 1914 Total |
|---|---|---|---|---|
| 1 | .......... | **$2,809 09** | .......... | **$3,078 28** |
| 2 | .......... | **$21,947 73** | .......... | **$21,780 73** |
| 3 | $64,798 45 | | $32,181 09 | |
| 4 | 20,862 81 | | 23,907 95 | |
| 5 | 20,604 09 | | 21,238 27 | |
| 6 | 16,988 95 | | 21,026 12 | |
| 7 | 22,803 93 | | 27,394 11 | |
| 8 | 25,492 49 | | 22,832 82 | |
| 9 | 31,969 55 | | 35,316 55 | |
| 10 | 31,810 92 | | 33,228 47 | |
| 11 | 65,662 33 | | 55,808 60 | |
| 12 | .......... | | 27,253 51 | |
| 13 | 31,931 39 | | 32,356 14 | |
| 14 | | **$332,924 91** | | **$332,543 63** |
| 15 | .......... | **$31,447 01** | .......... | **$40,740 26** |
| 16 | $31,258 24 | | $30,368 45 | |
| 17 | 38,237 99 | | 43,677 88 | |
| 18 | 21,596 60 | | 22,472 48 | |
| 19 | 20,078 48 | | 21,688 96 | |
| 20 | 36,875 35 | | 39,308 04 | |
| 21 | 24,374 26 | | 31,978 19 | |
| 22 | 9,247 09 | | 11,685 50 | |
| 23 | 27,740 80 | | 26,967 31 | |
| 24 | | **$209,408 81** | | **$228,146 81** |
| 25 | .......... | **$6,082 26** | .......... | **$6,428 33** |
| 26 | .......... | **$8,444 99** | .......... | **$10,555 86** |
| 27 | | **$613,064 80** | | **$643,273 90** |

# THE CITY OF NEW YORK

## DEPARTMENT OF CORRECTION

Comparative Summary for the Years 1913 and 1914, of Expenses Incurred in the Care of Prisoners and the Maintenance of Correctional Institutions.

| | 1913 | 1914 |
|---|---|---|
| General Administration and Undistributed Expenses: | | |
| Office of Commissioner | $22,339 56 | $24,549 93 |
| (b) Bureau of Registration and Passes | .......... | 3,922 18 |
| Audit and Accounts | 12,848 15 | 11,219 78 |
| Purchase and Storage of Supplies | 12,443 82 | 13,115 36 |
| Automobile Service | 6,171 21 | 7,465 84 |
| Operation and Maintenance of Stables | 37,820 88 | 38,623 06 |
| (c) Operation and Maintenance of Steamers and Launches | 78,359 74 | 65,791 77 |
| Operation and Maintenance of Piers and Docks | 716 10 | 2,135 81 |
| Miscellaneous | 19,669 95 | 22,677 28 |
| Total General Activities and Undistributed Expenses | **$190,369 41** | **$189,501 01** |
| Prison Service, Direct Expense: | | |
| City Prison, Manhattan | $165,527 15 | $145,756 03 |
| City Prison, Brooklyn | 83,580 36 | 82,408 17 |
| City Prison, Queens | 47,511 02 | 39,108 24 |
| Workhouse, Blackwell's Island | 217,339 42 | 228,938 31 |
| Workhouse, Hart's Island Branch | 158,769 60 | 138,290 14 |
| Workhouse, Riker's Island Branch | 47,812 80 | 55,351 01 |
| Reformatory, Hart's Island | 84,204 58 | 82,547 09 |
| (a) Penitentiary, Blackwell's Island | 263,485 00 | 255,883 40 |
| District Prisons | 78,417 56 | 76,883 13 |
| (d) New Hampton Farms | .......... | 11,613 01 |
| Brooklyn Disciplinary Training School | .......... | 169 28 |
| Total Prison Service, Direct Expense | **$1,146,647 49** | **$1,116,947 81** |
| Departmental Total | **$1,337,016 90** | **$1,306,448 82** |

(a) This cost does not include cost of materials consumed in the manufacturing industry.
(b) This function extended and segregated in 1914. In 1913 it was included with Office of Commissioner.
(c) Steamer "Massasoit" transferred on June 30, 1914, to Department of Public Charities.
(d) New activity in 1914.

# THE CITY OF NEW YORK

## DEPARTMENT OF CORRECTION

### Comparative Statement of Unit Costs for the Years 1913 and 1914

| Name of Institution | Units of Service | | | * Cost per Unit | |
|---|---|---|---|---|---|
| | Description | Number | | | |
| | | 1913 | 1914 | 1913 | 1914 |
| City Prison, Manhattan | Prisoner-Day | 249,537 | 262,776 | $0.748 | $0.635 |
| City Prison, Brooklyn | Prisoner-Day | 112,569 | 134,583 | .915 | .760 |
| City Prison, Queens | Prisoner-Day | 61,402 | 66,716 | .858 | .666 |
| Workhouse, Blackwell's Island Branch | Prisoner-Day | 340,975 | 455,657 | .748 | .583 |
| Workhouse, Hart's Island Branch | Prisoner-Day | 217,242 | 213,014 | .846 | .775 |
| Workhouse, Riker's Island Branch | Prisoner-Day | 65,194 | 77,047 | .852 | .848 |
| Reformatory, Hart's Island | Prisoner-Day | 123,908 | 145,058 | .788 | .691 |
| Penitentiary, Blackwell's Island | Prisoner-Day | 464,682 | 494,937 | .680 | .602 |
| District Prisons | Prisoner-Day | 89,493 | 88,875 | .961 | .945 |
| New Hampton Farms | Prisoner-Day | ....... | 10,545 | .... | 1.292 |
| Total | | **1,725,002** | **1,949,208** | **$ .775** | **$ .670** |

* Includes departmental overhead.

# SECTION III

## SUMMARY AND DETAILED STATEMENTS OF REVENUES COLLECTED AND OTHER CASH RECEIPTS

## Summary Statement of Revenues Collected and Other Cash Receipts

| General Character of Revenue | Refer to Page | Year 1910 | Year 1911 | Line No. |
|---|---|---|---|---|
| **I. Taxes and Assessments:** | | | | |
| Taxes, General Property | 204 | $133,590,299 94 | $135,023,685 61 | 1 |
| Taxes, Special | 204 | 10,799,056 52 | 10,656,948 55 | 2 |
| Assessments | 205 | 11,533,132 38 | 11,333,213 55 | 3 |
| Total Taxes and Assessments | | **$155,922,488 84** | **$157,013,847 71** | 4 |
| **II. Revenues Other than Taxes and Assessments;** | | | | |
| Apportionment of School Moneys by the State of New York | 205 | $1,953,667 08 | $1,850,438 45 | 5 |
| Payments by State for Costs of Bronx Parkway | 205 | .......... | 8,750 00 | 6 |
| Gifts, Legacies, Bequests and Unclaimed Moneys | 205 | .......... | .......... | 7 |
| Payments by Lessees of City Property for Cost of Construction of Property to be Leased | 206 | .......... | 27,339 40 | 8 |
| Interboro Rapid Transit Rentals | 206 | 2,200,772 62 | 2,272,838 03 | 9 |
| Dock and Slip Rents | 206 | 4,115,601 75 | 4,377,223 66 | 10 |
| Ferry Rents and Leases | 206 | 247,912 77 | 232,624 67 | 11 |
| Municipal Ferry Fares and Privileges | 206 | 942,596 10 | 983,181 93 | 12 |
| Water Revenues | 206 | 13,200,046 16 | 13,349,252 20 | 13 |
| Bridge Tolls | 206 | 791,455 16 | 636,703 47 | 14 |
| Revenues from Operation of Bus Line, Bartow to City Island | 206 | .......... | .......... | 15 |
| Revenues from Municipal Operation of Scow Trimming | 206 | .......... | .......... | 16 |
| Revenues from Operation of Municipal Baths and Comfort Stations | 206 | 18,924 75 | 22,711 42 | 17 |
| Receipts from Sales and Redemptions of Seized or Confiscated Property | 207 | 34,050 84 | 3,232 73 | 18 |
| Sale of Publications, Maps, Drugs, etc., and Articles Manufactured by City Departments | 207 | 192,386 65 | 174,118 95 | 19 |
| Sales of Ashes, Old Paper, Condemned Material and Equipment, and Other By-Products | 208 | 54,784 09 | 76,751 99 | 20 |
| Court Fees, Fines and Penalties (Other than Interest) and Forfeitures of Bail | 208 | 556,228 63 | 624,291 89 | 21 |
| Rents, Permits and Privileges Not Otherwise Classified | 209 | 637,734 31 | 616,560 86 | 22 |
| Franchises and Permits to Use Streets for Railways, Stage Lines, Tunnels, Conduits, Vaults, Bridges and Building Projections | 209 | 1,525,028 02 | 1,486,851 89 | 23 |
| Licenses | 210 | 604,775 00 | 621,355 25 | 24 |
| Fees, Commissions and Other Charges for Services Rendered, and Reimbursements for Costs Incurred | 211 | 1,526,262 26 | 1,643,434 53 | 25 |
| Interest on Overdue Payments (Accounts Receivable) | 212 | 4,394,183 45 | 3,306,286 87 | 26 |
| Interest on Deposits | 213 | 691,497 25 | 811,594 92 | 27 |
| Interest and Dividends on Investments other than New York City Bonds | 213 | 3,078 60 | 5,642 46 | 28 |
| Interest on Bonds of the City of New York Held by Sinking Funds | 213 | 7,209,938 70 | 7,893,987 32 | 29 |
| Recoveries for Damages, Settlements of Claims (Unclassified) and Forfeitures of Bonds and Security Deposits | 213 | 20,621 88 | 20,043 80 | 30 |
| Total Revenues Other than Taxes and Assessments | | **$40,921,546 07** | **$41,045,216 69** | 31 |
| **III. Other Receipts:** | | | | |
| Proceeds of Sales of Real Estate Owned by the City | 213 | $684,987 45 | $347,108 91 | 32 |
| Proceeds of Sales and Redemption of Bonds, Mortgages, Stocks and Other Securities Not Issued by the City of New York | 213 | 8,657 50 | 4,266 50 | 33 |
| Par Value of New York City Bonds Sold | 214 | 293,970,074 25 | 279,980,713 67 | 34 |
| Premium on Corporate Stock Sold | 214 | 637,922 89 | 542,548 60 | 35 |
| Refunds, Rebates, Returns of Advances and Accrued Interest on New York City Bonds Sold | 214 | 214,591 41 | 458,427 45 | 36 |
| Receipts of Security Deposits, Pledges, Bail, etc | 214 | 96 00 | 136 00 | 37 |
| Receipts of City as Agent or Administrator for Private Persons or Corporations and for Pension Funds Not Administered by the Finance Department | 214 | 14,149 92 | 21,524 29 | 38 |
| Redemption of Bonds of the City of New York held by the Sinking Funds | 214 | 8,256,000 00 | 11,244,309 76 | 39 |
| Transfers to Sinking Funds | 214 | 7,883,667 16 | 9,857,547 17 | 40 |
| Total Receipts Other than Revenues | | **$311,670,146 58** | **$302,456,582 35** | 41 |
| Total Receipts | | **$508,514,181 49** | **$500,515,646 75** | 42 |

NEW YORK

by the City of New York for the Years 1910 to 1914, Inclusive:

| Line No. | Year 1912 | Year 1913 | Year 1914 | Total | Distribution by Classes of Funds: General Fund | Special and Trust Funds | Sinking Funds |
|---|---|---|---|---|---|---|---|
| 1 | $149,490,658 15 | $148,556,847 55 | $142,994,191 25 | $709,655,682 50 | $709,655,682 50 | .......... | .......... |
| 2 | 10,500,429 76 | 10,785,858 80 | 10,318,726 15 | 53,061,019 78 | 23,924,524 46 | $29,136,495 32 | .......... |
| 3 | 10,161,069 93 | 9,765,523 27 | 10,688,369 01 | 53,481,308 14 | .......... | 53,266,664 99 | $214,643 15 |
| 4 | **$170,152,157 84** | **$169,108,229 62** | **$164,001,286 41** | **$816,198,010 42** | **$733,580,206 96** | **$82,403,160 31** | **$214,643 15** |
| 5 | $1,970,610 57 | $2,011,961 30 | $2,063,326 11 | $9,850,003 51 | $9,070,860 79 | $779,142 72 | .......... |
| 6 | .......... | 204,500 00 | 286,919 76 | 500,169 76 | .......... | 500,169 76 | .......... |
| 7 | 17,722 39 | 157 30 | 55 10 | 17,934 79 | 157 30 | 17,777 49 | .......... |
| 8 | .......... | 4,378,799 44 | 1,636,514 82 | 6,042,653 66 | .......... | 6,042,653 66 | .......... |
| 9 | 2,315,301 79 | 2,348,539 09 | 2,362,028 02 | 11,499,479 55 | .......... | 8,974,114 47 | $2,525,365 08 |
| 10 | 4,498,659 99 | 4,596,092 49 | 4,688,151 33 | 22,275,729 22 | .......... | .......... | 22,275,729 22 |
| 11 | 243,733 88 | 307,318 29 | 318,291 71 | 1,349,881 32 | .......... | .......... | 1,349,881 32 |
| 12 | 1,042,192 81 | 1,096,415 64 | 1,080,079 52 | 5,144,466 00 | .......... | .......... | 5,144,466 00 |
| 13 | 10,900,968 67 | 12,792,309 83 | 12,881,183 42 | 63,123,760 28 | 1,199,477 43 | 20,089,113 89 | 41,835,168 96 |
| 14 | 438,626 40 | 411,804 88 | 385,333 45 | 2,663,923 36 | 246,634 31 | 2,417,289 05 | .......... |
| 15 | .......... | .......... | 6,180 64 | 6,180 64 | .......... | 6,180 64 | .......... |
| 16 | .......... | 5,337 00 | 17,445 28 | 22,782 28 | 5,337 00 | 17,445 28 | .......... |
| 17 | 47,726 81 | 58,819 32 | 60,607 73 | 208,790 03 | 208,790 03 | .......... | .......... |
| 18 | 1,453 26 | 91 96 | 2,533 88 | 41,362 67 | 1,521 29 | 39,841 38 | .......... |
| 19 | 243,907 82 | 215,204 18 | 191,503 31 | 1,017,120 91 | 679,214 13 | 337,906 78 | .......... |
| 20 | 69,810 08 | 147,532 90 | 144,347 95 | 493,227 01 | 432,388 02 | 60,838 99 | .......... |
| 21 | 781,750 10 | 907,110 08 | 987,843 59 | 3,857,224 29 | 35,324 78 | 776,966 09 | 3,044,933 42 |
| 22 | 548,148 70 | 606,855 44 | 614,512 04 | 3,023,811 35 | 540,151 10 | 1,543 50 | 2,482,116 75 |
| 23 | 1,594,233 92 | 1,586,494 18 | 1,605,775 67 | 7,798,383 68 | 3,541,195 73 | 107,882 35 | 4,149,305 60 |
| 24 | 611,485 25 | 630,905 38 | 686,408 83 | 3,154,929 71 | 2,006,234 57 | .......... | 1,148,695 14 |
| 25 | 1,809,531 30 | 2,314,911 37 | 2,383,424 20 | 9,677,563 66 | 4,225,348 40 | 5,429,941 29 | 22,273 97 |
| 26 | 2,783,179 91 | 3,595,218 50 | 2,637,733 34 | 16,716,602 07 | 13,967,138 84 | 2,510,389 37 | 239,073 86 |
| 27 | 756,904 37 | 731,814 54 | 1,191,995 63 | 4,183,806 71 | 252,609 59 | 458 31 | 3,930,738 81 |
| 28 | 2,866 16 | 2,622 85 | 4,752 51 | 18,962 58 | 5,677 85 | .......... | 13,284 73 |
| 29 | 8,534,644 37 | 9,517,728 68 | 10,217,844 65 | 43,374,143 72 | .......... | .......... | 43,374,143 72 |
| 30 | 37,713 46 | 20,215 39 | 52,811 37 | 151,405 90 | 126,327 37 | 15,022 00 | 10,056 53 |
| 31 | **$39,251,172 01** | **$48,488,760 03** | **$46,507,603 86** | **$216,214,298 66** | **$36,544,388 53** | **$48,124,677 02** | **$131,545,233 11** |
| 32 | $205,285 72 | $332,575 60 | $159,640 61 | $1,729,598 29 | .......... | $1,258,949 40 | $470,648 89 |
| 33 | 4,480 00 | 3,605 00 | .......... | 21,009 00 | .......... | .......... | 21,009 00 |
| 34 | 333,963,184 92 | 552,364,512 17 | 405,117,358 64 | 1,865,395,843 65 | $1,087,980,869 93 | 777,414,973 72 | .......... |
| 35 | 476,236 36 | 61,651 77 | 942,500 00 | 2,660,859 62 | .......... | 2,660,859 62 | .......... |
| 36 | 112,974 14 | 296,499 89 | 670,268 04 | 1,752,760 93 | 32,603 98 | 1,720,056 95 | 100 00 |
| 37 | 3,060 00 | 149 77 | 10,052 00 | 13,493 77 | .......... | 13,493 77 | .......... |
| 38 | 64,644 48 | 89,868 45 | 140,604 84 | 330,791 98 | .......... | 330,791 98 | .......... |
| 39 | 38,097,666 05 | 58,914,000 00 | 29,587,493 57 | 146,099,469 38 | .......... | .......... | 146,099,469 38 |
| 40 | 9,492,762 23 | 10,167,765 06 | 9,965,838 20 | 47,367,579 82 | .......... | .......... | 47,367,579 82 |
| 41 | **$382,420,293 90** | **$622,230,627 71** | **$446,593,755 90** | **$2,065,371,406 44** | **$1,088,013,473 91** | **$783,399,125 44** | **$193,958,807 09** |
| 42 | **$591,823,623 75** | **$839,827,617 36** | **$657,102,646 17** | **$3,097,783,715 52** | **$1,858,138,069 40** | **$913,926,962 77** | **$325,718,683 35** |

DETAILED STATEMENT OF REVENUES COLLECTED AND OTHER CASH RECEIPTS BY THE CITY OF NEW YORK
ALSO SHOWING THE DISTRIBUTION

| Character of Revenue | Department, Bureau of Office Through Which Collected | Statute or Ordinance | Year | | LINE No. |
|---|---|---|---|---|---|
| | | | 1910 | 1911 | |
| 1. TAXES—GENERAL PROPERTY: | | | | | |
| Levies for 1898 and Previous Years | Comptroller | | $118,755 79 | $59,099 32 | 1 |
| Levies for 1899 and Subsequent Years | Comptroller | Secs. 249 and 900, G.N.Y.C. | 133,471,544 15 | 134,964,586 29 | 2 |
| Total | | | **$133,590,299 94** | **$135,023,685 61** | 3 |
| 2. TAXES, SPECIAL: | | | | | |
| Bank | Comptroller | Chap. 550, L. 1901, Sec. 24 of Tax Law | $3,443,279 28 | $3,566,858 32 | 4 |
| Mortgage | Chamberlain | Chap. 729, L. 1905, Sec. 253 and 261 of Tax Law | 1,336,115 37 | 1,316,286 87 | 5 |
| Mortgage | Chamberlain | Chap. 771, L. 1913, Sec. 253 and 261 of Tax Law | .......... | .......... | 6 |
| Excise | Chamberlain | Secs. 8, 9 and 10 Liquor Tax Law; Secs. 353, 789 and 1092 G. N. Y. C. | 6,019,661 87 | 5,773,803 36 | 7 |
| Total | | | **$10,799,056 52** | **$10,656,948 55** | 8 |
| 3. ASSESSMENTS: | | | | | |
| Street Improvement Fund | Comptroller | Secs. 181 and 942–964, G. N. Y. C. | | | |
| Work contracted for prior to Jan. 1, 1898 | | | $78,169 37 | $159,994 16 | 9 |
| Work contracted for after Jan. 1, 1898 | | | 6,476,007 28 | 6,941,362 60 | 10 |
| Fund for Street and Park Openings | Comptroller | Secs. 173 and 970–1011, G. N. Y. C. | 4,619,138 63 | 3,921,402 46 | 11 |
| Special Assessments | Comptroller | Secs. 942–964, G. N. Y. C., Chap. 383, L. of 1878 | | | |
| Brooklyn— | | | | | |
| Improving Ocean Parkway | | | .......... | .......... | 12 |
| Eighth Ward Improvement Fund | | | 30,002 94 | 7,249 26 | 13 |
| Principal and Interest on 26th Ward Bonds, 1906 and subsequent | | | 60,123 71 | 53,917 88 | 14 |
| Interest on 26th Ward Bonds, Levies for 1899 and subsequent years | | | 2,214 64 | 590 93 | 15 |
| Sewerage Fund | | Laws of 1892 and 1894 | 1,165 27 | 314 39 | 16 |
| 26th Ward Main Sewer | | | 22,000 61 | 19,627 60 | 17 |
| Assessment Fund | | | 1,226 58 | 71 49 | 18 |
| Assessments for Local Improvements, Town of New Lots | | | 3,847 16 | 2,020 86 | 19 |
| Board of Assessors Decisions | | Chapter 114, Laws 1883 | .......... | .......... | 20 |
| Flatbush Avenue Improvement, 29th Ward Instalments for 1900 and subsequent years | | | 31,945 17 | 31,852 68 | 21 |
| Flagging Tax Assessments, 30th Ward Instalments, 1897 and previous years | | | 105 87 | .......... | 22 |
| Flagging Tax Assessment, 30th Ward Instalments, 1900 and subsequent years | | | 165 48 | 163 62 | 23 |
| Opening and Grading, 31st Ward | | | 37,653 53 | 59,610 41 | 24 |
| Opening and Grading, Town of Gravesend | | | 16 85 | 19 94 | 25 |
| Sales of Unpaid Assessments, Town of New Utrecht | | | 173 73 | 680 47 | 26 |
| Sewer Assessments, 29th Ward Instalments for 1899 and subsequent years | | | 7,251 43 | 6,775 23 | 27 |
| Assessors' Arrearages | | Laws of 1883 | .......... | 16,422 66 | 28 |
| Local Improvements, Late Town of Utrecht | | | 10,491 41 | 10,512 10 | 29 |
| Local Improvements, Town of Flatlands | | | 26 95 | .......... | 30 |
| Sales of Unpaid Assessments, Town of Gravesend | | | 169 46 | 27 24 | 31 |
| Bond Street Sewer, Diary No. 4839 | | | .......... | .......... | 32 |
| Opening, Grading and Sewers, 30th Ward | | | 1,682 25 | 40 00 | 33 |
| Sackett Street Improvement Fund | | | .......... | .......... | 34 |
| Opening, Widening and Closing Streets | | | 1,728 46 | 67 94 | 35 |
| Assessment Fund | | Laws of 1886 | .......... | 182 31 | 36 |
| Unpaid Assessments, 30th Ward, New Utrecht, including default and interest to Nov. 15, 1895 | | | 161 50 | 9 80 | 37 |

# NEW YORK

FOR THE YEARS 1910 TO 1914, INCLUSIVE, GROUPED ACCORDING TO THE GENERAL CHARACTER THEREOF; THEREOF BY CLASSES OF FUNDS:

| LINE No. | Year | | | Total | Distribution by Classes of Funds | | |
|---|---|---|---|---|---|---|---|
| | 1912 | 1913 | 1914 | | General Fund | Special and Trust Funds | Sinking Funds |
| 1 | $32,702 53 | $27,076 02 | $33,738 80 | $271,372 46 | $271,372 46 | .......... | .......... |
| 2 | 149,457,955 62 | 148,529,771 53 | 142,960,452 45 | 709,384,310 04 | 709,384,310 04 | .......... | .......... |
| 3 | **$149,490,658 15** | **$148,556,847 55** | **$142,994,191 25** | **$709,655,682 50** | **$709,655,682 50** | .......... | .......... |
| 4 | $3,489,313 67 | $3,600,728 73 | $3,629,408 92 | $17,729,588 92 | $17,729,588 92 | .......... | .......... |
| 5 | 1,290,479 75 | 1,319,479 77 | 734,602 28 | 5,996,964 04 | 5,996,964 04 | .......... | .......... |
| 6 | .......... | 199,215 00 | 395,943 00 | 595,158 00 | 197,971 50 | $397,186 50 | .......... |
| 7 | 5,720,636 34 | 5,666,435 30 | 5,558,771 95 | 28,739,308 82 | .......... | 28,739,308 82 | .......... |
| 8 | **$10,500,429 76** | **$10,785,858 80** | **$10,318,726 15** | **$53,061,019 78** | **$23,924,524 46** | **$29,136,495 32** | .......... |
| 9 | $36,293 70 | $63,269 95 | $11,639 18 | $349,366 36 | .......... | $349,366 36 | .......... |
| 10 | 5,836,411 59 | 4,829,062 35 | 6,671,086 29 | 30,753,930 11 | .......... | 30,753,930 11 | .......... |
| 11 | 4,043,860 29 | 4,567,666 89 | 3,787,617 97 | 20,939,686 24 | .......... | 20,939,686 24 | .......... |
| 12 | 43 72 | 71 90 | .......... | 115 62 | .......... | 115 62 | .......... |
| 13 | 1,174 39 | 2,215 20 | 364 73 | 41,006 52 | .......... | 41,006 52 | .......... |
| 14 | 57,186 84 | 55,252 08 | 50,826 76 | 277,307 27 | .......... | 277,307 27 | .......... |
| 15 | 11 04 | 20 00 | 12 08 | 2,848 69 | .......... | 2,848 69 | .......... |
| 16 | 242 20 | 37 52 | 77 80 | 1,837 18 | .......... | 1,837 18 | .......... |
| 17 | 4,153 25 | 462 78 | 652 61 | 46,896 85 | .......... | 46,896 85 | .......... |
| 18 | .......... | 57 50 | 51 92 | 1,407 49 | .......... | 1,407 49 | .......... |
| 19 | 26 96 | 1,010 25 | 132 54 | 7,037 77 | .......... | 7,037 77 | .......... |
| 20 | 13 50 | 991 37 | 974 79 | 1,979 66 | .......... | 1,979 66 | .......... |
| 21 | 35,494 87 | 9,093 30 | 2,671 46 | 111,057 48 | .......... | 111,057 48 | .......... |
| 22 | .......... | 1 47 | 24 01 | 131 35 | .......... | 131 35 | .......... |
| 23 | 4 55 | .......... | .......... | 333 65 | .......... | 333 65 | .......... |
| 24 | 30,752 06 | 28,792 04 | 29,653 06 | 186,461 10 | .......... | 186,461 10 | .......... |
| 25 | .......... | 17 50 | 80 | 55 09 | .......... | 55 09 | .......... |
| 26 | 23 13 | 912 95 | 5,418 88 | 7,209 16 | .......... | 7,209 16 | .......... |
| 27 | 5,677 93 | 5,705 97 | 2,087 81 | 27,498 37 | .......... | 27,498 37 | .......... |
| 28 | 3,947 64 | 87,499 66 | 12,632 14 | 120,502 10 | .......... | 120,502 10 | .......... |
| 29 | 8,542 33 | 9,625 26 | 9,076 58 | 48,247 68 | .......... | 48,247 68 | .......... |
| 30 | 2 40 | .......... | .......... | 29 35 | .......... | 29 35 | .......... |
| 31 | .......... | 1 15 | .......... | 197 85 | .......... | 197 85 | .......... |
| 32 | .......... | .......... | 15 58 | 15 58 | .......... | 15 58 | .......... |
| 33 | .......... | .......... | 384 30 | 2,106 55 | .......... | 2,106 55 | .......... |
| 34 | .......... | .......... | 48 15 | 48 15 | .......... | 48 15 | .......... |
| 35 | 50 65 | .......... | 49 05 | 1,896 10 | .......... | 1,896 10 | .......... |
| 36 | 78 | 35 67 | .......... | 218 76 | .......... | 218 76 | .......... |
| 37 | .......... | .......... | .......... | 171 30 | .......... | 171 30 | .......... |

Detailed Statement of Revenues Collected and Other Cash Receipts by the City of New York also Showing the Distribution

| Character of Revenue | Department, Bureau or Office Through Which Collected | Statute or Ordinance | Year 1910 | Year 1911 | Line No. |
|---|---|---|---|---|---|
| 3. Assessments (Continued). Special Assessments (Continued): | | | | | |
| Brooklyn— | | | | | |
| Sewer Assessments, 29th Ward Instalments for 1897 and previous years | | | $32 94 | $14 29 | 1 |
| 26th Ward Street Improvement Fund | | | 725 61 | 79 36 | 2 |
| Grading Atlantic Avenue | | | 5,297 34 | 134 40 | 3 |
| Widening North Second Street | | | 4.08 | .......... | 4 |
| Assessments under $100 not sold, Town of Gravesend | | | 59 12 | .......... | 5 |
| Opening, Extending, Laying Out and Improving Bedford Ave | | | 11,700 89 | 11,715 94 | 6 |
| Prospect Park Improvements | | | 30,756 24 | 32,058 25 | 7 |
| Maintenance and Improvement of Public Parks, Brooklyn Heights | | | 550 08 | 550 08 | 8 |
| Queens— | | | | | |
| Long Island City, General Improvements | | Chap. 644, Laws of 1893 | 46,060 14 | 38,237 35 | 9 |
| Long Island City, Local Improvements | | | 3,011 60 | 158 96 | 10 |
| College Point, Local Improvements | | | 56 51 | .......... | 11 |
| Flushing, Local Improvements | | | 313 10 | 40 95 | 12 |
| Whitestone, Local Improvements | | | 148 94 | 235 75 | 13 |
| Various Villages, Local Improvements | | | .......... | 133 31 | 14 |
| Jamaica Avenue Improvement Fund | | | .......... | 67 40 | 15 |
| Richmond— | | | | | |
| Various Villages, Local Improvements | | | 3,708 57 | 460 84 | 16 |
| Manhattan and Bronx— | | | | | |
| Harlem River and Spuyten Duyvil Creek Improvement Fund | | | 17 09 | 21 41 | 17 |
| Williambridge Sewer Fund | | | 10,706 99 | 13,356 11 | 18 |
| 155th Street Viaduct | | | 1,307 87 | 26 19 | 19 |
| Towns of Westchester County | | Chap. 329, Laws of 1874; Chap. 934, Laws of 1895 | 5,382 31 | 2,328 40 | 20 |
| Assessments under Chap. 550, Laws of 1880 | | | 27,824 68 | 678 53 | 21 |
| Total | | | **$11,531,132 38** | **$11,333,213 55** | 22 |
| 4. Apportionment of School Moneys by the State of New York | Chamberlain | | | | |
| Common School Fund | | Article IX., Sec. 3—State Constitution; Sec. 1102—G. N. Y. C.; Secs. 490, 491, 492—Education Law. | $1,702,225 00 | $1,754,533 42 | 23 |
| Public School Library Fund | | Sec. 493—Education Law. | 92,716 00 | 32,200 00 | 24 |
| Special High School Fund | | Sec. 493—Education Law. | 99,703 72 | 7,584 00 | 25 |
| Hunter College, Special High School Fund | | | 3,978 43 | 2,322 90 | 26 |
| Maintenance of Training Schools | | Sec. 502—Education Law. | 55,043 93 | 53,798 13 | 27 |
| Vocational Training Schools | | Sec. 604—Education Law. Chap. 140, Laws of 1910, as amended | .......... | .......... | 28 |
| Total | | | **$1,953,667 08** | **$1,850,438 45** | 29 |
| 5. Payments by the State for Acquisition and Construction of Bronx Parkway | Comptroller | Chap. 594, Laws of 1907; Chap. 737, Laws of 1913 | .......... | **$8,750 00** | 30 |
| 6. Gifts, Legacies, Bequests and Unclaimed Moneys: | | | | | |
| Legacy of Betsy Head of Islip, N. Y. | Comptroller | | .......... | .......... | 31 |
| Bequest of Henry Harteau | Comptroller | | .......... | .......... | 32 |
| Amounts left by Deceased Patients | Dept. of Public Charities. | | .......... | .......... | 33 |
| Total | | | .......... | .......... | 34 |

# NEW YORK

FOR THE YEARS 1910 TO 1914, INCLUSIVE, GROUPED ACCORDING TO THE GENERAL CHARACTER THEREOF; THEREOF BY CLASSES OF FUNDS:

| LINE No. | Year | | | Total | Distribution by Classes of Funds | | |
|---|---|---|---|---|---|---|---|
| | 1912 | 1913 | 1914 | | General Fund | Special and Trust Funds | Sinking Funds |
| 1 | ... | ... | ... | $47 23 | ... | $47 23 | ... |
| 2 | ... | ... | ... | 804 97 | ... | 804 97 | ... |
| 3 | ... | ... | ... | 5,431 74 | ... | 5,431 74 | ... |
| 4 | ... | ... | ... | 4 08 | ... | 4 08 | ... |
| 5 | ... | ... | ... | 59 12 | ... | 59 12 | ... |
| 6 | $10,916 54 | $12,705 29 | $12,687 52 | 59,726 18 | ... | 59,726 18 | ... |
| 7 | 29,818 00 | 32,250 22 | 25,381 52 | 150,264 23 | ... | ... | $150,264 23 |
| 8 | 341 68 | 300 00 | 300 00 | 2,041 84 | ... | 2,041 84 | ... |
| 9 | 30,389 13 | 31,018 49 | 29,480 42 | 175,185 53 | ... | 175,185 53 | ... |
| 10 | 3,504 62 | ... | 1,320 23 | 7,995 41 | ... | 7,995 41 | ... |
| 11 | ... | ... | ... | 56 51 | ... | 56 51 | ... |
| 12 | ... | ... | ... | 354 05 | ... | 354 05 | ... |
| 13 | ... | ... | ... | 384 69 | ... | 384 69 | ... |
| 14 | 1,445 41 | 284 73 | 1,245 64 | 3,109 09 | ... | 3,109 09 | ... |
| 15 | ... | ... | ... | 67 40 | ... | 67 40 | ... |
| 16 | 849 41 | 1,238 36 | 128 02 | 6,385 20 | ... | 6,385 20 | ... |
| 17 | 39 33 | 16 58 | 228 11 | 322 52 | ... | 322 52 | ... |
| 18 | 7,931 64 | 16,013 10 | 4,478 38 | 52,486 22 | ... | 52,486 22 | ... |
| 19 | 205 21 | 167 37 | 21 30 | 1,727 94 | ... | 1,727 94 | ... |
| 20 | 3,117 27 | 6,324 79 | 3,723 12 | 20,875 89 | $3,723 12 | 17,152 77 | ... |
| 21 | 8,597 87 | 3,401 58 | 23,876 26 | 64,378 92 | ... | ... | 64,378 92 |
| 22 | **$10,161,069 93** | **$9,765,523 27** | **$10,688,369 01** | **$53,481,308 14** | ... | **$53,266,664 99** | **$228,909 36** |
| 23 | $1,812,325 00 | $1,878,752 37 | $1,923,025 00 | $9,070,860 79 | $9,070,860 79 | ... | ... |
| 24 | 32,834 00 | ... | 34,930 00 | 192,680 00 | ... | $192,680 00 | ... |
| 25 | 71,239 37 | 86,298 28 | 73,024 74 | 337,850 11 | ... | 337,850 11 | ... |
| 26 | 1,439 23 | 1,222 49 | 1,292 70 | 10,255 75 | ... | 10,255 75 | ... |
| 27 | 52,772 97 | 45,688 16 | 17,853 67 | 225,156 86 | ... | 225,156 86 | ... |
| 28 | ... | ... | 13,200 00 | 13,200 00 | ... | 13,200 00 | ... |
| 29 | **$1,970,610 57** | **$2,011,961 30** | **$2,063,326 11** | **$9,850,003 51** | **$9,070,860 79** | **$779,142 72** | ... |
| 30 | ... | **$204,500 00** | **$286,919 76** | **$500,169 76** | ... | **$500,169 76** | ... |
| 31 | ... | ... | $55 10 | $55 10 | ... | $55 10 | ... |
| 32 | $17,722 39 | ... | ... | 17,722 39 | ... | 17,722 39 | ... |
| 33 | ... | $157 30 | ... | 157 30 | $157 30 | ... | ... |
| 34 | **$17,722 39** | **$157 30** | **$55 10** | **$17,934 79** | **$157 30** | **$17,777 49** | ... |

DETAILED STATEMENT OF REVENUES COLLECTED AND OTHER CASH RECEIPTS BY THE CITY OF NEW YORK ALSO SHOWING THE DISTRIBUTION

| Character of Revenue | Department, Bureau or Office Through Which Collected | Statute or Ordinance | Year 1910 | Year 1911 | Line No. |
|---|---|---|---|---|---|
| 7. PAYMENTS TO CITY BY LESSEES OF CITY PROPERTY FOR COSTS OF CONSTRUCTION: | | | | | |
| Erection of Shed on Pier 4.......... | Dept. of Docks & Ferries. | ........................ | .......... | $27,339 40 | 1 |
| Construction of Rapid Transit Railroads.......................... | Comptroller.......... | ........................ | .......... | .......... | 2 |
| Total...................... | ........................ | ........................ | .......... | **$27,339 40** | 3 |
| 8. RAPID TRANSIT R. R. RENTALS..... | Comptroller........... | Contract. | | | |
| Amortization Instalments on Bonds, Manhattan and Bronx Division... | ........................ | ........................ | $452,284 04 | $462,816 00 | 4 |
| Amortization Instalments on Bonds, Brooklyn and Manhattan Division. | ........................ | ........................ | 37,595 65 | 39,117 32 | 5 |
| Interest on Bonds, Manhattan and Bronx Division............ | ........................ | ........................ | 1,568,963 86 | 1,618,017 33 | 6 |
| Interest on Bonds, Brooklyn and Manhattan Division............ | ........................ | ........................ | 141,929 07 | 152,887 38 | 7 |
| Total...................... | ........................ | ........................ | **$2,200,772 62** | **$2,272,838 03** | 8 |
| 9. DOCK AND SLIP RENTS............ | Dept. of Docks & Ferries | Secs. 825, 825a, 859–862, G. N. Y. C............ Chap. 2, Art. I, Sec. 4, C. O., 1915.............. | **$4,115,601 75** | **$4,377,223 66** | 9 |
| 10. FERRY RENTS AND LEASES......... | Dept. of Docks & Ferries | Sec. 826, G. N. Y. C...... | **$247,912 77** | **$232,624 67** | 10 |
| 11. MUNICIPAL FERRY FARES AND PRIVILEGES........................ | Dept. of Docks & Ferries | Secs. 818–826, G. N. Y. C. | | | |
| Staten Island Ferry, Fares.......... | ........................ | ........................ | $704,148 30 | $726,988 60 | 11 |
| Staten Island Ferry, Privileges...... | ........................ | ........................ | 47,138 98 | 52,863 97 | 12 |
| Thirty-ninth Street Ferry, Fares..... | ........................ | ........................ | 186,770 38 | 199,188 22 | 13 |
| Thirty-ninth Street Ferry, Privileges. | ........................ | ........................ | 4,538 44 | 4,141 14 | 14 |
| Total...................... | ........................ | ........................ | **$942,596 10** | **$983,181 93** | 15 |
| 12. WATER REVENUES: | | | | | |
| Manhattan and The Bronx........ | Dept. of W. S. G. & E. and Comptroller..... | Secs. 473, 475 and 476, G. N. Y. C............ Ch. 2, Art. I, Sec. 1, C.O., 1915.................. | $9,090,203 47 | $8,905,180 93 | 16 |
| Brooklyn........................ | Dept. of W. S. G. & E. and Comptroller..... | Secs. 473, 475 and 476, G. N. Y. C............ Ch. 396, Laws 1859...... | 3,609,955 82 | 3,872,411 27 | 17 |
| Queens......................... | Dept. of W. S. G. & E. and Comptroller.... | Secs. 473, 475 and 476, G. N. Y. C.......... | 317,583 51 | 331,720 25 | 18 |
| Richmond....................... | Dept. of W. S. G. & E. and Comptroller..... | Secs. 473, 475 and 476, G. N. Y. C............ | 178,520 60 | 201,443 16 | 19 |
| Flushing, Newtown and Jamaica..... | ........................ | ........................ | .......... | 38,496 59 | 20 |
| Building Purposes................ | Dept. of W. S. G. & E... | ........................ | 2,182 56 | .......... | 21 |
| Street Sprinkling................ | Dept. of W. S. G. & E... | ........................ | 1,600 20 | .......... | 22 |
| American Sugar Refining Co....... | ........................ | ........................ | .......... | .......... | 23 |
| Total...................... | ........................ | ........................ | **$13,200,046 16** | **$13,349,252 20** | 24 |
| 13. BRIDGE TOLLS: | | | | | |
| Brooklyn Bridge Revenues.......... | Dept. of Bridges........ | Sec. 242, G. N. Y. C...... | $369,154 25 | $339,983 76 | 25 |
| Williamsburgh Bridge (Maintenance). | Dept. of Bridges........ | Sec. 242, G. N. Y. C...... | 274,870 83 | 205,286 58 | 26 |
| Williamsburgh Bridge Revenues..... | Dept. of Bridges........ | Sec. 242, G. N. Y. C...... | .......... | .......... | 27 |
| Manhattan Bridge................ | Dept. of Bridges........ | Sec. 242, G. N. Y. C...... | .......... | .......... | 28 |
| Bridges not Specified.............. | Dept. of Bridges........ | Sec. 242, G. N. Y. C...... | 147,430 08 | 91,433 13 | 29 |
| Total...................... | ........................ | ........................ | **$791,455 16** | **$636,703 47** | 30 |
| 14. REVENUES FROM OPERATION OF BUS LINE, BARTOW TO CITY ISLAND.... | Dept. of Parks, Bronx... | ........................ | .......... | .......... | 31 |
| 15. MUNICIPAL OPERATION OF SCOW TRIMMING AND PICKING.............. | Dept. of Street Cleaning. | ........................ | .......... | .......... | 32 |
| 16. REVENUES FROM OPERATION OF MUNICIPAL BATHS AND COMFORT STATIONS: | | | | | |
| Municipal Bath, Coney Island....... | Borough Presidents..... | Sec. 383, G. N. Y. C...... | .......... | $2,190 80 | 33 |
| Use of Private Rooms, Towels, etc. Public Baths and Comfort Stations. | Borough Presidents..... | Sec. 383, G. N. Y. C..... | $18,924 75 | 20,520 62 | 34 |
| Total...................... | ........................ | ........................ | **$18,924 75** | **$22,711 42** | 35 |

# EW YORK

R THE YEARS 1910 TO 1914, INCLUSIVE, GROUPED ACCORDING TO THE GENERAL CHARACTER THEREOF; EREOF BY CLASSES OF FUNDS:

| Year | | | Total | Distribution by Classes of Funds | | |
|---|---|---|---|---|---|---|
| 1912 | 1913 | 1914 | | General Fund | Special and Trust Funds | Sinking Funds |
| .......... | .......... | .......... | $27,339 40 | .......... | $27,339 40 | .......... |
| .......... | $4,378,799 44 | $1,636,514 82 | 6,015,314 26 | .......... | 6,015,314 26 | .......... |
| .......... | **$4,378,799 44** | **$1,636,514 82** | **$6,042,653 66** | .......... | **$6,042,653 66** | .......... |
| $465,381 48 | $467,592 83 | $468,597 55 | $2,316,671 90 | .......... | .......... | $2,316,671 90 |
| 42,317 16 | 44,959 90 | 44,703 15 | 208,693 18 | .......... | .......... | 208,693 18 |
| 1,641,134 64 | 1,647,544 37 | 1,649,821 01 | 8,125,481 21 | .......... | $8,125,481 21 | .......... |
| 166,468 51 | 188,441 99 | 198,906 31 | 848,633 26 | .......... | 848,633 26 | .......... |
| **$2,315,301 79** | **$2,348,539 09** | **$2,362,028 02** | **$11,499,479 55** | .......... | **$8,974,114 47** | **$2,525,365 08** |
| **$4,498,659 99** | **$4,596,092 49** | **$4,688,151 33** | **$22,275,729 22** | .......... | .......... | **$22,275,729 22** |
| **$243,733 88** | **$307,318 29** | **$318,291 71** | **$1,349,881 32** | .......... | .......... | **$1,349,881 32** |
| $759,365 70 | $813,772 65 | $821,416 43 | $3,825,691 68 | .......... | .......... | $3,825,691 68 |
| 73,275 17 | 51,753 61 | 36,620 87 | 261,652 60 | .......... | .......... | 261,652 60 |
| 204,257 71 | 224,398 64 | 218,620 54 | 1,033,235 49 | .......... | .......... | 1,033,235 49 |
| 5,294 23 | 6,490 74 | 3,421 68 | 23,886 23 | .......... | .......... | 23,886 23 |
| **$1,042,192 81** | **$1,096,415 64** | **$1,080,079 52** | **$5,144,466 00** | .......... | .......... | **$5,144,466 00** |
| $7,259,486 22 | $8,167,941 88 | $8,412,356 46 | $41,835,168 96 | .......... | .......... | $41,835,168 96 |
| 3,131,302 73 | 3,711,011 43 | 3,778,608 01 | 18,103,289 26 | .......... | $18,103,289 26 | .......... |
| 274,307 18 | 353,064 30 | 410,578 98 | 1,687,254 22 | .......... | 1,687,254 22 | .......... |
| 185,370 41 | 215,248 43 | 217,952 57 | 998,535 17 | $985,698 92 | 12,836 25 | .......... |
| 50,502 13 | 59,309 63 | 61,665 71 | 209,974 06 | 209,974 06 | .......... | .......... |
| .......... | .......... | 21 69 | 2,204 25 | 2,204 25 | .......... | .......... |
| .......... | .......... | .......... | 1,600 20 | 1,600 20 | .......... | .......... |
| .......... | 285,734 16 | .......... | 285,734 16 | .......... | 285,734 16 | .......... |
| **$10,900,968 67** | **$12,792,309 83** | **$12,881,183 42** | **$63,123,760 28** | **$1,199,477 43** | **$20,089,113 89** | **$41,835,168 96** |
| $305,751 11 | $282,673 43 | $291,085 87 | $1,588,648 42 | .......... | $1,588,648 42 | .......... |
| 132,553 49 | .......... | 1,000 00 | 613,710 90 | .......... | 613,710 90 | .......... |
| .......... | 121,842 60 | 93,087 13 | 214,929 73 | .......... | 214,929 73 | .......... |
| 321 80 | 7,288 85 | 160 45 | 7,771 10 | $7,771 10 | .......... | .......... |
| .......... | .......... | .......... | 238,863 21 | 238,863 21 | .......... | .......... |
| **$438,626 40** | **$411,804 88** | **$385,333 45** | **$2,663,923 36** | **$246,634 31** | **$2,417,289 05** | .......... |
| .......... | .......... | **$6,180 64** | **$6,180 64** | .......... | **$6,180 64** | .......... |
| .......... | **$5,337 00** | **$17,445 28** | **$22,782 28** | **$5,337 00** | **$17,445 28** | .......... |
| $25,311 25 | $37,110 50 | $29,872 00 | $94,484 55 | $94,484 55 | .......... | .......... |
| 22,415 56 | 21,708 82 | 30,735 73 | 114,305 48 | 114,305 48 | .......... | .......... |
| **$47,726 81** | **$58,819 32** | **$60,607 73** | **$208,790 03** | **$208,790 03** | .......... | .......... |

**Detailed Statement of Revenues Collected and Other Cash Receipts by the City of New York also Showing the Distribution**

| Character of Revenue | Department, Bureau or Office Through Which Collected | Statute or Ordinance | Year | | LINE No. |
|---|---|---|---|---|---|
| | | | 1910 | 1911 | |
| **17. Receipts from Sales and Redemptions of Seized or Confiscated Property:** | | | | | |
| Redemption of Lands Purchased for Taxes and Assessments | | | $2,637 01 | $294 30 | 1 |
| Incumbrances Seized | Dept. of Street Cleaning | Sec. 545, G. N. Y. C. | 3,863 64 | 2,920 38 | 2 |
| Incumbrances Seized | Borough Presidents | | | | 3 |
| Confiscated Property | District Attorney | | 3 00 | 18 05 | 4 |
| Surplus on Sales of St. Incumbrances | Dept. of Street Cleaning | | 55 00 | | 5 |
| Redemption Fund, Boro. of Brooklyn | | | 27,179 43 | | 6 |
| Surplus Fund, Boro. of Brooklyn | | | 312 76 | | 7 |
| Total | | | **$34,050 84** | **$3,232 73** | 8 |
| **18. Sale of Publications, Maps, Drugs, Etc., and Articles Manufactured by Departments:** | | | | | |
| Disinfectants | Dept. of Charities | | | | 9 |
| Vaccine | Dept. of Health | Sec. 1226, G. N. Y. C. | $11,243 73 | $10,299 76 | 10 |
| Antitoxin | Dept. of Health | Sec. 1226, G. N. Y. C. | 51,226 51 | 35,718 18 | 11 |
| Manufactured Articles | Dept. of Corrections | Sec. 700, G. N. Y. C., Resolution of Board of Aldermen, Mar. 17, 1914 | 112,428 03 | 115,673 00 | 12 |
| Prints | Borough Presidents | | | 73 99 | 13 |
| Contract Maps | Public Service Com | | 4,619 20 | 1,108 66 | 14 |
| Maps, Plans, etc | Borough Presidents | | | | 15 |
| Forms | Borough Presidents | | | | 16 |
| City Record | Board of City Record | Sec. 1526, G. N. Y. C. | 12,749 73 | 11,245 36 | 17 |
| Manual of Accounting | Comptroller | | 119 45 | | 18 |
| Badges | Borough Presidents | | | | 19 |
| Caps and Badges | Dept. of Parks | | | | 20 |
| Total | | | **$192,386 65** | **$174,118 95** | 21 |
| **19. Sale of Ashes, Paper, Condemned Material and Equipment and Other By-Products:** | | | | | |
| Old Material, Equipment, etc. | Dept. of W. S. G. & E. | Sec. 1553, G. N. Y. C.; Chap. 396, Laws of 1859 | $4,688 84 | $1,447 83 | 22 |
| Old Material, Equipment, etc. | Dept. of Corrections | Sec. 1553, G. N. Y. C.; Chap. 396, Laws of 1859 | 1,212 02 | 5,417 37 | 23 |
| Old Material, Equipment, etc. | Bellevue and Allied Hos. | Sec. 1553, G. N. Y. C.; Chap. 396, Laws of 1859 | 2,276 05 | 2,174 96 | 24 |
| Old Material, Equipment, etc. | Dept. of Health | Sec. 1553, G. N. Y. C.; Chap. 396, Laws of 1859 | | | 25 |
| Old Material, Equipment, etc. | Dept. of Charities | Sec. 1553, G. N. Y. C.; Chap. 396, Laws of 1859 | 6,938 50 | 11,472 97 | 26 |
| Old Material, Equipment, etc. | Dept. of Bridges | Sec. 1553, G. N. Y. C.; Chap. 396, Laws of 1859 | | 617 00 | 27 |
| Old Material, Equipment, etc. | Dept. of Street Cleaning | Sec. 1553, G. N. Y. C.; Chap. 396, Laws of 1859 | 16,450 83 | 10,716 56 | 28 |
| Old Material, Equipment, etc. | Dept. of Education | Sec. 1066, G. N. Y. C. | 7 43 | | 29 |
| Old Material, Equipment, etc. | Borough Presidents | Sec. 1553, G. N. Y. C.; Chap. 396, Laws of 1859 | 6,170 87 | 4,663 33 | 30 |
| Old Material, Equipment, etc. | Board of Elections | Sec. 1553, G. N. Y. C.; Chap. 396, Laws of 1859 | | 1,795 45 | 31 |
| Old Material, Equipment, etc. | Board of Aldermen | Sec. 1553, G. N. Y. C.; Chap. 396, Laws of 1859 | | | 32 |
| Old Material, Equipment, etc. | B'd of City Magistrates | Sec. 1553, G. N. Y. C.; Chap. 396, Laws of 1859 | | | 33 |
| Old Material, Equipment, etc. | Exam. B'd of Plumbers | Sec. 1553, G. N. Y. C.; Chap. 396, Laws of 1859 | 26 19 | | 34 |
| Old Material, Equipment, etc. | Board of City Record | Sec. 1553, G. N. Y. C.; Chap. 396, Laws of 1859 | | | 35 |
| Old Material, Equipment, etc. | Commissioners of Acc'ts. | Sec. 1553, G. N. Y. C.; Chap. 396, Laws of 1859 | | 202 50 | 36 |
| Old Material, Equipment, etc. | Chamberlain | Sec. 1553, G. N. Y. C.; Chap. 396, Laws of 1859 | | | 37 |
| Old Material, Equipment, etc. | Comptroller | Sec. 1553, G. N. Y. C.; Chap. 396, Laws of 1859 | 16,045 91 | 30,194 29 | 38 |
| Old Material, Equipment, etc. | Com. of Jurors, N.Y.Co. | | | | 39 |
| Old Material, Court House Site | | | | | 40 |
| Old Material, 9th Artillery Armory | | | | | 41 |
| Old Material, B'klyn Disciplinary Sc'l. | | Sec. 1553, G. N. Y. C.; Chap. 396, Laws of 1859 | 77 70 | | 42 |
| Personal Property | Board of Education | Sec. 1066, G. N. Y. C. | | 6,729 84 | 43 |
| Unused Ballots | Board of Elections | Chap. 95, Laws of 1901 | | 163 06 | 44 |
| Ashes | Dept. W. S. G. & E. | Sec. 1553, G. N. Y. C.; Chap. 396, Laws of 1859 | 250 00 | 194 15 | 45 |
| Old Paper | Borough Presidents | Sec. 1553, G. N. Y. C.; Chap. 396, Laws of 1859 | | | 46 |

# NEW YORK

FOR THE YEARS 1910 TO 1914, INCLUSIVE, GROUPED ACCORDING TO THE GENERAL CHARACTER THEREOF; THEREOF BY CLASSES OF FUNDS:

| LINE No. | Year | | | Total | Distribution by Classes of Funds | | |
|---|---|---|---|---|---|---|---|
| | 1912 | 1913 | 1914 | | General Fund | Special and Trust Funds | Sinking Funds |
| 1 | $36 25 | $73 19 | $2,421 86 | $5,462 61 | .......... | $5,462 61 | .......... |
| 2 | .......... | .......... | .......... | 6,784 02 | .......... | 6,784 02 | .......... |
| 3 | 1,343 97 | .......... | .......... | 1,343 97 | $1,343 97 | .......... | .......... |
| 4 | 44 25 | .......... | 112 02 | 177 32 | 177 32 | .......... | .......... |
| 5 | 28 79 | 18 77 | .......... | 102 56 | .......... | 102 56 | .......... |
| 6 | .......... | .......... | .......... | 27,179 43 | .......... | 27,179 43 | .......... |
| 7 | .......... | .......... | .......... | 312 76 | .......... | 312 76 | .......... |
| 8 | **$1,453 26** | **$91 96** | **$2,533 88** | **$41,362 67** | **$1,521 29** | **$39,841 38** | .......... |
| 9 | .......... | $2,548 53 | $2,765 23 | $5,313 76 | $5,313 76 | .......... | .......... |
| 10 | $9,674 96 | 7,269 68 | 11,782 76 | 50,270 89 | .......... | $50,270 89 | .......... |
| 11 | 37,971 60 | 33,319 74 | 59,146 19 | 217,382 22 | .......... | 217,382 22 | .......... |
| 12 | 179,280 46 | 153,666 25 | 96,326 22 | 657,373 96 | 587,120 29 | 70,253 67 | .......... |
| 13 | 264 01 | 334 54 | 233 27 | 905 81 | 905 81 | .......... | .......... |
| 14 | 4,011 90 | 4,091 09 | 8,270 59 | 22,101 44 | 22,101 44 | .......... | .......... |
| 15 | 13 40 | 71 98 | .......... | 85 38 | 85 38 | .......... | .......... |
| 16 | .......... | 5 00 | .......... | 5 00 | 5 00 | .......... | .......... |
| 17 | 12,669 24 | 13,562 48 | 12,979 05 | 63,205 86 | 63,205 86 | .......... | .......... |
| 18 | 22 25 | 34 14 | .......... | 175 84 | 175 84 | .......... | .......... |
| 19 | .......... | 262 50 | .......... | 262 50 | 262 50 | .......... | .......... |
| 20 | .......... | 38 25 | .......... | 38 25 | 38 25 | .......... | .......... |
| 21 | **$243,907 82** | **$215,204 18** | **$191,503 31** | **$1,017,120 91** | **$679,214 13** | **$337,906 78** | .......... |
| 22 | $3,793 77 | $3,387 20 | $16,151 76 | $29,469 40 | $25,648 59 | $3,820 81 | .......... |
| 23 | 2,399 77 | 1,992 81 | 2,295 14 | 13,317 11 | 13,317 11 | .......... | .......... |
| 24 | 4,046 45 | 4,885 45 | 4,833 85 | 18,216 76 | 18,216 76 | .......... | .......... |
| 25 | 765 11 | 535 00 | 335 32 | 1,635 43 | 1,635 43 | .......... | .......... |
| 26 | 11,561 44 | 9,083 21 | 9,815 59 | 48,871 71 | 48,871 71 | .......... | .......... |
| 27 | 2,338 01 | 909 06 | 280 45 | 4,144 52 | 4,144 52 | .......... | .......... |
| 28 | .......... | .......... | .......... | 27,167 39 | 27,167 39 | .......... | .......... |
| 29 | 201 50 | .......... | .......... | 208 93 | 208 93 | .......... | .......... |
| 30 | 4,578 48 | 6,020 89 | 3,136 08 | 24,569 65 | 24,560 65 | .......... | .......... |
| 31 | .......... | .......... | 5 10 | 1,800 55 | 1,800 55 | .......... | .......... |
| 32 | .......... | .......... | 10 00 | 10 00 | 10 00 | .......... | .......... |
| 33 | .......... | .......... | 28 50 | 28 50 | 28 50 | .......... | .......... |
| 34 | .......... | .......... | .......... | 26 19 | 26 19 | .......... | .......... |
| 35 | .......... | 103 22 | .......... | 103 22 | 103 22 | .......... | .......... |
| 36 | .......... | .......... | .......... | 202 50 | 202 50 | .......... | .......... |
| 37 | .......... | .......... | 141 51 | 141 51 | 141 51 | .......... | .......... |
| 38 | 28,253 30 | 99,217 18 | 59,105 66 | 232,816 34 | 232,804 81 | 11 53 | .......... |
| 39 | .......... | .......... | 19 50 | 19 50 | 19 50 | .......... | .......... |
| 40 | .......... | 4,947 00 | 22,475 00 | 27,422 00 | 27,422 00 | .......... | .......... |
| 41 | .......... | .......... | 15 00 | 15 00 | 15 00 | .......... | .......... |
| 42 | .......... | .......... | .......... | 77 70 | 77 70 | .......... | .......... |
| 43 | 9,835 07 | 14,220 21 | 19,682 92 | 50,468 04 | .......... | 50,468 04 | .......... |
| 44 | 491 12 | .......... | 1,817 46 | 2,471 64 | .......... | 2,471 64 | .......... |
| 45 | 595 50 | 872 75 | 1,564 25 | 3,476 65 | 2,175 85 | 1,300 80 | .......... |
| 46 | .......... | .......... | 1,996 63 | 1,996 63 | 1,996 63 | .......... | .......... |

**Detailed Statement of Revenues Collected and Other Cash Receipts by the City of New York also Showing the Distribution**

| Character of Revenue | Department Bureau or Office Through Which Collected | Statute or Ordinance | Year | | LINE No. |
|---|---|---|---|---|---|
| | | | 1910 | 1911 | |
| 19. Sale of Ashes, Paper, Condemned Material, and Equipment and Other By-Products (Continued): | | | | | |
| Old Paper | Dept. of Finance | Sec. 1553, G. N. Y. C.; Chap. 396, Laws of 1859 | .......... | .......... | 1 |
| Auction Sale of Lead | Exam. B'd of Plumbers | Sec. 1553, G. N. Y. C.; Chap. 396, Laws of 1859 | .......... | $40 28 | 2 |
| Cement Bags | Dept. of Corrections | Sec. 1553, G. N. Y. C.; Chap. 396, Laws of 1859 | .......... | .......... | 3 |
| Removal of Ashes | Dept. of W. S. G. & E. | Sec. 1553, G. N. Y. C.; Chap. 396, Laws of 1859 | $120 00 | 240 00 | 4 |
| Zoological Garden Equipment | .......... | .......... | 519 75 | 482 40 | 5 |
| Allowance for Safe | Borough President | Sec. 1553, G. N. Y. C.; Chap. 396, Laws of 1859 | .......... | 200 00 | 6 |
| Total | .......... | .......... | **$54,784 09** | **$76,751 99** | 7 |
| 20. Court Fees, Fines and Penalties (Other than Interest) and Forfeiture of Bails: | | | | | |
| Fees, Stenographers' | .......... | .......... | $22,716 00 | $20,964 00 | 8 |
| Court Fees and Fines | Various City and County Courts | See Note No. 1, page 215 | 408,248 95 | 432,072 05 | 9 |
| Court Fees and Fines | District Attorney, Kings | .......... | .......... | .......... | 10 |
| Court Fees and Fines | County Clerk, Richmond | Sec. 161, County Law | .......... | .......... | 11 |
| Fines, License | .......... | .......... | 41 50 | 81 50 | 12 |
| Fines, Jurors' | Commissioner of Jurors | .......... | 2,144 41 | 331 11 | 13 |
| Fines, Abandonment | .......... | .......... | .......... | .......... | 14 |
| Fines and Penalties | Corporation Counsel | Sec. 259, G. N. Y. C. | 19,679 45 | 22,506 40 | 15 |
| Fines and Penalties | Sheriff, Bronx Co. | .......... | .......... | .......... | 16 |
| Fines and Penalties | Sheriff, Queens Co. | .......... | 1,293 00 | 710 00 | 17 |
| Fines and Penalties | Sheriff, Richmond Co. | .......... | 325 00 | 295 00 | 18 |
| Fines and Penalties, N. Y. County Penitentiary | Dept. of Correction | .......... | 3,200 00 | 3,760 00 | 19 |
| Fines and Penalties, City Prisons, Manhattan | Dept. of Correction | .......... | 5,429 00 | 8,059 00 | 20 |
| Fines and Penalties, District Prison, Manhattan and Bronx | Dept. of Correction | .......... | 29,153 50 | 24,500 00 | 21 |
| Fines and Penalties, Workhouse | Dept. of Correction | .......... | 3,950 00 | 3,249 00 | 22 |
| Fines and Penalties, Kings County Jail | Dept. of Correction | .......... | 6,671 50 | 5,010 00 | 23 |
| Fines and Penalties, City Prison, Queens | Dept. of Correction | .......... | .......... | .......... | 24 |
| Penalties | Tenement House Dept. | Chap. 78, Laws of 1902 | 4,633 75 | 6,546 47 | 25 |
| Penalties for Violation of Sunday Law | .......... | .......... | .......... | 500 00 | 26 |
| Fines and Penalties, in Trust for Various Societies | Various | .......... | 18,272 50 | 47,046 50 | 27 |
| Forfeited Recognizances | District Attorney | Secs. 593–598, Code of Criminal Procedure | 30,470 07 | 48,660 86 | 28 |
| Forfeited Bonds, Given for Good Behavior | .......... | .......... | .......... | .......... | 29 |
| Total | .......... | .......... | **$556,228 63** | **$624,291 89** | 30 |
| 21. Rents, Permits and Privileges Not Otherwise Classified: | | | | | |
| Ground | Comptroller | Sec. 205, G. N. Y. C.; Chap. 2, Art. I, Sec. 4, C. O., 1915 | $55,720 60 | $69,282 68 | 31 |
| House | Comptroller | Sec. 205, G. N. Y. C.; Chap. 2, Art. I, Sec. 4, C. O., 1915 | 109,440 52 | 124,869 65 | 32 |
| Water Lot | Comptroller | Sec. 205, G. N. Y. C.; Chap. 2, Art. I, Sec. 5, C. O., 1915 | 770 02 | 675 23 | 33 |
| Water Lot, Quit | Comptroller | Sec. 205, G. N. Y. C.; Chap. 2, Art. I, Sec. 5, C. O., 1915 | 32 73 | 45 60 | 34 |
| Common Lands | .......... | Sec. 205, G. N. Y. C. | 86 00 | 48 00 | 35 |
| Market Stands, Manhattan | Comptroller | Sec. 205, G. N. Y. C. | 209,612 70 | 206,159 56 | 36 |
| Market Stands | Comptroller | Sec. 205, G. N. Y. C. | 85 00 | 51 00 | 37 |
| Flower Market | Comptroller | Sec. 205, G. N. Y. C. | .......... | 800 00 | 38 |
| Market and Cellar, Manhattan | Comptroller | Sec. 205, G. N. Y. C.; Chap. 2, Art. I, Sec. 4, C. O., 1915 | 845 00 | 625 00 | 39 |
| Wallabout Market Lot, Brooklyn | Comptroller | .......... | 62,186 50 | 66,995 22 | 40 |
| Park Rents, etc., including Bay Window Permits | Dept. of Parks | Sec. 612, G. N. Y. C. | 70,356 90 | 56,646 85 | 41 |
| Bridge Rents | Dept. of Bridges | .......... | 2,100 00 | 2,100 00 | 42 |
| Commutation of Water Grants | Comptroller | .......... | 1,682 84 | .......... | 43 |
| Portion of Old Clinton Market | Dept. of Street Cleaning | .......... | 1,000 00 | .......... | 44 |
| Cloves Lake, S. I. | Borough President | .......... | 281 25 | .......... | 45 |
| Poles, License Fees, Rentals, etc. | .......... | .......... | .......... | 416 25 | 46 |

# NEW YORK

OR THE YEARS 1910 TO 1914, INCLUSIVE, GROUPED ACCORDING TO THE GENERAL CHARACTER THEREOF; HEREOF BY CLASSES OF FUNDS:

| LINE No. | Year 1912 | Year 1913 | Year 1914 | Total | Distribution of Classes by Funds: General Fund | Special and Trust Funds | Sinking Funds |
|---|---|---|---|---|---|---|---|
| 1 | $38 10 | .......... | .......... | $38 10 | $38 10 | .......... | .......... |
| 2 | 39 36 | .......... | .......... | 79 64 | 79 64 | .......... | .......... |
| 3 | .......... | $866 23 | .......... | 866 23 | 866 23 | .......... | .......... |
| 4 | 240 00 | .......... | .......... | 600 00 | 600 00 | .......... | .......... |
| 5 | 633 10 | 492 69 | $638 23 | 2,766 17 | .......... | $2,766 17 | .......... |
| 6 | .......... | .......... | .......... | 200 00 | 200 00 | .......... | .......... |
| 7 | **$69,810 08** | **$147,532 90** | **$144,347 95** | **$493,227 01** | **$432,388 02** | **$60,838 99** | .......... |
| 8 | $21,243 00 | $25,458 00 | $25,803 70 | $116,184 70 | .......... | .......... | $116,184 70 |
| 9 | 480,017 36 | 568,816 87 | 660,570 31 | 2,549,725 54 | .......... | .......... | 2,549,725 54 |
| 10 | .......... | 25 00 | 1,240 00 | 1,265 00 | .......... | .......... | 1,265 00 |
| 11 | .......... | 25 00 | 170 00 | 195 00 | .......... | .......... | 195 00 |
| 12 | 332 00 | 453 00 | 2,555 00 | 3,463 00 | .......... | .......... | 3,463 00 |
| 13 | 133 67 | 110 00 | 397 00 | 3,116 19 | .......... | .......... | 3,116 19 |
| 14 | .......... | .......... | 116 00 | 116 00 | $116 00 | .......... | .......... |
| 15 | 32,713 07 | 14,770 57 | 6,785 50 | 96,454 99 | .......... | .......... | 96,454 99 |
| 16 | .......... | .......... | 466 00 | 466 00 | .......... | .......... | 466 00 |
| 17 | 90 00 | .......... | 251 00 | 2,344 00 | .......... | .......... | 2,344 00 |
| 18 | 359 00 | 361 00 | .......... | 1,340 00 | 4 00 | .......... | 1,336 00 |
| 19 | 6,513 00 | 4,557 00 | 7,450 00 | 25,480 00 | .......... | .......... | 25,480 00 |
| 20 | 7,391 50 | 6,704 00 | 8,567 00 | 36,150 50 | .......... | .......... | 36,150 50 |
| 21 | 24,574 50 | 28,212 00 | 42,705 00 | 149,145 00 | .......... | .......... | 149,145 00 |
| 22 | 2,526 00 | 2,945 00 | 2,957 00 | 15,627 00 | .......... | .......... | 15,627 00 |
| 23 | 10,718 00 | 8,192 00 | 9,938 00 | 40,529 50 | .......... | .......... | 40,529 50 |
| 24 | 445 00 | 870 00 | 2,136 00 | 3,451 00 | .......... | .......... | 3,451 00 |
| 25 | 3,783 53 | 4,186 08 | 6,508 60 | 25,658 43 | 25,658 43 | .......... | .......... |
| 26 | .......... | .......... | .......... | 500 00 | 500 00 | .......... | .......... |
| 27 | 66,468 25 | 84,264 10 | 78,590 00 | 294,647 35 | .......... | $294,647 35 | .......... |
| 28 | 124,442 22 | 157,160 46 | 129,998 48 | 490,732 09 | 8,413 35 | 482,318 74 | .......... |
| 29 | .......... | .......... | 633 00 | 633 00 | 633 00 | .......... | .......... |
| 30 | **$781,750 10** | **$907,110 08** | **$987,843 59** | **$3,857,224 29** | **$35,324 78** | **$776,966 09** | **$3,044,933 42** |
| 31 | $63,396 42 | $59,230 11 | $72,147 23 | $319,777 04 | .......... | .......... | $319,777 04 |
| 32 | 102,788 22 | 166,529 05 | 185,180 95 | 688,808 39 | $2,170 00 | .......... | 686,638 39 |
| 33 | 677 55 | 676 39 | 675 23 | 3,474 42 | .......... | .......... | 3,474 42 |
| 34 | 7 36 | 7 36 | 7 36 | 100 41 | .......... | .......... | 100 41 |
| 35 | 82 00 | 144 00 | 151 50 | 511 50 | .......... | $511 50 | .......... |
| 36 | 204,900 77 | 200,357 77 | 155,410 02 | 976,440 82 | .......... | .......... | 976,440 82 |
| 37 | 45 00 | 45 00 | 27 00 | 253 00 | 253 00 | .......... | .......... |
| 38 | 750 00 | .......... | 800 00 | 2,350 00 | .......... | .......... | 2,350 00 |
| 39 | 750 00 | 750 00 | 750 00 | 3,720 00 | .......... | .......... | 3,720 00 |
| 40 | 67,803 56 | 69,640 37 | 69,144 68 | 335,770 33 | .......... | .......... | 335,770 33 |
| 41 | 61,799 28 | 63,629 08 | 85,477 68 | 337,909 79 | 337,909 79 | .......... | .......... |
| 42 | 2,500 00 | 2,500 00 | 2,500 00 | 11,700 00 | 11,700 00 | .......... | .......... |
| 43 | .......... | .......... | .......... | 1,682 84 | .......... | .......... | 1,682 84 |
| 44 | .......... | .......... | .......... | 1,000 00 | 1,000 00 | .......... | .......... |
| 45 | .......... | .......... | .......... | 281 25 | 281 25 | .......... | .......... |
| 46 | 278 65 | 1,876 50 | 1,918 33 | 4,489 73 | 3,457 73 | 1,032 00 | .......... |

**Detailed Statement of Revenues Collected and Other Cash Receipts by the City of New York also Showing the Distribution**

| Character of Revenue | Department, Bureau or Office Through Which Collected | Statute or Ordinance | Year 1910 | Year 1911 | Line No. |
|---|---|---|---|---|---|
| 21. Rents, Permits and Privileges Not Otherwise Classified (Con.): | | | | | |
| Market Wagon Fees | Comptroller | | $27,966 25 | $32,453 25 | 1 |
| Boot Black Stands | Comptroller | | | | 2 |
| Bridge Privileges | Dept. of Bridges | | 3,673 50 | 4,349 00 | 3 |
| Fountains—Drinking Water | Comptroller | | 108 00 | 36 00 | 4 |
| Lunch Counter | Comptroller | | | | 5 |
| Telephone Booths | Comptroller | | 600 00 | 600 00 | 6 |
| Possession of 83 Chambers St | Dept. of Street Cleaning | | | | 7 |
| Trimming Scows | Dept. of Street Cleaning | | 91,076 50 | 50,357 57 | 8 |
| Privileges not Specified | Dept. of Street Cleaning | | 60 00 | | 9 |
| Use of Playgrounds, High Schools, etc. | Dept. of Education | Sec. 1055, G. N. Y. C. | 50 00 | 50 00 | 10 |
| Use of Armory for Food Show (13th Artillery Dis.) | | | | | 11 |
| Public Stenographers | | | | | 12 |
| Total | | | **$637,734 31** | **$616,560 86** | 13 |
| 22. Franchises and Permits to Use Streets for Railways, Stage Lines, Tunnels, Conduits, Vaults, Bridges, and Building Projections: | | | | | |
| Duct | Comptroller | | $100 00 | $100 00 | 14 |
| Electrification | Comptroller | | | 124 93 | 15 |
| Foundation | Comptroller | | | | 16 |
| Use of Plaza, Union Railway Co. | Comptroller | | 1,500 00 | 2,500 00 | 17 |
| Platform Scales | Comptroller | | | 124 75 | 18 |
| Station Platforms | Comptroller | | | 624 18 | 19 |
| Trestle | Comptroller | | | | 20 |
| Tunnel, Privilege | | | | 623 90 | 21 |
| Connecting Bridge | Comptroller | | 72 88 | | 22 |
| Pipe, Privilege | Comptroller | | 116 64 | 2,116 30 | 23 |
| Poles, Wires, Cables and Conduits | Comptroller | | 6,200 00 | 1,200 00 | 24 |
| Canopy | Comptroller | | 16 00 | | 25 |
| Overhead Wire | Comptroller | | | | 26 |
| Street Vaults, Privilege | Borough Presidents | Sec. 391, G. N. Y. C.; Chap. 2, Art. I, Sec. 4, C. O., 1915 | 339,140 02 | 308,702 75 | 27 |
| Street Vaults, Privilege | Comptroller | | | 3,620 49 | 28 |
| Street Vaults, Privilege | Dept. of Parks | | 1,506 67 | 168 33 | 29 |
| Temporary Sheds and Roofs | Borough Presidents | Secs. 383 and 391, G. N. Y. C., Sec. 92, C. O. | 2,895 00 | 2,560 00 | 30 |
| Vaults, Privilege | Comptroller | | 4,649 62 | 4,755 25 | 31 |
| Electric Signs | City Clerk | | 8,688 12 | | 32 |
| Electric Signs | Borough Presidents | Secs. 383 and 391, G. N. Y. C., Sec. 92, C. O. | | 15,353 32 | 33 |
| Ornamental Projections | Borough Presidents | Secs. 383 and 391, G. N. Y. C., Sec. 92, C. O. | 11,796 23 | 1,484 78 | 34 |
| Bay Window | Borough Presidents | Secs. 383 and 391, G. N. Y. C., Sec. 92, C. O. | 19,080 92 | 7,076 86 | 35 |
| Street Encumbrances | Borough Presidents | Sec. 383, G. N. Y. C. | 748 91 | 1.413 91 | 36 |
| Tapping Water Pipes | Dept. W. S. G. & E. | Sec. 289, C. O., Chap. 396, Laws of 1859 | 38,220 00 | 34,753 91 | 37 |
| Tapping, Water Pipes | Borough Pres't, Queens | | | | 38 |
| Connecting Sewers and Drains | Borough Presidents | Secs. 383, 395, G. N. Y. C. | 124,662 72 | 140,337 99 | 39 |
| Street Railroad | Comptroller | Secs. 49 & 71–74, G.N.Y.C. | 750,257 19 | 726,534 29 | 40 |
| Street Car License Fees | Comptroller | | 71,720 00 | 95,364 17 | 41 |
| Railroad | | | 1,254 38 | | 42 |
| Stage and Omnibus | Comptroller | Sec. 1460, G. N. Y. C. | | | 43 |
| Electric Light and Power | Comptroller | Secs. 71–74, G. N. Y. C. | 10,249 04 | 11,501 22 | 44 |
| Gas Lighting | Comptroller | | 20,426 08 | 20,952 55 | 45 |
| New York Steam Co., Manhattan | Comptroller | Secs. 71–74, G. N. Y. C. | 61 23 | 52 20 | 46 |
| Subway at Webster Ave., N. Y. C. & H. R. R | Comptroller | Secs. 71–74, G. N. Y. C. | 4,500 00 | 4,500 00 | 47 |
| Public Service, Stock Quotation Telegraph, Etc. | Comptroller | Secs. 71–74, G. N. Y. C. | | | 48 |
| Bridges over Streets | Comptroller | | 6,939 79 | 10,814 43 | 49 |
| Pipe | Comptroller | Secs. 71–74, G. N. Y. C. | 49,122 52 | 51,199 83 | 50 |
| Tunnel, Pennsylvania R. R. Co. | Comptroller | Secs. 71–74, G. N. Y. C. | 35,352 69 | 16,974 11 | 51 |
| Tunnel, East River Gas Co. | | Secs. 71–74, G. N. Y. C. | | | 52 |
| Tunnels and Vaults | Comptroller | Secs. 71–74, G. N. Y. C. | 14,000 00 | 14,000 00 | 53 |
| Mail Tubes | Comptroller | | 1,751 37 | 1,617 44 | 54 |
| Fire and Burglar Alarm Conduits | | | | 5,700 00 | 55 |
| Total | | | **$1,525,028 02** | **$1,486,851 89** | 56 |
| 23. Licenses: | | Sec. 51, G. N. Y. C.; also see Note No. 2, page 215 | | | |
| Auctioneer | City Clerk | Sec. 34, G. N. Y. C. | $29,778 00 | $28,200 00 | 57 |
| Billiard Table | Bureau of Licenses | Secs. 305 and 307, C. O. | 13,062 00 | 14,193 50 | 58 |
| Bowling Alley | Bureau of Licenses | Secs. 305 and 307, C. O. | 5,127 50 | 6,025 00 | 59 |
| Concert Committee | Bureau of Licenses | | | | 60 |
| Dance Halls and Academies | Bureau of Licenses | Sec. 1490, G. N. Y. C. | 14,800 00 | 32,900 00 | 61 |

NEW YORK

FOR THE YEARS 1910 TO 1914, INCLUSIVE, GROUPED ACCORDING TO THE GENERAL CHARACTER THEREOF; THEREOF BY CLASSES OF FUNDS:

| LINE No. | Year | | | Total | Distribution by Classes of Funds | | |
|---|---|---|---|---|---|---|---|
| | 1912 | 1916 | 1914 | | General Fund | Special and Trust Funds | Sinking Funds |
| 1 | $31,570 50 | $29,897 50 | $30,275 00 | $152,162 50 | .......... | .......... | $152,162 50 |
| 2 | .......... | .......... | 213 00 | 213 00 | $213 00 | .......... | .......... |
| 3 | 3,788 88 | 5,014 62 | 4,872 52 | 21,698 52 | 21,698 52 | .......... | .......... |
| 4 | 352 00 | .......... | 504 00 | 1,000 00 | 1,000 00 | .......... | .......... |
| 5 | 1,957 50 | 2,727 50 | 176 00 | 4,861 00 | 4,861 00 | .......... | .......... |
| 6 | 1,516 51 | 2,903 25 | 3,057 54 | 8,677 30 | 8,677 30 | .......... | .......... |
| 7 | .......... | .......... | 10 00 | 10 00 | 10 00 | .......... | .......... |
| 8 | .......... | .......... | .......... | 141,434 07 | 141,434 07 | .......... | .......... |
| 9 | 2,925 00 | .......... | .......... | 2,985 00 | 2,985 00 | .......... | .......... |
| 10 | 259 50 | 433 50 | 414 00 | 1,207 00 | 1,207 00 | .......... | .......... |
| 11 | .......... | 493 44 | .......... | 493 44 | 493 44 | .......... | .......... |
| 12 | .......... | .......... | 800 00 | 800 00 | 800 00 | .......... | .......... |
| 13 | **$548,148 70** | **$606,855 44** | **$614,512 04** | **$3,023,811 35** | **$540,151 10** | **$1,543 50** | **$2,482,116 75** |
| 14 | $100 00 | .......... | $159 18 | $459 18 | $459 18 | .......... | .......... |
| 15 | 100 00 | $100 00 | 100 00 | 424 93 | 424 93 | .......... | .......... |
| 16 | 557 70 | 557 50 | 557 90 | 1,673 10 | 1,673 10 | .......... | .......... |
| 17 | 1,000 00 | 2,000 00 | 1,500 00 | 8,500 00 | .......... | .......... | $8,500 00 |
| 18 | 167 20 | 267 20 | 417 20 | 976 35 | 976 35 | .......... | .......... |
| 19 | 600 00 | 841 78 | 600 00 | 2,665 96 | 2,665 96 | .......... | .......... |
| 20 | .......... | .......... | 652 05 | 652 05 | 652 05 | .......... | .......... |
| 21 | .......... | .......... | .......... | 623 90 | 623 90 | .......... | .......... |
| 22 | .......... | .......... | .......... | 72 88 | 72 88 | .......... | .......... |
| 23 | .......... | .......... | .......... | 2,232 94 | 2,232 94 | .......... | .......... |
| 24 | 800 00 | 300 00 | .......... | 8,500 00 | 8,500 00 | .......... | .......... |
| 25 | .......... | .......... | .......... | 16 00 | 16 00 | .......... | .......... |
| 26 | 100 00 | .......... | .......... | 100 00 | 100 00 | .......... | .......... |
| 27 | 385,430 59 | 207,911 03 | 161,143 43 | 1,402,327 82 | .......... | .......... | 1,402,327 82 |
| 28 | 961 66 | 1,454 82 | 5,383 76 | 11,420 73 | .......... | .......... | 11,420 73 |
| 29 | 1,952 00 | .......... | 462 67 | 4,089 67 | .......... | .......... | 4,089 67 |
| 30 | 2,710 00 | 2,201 00 | 2,676 00 | 13,042 00 | 13,042 00 | .......... | .......... |
| 31 | 4,552 44 | 4,552 44 | 4,552 44 | 23,062 19 | .......... | .......... | 23,062 19 |
| 32 | 19,610 08 | 25,998 88 | 32,645 94 | 86,943 02 | 86,943 02 | .......... | .......... |
| 33 | .......... | .......... | 515 00 | 15,868 32 | 15,868 32 | .......... | .......... |
| 34 | 556 44 | 202 09 | 305 99 | 14,345 53 | 14,345 53 | .......... | .......... |
| 35 | 3,218 55 | 849 31 | 769 52 | 30,995 16 | 30,995 16 | .......... | .......... |
| 36 | 1,580 34 | 1,147 44 | 1,360 49 | 6,251 09 | 6,251 09 | .......... | .......... |
| 37 | 35,260 75 | 29,556 07 | 33,912 99 | 171,703 72 | 71,675 32 | $100,028 40 | .......... |
| 38 | 2,421 50 | 2,608 85 | 2,823 60 | 7,853 95 | .......... | 7,853 95 | .......... |
| 39 | 139,822 00 | 92,274 98 | 66,634 17 | 563,731 86 | 563,731 86 | .......... | .......... |
| 40 | 750,823 26 | 906,956 07 | 937,785 20 | 4,072,356 01 | 1,588,530 29 | .......... | 2,483,825 72 |
| 41 | 108,800 00 | 110,474 35 | 119,140 00 | 505,498 52 | 505,498 52 | .......... | .......... |
| 42 | .......... | .......... | .......... | 1,254 38 | .......... | .......... | 1,254 38 |
| 43 | .......... | .......... | 300 00 | 300 00 | 300 00 | .......... | .......... |
| 44 | 13,544 59 | .......... | 14,871 42 | 50,166 27 | 50,166 27 | .......... | .......... |
| 45 | 20,987 88 | 20,755 01 | 20,285 86 | 103,407 38 | .......... | .......... | 103,407 38 |
| 46 | 38 07 | 38 46 | 6 60 | 196 56 | .......... | .......... | 196 56 |
| 47 | 4,500 00 | 4,500 00 | 4,500 00 | 22,500 00 | .......... | .......... | 22,500 00 |
| 48 | 7,400 00 | 65,234 13 | 87,024 14 | 159,658 27 | 159,658 27 | .......... | .......... |
| 49 | 9,757 82 | 12,758 80 | 12,906 55 | 53,177 39 | 53,177 39 | .......... | .......... |
| 50 | 37,269 75 | 45,481 42 | 46,395 61 | 229,469 13 | 229,469 13 | .......... | .......... |
| 51 | 21,493 85 | 31,855 11 | 19,270 51 | 124,946 27 | 124,946 27 | .......... | .......... |
| 52 | 2,500 00 | .......... | .......... | 2,500 00 | 2,500 00 | .......... | .......... |
| 53 | 14,000 00 | 14,000 00 | 24,500 00 | 80,500 00 | .......... | .......... | 80,500 00 |
| 54 | 1,617 45 | 1,617 44 | 1,617 45 | 8,221 15 | .......... | .......... | 8,221 15 |
| 55 | .......... | .......... | .......... | 5,700 00 | 5,700 00 | .......... | .......... |
| 56 | **$1,594,233 92** | **$1,586,494 18** | **$1,605,775 67** | **$7,798,383 68** | **$3,541,195 73** | **$107,882 35** | **$4,149,305 60** |
| 57 | $27,700 00 | $26,600 00 | $27,900 00 | $140,178 00 | $140,178 00 | .......... | .......... |
| 58 | 14,586 00 | 14,116 50 | 12,106 50 | 68,062 50 | 68,062 50 | .......... | .......... |
| 59 | 5,290 00 | 4,711 50 | 4,595 00 | 25,749 00 | 25,749 00 | .......... | .......... |
| 60 | .......... | .......... | 150 00 | 150 00 | 150 00 | .......... | .......... |
| 61 | 31,150 00 | 32,650 00 | 38,700 00 | 150,200 00 | 150,200 00 | .......... | .......... |

DETAILED STATEMENT OF REVENUES COLLECTED AND OTHER CASH RECEIPTS BY THE CITY OF NEW YORK ALSO SHOWING THE DISTRIBUTION

| Character of Revenue | Department, Bureau or Office Through Which Collected | Statute or Ordinance | Year 1910 | Year 1911 | LINE No. |
|---|---|---|---|---|---|
| 23. LICENSES (Continued): | | | | | |
| Dirt Cart | Bureau of Licenses | Secs. 305 and 307, C. O. | $608 50 | $474 00 | 1 |
| Employment Agencies, Lodging Houses, etc. | Commissioner of Licenses | Chap. 20, Laws 1909 | .......... | 19,150 00 | 2 |
| Examining Board of Plumbers | Bureau of Licenses | Sec. 1573, G. N. Y. C. | 1,519 00 | .......... | 3 |
| Express | Bureau of Licenses | Secs. 305 and 307, C. O. | 9,842 50 | 9,625 00 | 4 |
| Express Driver | Bureau of Licenses | Secs. 305 and 307, C. O. | 516 50 | 461 25 | 5 |
| Gutterbridge | Bureau of Licenses | Sec. 530, C. O. | 786 00 | 750 00 | 6 |
| Hand Organ | Bureau of Licenses | Sec. 547, C. O. | 103 00 | 95 00 | 7 |
| Hoists, General | Bureau of Licenses | Secs. 305 and 307, C. O. | 6,012 50 | 6,462 50 | 8 |
| Hoists, Special | Bureau of Licenses | Secs. 305 and 307, C. O. | 24 50 | 37 00 | 9 |
| Junk Cart | Bureau of Licenses | Secs. 305 and 307, C. O. | 5,880 00 | 5,540 00 | 10 |
| Junk Boat | Bureau of Licenses | Secs. 305 and 307, C. O. | 270 00 | 257 50 | 11 |
| Junk Shop | Bureau of Licenses | Secs. 305 and 307, C. O. | 9,930 00 | 9,400 00 | 12 |
| Marriage | City Clerk | Secs. 13 and 14, Domestic Relations Law; Sec. 34, G. N. Y. C. | 53,621 00 | 56,656 00 | 13 |
| Moving Picture | Bureau of Licenses | Sec. 352-c, C. O. | .......... | .......... | 14 |
| Marconi Wireless Telegraph | .......... | .......... | .......... | .......... | 15 |
| Moving Picture, Open Air | Bureau of Licenses | Sec. 352-c, C. O. | .......... | .......... | 16 |
| Pawnbroker | Bureau of Licenses | Sec. 51, G. N. Y. C. | 93,050 00 | 93,550 00 | 17 |
| Peddler, Basket | Bureau of Licenses | Secs. 305 and 307, C. O. | 879 00 | 989 00 | 18 |
| Peddler, Horse and Wagon | Bureau of Licenses | Secs. 305 and 307, C. O. | 17,848 00 | 16,512 00 | 19 |
| Peddler, Push Cart | Bureau of Licenses | Secs. 305 and 307, C. O. | 7,036 00 | 5,834 00 | 20 |
| Public Cab | Bureau of Licenses | Secs. 305 and 307, C. O. | 1,213 00 | 1,151 00 | 21 |
| Public Drivers | Bureau of Licenses | Secs. 305 and 307, C. O. | 3,182 00 | .......... | 22 |
| Public Cart | Bureau of Licenses | Secs. 305 and 307, C. O. | 14,634 00 | 14,923 00 | 23 |
| Public Coach | Bureau of Licenses | Secs. 305 and 307, C. O. | 2,550 00 | 2,511 00 | 24 |
| Public Porter | Bureau of Licenses | Secs. 329-a, 329-b, and 329-c, C. O. | 190 50 | 174 00 | 25 |
| Public Hack Driver | Bureau of Licenses | Secs. 305 and 307, C. O. | 781 50 | 993 00 | 26 |
| Stage Coach | Bureau of Licenses | Chap. 41, Ord. of 1859 | 2,400 00 | 1,600 00 | 27 |
| Stands, Elevated R. R. | Bureau of Licenses | Secs. 305 and 307, G.N.Y.C. | 2,780 00 | 3,070 00 | 28 |
| Stands, Kiosk-Newspaper | Bureau of Licenses | Resolution of Oct. 20, '13, Bd. of Estimate and Apportionment | .......... | .......... | 29 |
| Stands, Newspaper | Bureau of Licenses | Secs. 305 and 307, C. O. | 4,115 00 | 6,250 00 | 30 |
| Stands, Newspaper | Comptroller | .......... | .......... | .......... | 31 |
| Stands, Newspaper and Fruit | Bureau of Licenses | Secs. 305 and 307, C. O. | 2,505 00 | 8,010 00 | 32 |
| Stands, Periodicals | Bureau of Licenses | Secs. 305 and 307, C. O. | .......... | 60 00 | 33 |
| Stands, Fruit | Bureau of Licenses | Secs. 305 and 307, C. O. | 27,780 00 | 30,260 00 | 34 |
| Stands, Bootblack | Bureau of Licenses | Secs. 305 and 307, C. O. | 19,905 00 | 19,730 00 | 35 |
| Taxicab, Driver | Bureau of Licenses | .......... | .......... | 4,322 00 | 36 |
| Taxicab, Little | Bureau of Licenses | .......... | .......... | .......... | 37 |
| Taxicab, Public | Bureau of Licenses | Sec. 316-B, C. O. | 810 00 | 4,610 00 | 38 |
| Theatrical | Bureau of Licenses | .......... | .......... | .......... | 39 |
| Theatrical Committee | Bureau of Licenses | .......... | .......... | .......... | 40 |
| Theatrical, Concert, Runners, etc. | Police Department | Secs. 1472-1475, G. N. Y. C.; Ord. Feb. 28, 1911. | 151,062 50 | 146,645 00 | 41 |
| Second-Hand Dealers | Bureau of Licenses | Secs. 305 and 307, C. O. | 14,650 00 | 15,587 50 | 42 |
| Show, Common | Bureau of Licenses | Secs. 305 and 307, C. O. | 20,262 50 | 24,062 50 | 43 |
| Street Railway Cars | Bureau of Licenses | .......... | 21,640 00 | .......... | 44 |
| Shooting Gallery | Bureau of Licenses | Secs. 305 and 307, C. O. | 245 00 | 250 00 | 45 |
| Sight-Seeing Car | Bureau of Licenses | Sec. 317, C. O. | .......... | .......... | 46 |
| Special Coach | Bureau of Licenses | .......... | 6,220 00 | 1,350 00 | 47 |
| Special Cab | Bureau of Licenses | .......... | 576 00 | 313 50 | 48 |
| Special Taxicab | Bureau of Licenses | .......... | 350 00 | 14,470 00 | 49 |
| Special Hackstand | Bureau of Licenses | .......... | 14,050 00 | 13,850 00 | 50 |
| Unclassified | Bureau of Licenses | .......... | 22,175 00 | .......... | 51 |
| Vehicles for Hire | Bureau of Licenses | .......... | 4 00 | 53 00 | 52 |
| Total | .......... | .......... | **$604,775 00** | **$621,355 25** | 53 |
| 24. FEES, COMMISSIONS AND OTHER CHARGES FOR SERVICES RENDERED AND REIMBURSEMENTS FOR COSTS: | | | | | |
| Cancellation | Corporation Counsel | .......... | .......... | .......... | 54 |
| Copies and Certification of Records, etc. | City Clerk | Sec. 28, G. N. Y. C. | $21,612 84 | $17,927 64 | 55 |
| | Comptroller | .......... | .......... | 6 88 | 56 |
| | Board of Estimate and Apportionment | .......... | 38 90 | 74 72 | 57 |
| | Surrogates | See Note No. 3, page 215 | 13,030 70 | 13,984 70 | 58 |
| | Borough Presidents | .......... | .......... | .......... | 59 |
| Coroners | Coroners | Sec. 3310, C. C. P. | 36 68 | .......... | 60 |
| County Clerks | County Clerks | See Note No. 4, page 215 | 121,520 42 | 125,302 15 | 61 |
| Examination | Exam. Board ot Plumb. | .......... | .......... | 1,307 00 | 62 |
| Land Title Registration | .......... | Chap. 444, L. 1908 | 40 75 | 63 30 | 63 |
| Leases, Issuance of | .......... | .......... | 765 00 | 480 00 | 64 |
| Marshals | Comptroller | .......... | .......... | 4 00 | 65 |
| Meter Tests, Gas and Electric | Public Service Com. | .......... | 3,609 00 | 3,600 25 | 66 |
| Receiving and Paying out Court Moneys | Chamberlain | Sec. 332, C. C. P., Sec. 198, G. N. Y. C. | 19,295 08 | 15,394 33 | 67 |
| Register, N. Y., Bronx and Kings Co's | Registers | See Note No. 5, page 215 | 335,314 86 | 321,152 06 | 68 |
| Searches | Comptroller | Sec. 1050, G. N. Y. C. | 307 35 | 268 70 | 69 |

NEW YORK

for the Years 1910 to 1914, Inclusive, Grouped According to the General Character Thereof; Thereof by Classes of Funds:

| LINE No. | Year | | | Total | Distribution by Classes of Funds | | |
|---|---|---|---|---|---|---|---|
| | 1912 | 1913 | 1914 | | General Fund | Special and Trust Funds | Sinking Funds |
| 1 | $412 50 | $411 00 | $333 00 | $2,239 00 | $2,239 00 | .......... | .......... |
| 2 | 19,775 00 | 20,875 00 | 19,253 00 | 79,053 00 | 79,053 00 | .......... | .......... |
| 3 | .......... | .......... | .......... | 1,519 00 | 1,519 00 | .......... | .......... |
| 4 | 8,210 00 | 7,827 50 | 6,377 50 | 41,882 50 | 41,882 50 | .......... | .......... |
| 5 | 229 00 | 224 50 | 87 50 | 1,518 75 | 1,518 75 | .......... | .......... |
| 6 | 393 00 | 4 00 | .......... | 1,933 00 | 1,933 00 | .......... | .......... |
| 7 | 96 00 | 86 00 | 227 00 | 607 00 | 607 00 | .......... | .......... |
| 8 | 6,825 00 | 7,462 50 | 8,262 50 | 35,025 00 | 35,025 00 | .......... | .......... |
| 9 | 35 00 | 45 00 | 38 00 | 179 50 | 179 50 | .......... | .......... |
| 10 | 5,677 50 | 5,517 50 | 4,832 50 | 27,447 50 | .......... | .......... | $27,447 50 |
| 11 | 230 00 | 332 50 | 392 50 | 1,482 50 | .......... | .......... | 1,482 50 |
| 12 | 10,370 00 | 11,490 00 | 11,170 00 | 52,360 00 | .......... | .......... | 52,360 00 |
| 13 | 60,561 00 | 62,876 00 | 64,940 50 | 298,654 50 | 298,654 50 | .......... | .......... |
| 14 | .......... | 21,000 00 | 76,971 07 | 97,971 07 | 97,971 07 | .......... | .......... |
| 15 | .......... | .......... | 596 77 | 596 77 | 596 77 | .......... | .......... |
| 16 | .......... | 175 00 | 13,387 48 | 13,562 48 | 13,562 48 | .......... | .......... |
| 17 | 95,500 00 | 98,025 00 | 94,577 00 | 474,702 00 | .......... | .......... | 474,702 00 |
| 18 | 1,031 00 | 1,087 00 | 1,329 00 | 5,315 00 | 5,315 00 | .......... | .......... |
| 19 | 16,520 00 | 16,024 00 | 18,042 00 | 84,946 00 | 84,946 00 | .......... | .......... |
| 20 | 5,765 00 | 5,754 00 | 14,398 00 | 38,787 00 | 38,787 00 | .......... | .......... |
| 21 | 1,752 00 | 2,785 50 | 4,242 50 | 11,144 00 | .......... | .......... | 11,144 00 |
| 22 | .......... | .......... | .......... | 3,182 00 | .......... | .......... | 3,182 00 |
| 23 | 15,081 00 | 15,187 00 | 19,583 00 | 79,408 00 | 79,408 00 | .......... | .......... |
| 24 | 2,206 50 | 1,765 00 | 2,547 50 | 11,580 00 | .......... | .......... | 11,580 00 |
| 25 | 81 75 | 92 75 | 134 00 | 673 00 | 673 00 | .......... | .......... |
| 26 | 897 00 | 3,015 13 | 4,749 01 | 10,435 64 | .......... | .......... | 10,435 64 |
| 27 | 1,620 00 | 2,120 00 | 2,520 00 | 10,260 00 | .......... | .......... | 10,260 00 |
| 28 | 3,000 00 | 2,980 00 | 3,550 00 | 15,380 00 | 15,380 00 | .......... | .......... |
| 29 | .......... | .......... | 495 00 | 495 00 | .......... | .......... | 495 00 |
| 30 | 4,075 00 | 3,380 00 | 3,335 00 | 21,155 00 | .......... | .......... | 21,155 00 |
| 31 | .......... | .......... | 231 00 | 231 00 | 231 00 | .......... | .......... |
| 32 | 9,165 00 | 9,150 00 | 10,860 00 | 39,690 00 | .......... | .......... | 39,690 00 |
| 33 | 10 00 | 10 00 | 20 00 | 100 00 | .......... | .......... | 100 00 |
| 34 | 30,460 00 | 28,875 00 | 29,640 00 | 147,015 00 | .......... | .......... | 147,015 00 |
| 35 | 20,295 00 | 18,215 00 | 18,175 00 | 96,320 00 | .......... | .......... | 96,320 00 |
| 36 | 5,286 00 | 2,232 00 | 980 00 | 12,820 00 | .......... | .......... | 12,820 00 |
| 37 | .......... | 390 00 | 830 00 | 1,220 00 | .......... | .......... | 1,220 00 |
| 38 | 5,510 00 | 12,485 00 | 22,225 00 | 45,640 00 | .......... | .......... | 45,640 00 |
| 39 | .......... | .......... | 11,000 00 | 11,000 00 | 11,000 00 | .......... | .......... |
| 40 | .......... | .......... | 1,600 00 | 1,600 00 | 1,600 00 | .......... | .......... |
| 41 | 127,565 00 | 132,662 50 | 102,287 50 | 660,222 50 | 660,222 50 | .......... | .......... |
| 42 | 15,937 50 | 18,212 50 | 18,475 00 | 82,012 50 | .......... | .......... | 82,912 50 |
| 43 | 25,212 50 | 24,387 50 | 9,150 00 | 103,075 00 | 103,075 00 | .......... | .......... |
| 44 | .......... | .......... | .......... | 21,640 00 | 21,640 00 | .......... | .......... |
| 45 | 267 50 | 292 50 | 245 00 | 1,300 00 | 1,300 00 | .......... | .......... |
| 46 | .......... | 180 00 | 865 00 | 1,045 00 | 1,045 00 | .......... | .......... |
| 47 | 1,030 00 | 297 50 | .......... | 8,897 50 | .......... | .......... | 8,897 50 |
| 48 | 223 50 | 66 00 | .......... | 1,179 00 | .......... | .......... | 1,179 00 |
| 49 | 14,950 00 | 10,660 00 | .......... | 40,430 00 | .......... | .......... | 40,430 00 |
| 50 | 16,325 00 | 4,000 00 | .......... | 48,225 00 | .......... | .......... | 48,225 00 |
| 51 | .......... | .......... | 2 50 | 22,177 50 | 22,175 00 | .......... | 2 50 |
| 52 | 129 00 | 170 00 | .......... | 356 00 | 356 00 | .......... | .......... |
| 53 | **$611,485 25** | **$630,905 38** | **$686,408 83** | **$3,154,929 71** | **$2,006,234 57** | .......... | **$1,148,695 14** |
| 54 | .......... | .......... | $4,009 67 | $4,009 67 | $4,009 67 | .......... | .......... |
| 55 | $20,291 08 | $21,541 97 | 22,200 02 | 103,573 55 | 103,573 55 | .......... | .......... |
| 56 | 3 50 | .......... | 4 00 | 14 38 | 14 38 | .......... | .......... |
| 57 | 36 25 | 59 00 | 360 25 | 569 12 | 569 12 | .......... | .......... |
| 58 | 16,110 60 | 16,285 20 | 17,211 05 | 76,622 25 | 76,622 25 | .......... | .......... |
| 59 | 35 | .......... | .......... | 35 | 35 | .......... | .......... |
| 60 | 27 34 | 14 65 | 23 40 | 102 07 | 102 07 | .......... | .......... |
| 61 | 131,387 80 | 197,202 98 | 200,559 36 | 775,972 71 | 775,972 71 | .......... | .......... |
| 62 | 1,853 70 | 1,645 26 | 4,923 00 | 9,728 96 | 9,728 96 | .......... | .......... |
| 63 | 35 50 | 66 40 | 57 75 | 263 70 | .......... | $263 70 | .......... |
| 64 | 174 00 | 19 00 | 9 00 | 1,447 00 | 1,447 00 | .......... | .......... |
| 65 | 5 25 | 8 00 | 10 00 | 27 25 | 27 25 | .......... | .......... |
| 66 | 3,445 08 | 2,794 50 | 2,896 00 | 16,344 83 | 16,344 83 | .......... | .......... |
| 67 | 21,026 16 | 17,642 05 | 16,153 53 | 89,511 15 | 89,511 15 | .......... | .......... |
| 68 | 310,279 90 | 286,887 76 | 270,854 97 | 1,524,489 55 | 1,524,489 55 | .......... | .......... |
| 69 | 210 70 | 215 60 | 246 20 | 1,248 55 | 1,248 55 | .......... | .......... |

DETAILED STATEMENT OF REVENUES COLLECTED AND OTHER CASH RECEIPTS BY THE CITY OF NEW YORK
ALSO SHOWING THE DISTRIBUTION

| Character of Revenue | Department Bureau or Office Through Which Collected | Statute or Ordinance | Year 1910 | Year 1911 | Line No. |
|---|---|---|---|---|---|
| 24. FEES, COMMISSIONS, ETC. (Continued) | | | | | |
| Searches, Transcripts, etc. (Vital Statistics) | Dept. of Health | Sec. 1241, G. N. Y. C. | $28,215 73 | $29,222 22 | 1 |
| Sheriff, N. Y. County | Sheriff | (See Note No. 6, page 215) | 100,567 75 | 91,784 44 | 2 |
| Sheriff, Bronx, Kings and Queens Cos. | Sheriffs | (See Note No. 6, page 215) | 13,151 11 | 14,400 15 | 3 |
| Transcripts of Tax Liens | | | .......... | .......... | 4 |
| Writs of Certiorari | | | .......... | 4 00 | 5 |
| Miscellaneous, Subpœna Fees, Copying, etc. | | | 352 15 | 437 58 | 6 |
| Commissions | Public Administrators | | 10,217 50 | 9,940 10 | 7 |
| Commissions on State Taxes | Chamberlain | | .......... | .......... | 8 |
| Subpœna Fees | Various | | 3 56 | 77 15 | 9 |
| Reimbursements, Fund for Street and Park Openings | | | 1,408 83 | 15,068 88 | 10 |
| Reimbursements, Street Improvement Fund (work contracted for before January 1, 1898) | | | .......... | .......... | 11 |
| Reimbursements, Street Improvement Fund (work contracted for after January 1, 1898) | | | 26,690 14 | .......... | 12 |
| Reimbursements from Railroad Companies for repaving between tracks | | Sec. 178, Railroad Law | 6,956 00 | 104,582 33 | 13 |
| Advertising Charges on Sales | | Secs. 1027, 1029, 1032, G. N. Y. C. | 18,285 46 | 17,052 66 | 14 |
| Construction of Private Sewers | | Sec. 395, G. N. Y. C., Sec. 157, C. O. | 3,136 56 | 7,873 25 | 15 |
| Board of Committed Children | Dept. of Public Charities. | Sec. 678, G. N. Y. C. | 39,899 48 | 37,438 75 | 16 |
| Board of Inmates of Institutions | Dept. of Corrections | | 70,829 37 | 104,217 99 | 17 |
| Board of Inmates of Institutions | Bellevue & Allied Hosp's. | Sec. 692, G. N. Y. C. | 1,926 73 | 13,510 00 | 18 |
| Board of Inmates of Institutions | Dept. of Public Charities. | Secs. 678, 683, 688, G. N. Y. C. | 53,548 69 | 64,718 96 | 19 |
| Unsafe Building Fund | | Sec. 158, Bldg. Code | 9,577 27 | 5,627 96 | 20 |
| Water Meter Funds | Water Reg. and Comp. | Sec. 475, G. N. Y. C. | 37,523 11 | 32,384 81 | 21 |
| Repairs to Scow | Dept. Street Cleaning | | .......... | .......... | 22 |
| Labor in Removing and Replacing Fire Alarm Telegraph Wires | Fire Dept. | | .......... | .......... | 23 |
| Costs of Various Litigations | Public Service Com. | | .......... | .......... | 24 |
| Charges on Arrears of Taxes | Comptroller | | 1,262 05 | 386 25 | 25 |
| Charges on Arrears of Assessments | Comptroller | | 82 50 | 98 50 | 26 |
| Charges on Sales, Boro. of Brooklyn. | | | 2,000 00 | .......... | 27 |
| Costs and Fees in Pending Litigations of the Public Service Commission, Suspense Account | | | .......... | .......... | 28 |
| Brooklyn Bridge, Materials and Labor, 1914 | | | .......... | .......... | 29 |
| Restoring and Repaving, Special Fund | | Sec. 391, G. N. Y. C., Secs. 148, 149, C. O. | 444,313 63 | 523,443 28 | 30 |
| Transportation of State Prisoners | Sheriffs | | 612 99 | .......... | 31 |
| Board of U. S. Prisoners | Sheriff, Richmond | | 57 00 | .......... | 32 |
| Costs of Condemnation Proceedings in Dock Construction, Lehigh Valley Railroad | | Agreement authorized, Dec. 17, 1913 | .......... | .......... | 33 |
| Dock Fund | | | 98,514 31 | 22,551 07 | 34 |
| Planting Trees in City Sts., Brooklyn. | | | .......... | .......... | 35 |
| Clothing for State Patients | Dept. of Public Charities. | | .......... | .......... | 36 |
| Sewer Inspection and Repairs, Borough of Richmond | | | 1,677 00 | 1,539 00 | 37 |
| Costs for Recovery of Penalties | Corporation Counsel | Sec. 259, G. N. Y. C. | 21,206 10 | 21,792 65 | 38 |
| Labor and Material | Dept. of W. S. G. & E. | Chap. 396, Laws 1859 | 13,365 18 | 16,786 48 | 39 |
| Labor and Material | Dept. of Bridges | | 9 00 | 54 86 | 40 |
| Labor and Material | Borough Presidents | | 565 60 | 489 64 | 41 |
| Labor and Material | Various | | .......... | .......... | 42 |
| Various Extradition Cases | District Attorneys | | .......... | .......... | 43 |
| Costs of Re-advertising | Comptroller | | 127 50 | 395 20 | 44 |
| Costs of Re-advertising | Various | | 344 22 | 50 00 | 45 |
| Restoring Pavements | | | 1,480 56 | 6,946 63 | 46 |
| Sundry Reimbursements | Various | | 2,783 60 | 994 01 | 47 |
| Total | | | **$1,526,262 26** | **$1,643,434 53** | 48 |
| 25. INTEREST ON OVERDUE PAYMENTS (ACCOUNTS RECEIVABLE): | | | | | |
| Interest on Taxes: | Comptroller | Secs. 916 and 1020, G.N.Y.C. | | | |
| 1898 and Prior | | | $110,366 82 | $52,805 48 | 49 |
| 1899 and Subsequent | | | 3,371,404 61 | 2,171,897 44 | 50 |
| Long Island City | | | 3,175 80 | 2,506 80 | 51 |
| Interest on Assessments: | Comptroller | | | | |
| Fund for Street and Park Openings | | | 270,546 43 | 328,897 91 | 52 |
| Street Improvement Fund, Work Contracted for Prior to January 1, 1898 | | Sec. 1020, G. N. Y. C. | 56,393 07 | 107,377 23 | 53 |
| Street Improvement Funds, Work Contracted for after Jan. 1, 1898. | | Sec. 1020, G. N. Y. C. | 428,654 54 | 522,298 17 | 54 |
| Opening, Laying Out and Improving Bedford Avenue, Brooklyn | | | 238 03 | 423 54 | 55 |

# NEW YORK

FOR THE YEARS 1910 TO 1914, INCLUSIVE, GROUPED ACCORDING TO THE GENERAL CHARACTER THEREOF; THEREOF BY CLASSES OF FUNDS:

| LINE No. | Year | | | Total | Distribution by Classes of Funds | | |
|---|---|---|---|---|---|---|---|
| | 1912 | 1913 | 1914 | | General Fund | Special and Trust Funds | Sinking Funds |
| 1 | $29,760 42 | $31,044 92 | $32,756 18 | $150,999 47 | $150,999 47 | .......... | .......... |
| 2 | 110,818 56 | 106,549 72 | 112,432 10 | 535,303 68 | 79,194 29 | $470,509 54 | .......... |
| 3 | 14,244 39 | 15,690 97 | 21,813 84 | 66,149 35 | 51,749 20 | .......... | .......... |
| 4 | 1 60 | 5 00 | .......... | 6 60 | 6 60 | .......... | .......... |
| 5 | 4 00 | 1 00 | .......... | 9 00 | 9 00 | .......... | .......... |
| 6 | 788 80 | 1,036 60 | 188 73 | 2,803 86 | 2,803 86 | .......... | .......... |
| 7 | 11,214 64 | 19,566 96 | 17,697 79 | 68,636 99 | 68,636 99 | .......... | .......... |
| 8 | 5,000 00 | 8,808 18 | 8,455 79 | 22,263 97 | .......... | .......... | $22,263 97 |
| 9 | 284 28 | 507 47 | 1,691 77 | 2,564 23 | 2,564 23 | .......... | .......... |
| 10 | 2,777 94 | 26,180 99 | 10,464 15 | 55,900 79 | .......... | 55,900 79 | .......... |
| 11 | 80 65 | .......... | .......... | 80 65 | .......... | 80 65 | .......... |
| 12 | 70 80 | 2,133 34 | 1,113 39 | 30,007 67 | .......... | 30,007 67 | .......... |
| 13 | 210 555 31 | 446 585 21 | 714,874 20 | 1,483,553 05 | 7,058 01 | 1,476,495 04 | .......... |
| 14 | 8,513 55 | 18,532 35 | 10,844 94 | 73,228 96 | 62,992 69 | 10,236 27 | .......... |
| 15 | 8,902 33 | 3,968 39 | 4,004 02 | 27,884 55 | .......... | 27,884 55 | .......... |
| 16 | 38,952 32 | 43,916 39 | 36,197 75 | 196,404 69 | 196,404 69 | .......... | .......... |
| 17 | 95,560 06 | 77,820 82 | 10,560 79 | 358,989 03 | 358,989 03 | .......... | .......... |
| 18 | 8,010 00 | 7,638 00 | 8,717 50 | 39,802 23 | 39,802 23 | .......... | .......... |
| 19 | 81,960 54 | 94,533 53 | 109,291 86 | 404,053 58 | 404,053 58 | .......... | .......... |
| 20 | 9,379 64 | 12,629 93 | 5,062 56 | 42,277 36 | .......... | 42,277 36 | .......... |
| 21 | 23,361 82 | 28,456 06 | 14,800 34 | 136,526 14 | .......... | 136,526 14 | .......... |
| 22 | 148 00 | 2,065 70 | .......... | 2,213 70 | 2,213 70 | .......... | .......... |
| 23 | 129 97 | 399 24 | .......... | 529 21 | 529 21 | .......... | .......... |
| 24 | .......... | 685 50 | .......... | 685 50 | 685 50 | .......... | .......... |
| 25 | .......... | .......... | .......... | 1,648 30 | 386 25 | 1,262 05 | .......... |
| 26 | .......... | .......... | .......... | 181 00 | 98 50 | 82 50 | .......... |
| 27 | .......... | .......... | .......... | 2,000 00 | .......... | 2,000 00 | .......... |
| 28 | .......... | 2,766 70 | .......... | 2,766 70 | .......... | 2,766 70 | .......... |
| 29 | .......... | .......... | 1,248 67 | 1,248 67 | .......... | 1,248 67 | .......... |
| 30 | 589,990 66 | 740,816 40 | 662,285 72 | 2,960,849 69 | .......... | 2,960,849 69 | .......... |
| 31 | .......... | .......... | .......... | 612 99 | 612 99 | .......... | .......... |
| 32 | .......... | .......... | .......... | 57 00 | 57 00 | .......... | .......... |
| 33 | .......... | .......... | 1,700 00 | 1,700 00 | .......... | 1,700 00 | .......... |
| 34 | 7,461 69 | 14,527 12 | 6,847 24 | 149,901 43 | .......... | 149,901 43 | .......... |
| 35 | .......... | .......... | 1,880 00 | 1,880 00 | .......... | 1,880 00 | .......... |
| 36 | .......... | 561 82 | 1,094 29 | 1,656 11 | 1,656 11 | .......... | .......... |
| 37 | 1,533 00 | 1,387 00 | .......... | 6,136 00 | .......... | 6,136 00 | .......... |
| 38 | 26,167 79 | 34,689 64 | 22,449 60 | 126,305 78 | 126,305 78 | .......... | .......... |
| 39 | 14,516 06 | 22,955 71 | 16,752 05 | 84,375 48 | 51,228 40 | 33,147 08 | .......... |
| 40 | 75 80 | 77 37 | 159 75 | 376 78 | 376 78 | .......... | .......... |
| 41 | 1,186 90 | 49 50 | 45 61 | 2,337 25 | 2,337 25 | .......... | .......... |
| 42 | .......... | 60 | 282 58 | 283 18 | 283 18 | .......... | .......... |
| 43 | .......... | .......... | 1,144 64 | 1,144 64 | 1,144 64 | .......... | .......... |
| 44 | 439 56 | 476 46 | 816 90 | 2,255 62 | 2,255 62 | .......... | .......... |
| 45 | 369 20 | 347 00 | 114 00 | 1,224 42 | 1,224 42 | .......... | .......... |
| 46 | 1,138 11 | 2,302 14 | 2,398 77 | 14,266 21 | .......... | 14,266 21 | .......... |
| 47 | 1,245 70 | 815 27 | 3,728 48 | 9,557 06 | 5,038 26 | 4,518 80 | .......... |
| 48 | **$1,809,531 30** | **$2,314,911 37** | **$2,383,424 20** | **$9,677,563 66** | **$4,225,348 40** | **$5,429,941 29** | **$22,273 97** |
| 49 | $33,048 29 | $21,916 35 | $31,522 19 | $249,659 13 | $249,659 13 | .......... | .......... |
| 50 | 1,934,425 05 | 2,681,573 56 | 1,788,065 00 | 11,947,365 66 | 11,947,365 66 | .......... | .......... |
| 51 | .......... | .......... | .......... | 5,682 60 | .......... | $5,682 60 | .......... |
| 52 | 261,590 87 | 257,650 23 | 181,117 87 | 1,299,803 31 | 1,299,803 31 | .......... | .......... |
| 53 | 28,072 20 | 53,456 05 | 12,621 84 | 257,920 39 | 6,732 72 | 251,187 67 | .......... |
| 54 | 438,843 56 | 440,666 08 | 475,193 64 | 2,305,655 99 | 220,055 55 | 2,085,600 44 | .......... |
| 55 | 365 24 | 526 71 | 679 87 | 2,233 39 | 2,233 39 | .......... | .......... |

**DETAILED STATEMENT OF REVENUES COLLECTED AND OTHER CASH RECEIPTS BY THE CITY OF NEW YORK ALSO SHOWING THE DISTRIBUTION**

| Character of Revenue | Department, Bureau or Office Through Which Collected | Statute or Ordinance | Year 1910 | Year 1911 | LINE No. |
|---|---|---|---|---|---|
| 25. INTEREST ON OVERDUE PAYMENTS (ACCOUNTS RECEIVABLE) (Con.) | | | | | |
| Interest on Assessments (Con.): | | | | | |
| For Local Improvements, Various Villages | ........ | ........ | $2,794 51 | $238 18 | 1 |
| For Local Improvements, Long Island City | ........ | ........ | 444 25 | 21 76 | 2 |
| Opening, Widening and Closing Streets, Brooklyn | ........ | ........ | 2,387 31 | 62 09 | 3 |
| Restoring Pavements | ........ | Sec. 391, G. N. Y. C. | 111 44 | 692 44 | 4 |
| Prospect Park Improvements | ........ | ........ | 2,703 79 | 1,712 86 | 5 |
| Board of Assessors Decisions, Brooklyn | ........ | Chap. 114, Laws of 1893 | ........ | ........ | 6 |
| Taxes and Charges, Westchester County | ........ | Chap. 329, Laws, of 1874 and Chap. 934, Laws of 1895. | 7,710 37 | 3,817 33 | 7 |
| Interest on Tax for Interest on 26th Ward Bonds | Comptroller | ........ | 1,031 44 | 312 81 | 8 |
| Interest on Taxes, 26th Ward Bonds, 1897 | Comptroller | ........ | 52 68 | 13 42 | 9 |
| Interest on Principal and Interest, 26th Ward Bonds, 1906 and Subsequent | Comptroller | ........ | 3,816 71 | ........ | 10 |
| Repaving Streets | ........ | ........ | ........ | ........ | 11 |
| Street Opening Refund Account | ........ | ........ | ........ | ........ | 12 |
| Brooklyn Assessments | ........ | Sec. 1020, G. N. Y. C. | 38,297 77 | 33,592 88 | 13 |
| Long Island City Assessments | ........ | Sec. 1020, G. N. Y. C. | 4,029 57 | 3,679 39 | 14 |
| West Farms Gas Tax | ........ | ........ | ........ | 24 24 | 15 |
| Local Improvements, Various Villages, Queens | ........ | ........ | 310 37 | 45 00 | 16 |
| Interest on Water Rents: | | | | | |
| Croton Water Rents | ........ | ........ | 36,308 21 | 45,693 13 | 17 |
| Brooklyn Water Rents | ........ | ........ | 44,771 89 | 19,746 69 | 18 |
| Queens Water Rents | ........ | ........ | 2,631 11 | 3,097 05 | 19 |
| Richmond Water Rents | ........ | ........ | ........ | 237 59 | 20 |
| Interest on Sundry Accounts: | | | | | |
| Interest on Deferred Payments | Comptroller | ........ | 2,141 43 | 1,209 92 | 21 |
| Interest on Deferred Payments | Dept. Docks & Ferries | ........ | ........ | ........ | 22 |
| Interest on Deferred Payments, Street Railroad Franchises | ........ | ........ | ........ | 1,133 57 | 23 |
| Interest on Recovery of Penalties | Corporation Counsel | Sec. 259, G. N. Y. C. | ........ | ........ | 24 |
| Interest on Tax Sale Liens Receivable | ........ | ........ | 3,023 20 | 3,568 63 | 25 |
| Interest on Excess Advertising Account, Brooklyn | ........ | ........ | 42 33 | 43 87 | 26 |
| Interest on Forfeited Recognizances | ........ | ........ | 98 00 | ........ | 27 |
| Interest on Attachments | Sheriff, N. Y. County | ........ | 69 05 | ........ | 28 |
| Interest on Lands Purchased | ........ | ........ | 628 72 | 589 99 | 29 |
| Interest on Reimbursement for Damages to Scow | Dept. Street Cleaning | ........ | ........ | ........ | 30 |
| Sundries | ........ | ........ | ........ | ........ | 31 |
| Interest on Bank Tax | ........ | ........ | ........ | 547 46 | 32 |
| Total | ........ | ........ | **$4,394,183 45** | **$3,306,286 87** | 33 |
| 26. INTEREST ON DEPOSITS: | | | | | |
| Board of City Record | ........ | ........ | $8 71 | $8 49 | 34 |
| Board of Estimate and Apportionment | ........ | ........ | ........ | 87 | 35 |
| Borough Presidents | ........ | ........ | 26 58 | ........ | 36 |
| County Clerks | ........ | ........ | 360 87 | 142 76 | 37 |
| County Registers | ........ | ........ | 317 56 | 196 19 | 38 |
| Courts of Special Sessions | ........ | ........ | ........ | 103 95 | 39 |
| City Clerk | ........ | ........ | 56 87 | 60 17 | 40 |
| City Court of New York | ........ | ........ | ........ | 131 73 | 41 |
| City Magistrates' Courts | ........ | ........ | ........ | ........ | 42 |
| City Treasury Balances | Chamberlain | Sec. 196, G. N. Y. C. | 537,591 79 | 662,892 51 | 43 |
| Criminal Bail Deposits | Chamberlain | ........ | 2,191 06 | 1,863 23 | 44 |
| Department of Corrections | ........ | ........ | 228 71 | ........ | 45 |
| Department of Education | ........ | ........ | ........ | ........ | 46 |
| Department of Parks, All Boroughs | ........ | ........ | ........ | 265 00 | 47 |
| Department of Public Charities | ........ | ........ | 534 98 | 662 80 | 48 |
| Police Department | ........ | ........ | ........ | 1 41 | 49 |
| Garnisheed Salaries | ........ | ........ | 980 26 | 1,161 95 | 50 |
| Mortgage Taxes | ........ | ........ | 4,680 24 | 4,100 93 | 51 |
| Mortgage Taxes | ........ | ........ | ........ | ........ | 52 |
| Municipal Courts | ........ | ........ | ........ | 952 37 | 53 |
| Sinking Fund Balances | ........ | ........ | 126,283 00 | 118,866 06 | 54 |
| Sheriffs | ........ | ........ | 183 66 | 152 34 | 55 |
| Stocks and Bonds Issued Abroad | ........ | ........ | ........ | ........ | 56 |
| Tax Sales | ........ | ........ | ........ | 287 94 | 57 |
| Interest on Security Deposit of Brooklyn-Manhattan Rapid Transit Construction | ........ | ........ | ........ | ........ | 58 |

# 'EW YORK

)R THE YEARS 1910 TO 1914, INCLUSIVE, GROUPED ACCORDING TO THE GENERAL CHARACTER THEREOF; HEREOF BY CLASSES OF FUNDS:

| o. | Year | | | Total | Distribution by Classes of Funds | | |
|---|---|---|---|---|---|---|---|
| | 1912 | 1913 | 1914 | | General Fund | Special and Trust Funds | Sinking Funds |
| 1 | $1,242 00 | $440 14 | $750 81 | $5,465 64 | .......... | $5,465 64 | .......... |
| 2 | 1,732 39 | .......... | 4,461 92 | 6,660 32 | .......... | 6,660 32 | .......... |
| 3 | .......... | .......... | 93 19 | 2,542 59 | .......... | 2,542 59 | .......... |
| 4 | 39 21 | 93 26 | 192 46 | 1,128 81 | .......... | 1,128 81 | .......... |
| 5 | 1,550 01 | 1,630 72 | 1,430 80 | 9,028 18 | .......... | .......... | $9,028 18 |
| 6 | 29 49 | .......... | 126 15 | 155 64 | $155 64 | .......... | .......... |
| 7 | 4,779 51 | 9,962 48 | 5,137 94 | 31,407 63 | 5,137 94 | 26,269 69 | .......... |
| 8 | 5 18 | .......... | 7 18 | 1,356 61 | 1,356 61 | .......... | .......... |
| 9 | .......... | .......... | .......... | 66 10 | .......... | 66 10 | .......... |
| 0 | 2,404 27 | 3,069 06 | .......... | 9,290 04 | 9,290 04 | .......... | .......... |
| 1 | 19 60 | .......... | .......... | 19 60 | 19 60 | .......... | .......... |
| 2 | .......... | .......... | 696 61 | 696 61 | 696 61 | .......... | .......... |
| 3 | 7,386 01 | 5,843 73 | 5,990 07 | 91,110 46 | 91,110 46 | .......... | .......... |
| 4 | 3,503 51 | 4,528 44 | 268 81 | 16,009 72 | 16,009 72 | .......... | .......... |
| 5 | 109 51 | .......... | 3 32 | 137 07 | .......... | .......... | 137 07 |
| 6 | .......... | .......... | .......... | 355 37 | .......... | 355 37 | .......... |
| 7 | 39,089 05 | 67,755 75 | 39,928 90 | 228,775 04 | .......... | .......... | 228,775 04 |
| 8 | 14,453 08 | 25,734 61 | 19,298 58 | 124,004 85 | .......... | 124,004 85 | .......... |
| 9 | 4,150 12 | 7,138 46 | 14,746 82 | 31,773 56 | 3,530 12 | 28,243 44 | .......... |
| 0 | 1,157 41 | 1,291 66 | 1,358 26 | 4,044 92 | 4,044 92 | .......... | .......... |
| 1 | 357 55 | 87 95 | 4,061 15 | 7,858 00 | 7,858 00 | .......... | .......... |
| 2 | .......... | 5,891 62 | .......... | 5,891 62 | 5,891 62 | .......... | .......... |
| 3 | .......... | .......... | .......... | 1,133 57 | .......... | .......... | 1,133 57 |
| 4 | .......... | .......... | 38,461 31 | 38,461 31 | 38,461 31 | .......... | .......... |
| 5 | 4,730 06 | 5,707 40 | 11,458 71 | 28,488 00 | 28,488 00 | .......... | .......... |
| 6 | 43 92 | 47 66 | 51 17 | 228 95 | 228 95 | .......... | .......... |
| 7 | .......... | .......... | .......... | 98 00 | 98 00 | .......... | .......... |
| 8 | .......... | .......... | .......... | 69 05 | 69 05 | .......... | .......... |
| 9 | .......... | 206 58 | .......... | 1,425 29 | .......... | 1,425 29 | .......... |
| 0 | 42 82 | .......... | .......... | 42 82 | 42 82 | .......... | .......... |
| 1 | .......... | .......... | 8 77 | 8 77 | 8 77 | .......... | .......... |
| 2 | .......... | .......... | .......... | 547 46 | 547 46 | .......... | .......... |
| 3 | **$2,783,179 91** | **$3,595,218 50** | **$2,637,733 34** | **$16,716,602 07** | **$13,967,138 84** | **$2,510,389 37** | **$239,073 86** |
| 4 | $9 29 | $8 86 | $11 68 | $47 03 | $47 03 | .......... | .......... |
| 5 | .......... | .......... | .......... | 87 | 87 | .......... | .......... |
| 6 | .......... | .......... | .......... | 26 58 | 26 58 | .......... | .......... |
| 7 | 103 73 | 132 54 | 227 83 | 967 73 | 967 73 | .......... | .......... |
| 8 | 345 98 | 149 83 | 229 58 | 1,239 14 | 1,239 14 | .......... | .......... |
| 9 | 20 60 | 33 09 | 48 07 | 205 71 | 205 71 | .......... | .......... |
| 0 | 104 85 | 100 49 | 110 42 | 432 80 | 432 80 | .......... | .......... |
| 1 | .......... | .......... | 30 97 | 162 70 | 162 70 | .......... | .......... |
| 2 | .......... | .......... | 8 02 | 8 02 | 8 02 | .......... | .......... |
| 3 | .......... | .......... | 884,268 63 | 2,084,752 93 | .......... | .......... | $2,084,752 93 |
| 4 | 2,449 62 | 2,386 96 | 3,120 70 | 12,011 57 | 12,011 57 | .......... | .......... |
| 5 | .......... | 390 74 | 4 74 | 624 19 | 624 19 | .......... | .......... |
| 6 | .......... | 128 93 | .......... | 128 93 | 128 93 | .......... | .......... |
| 7 | 167 11 | 29 17 | 74 33 | 535 61 | 535 61 | .......... | .......... |
| 8 | 775 86 | 927 88 | 764 41 | 3,665 93 | 3,665 93 | .......... | .......... |
| 9 | 308 15 | 23 98 | .......... | 333 54 | 333 54 | .......... | .......... |
| 0 | 1,427 13 | 1,469 97 | 1,523 34 | 6,562 65 | 6,562 65 | .......... | .......... |
| 1 | 4,101 91 | 7,612 57 | 10,085 22 | 30,580 87 | 30,580 87 | .......... | .......... |
| 2 | .......... | .......... | 1,929 21 | 1,929 21 | 1,929 21 | .......... | .......... |
| 3 | 1,097 26 | 1,208 46 | 1,060 99 | 4,319 08 | 4,319 08 | .......... | .......... |
| 4 | 730,761 52 | 696,004 18 | 174,071 12 | 1,845,985 88 | .......... | .......... | 1,845,985 88 |
| 5 | 191 66 | 175 23 | 44 72 | 747 61 | 747 61 | .......... | .......... |
| 6 | .......... | .......... | 582 53 | 582 53 | 582 53 | .......... | .......... |
| 7 | 1 26 | .......... | 166 04 | 455 24 | 455 24 | .......... | .......... |
| 8 | .......... | .......... | 97,231 85 | 97,231 85 | 97,231 85 | .......... | .......... |

## Detailed Statement of Revenues Collected and Other Cash Receipts by the City of New York also Showing the Distribution

| Character of Revenue | Department, Bureau or Office Through Which Collected | Statute or Ordinance | Year 1910 | Year 1911 | Line No. |
|---|---|---|---|---|---|
| 26. Interest on Deposits (Continued): | | | | | |
| Interest on Security Deposits, Miscellaneous | ........ | ........ | $14,317 81 | $14,614 21 | 1 |
| Interest on Redemption Deposits | ........ | ........ | 1,522 13 | 1,365 17 | 2 |
| Interest on Water Meter Funds | ........ | ........ | 1,922 00 | 2,599 30 | 3 |
| Interest on Contingent Fund for Snow Removal | Dept. of Bridges | ........ | ........ | ........ | 4 |
| Interest on License Account | Police Dept | ........ | ........ | ........ | 5 |
| Interest on Surplus Funds | Borough Pres., Brooklyn | ........ | 285 96 | 151 44 | 6 |
| Interest on Surplus, Sales of Merchandise | Chamberlain | ........ | 5 06 | 4 01 | 7 |
| Interest on Restoring and Repaving, Special Fund | ........ | ........ | ........ | 1,010 09 | 8 |
| Total | ........ | ........ | **$691,497 25** | **$811,594 92** | 9 |
| 27. Interest and Dividends on Investments | ........ | ........ | **$3,078 60** | **$5,642 46** | 10 |
| 28. Interest on Bonds of the City of New York Held by Sinking Funds | ........ | (See Note No. 8, page 215) | **$7,209,938 70** | **$7,893,987 32** | 11 |
| 29. Recoveries for Damages, Settlements of Claims (Unclassified) and Forfeiture of Bonds and Security Deposits: | | | | | |
| Damage to Departmental Property | Dept. W. S. G. & E. | ........ | $1,138 75 | $1,365 60 | 12 |
| Damage to Departmental Property | Borough Presidents | ........ | 13 95 | ........ | 13 |
| Damage to Departmental Property | Bellevue and Allied Hos. | ........ | 14 00 | 14 50 | 14 |
| Damage to Departmental Property | Dept. of Bridges | ........ | ........ | ........ | 15 |
| Damage to Departmental Property | Dept. of Charities | ........ | ........ | 440 00 | 16 |
| Damage to Departmental Property | Dept. of Street Cleaning | ........ | 79 70 | 136 83 | 17 |
| Damage to Departmental Property | Fire Department | ........ | 2,425 26 | 145 23 | 18 |
| Damage to Departmental Property | Police Department | ........ | 175 00 | 11 50 | 19 |
| Damage to Departmental Property | Sundry Departments | ........ | 227 71 | 24 50 | 20 |
| Recovery of Damages to Building occupied by Hook & Ladder Co. No. 2 | ........ | ........ | ........ | 865 67 | 21 |
| Recovery of Lost Property | Dept. of Street Cleaning | ........ | 3 50 | 3 00 | 22 |
| Damaged Text Books | College of City of N. Y. | ........ | ........ | 151 20 | 23 |
| Lost Text Books | Board of Education | ........ | ........ | 5 00 | 24 |
| Lost Badges | Dept. of Parks | ........ | ........ | ........ | 25 |
| Settlement of Default of Contract | Fire Department | ........ | 185 45 | ........ | 26 |
| Repaving Walcott St., Default on Contracts | Borough Presidents | ........ | 2,000 00 | ........ | 27 |
| Forfeit on Contract for Trimming Scows | Borough President | ........ | ........ | ........ | 28 |
| Amount Received from County Clerk for City's share in Award for Opening St. Nicholas Ave. and the Widening of Manhattan St., etc | ........ | ........ | ........ | ........ | 29 |
| Recovery of Damages for Defective Hose | Fire Department | ........ | 2,939 47 | ........ | 30 |
| Award in Condemnation Proceedings in Connection with Opening of Broadway | Chamberlain | ........ | ........ | ........ | 31 |
| Award in Proceeding entitled, "County of Westchester vs. Muench et al" | ........ | ........ | ........ | ........ | 32 |
| Forfeited Security Deposits to Cover Expenses in Demolition of Buildings | ........ | ........ | ........ | ........ | 33 |
| Forfeited Deposits, Tax Sales | Comptroller | ........ | 22 00 | 2,262 87 | 34 |
| Forfeited Special Deposit, Clarke Contracting Co. | Dept. of Street Cleaning | Sec. 420, G. N. Y. C. | ........ | ........ | 35 |
| Forfeited Security Deposits, Sundry | Comptroller | Sec. 420, G. N. Y. C. | 275 00 | 920 63 | 36 |
| Judgments and Sundry Settlements, Unclassified | ........ | ........ | 9,716 62 | 12,827 78 | 37 |
| Conscience Money | Various Departments | ........ | 1,405 47 | 869 49 | 38 |
| Total | ........ | ........ | **$20,621 88** | **$20,043 80** | 39 |
| 30. Proceeds of Sales of Real Estate Owned by the City: | | | | | |
| Real Estate | Comptroller | Sec. 205, G. N. Y. C., as amended by Chap. 259, Laws 1913; Secs. 72 to 76 of the Code of Ordinances | $22,424 39 | $335,972 91 | 40 |
| Real Estate | Public Service Com. | Sec. 39, Rapid Transit Act | 626,680 71 | 2,866 41 | 41 |
| Real Estate | Dept. of Corrections | ........ | 35,882 35 | 8,269 59 | 42 |
| Total | ........ | ........ | **$684,987 45** | **$347,108 91** | 43 |
| 31. Sales and Redemptions of Bonds, Mortgages, Stocks and Other Securities Not Issued by the City of New York | ........ | ........ | **$8,657 50** | **$4,266 50** | 44 |

# NEW YORK

FOR THE YEARS 1910 TO 1914, INCLUSIVE, GROUPED ACCORDING TO THE GENERAL CHARACTER THEREOF; THEREOF BY CLASSES OF FUNDS:

| LINE No. | Year | | | Total | Distribution by Classes of Funds | | |
|---|---|---|---|---|---|---|---|
| | 1912 | 1913 | 1914 | | General Fund | Special and Trust Funds | Sinking Funds |
| 1 | $11,770 14 | $13,726 96 | $13,915 20 | $68,344 32 | $68,344 32 | .......... | .......... |
| 2 | 1,092 89 | 1,232 64 | 1,346 26 | 6,559 09 | 6,559 09 | .......... | .......... |
| 3 | 1,841 77 | 4,571 64 | 885 30 | 11,820 01 | 11,820 01 | .......... | .......... |
| 4 | 187 30 | 210 24 | 107 59 | 505 13 | 505 13 | .......... | .......... |
| 5 | .......... | 169 29 | 146 88 | 316 17 | 316 17 | .......... | .......... |
| 6 | 20 91 | .......... | .......... | 458 31 | .......... | $458 31 | .......... |
| 7 | 6 95 | 8 75 | .......... | 24 77 | 24 77 | .......... | .......... |
| 8 | 118 48 | 1,112 14 | .......... | 2,240 71 | 2,240 71 | .......... | .......... |
| 9 | **$756,904 37** | **$731,814 54** | **$1,191,995 63** | **$4,183,806 71** | **$252,609 59** | **$458 31** | **$3,930,738 81** |
| 10 | **$2,866 16** | **$2,622 85** | **$4,752 51** | **$18,962 58** | **$5,677 85** | .......... | **$13,284 73** |
| 11 | **$8,534,644 37** | **$9,517,728 68** | **$10,217,844 65** | **$43,374,143 72** | .......... | .......... | **$43,374,143 72** |
| 12 | $2,555 92 | $1,125 14 | $601 67 | $6,787 08 | $6,787 08 | .......... | .......... |
| 13 | 380 20 | 417 14 | 58 69 | 869 98 | 869 98 | .......... | .......... |
| 14 | 268 50 | 14 00 | 15 50 | 326 50 | 326 50 | .......... | .......... |
| 15 | 43 40 | .......... | 189 82 | 233 22 | 233 22 | .......... | .......... |
| 16 | 145 00 | 199 40 | 300 00 | 1,084 40 | 1,084 40 | .......... | .......... |
| 17 | 114 56 | 55 00 | 109 81 | 495 90 | 495 90 | .......... | .......... |
| 18 | 443 97 | 2,165 95 | 2,789 16 | 7,969 57 | 7,969 57 | .......... | .......... |
| 19 | 325 00 | 81 20 | 57 53 | 650 23 | 650 23 | .......... | .......... |
| 20 | .......... | .......... | 20 00 | 272 21 | 272 21 | .......... | .......... |
| 21 | .......... | .......... | .......... | 865 67 | 865 67 | .......... | .......... |
| 22 | 9 48 | .......... | .......... | 15 98 | 15 98 | .......... | .......... |
| 23 | .......... | 128 23 | .......... | 279 43 | 279 43 | .......... | .......... |
| 24 | 12 25 | .......... | .......... | 17 25 | 17 25 | .......... | .......... |
| 25 | .......... | 7 00 | .......... | 7 00 | 7 00 | .......... | .......... |
| 26 | .......... | .......... | .......... | 185 45 | 185 45 | .......... | .......... |
| 27 | .......... | .......... | .......... | 2,000 00 | 2,000 00 | .......... | .......... |
| 28 | .......... | .......... | 3,035 76 | 3,035 76 | 3,035 76 | .......... | .......... |
| 29 | .......... | 5,371 82 | .......... | 5,371 82 | 5,371 82 | .......... | .......... |
| 30 | .......... | .......... | .......... | 2,939 47 | 2,939 47 | .......... | .......... |
| 31 | .......... | .......... | 11,308 26 | 11,308 26 | 11,308 26 | .......... | .......... |
| 32 | .......... | .......... | 4,791 72 | 4,791 72 | 4,791 72 | .......... | .......... |
| 33 | .......... | .......... | 52 50 | 52 50 | 52 50 | .......... | .......... |
| 34 | 74 21 | .......... | .......... | 2,359 08 | 2,337 08 | $22 00 | .......... |
| 35 | .......... | .......... | 15,000 00 | 15,000 00 | .......... | 15,000 00 | .......... |
| 36 | 491 33 | 6,714 00 | 6,847 82 | 15,248 78 | 5,192 25 | .......... | $10,056 53 |
| 37 | 32,633 46 | 3,511 70 | 7,280 70 | 65,970 26 | 65,970 26 | .......... | .......... |
| 38 | 216 18 | 424 81 | 352 43 | 3,268 38 | 3,268 38 | .......... | .......... |
| 39 | **$37,713 46** | **$20,215 39** | **$52,811 37** | **$151,405 90** | **$126,327 37** | **$15,022 00** | **$10,056 53** |
| 40 | $68,284 88 | $313,497 33 | $60,371 69 | $800,551 20 | .......... | $329,902 31 | $470,648 89 |
| 41 | 128,691 67 | 8,610 00 | 43,263 62 | 810,112 41 | .......... | 810,112 41 | .......... |
| 42 | 8,309 17 | 10,468 27 | 56,005 30 | 118,934 68 | .......... | 118,934 68 | .......... |
| 43 | **$205,285 72** | **$332,575 60** | **$159,640 61** | **$1,729,598 29** | .......... | **$1,258,949 40** | **$470,648 89** |
| 44 | **$4,480 00** | **$3,605 00** | .......... | **$21,009 00** | .......... | .......... | **$21,009 00** |

DETAILED STATEMENT OF REVENUES COLLECTED AND OTHER CASH RECEIPTS BY THE CITY OF NEW YORK
ALSO SHOWING THE DISTRIBUTION

| Character of Revenue | Department, Bureau or Office Through Which Collected | Statute or Ordinance | Year 1910 | Year 1911 | LINE No. |
|---|---|---|---|---|---|
| 32. PAR VALUE OF NEW YORK CITY BONDS SOLD: | | (See Note No. 9, page 215.) | | | |
| Corporate Stock | | | $63,021,795 77 | $61,789,941 68 | 1 |
| Corporate Stock Notes | | | .......... | 24,295,578 62 | 2 |
| Assessment Bonds | | | 1,000 00 | 500 00 | 3 |
| Special Revenue Bonds | | | 7,264,625 00 | 5,970,164 92 | 4 |
| Revenue Bonds | | | 206,682,653 48 | 104,455,855 20 | 5 |
| Revenue Bills | | | .......... | 65,968,673 25 | 6 |
| General Fund Bonds | | | 17,000,000 00 | 17,500,000 00 | 7 |
| Total | | | **$293,970,074 25** | **$279,980,713 67** | 8 |
| 33. PREMIUM ON CORPORATE STOCK SOLD | | | **$637,922 89** | **$542,548 60** | 9 |
| 34. REFUNDS, REBATES, RETURNS OF ADVANCES AND ACCRUED INTEREST ON CITY BONDS SOLD: | | | | | |
| Refunds of Overpayments on Contract for Final Disposition of Garbage in Borough of The Bronx | | | .......... | .......... | 10 |
| Refunds on Transportation | | | $40 96 | $1,020 27 | 11 |
| Refunds of Telephone Charges | Various | | 301 54 | 1,048 71 | 12 |
| Overcharge for Publication of City Record | | | 13,596 19 | .......... | 13 |
| Accrued Interest on Revenue Bonds Sold | | | .......... | .......... | 14 |
| Accrued Interest on Corporate Stock Notes for Water Supply and Various Municipal Purposes | | | .......... | .......... | 15 |
| Refunds to Corporate Stock Account | | | 199,669 69 | 455,659 45 | 16 |
| Sundry Refunds and Rebates | | | 983 03 | 699 02 | 17 |
| Total | | | **$214,591 41** | **$458,427 45** | 18 |
| 35. RECEIPTS OF SECURITY DEPOSITS, PLEDGES, BAIL, ETC.: | | | | | |
| Electric Meter Test Deposits | | | $96 00 | $136 00 | 19 |
| Restoration of Roadway, 17th and 18th Sts., between Broadway and Avenue A, Central Crosstown R. R. Co., of New York | | Sec. 391, G. N. Y. C., and Secs. 148, 149, C. O. | .......... | .......... | 20 |
| Security on Agreement with Rogers & Haggerty and Dept. of Parks. Subway Const., McCombs Dam Park | | | .......... | .......... | 21 |
| Deposit to Secure City for Payment of Salary in Disregard of Assignment (Suspense Account) | | | .......... | .......... | 22 |
| Total | | | **$96 00** | **$136 00** | 23 |
| 36. RECEIPTS OF THE CITY AS AGENT OR ADMINISTRATOR FOR PRIVATE PERSONS OR CORPORATION, AND FOR PENSION FUNDS NOT ADMINISTERED BY FINANCE DEPARTMENT: | | | | | |
| Collection by the Dept. of S. C. for N. Y. Disposal Co | | | .......... | .......... | 24 |
| Collection by the Dept. of S. C. for N. Y. Sanitary Utilization Co | | | .......... | .......... | 25 |
| Intestate Estates | | | $14,149 92 | $20,637 59 | 26 |
| Supreme Court Retirement Fund | | | .......... | .......... | 27 |
| Receipts of Street Cleaning Pension Fund | | | .......... | 886 70 | 28 |
| Total | | | **$14,149 92** | **$21,524 29** | 29 |
| 37. REDEMPTION OF BONDS OF THE CITY OF NEW YORK HELD BY THE SINKING FUNDS | | | **$8,256,000 00** | **$11,244,309 76** | 30 |
| 38. TRANSFER FROM GENERAL AND SPECIAL FUNDS TO THE SINKING FUNDS: | | | | | |
| Annual Instalments to Sinking Funds | | | $7,160,614 84 | $7,788,739 51 | 31 |
| Transfer from Water Revenue, Brooklyn, to Water Sinking Fund of the City of Brooklyn | | | 723,052 32 | 2,068,807 66 | 32 |
| Transfer from Corporate Debt Fund for Redemption of Permanent Water Loan Bonds, Brooklyn | | | .......... | .......... | 33 |
| Total | | | **$7,883,667 16** | **$9,857,547 17** | 34 |
| Total Revenues Collected and Other Cash Receipts | | (See Note No. 7, page 215.) | **$508,514,181 49** | **$500,515,646 75** | 35 |

# NEW YORK

FOR THE YEARS 1910 TO 1914, INCLUSIVE, GROUPED ACCORDING TO THE GENERAL CHARACTER THEREOF; THEREOF BY CLASSES OF FUNDS:

| LINE No. | Year | | | Total | Distribution by Classes of Funds | | |
|---|---|---|---|---|---|---|---|
| | 1912 | 1913 | 1914 | | General Fund | Special and Trust Funds | Sinking Funds |
| 1 | $68,400,000 00 | $60,423,079 49 | $72,096,444 50 | $325,731,261 44 | .......... | *$325,731,261 44 | .......... |
| 2 | 85,177,467 20 | 189,702,897 45 | 141,351,769 01 | 440,527,712 28 | .......... | *440,527,712 28 | .......... |
| 3 | 1,000 00 | 2,555,000 00 | 8,598,500 00 | 11,156,000 00 | .......... | *11,156,000 00 | .......... |
| 4 | 7,038,065 51 | 6,319,225 00 | 11,925,425 00 | 38,517,505 43 | $38,517,505 43 | .......... | .......... |
| 5 | 87,617,560 42 | 145,623,269 53 | 58,056,872 69 | 602,436,211 32 | 602,436,211 32 | .......... | .......... |
| 6 | 68,229,091 79 | 125,741,040 70 | 89,588,347 44 | 349,527,153 18 | 349,527,153 18 | .......... | .......... |
| 7 | 17,500,000 00 | 22,000,000 00 | 23,500,000 00 | 97,500,000 00 | 97,500,000 00 | .......... | .......... |
| 8 | **$333,963,184 92** | **$552,364,512 17** | **$405,117,358 64** | **$1,865,395,843 65** | **$1,087,980,869 93** | **$777,414,973 72** | .......... |
| 9 | **$476,236 36** | **$61,651 77** | **$942,500 00** | **$2,660,859 62** | .......... | **$2,660,859 62** | .......... |
| 10 | $4,041 66 | .......... | .......... | $4,041 66 | $4,041 66 | .......... | .......... |
| 11 | 311 43 | $49 44 | .......... | 1,422 10 | 1,422 10 | .......... | .......... |
| 12 | 2,094 04 | 2,177 44 | $1,874 12 | 7,495 85 | 7,495 85 | .......... | .......... |
| 13 | .......... | .......... | .......... | 13,596 19 | 13,596 19 | .......... | .......... |
| 14 | .......... | .......... | 71,666 62 | 71,666 62 | .......... | $71,666 62 | .......... |
| 15 | .......... | .......... | 53,330 02 | 53,330 02 | .......... | 53,330 02 | .......... |
| 16 | 105,398 94 | 293,491 00 | 540,385 28 | 1,594,604 36 | .......... | 1,594,604 36 | .......... |
| 17 | 1,128 07 | 782 01 | 3,012 00 | 6,604 13 | 6,048 18 | 455 95 | $100 00 |
| 18 | **$112,974 14** | **$296,499 89** | **$670,268 04** | **$1,752,760 93** | **$32,603 98** | **$1,720,056 95** | **$100 00** |
| 19 | $60 00 | $48 00 | $52 00 | $392 00 | .......... | $392 00 | .......... |
| 20 | .......... | .......... | 10,000 00 | 10,000 00 | .......... | 10,000 00 | .......... |
| 21 | 3,000 00 | .......... | .......... | 3,000 00 | .......... | 3,000 00 | .......... |
| 22 | .......... | 101 77 | .......... | 101 77 | .......... | 101 77 | .......... |
| 23 | **$3,000 00** | **$149 77** | **$10,052 00** | **$13,493 77** | .......... | **$13,493 77** | .......... |
| 24 | .......... | .......... | $183 50 | $183 50 | .......... | $183 50 | .......... |
| 25 | .......... | $910 25 | 7 75 | 918 00 | .......... | 918 00 | .......... |
| 26 | $19,082 18 | 33,710 36 | 13,597 18 | 101,177 23 | .......... | 101,177 23 | .......... |
| 27 | .......... | .......... | 8,808 00 | 8,808 00 | .......... | 8,808 00 | .......... |
| 28 | 45,562 30 | 55,247 84 | 118,008 41 | 219,705 25 | .......... | 219,705 25 | .......... |
| 29 | **$64,644 48** | **$89,868 45** | **$140,604 84** | **$330,791 98** | .......... | **$330,791 98** | .......... |
| 30 | **$38,097,666 05** | **$58,914,000 00** | **$29,587,493 57** | **$146,099,469 38** | .......... | .......... | **$146,099,469 38** |
| 31 | $8,366,206 93 | $8,725,597 17 | $7,451,778 88 | $39,492,937 33 | .......... | .......... | $39,492,937 33 |
| 32 | 1,126,555 30 | 1,439,167 89 | 2,514,059 32 | 7,871,642 49 | .......... | .......... | 7,871,642 49 |
| 33 | .......... | 3,000 00 | .......... | 3,000 00 | .......... | .......... | 3,000 00 |
| 34 | **$9,492,762 23** | **$10,167,765 06** | **$9,965,838 20** | **$47,367,579 82** | .......... | .......... | **$47,367,579 82** |
| 35 | **$591,823,623 75** | **$839,827,617 36** | **$657,102,646 17** | **$3,097,783,715 52** | **$1,858,138,069 40** | **$913,926,962 77** | **$325,718,683 35** |

*Corporate Stock and Assessment Bond Fund.

# THE CITY OF NEW YORK

Note No. 1. Fees and Fines, Various City and County Courts. (Page 208.)

The names of the various Courts through which these fees and fines are collected, and the authority therefor are as follows:

|  |  |
|---|---|
| City Court of the City of New York | Sections 331 and 3164-a, C. C. P. |
| City Magistrates' Courts. Courts of Special Sessions. | Section 110, Inferior Criminal Courts Act.<br>Section 291, Motor Vehicle Law.<br>Sections 38 and 39, Liquor Tax Law.<br>Section 132, G. N. Y. C.<br>Sections 203 and 174, Public Health Law. |
| Court of General Sessions of the Peace in and for the City and County of New York | Chapter 410, Laws 1882.<br>Sections 3301, 3302 and 3303, C. C. P. |
| Municipal District Courts | Sections 283, 347 and 349, Municipal Court Act. |
| County Courts | Sections 3301, 3302 and 3303, C. C. P. |
| Appellate Division of Supreme Court | Sections 3301, 3302 and 3303, C. C. P. |
| Supreme Court | Section 3301, C. C. P. and Section 253, Judiciary Law.<br>Section 161, County Law. |

Note No. 2. Licenses. (Page 209.)

As provided in Chapter XII-A of the Laws of 1914, during the latter half of 1914 certain licenses which had theretofore been issued by the Mayor's Bureau of Licenses, the Commissioner of Licenses and the Police Commissioner, were issued by the Department of Licenses. No attempt has been made in this statement to show separately the license fees collected by the Department of Licenses.

Note No. 3. Surrogate's Fees. (Page 210.)

Chapter 443, Laws of 1914; Chapter 530, Laws of 1884; Sections 961, 2499 and 2771, C. C. P.
Chapter 548, Laws of 1912; Resolution of Board of Aldermen, Jan. 23, 1912.
Resolution of Board of Supervisors, June 15, 1900.

Note No. 4. County Clerk's Fees. (Page 210.)

Sections 3304, 3305-a and 3306-a, C. C. P.; Section 161, County Law.
Chapter 446, Laws of 1906; Chapter 353, Laws of 1915; Chapter 540, Laws 1912.
Chapter 513, Laws 1909; Chapter 548, Laws 1912.

Note No. 5. Register's Fees (Page 210.)

Sections 3304, 3305 and 3306, C. C. P.; Section 234, Lien Law.
Chapter 365, Laws 1894; Chapter 706, Laws 1901; Chapter 548, Laws 1912.
Chapter 480, Laws 1906; Chapter 349, Laws 1889, as amended by Chapter 166, Laws 1890.
Chapter 376, Laws 1887; Chapter 665, Section 2, Laws 1901; Chapter 52, Laws 1909.
Section 161, County Law.

Note No. 6. Sheriff's Fees. (Page 211.)

Chapter 523, Laws 1890; Sections 3307 and 3308, C. C. P.; Chapter 166, Laws 1873; Chapter 439, Laws 1876.
Chapter 705, Laws 1901; Chapter 502, Laws 1909; Chapter 701, Laws 1911; Chapter 548, Laws 1912.

Note No. 7. Redemptions of Sinking Fund Investments. (Page 214.)

This total includes redemptions by one Sinking Fund of bonds held by another. ($2,646,500 in 1914.)

Note No. 8. Interest on Bonds of the City of New York Held by Sinking Funds. (Page 213.)

This total includes $5,526,558.04 paid by the "Sinking Fund for the Payment of Interest."

Note No. 9. Bonds Sold to Sinking Funds. (Page 214.)

Of the total par value of New York City Bonds sold, amounting to $1,865,395,843.65, there were purchased by the Sinking Funds bonds aggregating $292,658,580.08, consisting of the following:

| | 1910 | 1911 | 1912 | 1913 | 1914 | Total |
|---|---|---|---|---|---|---|
| Corporate Stock | $13,076,795 97 | $3,703,900 70 | $3,400,000 00 | $15,423,179 49 | $7,096,444 50 | $42,700,320 46 |
| Corporate Stock Notes | .......... | 6,837,166 05 | 37,168,500 00 | 44,350,000 00 | 21,625,993 57 | 109,981,659 62 |
| Assessment Bonds | 536,600 00 | 500 00 | 1,000 00 | 2,555,000 00 | 8,598,500 00 | 11,691,600 00 |
| Special Revenue Bonds | 200,000 00 | 1,155,000 00 | 4,400,000 00 | 3,550,000 00 | 4,980,000 00 | 14,285,000 00 |
| Revenue Bonds | 3,500,000 00 | 9,000,000 00 | 4,000,000 00 | .......... | .......... | 16,500,000 00 |
| General Fund Bonds | 17,000,000 00 | 17,500,000 00 | 17,500,000 00 | 22,000,000 00 | 23,500,000 00 | 97,500,000 00 |
| Total | **$34,313,395 77** | **$38,196,566 75** | **$66,469,500 00** | **$87,878,179 49** | **$65,800,938 07** | **$292,658,580 08** |

STATEMENT OF REVENUES COLLECTED WITHIN THE FIVE COUNTIES OF GREATER NEW

| General Character of Revenues | Collected by | To Whom Paid | Statute or Charter Reference | LINE No. |
|---|---|---|---|---|
| SUNDRY FEES (estimated). | Sheriff, Richmond County............ | Sheriff, Richmond County, applied to the payment of expenses.......... | ........................ | 1 |
| COMMISSIONS............ | Public Administrator, Richmond County... | Public Administrator, Richmond County, applied to the payment of expenses.......... | Chap. 486, Laws of 1899, and Chap. 412, Laws of 1910. ........................ | 2 |
| EXCISE TAXES: | Deputy Commissioners of Excise in the Counties of: | | | |
| Regular Liquor Licenses | New York and Bronx | State of New York | ........................ | 3 |
| | Kings.............. | | ........................ | 4 |
| | Queens.............. | | ........................ | 5 |
| | Richmond.......... | | ........................ | 6 |
| | | | Total Regular Liquor Licenses | 7 |
| All-Night Licenses..... | New York and Bronx | State of New York | ........................ | 8 |
| | Kings.............. | | ........................ | 9 |
| | Queens.............. | | ........................ | 10 |
| | Richmond.......... | | ........................ | 11 |
| | | | Total All-Night Licenses.... | 12 |
| | | | Total Excise Taxes.......... | 13 |
| MORTGAGE TAXES (See detailed statement, page 218) ............. | County Registers: .................... | State of New York .................... | ........................ | 14 |
| FIRE DEPARTMENT RELIEF FUND REVENUES (See detailed statement, page 219).......... | Treasurer, Fire Department Relief Fund. .................... | Fire Department Relief Fund. .................... | Sections 764–765, G. N. Y. C. | 15 |
| POLICE PENSION FUND REVENUES (See detailed statement, page 219)............... | Treasurer Police Pension Fund. .................... | Police Department Pension Fund. .................... | Section 353, G. N. Y. C. ........................ | 16 |
| NOTARIAL FEES......... | County Clerk: New York County... | State of New York | Section 7, Chap. 513, L. 1909. ........................ | 17 |
| | Kings County....... | | ........................ | 18 |
| | Queens County...... | | ........................ | 19 |
| | Richmond County... | | ........................ | 20 |
| | Bronx County....... | | ........................ | 21 |
| | | | Total................ | 22 |
| HUNTERS' LICENSES...... | County Clerk: New York County... | State of New York | Section 185, of the Conservation Law. ........................ | 23 |
| | Kings County....... | | ........................ | 24 |
| | Queens County...... | | ........................ | 25 |
| | Richmond County... | | ........................ | 26 |
| | | | Total................ | 27 |

NEW YORK

York, Which Did Not Go into the City Treasury, from January 1, 1910, to December 31, 1914

| LINE No. | Total | 1910 | 1911 | 1912 | 1913 | 1914 |
|---|---|---|---|---|---|---|
| 1 | **$7,500 00** | **$1,500 00** | **$1,500 00** | **$1,500 00** | **$1,500 00** | **$1,500 00** |
| 2 | **$1,684 55** | **$1,021 44** | **$88 92** | **$152 53** | **$103 78** | **$317 88** |
| 3 | $17,469,925 45 | $3,625,045 32 | $3,500,273 51 | $3,485,678 73 | $3,465,376 87 | $3,393,551 02 |
| 4 | 9,458,852 16 | 2,027,003 75 | 1,920,658 41 | 1,874,953 75 | 1,835,978 75 | 1,800,257 50 |
| 5 | 1,369,867 02 | 275,744 08 | 268,828 47 | 271,730 10 | 275,329 06 | 278,235 31 |
| 6 | 445,036 87 | 91,868 72 | 88,415 65 | 88,273 76 | 89,750 62 | 86,728 12 |
| 7 | **$28,743,681 50** | **$6,019,661 87** | **$5,778,176 04** | **$5,720,636 34** | **$5,666,435 30** | **$5,558,771 95** |
| 8 | $118,645 00 | $8,645 00 | $17,330 00 | $29,620 00 | $29,845 00 | $33,205 00 |
| 9 | 28,415 00 | 905 00 | 3,755 00 | 6,900 00 | 7,525 00 | 9,330 00 |
| 10 | 295 00 | .......... | 50 00 | 235 00 | 10 00 | .......... |
| 11 | 60 00 | .......... | 60 00 | .......... | .......... | .......... |
| 12 | **$147,415 00** | **$9,550 00** | **$21,195 00** | **$36,755 00** | **$37,380 00** | **$42,535 00** |
| 13 | **$28,891,096 50** | **$6,029,211 87** | **$5,799,371 04** | **$5,757,391 34** | **$5,703,815 30** | **$5,601,306 95** |
| 14 | **$5,975,545 49** | **$1,362,911 11** | **$1,348,358 76** | **$1,324,192 16** | **$1,155,814 77** | **$784,268 69** |
| 15 | **$1,608,012 51** | **$351,055 46** | **$326,027 20** | **$311,988 23** | **$291,418 08** | **$327,523 54** |
| 16 | **$307,914 15** | **$60,820 84** | **$65,181 10** | **$59,170 12** | **$66,431 01** | **$56,311 08** |
| 17 | $189,748 00 | $36,264 00 | $39,944 50 | $37,343 50 | $39,302 00 | $36,894 00 |
| 18 | 85,671 50 | 15,790 00 | 17,193 50 | 16,483 00 | 17,667 00 | 18,538 00 |
| 19 | 2,500 00 | *.......... | *.......... | *.......... | 1,250 00 | 1,250 00 |
| 20 | 2,003 00 | 414 00 | 368 00 | 395 00 | 374 00 | 452 00 |
| 21 | 3,684 00 | .......... | .......... | .......... | .......... | 3,684 00 |
| 22 | **$283,606 50** | **$52,468 00** | **$57,506 00** | **$54,221 50** | **$58,593 00** | **$60,818 00** |
| 23 | $23,668 00 | $3,819 00 | $4,171 00 | $4,515 00 | $5,395 00 | $5,768 00 |
| 24 | 9,525 00 | 1,691 00 | 1,780 00 | 1,854 00 | 2,090 00 | 2,110 00 |
| 25 | 2,550 00 | *.......... | *.......... | *.......... | 1,199 00 | 1,351 00 |
| 26 | 2,605 00 | 411 00 | 466 00 | 506 00 | 562 00 | 660 00 |
| 27 | **$38,348 00** | **$5,921 00** | **$6,417 00** | **$6,875 00** | **$9,246 00** | **$9,889 00** |

*No figures obtainable.

THE CITY OF

STATEMENT OF REVENUES COLLECTED WITHIN THE FIVE COUNTIES OF GREATER NEW YORK, WHICH

| General Character of Revenue | Collected by | To Whom Paid | Statute or Charter Reference | LINE No. |
|---|---|---|---|---|
| SUNDRY FEES........... | Surrogate, Queens Co.. | Surrogate, Queens Co., applied to the payment of expenses.......... | Resolution, Board of Supervisors, June 15, 1900. .......................... | 1 |
| DOG LICENSES, RENEWALS, TAGS AND REDEMPTIONS......... | American Society for the Prevention of Cruelty to Animals... | American Society for the Prevention of Cruelty to Animals | Chap. 88, Laws of 1909. .......................... | 2 |
| FINES AND PENALTIES.... | Health Department.... | Health Dept. Pension Fund....... | .......................... | 3 |
| | | | Grand Total............. | 4 |

NEW YORK

DID NOT GO INTO THE CITY TREASURY, FROM JANUARY, 1, 1910, TO DECEMBER 31, 1914:—*Continued*

| LINE No. | Total | 1910 | 1911 | 1912 | 1913 | 1914 |
|---|---|---|---|---|---|---|
| 1 | **$6,003 79** | **$790 60** | **$1,193 55** | **$1,227 89** | **$1,403 15** | **$1,388 60** |
| 2 | **$375,594 00** | **$61,088 00** | **$57,332 00** | **$84,010 00** | **$86,866 00** | **$86,298 00** |
| 3 | **$133,141 10** | ............ | ............ | ............ | **$66,042 10** | **$67,099 00** |
| 4 | **$37,628,446 59** | **$7,926,788 32** | **$7,662,975 57** | **$7,600,728 77** | **$7,441,233 19** | **$6,996,720 74** |

STATEMENT SHOWING TOTAL COLLECTIONS OF MORTGAGE TAX IN THE FIVE COUNTIES COMPRISING
1914. (CHAPETR 729, LAWS OF 1905

| | 1910 | | 1911 | | LINE No. |
|---|---|---|---|---|---|
| Collected by County Registers (less Refunds)................... | | $2,694,500 93 | | $2,662,747 38 | 1 |
| Interest Collected by City Chamberlain..................... | | 6,010 52 | | 5,999 18 | 2 |
| Gross Revenue........... | | **$2,700,511 45** | | **$2,668,746 56** | 3 |
| DEDUCTIONS: | | | | | |
| Expenses of Registers........... | $25,673 36 | | $26,708 47 | | 4 |
| Expenses of City Chamberlain.... | 1,122 36 | | 1,262 50 | | 5 |
| Total Deductions......... | | **26,795 72** | | **27,970 97** | 6 |
| Net Revenue......... | | **$2,673,715 73** | | **$2,640,775 59** | 7 |
| APPORTIONED AS FOLLOWS: | | | | | |
| To State of New York........... | | $1,336,115 39 | | $1,320,387 79 | 8 |
| To City of New York........... | | 1,337,600 34 | | 1,320,387 80 | 9 |
| | | **$2,673,715 73** | | **$2,640,775 59** | 10 |
| Total Amount of Collection of Mortgage Taxes which did not go into the City Treasury: | | | | | |
| Used for Expenses.............. | | $26,795 72 | | $27,970 97 | 11 |
| Apportioned to State of New York. | | 1,336,115 39 | | 1,320,387 79 | 12 |
| Totals, carried to page 216........ | | **$1,362,911 11** | | **$1,348,358 76** | 13 |

NEW YORK

Greater New York, and the Disposition Thereof for the Five Years Ending December 31, and Chapter 771, Laws of 1913.)

| LINE No. | 1912 | | 1913 | | 1914 | |
|---|---|---|---|---|---|---|
| 1 | | $2,613,622 78 | | $2,675,327 77 | | $1,921,235 80 |
| 2 | | 5,151 04 | | 6,794 34 | | 5,592 60 |
| 3 | | **$2,618,773 82** | | **$2,682,122 11** | | **$1,926,828 40** |
| 4 | $28,173 00 | | $28,229 52 | | $37,652 41 | |
| 5 | 1,437 50 | | 1,562 50 | | 1,928 77 | |
| 6 | | **29,610 50** | | **29,792 02** | | **39,581 18** |
| 7 | | **$2,589,163 32** | | **$2,652,330 09** | | **$1,887,247 22** |
| 8 | | $1,294,581 66 | | $1,126,022 75 | | $744,687 51 |
| 9 | | 1,294,581 66 | | 1,526,307 34 | | 1,142,559 71 |
| 10 | | **$2,589,163 32** | | **$2,652,330 09** | | **$1,887,247 22** |
| 11 | | $29,610 50 | | $29,792 02 | | $39,581 18 |
| 12 | | 1,294,581 66 | | 1,126,022 75 | | 744,687 51 |
| 13 | | **$1,324,192 16** | | **$1,155,814 77** | | **$784,268 69** |

THE CITY OF

STATEMENT OF REVENUES COLLECTED BY THE POLICE DEPARTMENT FOR

| General Character of Revenues | Total for the Five Years | LINE No. |
|---|---|---|
| Sale of Condemned Property | $37,692 93 | 1 |
| Violation of Coal Law | 194 00 | 2 |
| Violation of Agricultural Law | 200 00 | 3 |
| Sale of Manure | 130 00 | 4 |
| Donations | 2,313 93 | 5 |
| Unclaimed Cash | 9,037 37 | 6 |
| Interest | 24,230 00 | 7 |
| Boiler Inspections | 127,824 00 | 8 |
| Pistol Permits | 21,271 00 | 9 |
| Masked Ball Permits | 54,765 00 | 10 |
| Reverted Pensions | 28,174 76 | 11 |
| Percentage of Rewards | 1,713 41 | 12 |
| Penalties | 45 | 13 |
| Deposits on Unclaimed Runners' Shields | 148 00 | 14 |
| Identification Cards | 204 30 | 15 |
| Sale of Budget Exhibit Photos | 15 00 | 16 |
| Totals, carried to page 216 | **$307,914 15** | 17 |

THE CITY OF

STATEMENT OF REVENUES COLLECTED BY THE FIRE DEPARTMENT FOR

| General Character of Revenues | Total for the Five Years | LINE No. |
|---|---|---|
| Oil Licenses | $228,510 22 | 1 |
| Powder Licenses | 240 00 | 2 |
| Match Licenses | 555 00 | 3 |
| Penalties | 24,109 00 | 4 |
| Fireworks Permits | 1,322 00 | 5 |
| Permit for Sale and Use of Explosives | 59,701 00 | 6 |
| Special Permits | 318,876 05 | 7 |
| Fire in Street Permits | 270 73 | 8 |
| Sale of Fire Line Badges | 9,526 95 | 9 |
| Donations | 36,571 99 | 10 |
| Foreign Insurance Tax | 723,731 46 | 11 |
| Sale of Condemned Property | 54,183 33 | 12 |
| Sale of Seized Combustibles | 225 00 | 13 |
| Violation of Agricultural Law | 50 00 | 14 |
| Premiums and Discounts on Bonds | 14,189 50 | 15 |
| Interest | 135,950 28 | 16 |
| Totals, carried to page 216 | **$1,608,012 51** | 17 |

## NEW YORK

THE POLICE PENSION FUND FOR THE FIVE YEARS ENDED DECEMBER 31, 1914.

| LINE No. | 1910 | 1911 | 1912 | 1913 | 1914 |
|---|---|---|---|---|---|
| 1 | $5,377 74 | $8,555 38 | $7,913 69 | $9,342 79 | $6,503 33 |
| 2 | 176 50 | 12 50 | 5 00 | .......... | .......... |
| 3 | 200 00 | .......... | .......... | .......... | .......... |
| 4 | 50 00 | 50 00 | 30 00 | .......... | .......... |
| 5 | 1,182 11 | 390 28 | 125 50 | 123 35 | 492 69 |
| 6 | 2,320 33 | 1,349 90 | 712 60 | 2,798 79 | 1,855 75 |
| 7 | 4,818 98 | 5,034 58 | 2,799 43 | 5,301 90 | 6,275 11 |
| 8 | 27,014 00 | 25,916 00 | 25,132 00 | 24,994 00 | 24,768 00 |
| 9 | 1,230 00 | 6,642 50 | 3,552 50 | 5,496 50 | 4,349 50 |
| 10 | 12,940 00 | 12,025 00 | 11,240 00 | 9,995 00 | 8,565 00 |
| 11 | 5,098 93 | 4,785 01 | 7,222 30 | 7,957 74 | 3,110 78 |
| 12 | 397 25 | 419 50 | 255 50 | 264 74 | 376 42 |
| 13 | .......... | 45 | .......... | .......... | .......... |
| 14 | .......... | .......... | 24 00 | 124 00 | .......... |
| 15 | .......... | .......... | 157 60 | 32 20 | 14 50 |
| 16 | 15 00 | .......... | .......... | .......... | .......... |
| 17 | **$60,820 84** | **$65,181 10** | **$59,170 12** | **$66,431 01** | **$56,311 08** |

## NEW YORK

THE FIREMEN'S RELIEF FUND FOR THE FIVE YEARS ENDED DECEMBER 31, 1914.

| LINE No. | 1910 | 1911 | 1912 | 1913 | 1914 |
|---|---|---|---|---|---|
| 1 | $50,860 00 | $47,840 00 | $43,820 00 | $39,820 00 | $46,170 22 |
| 2 | 170 00 | 60 00 | 10 00 | .......... | .......... |
| 3 | 280 00 | 260 00 | 15 00 | .......... | .......... |
| 4 | 3,317 50 | 8,856 50 | 5,931 00 | 3,670 00 | 2,334 00 |
| 5 | 740 00 | 414 00 | 168 00 | .......... | .......... |
| 6 | 6,365 00 | 8,184 00 | 14,526 00 | 16,065 00 | 14,561 00 |
| 7 | 43,919 00 | 48,522 00 | 57,721 00 | 88,117 00 | 80,597 05 |
| 8 | 34 00 | 46 00 | 29 50 | 56 00 | 105 23 |
| 9 | 7,481 95 | 1,700 00 | .......... | 345 00 | .......... |
| 10 | 28,443 25 | 6,877 34 | 519 50 | 27 00 | 704 90 |
| 11 | 154,179 83 | 166,918 76 | 153,746 03 | 103,525 03 | 145,361 81 |
| 12 | 17,271 91 | 9,495 57 | 8,576 20 | 12,875 14 | 5,964 51 |
| 13 | .......... | 81 00 | 144 00 | .......... | .......... |
| 14 | 50 00 | .......... | .......... | .......... | .......... |
| 15 | 9,284 50 | .......... | .......... | .......... | 4,905 00 |
| 16 | 28,658 52 | 26,772 03 | 26,782 00 | 26,917 91 | 26,819 82 |
| 17 | **$351,055 46** | **$326,027 20** | **$311,988 23** | **$291,418 08** | **$327,523 54** |

# SECTION IV

## SUMMARY AND DETAILED STATEMENTS OF TAXES LEVIED AND COLLECTED AND OF DEFICIENCIES IN TAXES

GRAND SUMMARY OF REAL ESTATE AND PERSONAL

| Borough and Class of Tax | Amount of Levy | Collections | | | LINE No. |
|---|---|---|---|---|---|
| | | Total | Less Refunds and Over and Double Payments | Net | |
| MANHATTAN: | | | | | |
| Real Estate........... | $1,002,031,283 03 | $958,509,350 90 | $2,727,856 37 | $955,781,494 53 | 1 |
| Personal.............. | 108,188,631 26 | 69,045,196 00 | 212,709 59 | 68,832,486 41 | 2 |
| Total............. | **$1,110,219,914 29** | **$1,027,554,546 90** | **$2,940,565 96** | **$1,024,613,980 94** | 3 |
| THE BRONX: | | | | | |
| Real Estate........... | $92,555,996 40 | $85,930,837 12 | $147,584 54 | $85,783,252 58 | 4 |
| Personal.............. | 2,889,166 16 | 771,372 70 | 385 84 | 770,986 86 | 5 |
| Total............. | **$95,445,162 56** | **$86,702,209 82** | **$147,970 38** | **$86,554,239 44** | 6 |
| BROOKLYN: | | | | | |
| Real Estate........... | $300,867,653 01 | $279,922,949 56 | $587,262 89 | $279,335,686 67 | 7 |
| Personal.............. | 19,961,872 48 | 8,162,621 50 | 162,355 25 | 8,000,266 25 | 8 |
| Total............. | **$320,829,525 49** | **$288,085,571 06** | **$749,618 14** | **$287,335,952 92** | 9 |
| QUEENS: | | | | | |
| Real Estate........... | $64,074,804 27 | $57,398,200 74 | $169,266 29 | $57,228,934 45 | 10 |
| Personal.............. | 2,283,205 09 | 823,357 18 | 7,629 55 | 815,727 63 | 11 |
| Total............. | **$66,358,009 36** | **$58,221,557 92** | **$176,895 84** | **$58,044,662 08** | 12 |
| RICHMOND: | | | | | |
| Real Estate........... | $15,528,027 39 | $14,073,552 19 | $28,480 00 | $14,045,072 19 | 13 |
| Personal.............. | 1,271,844 61 | 609,461 96 | 637 05 | 608,824 91 | 14 |
| Total............. | **$16,799,872 00** | **$14,683,014 15** | **$29,117 05** | **$14,653,897 10** | 15 |
| TOTAL—ALL BOROUGHS: | | | | | |
| Real Estate........... | $1,475,057,764 10 | $1,395,834,890 51 | $3,660,450 09 | $1,392,174,440 42 | 16 |
| Personal.............. | 134,594,719 60 | 79,412,009 34 | 383,717 28 | 79,028,292 06 | 17 |
| Grand Totals..... | **$1,609,652,483 70** | **$1,475,246,889 85** | **$4,044,167 37** | **$1,471,202,732 48** | 18 |

NEW YORK

Tax Accounts—Levies 1899 to 1913—By Boroughs:

| LINE No. | Deficiencies | | | | Balance Uncollected at Dec. 31, 1913 | Percentages | | |
|---|---|---|---|---|---|---|---|---|
| | Discounts | Cancellations | Deductions Under Sec. 48 General Tax Laws | Total | | Net Collections to Levy | Total Deficiencies to Levy | Uncollected Balance to Levy |
| 1 | $3,231,342 35 | $17,292,275 95 | $5,936,569 98 | $26,460,188 28 | $19,789,600 22 | 95.38 | 2.65 | 1.97 |
| 2 | 319,666 19 | 6,280,065 66 | .......... | 6,599,731 85 | 32,756,413 00 | 63.62 | 6.10 | 30.28 |
| 3 | **$3,551,008 54** | **$23,572,341 61** | **$5,936,569 98** | **$33,059,920 13** | **$52,546,013 22** | **92.29** | **2.98** | **4.73** |
| 4 | $203,574 33 | $1,067,641 39 | $430,272 88 | $1,701,488 60 | $5,071,255 22 | 92.68 | 1.84 | 5.48 |
| 5 | 1,948 79 | 337,862 30 | .......... | 339,811 09 | 1,778,368 21 | 26.68 | 11.76 | 61.56 |
| 6 | **$205,523 12** | **$1,405,503 69** | **$430,272 88** | **$2,041,299 69** | **$6,849,623 43** | **90.68** | **2.14** | **7.18** |
| 7 | $741,513 82 | $3,530,910 87 | $3,456,165 23 | $7,728,589 92 | $13,803,376 42 | 92.84 | 2.57 | 4.59 |
| 8 | 29,731 44 | 2,034,424 81 | .......... | 2,064,156 25 | 9,897,449 98 | 40.08 | 10.34 | 49.58 |
| 9 | **$771,245 26** | **$5,565,335 68** | **$3,456,165 23** | **$9,792,746 17** | **$23,700,826 40** | **89.56** | **3.05** | **7.39** |
| 10 | $122,708 82 | $526,862 51 | $56,642 17 | $706,213 50 | $6,139,656 32 | 89.32 | 1.10 | 9.58 |
| 11 | 2,828 20 | 234,335 01 | .......... | 237,163 21 | 1,230,314 25 | 35.73 | 10.39 | 53.88 |
| 12 | **$125,537 02** | **$761,197 52** | **$56,642 17** | **$943,376 71** | **$7,369,970 57** | **87.47** | **1.42** | **11.11** |
| 13 | $37,168 12 | $192,046 53 | .......... | $229,214 65 | $1,253,740 55 | 90.45 | 1.48 | 8.07 |
| 14 | 2,414 18 | 28,867 68 | .......... | 31,281 86 | 631,737 84 | 47.87 | 2.46 | 49.67 |
| 15 | **$39,582 30** | **$220,914 21** | .......... | **$260,496 51** | **$1,885,478 39** | **87.23** | **1.55** | **11.22** |
| 16 | $4,336,307 44 | $22,609,737 25 | $9,879,650 26 | $36,825,694 95 | $40,057,628 73 | 94.38 | 2.50 | 3.12 |
| 17 | 356,588 80 | 8,915,555 46 | .......... | 9,272,144 26 | 46,294,283 28 | 58.72 | 6.89 | 34.39 |
| 18 | **$4,692,896 24** | **$31,525,292 71** | **$9,879,650 26** | **$46,097,839 21** | **$92,351,912 01** | **91.40** | **2.86** | **5.74** |

THE CITY OF

STATEMENT SHOWING STATUS OF REAL ESTATE

| Year of Levy and Class of Tax | Amount of Levy | Collections: Total | Collections: Less Refunds and Over and Double Payments | Collections: Net | Line No. |
|---|---|---|---|---|---|
| **1899** | | | | | |
| Real Estate | $72,805,838 36 | $71,710,238 04 | $227,622 68 | $71,482,615 36 | 1 |
| Personal | 13,374,238 37 | 8,502,931 50 | 23,393 64 | 8,479,537 86 | 2 |
| Total | **$86,180,076 73** | **$80,213,169 54** | **$251,016 32** | **$79,962,153 22** | 3 |
| **1900** | | | | | |
| Real Estate | $71,758,376 26 | $68,595,538 57 | $109,526 63 | $68,486,011 94 | 4 |
| Personal | 10,780,825 69 | 7,619,818 78 | 27,631 00 | 7,592,187 78 | 5 |
| Total | **$82,539,201 95** | **$76,215,357 35** | **$137,157 63** | **$76,078,199 72** | 6 |
| **1901** | | | | | |
| Real Estate | $75,632,264 78 | $72,473,934 67 | $268,740 04 | $72,205,194 63 | 7 |
| Personal | 12,609,537 08 | 7,232,915 29 | 205,932 51 | 7,026,982 78 | 8 |
| Total | **$88,241,801 86** | **$79,706,849 96** | **$474,672 55** | **$79,232,177 41** | 9 |
| **1902** | | | | | |
| Real Estate | $76,303,323 56 | $73,059,897 07 | $159,875 19 | $72,900,021 88 | 10 |
| Personal | 11,925,231 36 | 6,341,591 51 | 9,022 96 | 6,332,568 55 | 11 |
| Total | **$88,228,554 92** | **$79,401,488 58** | **$168,898 15** | **$79,232,590 43** | 12 |
| **1903** | | | | | |
| Real Estate | $67,927,923 61 | $66,084,244 98 | $127,463 34 | $65,956,781 64 | 13 |
| Personal | 9,703,850 94 | 4,955,446 62 | 1,270 45 | 4,954,176 17 | 14 |
| Total | **$77,631,774 55** | **$71,039,691 60** | **$128,733 79** | **$70,910,957 81** | 15 |
| **1904** | | | | | |
| Real Estate | $76,552,162 84 | $74,426,303 26 | $216,947 22 | $74,209,356 04 | 16 |
| Personal | 9,516,240 66 | 4,971,780 11 | 1,523 60 | 4,970,256 51 | 17 |
| Total | **$86,068,403 50** | **$79,398,083 37** | **$218,470 82** | **$79,179,612 55** | 18 |
| **1905** | | | | | |
| Real Estate | $78,625,859 34 | $76,084,799 03 | $231,007 53 | $75,853,791 50 | 19 |
| Personal | 10,354,826 68 | 4,791,072 78 | 99,807 82 | 4,691,264 96 | 20 |
| Total | **$88,980,686 02** | **$80,875,871 81** | **$330,815 35** | **$80,545,056 46** | 21 |
| **1906** | | | | | |
| Real Estate | $85,650,130 58 | $82,487,300 26 | $291,685 17 | $82,195,615 09 | 22 |
| Personal | 8,444,962 83 | 4,381,888 22 | 2,846 85 | 4,379,041 37 | 23 |
| Total | **$94,095,093 41** | **$86,869,188 48** | **$294,532 02** | **$86,574,656 46** | 24 |
| **1907** | | | | | |
| Real Estate | $93,635,303 09 | $89,388,103 83 | $452,480 55 | $88,935,623 28 | 25 |
| Personal | 8,312,366 93 | 4,503,585 39 | 1,018 90 | 4,502,566 49 | 26 |
| Total | **$101,947,670 02** | **$93,891,689 22** | **$453,499 45** | **$93,438,189 77** | 27 |
| **1908** | | | | | |
| Real Estate | $109,452,257 89 | $104,806,562 65 | $471,699 61 | $104,334,863 04 | 28 |
| Personal | 7,088,825 73 | 4,364,673 16 | 1,422 98 | 4,363,250 18 | 29 |
| Total | **$116,541,083 62** | **$109,171,235 81** | **$473,122 59** | **$108,698,113 22** | 30 |

NEW YORK

AND PERSONAL TAX ACCOUNTS—LEVIES 1899 TO 1913:

| LINE No. | Deficiencies | | | | Balance Uncollected at Dec. 31, 1913 | Percentages | | |
|---|---|---|---|---|---|---|---|---|
| | Discounts | Cancellations | Deductions Under Sec. 48 General Tax Laws | Total | | Net Ccllections to Levy | Total Deficiencies to Levy | Uncollected Balance to Levy |
| 1 | $371,375 50 | $694,007 44 | .......... | $1,065,382 94 | $257,840 06 | 98.18 | 1.46 | .36 |
| 2 | 53,061 95 | 453,118 96 | .......... | 506,180 91 | 4,388,519 60 | 63.41 | 3.78 | 32.81 |
| 3 | **$424,437 45** | **$1,147,126 40** | .......... | **$1,571,563 85** | **$4,646,359 66** | **92.79** | **1.81** | **5.40** |
| 4 | $369,340 02 | $2,239,989 10 | $274,482 05 | $2,883,811 17 | $388,553 15 | 95.44 | 4.02 | .54 |
| 5 | 55,432 23 | 482,472 11 | .......... | 537,904 34 | 2,650,733 57 | 70.42 | 4.99 | 24.59 |
| 6 | **$424,772 25** | **$2,722,461 21** | **$274,482 05** | **$3,421,715 51** | **$3,039,286 72** | **92.17** | **4.15** | **3.68** |
| 7 | $366,795 49 | $2,258,766 34 | $551,372 53 | $3,176,934 36 | $250,135 79 | 95.46 | 4.20 | .34 |
| 8 | 42,499 93 | 1,133,757 04 | .......... | 1,176,256 97 | 4,406,297 33 | 55.73 | 9.33 | 34.94 |
| 9 | **$409,295 42** | **$3,392,523 38** | **$551,372 53** | **$4,353,191 33** | **$4,656,433 12** | **89.79** | **4.93** | **5.28** |
| 10 | $388,875 36 | $2,204,873 35 | $564,918 12 | $3,158,666 83 | $244,634 85 | 95.53 | 4.14 | .33 |
| 11 | 40,053 18 | 1,313,562 61 | .......... | 1,353,615 79 | 4,239,047 02 | 53.10 | 11.35 | 35.55 |
| 12 | **$428,928 54** | **$3,518,435 96** | **$564,918 12** | **$4,512,282 62** | **$4,483,681 87** | **89.80** | **5.12** | **5.08** |
| 13 | $366,006 33 | $797,639 73 | $539,940 30 | $1,703,586 36 | $267,555 61 | 97.10 | 2.51 | .39 |
| 14 | 32,553 28 | 859,075 86 | .......... | 891,629 14 | 3,858,045 63 | 51.06 | 9.19 | 39.75 |
| 15 | **$398,559 61** | **$1,656,715 59** | **$539,940 30** | **$2,595,215 50** | **$4,125,601 24** | **91.34** | **3.34** | **5.32** |
| 16 | $445,608 05 | $966,042 40 | $560,684 08 | $1,972,334 53 | $370,472 27 | 96.94 | 2.58 | .48 |
| 17 | 35,587 65 | 200,960 79 | .......... | 236,548 44 | 4,309,435 71 | 52.23 | 2.48 | 45.29 |
| 18 | **$481,195 70** | **$1,167,003 19** | **$560,684 08** | **$2,208,882 97** | **$4,679,907 98** | **92.00** | **2.57** | **5.43** |
| 19 | $476,779 66 | $1,263,120 82 | $599,032 55 | $2,338,933 03 | $433,134 81 | 96.47 | 2.97 | .56 |
| 20 | 36,297 77 | 1,108,804 27 | .......... | 1,145,102 04 | 4,518,459 68 | 45.31 | 11.06 | 43.63 |
| 21 | **$513,077 43** | **$2,371,925 09** | **$599,032 55** | **$3,484,035 07** | **$4,951,594 49** | **90.52** | **3.92** | **5.56** |
| 22 | $494,683 94 | $1,787,815 23 | $648,013 68 | $2,930,512 85 | $524,002 64 | 95.97 | 3.42 | .61 |
| 23 | 31,668 71 | 663,915 74 | .......... | 695,584 45 | 3,370,337 01 | 51.85 | 8.24 | 39.91 |
| 24 | **$526,352 65** | **$2,451,730 97** | **$648,013 68** | **$3,626,097 30** | **$3,894,339 65** | **92.01** | **3.85** | **4.14** |
| 25 | $460,398 70 | $2,499,524 75 | $756,770 40 | $3,716,693 85 | $982,985 96 | 94.98 | 3.97 | 1.05 |
| 26 | 29,434 10 | 665,095 78 | .......... | 694,529 88 | 3,115,270 56 | 54.17 | 8.36 | 37.47 |
| 27 | **$489,832 80** | **$3,164,620 53** | **$756,770 40** | **$4,411,223 73** | **$4,098,256 52** | **91.65** | **4.33** | **4.02** |
| 28 | .......... | $2,875,717 87 | $880,368 83 | $3,756,086 70 | $1,361,308 15 | 95.33 | 3.43 | 1.24 |
| 29 | .......... | 554,555 25 | .......... | 554,555 25 | 2,171,020 30 | 61.55 | 7.82 | 30.63 |
| 30 | .......... | **$3,430,273 12** | **$880,368 83** | **$4,310,641 95** | **$3,532,328 45** | **93.27** | **3.70** | **3.03** |

STATEMENT SHOWING STATUS OF REAL ESTATE AND PERSONAL

| Year of Levy and Class of Tax | Amount of Levy | Collections: Total | Collections: Less Refunds and Over and Double Payments | Collections: Net | LINE No. |
|---|---|---|---|---|---|
| **1909** | | | | | |
| Real Estate | $115,245,613 96 | $110,809,656 39 | $350,185 38 | $110,459,471 01 | 1 |
| Personal | 7,497,019 70 | 4,555,176 26 | 1,559 03 | 4,553,617 23 | 2 |
| Total | **$122,742,633 66** | **$115,364,832 65** | **$351,744 41** | **$115,013,088 24** | 3 |
| **1910** | | | | | |
| Real Estate | $124,884,960 78 | $119,143,779 01 | $393,796 38 | $118,749,982 63 | 4 |
| Personal | 6,589,809 14 | 4,620,520 62 | 1,250 32 | 4,619,270 30 | 5 |
| Total | **$131,474,769 92** | **$123,764,299 63** | **$395,046 70** | **$123,369,252 93** | 6 |
| **1911** | | | | | |
| Real Estate | $136,052,014 88 | $128,903,178 07 | $186,055 20 | $128,717,122 87 | 7 |
| Personal | 6,185,744 49 | 4,383,434 68 | 3,252 54 | 4,380,182 14 | 8 |
| Total | **$142,237,759 37** | **$133,286,612 75** | **$189,307 74** | **$133,097,305 01** | 9 |
| **1912** | | | | | |
| Real Estate | $144,658,761 00 | $135,439,901 20 | $125,801 34 | $135,314,099 86 | 10 |
| Personal | 6,297,944 75 | 4,398,876 09 | 2,515 78 | 4,396,360 31 | 11 |
| Total | **$150,956,705 75** | **$139,838,777 29** | **$128,317 12** | **$139,710,460 17** | 12 |
| **1913** | | | | | |
| Real Estate | $145,872,973 17 | $122,421,453 48 | $47,563 83 | $122,373,889 65 | 13 |
| Personal | 5,913,295 25 | 3,788,298 33 | 1,268 90 | 3,787,029 43 | 14 |
| Total | **$151,786,268 42** | **$126,209,751 81** | **$48,832 73** | **$126,160,919 08** | 15 |
| Grand Totals | **$1,609,652,483 70** | **$1,475,246,899 85** | **$4,044,167 37** | **$1,471,202,732 48** | 16 |

# NEW YORK

Tax Accounts—Levies 1899 to 1913:—*Continued.*

| Line No. | Deficiencies | | | | Balance Uncollected at Dec. 31, 1913 | Percentages | | |
|---|---|---|---|---|---|---|---|---|
| | Discounts | Cancellations | Deductions Under Sec. 48 General Tax Laws | Total | | Net Collections to Levy | Total Deficiencies to Levy | Uncollected Balance to Levy |
| 1 | .......... | $2,462,656 74 | $982,450 61 | $3,445,107 35 | $1,341,035 60 | 95.85 | 2.99 | 1.16 |
| 2 | .......... | 547,675 21 | .......... | 547,675 21 | 2,395,727 26 | 60.73 | 7.31 | 31.96 |
| 3 | .......... | **$3,010,331 95** | **$982,450 61** | **$3,992,782 56** | **$3,736,762 86** | **93.70** | **3.25** | **3.05** |
| 4 | .......... | $1,362,026 25 | $928,391 24 | $2,290,417 49 | $3,844,560 66 | 95.09 | 1.83 | 3.08 |
| 5 | .......... | 492,221 02 | .......... | 492,221 02 | 1,478,317 82 | 70.10 | 7.47 | 22.43 |
| 6 | .......... | **$1,854,247 27** | **$928,391 24** | **$2,782,638 51** | **$5,322,878 48** | **93.83** | **2.12** | **4.05** |
| 7 | .......... | $793,745 13 | $978,762 75 | $1,772,507 88 | $5,562,384 13 | 94.61 | 1.30 | 4.09 |
| 8 | .......... | 341,812 40 | .......... | 341,812 40 | 1,463,749 95 | 70.82 | 5.51 | 23.67 |
| 9 | .......... | **$1,135,557 53** | **$978,762 75** | **$2,114,320 28** | **$7,026,134 08** | **93.57** | **1.49** | **4.94** |
| 10 | $317,518 77 | $283,569 02 | $646,945 98 | $1,248,033 77 | $8,096,627 37 | 93.54 | .86 | 5.60 |
| 11 | .......... | 60,170 16 | .......... | 60,170 16 | 1,841,414 28 | 69.81 | .96 | 29.23 |
| 12 | **$317,518 77** | **$343,739 18** | **$646,945 98** | **$1,308,203 93** | **$9,938,041 65** | **92.55** | **.87** | **6.58** |
| 13 | $278,925 62 | $120,243 08 | $967,517 14 | $1,366,685 84 | $22,132,397 68 | 83.89 | .93 | 15.18 |
| 14 | .......... | 38,358 26 | .......... | 38,358 26 | 2,087,907 56 | 64.05 | .65 | 35.30 |
| 15 | **$278,925 62** | **$158,601 34** | **$967,517 14** | **$1,405,044 10** | **$24,220,305 24** | **83.12** | **.93** | **15.95** |
| 16 | **$4,692,896 24** | **$31,525,292 71** | **$9,879,650 26** | **$46,097,839 21** | **$92,351,912 01** | **91.40** | **2.86** | **5.74** |

THE CITY OF

STATEMENT SHOWING BY BOROUGHS AND FOR EACH LEVY THE AMOUNT

| Levies of | Manhattan | LINE No. |
|---|---|---|
| 1898 and prior | ............ | 1 |
| 1899 | $3,728,831 10 | 2 |
| 1900 | 1,988,925 01 | 3 |
| 1901 | 2,908,452 86 | 4 |
| 1902 | 2,904,765 39 | 5 |
| 1903 | 2,787,656 66 | 6 |
| 1904 | 3,204,683 79 | 7 |
| 1905 | 3,519,107 29 | 8 |
| 1906 | 2,407,372 48 | 9 |
| 1907 | 2,153,712 44 | 10 |
| 1908 | 1,178,260 17 | 11 |
| 1909 | 1,301,789 70 | 12 |
| 1910 | 961,016 91 | 13 |
| 1911 | 973,597 19 | 14 |
| 1912 | 1,261,707 39 | 15 |
| 1913 | 1,476,534 62 | 16 |
| Total Uncollected | **$32,756,413 00** | 17 |

THE CITY OF

STATEMENT SHOWING NET COLLECTIONS OF PERSONAL TAXES, LEVIES 1899 TO 1913; ALSO AMOUNT
(b) DURING SUCCEEDING TWELVE MONTHS, (c) DURING REMAINING

| Year of Levy | Collections | | | LINE No. |
|---|---|---|---|---|
| | Amount of Levy | First 3 Months of Imposition, Oct. to Dec. 31 of Each Year | | |
| | | Amount | Per Cent. | |
| 1899 | $13,374,238 37 | $7,335,533 36 | 54.85 | 1 |
| 1900 | 10,780,825 69 | 6,689,831 18 | 62.05 | 2 |
| 1901 | 12,609,537 08 | 5,929,471 57 | 47.02 | 3 |
| 1902 | 11,925,231 36 | 5,601,909 95 | 46.98 | 4 |
| 1903 | 9,703,850 94 | 4,346,476 44 | 44.79 | 5 |
| 1904 | 9,516,240 66 | 4,442,472 45 | 46.68 | 6 |
| 1905 | 10,354,826 68 | 4,217,726 40 | 40.73 | 7 |
| 1906 | 8,444,962 83 | 3,856,659 12 | 45.67 | 8 |
| 1907 | 8,312,366 93 | 3,933,844 29 | 47.32 | 9 |
| 1908 | 7,088,825 73 | 3,867,200 66 | 54.55 | 10 |
| 1909 | 7,497,019 70 | 4,055,233 14 | 54.09 | 11 |
| 1910 | 6,589,809 14 | 4,352,344 03 | 66.05 | 12 |
| 1911 | 6,185,744 49 | 4,124,719 80 | 66.68 | 13 |
| 1912 | 6,297,944 75 | 4,237,469 75* | 67.29 | 14 |
| 1913 | 5,913,295 25 | 3,787,029 43* | 64.05 | 15 |
| Totals | **$134,594,719 60** | **$70,777,921 57** | **52.58** | 16 |

* Covers a period of eight months from May 1 to December 31.

## NEW YORK

OF UNCOLLECTED PERSONAL TAXES AS AT DECEMBER 31, 1913.

| LINE No. | The Bronx | Brooklyn | Queens | Richmond | Totals |
|---|---|---|---|---|---|
| 1 | .............. | $740,144 96 | .............. | ............ | $740,144 96 |
| 2 | $106,964 61 | 426,868 46 | $87,498 25 | $38,357 18 | 4,388,519 60 |
| 3 | 128,125 47 | 388,716 31 | 68,121 21 | 76,845 57 | 2,650,733 57 |
| 4 | 166,369 22 | 1,049,528 52 | 125,585 63 | 156,361 10 | 4,406,297 33 |
| 5 | 192,801 65 | 939,089 75 | 101,720 66 | 100,669 57 | 4,239,047 02 |
| 6 | 140,429 14 | 815,447 72 | 60,743 58 | 53,768 53 | 3,858,045 63 |
| 7 | 176,828 88 | 802,177 70 | 70,551 68 | 55,193 66 | 4,309,435 71 |
| 8 | 169,170 54 | 702,620 07 | 80,255 26 | 47,306 52 | 4,518,459 68 |
| 9 | 175,943 04 | 663,855 07 | 89,184 14 | 33,982 28 | 3,370,337 01 |
| 10 | 117,637 03 | 718,507 66 | 102,860 67 | 22,552 76 | 3,115,270 56 |
| 11 | 100,114 20 | 767,553 66 | 109,778 48 | 15,313 79 | 2,171,020 30 |
| 12 | 114,862 74 | 849,678 96 | 114,513 96 | 14,881 90 | 2,395,727 26 |
| 13 | 58,394 74 | 418,323 41 | 35,883 06 | 4,699 70 | 1,478,317 82 |
| 14 | 32,601 79 | 415,043 31 | 40,293 74 | 2,213 92 | 1,463,749 95 |
| 15 | 43,401 93 | 469,997 60 | 63,520 48 | 2,786 88 | 1,841,414 28 |
| 16 | 54,723 23 | 470,041 78 | 79,803 45 | 6,804 48 | 2,087,907 56 |
| 17 | **$1,778,368 21** | **$10,637,594 94** | **$1,230,314 25** | **$631,737 84** | **$47,034,428 24** |

## NEW YORK

AND PERCENTAGE OF PERSONAL TAXES COLLECTED (a) DURING FIRST THREE MONTHS OF IMPOSITION, YEARS TO DECEMBER 31, 1913, AND (d) TOTAL TO DECEMBER 31, 1913.

| LINE No. | Collections | | | | | | |
|---|---|---|---|---|---|---|---|
| | Second Year of Imposition (Succeeding 12 Months) | | Remaining Years to December 31, 1913 | | | Total | |
| | Amount | Per Cent. | Number of Years | Amount | Per Cent. | Amount | Per Cent. |
| 1 | $776,507 32 | 5.81 | 13 | $367,497 18 | 2.75 | $8,479,537 86 | 63.41 |
| 2 | 673,315 96 | 6.25 | 12 | 229,040 64 | 2.12 | 7,592,187 78 | 70.42 |
| 3 | 886,307 54 | 7.03 | 11 | 211,203 67 | 1.68 | 7,026,982 78 | 55.73 |
| 4 | 580,642 26 | 4.87 | 10 | 150,016 34 | 1.25 | 6,332,568 55 | 53.10 |
| 5 | 481,438 25 | 4.97 | 9 | 126,261 48 | 1.30 | 4,954,176 17 | 51.06 |
| 6 | 432,782 09 | 4.55 | 8 | 95,001 97 | 1.00 | 4,970,256 51 | 52.23 |
| 7 | 370,920 85 | 3.59 | 7 | 102,617 71 | .99 | 4,691,264 96 | 45.31 |
| 8 | 433,939 80 | 5.14 | 6 | 88,442 45 | 1.04 | 4,379,041 37 | 51.85 |
| 9 | 471,902 18 | 5.68 | 5 | 96,820 02 | 1.17 | 4,502,566 49 | 54.17 |
| 10 | 443,716 29 | 6.26 | 4 | 52,333 23 | .74 | 4,363,250 18 | 61.55 |
| 11 | 450,335 30 | 6.00 | 3 | 48,048 79 | .64 | 4,553,617 23 | 60.73 |
| 12 | 231,018 91 | 3.50 | 2 | 35,907 36 | .55 | 4,619,270 30 | 70.10 |
| 13 | 221,157 83 | 3.58 | 1 | 34,304 51 | .56 | 4,380,182 14 | 70.82 |
| 14 | 158,890 56 | 2.52 | .. | ........... | .... | 4,396,360 31 | 69.81 |
| 15 | ........... | .... | .. | ........... | .... | 3,787,029 43 | 64.05 |
| 16 | **$6,612,875 14** | **5.14** | .. | **$1,637,495 35** | **1.34** | **$79,028,292 06** | **58.72** |

STATEMENT OF DEFICIENCIES IN TAXES, SHOWING ALL LOSSES, KNOWN AND ESTIMATED, TOGETHER TO DECEMBER

LOSSES

| | | | | |
|---|---|---|---|---|
| Tax Levies, 1898 and Prior: | | | | |
| Discounts | | | $244,159 85 | |
| Cancellations | | | 2,237,742 70 | |
| Personal taxes, years 1875 to 1898, written off | | $10,957,131 90 | | |
| Less amount subsequently cancelled and now included under the caption "Cancellations" | | 266,235 96 | | |
| | | | 10,690,895 94 | |
| *Personal taxes, levies 1896 to 1897, former City of Brooklyn, estimated to be uncollectible | | | 740,144 96 | |
| Cancellations from January 1, 1898, to December 31, 1913, of taxes levied by the former municipalities consolidated at January 1, 1898, and now comprised within the Boroughs of Brooklyn, Queens and Richmond, included in this statement pending the completion of an examination of the respective borough accounts to ascertain whether it shall be necessary to fund these deficiencies by budget provision | | | 682,616 42 | |
| Total losses, levies, 1898 and prior | | | | **$14,595,559 87** |
| TAX LEVIES, 1899 AND SUBSEQUENT (see detailed statement, page 225) | | | | |
| Discounts: | | | | |
| Real Estate | $4,336,307 44 | | | |
| Personal | 356,588 80 | | | |
| | | **$4,692,896 24** | | |
| Cancellations: | | | | |
| Real estate | $22,609,737 25 | | | |
| Personal | 8,915,555 46 | | | |
| | | **31,525,292 71** | | |
| | | | **$36,218,188 95** | |
| *Personal taxes estimated to be uncollectible | | | **41,259,855 04** | |
| Total losses, levies, 1899 and subsequent | | | | **77,478,043 99** |
| Taxes on city-owned property | | | | **1,915,687 53** |
| Levies, 1898 and prior | | | $504,127 28 | |
| Levies, 1899 to 1904 | | | 595,024 80 | |
| Levies, 1905 and subsequent | | | 816,535 45 | |
| Total known and estimated losses | | | | **$93,989,291 39** |

* NOTE—Total amount of outstanding personal taxes at December 31, 1913, was $47,034,428.24, (see detailed statement, page 223), of which $42,000,000 is deemed to be uncollectible.

# NEW YORK

WITH ALL RESERVATIONS AND PROVISIONS MADE TO FUND DEFICIENCIES, FROM JANUARY 1, 1898, 31, 1913.

## CREDITS

| | | | |
|---|---|---|---|
| Balance, January 1, 1898 | | $787,113 81 | |
| Less remissions and cancellations entered on tax rolls prior to consolidation, but not recorded on the General Journal of the Department until 1908. | | 582,033 90 | |
| Adjusted balance as of January 1, 1898 | | | **$205,079 91** |
| CONSOLIDATED DEBT FUND: | | | |
| Being balance formerly carried to the credit of an account entitled "Adjustment Account," which amount appears to be the balance of bonds issued for the purpose of providing for deficiencies in taxes prior to consolidation | | | **4,183,000 00** |
| Total Provision from 1899 to 1914 to Fund Estimated Deficiencies in the Product of Taxes: | | | |
| (a) From 1899 to 1906, added directly to the tax levy. | $13,564,293 99 | | |
| (b) From 1907 to 1914, included in the annual budget. | 31,009,813 82 | | |
| Total tax levy and budget provision (see detailed statement, page 226) | | **$44,574,107 81** | |
| (c) Corporate stock authorized under Chapter 208 of the Laws of 1906, to fund estimated deficiencies in the product of tax levies of 1904 and prior (see detailed statement, page 227), $36,000,000: | | | |
| Issued and allotted | $23,000,000 00 | | |
| Premiums | 130,804 98 | | |
| Total provided to date under Chapter 208, Laws of 1906 | | **23,130,804 98** | |
| | | | **67,704,912 79** |
| Balance of corporate stock authorized under Chapter 208, Laws of 1906, but unallotted. | | | **13,000,000 00** |
| General Fund Reserve: | | | |
| To provide for deficiencies arising out of deductions under Section 48 of the General Tax Law, transferred from the General Fund to this account, in accordance with Chapter 31, Laws of 1913 | | $10,120,000 00 | |
| Less total deductions of special franchise taxes under Section 48 of the General Tax Law, from 1899 to and including 1913 (see detailed statement, page 227) | | 9,879,650 26 | |
| Surplus applicable only to further deductions under Section 48 of the General Tax Laws | | **$240,349 74** | |
| Net gain by fractions in the product of taxes (see detailed statement, page 228) | | | **596,828 64** |
| Total available to fund deficiencies | | | **$85,689,821 34** |
| **Estimated Deficit** | | | **8,299,470 05** |
| Total | | | **$93,989,291 39** |

STATEMENT SHOWING THE DEFICIENCIES IN EACH TAX LEVY FROM 1899 TO 1913, INCLUSIVE, CAUSED
48 OF THE GENERAL

| Year of Levy | Discounts | | | Line No. |
|---|---|---|---|---|
| | Real Estate | Personal | Total | |
| 1899 | $371,375 50 | $53,061 95 | $424,437 45 | 1 |
| 1900 | 369,340 02 | 55,432 23 | 424,772 25 | 2 |
| 1901 | 366,795 49 | 42,499 93 | 409,295 42 | 3 |
| 1902 | 388,875 36 | 40,053 18 | 428,928 54 | 4 |
| 1903 | 366,006 33 | 32,553 28 | 398,559 61 | 5 |
| 1904 | 445,608 05 | 35,587 65 | 481,195 70 | 6 |
| 1905 | 476,779 66 | 36,297 77 | 513,077 43 | 7 |
| 1906 | 494,683 94 | 31,668 71 | 526,352 65 | 8 |
| 1907 | 460,398 70 | 29,434 10 | 489,832 80 | 9 |
| 1908 | .......... | .......... | .......... | 10 |
| 1909 | .......... | .......... | .......... | 11 |
| 1910 | .......... | .......... | .......... | 12 |
| 1911 | .......... | .......... | .......... | 13 |
| 1912 | 317,518 77 | .......... | 317,518 77 | 14 |
| 1913 | 278,925 62 | .......... | 278,925 62 | 15 |
| | **$4,336,307 44** | **$356,588 80** | **$4,692,896 24** | 16 |

## NEW YORK

THROUGH DISCOUNTS, AND REMISSIONS AND CANCELLATIONS OTHER THAN DEDUCTIONS UNDER SECTION TAX LAW.

| LINE No. | Cancellations | | | Total |
|---|---|---|---|---|
| | Real Estate | Personal | Total | |
| 1 | $694,007 44 | $453,118 96 | $1,147,126 40 | $1,571,563 85 |
| 2 | 2,239,989 10 | 482,472 11 | 2,722,461 21 | 3,147,233 46 |
| 3 | 2,258,766 34 | 1,133,757 04 | 3,392,523 38 | 3,801,818 80 |
| 4 | 2,204,873 35 | 1,313,562 61 | 3,518,435 96 | 3,947,364 50 |
| 5 | 797,639 73 | 859,075 86 | 1,656,715 59 | 2,055,275 20 |
| 6 | 966,042 40 | 200,960 79 | 1,167,003 19 | 1,648,198 89 |
| 7 | 1,263,120 82 | 1,108,804 27 | 2,371,925 09 | 2,885,002 52 |
| 8 | 1,787,815 23 | 663,915 74 | 2,451,730 97 | 2,978,083 62 |
| 9 | 2,499,524 75 | 665,095 78 | 3,164,620 53 | 3,654,453 33 |
| 10 | 2,875,717 87 | 554,555 25 | 3,430,273 12 | 3,430,273 12 |
| 11 | 2,462,656 74 | 547,675 21 | 3,010,331 95 | 3,010,331 95 |
| 12 | 1,362,026 25 | 492,221 02 | 1,854,247 27 | 1,854,247 27 |
| 13 | 793,745 13 | 341,812 40 | 1,135,557 53 | 1,135,557 53 |
| 14 | 283,569 02 | 60,170 16 | 343,739 18 | 661,257 95 |
| 15 | 120,243 08 | 38,358 26 | 158,601 34 | 437,526 96 |
| 16 | **$22,609,737 25** | **$8,915,555 46** | **$31,525,292 71** | **$36,218,188 95** |

# THE CITY OF NEW YORK

STATEMENT SHOWING THE ANNUAL AMOUNTS ADDED TO TAX LEVIES OR INCLUDED IN BUDGETS FROM 1899 TO 1914, TO PROVIDE FOR DEFICIENCIES IN THE PRODUCT OF TAXES, NOT INCLUDING CORPORATE STOCK PROVIDED BY CHAPTER 208 OF THE LAWS OF 1906.

| Year | Added Directly to Tax Levy, Chap. 466, Laws 1901, as Amended | Included in the Annual Budgets, Chap. 209, Laws 1906 |
|---|---|---|
| 1899 | $1,689,877 81 | ............ |
| 1900 | 1,618,473 98 | ............ |
| 1901 | 1,726,169 24 | ............ |
| 1902 | 1,730,018 42 | ............ |
| 1903 | 1,522,209 07 | ............ |
| 1904 | 1,687,667 20 | ............ |
| 1905 | 1,744,816 56 | ............ |
| 1906 | 1,845,061 71 | ............ |
| 1907 | ............ | $3,000,000 00 |
| 1908 | ............ | 3,000,000 00 |
| 1909 | ............ | 2,922,447 08 |
| 1910 | ............ | 4,000,000 00 |
| 1911 | ............ | 10,000,000 00 |
| 1912 | ............ | 3,287,366 74 |
| 1913 | ............ | 2,300,000 00 |
| 1914 | ............ | 2,500,000 00 |
| | **$13,564,293 99** | **$31,009,813 82** |

SUMMARY

| | |
|---|---|
| Added directly to Tax Levy, years 1899 to 1906 | $13,564,293 99 |
| Included in the Annual Budget, years 1907 to 1914 | 31,009,813 82 |
| Total provision to date exclusive of $36,000,000 provided by Chapter 208, Laws of 1906 | **$44,574,107 81** |

## THE CITY OF NEW YORK

Statement Showing the Several Amounts of Corporate Stock Issued to Fund Deficiencies in Taxes in Accordance with Chapter 208 of the Laws of 1906, Together with the Premiums Realized, and the Amount Unissued at December 31, 1913.

| Year of Issue | Amount of Corporate Stock Issued | Premiums | Total |
|---|---|---|---|
| 1908 | $3,000,000 00 | $10,120 59 | $3,010,120 59 |
| 1910 | 3,000,000 00 | 38,303 75 | 3,038,303 75 |
| 1911 | 7,000,000 00 | 45,529 04 | 7,045,529 04 |
| 1912 | 5,000,000 00 | 36,851 60 | 5,036,851 60 |
| 1913 | 5,000,000 00 | .......... | 5,000,000 00 |
| | **$23,000,000 00** | **$130,804 98** | **$23,130,804 98** |

| | |
|---|---|
| Total amount of Corporate Stock authorized to be issued pursuant to Chapter 208 of the Laws of 1906 to provide for Deficiencies in Tax Levies of 1904 and prior, deemed to be uncollectible January 1, 1905 | $36,000,000 00 |
| Corporate Stock issued to December 31, 1913, in accordance with authority quoted above | 23,000,000 00 |
| Authorized but unissued | **$13,000,000 00** |

## THE CITY OF NEW YORK

Statement Showing Amount of Deductions of Special Franchise Taxes Under Section 48 of the General Tax Law on Levies 1899 to 1913, from October, 1899, to December 31, 1913, Provided for by Special Reservation Out of General Fund Pursuant to Chapter 31, Laws of 1913.

| Year of Levy | Amount |
|---|---|
| 1900 | $274,482 05 |
| 1901 | 551,372 53 |
| 1902 | 564,918 12 |
| 1903 | 539,940 30 |
| 1904 | 560,684 08 |
| 1905 | 599,032 55 |
| 1906 | 648,013 68 |
| 1907 | 756,770 40 |
| 1908 | 880,368 83 |
| 1909 | 982,450 61 |
| 1910 | 928,391 24 |
| 1911 | 978,762 75 |
| 1912 | 646,945 98 |
| 1913 | 967,517 14 |
| Total | **$9,879,650 26** |

# THE CITY OF NEW YORK

STATEMENT SHOWING AMOUNT OF EACH YEAR'S TAX AS IMPOSED BY ORDINANCE, AS EXTENDED ON THE TAX ROLLS AND THE RESULTING GAIN OR LOSS BY FRACTIONS, ETC., IN THE PRODUCT OF TAXES.

| Year of Levy | Total of Tax Levy as Imposed | Tax Levy as Extended on Tax Rolls | Losses in the Product of Taxes | Gain in the Product of Taxes |
|---|---|---|---|---|
| 1898 | .......... | .......... | $2,771 93 | .......... |
| 1899 | $86,183,768 58 | $86,180,076 73 | 3,691 85 | .......... |
| 1900 | 82,542,173 75 | 82,539,201 95 | 2,971 80 | .......... |
| 1901 | 88,238,075 51 | 88,241,801 86 | .......... | $3,726 35 |
| 1902 | 88,230,940 08 | 88,228,554 92 | 2,385 16 | .......... |
| 1903 | 77,632,663 94 | 77,631,774 55 | 889 39 | .......... |
| 1904 | 86,071,028 27 | 86,068,403 50 | 2,624 77 | .......... |
| 1905 | 88,985,645 75 | 88,980,686 02 | 4,959 73 | .......... |
| 1906 | 94,098,147 42 | 94,095,093 41 | 3,054 01 | .......... |
| 1907 | 101,950,253 58 | 101,947,670 02 | 2,583 56 | .......... |
| 1908 | 116,542,896 09 | 116,541,083 62 | 1,812 47 | .......... |
| 1909 | 122,745,210 17 | 122,742,633 66 | 2,576 51 | .......... |
| 1910 | 131,478,283 11 | 131,474,769 92 | 3,513 19 | .......... |
| 1911 | 142,240,654 56 | 142,237,759 37 | 2,895 19 | .......... |
| 1912 | 150,506,057 47 | 150,956,705 75 | .......... | 450,648 28 |
| 1913 | 151,607,084 85 | 151,786,268 42 | .......... | 179,183 57 |
| Total | **$1,609,052,883 13** | **$1,609,652,483 70** | **$36,729 56** | **$633,558 20** |

SUMMARY

| | |
|---|---|
| Gains in the product of Taxes | $633,558 20 |
| Losses in the product of Taxes | 36,729 56 |
| Net gain in the product of Taxes | **$596,828 64** |

# THE CITY OF NEW YORK

STATEMENT DIVIDING THE TOTAL DEFICIENCIES IN TAXES INTO THREE PERIODS, AND SHOWING THE APPLICATION OF ALL RESERVATIONS AND PROVISIONS TO FUND THESE DEFICIENCIES, FROM JANUARY 1, 1898, TO DECEMBER 31, 1913:

| | | | |
|---|---|---|---|
| 1. TAX LEVIES, 1898 AND PRIOR: | | | |
| Total Losses, as Per Statement "A," Consisting of: | | | |
| Discounts, levy of 1898 | $244,159 85 | | |
| Cancellations | 2,920,359 12 | | |
| Personal taxes written off (levies 1875 to 1898) | 10,690,895 94 | | |
| *Personal taxes, estimated to be uncollectible | 740,144 96 | | |
| | | $14,595,559 87 | |
| Loss by fractions in the product of taxes | $2,771 93 | | |
| Taxes on city-owned property | 504,127 28 | | |
| | | 506,899 21 | |
| Total losses, levies 1898 and prior | | **$15,102,459 08** | |
| Amounts Available to Fund Above Deficiencies: | | | |
| Balance to credit of deficiency account on January 1, 1898 | $205,079 91 | | |
| Balance of Consolidated Debt Fund | 4,183,000 00 | | |
| Part of $36,000,000 corporate stock authorized by Chapter 208, Laws 1906, directly applicable to these tax levies | 8,029,841 59 | | |
| Total credits | | **12,417,921 50** | |
| Total unfunded deficiency, tax levies, 1898 and prior | | | **$2,684,537 58** |

## THE CITY OF NEW YORK

Statement Dividing the Total Deficiencies in Taxes into Three Periods—*Continued*

| | | | |
|---|---|---|---|
| Amount brought forward | | | **$2,684,537 58** |
| 2. Tax Levies, 1899 to 1904: | | | |
| Discounts | $2,567,188 97 | | |
| Cancellations | 13,604,265 73 | | |
| *Personal taxes deemed to be uncollectible, being total outstanding on these levies at December 31, 1913 | 23,852,078 86 | | |
| Loss by fractions in the product of taxes | 8,836 62 | | |
| Taxes on city-owned property | 595,024 80 | | |
| Total losses, levies 1899 to 1904 | | **$40,627,394 98** | |
| Amounts Available to Fund Above Deficiencies: | | | |
| Provided by addition to tax levies, 1899 to 1904 | $9,974,415 72 | | |
| Part of $36,000,000 corporate stock authorized by Chapter 208, Laws 1906, directly applicable to these tax levies | 27,694,922 46 | | |
| Total provisions | | **37,669,338 18** | |
| Total unfunded deficiency, tax levies, 1899 to 1904 | | | **2,958,056 80** |
| Total unfunded deficiency, tax levies, 1904 and prior years | | | **$5,642,594 38** |
| Additional Items Available to Fund These Deficiencies: | | | |
| Premium on corporate stock issued | $130,804 98 | | |
| Remainder of $36,000,000 corporate stock authorized by Chapter 208, Laws 1906, applied to tax levies of 1904 and prior years | 275,235 95 | | |
| Total additional credits | | | **406,040 93** |
| Net unfunded deficiency in tax levies, 1904 and prior years | | | **$5,236,553 45** |
| 3. Tax Levies, 1905 to 1913: | | | |
| Discounts | $2,125,707 27 | | |
| Cancellations | 17,921,026 98 | | |
| *Personal Taxes—Proportion of outstanding personal taxes amounting to $22,442,204.42, deemed to be uncollectible | 17,407,776 18 | | |
| Taxes on city-owned property | 816,535 45 | | |
| Total losses, levies, 1905 to 1913 | | **$38,271,045 88** | |
| Amounts Available to Fund Above Deficiencies: | | | |
| Provided by addition to tax levies, 1905 and 1906 | $3,589,878 27 | | |
| Provided in annual budgets | 31,009,813 82 | | |
| Gain by fractions in the product of taxes | 608,437 19 | | |
| Total provisions | | **35,208,129 28** | |
| Net unfunded deficiency in tax levies, 1905 to 1913 | | | **3,062,916 60** |
| Total Net Unfunded Deficiency at December 31, 1913 | | | **$8,299,470 05** |

* Total amount outstanding personal taxes deemed to be uncollectible is $42,000,000.